WINDOWS™ INTERNALS

"Every experienced Windows programmer should read *Windows Internals* and keep it on the shelf for future reference."

– BYTE Magazine

"This is the first book of its kind to explore the inner workings of Windows, and contains material you will not find in any other book."

– Paul Bonneau, Q&A Columnist,
WINDOWS/DOS DEVELOPER'S JOURNAL

"*Windows Internals* is an absolute must-read for Windows programmers. Nobody does it better – or in more detail – than Matt. The only way you'll learn more about how Windows works is to steal a peek at the source code."

– Jeff Prosise, Contributing Editor, PC MAGAZINE

"*Windows Internals*, by Matt Pietrek, belongs on the reference shelf of every serious Windows programmer."

– "Book O' the Month," WINDOWS MAGAZINE

"... *Windows Internals* is another victory for reverse engineering, telling it how it really is so that we can be more effective developers of Windows software."

– "Read Only," PC MAGAZINE

Windows™ Internals

The Implementation of the Windows Operating Environment

Matt Pietrek

Series Editor:
Andrew Schulman

Addison-Wesley Publishing Company

Reading, Massachusetts   Menlo Park, California   New York
Don Mills, Ontario   Wokingham, England   Amsterdam   Bonn
Sydney   Singapore   Tokyo   Madrid   San Juan
Paris   Seoul   Milan   Mexico City   Taipei

Library of Congress Cataloging-in-Publication Data

Pietrek, Matt.
Windows internals : the implementation of the Windows operating environment / Matt Pietrek.
p. cm.
Includes index.
ISBN 0-201-62217-3
1. Windows (Computer programs) 2. Microsoft Windows (Computer file) I. Title
QA76.76.W56P55 1993
005.4'3--dc20 92-46133
CIP

Series Editor: Andrew Schulman
Managing Editor: Amorette Pedersen
Puppy illustration by Lynn Hunt Illustration, Capitola, CA.
Interior Design by Richard DeFeo, Hamlet Studios, Hamilton, MA.
Set in 10.5-point Galliard by Benchmark Productions

4 5 6 7 8-MA-97969594
Fourth printing, April 1994

Contents

CHAPTER 1 (Cont.)

CHAPTER 2

CHAPTER 2 (Cont.)

CHAPTER 2 (Cont.)

CHAPTER 2 (Cont.)

CHAPTER 3

CHAPTER 3 (Cont.)

CHAPTER 7
The Windows Messaging System 429

CHAPTER 8
Dynamic Linking 463

Foreword

The Microsoft Windows operating environment is used by millions, and programmed by thousands, every day. And thousands of Windows programmers have to ask themselves several times each day how Windows will behave in a given situation. Windows is such a large, complex, and flexible environment that Microsoft's documentation can only scratch the surface of how this beast behaves.

Is there some way to learn the answer to every possible question about how Windows will behave in a given circumstance? Of course there is: in the odd world of UNIX this is known as UTSL or "Use the Source, Luke":

> "UTSL. On-line acronym for 'Use the Source, Luke' (a pun on Obi-Wan Kenobi's 'Use the Force, Luke!' in Star Wars)... This is a common way of suggesting that someone would be best off reading the source code that supports whatever feature is causing confusion, rather than making yet another futile pass through the manuals or broadcasting questions that haven't attracted wizards to answer them." —*The New Hacker's Dictionary*

Truly, any question you could possibly have about Windows is answered in the source code for Windows, that is, in files such as krnl386\winexec.c (or is it winexec.asm?), user\wmvisrgn.c, and gdi\meta.c.

The problem is, the source code resides somewhere on Microsoft's "campus" in Redmond, WA, and, most likely, you don't. While Microsoft has been talking about releasing the source code to its new Windows NT operating system to universities, there never has been much discussion of making the Windows source code available to anyone outside a small handful of OEMs (original equipment manufacturers) and ISVs (independent software vendors). Two small pieces of Windows source code (user\defwnd.c and user\defdlg.c) are included with the Windows software development kit (SDK), and the source code for many Windows device drivers is included with the device development kit (DDK), but that's it.

This is unfortunate, but it is not an enormous obstacle. Anyone can walk into their friendly neighborhood software store, buy a copy of Windows, take it home, and reverse-engineer or disassemble it. As almost any textbook on computer law or trade secrets will tell you (see Raymond T. Nimmer's *The Law of Computer Technology*, for example), a purchaser is free to disassemble a computer program; this "capability of discovery through reverse-engineering" is particularly strong when there is the kind of widespread mass-market distribution we've seen with Windows. Microsoft even provides tools such as EXEHDR, CodeView, and debug versions of Windows, that make disassembly easy and almost unavoidable.

In *Windows Internals*, Matt has provided a kind of Windows source code "for the rest of us." Matt doesn't have the Windows source code, but he has used the time-honored technique of reverse-engineering to provide us with a rare inside look at what really goes on in Windows. This book gives detailed (and I mean *detailed!*) pseudocode for many of the key functions that make up the Windows API. For example, while most Windows programming books will tell you what parameters the function CreateWindow expects, will tell you what values it returns, and will tell you roughly what the function does, Matt shows you *exactly* what it does, in about 500 lines of C-like pseudocode. (See Chapter 4.)

The big question, I suppose, is "Do I need this information?" Certainly, it would be very nice if you *didn't* need to know what goes on under the hood when you do Windows programming. "Information hiding" is one of the key principles of what is optimistically called software engineering. Unfortunately, the software industry is still very far from being able to say that programming interfaces like the Windows API can be used as black-box components. Time and again, Windows programmers find themselves having to ask what CreateWindow or GetMessage or GlobalAlloc will do in a given situation. With Matt's book, they now have a good shot at finding the answers.

To take one example, look at Microsoft's documentation for the GlobalAlloc function. Notice that you can call GlobalAlloc with a GMEM_FIXED option, to tell Windows that the newly allocated block of memory shouldn't be moved around in the linear address space. Now turn to Chapter 2 and look at the psuedocode for GbTop, which is called by GlobalAlloc. The pseudocode shows, as plain as day, that in Windows 3.1 GbTop will simply turn this flag *off* if it's coming from something other than a DLL. Period. As Matt puts it in one of his comments to the pseudocode, "KERNEL knows best!" Do you still feel safe programming for Windows without knowing this sort of thing?

I think there is another reason to examine Windows at this level. In the arcane language of the law, computer programs are regarded as "literary works," but unfortunately this idea is never taken to its logical conclusion: that the source code for computer programs such as Windows should be available to read as *books*. The fact is, only a handful of large computer programs have ever been publicly examined or subjected to what literary critics call "close reading." This handful includes the UNIX operating system, which has been examined (in psuedocode form) in books such as Bach's *Design of the UNIX Operating System* and Leffler et al.'s *Design and Implementation of the 4.3BSD UNIX Operating System*. Donald Knuth has treated two of his own large programs this way in *TEX: The Program* and *METAFONT: The Program*, and in fact Knuth has put forward a whole methodology called "literate programming," which takes seriously this idea of the computer programs as essentially books to be read. In *Windows Internals*, Matt has for the first time subjected one of Microsoft's messy mass-market operating environments to such examination and dissection. His book should move the understanding of, and writing about, Windows to a new level.

Since Matt was, along with David Maxey and myself, one of the coauthors of the infamous book *Undocumented Windows*, it is natural to ask how *Windows Internals* differs from *Undocumented Windows.* In fact, there is surprisingly little overlap between the two books. Where the books do overlap, *Windows Internals* is more accurate because it reflects the many things Matt has discovered about Windows since we finished *Undocumented Windows.*

Mostly, though, the two books cover very different subjects: *Undocumented Windows* focuses on those functions that Windows happens to export, yet the Windows documentation does not mention. This is a motley crew, combining functions that are absolutely essential to Windows programming with ones that are of no earthly use to anyone. They are all included in *Undocumented Windows* because they happen to be exported from some DLL (making them at least potentially callable from your programs). *Windows Internals* in contrast covers the core *documented* functions that Windows programmers use many times every single day, and shows how these functions are actually implemented. This is an entirely different topic from the one that Matt, David, and I smashed our heads against in *Undocumented Windows.*

This distinction between "Internals" and "Undocumented" is important, because there will be more "Internals" and "Undocumented" books in this series. Geoff Chappell's *DOS Internals* is quite different from Matt's book, yet it shares the perspective that, to understand programs like DOS or Windows, you have to look at the code. Use the Source, Luke!

Interestingly, Chappell's *DOS Internals* includes a lot of new material on Windows, and provides even more detailed coverage of some of the topics that Matt discusses in Chapter 1 of this book ("The Big Bang: Starting Up and Shutting Down Windows"). Increasingly, DOS is being used as a platform from which to boot Windows, so if you are looking for more information on some of the topics that Matt covers, particularly in Chapter 1, you will definitely want to look at Geoff's book. Likewise, the second edition of *Undocumented DOS* has a lengthy new chapter on DOS/Windows interaction. This is a fascinating, important topic that has not been adequately covered before. It is also such a large topic that, surprisingly, there is little overlap between what Matt, Geoff, and myself say about it. But this merely reflects the increasing complexity of programming for DOS, Windows, and the PC. Which brings me to...

The Series

You may have noticed on the cover that this book is part of what we are calling, for want of a better name, "The Andrew Schulman Programming Series." The goal of this series is to present information or approaches that weren't in the manuals. The increasing complexity of programming for DOS, Windows, and the PC, makes this type of book more necessary than ever. In some cases, the information is of the "Undocumented" or "Internals" type, and is the product of disassembly. In other cases, the book puts forward an approach to programming that the manuals and all the other books have missed.

For example, Woody Leonhard's irreverent and wacky *Windows 3.1 Programming for Mere Mortals* and Paul DiLascia's beautifully written *Windows++* both present methods of programming Windows that are radically different from the "look, I can write a fourteen-page switch statement" method put forward in the Windows SDK and in most books on Windows programming. Woody shows how simple tools like WordBasic (the macro language in a word processor, for heaven's sake!) can be used to accomplish serious work in Windows. Paul shows how to write your own C++ application framework—not how to use an existing one like Borland's OWL or Microsoft's MFC, mind you, but how to write your own. Even if you are using OWL or MFC, Paul's book will show you how these things really *work*. "No mysteries!" is one of the slogans for this series.

Of course, books like *Undocumented Windows*, *Windows Internals*, *DOS Internals*, and the forthcoming *Undocumented PC* by Frank van Gilluwe (of Sourcer fame), provide crucial programming information you won't find anywhere else. Why aren't there more books like this? Because it's hard work! It is difficult finding talented programmers masochistic enough to commit to reverse-engineering some enormous system, and then writing up their findings in a useful form. But somehow we at the Addison-Wesley test kitchens manage to find these programmer/writers and we put them to work, sifting through mountains of disassembly listings to cook up useful and unique books.

Another useful type of book in this series gathers together previously disparate material into one easy-to-reach volume. For example, Ralph Davis's *Windows Network Programming: How to Survive in a World of Windows, DOS, and Networks* brings together just about everything you would want to know about network programming under Windows, including lengthy chapters on Windows for Workgroups, the Windows network device drivers, NetBios, Novell NetWare, the Windows Sockets API, LAN Manager, the Win32 networking API in Windows NT, and Banyan Vines. There's even a very nice chapter on API translation with DPMI, for those times when you have to "roll your own" Windows programming interface.

Similarly, Al Williams's *DOS and Windows Protected Mode* covers many topics that haven't made it into other books on DOS or Windows programming (not even the excellent collection *Extending DOS*). These topics include protected mode interrupt handling, real mode callbacks, exception handling, calling real mode code from protected mode, virtual memory, mixing 16-bit and 32-bit code, protected mode performance issues, and so on. Al treats Windows as essentially a big DPMI server and protected mode DOS extender.

My role in this series is to act as an advocate for the reader. I read the manuscript for each book several times, and push the authors to go into more detail (I love details), to cover more topics (I hate the phrase "outside the scope of this book"), and to anticipate the reader's questions (I can't stand when a book leaves me asking "But wait a minute, what about...?" without even trying to answer the question—I figure it's the author's job to know what questions I'm going to have). I also sometimes try to inject my own feeble sense of humor into the books. Each book goes through several iterations of this process, with me pounding on the author, the author doing a great job of supplying the new material I've asked for, and then me asking for *yet more*, until we're all exhausted, and the book is done.

Please let me know what you think of this book, other books in the series, and other books you would like to see.

Andrew Schulman
Series Editor
March 1993
Addison-Wesley Publishing
One Jacob Way
Reading, MA 01867

Introduction

It's Just Code

Despite the phenomenal success of Microsoft Windows, its inner workings remain a mystery to most programmers. At an intellectual level, we know that Windows uses data structures and algorithms, just like our own code. However, when faced with the sheer number of APIs, messages, handles, callback functions, etc., there's a tendency to forget that. Windows can seem like a monolithic entity that you deliver your handles to on command, and if you do well, Windows rewards you by carrying out your small request. If you anger Windows, it condemns your program with an Unrecoverable Application Error (UAE). In other words, the mental model that many Windows programmers work with is that Windows is a beast, rather than just a big library of code that you call, and that calls you.

In this book, I will attempt to strip away the layers and reveal *how Windows works.* The goal is to provide you with some degree of orderliness and predictability. If you can see and understand how Windows creates and maintains its objects, you can often think through problems, rather than trying different approaches until something works.

There are now numerous books available on how to write Windows programs. Although there are many good ones, they almost all concentrate on giving you inputs to a "black box." You want to put pictures on your buttons? Well, you plug this in here, that in there, turn the crank, and there's your button. This book has a different approach. The focus is on opening the black box to reveal what's inside, and to let you see *how and why* the techniques described in other books work.

A coworker of mine is of the opinion that you shouldn't need to know what's inside the black box. The assumption is that if you design a black box well, the users don't need to know what's happening under the hood. While we differ on the validity of this premise, we both agree that the Windows black box doesn't work very well. To do anything of significance, you have to understand things at a deeper level than the documentation provides. This is not to denigrate the work of the documentation writers at Microsoft. Instead, it's a by-product of the incredible number of applications that "push the limit," along with a slightly eccentric CPU architecture.

What We'll Cover

In the chapters that follow, we'll select a few broad operating system concepts, and discuss in detail how Windows implements them. For example, we'll see how an executable file on disk becomes a running process with windows that you interact with. The chapter on memory management is especially lengthy, as this particular area underpins almost everything else in Windows.

When I set out to write this book, I knew there was absolutely no way to cover all the various aspects of Windows. I therefore had to select just a few areas I felt were especially critical, which I knew the most about, and which would be of use to the largest number of programmers. Even with this narrowed down topic list, there was still too much to cover. Specifically, there are numerous "varieties" of Windows that are available. Consider the following list:

- Windows 3.0 versus Windows 3.1
- Standard versus Enhanced mode
- Far East editions of Windows
- WINOS2 (the version of Windows included with OS/2 2.0)
- Windows for Workgroups
- Win32s (runs 32-bit applications on top of Windows 3.1)

It would be nearly impossible to include all the possible permutations. I therefore made a conscious decision to base the book on Enhanced mode Windows 3.1, as released in March, 1992. Where appropriate, I do discuss some of the other permutations (e.g., the discussion of what the Windows 3.1 loader does when it encounters a Win32 application). Although Windows for Workgroups is not specifically mentioned in the chapters that follow, all of the discussions apply equally as well to it, as to Windows 3.1. The "core" of Windows that this book focuses on is unchanged between Windows 3.1 and Windows for Workgroups.

Because Windows is such a huge topic, there's quite a list of things that there just wasn't time to cover. For instance, there's the entire area of Virtual Device Drivers, the Virtual Machine Manager, and running DOS applications under Windows. At a higher level, I had to forgo discussions of the inner workings of dialogs, custom controls, DDE, and OLE. Nor was I able to cover the network APIs, the multimedia extensions, and many of the new functionality added to Windows 3.1 and Windows for Workgroups. This book focuses on the *core* of Windows that's beneath all of these areas. Fortunately, there are other books planned for this series that will encompass some of the topics I couldn't cover in this book.

In order to do justice to the topics that I was able to cover, I built in a set of assumptions about you, the reader. In writing the book, I assumed that you were at least somewhat familiar with the concepts of segmentation, selectors, and protected mode. Rather than trying to provide yet another tutorial on these topics, I decided that I would rather use the space to cover more topics, and give you more details. The bibliography lists some books I feel are helpful if you're not familiar with these topics.

Another assumption I made is that you either have the Windows SDK documentation, or some reasonably complete substitution (e.g., the Windows documentation that comes with Borland C++). For instance, in the description of the implementation of GlobalAlloc(), in the memory management chapter, I don't repeat all the details that can be found in the SDK documentation. The goal is to provide you with *new* information.

Lastly, it will help if you understand the basic concepts of operating systems (e.g., what multitasking is, an idea of how virtual memory works at a high level, etc.) You certainly don't need a degree in computer science to read this book, but we won't be dwelling for too long on general operating system concepts. The implementation of those concepts *in Windows* is our objective. If you're interested in learning more about general operating-system principles, check out Andrew Tanenbaum's book *Modern Operating Systems*, or any of the numerous books available on Unix internals.

In short, this book won't teach you how to write Windows programs. Instead, it should teach you about how Windows works, and how you can apply it to your current knowledge.

Methods of Investigation

Unlike operating systems like Unix (or its variations), the source for Windows is generally kept under wraps within Microsoft. Thus, finding out how Windows works took some effort on my part (along with some wonderful assistance from people we'll mention later). As with the previous book I coauthored (*Undocumented Windows*), I used two methods of breaking Windows apart and determining how it works.

The primary method used was analysis of assembly language listings of the Windows files. These listings were generated by a program of my own devising called WINDIS. (Little did I know how much my life would change when I concocted it several years ago!)

To give an example of what WINDIS produces, consider the following excerpt from the IsTask() function in KRNL386.EXE. The IsTask() function is a documented Windows 3.1 function that takes an hTask argument, and determines if the argument really is a task handle:

```
ISTASK proc
881E:   MOV     BX,SP
8820:   MOV     AX,WORD PTR SS:[BX+04]  ; Get the parameter off
                                        ; the stack, and into AX

8824:   OR      AX,AX        ; Is the parameter == 0 ?
8826:   JE      8840         ; 8840 is where failures jump to
```

```
8828:   LSL     BX,AX        ; Get the selector limit into BX.
882B:   JNE     8840         ; Return 0 if not a valid selector

882D:   CMP     BX,00FC      ; Make sure the segment limit is big
8831:   JL      8840         ; enough to allow the read below

8833:   MOV     ES,AX                       ; Look for the TDB
8835:   CMP     WORD PTR ES:[00FA],4454 ; signature ('TD') at
883C:   JNE     8840                        ; offset 00FA. Return 0
                                            ; if not found

883E:   JMP     8842      ; AX still contains the parameter. Jump
                          ; over the next instruction, which puts
                          ; 0 in AX to make IsTask() return FALSE

8840:   XOR     AX,AX     ; All failed tests jump to here

8842:   RETF    0002      ; Return whatever's in AX (a TDB, or 0)
ISTASK endp
```

While it would be nice if WINDIS were able to add the very verbose comments, it currently doesn't. What you see above is the raw output from WINDIS, with some comments and line feeds I added to make it more readable.

Since very little Windows programming is done in assembler these days, I felt the book would be more accessible if I translated my assembler listings into C pseudocode. For the IsTask() code above, I would translate it into the following C pseudocode:

```
Pseudo code for IsTask() - CONTEXT.OBJ
// Parameters:
//      WORD    hTask       // A potential hTask (a TDB selector)
// Locals:
        WORD    segLimit    // Limit of the passed selector

    if ( hTask == 0 )
        return 0

    segLimit = LSL hTask     // Get the segment limit using LSL

    if ( LSL returned failure because of an invalid selector )
        return 0

    if ( segLimit < 0xFC )   // Make sure we won't GP fault by
        return 0             // trying to read past the limit

    if ( hTask->TDBsig != 'TD' )
```

```
        return 0;

    return hTask
```

Translating into C pseudocode also has the advantage of cutting out a lot of repetitive code such as function prologues, segment register loads, and so on. Additionally, much of Windows appears to be written in highly optimized assembler, or in C with the optimizer turned on. Following all the conditional jumps is very tedious. There's also heavy use of register variables and parameters that are passed in registers. In my C pseudocode, I've placed more emphasis on showing the algorithms and steps, rather than exact adherence to the binary code as it exists in the Windows DLLs.

Chapter 3 of *Undocumented Windows* has a comprehensive discussion of how you can methodically work a disassembly listing into something that's readable, with regards to determining what the code does at a high level. While my WINDIS program is not currently available, the tool Andrew Schulman wrote and uses (Windows Source, from V Communications) is. Chapter 3 of *Undocumented Windows* uses Windows Source for its examples, but in my experience, listings from either disassembler are usually identical in content.

Crucial to the success of the assembly listings was the availability of comprehensive CodeView debug information. Certain versions of the core Windows DLLs (e.g., USER, KRNLx86, and GDI) have the names and addresses of all public symbols in the module. Knowing descriptive symbolic names for internal (i.e., non-exported) functions and global variables made analysis several orders of magnitude easier. It was much easier to guess what the code was doing when I saw variables called names like "NUM_TASKS", rather than "[026A]".

In the pseudocode that's presented in this book, the names of functions and global variables are taken straight out of the CodeView information (with a little bit of "case" translation to make them more readable). I made up the names of all local variables, and almost all labels, as they were not included in the debugging information in most cases.

The second method of inquiry involved the wonderful Soft-ICE/W debugger, from Nu-Mega Technologies. Unlike more traditional debuggers like Turbo Debugger, CodeView, or Multiscope, Soft-ICE/W is a kernel debugger. It trades a flashy user interface for the ability to get at the lowest level of the operating system, where traditional debuggers can't dream of going. When an assembly listing wasn't revealing the true nature of the code, stepping through it in Soft-ICE/W, and examining registers and memory was just the ticket. There's no other way I could have figured out the Windows scheduler, for instance. And since Soft-ICE/W recognizes the aforementioned CodeView debug info, it was a double dose of a good thing.

On Modes

When discussing modes of the Intel architecture, I have used lowercase (e.g., real mode, protected mode, and virtual 86 mode). I have capitalized the modes of Windows in discussion (e.g., Standard, Enhanced and, in the case of Windows 3.0, Real mode).

Relationship to *Undocumented Windows*

In the ensuing chapters, there are many spots where I refer to *Undocumented Windows*. The goal of *Undocumented Windows* was to provide a guide to the functions that were *both* undocumented *and* exported from the Windows DLLs. The goal of this book is to examine *how Windows works* without restricting the discussion to the undocumented functions.

To give an example, *Undocumented Windows* describes the SetPriority() function. Unfortunately, *Undocumented Windows* didn't have the time or space to show you in any detail how a task's priority affects its execution. I can do that here. I had the freedom to examine how Windows works, without being bound by whether a function was documented, undocumented, exported, or internal. They're all treated equally.

Both Andrew Schulman (the editor of this book) and I (along with David Maxey) were coauthors of *Undocumented Windows*. The frequent mentions are not intended as "plugs" of *Undocumented Windows*. Instead, the intent was to offer you additional sources of information for paths I didn't have the time or space to travel down.

In writing this book, I've tried to make it stand alone as much as possible. It was a very tough balancing act deciding what areas that were covered in *Undocumented Windows absolutely had* to be repeated here. Since this book was written after *Undocumented Windows*, I was generally able to improve in some manner the small amount of material that originally appeared in the prior book.

To sum up this section, I consider *Undocumented Windows* and this book to be complementary. Neither one *needs* the other, but the combination can be greater than the sum of the individual parts.

Thank Yous

This is my favorite part of the entire book. Here I have the opportunity to thank the many people who helped and encouraged me along the way.

For starters, there's my editor, Andrew Schulman. This book would not have been possible without him. When we dreamed up this book, it looked impossibly daunting. Only because I knew he'd help me through it did I take it on. In addition to being tremendously knowledgeable in almost everything I wrote about, he has an attention to detail that boggles the imagination. Every time I thought I'd covered a chapter in exhaustive detail, he'd send me back literally hundreds of comments, pushing for even more details. I can't imagine having a better editor.

The fine folks at Benchmark, including Chris Williams, Amy Pedersen, and Andrew Williams. They've gone out of their way to show me the ropes and make things easy for me. Judging from their previous books, I know I've gone top of the line with this book.

My technical reviewers: Orin Eman, Mike Geary, Scott Kliger, Eli Boling, and of course, Andrew Schulman. Every one of them is unquestionably one of *the* experts in their particular field(s). The insights and technical corrections provided by them were invaluable. It would be virtually impossible to select a more qualified and helpful group of programmers to review this book.

The journal editors: Ron Burk ("Windows/DOS Developers Journal"), Jon Erickson and Ray Valdés ("Dr. Dobb's Journal"), and Gretchen Bilson ("Microsoft Systems Journal"). Not only did they encourage me to write, they put up with the fact that I'm more of a programmer than a writer. They also put in a tremendous amount of work to help me adapt and condense certain chapters into articles. Chapter 6 (the scheduler) appeared in an earlier form in the August 1992 "Dr. Dobb's Journal." Chapter 7 (the messaging system) is condensed in the February 1993 "Dr. Dobb's Journal," and portions of Chapter 2 (memory management) are in the March 1993 "Microsoft Systems Journal."

My family, especially my mother and father, my mother- and father-in-law, and my grandmother-in-law. They all were overwhelmingly supportive, even though they understand about .001% of what I wrote. (Listening to my mother try to read one of my chapters aloud is hilarious!)

My "boys," Theodore and Gunther (they're really twin Dachshund brothers). It may seem a bit strange to thank a pair of dogs, but they were critical to my completing this book. Too many times to count, I would look over from my writing, and see them flopped out on the sofa, a perfect demonstration of entropy. I had no choice but to stop what I was doing, and go play with them. They really helped keep things in perspective.

Finally, and most importantly of all, my wife April. I could never hope to repay her for putting up with me while I wrote this book. It was a rare night indeed when she didn't go to bed by herself (with Gunther and Theodore at her feet). She essentially ran the house single-handedly while I worked seven days a week on the book (on top of my real job at Borland). She's threatened to write a book on computer widowhood, so I'm especially looking forward to spending time with her, now that the book is finished. Mere words cannot express my gratitude to her.

Matt Pietrek
March, 1993

(CIS ID: [71774,362])
Capitola, CA

CHAPTER 1

The Big Bang: Starting Up and Shutting Down Windows

Among most astronomers and astrophysicists, there is consensus that the universe as we know it was once an infinitely dense, infinitely small point. This point exploded, sending out matter and energy and creating the galaxies and stars. What astronomers know is that the state of the universe underwent a transition from one form to another. What they don't know, however, is what occurred at the very *moment* of the explosion.

In contrast, DOS and Windows allow the programmer to uncover in detail what goes on when the computer transforms itself from a mild-mannered DOS machine to a protected mode, event-driven, multitasking, graphical user interface computer.

This chapter strips away the mystique of what goes on during those seconds after you type WIN, but before you can begin work in Windows. On a more general level, this chapter serves as a road map for the subsequent chapters of the book. The discussion of what happens when you boot Windows includes mention of things that are examined in more detail in their own chapters. You'll cover all the major bases by studying the following Windows subsystems.

- Tasks and Modules: Explains how they're related to each other. In addition, this section shows how the Windows loader creates a new task, and how it dynamically links to dynamic link libraries (DLLs).
- Windows memory management: Examines the structure of the global and local heaps and looks at what the various memory attributes mean. This chapter includes detailed descriptions of all memory management functions. Best of all, real mode is *not* included.

- Dynamic linking: Discusses how applications and DLLs link up to routines that aren't present at link time. This chapter covers both implicit (load time) loading and runtime dynamic linking (GetProcAddress()). In addition, it covers such topics as MakeProcInstance() and function exports.
- The Windows messaging system: Looks at the various kinds of messages and their relative priorities. This chapter discusses the application and system message queues and the way messages move through the system.
- The windowing system: Shows the relationship between parent and child windows, between parents and owners, and between windows and classes. This chapter takes an in-depth look at the process of creating and destroying windows, as well as at registering new classes in the system.
- The Graphics Device Interface: Looks into the data structures and the methods by which Windows can output text, lines, bitmaps, and so forth, in a device-independent manner.
- The Windows Scheduler: Examines how Windows decides which task will run next while keeping all other tasks in a suspended state.

This chapter's discussion of these areas includes references to the appropriate chapters so that you can do further investigation.

The goal of this chapter is to focus on the link between real mode DOS and protected mode Windows. It is by far the most conceptual chapter in the book.

A Word or Two About Protected Mode and DOS Extenders

Before beginning this journey into the caverns of Windows, you might want to read through this overview of what lies ahead.

Speaking in the most general terms, Windows consists of two major parts: A DOS extender and an operating environment. This book primarily focuses on the operating environment aspect of Windows. However, it's unavoidable to encounter portions of Windows that are unquestionably part of the DOS extender. Several chapters (but especially this chapter and Chapter 2 which deals with memory management assume that you're at least somewhat familiar with concepts of protected mode on the Intel CPU, including such areas as the differences between real and protected mode, the DOS Protected Mode Interface (DPMI), and DOS extenders in general. It also helps if you're familiar with operating system concepts such as virtual memory.

Quite a few good books discuss these topics. Rather than give you yet another five-page tutorial on protected mode, selectors, Local Descriptor Tables (LDTs), and so on, this book assumes that the mention of these terms doesn't bring you to a quiver, preferring to use the available space to explore new and uncharted territories in Windows. If you're not familiar with these topics, read *Extending DOS, Second Edition,* edited by Ray Duncan (Addison-

Wesley, 1992) or another book on the topic, *DOS and Windows Protected Mode: Programming with DOS Extenders in C*, by Al Williams (Addison-Wesley, 1993). Several other books in our bibliography also cover these topics.

Although most developers are vaguely aware that Windows runs on top of DOS, the extent to which Windows relies on DOS and is structured around DOS cannot be emphasized enough. To put it simply, Windows is not an operating system in the true sense of the word. You cannot yet boot a PC with just Windows on the hard drive. Windows relies on the underlying DOS to perform all file operations (Windows 3.1 FastDisk and the forthcoming VFAT.386 notwithstanding). The vague techspeak of marketing calls Windows an "operating *environment*," but only the combination of DOS capabilities with Windows results in a genuine operating *system*. In fact, some people contend that DOS is the operating system and that Windows is just an unusually fancy DOS extender that runs in graphics mode. On the other hand, Windows provides many services traditionally associated with operating systems, including memory management, task management, dynamic linking, and so on; from this perspective, Windows looks much more like a genuine operating system than does DOS. This chapter shows how Windows bootstraps itself up from a DOS program, and later returns things back to normal, making it appear that just another DOS program has run.

The First Step: WIN.COM

The initial step of bringing Windows up is to type WIN, followed optionally by additional parameters. This command invokes WIN.COM, an exclusively real mode program. WIN.COM is created when SETUP.EXE combines three files in the WINDOWS\SYSTEM directory: WIN.CNF, VGALOGO.RLE, and VGALOGO.LGO. (The latter two files may have different names, based upon your video configuration and the settings in the SETUP.INF file.) WIN.COM serves three primary purposes:

1. It pokes around in your system and decides in which mode to run Windows (Standard or Enhanced). Once it decides upon a mode, WIN.COM invokes the appropriate programs to start up Windows in the selected mode. The WIN.CNF file, which is really just a .COM file without the .COM extension, contains all of this code. More on the WIN.CNF code in a moment.
2. WIN.COM hangs around in the DOS memory space to provide certain real mode services—discussed in detail in a later section. Windows cannot perform these services itself, because there is no real mode code after the initial start up section of Windows. These services are not related to the real mode DOS file I/O that KERNEL manages.
3. WIN.COM puts up the initial splash screen—typically the Windows logo—that you see before WIN.COM initializes the Windows desktop. The VGALOGO.LGO and VGALOGO.RLE files (or whatever they happen to be named on your particular machine) perform this job. VGALOGO.LGO, a short binary

image similar to a .COM file, switches the screen into graphics mode and displays the VGALOGO.RLE file. The .RLE extension stands for "run length encoded." Programs such as WINGIF can produce .RLE files.

The WIN.CNF portion of WIN.COM performs several tasks:

It processes the WIN command line switches and acts accordingly. For instance /s sets a flag that indicates that Windows should run in Standard mode, even if it's possible for the machine to run in Enhanced mode. On the other hand, a /r causes an INT 21h, function 9 (write string to standard output) that tells DOS to print out an error message saying that this version of Windows can't run in real mode, before INT 21h, function 4Ch terminates the program. The /r switch is a holdover from the dark ages of Windows 3.0, which for some perverse reason lets you run Windows in real mode.

WIN.COM encounters and processes its own switches (leaving alone switches that KERNEL will later process) replacing each slash and the following character with two spaces. This step allows WIN.COM to pass the original command line buffer to the subsequently launched programs (WIN386, DOSX, or KRNLx86) rather than having to create a separate command line buffer for them.

WIN.COM determines what type of CPU the machine has. Windows 3.1 can run in Standard or Enhanced mode, with Standard mode requiring at least an 80286, and Enhanced mode requiring an 80386 or better. The CPU test involves moving values into the flags register using PUSH and POP, and then testing which bits are set in the CPU flags register. The only distinction the test makes between CPUs at this point is between 8086/8, 80286, and 80386 machines. Much later on in the startup process, KERNEL obtains the real CPU type using a DPMI function. The results from the DPMI call, rather than the value obtained here in WIN.COM, determine the values of the WF_xxx flags returned by the Windows function GetWinFlags().

WIN.COM determines what memory management system is on the machine and the amount of available and total memory. Windows requires an Extended Memory Specification (XMS) driver, either HIMEM.SYS or a more advanced memory manager that provides XMS services, such as QEMM386 or 386MAX. If WIN.COM doesn't find an XMS driver, it uses INT 15h, function 88h (Get Extended Memory Size) to determine if there is any extended memory at all on the machine. If extended memory is present, the function displays the message, "Missing HIMEM.SYS..." If no extended memory is present, the message instead reads, "Your computer cannot run Windows in either Standard or 386 Enhanced mode." WIN.COM also checks for the presence of Virtual Control Program Interface (VCPI) services using INT 67h, function 0DE00h (VCPI Installation Check). Oddly enough, this test has nothing to do with the availability of VCPI services for Standard mode Windows. Instead, the presence of VCPI services plays a role in determining whether to reduce the SMARTDRV cache size. If you're wondering about all these INT functions, see the book *PC Interrupts* by Ralf Brown and Jim Kyle (Addison-Wesley, 1991).

Also included in these memory checks is a test for Global EMM Importation, a Microsoft interface that allows WIN386 to import the page mapping tables from a virtual 8086 memory manager, such as QEMM386 or 386MAX. Without this specification, trying to run Windows on top of a 386 memory manager would be a horrendous mess because both programs want complete control of the 80386 page tables.

A smaller disk cache is often advantageous in freeing extended memory for the Windows global heap. To facilitate the creation of a smaller disk cache, the Microsoft disk cache, SMARTDRV, allows the user to specify a minimum and maximum cache size on its command line. SMARTDRV provides an application programming interface (API) for adjusting these values dynamically. WIN.COM uses this API to shrink the SMARTDRV cache down to its minimum size before starting the protected mode portion of Windows. WIN.COM starts this process by attempting to open the DOS file SMARTAAR, which is the device name that SMARTDRV uses. (DOS device drivers can be opened as files, for example, CON, LPT1, or PRN.) If WIN.COM finds SMARTAAR, it queries its status and modifies it, using IOCTL functions (INT 21h, functions 4402h and 4403h). In order to be compatible with SMARTDRV, other disk caches, such as HyperDisk, have taken to responding to WIN.COM as if they too were SMARTDRV.

WIN.COM counts the number of files in the system file table, using the still undocumented INT 21h, function 52h (Get List of Lists) to find the first block of entries in the system file table. WIN.COM then walks the list of file entry blocks, keeping a running total as it goes. If the total number of file entry blocks is less than 30, WIN.COM displays an error, "Insufficient file handles available; increase file= statement in config.sys to 30 or greater." Windows needs as many file handles—up to 255—as it can get its hands on because Windows can run several programs simultaneously. Each of these programs might want to open up numerous files. Later on, you'll see that KERNEL actually *grows* the number of available file handles. Real operating systems like OS/2 or Windows NT don't have this problem because they don't sit on top of DOS, the way Windows does.

Every time WIN.COM is run, it checks to see if Windows is already running. The initial test for this is with INT 2Fh, function 160Ah (Get Windows Mode). This interrupt subfunction is new for Windows 3.1 and works as follows. WIN.COM hooks INT 2Fh, and when it sees a call to this subfunction, it returns a value in CX that indicates the current Windows mode. If you try to run WIN.COM a second time from inside a DOS box, the first instance of WIN.COM will respond to this interrupt, indicating to the second instance of WIN.COM that Windows is already running. Under Windows 3.0, this check wasn't made, so it was possible to start another real mode copy of Windows while running in a DOS box. If there is no response to the INT 2Fh, function 160Ah subfunction call, the code falls back to the INT 2Fh calls that were present in Windows 3.0. INT 2Fh, function 1600h tests for Enhanced mode operation, while INT 2Fh, function 4680h detects Real and Standard modes. In addition, INT 2Fh, function 4B02h checks for the presence of the DOS 5 task switcher. If responses to any of these subfunction calls indicate Windows is loaded, WIN.COM refuses to load Windows again.

WIN.COM looks for the presence of network software. First, it examines the interrupt 5Ch vector to see if it is nonzero. If the vector is nonzero, WIN.COM generates an INT 5Ch (NetBIOS interface), with ES:BX pointing to a Network Control Block (NCB). The first byte in the buffer, the command code, is set to 7Fh (a NetBIOS invalid command code). A return code of anything besides 3 (the NetBios invalid-command error code) indicates that something besides NetBIOS has taken over the interrupt.

Most important, WIN.COM uses INT 21h, function 4Bh (EXEC) to load the DPMI servers that Windows is based upon. In Standard mode, WIN.COM spawns WSWAP.EXE, the Standard mode task switcher, which is very similar to the DOS 5.0 DOSSHELL task switcher. WSWAP in turn loads DOSX.EXE, the Standard mode DPMI host and DOS extender. DOSX then runs either KRNL286.EXE or KRNL386.EXE, which switches the machine into protected mode, and sets up the Windows environment. In Enhanced mode, WIN.COM runs WIN386.EXE, which in turn loads KRNL386.EXE. We'll come back to the task switchers in a moment.

Besides the chore of checking out the system in preparation for running protected mode Windows, WIN.COM, along with WSWAP.EXE in Standard mode, remains behind to mind the real mode store. The most obvious use of WIN.COM is to assist Windows in restarting itself after exiting. (See the SDK documentation for ExitWindows (EW_RESTARTWINDOWS)). For example, an install program may wish to exit Windows, run a DOS program, and then start up Windows again (ExitWindowsExec()).

How does WIN.COM assist in this process of restarting Windows? Exiting Windows causes a series of program terminations, which eventually culminates in the completion of the INT 21h, function 4Bh (EXEC) that WIN.COM performed to start the ball rolling. It is a simple matter for WIN.COM to check the return (exit) code from the EXEC. An exit code of 0x42 (0x42 is the value of EW_RESTARTWINDOWS, or the answer to life, the universe, and everything) alerts WIN.COM to execute the appropriate program again. An exit code of 0x44 tells WIN.COM to first execute the program specified in the ExitWindowsExec() call and then restart Windows.

How does WIN.COM get that other program's filename? Simple. WIN.COM hooks INT 2Fh, and when it sees a 4B20h subfunction code, it returns the address of a buffer inside WIN.COM. When WIN.COM sees a return code of 0x44 from the INT 21h, function 4Bh call that started protected mode Windows, WIN.COM uses the contents of the buffer as a program name that it should run. Thus, the code for ExitWindowsExec() simply calls INT 2Fh, function 4B20h, and copies the passed filename into the real mode buffer that's returned by WIN.COM. It then exits Windows (KERNEL) with an exit code of 0x44. Pseudocode for this process looks like this:

```
// -- In real mode WIN.COM --

    INT 21h, fn. 4Bh to start WIN386 or WSWAP. This interrupt
    doesn't return until KERNEL shuts down.

// - In protected mode KERNEL (ExitWindowsExec) --

    Invoke INT 2Fh, fn. 4B20h. When it returns, the registers
    contain the address of a real mode buffer. Copy the
    filename to execute in real mode into the buffer.
```

```
// - In INT 2Fh handler of real mode WIN.COM --

    Receive INT 2F, fn. 4B20h. Return the address of a buffer
    in a register pair.

// - In real mode WIN.COM --

    Return from INT 21h, fn. 4Bh. Examine the return code. If
    it's 42h, exec WIN386 or WSWAP again. If it's 44h, exec
    the filename in the buffer, then exec WIN386
    or WSWAP again.
```

In addition to providing support for restarting Windows, the INT 2Fh handler that WIN.COM installs performs other useful tasks. There are actually two different INT 2Fh handlers in WIN.COM. Depending on which mode Windows will run in, WIN.COM installs one handler or the other. In Enhanced mode, the INT 2Fh handler processes subfunctions 160Ah and 4B20h, both discussed previously.

When WIN.COM starts Windows in Standard mode, the INT 2Fh handler deals with the above two subfunctions and adds a few more as well. For instance, INT 2Fh provides the 4A05h subfunction as an interface to the Standard mode task switcher. The 4B06h subfunction gives an entry point for a function that can manipulate DOS memory control blocks (MCBs) in real mode. For a further discussion of these subfunctions, see Geoff Chappell's forthcoming book, *DOS Internals.*

The last bits of the WIN.COM startup to discuss are the swappers. To support the DOS 5 task switching interface (see Microsoft's *MS-DOS Programmer's Reference*), Standard mode Windows uses two programs, WSWAP and DSWAP, both which are remarkably free of any sort of documentation. Some good old trial and error experimentation yields the following observations:

- WIN.COM loads WSWAP.EXE for Standard mode. If WIN.COM can't find the program, it displays an error message to the effect of, "can't find executable," and returns to a DOS prompt.
- You can rename WSWAP and still run Standard mode if, rather than running WIN.COM, you invoke SYSTEM\DOSX.EXE directly (described below). Once in Standard mode however, you can't run a DOS box. You receive a dialog box with the message, "Standard-mode switcher is not running. Cannot start application."
- DSWAP *appears* to run as part of the startup of the Standard mode DOS box. You can rename DSWAP so that startup can't find it, and still start Windows in Standard mode. However if you try to start a DOS box, the screen switches to text mode and shows you the faintest glimmer of a prompt before the screen switches back to Windows. Windows generates no error messages in this situation.

The Next Step: Loading the DPMI Hosts

At this point, WIN.COM has determined that there's a suitable CPU, that Windows isn't already running and that XMS services are present. WIN.COM has done its preflight checkout of the system and has decided that all systems are GO! It now loads the appropriate DPMI host program.

DPMI is not a DOS extender. Instead, DPMI is a set of services that DOS extenders can use to coexist. DPMI provides core memory management, interrupt and exception handling, and real/protected mode transitions for DOS extenders that adhere to the DPMI specification. (See Chapter 2 for more detail.) In the case of Windows, there are actually two layers of DOS extenders resting on top of the DPMI services. DOSX.EXE and WIN386.EXE provide the DPMI services, hence the term DPMI host. In addition, DOSX and WIN386 also have DOS extender portions. These DOS extenders take care of things like switching back and forth between real and protected mode in order to pass things to DOS. They provide reasonable default handling for the various INT 21h calls that a protected mode program might make. On top of this layer rest KRNL286 and KRNL386, which are the 286 and 386 versions of the Windows KERNEL. These programs selectively handle exceptions and interrupt calls that KERNEL needs to handle differently than the default DOSX/WIN386 handlers would. You can think of this selective handling as a form of subclassing, or in Object-Oriented Programming (OOP) parlance, derivation.

It's important to note that DPMI is not tied to Windows, although it came about as a result of needing a more flexible and secure environment for DOS extenders under Windows than VCPI could provide. WIN386 and DOSX are the most prominent examples of DPMI hosts, but there are numerous other DPMI implementations as well. Current versions of 386MAX from Qualitas are DPMI hosts, as is QDPMI for use with QEMM386, from Quarterdeck. The Borland language compilers ship with a DPMI server (DPMI16BI.OVL) since some of the tools run only in protected mode. And don't forget OS/2 2.0 and Windows NT, which provide DPMI services in their DOS boxes.

As mentioned earlier, one of the tasks of WIN.COM is to determine which DPMI host to run. The algorithm WIN.COM uses is simple: If the machine is a 386 with 2Mb or more of memory, WIN.COM selects WIN386 as the DPMI host. If the machine is a 286, or if it has less than 2Mb of memory, then WIN.COM selects DOSX. You can force the selection of DOSX as the DPMI host by using /S or /2 on the WIN.COM command line. An important point to remember here is that it is not whether Windows 3.1 uses KRNL286 or KRNL386 that determines which mode Windows 3.1 runs in. Instead, it's which DPMI host Windows uses, WIN386.EXE for Enhanced mode or DOSX.EXE for Standard mode. Under Windows 3.0, the story is different because Standard mode Windows 3.0 always used KRNL286, even on 386 machines.

Both DOSX and WIN386 start out executing as real mode programs, doing whatever initialization needs to be done and then invoking the appropriate Windows KRNLx86 file *while still in real mode* (in Enhanced mode, it is actually virtual-8086 mode). Under Windows 3.1, the switch to protected mode occurs inside the KRNLx86 files and is one of the highlights of our later tour through the KRNLx86 startup sequence. In Windows 3.0, KRNLx86 began life already running in protected mode.

On an 80286, DOSX uses INT 21h, function 4Bh to load KRNL286. On a 386, DOSX first tries to load KRNL386. If unsuccessful, DOSX tries again, using KRNL286. WIN386, on the other hand, only loads KRNL386, and aborts if it cannot find the file. For the remainder of this chapter, KRNLx86 refers to both KRNL286 and KRNL386.

It is easy to prove the above assertions with a couple of experiments. First, to see that WIN.COM really does in fact run WIN386 or (eventually) DOSX, go to the WINDOWS directory (for example, C:\WINDOWS). Try running Windows in either Standard or Enhanced mode by giving the command SYSTEM\DOSX.EXE or SYSTEM\WIN386.EXE, respectively. No need to run WIN.COM anymore, right? Not so fast. Using SYSTEM\DOSX.EXE to start Windows prevents you from running a DOS box once you're in Windows. Why? Because this command bypassed the loading of WSWAP by WIN.COM.

To prove that DOSX first tries to load KRNL386 before settling for KRNL286, rename KRNL286 to something else temporarily (this experiment assumes you have at least a 386). Then, run SYSTEM\DOSX.EXE. Windows loads normally. Now run HEAPWALK, or a program that lists system modules, such as WINMOD from the book *Undocumented Windows* (Schulman, Pietrek, Maxey, Addison-Wesley, 1992), and note that KRNL386 has run, rather than KRNL286. To prove that DOSX settles for running KRNL286, on the other hand, just restore the renamed KRNL286 to its original name; then rename KRNL386 to something else. Running SYSTEM\DOSX.EXE still works, but notice that KRNL286 is now the KERNEL file, rather than KRNL386. Who cares? Well, this is the only way to test your programs under 286-style Standard mode in Windows 3.1 without a 286 machine.

Finally, to show that there's no special magic between the DPMI host and KRNLx86 (besides DPMI services), temporarily rename KRNL286 and KRNL386. Then, copy another program to the WINDOWS\SYSTEM directory (COMMAND.COM does nicely) and rename that file KRNL386.EXE. Last, run WIN.COM. Your program should run just as if it were run from the DOS prompt. But running COMMAND.COM, or the DOS shell of your choice, this way gives it DPMI services!

If WIN386 and DOSX are both DPMI hosts, what's the difference between them? DOSX weighs in at around 32K, while WIN386 takes up somewhere in the neighborhood of 530K. The key difference is that DOSX is predominantly a DPMI server and a minimal DOS extender, with very little code devoted to other things. Microsoft claims that there are only seven DPMI functions that DOSX supports. Don't you believe it. The fact is, DOSX is almost a complete DPMI 0.9 implementation. It lacks the ability to do paged virtual memory, so it's not as complete as WIN386. However, DOSX does support enough of the DPMI specification so that KRNL386 can run on top of it.

The roughly 500K difference between DOSX and WIN386 can't all be due to code for supporting virtual memory, can it? Luckily, the answer is no. The vast majority of WIN386 consists of virtual device drivers (VxDs) and support of multiple DOS sessions on the same CPU.

The real mode DOS stub of WIN386 switches into protected mode after loading all the VxDs. After the VxDs load, the stub jumps to the Windows Virtual Machine Manager (VMM), which begins execution in protected mode. In addition to managing the virtual machines, the VMM is also where the Enhanced mode DPMI server code resides. Both KRNL286 and KRNL386 in Windows 3.1 start out running in real mode and must call

DPMI to switch into protected mode. How then, does the CPU switch back to real mode before loading KRNLx86?

It doesn't. As it turns out, the Virtual Machine Manager creates a virtual 8086 (V86) session, which *simulates* real mode. This session is called the System Virtual Machine (VM). A VM is a virtual 8086 session as implemented on 80386s and higher. All Windows programs run in the same virtual machine, the System VM. Each DOS session started within Windows in Enhanced mode runs in its own distinct VM.

Once VMM has created the System VM, it runs the WINSTART.BAT file. Afterwards, it runs KRNL386 just like any other real mode program, though it is in fact running in V86 mode. Since this book focuses on the 16-bit code in the Windows DLLs (KERNEL, USER, and GDI), the book doesn't cover WIN386 or VxDs any further, except in passing. VxDs are extremely important, but it's not necessary to go into the details of VxDs to understand how Windows starts itself up. For the purposes of this book, DOSX and WIN386 are functionally equivalent. The book ignores the incredible wealth of additional functionality in WIN386. For those interested in VxDs, there's no substitute for having the Microsoft Windows Device Driver Kit (DDK), although books and articles on VxDs are slowly coming forth. Look for Dan Norton's book, *Writing Windows Device Drivers* (Addison-Wesley, 1992).

The Fun Begins: Loading the KERNEL Module

At this juncture, the DPMI server has done the required initialization. If WIN386 is running, it has set up a virtual machine and initialized the VMM.

With the DOS extender and virtual machine initialization out of the way, WIN386 or DOSX loads the KERNEL module into memory. The remainder of this chapter focuses on what goes on in the KRNLx86 file as it builds the Windows environment from just some real mode code and DPMI services.

In Windows 3.0, the DPMI host switches the CPU into protected mode before the code in KRNLx86 begins running. In Windows 3.1, the KERNEL module begins execution in real (or V86) mode. Even though the two KRNLx86 files look like New Executable (NE) files (see Chapter 3 on modules) and quack like NE files, they are not loaded like normal NE files. If you think about it, the KERNEL module provides NE loading services for the other Windows modules through the WinExec() and LoadModule() APIs. How can it load itself? There must be an NE loader in the DPMI hosts, right? Not so. The process just involves some bootstrap code.

In all NE files, there is a real mode *stub* program that precedes the actual new executable portion of the file. In most programs, the stub program just prints out a message like, "This program requires Microsoft Windows." The stub programs in the KRNLx86 files are completely different. Simply put, in Windows 3.1, KRNL286 and KRNL386 begin life as ordinary, real mode DOS programs. This point should be emphasized again because it is critical to understanding the early stages of Windows' bootstraps activity. *The DOS loader loads KRNL286 and KRNL386,* which begin execution as DOS programs. In fact, rumor has it that a non-Windows DPMI server, which can handle all the DPMI functions that WIN386 handles (including the undocumented and obsolete ones), makes it possible to run KRNL386 directly from the DOS command line without WIN386!

The following pseudocode for the KRNL386 real mode stub shows the first steps of KERNEL's journey to protected mode nirvana. The code uses details of the NE file format. If you're not at least somewhat familiar with the NE format, see the *Programmer's Reference, Volume 4: Resources* in the Windows 3.1 Software Development Kit (SDK). In the following example, notice how the DOS MZ portion of KRNL386.EXE (all DOS executables have an 'MZ' signature, the initials of Microsoft's legendary Mark Zbikowski) loads the Windows NE portion of the same file.

```
pseudocode for the KRNL386 real mode loader
// Locals:
//      NEW_EXE *ne_ptr          // points at KRNL386's 'NE' header
//      WORD    DGROUP_index     // Index of the DGROUP segment
//      WORD    *DGROUP_segtable_ptr
//      WORD    DGROUP_sector    // Sector offset of DGROUP start
//      WORD    EntrySeg_index   // Index of the entry point segment
//      WORD    *EntrySeg_segtable_ptr
//      WORD    EntrySeg_sector // Sector offset of entry segment

    // The real mode stub "loader" has its load image size set
    // in the DOS 'MZ' header to a value large enough to cause
    // the entire KRNLx86.EXE file to be read into memory.
    // Thus, execution begins with the contents of the entire
    // KRNLx86.EXE file residing in a DOS memory block.

    // point "ne_ptr" at the 'NE' header read in by the DOS loader
    // (along with everything else in the file). The header should
    // be immediately after the code for this real mode stub.
    ne_ptr = MK_FP(CS, 0x200)

    if ( ne_ptr->ne_magic != 'NE' ) // Found the 'NE' header
        goto LoadingError           // in memory?

    SS = DS             // Point SS:SP at a region after the end of
    SP = 0x0160         // the real mode code. A Temporary stack.

    // Get the segment number of the DGROUP segment out of the
    // 'NE' header. Subtract 1 because segment numbering
    // starts at 1, and we'll be looking up the segment's
    // information in a table that's 0 based.
    DGROUP_index = ne_ptr->ne_autodata - 1

    if ( DGROUP_index )       // Is there a DGROUP segment?
    {
        // Convert DGROUP index to an offset into the segment table
        // (each segment-table entry is 8 bytes).

        DGROUP_segtable_ptr = DGROUP_index << 3
```

```
    // Add in the offset of the segment table itself
    DGROUP_segtable_ptr += ne_ptr->ne_segtab

    // Get the file sector of the DGROUP segment
    DGROUP_sector = DGROUP_segtable_ptr->ns_sector

    // Set alignment shift count to 9 (512) bytes, if none
    // specified in the 'NE' header
    if ( ne_ptr->ne_align == 0 )
        ne_ptr->ne_align = 9

    // Set DI to the paragraph address in memory of the
    // DGROUP segment. Subtract 0x20 from the current CS
    // because the first 0x20 paragraphs (512 bytes) of the
    // file weren't loaded into memory. The first 512 bytes
    // of the file are the old EXE header & fixup table.
    DI = (CS-0x20) + DGROUP_sector << (ne_ptr->ne_align - 4)
}

// Now start the process of finding the entry point
// segment, which is just the initial CS value given in the
// header of the 'NE' file. See DGROUP segment above for
// why we subtract 1.
EntrySeg_index = FP_SEG( ne_ptr->ne_csip ) - 1

if ( EntrySeg_index < 0 )  // There must be an entry point
    goto LoadingError

// Convert EntrySeg index to an offset in the segment table
EntrySeg_segtable_ptr = EntrySeg_index << 3

// Add in the offset of the segment table itself
EntrySeg_segtable_ptr += ne_ptr->ne_segtab

// Get the file sector of the EntrySeg segment
EntrySeg_sector = EntrySeg_segtable_ptr->ns_sector

// Point DX at the paragraph address in memory of the
// EntrySeg segment. See above for the (CS-0x20) term.
DX = (CS-0x20) + EntrySeg_sector << (ne_ptr->ne_align - 4)

// Push the entry point address (from the 'NE' header) onto
// the stack. Note: the address put on the stack is an actual,
// real mode address. Then, set up the DS segment to point
// at the DGROUP segment (as loaded by DOS).
```

```
    PUSH     DX
    PUSH     FP_OFF( ne_ptr->ne_csip )

    DS = DI      // Point DS at the DGROUP segment (see above)
    CX = ne_ptr + 0x200      // CX = offset of 'NE' header in file

    // Put a signature word in AX, and RETF, thereby causing
    // execution to transfer to the 'NE' file entry point. We're
    // still running in real mode at this point.
    mov      AX, 4B4Fh              // 4B4Fh -> "OK"
    RETF                            // "JMP" to KERNEL Entry point

LoadingError:

    INT 21h, fn. 9, to print out: "KERNSTUB: Error during boot"

    INT 21h, fn. 4C, AL =1. Terminate with exit code 1.
```

Notice that the program uses the DOS loader as a convenient mechanism for bringing the entire KRNL386 file into memory. The DOS loader blindly reads NE fixups, padding, debug information, in fact, *everything* into memory before transferring control to the stub at the beginning of the code. The stub program has some smarts and knows where to find the NE header amongst the raw image. The stub can therefore do some calculations, based on knowledge of the NE format, and find the location of the Windows portion's entry point, as specified in the NE header. Besides the entry point, the stub also calculates where the KERNEL data segment was loaded and sets DS to point at that paragraph. Finally, the stub transfers control to the real NE header entry point, which will be known hereafter as BootStrap.

The KERNEL BootStrap() Routine

After receiving control from the KRNLx86 stub loader, the BootStrap() routine has a real mode code segment in CS, a real mode data segment in DS, and a small stack. Keeping in mind that Windows is still running in real mode, see Figure 1-1 for the layout of memory at this time.

Figure 1-1: The Low Memory Layout, Real Mode.

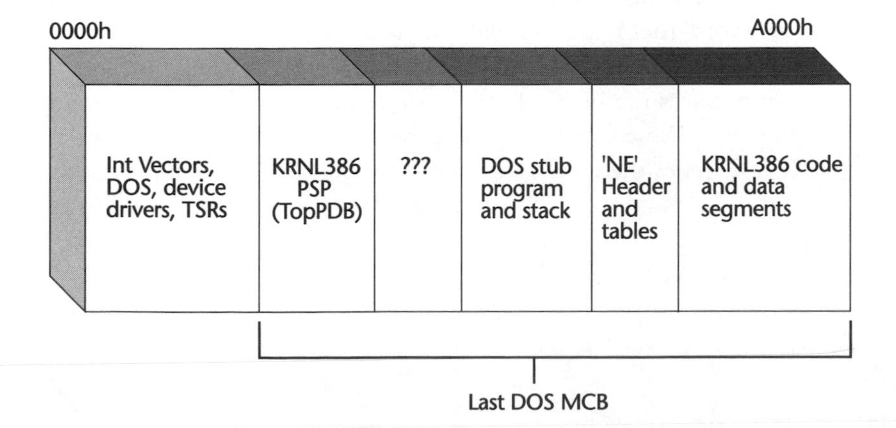

It's now time for KERNEL to go out into the real (or should we say, protected?) world and make its fortune. The BootStrap() routine is quite large in scope, and calls a few interesting functions that we will want to examine. Thus, the BootStrap() pseudocode is broken up into manageable chunks that we'll discuss individually. The first section of BootStrap() is as follows:

```
pseudocode for BootStrap() - LDBOOT.OBJ

    if (debug KERNEL)
        if ( real INT 68h vector != 0 )
        {
            ES:SI = "Windows Kernel Entry\r\n"
            INT 68h, AH = 47H    // Tell the KERNEL debugger that
        }                        // we're starting up

    if ( AX != 0x4B4F )          // Verify the signature word (from
    {                            // WIN.COM) in AX, and abort if not
        AX = 0                   //  "OK". 0x4B4F = "OK"
        RETF
    }

    MyCSSeg = CS    // Store the real mode CS & DS values into
    MyDSSeg = DS    // MyCSSeg & MyDSSeg (KERNEL global variables)

    SwitchToPmode() // Switch into protected mode via DPMI
```

First the BootStrap() routine informs the system level debugger, such as WDEB386 or Soft-ICE/W, that the KERNEL BootStrap() routine is running. This procedure only occurs with the debugging versions of KERNEL and presumably allows the system debugger to stop very early on in the KERNEL initialization. The interface for this procedure uses INT 68h.

The real mode stub portion of KERNEL sets AX to a special value, the characters for "OK". KERNEL now checks the value in AX to see if it contains this value, a form of validity testing that ensures the KERNEL stub code executed properly. For instance, this test prevents problems when curious people run the Windows File Manager and double click on the KRNL386 file to see what happens.

Next, the BootStrap() routine saves the original real mode values of CS and DS into variables in the KERNEL data segment. These values will be needed later. With this very minimal setup out of the way, KERNEL switches the CPU into protected mode and improves its lot in life by an order of magnitude:

```
pseudocode for SwitchToPMode() - 3PROTECT.OBJ
// Locals
// LPFN    LpProc()    // A utility function pointer

    INT 2Fh, AX = 1687  // DPMI get entry point address

    if ( AX != 0 )      // Couldn't get DPMI entry point
        goto NoPMode

    if ( CL < 3 )       // Is it at least a 386?
        goto NoPMode    // CL < 2 for KRNL286.EXE

    if ( CL == 3 )              // Set the WinFlags global
        WinFlags = WF_CPU386    // to an appropriate value
    else                        // See GetWinFlags() API.
        WinFlags = WF_CPU486    // What about Pentium aka P5 aka 586?

    LpProc = ES:DI  // ES:DI is DPMI "switch to pmode" addr from 2F/1687

    // The DPMI spec says that ES points to a real mode buffer
    // for DPMI host's private data. Apparently the first portion
    // of the program (after the PSP) will be used as the buffer.
    // SI contains the number of paragraphs need for the host
    ES = (PSP at KERNEL entry + 10h )
    SI = (PSP at KERNEL entry + 10h ) + SI  // First segment after
                                            // DPMI host buffer

    AX = 0  // Windows is a 16 bit program. Bit 0 on for 32 bit program

    LpProc()    // Call the DPMI "switch to protected mode entry
                // point. When we return, we're in protected
                // mode (if everything went according to plan!)

    if ( carry flag set after call )
        goto NoPMode    // Still in real mode. Time to complain

    // From this point on, we're running in protected mode. The
    // DPMI host has graciously provided us with selectors that
    // we can use while setting up shop in protected mode.

    if ( bottom 3 bits of CS != 7 ) // Our selector must be a ring
        goto DPMI_is_screwy         // 3 selector in the Local
                                    // Descriptor Table (LDT)
    BX = CS       // Create a writeable DS alias for the read-only CS segment
    AX = 000Ah    // and store away in MyCSAlias
    MyCSAlias = DPMIProc()  // A wrapper around an INT 31h call
```

```
// Use the newly created writeable CS alias to store the DS value (from
// DPMI) into a variable in the protected mode code segment.

BX = DS             // Save value of DS into BX
DS = MyCSAlias      // Load DS with CS alias
MyCSDS = BX         // Plug MyCSDS variable with the original DS value
DS = BX             // Put the original DS value back

INT 2Fh, fn. 168A, DS:SI = "MS-DOS" // Get DPMI vendor extensions
if ( AL = 8Ah )     // Did the call fail?
    goto DPMI_is_screwy

LpProc = ES:DI      // Save the "Extensions" address. The old
                    // value (the PMode entry point) is lost
AX = 0x100
LpProc()            // Get LDT selector into AX

// If the call succeeded, store away the LDT selector where
// we can get at it later so that we can manipulate the LDT.
// Note that GDTDsc is the selector of the  _LOCAL_
// descriptor table. What a confusing name!!!
// VERW verifies that selector is writeable
if ( Carry flag not set, and VERW AX returns Zero flag )
    GDTDsc = AX

// Convert the start of the usable DOS memory region to a
// linear address for a subsequent DPMI call. A typical
// paragraph address would be 0948h.
// Note use of 32-bit registers (EBX, ESI)

EBX = (First paragraph address after DPMI host buffer) << 4

ESI = ES:block_end << 4 // ES is the PSP block. Convert the
                        // block end value from paragraphs to a
                        // byte offset. The block_end value
                        // is usually A000h.

ESI -= EBX  // Subtract the starting address from the ending
            // address, leaving the block length in ESI
// Mark the region above where Windows starts, to the
// end of DOS memory, as pageable (not locked).
Convert ESI to be in SI:DI  // Put the size in SI:DI
Convert EBX to be in CX:DX  // Put the start address in CX:DX

INT 31h, 0602   // DPMI mark region as pageable.
```

```
    // Get protected-mode selector to real mode (conventional) memory.
    SI = First paragraph address after the DPMI host private data
    INT 31h, AX = 2     // Allocate selector to real mode seg

    SI = AX     // Put "real mode" selector in SI for return

    return to caller

DPMI_is_screwy:     // Only error states come through here

    // There's a static buffer that acts as a DPMI real mode call
    // structure. Here we call it "RealModeCallStruc"
    RealModeCallStruc._DS_ = MyCSSeg
    RealModeCallStruc._ES_ = 0
    RealModeCallStruc._CS_ = MyCSSeg
    RealModeCallStruc._IP_ = do_error_msg_in_real_mode  // Below
    ES:DI = &RealModeCallStruc

    INT 31h, 0301h      // DPMI call real mode procedure

    INT 21h, fn. 4CFFh  // Terminate program

do_error_msg_in_real_mode:  // This executes in real mode via 31/0301!

    DX = KERNEL: "Inadequate DPMI Server\r\n"
    INT 21h, fn. 9      // Print out above error message
    retf                // Return to protected mode caller

NoPMode:    // This executes in real mode!

    DX = KERNEL: "KERNEL: Unable to enter protected mode\r\n"
    INT 21h, fn. 9      // Print out above error message

    INT 21h, fn. 4CFFh  // Terminate program
```

The SwitchToPMode() function does a bit more than its name implies. The code begins by calling the requisite DPMI INT 2Fh, 1687h function to get the address that SwitchToPMode() calls to switch into protected mode. A program can switch into protected mode simply by making a FAR CALL to this address. Besides returning a function pointer, the interrupt returns the CPU type as well. SwitchToPMode() checks the returned CPU type to ensure that Windows is running on at least a 386 and stores the CPU type as the initial value for the WinFlags global variable. As the bootstrapping process continues, it turns on other bits in WinFlags.

INT 2Fh, function 1687h also returns the value for the number of paragraphs the DPMI host needs for a private data area. SwitchToPMode() uses the region starting immediately after KRNL286's or KRNL386's real mode PSP as the data area. You might be thinking that the region right after the PSP is program code and that using the space for the DPMI data area overwrites the code. As it turns out, the KRNLx86 image loads at the very high end of its MCB block through the little known trick of setting to zero both the *min* and *max* paragraphs required fields in KRNLx86's MZ header. Unless the DPMI private data area is truly huge, the start of the KRNLx86 image is safe from being overwritten. Figure 1-1 shows the situation graphically. This function call also calculates and remembers the next available paragraph after the private data area, using it later as the base address of the global heap.

Assuming everything checks out, the SwitchToPMode() function's next step is to make a FAR CALL to the DPMI "switch to protected mode" entry point described above. Although many interesting things go on when switching to protected mode, this section focuses on KERNEL. So just take it on faith that, unless something went wrong inside the DPMI host, the function call completes its task and KERNEL begins running in protected mode. If the DPMI host is able to switch to protected mode, it also changes the CS and DS values, creating protected mode descriptors and selectors. These descriptors map to the same memory locations that CS and DS referenced before the switch to protected mode. In other words, the DPMI host changes CS and DS right out from under the program.

One of the fun things that KERNEL does is store certain global variables in its code segment. In order to write to these variables, KERNEL needs an alias selector for the code segment (remember, Windows is in protected mode now). Very soon after switching into protected mode, SwitchToPMode() creates an alias descriptor for KERNEL's first code segment using DPMI function 000Ah (Create Alias Descriptor). SwitchToPMode() then uses this alias descriptor to store the value of the DS selector into a code segment variable. Now, no matter what happens, KERNEL can gain access to its data segment selector simply by looking up the value in its code segment.

After a relatively wholesome stretch of code that got us into protected mode, the monkey business begins. The DPMI specification allows for vendor-specific extensions to the DPMI servers. In this case, the Microsoft DPMI hosts, DOSX and WIN386, have an extension that allows them to obtain the selector of the protected mode local descriptor table (LDT), a horrifying development from a purist's point of view. The whole point of DPMI was so that DPMI servers would provide a well-rounded API, which would prevent the need for DOS extenders to muck about with extremely sensitive system resources such as the LDT. The DPMI interface purposefully does not give you direct access to the LDT. Here, we have KERNEL willfully violating this rule. Chapter 2 explains in more detail the reasons why the developers at Microsoft did this. In short, the reason was performance. The selector of the LDT is saved into a wonderfully confusing variable called GDTDSC, perhaps named this because the selector of the LDT must be a selector in the Global Descriptor Table (GDT).

Before returning to BootStrap(), assuming things are still going well, SwitchToPMode() calculates the base address and length of the region that starts at the end of the DPMI host area and extends to the end of contiguous DOS memory (for example, A000h). SwitchToPMode() sends this address to the DPMI server as part of a command to mark the region as pageable. Paging is a joint project between the WIN386 memory manager and the

80386 hardware that allows Windows to create virtual memory. Chapter 2 discusses this subject in more detail.

At the end of SwitchToPMode(), an interesting section of code deals with the case in which SwitchToPMode() discovers something wrong only after switching the CPU into protected mode. In this situation, the KERNEL hasn't yet had a chance to initialize all of its DOS extender components. Thus, to print out an error message, it switches back into real mode. INT 31h, function 0301h (DPMI Call Real Mode Procedure with FAR Return Frame) performs this chore. After displaying the error message in real mode, SwitchToPMode() doesn't just terminate the program on the spot. Instead, SwitchToPMode() returns to protected mode and calls INT 21h, function 4C (DOS Exit), in protected mode. This is the only way to prevent the DPMI host from getting completely confused.

```
Continuation of code for BootStrap() - LDBOOT.OBJ

    BaseDsc = SI        // SI contains a selector that references the
                        // region between where KRNL386 was loaded,
                        // and A000h

    LDT_init()          // Initialize the LDT free list, and get some
                        // selectors that KERNEL will use for various
                        // purposes later on.
```

After SwitchToPMode() executes, the SI register in the KERNEL data segment contains a selector that references the large free memory block between the positions of WIN.COM and paragraph A000h. KERNEL will use this selector later to initialize the global heap. After the switch into protected mode, memory below 1Mb looks like Figure 1-2.

Figure 1-2: The Low Memory Layout, Protected Mode.

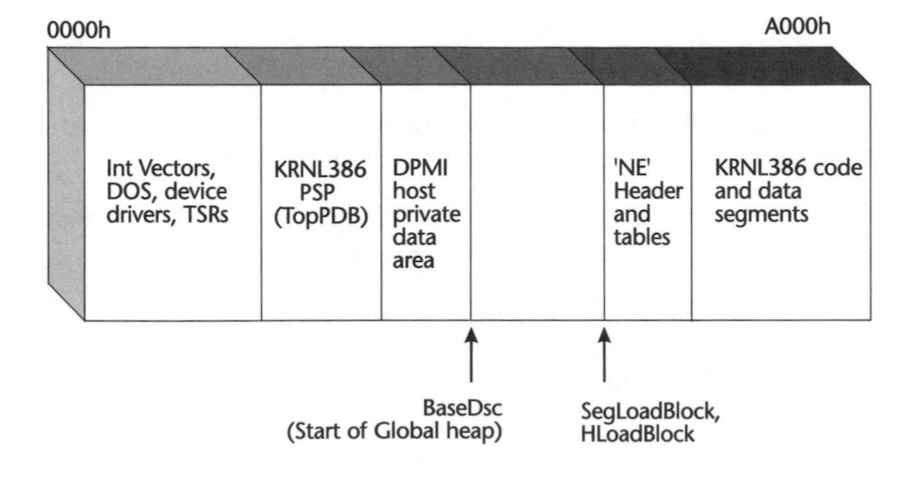

In the LDT_Init() routine KERNEL uses the "illicitly" obtained LDT selector to set up its own private domain in the Local Descriptor Table:

```
pseudocode for LDT_Init() - 3PROTECT.OBJ

    if ( GDTDsc == 0 )                       // If we didn't get the LDT
        goto allocate_kernel_selectors  // selector, we can't play
                                             // with the LDT!

    INT 31h, AX=0, CX = 1           // Allocate 1 selector from DPMI

    AND AL, NOT 8    // Clear out LDT and privilege level bits,
                     // since we're going to use it as a near ptr
                     // into the LDT. Each LDT entry is 8 bytes.

    FirstFreeSel = AX    // Initialize the head ptr of the free
                         // selector list maintained by KERNEL

    SI = AX          // Copy ptr into SI for accessing the LDT

    Turn on bits 16-19 in the limit field of the descriptor
    referenced by FirstFreeSel. This indicates that the selector
    is in use, and should not be allocated again.

    Use LSL to get the limit of the LDT segment into CX

    while ( SI < CX )    // While not at the end of the LDT segment
    {
        SI += 8          // Advance to the next descriptor

        if ( the 8 bytes pointed to by SI are all 0's )
        {
            // The descriptor is free. Take it for ourselves

            Turn on bits 16-19 of the limit field of the
            descriptor pointed to by ES:SI, indicating that it's
            free for use by KERNEL, but not by WIN386

            CountFreeSel++  // Another selector for ourselves!

            Update the "next" field (AKA the "limit" field) of
            the previous free selector to point to the selector
            we just grabbed for ourselves.
        }
    }
```

```
allocate_kernel_selectors:

    CX = 1          // Get_Sel() takes the count parameter in CX

    Get_Sel()       // returns selector value (no Table or
                    // privilege level bits) in SI
    OR  SI, 7       // Turn on the LDT bit and ring level 3 bits
    KR1Dsc = SI     // used as a "utility" descriptor in
                    // MakeProcInstance() / FreeProcInstance()

    Get_Sel()       // Do the same thing for KR2Dsc
    OR  SI, 7       // Turn on the LDT bit and ring level 3 bits
    KR2Dsc = SI     // Seems to be a "utility" descriptor in
                    // Get_Rover_2xx() heap routines

    Get_Sel()       // Do the same thing for BlotDsc
    OR  SI, 7       // Turn on the LDT bit and ring level 3 bits
    BlotDsc = SI    // used to zero out allocated memory blocks

    Get_Sel()       // Do the same thing for DemandLoadSel
    OR  SI, 7       // Turn on the LDT bit and ring level 3 bits
    DemandLoadSel=SI // Demand loading of not present segments
```

LDT_Init() initializes the local descriptor table by checking every descriptor, looking for entries that are all zeros. This function adds each free descriptor it finds to a linked list of free descriptors. Since each descriptor has a bit which indicates if it's in use or not, the fields of a descriptor that would normally be used for things like the segment limits are available for use by the operating system. In this case, the lower 16 bits of the limit field serve as a 16-bit offset to the next free descriptor. As described in Chapter 2 on memory management, various routines in KERNEL use the free list to grab a selector, rather than always allocating from the slower DPMI services.

After tweaking the LDT to its liking, LDT_Init() wastes no time in using the LDT. LDT_Init() calls the Get_Sel() routine (see Chapter 2) several times to obtain permanent utility selectors that KERNEL uses for various things, such as code segments for demand loading.

The next portion of the BootStrap() process relates to KERNEL debugging support:

```
Continuation of code for BootStrap() - LDBOOT.OBJ

    DebugInit()     // Look for a system level debugger

    // Tell the KERNEL debugger about the CS and DS segment
    DebugDefineSegment("KERNEL", 0, CS, 0, 0 )
    DebugDefineSegment("KERNEL", 3, DS, 0, 1 )
```

The DebugInit() function (see the pseudocode on the following page) looks for the presence of a system-level debugger, such as WDEB386 or Soft-ICE/W, and sets some internal bits accordingly. The two DebugDefineSegment() calls tell the debugger about the presence of the first KERNEL code segment and the KERNEL data segment by using the INT 41h interface. This interface is virtually identical to the RegisterPtrace() and ToolhelpHook() notifications described in Chapter 5 of *Undocumented Windows.*

```
pseudocode for DebugInit() - LDDEBUG.OBJ

    int 41h, AX = 4Fh
    if ( AX == 0F386h ) // AX set to 0F386h if debugger present
    {
        Increment a static variable used in DebugSysReq()
        Turn on bit 0x0008 of [Kernel_Flags + 2]
    }
```

```
Continuation of code for BootStrap() - LDBOOT.OBJ

    if ( !InitDosVarP() )   // If couldn't initialize, abort
    {
        KOutDSstr("KERNEL: InitDosVarP failed");
        AX = 0x4CFF             //Terminate with exit code 0xFF
        INT 21h
    }
```

BootStrap() now turns its attention toward the task of poking around in DOS to obtain and save critical values. At the same time, BootStrap() saves the original vectors for the interrupts that KERNEL manages on a per-task basis. The following pseudocode is ample evidence that Windows really does rest on top of DOS. The code also demonstrates that the Microsoft programmers use many of the same tricks that the rest of the programming world has to find out about in books like *Undocumented DOS*:

```
pseudocode for InitDosVarP() - DOSINIT.OBJ

    // On entry, ES contains a selector for the PSP of KRNL386.EXE
    // TopPDB and HeadPDB are heavily used KERNEL variables.
    // In Windows, a PDB is the same thing as a PSP. Chapter 3
    // covers this in detail.

    TopPDB = HeadPDB = ES

    ES:[0042] = 0   // Offset 42h in the PSP is not documented

    Cur_DOS_PDB = Win_PDB = ES  // Save PSP in a few more places.

    CurDTA = ES:80h     // Save the current Disk Transfer Area
```

```
INT 21h, AX = 3300h // Get Ctrl-C state into DL
FBreak = DL         // ...and remember it for later

// Set Ctrl-C & Ctrl-Bk handling to only check console funcs.
INT 21h, AX = 3301, DL = 0

INT 21h, AH = 34h       // Get InDOS pointer into ES:BX
InDOS = ES:BX

INT 21h, AH = 19h       // Get current drive into AL
CurDOSDrive = AL

DL = AL                 // Log into the current drive
INT 21h, AH = 0Eh       // Gets number of drives (LASTDRIVE) in AL
DOSDrives = AL

INT 21h, AX = 3521h     // Get INT 21h vector into ES:BX
PrevInt21Proc = ES:BX   // Windows calls through this often,
                        // rather than using INT 21h.

// Use our new method of calling DOS ( PrevInt21Proc() ) to
// save off the original values of some other INT handlers
// that will be changed. Each of these interrupts, with the
// exception of 2Fh, is managed on a per-task basis. Each
// Windows task can set these vectors, with the resulting
// handler address being stored in its Task Database.
// Interrupts not in this list (as well as INT 2Fh), are
// handled by the standard, system wide interrupt handlers.
PrevInt02Proc = PrevInt21Proc(AX = 3502h),  // NMI
PrevInt04Proc = PrevInt21Proc(AX = 3504h),  // INTO
PrevInt06Proc = PrevInt21Proc(AX = 3506h),  // Invalid Opcode
PrevInt07Proc = PrevInt21Proc(AX = 3507h),  // No 80x87
PrevInt3EProc = PrevInt21Proc(AX = 353Eh),  // 80x87 emulator
PrevInt75Proc = PrevInt21Proc(AX = 3575h),  // 80x87 error
PrevInt2FProc = PrevInt21Proc(AX = 352Fh),  // Multiplex

INT 21h, AH = 0DCh  // Novell Get Station # in AL. Nonzero
FNovell = AL        // if running under Novell. This flag
                    // affects how file opens are performed.

INT 21h, AH = 30h   // Get DOS version # in AL:AH. There are
                    // more accurate ways to get the version
                    // number, such as INT 21h, fn. 3306h

// This next section is related to finding the size of an
// entry in the System File Table (SFT). Since this value
```

```
    // changes from version to version of DOS, the following
    // code is fairly convoluted, and goes to some lengths
    // to deal with the case of Windows running atop OS/2.
    // We want to know the size of an SFT entry so that we can
    // grow the system file table. Typically, a user running DOS
    // only needs to have 30-40 file handles available. When you
    // start multitasking applications like Windows does, the need
    // for available file handles can increase dramatically.

    // The first step is to make sure we're running on at least
    // DOS 3.1.
    if ( AL > 10 )                  // OS/2 1.X returns 10
        goto store_DOS_version      // OS/2 2.0 returns 20
                                    // NT returns 30

    if ( AL > 4 )    // DOS version > 4.0?
        goto store_DOS_version

    if ( (AL < 3) || (AH = 10) ) // Windows requires at least 3.1
        goto incorrect_DOS_version  // Abort now if this isn't so

store_DOS_version:  // We get here if the DOS version is O.K.

    DOS_Version = AL, DOS_Revision = AH     // Global variables

    BX = 0      // Default file entry size is 0 ("Don't know")

    if  (DOS_Version >= 10 )    // Can't do anything for OS/2
        goto Store_FileEntrySize

    if ( DOS_Version == 3 )
    {
        BX = 56         // File entry size is 56 bytes
        if ( AH == 0 )  // DOS 3.0???
            goto Store_FileEntrySize

        BX = 53         // File entry size is 53 bytes
        if ( AH <= 31 ) // DOS 3.31 and below???
            goto Store_FileEntrySize
    }

    // Get the file entry size by poking around in DOS. DOS
    // versions > 3.31 come through this code. GetFileSize()
    // is a function that opens the CON file
    // several times, then searches through memory looking for
    // successive "CON" strings. The difference between
    // successive "CON"s is the SFT entry size. Brrrr!!!!!
```

```
    BX = GetFileSize( AX )  // Pass the DOS version.
    if ( BX == -1 )
        goto incorrect_DOS_version

Store_FileEntrySize:

    FileEntrySize = BX  // Used to grow the number of system file
                        // table entries. Used by GrowSFTToMax().

    AX = -1
    return to caller

incorrect_DOS_version:

    INT 21h, AH = 9, DX =          // DOS writes to standard output.
    "Incorrect MS-DOS version. MS-DOS 3.1 or greater required.\r\n"

    AX = 0
    return to caller
```

After InitDOSVarp() finishes, BootStrap() resumes execution and sets some more general purpose global variables:

```
Continuation of code for BootStrap() - LDBOOT.OBJ

    // We start out this section by setting some more flags in
    // the WinFlags global variable ( See GetWinFlags() API )

    INT 11h                     // Get Equipment List bits into AX
    if ( bit 1 set in AX )      // This is not the most reliable way
    {                           // to check for an 80x87!
        turn on WF_80x87 flag in WinFlags
    }

    INT 2Fh, AX = 1600  // Enhanced mode installation check

    if ( AL == 3 )
    {
        turn on bit 0x0100 of Kernel_Flags
        turn on WF_PMODE and WF_ENHANCED bits in WinFlags
    }
    else
    {
        turn on bit 0x0020 of [Kernel_Flags+2]
        turn on WF_PMODE and WF_STANDARD bits in WinFlags
    }
```

```
// Initialize WOAname[] with the name of the program that
// will be used to create and manage DOS applications. WOA=WinOldAp.
if ( running under Standard mode )
    strcpy(WOAname, "WINOLDAP.MOD");      // in 3.0, WINOA286.MOD
else
    strcpy(WOAname, "WINOA386.MOD")
```

The next step is for BootStrap() to start getting its memory act together.

```
Continuation of code for BootStrap() - LDBOOT.OBJ

    // Get a selector for the memory that starts at the current
    // SS:SP. This selector is called the SegLoadBlock selector.
    // At the SS:SP, it seems you will find the 'NE' header
    // of KRNL386.EXE that was read in by the DOS loader. This
    // happened when all of KRNL386.EXE was loaded into memory
    // earlier. Later on, the SegLoadBlock selector will be used
    // to reference the values in the KRNL386.EXE 'NE' header so
    // that a "proper" Windows module table can be built for it.
    DX:AX = Get_Physical_Address( SS ) + SP
    SegLoadBlock = Alloc_Data_Sel(DX:AX, 0FFFFh)

    A sequence of steps related to creating a new SS selector,
    and switching stacks around. The "GMove" stack, which is
    a small KERNEL stack, comes into play here.

    // It's now time to initialize the global heap
    AX = BaseDsc                // Selector for region between the
                                // KRNL386 load point & A000h.
    BX = SegLoadBlock           // Block used to access 'NE' header
    CX = TopPDB.end_of_block    // Offset 2 in the PSP. TopPDB
    DX = 0x200                  // was set in InitDosVarP()

    GlobalInit( DX, BX, AX, CX )    // See Chapter 2

    if ( GlobalInit() returned with carry flag set or AX == 0)
    {
        INT 21h, fn. 9, to print out:
            "KERNEL: Unable to initialize heap\r\n"

        INT 21h, fn. 4Ch, AL = FFh. //Exit with error code FFh
    }

    HLoadBlock = AX // AX returned from GlobalInit(). This is the
                    // handle associated with the SegLoadBlock
                    // selector, which points to the 'NE' header
                    // for KRNL386 in memory.
```

The preceding portion of BootStrap() starts out by calculating where the NE header is in memory. Remember, the DOS loader loaded it along with KRNLx86. BootStrap() then assigns a selector to the region where the NE header starts. Later on, KERNEL officially loads its segments using the standard NE loader mechanisms that load regular Windows EXEs and DLLs. The selector pointing to the NE header is a sort of foundation that the BootStrap() code builds everything else upon. After finding the NE header, the code switches stacks away from the stack that was in use when KERNEL started up. The new stack is a small stack within the KERNEL data segment.

Things are now sufficiently set up and stabilized that the GlobalInit() function can initialize the global heap. Chapter 2 on memory management gives the pseudocode for GlobalInit(). When GlobalInit() returns, it has established the global heap, which encompasses the conventional memory region between the KRNL386.EXE PSP and the end of the contiguous DOS memory (typically, paragraph 0A000h). Memory allocated by GlobalDOSAlloc() comes from this region. As KERNEL allocates more memory from the global heap, the global heap code starts allocating additional memory from the DPMI server. GlobalInit() marks the region starting with the NE header as an in-use block, so that it doesn't get overwritten while in use. The global heap handle for the block is saved into the global variable HLoadBlock.

```
Continuation of code for BootStrap() - LDBOOT.OBJ
// Locals:
// OFSTRUCT KernelOFStruct      // An OFSTRUCT
// WORD    Final_CS, Final_DS  // protected mode selectors

    PExitProc = CS:ExitKernel  // Set up the KERNEL exit fn. ptr

    Scan though the environment of TopPDB, looking for the double
    0's. The double 0's indicate the end of the environment, and
    the start of the complete path for the program (KRNLx86.EXE
    in this case). If success, DS:SI point at KRNL386 path
    at the end of the environment.

    Get_WinDir()       // Scans through the KRNL386 environment,
                       // looking for the string "windir=". The
                       // environment variable was put there by
                       // either DOSX or WIN386.

    if ( Get_WinDir() returned DI != 0 )
    {
        LpWindowsDir = ES:DI // Found it!!!  Now remember it.
        CBytesWinDir = CX    // length of Windows dir string

        copy LpWindowsDir to SZUserPro, then add on "\WIN.INI"
    }
```

```
// Try to open the KRNL386.EXE file (ourselves: argv[0]) with OpenFile()
if ( OpenFile( path to KRNL386.EXE, &KernelOFStruct,
               OF_EXIST ) == -1  )    // -1 indicates an error.
{
    TextMode()  // Switches back to text mode, either via
                // calling PDisableProc (if it's != 0 ),
                // or using INT 10h, fn. 0003 (set to
                // video mode 3)

    INT 21h, fn. 9, to print out:
        "KERNEL: Unable to open KERNEL executable\r\n"

    INT 21h, fn. 4Ch, AL = FFh.   //Exit with error code FFh
}

// Build a module table for the KERNEL module. Every other
// module that will be subsequently loaded will have a module
// table created for it. So KERNEL should have one as well. The
// LkExeHeader() module looks like a very stripped down version
// of LoadExeHeader(), which is a helper function for
// LoadModule() (see Chapter 3). LkExeHeader() (Load Kernel EXE Header?)
// makes many assumptions about the KERNEL module (to eliminate
// code that's not necessary for loading KERNEL?)  For example,
// instead of reading in KERNEL's information from the .EXE file,
// it uses the memory image of KRNLx86.EXE that was read in
// by the DOS loader before transferring to the KERNEL stub.
HExeHead = LkExeHeader(SegLoadBlock, &KernelOFStruct)

if ( HExeHead == 0 )    // Couldn't "load" KERNEL
{
    TextMode()       // See above description

    INT 21h, fn. 9, to print out:
        "KERNEL: Unable to load KERNEL EXE header\r\n"

    INT 21h, fn. 4Ch, AL = FFh.   //Exit with error code FFh
}

LPSystemDir = pathname of KRNL386.EXE stored in the OFSTRUCT
of the newly created KERNEL module table.

// GetPureName() returns a pointer to just the filename.ext
// portion of a full pathname. By subtracting the start of
// the path from the filename.ext part, you can obtain the
// length of just the path portion. Store in CBytesSysDir.
CBytesSysDir = GetPureName() - LPSystemDir
```

```
Add 0xE00 bytes to the ns_minalloc field of the 4th segment
in KERNEL's module table. This is the DGROUP segment.

Loop through all of the KERNEL's segments, looking for the
largest discardable segment. If its size is greater than
the ne_swaparea field in KERNEL's module table, then put
the size into the ne_swaparea field.

// LkAllocSegs() allocates the segments for the KERNEL module,
// via GlobalAlloc(). It uses SetOwner() to associate each of
// the segments with the KERNEL module. The first segment
// is allocated LOW (and hence fixed). The other 2 code
// segments are MOVEABLE, DISCARDABLE, and SHAREABLE. The
// DATA segment is FIXED (allocation flags == 0 )
LkAllocSegs(ES) // ES = HExeHead = module table of KERNEL

DebugFreeSegment( CS, -1 )      // Tell KERNEL debugger that
DebugFreeSegment( MyCSDS, -1 )  // the original segs given to
                                // us by DPMI are being freed.

// The 3rd argument to LoadSegment() can either be a file
// handle from which to load the segment, or a selector whose
// data will be used to create the new segment. The 4th
// parameter indicates if it's a file handle or selector.
// Final_CS and Final_DS are the selectors that KERNEL
// ends up using after all the bootstrap work is out of
// the way.
Final_CS = LoadSegment(HExeHead, 1, CS, -1)
if( !Final_CS )         // If we couldn't create the segment,
    ExitKernel( 1 )     // get out now!

Final_DS = LoadSegment(HExeHead, 4, DS, -1)
if( !Final_DS )         // If we couldn't create the segment,
    ExitKernel( 1 )     // get out now!

DX:AX = Get_Physical_Address(AX) // Get physical address of
                                 // segment just loaded

// Some more mucking about with the stack. Maybe where the
// "final" SS:SP is established?

Add and subtract some values from DX:AX (above). Why???
Prev_GMove_SS = SS  // Get the current SS into a global var
SS = DS             // Now switch away to another stack
SP = &GMove_Stack
```

```
    // The original SS selector will now be modified to have a
    // new base and limit. Set_Physical_Address() uses the DX:AX
    // calculated above as the new base address of the segment.
    Set_Physical_Address( Prev_GMove_SS )   // New linear address
    Set_Sel_Limit( Prev_GMove_SS )          // New segment limit
    SS = Prev_GMove_SS       // Put the modified selector back

    Prev_GMove_SS = 0
    SP = SI                            // 0x200 + 0xE00
```

After GlobalInit() initializes the global heap, KERNEL can be reloaded into memory, just as any other NE file would be. Why is it necessary to reload KERNEL if it's already in memory and already running? Because once Windows is up and running, it must be able to treat KERNEL just like any other EXE or DLL module. For instance, programs can use exported functions from KERNEL, just like they can use exported functions from USER, GDI, or any other DLL. It wouldn't do for the dynamic linking mechanism to work one way for KERNEL and another way for all other DLLs. Therefore, KERNEL needs a module table just like all the other DLLs (Chapter 8 describes dynamic linking and the module table in more detail). The simplest way to make KERNEL look like any other DLL is to load it like any other DLL. In the preceding pseudocode, the original copy of the KERNEL code, which was loaded by the DOS loader, loads another copy of KERNEL. This time however, KRNLx86 is loaded as a Windows NE file, rather than as a DOS MZ file.

The first step of reloading KRNLx86 is to find the complete path to the KRNLx86.EXE file. Get_WinDir() scans the environment segment, looking for the windir= variable, which the DPMI host placed there before EXEC'ing KRNLx86. OpenFile() then opens the KRNLx86 file and passes the resulting OFSTRUCT to LkExeHeader(). LkExeHeader() seems to be a stripped down version of the LoadExeHeader() function. The Windows loader uses this function to transform an NE header on disk into an in-memory module table (see Chapter 3). Using the new KERNEL module table, BootStrap() now allocates selectors for the KERNEL segments with LkAllocSegs(). With the selectors firmly in place in the module table, LoadSegment() reads in the first KERNEL segment (the same code that Windows is currently executing in), as well as the KERNEL data segment. In the last portion of this section the stack switches to another location in the final KERNEL data segment.

```
Continuation of code for BootStrap() - LDBOOT.OBJ
// Locals:
//      WORD    TDB_sel          // Selector for a Task database

    // Get physical address of KERNEL segment 4 (DGROUP) in memory.
    // AX currently contains the "final" KERNEL DS selector
    DX:AX = Get_Physical_Address( AX )
    DX:AX += some value stored in a KERNEL static variable

    // The selector allocated here is used to create some
    // sort of a "dummy" task database.
    TDB_sel = Alloc_Data_Sel(DX:AX, 0, 100h)
```

```
Zero out the memory referenced by the selector just allocated.

    BP = 0                    // Initialize the variables at the
    SS:[PStackBot] = SP       // base of all segments containing
    SS:[PStackMin] = SP       // a local heap
    SS:[PStackTop] = 10h
    SS:[0] = BP               // BP is 0
    SS:[00ldSP] = BP
    SS:[H0ldSS] = BP

    SP -= 0x16

    TDB_sel.TDB_taskSS = SS           // Set up fields in the
    TDB_sel.TDB_taskSP = SP           // dummy Task Database
    TDB_sel.TDB_PDB = TopPDB          // that's being created.
    TDB_sel.TDB_DTA = 0x80
    TDB_sel.TDB_DTA = TopPDB
    TDB_sel.TDB_nEvents = 1
    TDB_sel.TDB_pModule = -1
    TDB_sel.TDB_ExpWinVer = WinVer
    TDB_sel.TDB_sig = 'TD'
```

The above section of BootStrap() creates what appears to be a dummy task database (TDB), described in Chapter 3. A TDB is necessary, since many KERNEL routines assume that there is always at least one task running in the system. A bit later, the shell program (usually PROGMAN.EXE) will be loaded and a TDB created for it. Once the shell program is up and running, the dummy TDB's mission is accomplished, and BootStrap() is free to delete it.

```
Continuation of code for BootStrap() - LDBOOT.OBJ

    DS = Final_DS          // Start using DS from LoadSegment()

    push CS on stack       // Save original CS on stack

    push Final_CS             // Push far return address on stack,
    push OFFSET New_Code      // then RETF to it, thereby loading
    RETF                      // the Final_CS selector into CS

New_Code:

    POP AX  // Get the original CS value into AX

    Free_Sel( AX )  // Free the original CS selector
    PrestoChangoSelector(CS, MyCSAlias) // Create an alias sel
```

```
AX = MyCSDS       // Free the original DS->CS alias selector,
MyCSDS = DS      // and replace with the new DS
Free_Sel(AX)

DebugDebug()     // Tell the system debugger what version of
                 // Windows we're using, as well as giving it
                 // a pointer to internal KERNEL variables.

// We've changed the CS selector we're running on. However,
// the PExitProc function pointer we initialized earlier
// still contains the old CS value. We therefore need to
// update the segment portion of it to contain the new CS
// selector that we're using.
FP_SEG( PExitProc ) = CS

// Store off the real mode segment addresses of our CS and DS
// selectors. SelToSeg() uses Get_Physical_Address() to get
// the linear address that the selector references. It then
// divides by 16 to get a real mode paragraph value.
MyDSSeg = SelToSeg( DS )
MyCSSeg = SelToSeg( CS )

MaxCodeSwapArea = 0xFFFFFFFF   // Maximum swap area size?
AX = GlobalAlloc(GMEM_SHARE|GMEM_MOVEABLE, 0) // Allocate
if ( AX != 0 )                                // DISCARDABLE
{                                             // block
    BX = AX
    AX = HExeHead
    Set_Discarded_Sel_Owner()    // Uses AX and BX
                                 // Sets "owner" of block BX
    WinIniInfo = DS:SZUserPro
}

AX = GlobalAlloc(GMEM_SHARE|GMEM_MOVEABLE, 0) // Allocate
if ( AX != 0 )                                // DISCARDABLE
{                                             // block
    BX = AX
    AX = HExeHead
    Set_Discarded_Sel_Owner()    // See above
}

Some non-understood code. It appears to have something to
do with "shrinking" the memory usage of KERNEL in memory.

AX = MyLock( HLoadBlock )   // Get selector from handle

// Load a segment from the KERNEL module, using the KERNEL
```

```
    // loader. SI always appears to contain 2 here. A seg number?
    if ( !LoadSegment( HExeHead, SI, AX, -1 ) )
        ExitKernel( 1 )       // Abort out of Windows
```

This phase of the KERNEL bootstrap process starts by switching to the final CS and DS selectors obtained when LoadSegment() officially brought the KERNEL segments into memory. After switching to the new selectors, the code frees the old selectors that were assigned when the code switched into protected mode. BootStrap() then calls DebugDebug() to give system level debuggers critical information needed to probe the system effectively. Pseudocode for DebugDebug() follows. Pressing on for a moment, BootStrap() allocates two DISCARDABLE segments from the global heap. One of them appears to be related to the WIN.INI file. It is not known conclusively what Windows uses the other segment for, although it may be for private profile data. BootStrap() finishes this section by calling LoadSegment() to load the second CODE segment from the KRNLx86 file.

```
pseudocode for DebugDebug() - LDDEBUG.OBJ

    // The 0x0010 bit indicates if the RegisterPtrace/ToolhelpHook
    // notifications should be sent out, rather than swallowed.
    if ( 0x0010 or 0x0008 bits are set in [Kernel_Flags + 2] )
    {
        BX = WinVer
        DX:CX = &THHOOK      // DX:CX is a far pointer to THHOOK

        INT 41h, AX = 0x5A   // System Debugger interrupt
    }
```

THHOOK is the starting address of a block of KERNEL variables that are critical for a system debugger to know. Presumably, the variables are fixed in their ordering, otherwise the KERNEL debugger would become thoroughly confused. THHOOK gets its name from the ToolHelp DLL, which gets the address of THHOOK and uses it to access the variables in the following list.

Chapters 2 and 3 cover these variables in more detail.

```
HGlobalHeap // Handle of the Burgermaster segment
PGlobalHeap // Selector of the Burgermaster segment
HExeHead    // Head of the list of modules (i.e., KERNEL)
HExeSweep   // Appears to be unused. For LRU sweeping???
TopPDB      // The PSP of KRNLx86.EXE
HeadPDB     // First PDB in linked list of PDBs
TopSizePDB  // Size of KRNLx86.EXE's PDB
HeadTDB     // First Task Database in the list (highest priority)
CurTDB      // Currently running task
```

```
LoadTDB     // Nonzero if a task is loading. Contains its TDB.
LockTDB     // Contains TDB if a task has "locked" itself.
SelTableLen     // Length of the selector table in Burgermaster.
SelTableStart   // Offset of the selector table in Burgermaster.
```

Continuation of code for BootStrap() - LDBOOT.OBJ

```
    GEnter()    // "Lock" the global heap. See Chapter 2.

    CurTDB = DS     // Set the "current" task
    HeadTDB = DS    // The head of the task (TDB) list.

    DI = 0x32       // start of interrupt table in the TDB

    INT 21h, fn. 3500h          // Get INT 00h vector (Divide by Zero)
    *(DWORD *)DS:DI = ES:BX     // Save in TDB int vector table
    DI += 4                     // Move DI to next slot

    INT 21h, fn. 3502h          // Get INT 02h vector (NMI)
    *(DWORD *)DS:DI = ES:BX     // Save in TDB int vector table
    DI += 4                     // Move DI to next slot

    // Continue this same sequence with:
    // INT 4h  (INTO)
    // INT 6h  (Invalid Opcode)
    // INT 7h  (80x87 Not Available)
    // INT 3Eh (80x87 Emulator)
    // INT 75h (80x87 Error)

    SaveState( DS ) // Save the current Drive/Directory and 80x87
                    // state in the "fake" TDB that we're making.
                    // See Chapter 6 (scheduler) for details.

    GLeave()    // Unlock the global heap.

    SetHandleCount( 0x20 )  // Bump the MS-DOS handles up to 0x20

    LPInt21 = CS:Int21Handler   // LPInt21 is a global fn. ptr

    // We now start a strange sequence that culminates by
    // intentionally generating an invalid opcode, and handling
    // the exception ourselves.
    INT 31h, fn 0202h, BL = 6   // DPMI call. Return exception
                                // 6 handler in CX:DX
```

```
    PUSH CX, DX         // Save original handler address on stack

    CX:DX = CS:ExceptionLabel    // Point the Exception 6 handler
    INT 31h, fn. 0203h, BL = 6 // At 'ExceptionLabel' (below)

    POP DX, CX          // Restore original handler address to CX:DX

    DB  0Fh, FFh        // Cause an exception 6 (invalid opcode)

ExceptionLabel:         // Exception 6 is handled here

    INT 31h, fn. 0203h, BL = 6 // First, restore the original
                               // exception 6 handler (still
                               // in CX:DX)

    Patch the return CS:IP on the DPMI exception frame with the
    address of ExceptionLabel_2

    SS:[PStackBot] = BP + 0x10
    SS:[PStackMin] = SP
    SS:[PStackTop] = 0x00A4

    RETF            // Returns control to ExceptionLabel_2 (below)

ExceptionLabel_2:

    // Save and hook Exception 0Bh (Segment not present)
    INT 31h, fn. 0202h, BL = 0BH
    Save old handler (CX:DX) into PrevInt3FProc // Note: 3Fh, not 0Bh!
    CX:DX = CS:SegmentNotPresentFault
    INT 31h, fn. 0203h, BL = 0BH

    // Save and hook Exception 0Dh (General Protection)
    INT 31h, fn. 0202h, BL = 0DH
    Save old handler (CX:DX) into PrevInt0DProc
    CX:DX = CS:GPFault
    INT 31h, fn. 0203h, BL = 0DH

    Ditto for INT 06h (Invalid_Op_Code_Exception)
    Ditto for INT 0ch (Stack Fault)
    Ditto for INT 0Eh (Page_Fault)
```

This section of BootStrap() continues the initialization of the dummy task database started earlier. First, INT 21h, function 35xxh, obtains the interrupt handler addresses for the interrupts/exceptions that are handled on a per-task basis. The code stores each of these handler addresses in the appropriate slot in the dummy task database. SaveState() then fills in the current drive and directory fields, as well as the 80x87 state. Chapter 6, which discusses the scheduler, gives pseudocode for SaveState().

The next sequence of code is somewhat strange because it sets the DPMI invalid opcode exception handler to a label just past the executing code. BootStrap() then intentionally causes an exception 6, which causes execution to begin at the label while running on a DPMI exception handler stack. The exception 6 handler resets the exception 6 vector back to its original address and then mucks with the return address on the DPMI exception stack frame. The exception handler then RETFs, causing execution to begin at yet another label, just past the exception handler code. The reason for jumping through these hoops is not clear, although it may have something to do with setting up stack limits for the DPMI stack used during exceptions.

With these DPMI contortions behind us, the BootStrap() code now revectors several exceptions KERNEL does not deal with on a per-task basis. For instance, BootStrap() sets Exception 0Bh (segment not present) to the routine that demand loads segments which are not present (discarded). For every exception that BootStrap() revectors, the exception's original handler address is saved in a KERNEL global variable. KERNEL will handle each of these exceptions the same way, regardless of which task the exception occurred in.

Before we go on, let's digress for a few moments to talk about the Exception 0Bh handler. With protected mode comes the ability to demand load segments, particularly discarded code segments, as necessary. When the CPU executes an instruction that would transfer control to a segment that's not present in memory, the CPU generates an Exception 0Bh. The Windows KERNEL handler handles this exception by loading the segment and restarting the instruction. The Exception 0Bh handler has to determine which module the segment belongs to by using the non-present CS value. (Chapter 3 discusses the structures that allow KERNEL to map a CS value into a module handle and logical segment.) The exception handler then calls routines to load the segment from the module's NE file and perform any needed fixups, before restarting the instruction.

You might be wondering why the old Exception 0Bh handler is stored in a global variable named PrevInt3FProc. What does INT 3Fh have to do with this? The answer involves a bit of history. Before Windows could use protected mode (that is, before Windows 3.0), there was still a need to demand load segments as needed. Real mode DOS just didn't have enough memory to do what Windows asked of it. The solution was to use *far-call thunks*. In this scheme, far calls didn't go directly to the intended destination segment. Instead, they went through a thunk that just JMP'ed to the real destination. These far-call thunks are completely unrelated to the instance thunks created by MakeProcInstance(). If the destination segment of the thunk wasn't in memory, KERNEL replaced the JMP in the thunk with an INT 3Fh instruction. The INT 3Fh handler did the same thing as the Exception 0Bh handler does now. It loads the segment and patches the thunk back to a JMP instruction. You can think of this scheme as a poor man's protected mode. The DOS overlay managers available from Borland and Microsoft work in a very similar way, even down to their usage of INT 3Fh.

The next section of BootStrap() pseudocode puts runtime dynamic linking to the test:

Continuation of code for BootStrap() - LDBOOT.OBJ

```
// Now "fix up" the "constant" values such as __WINFLAGS,
// __0000H, etc. This section of code relies on the
// undocumented fact that GetProcAddress() can return a far
// pointer (ES:BX) to the entry in the module's entry table.
// This is only true for "constants" (those with segment
// values of 0FEh). Using the far pointer to the entry,
// BootStrap() "plugs" selector values into the "offset"
// portion of the entry point. GetProcAddress() returns these values
// when an application calls GetProcAddress() for
// one of the constant entry points.

GetProcAddress(HExeHead, 0, 178 ) // KERNEL.178 = __WINFLAGS
*(ES:BX) = WinFlags

GetProcAddress(HExeHead, 0, 183 ) // KERNEL.183 = __0000H
SI = BX      // Put BX into SI, since BX is needed below
BX = 0000h   // Segment value -> 0000h
AX = 2       // DPMI create selector for real mode segment
INT 31h
*(ES:SI) = AX    // Selector returned in AX

continue this process for these other "constant" exported
symbols:

KERNEL.193 = __0040H
KERNEL.173 = __ROMBIOS
KERNEL.194 = __F000H
KERNEL.174 = __A000H
KERNEL.181 = __B000H
KERNEL.182 = __B800H
KERNEL.195 = __C000H
KERNEL.179 = __D000H
KERNEL.190 = __E000H
```

This section of BootStrap() sets up the constant values, for example, the __A000H selector. Chapter 2 on memory management covers constant selectors in a bit more detail. For now, it will suffice to say that KERNEL needs to patch things so that when an application calls GetProcAddress() for one of the predefined selectors, the returned *offset* is actually a selector or constant value.

Getting the selector values for the real mode segments (for example, the segment A000h for __A000H) is the easy part. DPMI function 0002h returns a selector for a real mode segment with a minimum of fuss. The sneaky part is that ES:BX in GetProcAddress() can, in this situation, return a pointer to the offset portion of the address of the symbol in KERNEL's entry table. Thus, it's a simple matter of using ES:BX as a far pointer and writing the selector returned from DPMI to that location.

Continuation of code for BootStrap() - LDBOOT.OBJ

```
    // Look for the string "WININI=" in the environment. If
    // found, overwrite the default string in SZUserPro with the
    // portion after the '=' character. The default string in
    // SZUserPro is "WIN.INI". By setting the WININI variable
    // in the environment, you can select which WIN.INI file
    // you want to use.
    SetUserPro()

    // Free up the block of memory (SegLoadBlock/HLoadBlock) that
    // was used to reference the KRNL386.EXE 'NE' header loaded
    // by the real mode DOS loader. The return value from the
    // GlobalFree() call should be 0, so HLoadBlock should end
    // up set to 0.
    HLoadBlock = GlobalFree( HLoadBlock )

    FS = GS = 0        // Actually set to AX, which is 0 from the
                       // call to the above GlobalFree().

    // If there's no Windows directory string yet, retrieve it
    // from the path to the WIN.INI file.
    if ( FP_SEG(LpWindowsDir) == 0 )
    {
        OpenFile( SZUserPro, &some_OFSTRUCT, OF_PARSE )

        FP_SEG(LpWindowsDir) = DS
        FP_OFF(LpWindowsDir) = &some_OFSRUCT.szPathName

        // GetPureName() returns a pointer to just the filename
        // portion of a full pathname. See the above usage for
        // CBytesSysDir for more details on this.
        CBytesWinDir = GetPureName() - &some_OFSRUCT.szPathName
    }

    // Start scanning the command line, looking for ":" and
    // "/b". Remember, WIN.COM extracted its command line, and
    // removed the things it was interested in before passing it
    // to KRNLx86.EXE
    DS:SI = TopPDB:80h  // First byte is command line length

    Scan the command line, looking for a "/b" or "-b"
    argument. If found, replace the argument with "  ", and
    call DiagInit(). DiagInit() creates (if necessary) the
    BOOTLOG.TXT file, and sets the FDiagMode global variable
    to 1 (TRUE).
```

```
    // GrowSFTToMax() appears to "grow" the system file table by
    // adding a new cluster of file table entries to the end
    // of the list. Walking the system file table, and mucking
    // about with it is described in "Undocumented DOS." If
    // the amount of memory returned by GetFreeSpace() is
    // less than 512K, then the system file table is grown to
    // 100 entries. If more than 512K, then it's grown to 127
    // entries. As described in "Undocumented DOS," the system
    // file table is found via INT 21h, fn. 52h. The memory
    // for the new handle table entries is allocated via
    // GlobalDOSAlloc(), thereby ensuring that it is below
    // 1Mb, and accessible to real mode DOS.
    GrowSFTToMax()      // Grow the DOS system file table

    DS:SI = TopPDB:80h  // First byte is command line length

    LODSB               // Get the first byte, and increment SI
    if ( AL == 0 )      // Any command line at all???
        goto set_graphics

    CL = AL             // CL now has command line length

    // If "::" is specified on the command line after WIN.COM,
    // the variable Graphics gets set to 0. This causes KERNEL
    // to load differently than normal. It's not understood
    // what the reason for this command line argument is.
    if ( string pointed to by DS:SI != " ::" )
    {
        AX = 0
        goto set_graphics
    }

    copy the remaining portion of the string (after "::") to a
    static buffer. When done, AX != 0 (see below)

set_graphics:

    if ( AX != 0 )       // Graphics starts out == 1. It will be
        Graphics = 0     // set to 0 only if "::" appears on the
                         // command line.

    goto SlowBoot        // Continue on with more startup code
```

This last portion of BootStrap() consists of miscellaneous other initializations before BootStrap() jumps to the SlowBoot() routine. The first major highlight of this portion is the processing of the command-line arguments to KRNLx86. As you recall, WIN.COM has already parsed the original command line and replaced any options that it handles with spaces. Thus, KRNLx86 doesn't have to look for much. First off, there is the /B switch, which causes a diagnostic file to be written. The routine that creates this diagnostic file is called DiagInit(), (see the pseudocode below). In addition, KRNLx86 checks for two colons in a row (::). There is no known information on this option, but it does seem to have a rather dramatic impact on what happens later on in the bootstrapping process. The switch appears to be tied to the variable "Graphics".

The other major highlight is to call GrowSFTToMax(), which adds additional System File Table (SFT) entries to the linked list of SFT entry blocks. This function is similar to programs like Quarterdeck's FILES. Before BootStrap() calls GrowSFTToMax(), it gets the number of SFT entries (the FILES= line in the CONFIG.SYS file). *Undocumented DOS* describes the layout and use of the System File Table.

```
pseudocode for DiagInit() - DIAG.OBJ
// Locals:
//      WORD    fileHandle
// Statics:
//      char    LogFileName[]   // Stores path to BOOTLOG.TXT

    copy the LpWindowsDir string into LogFileName[], and
    append a '\' to it.

    Append "BOOTLOG.TXT" to LogFileName[]. The resulting string
    in LogFileName[] is typically: "C:\WINDOWS\BOOTLOG.TXT"

    if debug KERNEL
    {
        OutputDebugString
            ( "Diagnostic mode startup.  Log file is:  " )

        OutputDebugString( LogFileName )
        OutputDebugString("\r\n")           // Append a linefeed
    }

    // Call the Windows INT 21h routine directly. The command
    // is to open the file (given in DS:DX) for read/write, and
    // deny writing to others.
    Int21Handler( AX = 3D22h, CX = 0, DS:DX = LogFileName )

    if ( carry flag not set )
    {
        fileHandle = AX

        // Seek to the end of the file
        Int21Handler( AX = 4202h, BX = fileHandle, CX:DX = 0 )
    }
```

```
else    // Carry flag is set. We need to create the file
{
    Int21Handler( AH = 3Ch, CX = 0, DX = LogFileName )

    fileHandle = AX
    if ( carry flag set ) // If we couldn't create the file
        return            // return, and don't set FDiagMode
}

FDiagMode = 1  // Global variable indicating diagnostic mode

Int21Handler( AH = 3Eh, BX = fileHandle )   // Close file

// DiagOutput() is the method by which diagnostic strings
// are written to BOOTLOG.TXT. The file is always opened
// before writing the string, and closed afterwards,
// thereby guaranteeing that the files will be flushed to
// disk. This saves any strings that would
// be lost if Windows crashed during the boot process.
DiagOutput( "[boot]\r\n" );
```

DiagInit() first determines where the BOOTLOG.TXT file will be written to (for example, into the C:\WINDOWS directory), then DiagInit() opens or creates the file in this location. Next, a series of INT 21h calls opens BOOTLOG.TXT, seeks to the end of the file, and then closes the file. The final step is to call DiagOutput(), which writes a header for the file ([BOOT]). To be as safe as possible, DiagInit() always opens, writes to, and then closes the BOOTLOG.TXT file during each call to DiagOutput(). This is an attempt to prevent data from being lost if it is still in the DOS buffers, rather than safely on disk, when the machine crashes.

SlowBoot()

After BootStrap(), the next part of booting KERNEL is the SlowBoot() function. The SlowBoot name is a relic from pre-Windows 3.0 days. In order to speed up the loading of Windows, early versions combined the USER, KERNEL, and GDI modules into one big file. However, there were good reasons, such as needing symbol table information, to have separate USER, KERNEL, and GDI files. The option of having separate Windows modules was termed "slow boot." Since version 3.0, Windows always uses this slow boot option.

For the most part, the code in SlowBoot() operates at a slightly higher level than BootStrap(). It seems more focused on the goal of getting the rest of the Windows DLLs into memory. However, it's not immediately obvious why BootStrap() and SlowBoot() are two different procedures. If you look at BootStrap() and SlowBoot() as one uninterrupted blob of code it's difficult to see why it was broken into two pieces. Keep in mind as we dive back into more pseudocode that, in general, the code, like much of the Windows code, looks like it has been created piecemeal over the years. Code that is obviously new for Windows 3.1 appears intermixed with code that must be much older. For the most part, there doesn't appear to be any sort of natural order for these various steps.

```
pseudocode for SlowBoot() - LDBOOT.OBJ

    // Should Dr. Watson allow faulting instructions to be skipped
    // over?  Default value for GPEnable is 1. Only in KRNL386
    GPEnable = GetProfileInt("KERNEL", "GPCONTINUE", GPEnable)

    // Get filename to send debugging messages to instead of AUX.
    // "buffer" is a static array of 80 characters in KERNEL.
    GetPrivateProfileString("DEBUG", "OUTPUTTO",
                            buffer, 0x50, "SYSTEM.INI" )

    // If we got a filename, open it, then force AUX to be a
    // duplicate of it. This allows the KERNEL to write to AUX,
    // while DOS handles the redirection.
    if ( return value != 0 )
    {
        if ( return value != 0x4E )     // ??
        {
            // Create/truncate new file with the name in "buffer"
            INT 21h, fn. 3Ch, DX = buffer

            INT 21h, fn. 3Eh    // Close the file

            INT 21h, fn. 3Dh, AL = 42   // Open existing file.
                                        // Read/Write, DENYNONE

            // Force AUX file handle to be a duplicate of the
            // opened file. All writes to AUX will now go to
            // whatever file was specified in OUTPUTTO=.
            INT 21h, fn. 4h, CX = 3

            INT 21h, fn. 3Eh    // Close the file

            WDefRip = 'i' // Default RIP response -> i(gnore)?
        }
    }

    // Get the number of open file handles that KERNEL should keep
    // cached. These are file handles for EXEs/DLL, and help
    // speed up demand loading of segments and resources.
```

```
AX = GetPrivateProfileInt("BOOT", "CACHEDFILEHANDLES", 0xC,
                                  "SYSTEM.INI")
if ( AX < 2 )    // Ensure that the value is at least 2
    AX = 2
if ( AX > 0xC ) // Ensure that the value is at most 12
    AX = 0xC

FHCacheLen = AX          // Store away the value
FHCacheEnd = AX << 2     // Each entry is 4 bytes???

// Should boot time segments be loaded when idling inside
// the scheduler?  Default is 1 (yes).

FPokeAtSegment = GetPrivateProfileInt("BOOT",
                            "LOADSEGMENTSATIDLE",1,"SYSTEM.INI")
```

SlowBoot() begins by using the GetPrivateProfileXXX() functions to read various configuration options from the SYSTEM.INI file. Of particular interest is the OUTPUTTO= setting in the [DEBUG] section. The debugging version of Windows sends quite a bit of diagnostic information to the AUX file. Traditionally, developers using the debug version of Windows would need a terminal connected to the serial port to receive this information. Without this connection, the debug KERNEL would complain early on in the startup and go no further. Simply put, the debug KERNEL was useless without another terminal or a device driver that redirected the AUX file to something such as a monochrome monitor. OX.SYS, by Michael Geary, is the prototypical example of this. With the growing popularity of Windows, quite a few developers wish to use the debug KERNEL, but don't have the additional hardware. A minimalist solution to this problem sets the OUTPUTTO= section of the SYSTEM.INI file to a valid DOS filename, even a file on disk, that can receive the diagnostic information. Perhaps to minimize its effect on existing Windows code, the author(s) of this section of SlowBoot() implemented the OUTPUTTO= feature in a rather clever way. Since the existing code for KERNEL diagnostics assumes that AUX is the output device, the easiest way to redirect this stream is to cause the AUX device to be a duplicate file handle of whatever file the OUTPUTTO= line specified. DOS does all the hard work of redirecting the data, and the KERNEL code blissfully writes to AUX, unaware of what's really happening.

The preceding section of SlowBoot() pseudocode also sets the number of cached file handles. KERNEL keeps around a certain number of open file handles for the most recently used NE files in order to speed up demand loading. Chapter 3 discusses the open file handles in more detail. Another KERNEL global variable set at this point is FPokeAtSegments. FPokeAtSegments determines if segments from the boot time modules should be loaded into memory during times when the system is idle (a performance enhancement). Chapter 6 on the scheduler covers this topic in more detail.

Monochrome Monitors and Windows Diagnostics

As a side note to the topic of the debug version and diagnostics, I consider having a secondary monochrome monitor for your system to be an extremely worthwhile investment. For less than $100 (usually), a secondary monochrome monitor setup makes life much easier. Besides using it to display diagnostic messages, you can use it with debuggers such as TDW, CVW, and Soft-ICE/W, thereby eliminating the annoying switches between the text-mode debugger and graphics-mode Windows. For anyone who's had to debug on a single monitor system for more than five minutes, it's money well spent.

The following section of SlowBoot() is where Windows really comes alive. The LoadNewExe() routine takes the module name of a Windows DLL and loads it into memory. This is how KERNEL brings the SYSTEM, USER and GDI modules, the hardware device drivers, and fonts into memory. In the case of the hardware device drivers, the DLL file may have a different name than the standard module name. For instance, most machines use the SYSTEM.DRV DLL. However, Hewlett-Packard machines use HPSYSTEM.DRV instead. LoadNewExe() takes care of these details, as shown in the pseudocode after this section of the SlowBoot() code. Also, loading the USER module involves quite a bit of interesting initialization in its own right, which this chapter discusses in detail later on.

```
Continuation of code for SlowBoot() - LDBOOT.OBJ

    // Set up an EXEC Block for loading the boot time DLLs.
    // Win_Show is initialized to { 2, 1 }, where 1==SW_SHOWNORMAL
    // See the LoadModule() documentation for details.
    BootExecBlock.lpCmdShow = DS:Win_Show
    BootExecBlock.lpCmdLine = TopPDB:80h // points at our cmd line

    if ( graphics == 1 )            // Normally, graphics == 1
        LpBootApp = "PROGMAN.EXE"   // PROGMAN can be overridden with
                                    // the "shell=" option in
                                    // SYSTEM.INI (shown later).

    // Load the SYSTEM module into memory, via LoadNewExe().
    // LoadNewExe() loads the specified module into memory, after
    // first looking it up in SYSTEM.INI to see if it has been
    // renamed. See the pseudocode for details.
    LoadNewExe( "SYSTEM.DRV" )

    if ( graphics == 1 )    // graphics normally == 1
    {
        LoadNewExe( "KEYBOARD.DRV" )
```

```
        // Immediately after loading KEYBOARD.DRV, do the
        // following fixups, before loading the other modules:
        // #5 = AnsiToOem()  #6 = OemToAnsi()
        PKeyProc = GetProcAddress( hInstKEYBOARD, "#5" )
        PKeyProc1 = GetProcAddress( hInstanceKEYBOARD, "#6" )

        // Continue loading the rest of the boot modules
        // via LoadNewExe(). Each one of these is really
        // a DLL, and may contain an initialization routine.
        // Later on, we'll cover the USER initialization.
       "MOUSE.DRV"
       "DISPLAY.DRV"
       "SOUND.DRV"
       "COMM.DRV"
       "FONTS.FON"
       "OEMFONTS.FON"
       "GDI.EXE"
       "USER.EXE"            // USER needs many of the previous DLLs,
                             // which might be why it loads last.
    }

pseudocode for LoadNewExe() - LDBOOT.OBJ
// Parameters:
//      NPSTR   filename    // Near *. Assumes current DS
// Locals:
//      WORD    LoadModuleReturnCode

    // Get the actual name of the DLL from the [boot] section of
    // the SYSTEM.INI file. The result ends up in a static buffer
    // that we call "static_buffer" here.
    //
    // For instance, when LoadNewExe() is called with the
    // "SYSTEM.DRV" string, it calls GetPrivateProfileString()
    // with "SYSTEM.DRV" as the key. If the SYSTEM.INI has
    // some other string (say, "SYSTEM.DRV=HPSYSTEM.DRV"), then
    // static_buffer will be filled with e.g. "HPSYSTEM.DRV". If
    // there is no string for the passed-in key, then
    // static_buffer is filled with the default string (the
    // string that was passed to LoadNewExe())
    //
    // This is the mechanism that allows KERNEL to "hardcode" in
    // driver DLL names, while still allowing the names to be
    // overridden in the SYSTEM.INI file. For example, DISPLAY.DRV=VGA.DRV.

    GetPrivateProfileString( "BOOT", filename, filename,
                         &static_buffer, 0x50, "SYSTEM.INI" )
```

```
    // Use LoadModule() to bring the driver DLL into memory
    LoadModuleReturnCode = LoadModule( static_buffer, 0 )

    // If the LoadModule() failed, print out different error
    // messages for different error conditions. See the
    // LoadModule() documentation for the list of error codes.
    if ( LoadModuleReturnCode == 2 )
    {
        _KRDebugTest( "Kernel: Can't find @DS:DI" )
        goto LoadModule_failed
    }
    if ( LoadModuleReturnCode == 11 )
    {
        _KRDebugTest( "Kernel: Invalid EXE file @DS:DI" )
        goto LoadModule_failed
    }
    if ( LoadModuleReturnCode == 15 )
    {
        _KRDebugTest("Kernel: Invalid protect mode EXE file @DS:DI")
        goto LoadModule_failed
    }
    if ( LoadModuleReturnCode == 4 )
    {
        _KRDebugTest(
        "Kernel: Out of files (set FILES=30 in CONFIG.SYS) @DS:DI")
        goto LoadModule_failed
    }
    if ( LoadModuleReturnCode >= 32 )     // Success!
        return to caller

LoadModule_failed:

    LoadFail( static_buffer )    // Call TextMode(), and display:
                                 // "Error loading <filename>"
    ExitKernel( 1 )              // Abort out of Windows
```

If you've ever wondered about the entries in the [BOOT] section of SYSTEM.INI, LoadNewExe() is where they're put to use. Instead of forcing a name on certain DLLs (for example, MOUSE.DRV for mouse drivers), the boot section defines the boot time DLLs and what their actual filenames are. Once LoadNewExe() knows the real name of the DLL file, it uses LoadModule() to bring the DLL into memory. If LoadModule() fails for some reason, the debug KERNEL examines the return code and print out a meaningful message before aborting the bootstrap process. Chapter 3 discusses the inner workings of LoadModule() in more detail.

```
Continuation of code for SlowBoot() - LDBOOT.OBJ

    InitFwdRef()      // Initialize function pointers that KERNEL
                      // uses to call routines in other modules.
                      // KERNEL can't implicitly link to them, since
                      // KERNEL loads before the other modules.

    InternalEnableDOS() // Hook exceptions for the DOS layer
                        // and grow the System File Table (SFT)

    Check_Temp()      // Examines the TEMP= environment string,
                      // and creates the TEMP file, which is used
                      // by the print spooler.
```

Despite its name, KERNEL is not really as self-sufficient as you might think. In the normal course of events, the KERNEL module needs to call routines in USER, the DISPLAY driver, the SYSTEM driver, and so on. For instance, when the global heap management code in KERNEL is spending too much time compacting segments, it needs to send a message to all the running programs, directing them to free up whatever memory they can. Since the message posting routines are in the USER module, KERNEL needs to link to the USER module. However, because KERNEL loads before any of the other DLLs, it would be extremely difficult to fix up KERNEL's calls to the USER module at the time that KERNEL loads. To circumvent this problem, KERNEL maintains a collection of global variables. These variables are function pointers and are initialized by the InitFwdRef() routine, which in turn relies on the KERNEL run-time dynamic linking function, GetProcAddress(). The Windows SDK documentation fails to note it, but the string representation of an ordinal number, such as "#1", can be passed to GetProcAddress() just like DosGetProcAddr() in OS/2.

```
pseudocode for InitFwdRef() - DOSINIT.OBJ
// Locals:
//      WORD    hModSystem      // Module handle for "SYSTEM"
//      WORD    hModDisplay     // Module handle for "DISPLAY"
//      WORD    hModMouse       // Module handle for "MOUSE"
//      WORD    hModKeyboard    // Module handle for "KEYBOARD"

    PrevInt21Proc( AX = 352Fh ) // Get the INT 2Fh vector in ES:BX
    MyInt2F = ES:BX             // Store away in a global variable

    PrevInt00Proc = PrevInt21Proc( AX = 3502h ) // Div by zero
    PrevInt24Proc = PrevInt21Proc( AX = 3502h ) // Critical error

    // Get the address of SYSTEM.InquireSystem()
    hModSystem = GetModuleHandle( "SYSTEM" )
    PSysProc= GetProcAddress(hModSystem, "#1")
```

```
    // The following is a rather convoluted way to call
    // Get80x87SaveSize(), which returns the size of the coprocessor
    // "save state" buffer. The code starts out by pushing
    // a far address (inside this routine) on the stack.
    // It then gets the address of Get80x87SaveSize(), and
    // pushes it on the stack as well, before RETF'ing to it.
    // When Get80x87SaveSize() returns, it will RETF to the
    // "After_80x87_check" label. Is all this worth avoiding a
    // function pointer local variable for???
    push CS     // Push a far return address (the label below)
    push offset After_80x87_check
    GetProcAddress(hModSystem, "#7")
    push DX:AX  // Address of Get80x87SaveSize()
    retf        // Essentially a JMP to Get80x87SaveSize()
After_80x87_check:
    F8087 = AX  // Set to return value from Get80x87SaveSize()

    // The next section of code involve numerous calls to
    // GetModuleHandle() to get the module handles of the DLLs
    // that were loaded earlier. GetProcAddress() is used
    // repeatedly to get the address of routines that KERNEL
    // needs, and store them in KERNEL global variables.
    // The following modules are needed by KERNEL:
    // SYSTEM, DISPLAY, MOUSE, GDI, USER, and KEYBOARD

    // System.2 = CreateSystemTimer()
    PTimerProc = GetProcAddress( hModSystem, "#2" )

    // System.5 = DisableSystemTimers()
    PSystemTermProc = GetProcAddress( hModSystem, "#5" )

    if ( graphics == 0 )     // Usually, graphics == 1
        goto graphics_0      // Skip many of these if not.

    hModDisplay = GetModuleHandle( "DISPLAY" )

    // DISPLAY.500 = UserRepaintDisable()
    PDisplayCritSec = GetProcAddress( hModDisplay, "#500")

    hModMouse = GetModuleHandle( "MOUSE" )
    PMouseTermProc = GetProcAddress(hModMouse, "#3") // Disable()

    HGDI =  GetModuleHandle( "GDI" )    // HGDI is a global var
    HUser = GetModuleHandle( "USER" )   // HUser is a global var
```

```
PMBoxProc = GetProcAddress(HUser, "#1") // USER.1=MessageBox()

// USER.320 = SysErrorBox()
PSErrProc = GetProcAddress(HUser, "#320" )
// USER.7=ExitWindows()

PExitProc = GetProcAddress(HUser, "#7")

// USER.4 = DisableOEMLayer()
PDisableProc = GetProcAddress(HUser, "#4")

// USER.332 = UserYield()
PYieldProc = GetProcAddress(HUser, "#332")

// USER.400 = FinalUserInit()
PUserInitDone = GetProcAddress(HUser, "#400")

// USER.110 = PostMessage()
PPostMessage = GetProcAddress(HUser, "#110")

// USER.314 = SignalProc()
PSignalProc = GetProcAddress(HUser, "#314")

// USER.333 = IsUserIdle()
PIsUserIdle = GetProcAddress(HUser, "#333")

// USER.284 = GetFreeSystemResources()
PGetFreeSystemResources = GetProcAddress(HUser, "#284")

// USER.470 = StringFunc()
PStringFunc = GetProcAddress(HUser, "#470")

// USER.23 = GetFocus()
PUserGetFocus() = GetProcAddress(HUser, "#23")

// USER.224 = GetWindowTask()
PUserGetWinTask = GetProcAddress(HUser, "#224")

// USER.47 = IsWindow()
PUserIsWindow = GetProcAddress(HUser, "#47")

hModKeyboard = GetModuleHandle( "KEYBOARD" );

// KEYBOARD.3 = Disable()
PKeyboardTermProc = GetProcAddress( hModKeyboard, "#3" )

// KEYBOARD.136 = EnableKBSysReq()
PKeyboardSysReq = GetProcAddress( hModKeyboard, "#136" )
```

```
    PKeyboardSysReq( 4 )    // Enable CTRL-ALT-SYSREQ processing

    // Another instance of the strange calling method
    // described earlier. See Get80x87SaveSize(), above
    push CS
    push offset After_KEYBOARD_inquire
    GetProcAddress(hModKeyboard, "#1") // KEYBOARD Inquire()
    push DX:AX
    retf
After_KEYBOARD_inquire:
    Reads some WORDS starting at the "KeyInfo" label in the KERNEL
    data segment. Depending on the values there, KERNEL may
    increment the FFarEast flag, indicating a Japanese, Korean,
    or Chinese version of Windows. (For more information on Far
    East versions of Windows, see Microsoft's developer white paper,
    "Microsoft Windows Far East Editions," available from Microsoft Far
    East Developer Services in Redmond.) In all cases, control jumps
    past the graphics_0: label, to the call_DebugSysReq: label.

graphics_0:     // Never reached normally (Graphics must be 0)

    PYieldProc = CS:OldYield    // Set to OldYield() in KERNEL

call_DebugSysReq:

    DebugSysReq() // If PKeyboardSysReq is nonzero, and if not
                  // running under a system debugger,
                  // DebugSysReq() calls PKeyboardSysReq(1),
                  // (meaning: Don't generate INT 2's (NMI))
```

The second important task in the preceding SlowBoot() pseudocode is to call InternalEnableDOS(). During this process, KERNEL hooks into the standard DOS layer so that KERNEL can perform the tricky task of running multiple, protected mode applications on an operating system that was intended to run real mode applications one at a time.

```
pseudocode for InternalEnableDOS() - ENABLE.OBJ

    if ( FInt21 != 0 )  // FInt21 starts out == 0.
        return          // Don't "enable" DOS if it already is!

    FInt21 = 1          // KERNEL INT 21h hooks are now installed

    if ( FP_SEG( LpWinSFTLink ) != 0 ) // Something having to do
        *PSFTLink = *(LpWinSFTLink)    // with the SFT chain
```

```
    // Real_DOS() is a way to call INT 21h at a low level.
    // It bypasses much of KERNEL's normal INT 21h handler code
    // that "multiplexes" INT 21h calls from multiple protected
    // mode applications. This is so that they can run atop one
    // copy of real mode DOS.
    Real_DOS( AX = 0x3301, DL = 0 ) // Disable Ctrl-C checking

    Real_DOS( AH = 0x50, BX = TopPDB )  // Set current PSP

key_loop:       // Empty out the keyboard buffer

    Real_DOS( AH = 6, DL = 0FFh )   // Read a char from STDIN

    if ( zero flag not set )     // Keep looping until there are no
        goto key_loop            // no more chars left. Empty the
                                 // keyboard buffer so we don't
                                 // get "typeahead" problems with
                                 // the KEYBOARD driver.

    BX = CurTDB.TDB_PDB // Set BX to the PDB of the current task
    INT 21h, fn. 50h    // Set PSP to BX

    DS:DX = MyInt2F     // Set INT 2Fh handler to old INT 2Fh
    INT 21h, AX = 252Fh // handler obtained in InitFWDRef()

    // Install default KERNEL handlers for the interrupts that
    // can be overridden on a per-task basis. Each task starts
    // out with a small "interrupt table" in its TDB. The
    // default handler addresses are those set below.
    PrevInt21Proc( AX = 2524h, DX = Int24Handler )
    PrevInt21Proc( AX = 2500h, DX = Int00Handler )
    PrevInt21Proc( AX = 2502h, DX = Int02Handler )
    PrevInt21Proc( AX = 2504h, DX = Int04Handler )
    PrevInt21Proc( AX = 2506h, DX = Int06Handler )
    PrevInt21Proc( AX = 2507h, DX = Int07Handler )
    PrevInt21Proc( AX = 253Eh, DX = Int3EHandler )
    PrevInt21Proc( AX = 2575h, DX = Int75Handler )

    PSysProc( 2, 0 )    // PSyProc = InquireSystem: Disable "one-drive" logic

    loop backwards though the 26 possible drive letters,
    calling PSysProc( 1, drive_number ). This function
    returns whether the drive physically exists. The results
    are stored in an array called the "PHantArray". PSyProc is
    actually InquireSystem (see the earlier discussion of InitFwdref).
    DS:DX = LPInt21 // LPInt21 was initialized to CS:Int21Handler
                    // previously, in BootStrap().

    INT 21h, AX = 2521h     // Set INT 21h vector to DS:DX
```

Continuing along in the SlowBoot() code, we finally come to the spot where Windows loads its shell program. This program's name is normally PROGMAN.EXE, but to load a different shell, modify the SHELL= line in the SYSTEM.INI file.

```
Continuation of code for SlowBoot() - LDBOOT.OBJ

    // Get the name of the Windows "shell". Normally PROGMAN.EXE
    GetPrivateProfileString("BOOT", "SHELL", LpBootApp,
                            DS:some static buffer, 0x50, "SYSTEM.INI")

    // Set up the command line for the shell program. If
    // possible, use OemToAnsi() to convert the command line
    // to its "proper" form.
    if ( FP_SEG( PKeyProc1 ) != 0 ) // PKeyProc1 -> OemToAnsi()
    {
       Null terminate the command line string pointed at by
       BootExecBlock.lpCmdLine

       PKeyProc1( BootExecBlock.lpCmdLine ) // call OemToAnsi()
    }

    // Now that we have a program name and a command line, it's
    // time to load the first program (e.g., PROGMAN)
    if ( !graphics )     // Normally, this isn't executed
    {
        AX = LoadModule( LpBootApp, &BootExecBlock )
        FBooting = 0
    }
    else                 // This code usually is executed
    {
        // We no longer needs USER's file handle around in the
        // file/module cache, so get rid of it (close it)
        FlushCachedFileHandle( HUser )  // USER's module handle
                                        // Set in InitFwdRef()

        // Load the first program (usually PROGMAN.EXE)
        AX = LoadModule(LpBootApp, some buffer)    //See Chapter 3.
    }

    if ( return value from LoadModule() > 32 )  // Loaded OK?
    {
        HShell = GetExePtr( AX )    // Store the shell's hModule
        goto BootDone
    }
```

```
    // If we get here, the SHELL couldn't be loaded.
    if debug KERNEL
        output a message: "Kernel: BOOT: unable to load @ES:BX",
        where ES:BX are replaced by the LpBootApp string.

    LoadFail( LpBootApp )    // Call TextMode(), and display:
                             // "Error loading <filename>"
    ExitKernel( 1 )          // Abort out of Windows

    // The LoadNewExe() procedure sits here, in the middle of
    // the bootstrap code. Why???
BootDone:
```

The preceding section of SlowBoot() gets the name of the SHELL application from the SYSTEM.INI file and loads it. Although PROGMAN is the default shell program, there is quite a growing market for replacement shells, such as the Norton Desktop. If for some reason, the shell program did not load, SlowBoot() aborts the loading process and kicks Windows back to a DOS prompt.

Further Windows initialization occurs in this call to LoadModule() for what will become the first task in the system. (See the discussion of InitApp() in Chapter 3.)

SlowBoot() now continues initializing various KERNEL variables, setting a few values related to the debug KERNEL and debugging first. Next comes a small section of code relating to the math coprocessor and Windows 80x87 emulator. Afterwards, SlowBoot() sets up the LRU sweeping, if needed. As described in Chapter 2 on memory management, LRU sweeping uses a system timer to periodically scan all the discardable segments in memory and mark which ones were recently used. These marks enable the global heap management code to be more intelligent when it comes time to discard memory.

```
Continuation of code for SlowBoot() - LDBOOT.OBJ

    DebugOptions = GetProfileInt("WINDOWS", "DebugOptions",
                     DebugOptions )  // DebugOptions defaults to 0

    DebugFilter = GetProfileInt("WINDOWS", "DebugFilter",
                     DebugFilter )   // DebugFilter defaults to 0

    if ( DBO_CHECKHEAP flag set in DebugOptions )
        increment hi_check field in the GlobalInfo structure

    if ( DBO_DISABLEGPTRAPPING flag set in DebugOptions )
    {
        INT 31h, fn. 0203h,      // Undo exception 0Dh handler
        BL = 0Dh, CX:DX = PrevInt0Dproc
```

```
    INT 31h, fn. 0203h,     // Undo exception 06h handler
    BL = 06h, CX:DX = PrevIntx6proc

    INT 31h, fn. 0203h,     // Undo exception 0Eh handler
    BL = 0Eh, CX:DX = PrevInt0Eproc
}

// Get the value of FChkSum, which presumably has something
// to do with the real mode ValidateCodeSegments(). It does
// not appear to be used anywhere in the 3.1 KERNEL.
FChkSum = GetProfileInt("KERNEL", "EnableSegmentChecksum", 1)

// See if the user wants to use the 80x87 emulator, even if
// an 80x87 chip is present. Useful for testing; similar to the
// NO87 = environment variable.
if ( GetProfileInt("KERNEL", "NoUse80x87", 0) != 0 )
{
    F8087 = 0;
    Turn off WF_80x87 in WinFlags
}

// FastFP affects how 80x87 fixups are applied when segments
// are loaded. If nonzero, the FWAIT instruction preceding
// an 80x87 instruction will be NOP'ed out, since it's not
// needed on 80287s and greater. This setting only has an
// effect if there is an 80x87 installed in the system.
FastFP = GetProfileInt("KERNEL", "FastFP", 1 )

// Get the LRU sweep frequency rate.
if debug KERNEL
    AX = GetProfileInt("KERNEL", "LRUSweepFrequency", 500)
else
    AX = 500    // 500 Milliseconds

// Only do LRU sweeping if not paging, and there's a
// nonzero sweep frequency. No paging in Standard mode,
// or if SYSTEM.INI Paging = off in Enhanced Mode.
if ( ( AX != 0 ) && (WF_PAGING bit not set in WinFlags) )
{
    // Call CreateSystemTimer() to set up a hardware timer
    // that calls LRUSweep() at intervals specified by AX
    PTimerProc( AX, LRUSweep )
}

// "EnableEMSDebug" is presumably dead code from the real
// mode KERNEL.EXE. EMS is irrelevant in protected mode
```

```
if ( GetProfileInt("KERNEL", "EnableEMSDebug", 0) != 0 )
    turn on a bit in the Kernel_Flags

FCheckFree = 0  // FCheckFree Starts out with a value of 1.
                // Used inside the check_free_list() routine
                // in 3GALLOC.OBJ. If the value is 0, it
                // appears that check_free_list() will walk
                // the global heap free list, probably to
                // verify its integrity.

// Get the name of the "386GRABBER" from the SYSTEM.INI file.
// The grabber is essential to running DOS apps in a window.
GetPrivateProfileString("BOOT", "386GRABBER", "386GRABBER",
            Grab_Name, 0x80, "SYSTEM.INI" )
```

The last section of SlowBoot() makes final preparations for jumping into the main scheduler loop, to be described in Chapter 6. The initial dummy task, described previously, is no longer necessary, so DeleteTask() removes it from the list of tasks, leaving the shell program as the only task. SlowBoot() then switches the stack yet again, and shrinks the main KERNEL code segment, as well as its data segment down to the final size. The last act of the KERNEL bootstrap process is a somewhat funny jump into the scheduler loop. Once this happens, Windows never needs the bootstrap code again. Windows is now up and running, putting a graphical, protected mode, multitasking operating environment at your disposal. Now you can begin that game of Solitaire!

```
Continuation of code for SlowBoot() - LDBOOT.OBJ

    DeleteTask( CurTDB )      // Kill the fake task created earlier

    CurTDB = 0                // No more current task

    SP = Gmove_Stack          // Switch the stack. Unclear as to
    Free_Sel( SS )            // why the SS selector is deleted.

    GlobalRealloc( DS, 0x2610, 0 )  // Shrink the DGROUP

    push CS          // Put arguments to GlobalRealloc()
    push 00          // on the stack, just as if we were to
    push 0xCC80      // call it normally. We're going to
    push 00          // be resizing the main KERNEL code segment.

    // Make BootSchedule() the "return address" on the stack.
    // Instead of coming back to this code, GlobalRealloc() will
    // "return" into the scheduler. Thus begins the normal
    // process of waiting for events and scheduling tasks.
    push offset BootSchedule

    jmp near GlobalRealloc  // Jump to GlobalRealloc().
```

USER Initialization

The preceding code for BootStrap() and SlowBoot() highlights the protected mode, DOS extending, multitasking aspect of Windows. What Windows is most known for, however, is the graphical face that it puts on top of character mode DOS. The USER module is the central component of this aspect of Windows. For instance, the USER startup sequence sets up the window manager, which keeps track of all windows, visible and invisible. Therefore, to learn even more about Windows, examine now in more detail some of the highlights of USER initialization. This sequence started with the call to LoadNewExe ("USER.EXE"), that SlowBoot() performed.

Like almost every other DLL, USER has an entry point that Windows calls when loading the DLL. In normal programs, this function's name is LibMain(). However, the name LibMain is nothing special. The USER version of LibMain() is USEREntry(), and the pseudocode is presented below. Like any standard DLL, USER first initializes its local heap (see Chapter 2 for the details of LocalInit()). In the case of both USER and GDI, the local heap is especially important because many of the Windows handles are just handles for the USER and GDI local heaps. After USEREntry() initializes the USER local heap, USEREntry() uses GlobalWire(), GlobalFix(), and GlobalPageLock() to move the second USER data segment down as low as possible and pagelock it (again, see Chapter 2). This is necessary because the code inside an interrupt handler may call USER functions, and it's important that none of this segment's memory be paged out (not present) at a critical moment. Then the LoadWindows() routine does the real work of setting up USER. This routine is examined in the next section. After the LoadWindows() routine, USEREntry() GlobalUnlocks the DGROUP segment, which is another standard step in DLL startup code. Finally, if running under Enhanced mode, INT 2Fh, function 1684h, obtains the entry point for the VDD (virtual display driver) enable/disable routine.

```
pseudocode for USEREntry() - INENTRY.OBJ
// On entry, CX = heap size, ES:SI = command line offset,
// DS = library data segment, DI = instance handle

    if ( heap size == 0 )        // We must have a heap!
        return 0

    if ( !LocalInit( 0, heap size ) ) // Did LocalInit() succeed?
        return 0

    AX = USER's second data segment (not the DGROUP segment)

    GlobalWire( AX ) // Wire down and fix the segment, possibly
    GlobalFix( AX )  // because it's used at interrupt time?

    // Pagelock the segment if running in Enhanced mode
    if ( WF_WIN386 bit set in WinFlags )
        GlobalPageLock( AX )     // AX still the non DGROUP data seg
```

```
LoadWindows( DI )    // Do the real work of initializing USER.
                     // DI is the USER hInstance

GlobalUnlock( DS )      // Unlock the DGROUP segment

if ( WF_WIN386 bit set in WinFlags )
{
    GlobalPageLock( DS )    // Pagelock the DGROUP as well

    INT 2Fh, AX=1684h, BX = 17h       // Get device API entry
    LpWin386ShellCritSection = ES:DI // point for SHELL device
}

return 1         // Successful load
```

LoadWindows()

LoadWindows() is a top level routine that invokes more specific routines to perform the desired initializations. Some additional initialization is done inline as well. After covering LoadWindows() as a whole, this section examines pseudocode for some of the more interesting subfunctions.

LoadWindows() first checks for the presence of the Edsun chip set. Presumably, Microsoft felt the Edsun chip set important enough to implement special code for it, although this special code appears to occur in only one spot. After LoadWindows() checks for the chip, LW_LoadSomeStrings() initializes various global string variables needed by USER. In the pseudocode for this function, and in numerous other spots, notice the heavy use of LoadString(). LoadString() obtains a string from a stringtable resource in the DLL file. Why go through this hassle? The most compelling answer is to make internationalization easier. Putting strings that require internationalization into resources makes creating a foreign language version of USER almost trivial. This trick makes it unnecessary to recompile the source code. Just run a different .RC file, customized for the desired language, through the resource compiler and bind it to the USER DLL.

LoadWindows() next obtains the default number of entries in the system and message queues. Chapter 7 on the messaging system discusses both types of queues. The default for the shared system queue is 120 entries, while each application gets its own queue of eight entries. As described in Chapter 7, changing entries in the WIN.INI file allows you to override these values at boot time. Once LoadWindows() establishes the queue sizes, it creates an application message queue, thus allowing the creation of windows (each window is associated with a queue).

LoadWindows() uses a helper function, UT_GetIntFromProfile(), to obtain the aforementioned queue sizes, as well as many other values. UT_GetIntFromProfile() accepts a stringtable ID as a parameter and extracts the string from USER with LoadString().

UT_GetIntFromProfile() uses this string as a key value in a call to GetProfileInt(). The second parameter to UT_GetIntFromProfile() is the default value, if there is no corresponding entry in the .INI file.

Following the queue initialization section, LoadWindows() determines the minimum border width of a window. Then a long sequence of calls to functions constructs individual pieces of the USER machinery. For instance, LW_DriversInit() sets up the system message queue (Chapter 7) and then calls the inquire routines of the various drivers, like KEYBOARD or MOUSE. Later chapters examine some of these routines. For now, it's sufficient to say that these routines register the system windows classes, and enable the various input/output devices, like the mouse and keyboard. After these routines run, LoadWindows() creates the global atom table and adds two atoms to it. The EnumProps() API uses these atoms.

A major problem in 3.0, and to some extent in 3.1, is that Windows runs out of the badly named Free System Resources. A better name (at least for programmers) would be "Space Left in the USER and GDI Heaps." Since the 16-bit segments that Windows runs in limit these heaps to at most 64K in size, the amount of free memory in the heaps often shrinks down to where no more applications can run. To alleviate this problem, Windows 3.1 distributes the items that would normally go into the single USER heap across three separate heaps. The first heap is the USER DGROUP. LoadWindows() uses GlobalAlloc() to allocate memory for two more heaps and then uses the LocalInit() function to create heaps in both segments.

After LoadWindows() sets up the additional USER heaps, it calls a second set of initialization functions. Of particular interest is the LW_LoadTaskmanAndScreenSaver() function. Despite its name, it does not actually load these modules. Instead, LW_LoadTaskmanAndScreenSaver() simply obtains the default configuration values each Windows program uses.

```
pseudocode for LoadWindows() - INLOADW.OBJ
// Parameters:
//      WORD    hInstance    // hInstance of USER

    // Save the module and instance handles away in global vars
    HInstanceWin = hInstance     // The USER DGROUP
    HModuleWin = GetModuleHandle( 0, hInstance )

    // Is there an Edsun chip installed?  The Edsun chip set is a
    // video chip that uses anti-aliasing techniques to get better
    // display quality.
    FEdsunChipSet = GetProfileInt("Windows, "Edsun", 0)

    LW_LoadSomeStrings()     // Loads USER strings variables
                             // from resources

    // Get the number of entries in the system message queue
    CQEntries = Ut_GetIntFromProfile(7, 0x3C) << 1

    // Get the default number of messages in a task queue
```

```
DefQueueSize = Ut_GetIntFromProfile(OxF, 8)

CreateQueue( DefQueueSize ) // Create an application message
                            // queue. This is needed to
                            // create windows (chapter 7).

// Get the default border width for a window. Default is 3.
ClBorder = Ut_GetIntFromProfile(OxE, 3)
if ( ClBorder < 1 )       // Make sure it's got a reasonable
    ClBorder = 1          // value.
if ( ClBorder > 0x32 )
    ClBorder = 0x32

LW_DriversInit()    // Setup and initialize the Keyboard,
                    // mouse, and COMM drivers. The system
                    // message queue is created here (in
                    // DI_EventInit(), which is called from
                    // LW_DriversInit()).

// LW_DCInit() is where the 5 DISPLAY device contexts are
// created. Chapter 5 covers device contexts (DCs) in
// detail. LW_DCInit() also calls @InitCreateRgn(),
// GetDCState(), CreateCompatibleDC(), and GetStockObject().
// The HFontSys and HFontSysFixed global vars are set here.
LW_DCInit()

LW_BrushInit() // Calls GetStockObject() to set the variables
               // HBrWhite and HBrBlack. Calls CreateBitmap(),
               // CreatePatternBrush(), DeleteObject(),
               // and MakeObjectPrivate().

// Perform various initialization required by the DISPLAY
// driver. Sets HInstanceDisplay variable by calling
// GetModuleHandle("DISPLAY"). LW_OemDependentInit() is a very
// large function, with numerous calls to routines such as
// GetDeviceCaps(), GetStockObject(), SetResourceHandler(),
// FindResource(), ODI_CreateBits(), and so on.
LW_OEMDependentInit()

LW_OEMCursorInit()  // Sets HBmCursorBitmap and
                    // HPermanentCursor variables.

// Set the global variables: CLBorder, CXBorder, CXSzBorder,
// CXSzBorderPlus1, CYBorder, CYSzBorder, CYSzBorderPlus1,
```

```
// CXCwMargin, and CYCwMargin. Presumably these deal with
// the size of the borders around Windows.
InitSizeBorderDimensions()

LW_LoadResources()   // Loads lots of icons and cursors. See
                     // the pseudocode for more details.

HWndFocus = 0        // Start out with no focus

LW_InitSysMetrics() // Loads values into the RGWSYSMet array.
                    // These values can be retrieved via the
                    // GetSystemMetrics() API

LW_RegisterWindows()    // Register the windows classes for
                        // "predefined" windows, such as
                        // edit controls, etc. We'll come
                        // back to this routine later.

// Allocate some memory for an internal buffer.
// UserLocalAlloc() is a special version of LocalAlloc().
// The first parameter "marks" each item in the USER local
// heap with a value that indicates what it is. This
// "tagging" of blocks only occurs in the debug version of
// USER. See the TOOLHELP LocalEntry documentation for
// a list of the various "tag" values.
PState = UserLocalAlloc(LT_USER_STRING, 0x40, some_static_var + 0x10 )

LW_MouseInit()  // Sets X_Mickey_Rate, Y_Mickey_Rate, and
                // calls ClipCursor( 0 )

EnableInput()   // Call the "enable" routine for various
                // input/output devices. We'll look at this
                // routine a bit later on.

SetCursor( some x, some y )     // Middle of the screen???
AX = LoadCursor( 0, IDC_WAIT )  // Get the hourglass cursor
SetCursor( AX )                 // show it

LW_InitWndMgr( hInstance )  // Register the Desktop and
                            // switch windows classes, and
                            // create the windows. We'll
                            // come back to this routine
                            // in a bit.

SelectObject( HDCBits, some value )         // ???
SelectObject( HDCMonoBits, some value )
```

```
WMaxBtnSize = MB_FindLongestString() // Max button size???

GlobalInitAtom()    // Create the global atom table.

AtomCheckPointProp = GlobalAddAtom("SysCP") // Used by
AtomBwlProp = GlobalAddAtom( "SysBW" )      // EnumProps()

MsgWinHelp = RegisterWindowMessage( "WM_WINHELP" )

// Allocate another local heap for menus
MenuBase = HMenuHeap = GlobalAlloc( GMEM_DDESHARE |
                    GMEM_MOVEABLE | GMEM_ZEROINIT, 0x418 )

// Allocate another local heap for menu strings
MenuStringBase = HMenuStringHeap = GlobalAlloc( GMEM_DDESHARE |
                    GMEM_MOVEABLE | GMEM_ZEROINIT, 0x418 )

// Initialize the menu and menu string heaps. The heaps
// start out small (0x417 bytes), but can grow as needed.
LocalInit( HMenuHeap, 0x12, 0x417 )
LocalInit( HMenuStringHeap, 0x12, 0x417 )

// Load the "system" menu ("Restore", "Move", "Size", etc.)
HSysMenu = LoadMenu( HInstanceWin, MK_FP(0,1) )

LW_DisplayDriverInit() // Gets entry points in display driver

LW_LoadFonts()  // Uses AddFontResource() to load all the
                // fonts in the "fonts" section of WIN.INI

LW_DesktopIconInit( 0 ) // Initialize things related to
                        // desktop icons/fonts

LW_DrawIconInit()   // Initializes HBmDrawIconMono and
                    // HMbDrawIconColor

LW_LoadTaskmanAndScreenSaver()  // Doesn't _load_ them. Just
                                // gets configuration values.
return 1
```

The LoadWindows() Helper Routines

As you can see from the LoadWindows() code, the function uses a variety of helper functions. The following sections of pseudocode present some of the more interesting helper routines.

LW_LoadSomeStrings()

LW_LoadSomeStrings() does precisely what its name implies. The second parameter to LoadString() is a stringtable resource ID in USER. You can see these strings yourself by using programs such as Borland's Resource Workshop or RESDUMP from *Undocumented Windows.* The third parameter is a buffer that holds the string. For the most part, the names of the buffers are self-explanatory.

```
pseudocode for LW_LoadSomeStrings() - INLOADW.OBJ

    LoadString(HInstanceWin, 0x4B, SzSysError, 0x14)

    Continue making calls similar to the above, to load the
    following message strings:  SzDivZero, SzUntitled, SzError,
    SzOK, SzCancel, SzAbort, SzRetry, SzIgnore, SzYYes, SzNo,
    SzClose, SzAM, SzPM.
```

LW_LoadResources()

LW_LoadResources() does more than what its name suggests. The initial sequence of code is a hodgepodge of variable initializations unrelated to resources. For instance, this function establishes the cursor blink rate and double click threshold. The Control Panel applet normally sets these values. Other variables this function sets include the amount of slop when double clicking. The slop establishes how many pixels the mouse can move between double clicks, yet still be considered a double click.

After LW_LoadResources() establishes all the various configuration values, it finally gets down to the business of loading resources. It loads commonly used cursors, such as the default arrow cursor and the sizing cursors. These cursor resources reside in the display driver DLL. Then the LoadIcon() function call pulls in the standard set of icons in for system dialog boxes. This set includes, for example, the hand icon.

```
pseudocode for LW_LoadResources() - INLOADW.OBJ
// Locals:
//      char    szWindows[0x14]
//      char    szBeep[0x14]
//      char    szSwapMouseButtons[0x14]

    // Get some strings out of the USER resources, for use as
    // section and key strings in GetProfileInt() calls
    LoadString(HInstanceWin, 0, szWindows, 0x14);
    LoadString(HInstanceWin, 5, szSwapMouseButtons, 0x14);
    LoadString(HInstanceWin, 9, szBeep, 0x14);

    AX = Ut_GetIntFromProfile(4, 0x1F4) // 4 = "CursorBlinkRate"
    SetCaretBlinkTime( AX )

    AX = Ut_GetIntFromProfile(6, 0)     // 6 = "DoubleClickSpeed"
    SetDoubleClickTime( AX )
```

```
// The next three fetched values are stored in static vars
Ut_GetIntFromProfile(0x61, 4)   // 0x61 = "DoubleClickWidth"
Ut_GetIntFromProfile(0x62, 4)   // 0x62 = "DoubleClickHeight"
Ut_GetIntFromProfile(0x60, 0)   // 0x62 = "MenuDropAlignment"

// Get the delay times related to displaying menus.
// 0x5E = "MenuShowDelay", 0x5F = "MenuHideDelay". The
// default value is seemingly related to whether the
// WF_CPU286 flag is set. Perhaps there's some sort of
// timing issue?
IDelayMenuShow = Ut_GetIntFromProfile(0x5E, defaultVal)
IDelayMenuHide = Ut_GetIntFromProfile(0x5F, defaultVal)

// Set the value of FSwapButtons, which indicates if the left
// and right mouse buttons should be swapped
GetProfileString( szWindows, szSwapMouseButtons,
                  szNullString, &someLocalVar, 2 )
FSwapButtons = some calculation involving szYes, the buffer
    filled by GetProfileString(), and a call to AnsiLower().

// Set the value of FBeep. Used by MessageBeep() to
// determine if a sound should be produced.
GetProfileString( szWindows, szBeep, szNullString,
                  &someLocalVar, 2 )
FBeep  = some calculation involving szYes, the buffer
    filled by GetProfileString(), and a call to AnsiLower().

// 0x6B = "DragFullWindows". Drag around the entire window
// contents, rather than just the frame???
FDragFullWindows = Ut_GetIntFromProfile(0x6B, 0)

// 0x6F = "CoolSwitch". This has to do with fast ALT-TAB
// switching between different tasks.
FFastAltTab = Ut_GetIntFromProfile(0x6F, 1)

// Get the Grid granularity of the desktop. 0x50 = "Desktop"
// 8 = "GridGranularity". It appears that szBeep[] and
// szWindows[] are being reused, rather than creating
// additional char arrays on the stack.
LoadString(HInstanceWin, 0x50, szWindows, 0x14)
LoadString( HInstanceWin, 8, szBeep, 0x14 )
CXYGranularity =
    GetProfileInt( "Desktop", "GridGranularity", 0) << 3
if ( !CXYGranularity )  // Make sure CXYGranularity is at
    CXYGranularity++    // least 1.
```

```
    // Load some heavily used cursors
    HCursNormal = LoadCursor( 0, IDC_ARROW )
    HCursIBeam  = LoadCursor( 0, IDC_IBEAM )
    HCursUpArrow= LoadCursor( 0, IDC_UPARROW )
    HIconSample = LoadIcon( 0, IDI_APPLICATION )

    // Set the "resource handler" address for cursors & icons.
    SetResourceHandler( HInstanceWin, 1, LoadDIBCursorHandler )
    SetResourceHandler( HInstanceWin, 3, LoadDIBIconHandler )

    HIconWindows = LoadIcon( HInstanceWin,  // The Windows logo
                    MAKEINTRESOURCE( 0, OCR_ICOCUR) )

    // Load the "resizing" cursors (when cursor is over a border)
    LoadCursor( 0, IDC_SIZENWSE )
    LoadCursor( 0, IDC_SIZENESW )
    LoadCursor( 0, IDC_SIZENS )
    LoadCursor( 0, IDC_SIZEWE )

    // Load some icons used by various dialog boxes
    HIconHand = LoadIcon( 0, MAKEINTRESOURCE( OIC_HAND ) )
    HIconHand = LoadIcon( 0, MAKEINTRESOURCE( OIC_QUES ) )
    HIconHand = LoadIcon( 0, MAKEINTRESOURCE( OIC_BANG ) )
    HIconHand = LoadIcon( 0, MAKEINTRESOURCE( OIC_NOTE ) )

    HCursSizeAll =              // The "4 directions" icon
        LoadCursor(HInstanceWin, MAKEINTRESOURCE( OCR_SIZEALL))
```

LW_RegisterWindows()

If you've ever snooped around in Windows with such tools as WinSight or SPY from the SDK, you may have noticed that all of the standard windows like buttons and listboxes have their own classes, just like any other window. These classes are not hardcoded into USER. Instead, LW_RegisterWindows() registers them just like any other class. A small helper routine registers each of the predefined windows classes by simply filling in a WNDCLASS structure before passing the structure to RegisterClass(). Of special interest are the menu and dialog box classes. Rather than having standard string names, they use integer resource ID naming, wherein the segment portion of the string is zero, and the offset portion is an ordinal value that is greater than or equal to 0x8000. The MAKEINTATOM macro makes it easy to create integer resource IDs.

```
pseudocode for LW_RegisterWindows() - INLOADW.OBJ

    RW_RegisterMenus()          // Class = MAKELP(0, 0x8000)
    RW_RegisterButton()         // Class = "Button"
```

```
RW_RegisterStatic()          // Class = "Static"
RW_RegisterDlg()             // Class = MAKELP(0, 0x8002)
RW_RegisterEdit()            // Class = "Edit"
RW_RegisterLBoxCtl()         // Class = "ListBox"
RW_RegisterSB()              // Class = "ScrollBar"
RW_RegisterComboLBoxCtl()    // Class = "ComboLBox"
RW_RegisterCBoxCtl()         // Class = "ComboBox"
RW_RegisterMDIClient()       // Class = "MDIClient"
```

EnableInput()

EnableInput() brings the various hardware drivers to life so that Windows is more than just a pretty picture on the screen. The first task is to turn on the undocumented system timers that are critical to much of Windows (see EnableSystemTimer() in the SYSTEM DLL). Then EnableInput() initializes the keyboard driver followed by the mouse driver. If a sound driver was loaded previously, EnableInput() brings it to life as well. The last driver it initializes, if one exists, is the network driver. When EnableInput() has initialized all drivers, it calls InternalBroadcastDriverMessage(). From its name, this function apparently has something to do with broadcasting some sort of message to all installed drivers in the system.

```
code for EnableInput() - INENABLE.OBJ
// Locals:
//      WORD    HModSound
//      LPFN    lpfnSoundEnable

    EnableSystemTimers()    // See "Undocumented Windows"

    Initialize some memory starting at RGBKeyState to 0. Maybe
    some sort of an array. Do the same for RGBAsyncKeyState.

    Enable( Keybd_Event, RGBKeyState )  // KEYBOARD.2. See the
                                        // DDK examples for
                                        // source code for the
                                        // Enable() routines.

    CopyKeyState()      // copies keyboard state tables?

    if ( some static variable )
        Enable( Mouse_Event )       // MOUSE.2

    // Look for the presence of a SOUND driver. If found, get
    // the address of its enable() function, and call it.
    HModSound = GetModuleHandle("SOUND")
    if ( HModSound )
        lpfnSoundEnable = GetProcAddress(HModSound, "enable")
    if ( lpfnSoundEnable )
        lpfnSoundEnable()
```

```
// Call WNetEnable() to initialize the network module,
// if a network is present. See FarCallNetDriver() entry
// in "Undocumented Windows," and "Windows Network
// Programming" by Ralph Davis.
if ( PNetInfo && *(&PNetInfo + 0x50) )
    (&PNetInfo + 0x50)()     // Call through a function pointer

// Broadcast a message to the installable device drivers?
// 2 = DRV_ENABLE??
InternalBroadcastDriverMessage(0, 2, 0, 0, 0, 0, 0, 4)
```

LW_InitWndMgr()

LW_InitWndMgr() is a key player in bringing up the windowing system. The first task is to assign values to variables related to screen widths, border sizes, and so on. The fun part begins with registering the classes for the desktop and switch windows. The desktop window is the granddaddy of all windows. All other windows in the system are its descendants (see Chapter 4 for details). The switch window is normally an invisible window that resides in the center of the screen and its job is to switch between various tasks in the system. It is visible when you repeatedly ALT-TAB between the running Windows programs. At the same time, LW_InitWndMgr() creates the window class for icon title windows. The descriptive text you see beneath each icon on the Windows desktop is an instance of an icon title window. This function call registers each of the window classes described here with the name of an integer resource ID form. (See the description of this process in LW_RegisterWindows() above.)

LW_InitWndMgr() next creates instances of the windows classes it just registered by using CreateWindowEx(). CreateWindowEx() creates the desktop window, as you might expect, with a size equal to the entire screen. After creating the switch window, the CreateWindowEx() moves the switch window to the center of the screen and gives it attributes that maintain the window's size and position.

Now that there is a desktop, LW_InitWndMgr() sets the desktop wallpaper and pattern. Normally, you use the Control Panel applet to select the bitmaps. The parameter to both functions is -1, indicating that the Control Panel applet should retrieve the bitmap names from WIN.INI. After the Control Panel applet selects the wallpaper, the code sends a WM_SYSCOLORCHANGE message to the desktop window because the wallpaper bitmap may have a different palette than the default system palette. The LW_InitWndMgr()'s last step is to invalidate the entire desktop window, and call UpdateWindow(), which draws the selected wallpaper.

```
pseudocode for LW_InitWndMgr() - INLOADW.OBJ
// Parameters:
//      WORD    hInstance
// Locals:
//      WNDCLASS * pWndClass     // For use in registering classes
```

```
Initialize the following variables from static variables:
CXSize, CYSize, CYCaption, CXBorder, CYBorder, CYHScroll,
and CXVScroll

SetMinMaxInfo() // Appears to initialize some static vars.
                // Uses CXScreen, CYScreen, CXBorder, etc...

pWndClass = UserLocalAlloc( LT_USER_CLASS, 0x40, 0x1A ) // Allocate 0x1A
                                                         // bytes.

pWndClass->lpszClassName = MAKELP( 0, 0x8001)
pWndClass->hCursor = LoadCursor(0, IDC_ARROW)
pWndClass->lpfnWndProc = DeskTopWndProc
pWndClass->hInstance = hInstance
pWndClass->style = CS_DBLCLKS
pWndClass->hBrBackground = 2
RegisterClass( pWndClass )   // Register the DeskTop class

// Register the "switch window" class
pWndClass->lpszClassName = MAKELP( 0, 0x8003 )
pWndClass->hCursor = LoadCursor(0, IDC_ARROW)
pWndClass->lpfnWndProc = SwitchWndProc
pWndClass->hInstance = hInstance
pWndClass->style = CS_SAVEBITS | CS_VREDRAW | CS_HREDRAW
pWndClass->hBrBackground = 2
RegisterClass( pWndClass )

// Register the icon title class
pWndClass->lpszClassName = MAKELP( 0, 0x8004 )
pWndClass->hCursor = LoadCursor(0, IDC_ARROW)
pWndClass->lpfnWndProc = TitleWndProc
pWndClass->hInstance = hInstance
pWndClass->style =  0
pWndClass->hBrBackground = 0
RegisterClass( pWndClass )

LocalFree( pWndClass )  // Don't need WNDCLASS anymore!

// Create the desktop and switch windows
HWndDesktop = CreateWindowEx( 0, MAKELP(0, 0x8001),
                0, WS_CLIPCHILDREN | WS_POPUP, 0, 0,
                CXScreen, CYScreen, 0, 0, hInstance, 0)

HWndSwitch = CreateWindowEx( 0, MAKELP(0, 0x8003),
                0, WS_DISABLED | WS_POPUP, 0, 0, 0xA, 0xA,
                0, 0, hInstance, 0 )
```

```
// Move the switch window to the center of the screen
SetWindowPos( HWndSwitch, 0xFFFF, 0, 0, 0, 0,
    SWP_NOSIZE | SWP_NOMOVE | SWP_NOREDRAW | SWP_NOACTIVATE )

HWndRealPopup = CreateWindowEx( 0, MAKELP(0, 0x8000), 0,
                WS_POPUP, 0, 0, 0x64, 0x64, 0, 0,
                hInstance, 0 )      // Pop-up menu???

SetDeskPattern( -1 )    // Set the wallpaper and pattern
SetDeskWallpaper( -1 )  // Read names from the WIN.INI file

// Tell the desktop that the palette may have changed from
// loading the wallpaper image.
SendMessage(HWndDesktop, WM_SYSCOLORCHANGE, 0, 0)

Toggle a bit in the HWndDesktop flags   // ?

InvalidateDCCache( HWndDesktop, 0 ) // Force the entire
InvalidateRect( HWndDesktop, 0, 1 ) // desktop to be
UpdateWindow( HWndDesktop )         // refreshed
```

GlobalInitAtom()

Atom tables are a quick way to store a string in a hash table and then reference it by an integer handle. The USER module stores window class names, registered using RegisterClass() (see Chapter 4) in an atom table. Each application can have its own local atom table. However, class names are at system level scope, so a global atom table is necessary, as well. GlobalInitAtom() creates the global atom table.

GlobalInitAtom() starts by allocating a global memory block to hold the table and then stores the block's selector value into a USER global variable, HWinAtom. LocalInit() then creates a local heap within the HWinAtom memory block. Finally, InitAtomTable() sets up the atom table's internal data.

```
pseudocode for GlobalInitAtom() - WINATOM.OBJ

    HWinAtom = GlobalAlloc( GMEM_MOVABLE | GMEM_ZEROINIT |
                            GMEM_DDESHARE, 0xFA )
    if ( HWinAtom == 0 )
        return 0

    HWinAtom = HIWORD( GlobalLock( HWinAtom ) )

    Call a function that sets DS to HWinAtom, if it's nonzero.

    LocalInit( 0, 0, 0xEA ) // First 0 means use current DS
                            // See Chapter 2 for LocalInit()
```

```
    InitAtomTable( 0x25 )    // 37 entries in atom table. 37 is a
                             // prime number, which increases hash
                             // efficiency. (See Knuth.)

    GlobalUnlock( HWinAtom )    // does nothing, since the memory
                                // is MOVABLE. See Chapter 2.
```

LW_DisplayDriverInit()

LW_DisplayDriverInit() gets the addresses of two routines in the DISPLAY driver. If the DISPLAY driver knows how to save bitmaps internally, LW_DisplayDriverInit() sets the LpSaveBitmap global variable to point at the routine. The other function pointer LW_DisplayDriverInit() initializes here is for the DISPLAY function, which turns screen repainting on or off. The Windows scheduler calls this function when exiting the scheduling routine. Sometimes doing screen updates causes serious stability problems. To circumvent this, the DISPLAY driver exports a function that allows you to enable/disable screen repainting as necessary.

```
pseudocode for LW_DisplayDriverInit() - INLOADW.OBJ
// Locals:
//      HDC     hDC

    hDC = GetScreenDC()     // Need a device context below

    // If the display driver can save bits, get a function ptr
    // to the routine that does it. The function has an entry
    // ordinal of 92 (0x5C)
    FOnBoardBitmap = GetDeviceCaps( hDC, RASTERCAPS ) & 0x0040
    if ( FOnBoardBitmap )
        LpSaveBitmap=GetProcAddress(HInstanceDisplay,MAKELP(0,92))

    ReleaseCacheDC( hDC, 0 )    // Done with the device context

    // DISPLAY.500 -> UserRepaintDisable(). This function
    // tells the display driver when screen updates should be
    // enabled or disabled.
    LpDisplayCriticalSection =
        GetProcAddress( HInstanceDisplay, MAKELP(0, 500) )
```

LW_LoadTaskmanAndScreenSaver()

LW_LoadTaskmanAndScreenSaver() loads neither TASKMAN.EXE nor a screen saver module (Windows 3.1 has a documented API for writing screen savers). The function starts by retrieving the name of the TASKMAN file, or its replacement, from the SYSTEM.INI file. Double clicking on the desktop window or hitting CTRL-ESC loads TASKMAN. The function also gets the length of idle time that's required before activating the screensaver, as well as the status (enabled/disabled) of screensaving. When it's time to invoke the screensaver, USER loads the saver program's name (for example, SSMYST.SCR) from SYSTEM.INI and passes it as the argument to WinExec(). This process happens deep inside the default message handling code in USER.

```
pseudocode for LW_LoadTaskmanAndScreenSaver() - INLOADW.OBJ
// Locals:
//      char    szBoot[0xA]
//      char    szTaskMan[0xD]
//      char    szSysIni[0x14]

    // Get some strings out of the USER string tables.
    // 0x48 -> "BOOT", 0x4F -> "TASKMAN.EXE, 0x4A -> "SYSTEM.INI"
    LoadString( HInstanceWin, 0x48, szBoot, 0xA )
    LoadString( HInstanceWin, 0x4F, szTaskMan, 0xD )
    LoadString( HInstanceWin, 0x4A, szSysIni, 0x14 )

    // Get 0x82 bytes for use as the string buffer in the call to
    // GetPrivateProfileString(), below.
    PTaskManName = UserLocalAlloc( LT_USER_STRING, 0x40, 0x82 )

    // Get the "final" name of TASKMAN.EXE from the boot section
    // of the SYSTEM.INI file. The default is taskman.exe=taskman.exe.
    GetPrivateProfileString( szBoot, szTaskMan, szTaskMan,
            pTaskManName, 0x82, szSysIni )
    // Get rid of the excess memory that was allocated previously.
    LocalRealloc( PTaskManName, lstrlen(PTaskManName)+1, 0 )

    // The screen saver timeout value. 0x63 = "ScreenSaveTimeOut"
    IScreenSaveTimeOut = Ut_GetIntFromProfile(0x63, 0)

    // Screen saver active? 0x64 = "ScreenSaveActive"
    if ( Ut_GetIntFromProfile( 0x64, 0 ) == 0 )
    {
        if ( IScreenSaveTimeOut > 0 )
            IScreenSaveTimeOut = -IScreenSaveTimeOut     // ???
    }
```

This concludes the brief tour through the USER initialization. Although many routines and areas weren't touched upon, hopefully you now have an idea of Windows' incredible complexity, flexibility, and configurability, and can use it to your advantage.

Shutting Things Down

So far, this chapter has focused on the steps involved in turning a real mode DOS machine into a protected mode, multitasking, GUI environment. It has been said that the designers of the 286 chip felt it wasn't necessary to go back to real mode once the chip was in protected mode. The designers of Windows didn't have this luxury. Windows starts out from the DOS prompt and must return gracefully to the DOS prompt, whereupon the user may turn off the machine. The next few sections examine the mercifully shorter journey back to real mode DOS.

Shutting Down USER

You now know that the USER initialization code concentrates on the graphical user interface aspect of Windows, while KERNEL specializes in areas related to memory management, tasking, and so on. The shutdown process is no different. Except for when you ignominiously leave Windows with CTRL-ALT-DELETE (also known as the Big Red Switch or Vulcan Nerve Pinch), you normally exit Windows through the ExitWindows() API. ExitWindows() is usually invoked using PROGMAN, but your own programs can call ExitWindows() as well.

ExitWindows() starts by enumerating all the top-level windows, using EnumWindows(). The enumeration callback function sends a message to each window, which either asks if it's OK to shut down, or which says that things *are* shutting down. See the pseudocode for the callback function after the ExitWindows() code.

Assuming that nobody vetoes the idea of shutting down, ExitWindows() broadcasts another message to all the installed drivers. After this, it destroys the data in the clipboard and turns the cursor off. Also, at this point ExitWindows() changes the KERNEL fault handler from the standard handler to a different, exit time handler. This special handler just displays a message, "Fault at Exit Time!!!" in the debug KERNEL. Presumably there's little else that can be done for the patient at this stage.

In the next step, ExitWindows() disables input from the hardware drivers, using DisableInput(). The pseudocode for DisableInput() follows the other pseudocode below. With the drivers disabled, it's safe to free them as well. Nearing the end of the USER shutdown, Death(), a GDI function described in *Undocumented Windows*, puts the screen back into text mode. In a final dying gasp USER calls ExitKernel(), which is the KERNEL equivalent of ExitWindows().

```
pseudocode for ExitWindows() - ENABLE.OBJ

    if ( FEndSession )  // Prevent ExitWindows() from being
        return 0;       // re-entered???
    FEndSession = 1;

    @fQueryQuit()    // Calls EnumWindows(), with QueryQuitEnum()
                     // as the callback function

    if ( @fQueryQuit() == 0 )
    {
        FEndSession = FALSE
        SetSysModalWindow( 0 )  // Undo system modal window if
        return 0                // there is one.
    }
```

```
// Broadcast a message to installable drivers?
// 0xB = DRV_EXITSESSION???
InternalBroadcastDriverMessage( 0, 0xB, 0, 0, 0, 0, 0, 6 )

DestroyClipboardData()      // Trash the clipboard

ShowCursor( 0 )     // Turn off the cursor

Bunny_351() // Changes the KERNEL interrupt handler to
            // a different, exit-time, exception handler.

DisableInput()  // Do the opposite of EnableInput()

while (IDLastDriver != 0xFF) // Free all installed drivers?
    InternalFreeDriver( IDLastDriver + 1, 0 )

Death( PdceFirst->hDC ) // GDI function that switches the
                        // display back to text mode.

ExitKernel( ExitCode )  // Do KERNEL cleanup before
                        // returning to DOS.
```

QueryQuitEnum()

ExitWindows() calls QueryQuitEnum() for every top-level window in the system. Depending on the value of each window's lParam, QueryQuitEnum() sends either a WM_QUERYENDSESSION or a WM_ENDSESSION to the window specified by the HWND parameter. When this function sends the WM_QUERYENDSESSION message, it returns the value returned by the window. If an application window handles that message and returns zero, QueryQuitEnum() returns zero, causing the enumeration of windows to stop and ExitWindows() to abandon the shutdown procedure.

```
pseudocode for QueryQuitEnum() - INEXIT.OBJ
// Parameters:
//      HWND    hwnd
//      LPARAM  lparam

    if ( hwnd->hq == HQCurrent() )  // Don't bother with windows
        return 1                    // in the current task/queue

    if ( LOWORD( lparam ) == 2 )
    {
        // Be nice and ask the window if it's O.K. to quit
        // REvalSendMessage() is just a "wrapper" routine around
        // a SendMessage() call in the debug KERNEL. In the
        // retail KERNEL, it's just a SendMessage().
        return REvalSendMessage( hWnd, WM_QUERYENDSESSION, 0, 0 )
    }
```

```
    else
    {
        // Be firm, and tell the window that it will be shut down.
        REvalSendMessage( hwnd, WM_ENDSESSION, LOWORD(lparam), 0 )
        return 1
    }
```

DisableInput()

DisableInput() is almost identical to EnableInput(), but in reverse. First, DisableInput() broadcasts a message (DRV_DISABLE?) to all the installed drivers. Then, it disables the network and sound drivers, if present. Next in line is the mouse driver, followed by the keyboard driver. The system timer is the last driver disabled. The final bit of cleanup is to read in and toss all the messages in the system queue, thereby ensuring that it's empty.

```
pseudocode for DisableInput() - INENABLE.OBJ
// Locals
//      WORD    HSoundDriver
//      LPFN    lpfnSoundDisable
//      MSG     msg

    // Broadcast message to installable drivers.
    // 5 = DRV_DISABLE???
    InternalBroadcastDriverMessage( 0, 5, 0, 0, 0, 0, 0, 6 )

    // Call WNetDisable(). See the entry for FarCallNetDriver()
    // in Undocumented Windows.
    if ( PNetInfo && ( *(DWORD *)(PNetInfo + 0x54) ) )
        (PNetInfo + 0x54)() // Call through a function pointer

    HSoundDriver = GetModuleHandle( "sound" )   // Disable the
    if ( HSoundDriver )                         // SOUND driver,
    {                                           // if present.
        lpfnSoundDisable = GetProcAddress(HSoundDriver, "disable")
        if ( lpfnSoundDisable )
            lpfnSoundDisable()
    }

    if ( some static var )      // Say goodbye to the mouse
        DisableMouse()

    Disable()       // Disable the keyboard driver

    DisableSystemTimers()   // See "Undocumented Windows"

EmptyMessages:  // Keep reading system messages till the system
                // message queue is empty.

    if ( ReadMessage( HQSysQueue, &msg, 0, 0, 0xFFFF, 1 ))
        goto EmptyMessages
```

Exiting KERNEL—The Last Hurrah

The first major task of ExitKernel() is to call the WEP (Windows Exit Procedure) routine for each DLL in the system. KillLibraries() handles this chore and calls the WEP routines. KillLibraries() does not actually unload the DLLs however. ExitKernel() next calls the disable routine for the mouse, keyboard, and system drivers. This is somewhat strange because USER has already called these routines in its DisableInput() function. Perhaps this code exists in case a program calls ExitKernel() directly, instead of through an intervening call to ExitWindows().

The next step is for ExitKernel() to write out any profile (.INI) buffers that are not up-to-date with what's in the disk file. ExitKernel() then calls DisableKernel() to reset all the interrupt handlers that KERNEL installed, as well as to close file handles that various Windows tasks may have opened.

The final sequence of ExitKernel() is related to the way KERNEL should terminate itself. In most cases, KERNEL does a simple INT 21h, function 4Ch. Since KERNEL is running as a protected mode DPMI client, this function call does not cause the machine to immediately return to the DOS prompt. Instead, the DPMI host (WIN386 or DOSX) receives the interrupt and cleans up its own internal state of affairs. After completing this task, the DPMI host switches the machine back to either real or virtual 8086 mode, and you wind up back at the DOS prompt. The other way of leaving ExitKernel() is to reboot the machine (for example, call ExitWindows() with the EW_REBOOTSYSTEM return code). Depending on which mode Windows is running in, this function either calls the REBOOT VxD or it invokes INT 19h. The REBOOT VxD is responsible for the local reboot option in Windows 3.1. (INT 19h is discussed in detail in Geoff Chapell's forthcoming *DOS Internals*.)

```
pseudocode for ExitKernel() - ENABLE.OBJ
// Parameters:
//      WORD    exitCode

    Set a bit in [Kernel_Flags + 2]     // Exiting bit???

    // Loop through all the modules in the system, invoking
    // CallWEP() for each one (even for program modules). The
    // first module (KERNEL) is skipped.
    KillLibraries()

    if ( PMouseTermProc )   // Call mouse driver Disable(), if
        PMouseTermProc()    // we've got a valid ptr to it.

    if (PKeyboardTermProc)  // Call keyboard driver Disable(),
        PKeyboardTermProc() // if we've got a valid ptr to it.

    if (PSystemTermProc)    // Call system driver Disable(),
        PSystemTermProc()   // if we've got a valid ptr to it.
```

```
    WriteOutProfiles()      // Write out any profiles that are
                            // out of date with the disk
    FProfileMayBeStale = 1  // We just wrote it out???

    Enter_Gmove_Stack()     // Switches to a different stack

    DisableKernel() // Reset the exception handlers back to their
                    // original address, and close down open
                    // files in running tasks.

    if ( exitCode != 0x43 )     // 0x43 = EW_REBOOTSYSTEM
        goto exit_via_DOS

    INT 2F, AX = 1600           // Enhanced mode Windows running?
    if ( the bottom 7 bits in AL are zero )
        goto exit_via_INT_19

    if ( (AL == 1) || (AL == 0xFF) ) // Windows/386 2.x running???
        goto exit_via_DOS

    // Get the REBOOT VxD (9) API entry point in ES:DI
    INT 2Fh, AX = 1684h, BX = 9, ES:DI = 0:0
    if ( ES:DI == 0 )           // Couldn't get the entry point
        goto exit_via_DOS

    Call through ES:DI, with AX = 0x0100    // Reboot ourselves

    goto exit_via_DOS   // If we're still alive, exit to DOS

exit_via_INT_19:

    INT 21h, AH = 0Dh       // DOS Disk reset. Flushes buffers.

    AX = 0xFE03, SI = 0x4346, DI = 0x4E55   // Signature WORDS ?
    STC
    INT 2Fh         // Unknown what this is for

    INT 19h         // Reboot the system.

exit_via_DOS:

    AH = 4CH, AX = exitCode
    INT 21h         // Exit "to DOS".
```

DisableKernel()

DisableKernel() is the complementary function to EnableKernel(), resetting all of the exception handlers that KERNEL installed in EnableKernel() back to their original values. In addition, DisableKernel() iterates through the list of PSPs (PDBs), closing every file in each PSP's job file table that's not one of the standard files, such as CON. The last portion of DisableKernel() appears to have something to do with unlinking entries in the system file tables. This code is probably undoing the work done at startup time by GrowSFTToMax().

In addition to DisableKernel(), there's a corresponding EnableKernel() function in KERNEL. However, if you try to invoke it, the debug KERNEL displays the message, "Don't call EnableKernel." Nothing else is done in EnableKernel(). In the Windows 3.0 KERNEL, the function does the opposite of DisableKernel().

```
pseudocode for DisableKernel() - ENABLE.OBJ

    Turn on bit 0x0002 in [Kernel_Flags+2]

    // Restore some interrupt handlers (0, 24h, 2Fh, 2,
    // 4, 6, 7, 3E and 75h) to their previous handlers.
    if ( FP_SEG( PrevInt21Proc ) != 0 )
        InternalDisableDOS()

    CX:DX = PrevInt3FProc   // Set the old INT 3Fh handler back
    INT 31h, AX = 0203h, BL = 0Bh

    CX:DX = PrevInt0CProc   // Set the old Exc. 0Ch handler back
    INT 31h, AX = 0203h, BL = 0Ch

    CX:DX = PrevInt0DProc   // Set the old Exc. 0Dh handler back
    INT 31h, AX = 0203h, BL = 0Dh

    CX:DX = PrevIntx6Proc   // Set the old Exc. 06h handler back
    INT 31h, AX = 0203h, BL = 06h

    CX:DX = PrevInt0EProc   // Set the old Exc. 0Eh handler back
    INT 31h, AX = 0203h, BL = 0Eh

    Iterate through the TDB list (HeadPDB is the head ptr). Call
    TerminatePDB() for each task besides the TopPDB (the KERNEL
    boot time PSP). TerminatePDB() closes any file handles that
    the PDB has open.

    INT 21h, AH=50h, BX = TopPDB    // Switch the current PDB to
                                    // the KERNEL startup PSP

    Turn off bit 0x0002 in [Kernel_Flags+2], which was turned
    on when we entered the function.

    Iterate through all of the files in KERNEL's PSP (TopPDB).
    If the file handle is greater than 5, close it via INT 21h,
```

```
fn. 3Eh. This leave all the "standard" file handles open.

// Do something related to unlinking additional system file
// table entries that may have been added by GrowSFTToMax()
if ( PSFTLink != 0 )
{
    CX:DX = *PSFTLink
    *PSftLink = 0:0xFFFF
    LpWinSFTLink = CX:DX
}
```

InternalDisableDOS()

InternalDisableDOS() resets several values to their pre-InternalEnableDOS() settings. The first job is to reset the "one-drive logic" for floppy drives to its original state. Next, InternalDisableDOS() restores the original value of the INT 21h handler, as well as several more exception handlers that were hooked by InternalEnableDOS(). The final bit of code in the routine sets the CTRL-C checking state back to its pre-Windows setting.

```
pseudocode for InternalDisableDOS() - ENABLE.OBJ

    AX = FInt21
    FInt21 = 0              // Indicating that we've "disabled" DOS?

    if ( AX == 0 )          // Was DOS "disabled" already???
        return

    PSysProc( 2, 1 ) // Enable 1 drive logic, via InquireSystem()

    PrevInt21Proc( AX = 3301h, DL = 0 ) // Disable CTRL-C checking

    // Set the INT 21h handler address back to its old value
    PrevInt21Proc( AX = 2521, DS:DX = PrevInt21Proc )

    INT 21h, AX = 352Fh     // Get the current INT 2Fh handler
    MyInt2F = ES:BX

    // Restore the original interrupt/exception handlers for
    // the usual cast of hooked vectors.
    INT 21h, AX = 2500h, DS:DX = PrevInt00Proc
    INT 21h, AX = 2524h, DS:DX = PrevInt24Proc
    INT 21h, AX = 252Fh, DS:DX = PrevInt2FProc
    INT 21h, AX = 2502h, DS:DX = PrevInt02Proc
    INT 21h, AX = 2504h, DS:DX = PrevInt04Proc
    INT 21h, AX = 2506h, DS:DX = PrevInt06Proc
    INT 21h, AX = 2507h, DS:DX = PrevInt07Proc
    INT 21h, AX = 253Eh, DS:DX = PrevInt3EProc
```

```
INT 21h, AX = 2575h, DS:DX = PrevInt75Proc

// Set the CTRL-C checking state back to what it was when
// KERNEL started ( in InitDOSVarP() ).
INT 21h, AX = 3301h, DL = FBreak
```

Summary

Working through the mechanics of a Windows startup and shutdown exposes many different aspects of Windows. To describe the inner workings of each aspect would be a truly enormous task. This chapter is intended to serve as a sort of road map to the rest of this book. Don't hesitate to go off and study the parts of Windows that this book does cover and then come back to this chapter. Understanding Windows is not an all or nothing proposition. Rather, the purpose of reading this book is to continually refine your working model of Windows.

CHAPTER 2

Windows Memory Management

The most fundamental function of any operating system is memory management, which is the foundation of almost all other operating systems services. Poorly written memory management code results in operating systems that are both unreliable and difficult to program for. Just look at the state of MS-DOS programming today! Large portions of the KERNEL code address the complex task of managing memory on a CPU architecture that can at best be described as quirky. A fair amount of the KERNEL memory management code deals with the restrictions of the Intel 80x86 CPU's segmented architecture.

This chapter examines in detail how KERNEL orchestrates all the complex actions that go on in the global and local heaps, emphasizing Windows 3.1 Enhanced mode, but mentioning Standard mode and Windows 3.0 where appropriate. This chapter starts out with an overview of Windows memory management. Next, it dives into the low level selector APIs that support the higher level memory management. After that it goes through the heap functions in detail and gives the pseudocode for the various functions, including documented, undocumented and internal functions. This chapter is not a substitute for the actual documentation, but instead, shows you what actually goes on inside the heap functions. The functions' use determine their order, rather than their alphabetical order. The chapter finishes with a look at memory management at the application level.

Outline of the Memory Management Functions

A quick glance at the table of contents tells you that this chapter is well over 100 pages in length. It covers a phenomenal amount of information, mainly because Windows provides dozens of memory management APIs. There is definitely more going on here than malloc() and free() calls! Because there are so many functions, it's not absolutely necessary to read this chapter from beginning to end. Consider much of this chapter to be a reference to use when you need to know the details of a particular memory management API.

Many of the functions covered here call helper functions. In many cases, this chapter provides pseudocode for those functions as well. Because paper is a two-dimensional medium, it is necessary to string the function descriptions one after the other. This increases the difficulty of seeing the surrounding context of a function when you're several layers deep inside a function call hierarchy. To attempt to remedy this, Table 2-1 shows the functions and data structures in outline form. Note that many of the routines are called by several different routines. In each case, however, the routine only appears once in the outline. The top level function entries appear in a logical order, working from most to least important (although you might have grouped them differently).

You may be wondering why the selector functions come first, before the more familiar global heap functions. Ordering the chapter in this manner allows each section to build upon the previous section. The global heap functions absolutely depend on the selector functions. The local heap functions depend on the global heap functions. The idea, while not 100% achievable, is to avoid as many forward references as possible.

Table 2-1: Outline of Functions and Data Structures.

The selector functions

- AllocSelector()
- AllocSelectorArray()
    - Get_Sel()
- FreeSelector()
    - FreeSelArray()
        - Free_Sel()
- GetSelectorLimit()
- SetSelectorLimit()
- GetSelectorBase()
    - Get_Physical_Address()
- SetSelectorBase()
- PrestoChangoSelector()
- AllocDStoCSAlias()
    - AKA()
- AllocCStoDSAlias()

The global heap data structures

- The Burgermaster segment
    - GlobalInfo structure
    - GlobalInfo structure
    - Global heap arenas
    - Selector table (not the LDT)
- Memory blocks

Table 2-1: Outline of Functions and Data Structures. (continued)

The global heap functions

- GlobalInit()
  - GInit()
- GlobalAlloc()
  - GbTop()
  - GAlloc()
    - GSearch()
      - GrowHeap()
      - GCompact()
- GlobalFree()
  - GFree()
    - Free_Object()
- GlobalLock()
- GlobalUnlock()
- GlobalHandle()
  - MyLock()
    - XHandle()
- GlobalReAlloc()
- GlobalDOSAlloc()
- GlobalDOSFree()
- GlobalCompact()
  - InnerShrinkHeap()
    - UnlinkWin386Block()
- GlobalFix()
- GlobalUnfix()
  - GUnLock()
- LockSegment()
- UnlockSegment()
- GlobalPageLock()
- GlobalPageUnlock()
- GlobalWire()
  - GWire()
- GlobalUnwire()
- LRUSweep()
- GlobalLRUNewest()
- GlobalLRUOldest()
- GlobalFlags()
- GlobalSize()
- GlobalNotify()
- GetFreeSpace()
  - GetDPMIFreeSpace()
- GetFreeMemInfo()
- SetSwapAreaSize()
  - CalcMaxNRSeg()
    - GReserve()

The local heap data structures

- The LocalInfo structure
- Arenas
- handle tables

The local heap functions

- LocalAlloc()
  - LAlloc()
- LocalFree()
- LocalRealloc()
- LocalLock()
- LocalUnlock()
- LocalHandle()
- LocalSize()
- LocalFlags()
- LocalInit()
- LocalHeapSize()
- LocalHandleDelta()
- LocalShrink()
- LocalCompact()
- LocalNotify()
  - LocalNotifyDefault()

This chapter assumes that you are at least passingly familiar with 80x86 protected mode, for example with such concepts as segments, selectors, descriptors, and privilege levels. If not, you might want to find a book or two on these concepts (see the bibliography for some suggestions), and become familiar with them. This book doesn't cover these topics, as they've already been done to death in other books; it uses the available space to cover memory management, rather than CPU architecture.

Windows 3.1 works on both 80286s and 80386s. (From this point on, references to 386s also include the 486s and above.) Because the 386 has vastly improved memory capabilities like 32-bit addressing and paging, the designers of Windows felt that it was important to have two interchangeable KERNEL modules to take advantage of both chips, rather than one KERNEL module for the lowest common denominator, the 286. The two different KERNEL DLL files are KRNL286.EXE and KRNL386.EXE. Examine the debugging information that's included with the debugging versions of the two KRNLx86 files and note that there are entirely different source files for the memory management code in KRNL286 and in KRNL386. The local heap code and all other files unrelated to memory management (for example, the program loader) are the same in each DLL. The memory management source files have names like 2GINTERF.ASM for KRNL286 and 3GINTERF.ASM for KRNL386. The functions inside the various files have the same names in both the 286 and 386 versions. The idea is that the code provides one consistent memory management API to the rest of Windows, but optimizes the internals of each routine for the particular CPU it runs on.

The first thing to note when discussing Windows memory management is that Windows is just a DOS extender with a graphical user interface. During the design of Windows 3.0, Microsoft and various other companies hammered out an interface that would allow the Windows DOS extender, KERNEL, to coexist with other DOS extenders. This agreement resulted in the DOS Protected Mode Interface (DPMI) specification. It is important to realize that DPMI itself is *not* a DOS extender. Instead, it is a common foundation on which to build DOS extenders. A device driver or program that provides DPMI services is henceforth called a DPMI server. Protected mode Windows is a DPMI client. We won't dwell on the specifics of DPMI here because numerous good magazine articles and sample programs cover this subject. However, because of the crucial role DPMI plays in Windows memory management, it is highly recommended that you at least be somewhat familiar with it.

Windows ships with two different DPMI servers. The DOSX.EXE file in the Windows SYSTEM directory is a fairly simple DPMI server that works on 286s and above. Standard mode Windows uses DOSX, which provides a subset of the DPMI 0.9 specification and no support for virtual memory or paging. Windows 3.0 Standard mode loads DOSX first and then loads KRNL286 on top of it (see Chapter 1). In Windows 3.1, specifying Standard mode with the /S switch to WIN.COM, while running on a 386 or higher, loads DOSX, but KRNL386 loads instead of KRNL286. In this case, the memory management is the same as Windows 3.1 Enhanced mode, but there is no virtual memory available. To get Standard mode KERNEL memory management in Windows 3.1 (such as for testing), either run on a 286 machine or delete or rename KRNL386.EXE so that DOSX cannot find it.

The other DPMI server provided with Windows is inside the Virtual Machine Manager (VMM), which in turn is inside WIN386.EXE. It provides a full 32-bit DPMI 0.9 implementation—minus a few bugs—and supports disk-based virtual memory by utilizing the paging architecture of the 386. Setting "Paging=0" in the [386Enh] section of the SYSTEM.INI disables the virtual memory feature, which you might consider doing for performance reasons if you have enough RAM in your machine.

Later examples show that many of WIN386's DPMI functions are implemented in terms of functions in the VMM. The Windows Device Driver Kit (DDK) documents these functions, which allows you to dig even deeper into the memory management mechanics. A good source of information on these issues is Andrew Schulman's article on demand-paged virtual memory in the December 1992 *Microsoft Systems Journal.* Besides 386 memory management, WIN386 provides other services, but this book only discusses memory management, not DOS extenders.

It is very important to note that WIN386's and DOSX's memory management is entirely distinct from the KERNEL memory manager and is not dependent on KERNEL for anything. In general, KERNEL itself does not manipulate the global descriptor table or handle page faults, things which DOSX or WIN386 handle entirely. KERNEL leaves almost all of the really low level contortions to DOSX and WIN386 and usually uses the DPMI interface to direct them what to do. Proof of this separation is evidenced by the fact that KRNL386 can run on top of either DOSX or WIN386, using INT 31h, the DPMI interrupt, to communicate with them.

The discussion of the modes of Windows would not be complete without at least mentioning Windows 3.0 real mode. Real mode Windows deserves no more than a mention because it was a complete waste of time. Hardly anyone used it, mostly because it was unusable. Unfortunately, many of the idiosyncrasies and horrible things that real mode Windows required carried over to new Windows programmers as the gospel truth. This generation of programmers' knowledge of Windows memory management is, therefore, a hodge-podge of myths and lore picked up from various books and from conversations with other programmers. Programmers often overlook the fact that Standard and Enhanced mode don't require most of these atrocious practices; realizing that real mode Windows no longer exists facilitates a true understanding of what goes on under the hood.

A source of confusion among many programmers is the distinction between paging and segmentation, and how this distinction affects their program. Many of their questions presuppose that KERNEL plays with both pages and segments. This is quite simply not true. KERNEL deals with memory in terms of segments and blocks of memory allocated by using DPMI. WIN386 provides the necessary DPMI services and deals with memory in terms of pages. The virtual memory WIN386 provides is exactly what the name implies, virtual. Using the paging mechanism of the 386, WIN386 creates large spans of linear memory addresses that may or may not have physical memory mapped to them. It is important to understand that a linear address which KERNEL deals with does not necessarily correspond to the physical address that the CPU puts on the address bus. WIN386 and the paging unit of the CPU handle all of the address translations in order to provide large contiguous blocks of linear—not necessarily physical—memory. KERNEL in turn allocates large blocks of linear memory from DOSX or WIN386, through DPMI, and manages them with fairly standard heap algorithms. The fact that the memory allocated from WIN386 may not all be physically present is not important to KERNEL.

Think of physical memory as a sandbox that Windows and your programs play in. The virtual memory WIN386 provides simply creates a bigger sandbox, but it contains no more sand (physical memory). Put another way, physical memory is the amount of sand you have, while linear memory is the size of the sandbox. The virtual memory manager of WIN386 makes sure that there is adequate sand in the spots where play is going on (that is, in the most recently used memory). In the areas where nobody is playing (the least recently used memory), there's no sand (the memory is paged to disk). At any given time, there are regions of linear memory (the sandbox) that don't have any physical memory (sand) associated with them. A linear memory address, which corresponds to a particular spot in the sandbox, never changes. On the other hand, a physical address (the sand) needs to move around in order to be in the most recently used spots in the sandbox. The physical address moves around through the paging mechanism of the 386 architecture, which allows a physical address to map to any given logical address.

To stretch the analogy a bit further, for spots where you want to always have sand, regardless of where you're currently playing, you can prevent the paging mechanism from moving sand away from that area (pagelock the memory). The point is that the KERNEL memory management layer doesn't really care about the mechanisms of paging and virtual memory. It just knows that wherever it goes, there will be sand.

Two Kinds of Heaps

KERNEL allocates large regions of memory, typically 64K or 128K each, from the DPMI layer and maintains a global heap that divides these regions up into smaller areas, accessible by selectors. As we'll see later, a similar process happens on a smaller scale when global heap blocks are carved up for the local heap. For each global heap block that is carved out of the larger DPMI block, there is an associated selector. Your program sees these smaller blocks as segments and manipulates them with APIs such as GlobalAlloc() and GlobalFree().

Unfortunately, this process by itself is insufficient. Due to the architecture of the 80x86 CPUs, KERNEL needs to provide two kinds of memory management. Specifically, the segmented architecture and descriptor tables only allow for a maximum of 8,192 segments, which is prohibitively small. A program that allocated all of its memory from the global heap would use a new selector each time. WIN386 or DOSX would very quickly run out of available selectors. To remedy this situation, your program can allocate memory in small chunks from within a global heap block, without allocating a new selector for it. In Windows this is called a local heap. KERNEL provides a full set of local heap functions that are very similar to the global heap functions, and that allow you to create and manage local heaps within global heap blocks.

In DOS, INT 21h, function 48h allocates memory which is the equivalent of a global heap block. DOS has no equivalent for a local heap block, but the run-time libraries of many compilers provide functions (like the C malloc() function) that create and manage heaps within a block allocated from DOS. The main reason for doing this is because of the much higher overhead associated with allocating a system block than with maintaining a sub-heap. The same is true in Windows. Blocks allocated from a Windows local heap do not cause the allocation of a new selector; and the maintenance of each block requires much less space than a global heap allocated block would.

Surprisingly, OS/2 2.0 maintains this notion of global and local heaps, even though it's a flat model operating system and doesn't use selectors at the application level. Instead, the operating system allocate global heap blocks in chunks that are multiples of 4K for paging purposes. Each of these blocks has a fairly large administrative overhead. When your program needs to make numerous small allocations, it uses suballocation functions like DosSubSetMem() to manage local heaps within the larger global heap blocks.

Memory Attributes

The 80x86 architecture allows (nay, forces) protected mode segments to specify whether they contain code or data. While a good start, KERNEL needs more information to manage segments and local heap blocks effectively. Thus, each block that's allocated from a global or local heap has additional attributes associated with it.

One of the problems with most heap schemes, including KERNEL's, is that many allocations and deallocations can fragment the heap. To help alleviate this situation, KERNEL uses MOVEABLE blocks. When you allocate a block of memory or specify a segment attribute in a .DEF file, MOVEABLE is one of the possible attributes. However, if a block is MOVEABLE, its address can't be given to you when you allocate the block. Instead, you need to tell the operating system when you want to use the memory by calling a function (GlobalLock() or LocalLock()). The operating system at this point gives you back an actual address for the block and promises not to move it (at least, not in a way that will affect you) until you call the corresponding unlock function. Early programming guides for Windows recommend that you lock and unlock your block each time you use it, suggesting that keeping a block locked across different Windows messages is risky. Obviously this major inconvenience causes major headaches for new Windows programmers. Fortunately, this advice was written with real mode Windows in mind, so programmers can now ignore it. Assuming that your program only runs in protected mode (Standard or Enhanced), forget most of the advice and dramatically simplify your code by keeping your MOVEABLE blocks locked. In the vast majority of programs, you can mark the code and data segments as MOVEABLE; and that's all you need to think about. More on this later.

The opposite of a MOVEABLE block is a FIXED block. A block that does not have the MOVEABLE attribute set is implicitly FIXED. FIXED blocks do not move in linear memory. Therefore, when KERNEL allocates a FIXED block it returns the block's address to you at that time. A global heap allocation returns a selector to reference the memory. A local heap allocation returns the offset of the block within the segment. The downside to FIXED blocks is that because Windows cannot move them around, they can become "sandbars" in linear memory, preventing heap compaction from freeing up the maximum possible memory. Except in a few special cases, discussed a bit later, there's really no reason to use FIXED global heap blocks.

Another attribute available to heap blocks in Windows is DISCARDABLE. DISCARDABLE memory can be thrown away when the local or global heap manager needs to free up some space. When the previously discarded memory is needed again, it must be reloaded from disk or somehow be re-created. The most common use of DISCARDABLE memory is in application code segments and resources. Since code segments and resources are typically never written to, the program can reload them from the original .EXE or .DLL file as needed. KERNEL takes advantage of the "segment not present" fault to detect when it needs to reload a segment or resource from disk, thereby relieving you of the need to worry about discarded code or resources.

It is possible to have DISCARDABLE data in both the local and global heap. However, KERNEL does not swap anything to disk when it discards memory, as many people assume. Whatever was in the segment is simply gone, and it is up to you, the programmer, to somehow re-create the memory in the segment when you need it. For this reason, most programmers forgo using DISCARDABLE data, as it's not worth the effort. If you do want to use DISCARDABLE memory, you can take advantage of the KERNEL facilities that notify you when KERNEL is about to discard a block of memory. More on this subject later.

One wrinkle in the above discussion bears examination. Don't confuse the fact that KERNEL does not swap memory segments to disk with the virtual memory paging in Enhanced mode Windows. Previously, we mentioned the two separate layers of memory management, WIN386 and KERNEL. The KERNEL memory manager never swaps segments to disk. It may *discard* segments in tight memory conditions, but it does not *write* anything out to the disk. The PageSwap VxD in WIN386, on the other hand, copies memory out to its swap file for later retrieval, as needed. The key point is that there is almost no coordination going on here between KERNEL and WIN386. Thus, using virtual memory in Enhanced mode allows PageSwap to be able to swap your memory to disk, even if the memory is not marked as MOVEABLE or DISCARDABLE. Just remember, it's not KERNEL that's doing it. And if you run your application either in Enhanced mode without virtual memory or in Standard mode, then KERNEL will never swap your data to disk. Since it's not safe to assume that everyone runs Enhanced mode Windows with a large swap file, understanding these concepts will help you design your application to be memory friendly.

The Selector Functions

Later on, this chapter examines the functions and workings of the global heap, including such familiar faces as the GlobalAlloc() and GlobalLock() API calls. In order to really understand the global heap, it's important to have a firm grounding in the selector functions. Allocating memory from the global heap, actually allocates *two* things, the actual memory and the selector for referencing the memory. The selector corresponds to a descriptor in the LDT; it is this space in the LDT which must be allocated. In the beginning, there is no implicit connection between memory in the global heap and any given selector. As you'll see later, a fair amount of global heap code works to weld a usable block of memory and a selector together. Because this is so important, you need to be familiar with the selector functions before tackling the global heap.

Windows was supposed to be a break from the "bad old days" of DOS programming, when every part of the program was somehow tied to the architecture of the machine. The idea was that Windows programs would use the nice set of global and local heap allocation functions, and would never need to know about selectors and such. As has happened time and again, Microsoft underestimated the need to provide programmers with documented methods for getting at the lower levels of things. The selector functions are one such example.

The global heap manager in KERNEL needs to allocate and manipulate selectors and descriptors. Unfortunately, Microsoft overlooked the need for certain classes of application programs to do the same thing. Thus, several extremely useful selector manipulation functions in KERNEL were not documented until Windows 3.1.

Besides the selector manipulation functions, KERNEL also provides access to certain commonly accessed spaces within the lower 1Mb of memory. For instance, there is the ROM BIOS data area at real mode segment 40h, or the machine ID byte at the end of the real mode segment F000h. In fact, text-based Windows debuggers, such as TDW and CVW, use these selectors to write to their text mode screen. KERNEL allows access to this memory by creating a selector that maps the memory, starting at the desired address. The selectors have symbolic names associated with the region they map to. KERNEL provides (or exports) the following predefined selectors:

```
__ROMBIOS // Maps to segment 0F000h
__0000H
__0040H    // limit is 2FFh (300h bytes), rather than FFFFh (64K) like the others
__A000H
__B000H
__C000H
__B800H
__D000H
__E000H
__F000H
```

The *offset* of the address obtained by calling GetProcAddress() on these symbols is the *selector* value. For instance, to get the selector for __F000H, you could use:

```
selector = LOWORD( GetProcAddress( hModKernel, "__F000H" ));
```

where hModuleKernel is the module handle for KERNEL. You can obtain other techniques and details from the Windows 3.1 SDK documentation or from books like *Undocumented Windows.*

When studying the selector functions—as well as the global heap functions later on—it is important to understand selector tiling. Tiling is a convention that allows KERNEL and your programs to access spans of memory greater than 64K, even though they only can access 64K at a time. When a program reaches the end of a 64K block of memory, it switches to another selector to access the memory beyond that. How does it know which selector to use? The answer is selector tiling. Each successive 64K region of a memory block is accessed by the next descriptor in the LDT. Since the bottom three bits of a selector value aren't used to index the descriptor, simply adding one to the selector value doesn't work. Instead, you must add at least eight, which is the next value that has the same bottom three bits. For instance, allocating a 200K block of memory, with the first selector being 097Fh, would result in the following tiling layout:

Selector	Memory Region
097Fh	0 -> (64K -1)
0987h	64K -> (128K -1)
098Fh	128K -> (192K -1)
0997h	192K -> (200K -1)

Most compilers for Windows automatically load the right selector value because they have knowledge of this selector tiling scheme. In C and C++, declaring arrays with the _huge modifier causes selector tiling to be used. It's important to note that the value of 8 is not hard coded, but is instead obtained from the value of __AHINCR, which is a KERNEL constant similar to the predefined selector values just mentioned. Bear in mind that you must be careful when using huge arrays. If you have an array of structures, and one of the structure elements straddles the boundary between two 64K regions, a GP fault results when you try to access the element doing the straddling. Make sure that your data elements are always a power of two in size, thereby ensuring that they never straddle the boundary.

A final note before jumping into the discussion of the selector functions; Microsoft has warned repeatedly that future operating systems, such as Windows NT, will not support these functions, mostly because they allow your program to violate system security. Therefore, if you use these functions, it's probably a good idea to design your code so as to isolate these functions in a specific module. If you have to port your program, you should only need to change the isolated code.

AllocSelector()

AllocSelector(), a top level routine, uses Get_Sel() (see below) to actually allocate one or more tiled selectors. When AllocSelector() receives a valid selector handle, the routine uses the 80x86 Load Segment Limit (LSL) instruction to determine how big the segment is and allocate an appropriate numbers of selectors. The routine then copies the passed segments' attributes to the descriptors for the newly allocated selectors, and tiles the base address of each selector so that it comes directly after the end of the preceding selector's 64K memory range.

```
pseudocode for AllocSelector() - 3PROTECT.OBJ
// Parameters:

//      WORD    copy_sel            // Selector to copy, or 0
// Locals:
//      DWORD   limit               // segment limit of copy_sel
//      WORD    selectors_needed    // actually in CX register
//      WORD    return_selector     // Selector we'll return
//      char    copy_descriptor[8]

    selectors_needed = 1    // default to just 1 selector

    limit = LSL copy_sel    // Sets Zero flag is successful
```

```
    if ( not Zero flag )    // passed selector was 0 or no good
    {
        // Get just 1, "raw" selector. The attributes and RPL
        // fields will be filled in later.
        return_selector = Get_Sel( selectors_needed )
    }
    else
    {
        selectors_needed = (limit >> 16) + 1    // 1 selector=64K
        return_selector = Get_Sel(selectors_needed)
        if ( return_selector )  // Make sure we got the selectors
        {
            make a copy of copy_sel's descriptor table into the
            copy_descriptor local variable

            // Fill in the 1 or more new descriptors, using the
            // data in copy_descriptor as the model
            Fill_In_Selector_Array( return_selector )
        }
    }

    return return_selector
```

AllocSelectorArray()

AllocSelectorArray(), an undocumented function, uses the same Get_Sel() routine that AllocSelector() uses, and which this chapter covers below. After obtaining the desired number of tiled selectors, AllocSelectorArray() fills in their associated descriptors with the DATA and PRESENT attributes.

```
pseudocode for AllocSelectorArray() - 3PROTECT.OBJ
// Parameters:
//      WORD    selectors_needed
// Locals:
//      WORD    selector

    // Get_Sel() will try and find 'selectors_needed' free
    // contiguous selectors. It's important that the selectors
    // be contiguous so that they can be "tiled" for blocks > 64K
    selector = Get_Sel(selectors_needed)

    Starting with 'selector', and continuing for
    'selectors_needed' descriptors, fill in each LDT descriptor
    with the DATA and PRESENT attributes
    return selector;    //return first selector in array
```

Get_Sel()

Get_Sel(), a low level internal routine that is at the core of the selector management system, is a strange routine, in that it bypasses some of the DPMI services and does its own thing.

The low level KERNEL routines are not shy about considering the LDT to be their own little playpen. Get_Sel() allocates large blocks of selectors from DPMI and maintains them in a linked free-list, storing the link pointers in the descriptors themselves. See the pseudocode for details on this.

Why does KERNEL bypass DPMI? Wasn't DPMI created to prevent this kind of mucking with sensitive system resources? The answer is yes. However, there often comes a point where proper code and performance clash head to head. The KERNEL developers built and tested a version of KERNEL that allocated each and every selector from DPMI. The developers saw enough of a performance hit with this KERNEL that they felt hacking the code to access the LDT directly was worth it. The code is compatible with DOSX and WIN386, in that it still allows other programs to allocate selectors from the DPMI server. Unfortunately, this version of KERNEL creates a hidden assumption about the way the DPMI host manages the LDT. If another DPMI host wishes to replace WIN386 or DOSX, it must organize the LDT in the same manner. However, the DPMI specification doesn't tell a DPMI host to manage the LDT in a particular manner, which creates another ambiguity between the written and real DPMI specifications.

If just one selector is required, Get_Sel() grabs the first entry in the free list. If the caller requests more than one selector, Get_Sel() must find a block of contiguous selectors, so that they can later be tiled to access memory blocks greater than 64K. In this case, Get_Sel() searches the free list of selectors for a block of contiguous selectors that's big enough. If for some reason Get_Sel() cannot allocate a selector or selectors, Get_Sel() makes a request to the DPMI server for the desired number of selectors.

Once Get_Sel() finds a selector, there's still some housekeeping to do. If the number of free selectors drops below 256 in Enhanced mode, Get_Sel() calls DPMI to allocate another 256 selectors and adds them to the free list.

Finally, Get_Sel() makes sure that the highest selector allocated is mappable by the selector table. The global heap discussion covers details of the selector table. For now, just say that it's an array of offsets to information about each allocated selector/segment. The selector value is an index into this array. If the selector value indexes to a location past the end of the array, Get_Sel() gives up and frees the selectors back to DPMI.

A selector returned by Get_Sel() has none of its attributes (for example, code or data), descriptor tables, or privilege level bits set; the selector and corresponding descriptor is a clean slate. The higher level routines that call Get_Sel() are responsible for setting the bits to appropriate values before returning the selector to the application.

```
pseudocode for Get_Sel() - 3PROTECT.OBJ
// Parameters:
//      WORD    selectors_needed
// Locals:
//      WORD    Return_Selector
```

```
    // FirstFreeSel is a pointer to the first free
    // selector/descriptor in the LDT. For a non-present selector,
    // most of the 8 bytes in a descriptor are available for
    // whatever the operating system wants. KERNEL uses the first
    // 2 bytes (bit 0-15 of the limit field) to maintain a linked
    // list of the free selectors. The "first" free selector
    // doesn't really get allocated. Instead, the selector that
    // comes next in the list is the one that's allocated and
    // removed from the free list.
    if ( *FirstFreeSel == -1 )
        goto try_DPMI

    if ( selectors_needed == 1 )
    {
        // Mark the selector as "in-use" by KERNEL
        Put 0Fh into the "type" bits of the "access rights" field

        // remove the allocated selector from the free list
        Return_Selector = FirstFreeSel->next
        FirstFreeSel->next = Return_Selector->next

        goto have_a_selector
    }

    //selectors needed > 1
    Walk the free list of selectors. For each selector, see
    if there are enough contiguous free selectors to satisfy
    the requested number of selectors.

    If ( large enough block of selectors is not found )
        goto try_DPMI
    else
        Return_Selector = first selector of contiguous block

    loop through each of the selectors in the contiguous group
    that was found, and put 0Fh into the "type" portion of the
    "access rights" field. KERNEL uses this to indicate an
    in-use selector

    goto have_a_selector

try_DPMI:

    call INT 31h, fn. 0000h to allocate the number of selectors
    given by 'selectors_needed'. Store the selector that DPMI
    gives back into Return_Selector.
```

```
    if ( couldn't allocate selectors from DPMI )
    {
        Return_Selector = 0

        if debug KERNEL
            output a message: "Out of selectors"

        goto Get_Sel_done
    }

have_a_selector:

    CountFreeSel -= selectors_needed    // Update global variable

    // If we're in Enhanced mode, and we start getting low on
    // free selectors in our list, go allocate some more and
    // put them in the list
    if ( WF_ENHANCED bit set in WinFlags )
    {
        if ( CountFreeSel < 0100h )
        {
            // If the LDT hasn't been grown to its fullest
            // size yet, then allocate more selectors
            if ( segment limit of LDT < 0F000h )
            {
                INT 31h, fn. 0000 to allocate 100h selectors

                // put the new selectors in the free list
                if ( allocation succeeded )
                    call Free_Sel() for each of the 256 selectors
            }
        }
    }

check_selector_table_len:

    if ( SelTableLen != 0 )
    {
        // Make sure the handle->arena mapping table is big
        // enough to hold the data for the most recently
        // allocated selectors
        if ( address of selector table entry for the highest
             numbered selector is greater than SelTableLen )
        {
            loop through all the allocated selectors, calling
            INT 31h, fn. 0001h to free it up to DPMI, since it
            won't be mappable by the selector table.
        }
    }
```

```
Get_Sel_done:

    return Return_Selector
```

FreeSelector()

This documented API is just a wrapper around the FreeSelArray() routine, described below.

```
pseudocode for FreeSelector() - 3PROTECT.OBJ
// Parameters:
//      WORD    SelToFree

    FreeSelArray( SelToFree )
```

FreeSelArray()

FreeSelArray() takes the first selector in an array of tiled selectors and frees up the whole array. It first does some sanity checking, including the 80x86 Load Access Rights (LAR) instruction, on the passed-in selector. A strange selector catches the attention of FreeSelArray(), which calls Free_Sel() on just that one selector. On the other hand, if the selector looks good, FreeSelArray() calculates the number of selectors in the group and then calls Free_Sel() on each selector in turn. Free_Sel() is described below.

```
pseudocode for FreeSelArray() - 3PROTECT.OBJ
// Parameters:
//      WORD    SelToFree
// Locals:
//      WORD    freeUpCount (in CX)

    freeUpCount = 1

    OR on bottom bit of SelToFree, to convert to a selector value
    in case it's a handle.

    if ( using LAR on SelToFree failed (ZF set) )  // Valid selector?
        goto call_Free_Sel      // Just 1 selector

    if ( SelToFree's selector indicates it's a "system" segment)
        goto call_Free_Sel      // Just 1 selector

    // Calculate the number of selectors to be freed
    if ( SelToFree's segment is present in memory )
    {
        length = LSL SelToFree  // First selector has 32-bit limit
        if ( LSL failed )       // Something bad happened...
            goto call_Free_Sel
```

```
        // Calculate how many tiled selectors there are by
        // assuming 64K per selector.
        freeUpCount = (length >> 16) + 1
    }
    else    // segment not present. Get number of sels via DPMI
    {
        INT31, fn. 0006 on SelToFree -> linear address of segment

        // The number of selectors for a discarded segment is
        // kept in the base address field of descriptor
        freeUpCount = LOWORD(linear address) >> 8
    }

call_Free_Sel:

    // Iterate though each of the selectors in the array, freeing
    // each up in turn.
    for ( i=0; i < freeUpCount; i++ )
    {
        Free_Sel( SelToFree )
        SelToFree+= 8   // Point at next selector in array
                        // __AHINCR == 8
    }
```

FreeSel()

FreeSel() examines the passed-in selector. If the selector's value is too high for it to have been mapped through the selector table, it must have been allocated directly from DPMI. Thus, FreeSel() frees the selector back to DPMI. Otherwise, the function simply adds the selector to the front of the free list of selectors in the LDT.

```
pseudocode for Free_Sel() - 3PROTECT.OBJ
// Parameters:
//      WORD    SelToFree

    if ( GDTDsc == 0 )      // GDTDsc is the selector for the
        goto Free_to_DPMI   // memory containing the LDT.
                            // What a confusing name!

    // Convert SelToFree into a selector table offset
    turn off bottom 3 bits of SelToFree. WARNING!  This assumes
    that the selector is from the LDT, and not from the GDT.

    // Determine if the selector is a "normal" one that has its
    // arena pointer stored in the selector table. If not, free
    // the selector to DPMI, rather than putting it back in
    // the selector free-list.
```

```
    if ( (SelToFree >> 1) > SelTableLen )
        goto Free_to_DPMI

    CountFreeSel++  // We have 1 more free selector!

    Insert SelToFree in the LDT free list. FirstFreeSel->next
    now points at SelToFree's descriptor entry. Set bits
    in the descriptor entry to indicate that the selector is
    now available for reuse.

    return to caller

Free_to_DPMI:

    OR on the bottom bit of SelToFree to make sure it's a
    selector, rather than a handle

    INT 31h, fn. 0001 on SelToFree  // Free it to DPMI server

    return to caller
```

GetSelectorLimit()

A selector's limit is its last valid *byte* offset. For example, a 16-byte segment has a limit of 15, reading a byte from offset 15 is fine, but reading a two-byte word causes a GP fault. Although there is a DPMI function to set the selector limit, no DPMI function just *gets* the selector limit. However, the Intel protected mode architecture provides a Load Segment Limit (LSL) instruction, and the KERNEL GetSelectorLimit() function is essentially just a wrapper around this. Note that both GetSelectorLimit() and SetSelectorLimit() ignore the page granularity bit. The 32-bit limit is stuffed into DX:AX for the benefit of 16-bit code.

```
pseudocode for GetSelectorLimit() - 3PROTECT.OBJ
//  Parameters:
//      WORD    selector

    XOR     EAX, EAX            ; If LSL fails, return 0
    LSL     EAX, selector       ; Get the limit in EAX

    MOV     EDX, EAX            ; Put the high WORD in EDX,
    SHR     EDX, 16             ; then shift it down to DX

    return DX:AX
```

SetSelectorLimit()

Rather than call the DPMI function to set the limit of a selector, the code instead directly bashes the new limit into the Local Descriptor Table (LDT) entry, yet another example of performance taking precedence over correct code.

```
pseudocode for SetSelectorLimit() - 3PROTECT.OBJ
//  Parameters:
//      WORD    selector
//      DWORD   newLimit

    AND off the bottom three bits of selector to get the offset
    of the descriptor in the LDT. Each descriptor is 8 bytes, so
    ANDing off the bottom 3 bits of a selector turns it into a
    descriptor-table offset. This trick is used throughout KERNEL.
    WARNING!  This assumes that the selector is from the LDT, and
    not from the GDT. Bit number 2 determines if the selector is for
    the LDT or the GDT. Since it's not being paid attention to
    here, someone could pass in a GDT selector, and the code would
    blindly bash an innocent selector in the LDT.

    AND selector, not 7

    // Store the bottom 16 bits of the limit
    AX = LOWORD(newLimit)
    WORD at ( GDTDsc + selector ) = AX

    // Get the high 16 bits of newLimit. Since limits are only 20
    // bits long, only the bottom 4 bits matter here
    AX = HIWORD(newLimit)

    // Leave only the bottom 4 bits of the HIWORD() portion of
    // the selector's limit.
    AND     AL,0F

    // Zero out bits 16-19 in the limit portion of the descriptor
    AND     WORD at ( GDTDsc + selector + 6 ), F0

    // Use OR to copy the high 4 bits of limit, rather than MOV
    OR      WORD at ( GDTDsc + selector + 6 ), AL

    return AX = 0
```

GetSelectorBase()

GetSelectorBase() is just a direct call to the Get_Physical_Address() routine, below.

Get_Physical_Address()

This internal workhorse routine, which is used throughout the memory management code, takes a selector and returns the base address stored in its descriptor—once again, an example of a routine that bypasses the DPMI services. Note that the word physical in the function's name is misleading, since in fact it returns *linear* addresses, which aren't equivalent to physical memory locations if paging is enabled.

```
pseudocode for Get_Physical_Address() - 3PROTECT.OBJ
//  Parameters:
//      WORD    theSelector

    AND off the bottom three bits of theSelector. See the warning
    in SetSelectorLimit(). AND theSelector, NOT 7

    // The base address for a segment is stored in three different
    // parts of the descriptor. Extract the 3 fields, and put
    // into DX:AX (which is the convention for returning DWORDs)
    AX = WORD at ( GDTDsc + theSelector + 2 )
    DL = BYTE at ( GDTDsc + theSelector + 4 )
    DH = BYTE at ( GDTDsc + theSelector + 7 )

    return DX:AX
```

SetSelectorBase()

This code is almost the mirror image of the Get_Physical_Address() routine. It bypasses DPMI in favor of plugging the new base address directly into the fields of the designated descriptor.

```
pseudocode for SetSelectorBase() - 3PROTECT.OBJ
//  Parameters:
//      WORD    theSelector
//      DWORD   baseAddress

    AND off the bottom three bits of theSelector. See the warning
    in SetSelectorLimit(). AND theSelector, NOT 7

    CX = HIWORD(baseAddress)
    DX = LOWORD(baseAddress)

    // The base address for a segment is stored in three different
    // parts of the descriptor.
    WORD at ( GDTDsc + theSelector + 2 ) = DX
    BYTE at ( GDTDsc + theSelector + 4 ) = CL
    BYTE at ( GDTDsc + theSelector + 7 ) = CH

    return AX = theSelector
```

PrestoChangoSelector()

This function has a somewhat interesting story behind it. The Windows 3.0 documentation describes the function ChangeSelector() as toggling a descriptor between CODE and DATA. Unfortunately, KERNEL exported no such function. Strangely enough, however, an undocumented function called PrestoChangoSelector() did the things which were described in the

ChangeSelector() documentation. But wait, there's more! The arguments to PrestoChango-Selector() were reversed from the ChangeSelector description. Eventually, Microsoft 'fessed up and admitted that you could use the undocumented PrestoChangoSelector() function. Most likely, in the mad rush to get Windows 3.0 out the door, the coders at Microsoft forgot to change the name of PrestoChangoSelector() to ChangeSelector(); and the documentation people probably thought that this name change had occurred. On the other hand, developers often like to personalize their code, so perhaps they didn't forget! In Windows 3.1, ChangeSelector() has mysteriously disappeared, while PrestoChangoSelector() has taken its place.

The rather simple code for PrestoChangoSelector() copies the source selector's descriptor into the destination selector's descriptor, and then XORs the CODE bit in the destination descriptor. This has the effect of creating a segment with a code or data attribute which is the opposite of the source segment's.

```
pseudocode for PrestoChangoSelector() - 3PROTECT.OBJ
// Parameters:
//      WORD    srcSelector, destSelector

    AND off the bottom three bits of srcSelector & destSelector.
    See the warning in SetSelectorLimit().

    copy the src descriptor to the destination descriptor (MOVSD)

    Toggle the CODE/DATA bit in the destination descriptor,
    using the XOR instruction.  presto chango!

    OR on the bottommost bit in destSelector, thereby converting
    it to a selector if it started out as a handle.

    return AX = destSelector
```

AllocDStoCSAlias()

Besides PrestoChangoSelector, another Windows function that plays code and data tricks is AllocDStoCSAlias(). AllocDStoCSAlias() does some setting up and then jumps to the AKA() routine, described on the next page. AKA() does the real work of allocating the alias descriptor. Primarily programs that generate code into a data segment and then wish to execute it use AllocDStoCSAlias(). Because KERNEL can move segments around in linear memory, the possibility exists for a code segment alias to get out of synch with its data segment. AllocDStoCSAlias() checks to see if the data segment is FIXED, which prevents problems with moving memory around. If the segment is not FIXED, AllocDStoCSAlias() checks to see if the segment has been locked to prevent it from moving, calling GlobalFix() to lock the memory down, if necessary. Finally, AllocDStoCSAlias() calls AKA() to actually create the alias selector and descriptor.

```
pseudocode for AllocDStoCSAlias() - 3PROTECT.OBJ
// Parameters:
//      WORD    dataSel
// Locals:
//      WORD    dataHandle

    setup standard stack frame

    if debug KERNEL
        dataHandle = GlobalHandleNoRip(dataSel)
    else
        dataHandle = GlobalHandle(dataSel)

    if ( low bit of dataHandle is set )
        goto block_is_fixed

    // LOBYTE of GlobalFlags() is the lock count
    if ( LOBYTE( GlobalFlags(dataHandle) ) > 0 )
        goto block_is_fixed

    // Fix the block if not FIXED already, or at least locked
    // This prevents the block from moving. This is probably
    // done so that Windows can't move the block, and thereby
    // invalidate any alias selectors.
    GlobalFix( dataHandle )

block_is_fixed:

    remove standard stack frame

    DL = 1  // register parameter to AKA()

    goto AKA()
```

AKA()

AllocDStoCSAlias() and AllocCStoDSAlias() use AKA(). The name is a theatrical term that stands for "also known as." AKA() allocates a new descriptor, using the Get_Sel() routine described earlier, and copies the source selector into the descriptor for the destination selector. Then, based upon the value of the DL register passed to it, AKA() either sets or turns off the CODE bit in the descriptor, thereby creating a code segment alias for a data segment, or vice versa.

```
pseudocode for AKA() - 3PROTECT.OBJ
// Parameters:
//      WORD    srcSelector
//      BYTE
```

```
// Locals:
//      BYTE    isData          // True if srcSelector is DATA
//      WORD    aliasSelector

    isData = DL

    aliasSelector = Get_Sel(1)  // Get a new selector for alias

    OR on bottom 3 bits of aliasSelector // Make ring 3, LDT sel

    Save aliasSelector in BX

    AND off the bottom three bits of srcSelector & aliasSelector.
    See the warning in SetSelectorLimit().

    copy the src descriptor to the alias descriptor (MOVSD)

    Turn off the CODE bit in the alias descriptor

    if ( isData )
        Turn on the CODE bit in the alias descriptor

    DX = srcSelector

    return AX = BX  // BX = the alias descriptor
```

AllocCStoDSAlias()

AllocCStoDSAlias() is an undocumented function, a strange state of affairs since its corresponding function, AllocDStoCSAlias(), *is* documented. Perhaps it's because part of the Windows "religion" is that code segments are pure and can be shared between multiple instances of a program. Writing into a code segment puts this idea on very shaky ground, also causing problems with the idea that the contents of a code segment are read-only and can be discarded and then reloaded from the executable file.

The AllocCStoDSAlias() function, only one instruction long, sets DL to zero, and then falls through to the AKA() function, which expects the same arguments on the stack. Setting DL to zero indicates to AKA() that it should create a data segment that's aliased to the passed code segment.

The Global Heap

The most significant portion of the Windows memory management code involves the global heap code. The global heap code allocates and manipulates memory in terms of 16-bit global handles. It is now fairly common knowledge that some relationship exists between a global handle and the actual selector it represents. However, programmers often misunderstand the relationship. Thus, a lot of half-truths and mythical information float freely around. This section puts these issues to rest and takes advantage of the glorious freedom that arises from not having to contend with real mode Windows. Afterwards, we'll examine the global heap in detail.

Every block allocated from the global heap has a selector associated with it. The handle of a FIXED block is exactly the same as the selector. The internals of the global heap depend on this. However, a block that is MOVEABLE, which most blocks are, has a mathematical relationship between the handle and the selector. It is not safe, though, to assume what the relationship is without completely understanding the entire situation.

What then, is the relationship between a selector and its handle? To answer this question, let's first do a very quick review of what a selector looks like. The bottom two bits are the requested privilege level (or RPL) of the selector. The bit above those, bit 2, defines which descriptor table, local or global, that the selector references. The remaining top 13 bits are an index into the descriptor table.

Windows 3.0 runs the application code and data segments at ring level 1, making the bottom two bits of the selectors 01. All selectors from the global heap are from the local descriptor table (represented by a value of '1' in bit 2). Thus, the bottom most three bits of a normal Windows 3.0 selector are always 101. Translating these bits into hex numbering means that the values of all selectors end with a 5 or a D, for instance, 0x0835 or 0x097D. In Windows 3.0, the handle for a MOVEABLE block is the selector value plus one. In the above examples, the corresponding handles would be 0x0836 and 0x097E. Some applications took advantage of this relationship and simply subtracted one from the returned global handles to get the corresponding selector value, rather than calling the GlobalLock() function.

When Windows 3.1 came out, this bad practice came back to haunt them. In Windows 3.1, an application runs at RPL 3. Thus, all three of the bottommost bits are set to 1. Typical selector values in Windows 3.1 would be 0x0837 and 0x097F. It's no longer possible to have the handle of a segment be the selector plus one, because the bottom three bits would roll over, and the top 13 bits would index a different descriptor than the selector value does. To accommodate this change in ring levels, Microsoft changed the handle-to-selector algorithm so that you *subtract* one from the selector value to get the handle value. In the above examples, the handle values would be 0x0836 and 0x097E.

The moral of the story here is that it's not a good idea to assume relationships between handles and selectors. To safely deal with this situation, allocate your global memory and then call GlobalLock() to obtain a far pointer to the memory. Conventional wisdom at this point says, go ahead, keep the memory locked, and then unlock it before you free the handle. But this can be a nuisance because you need to keep around both the original handle and the far pointer for accessing the memory. To handle this situation in an easier, entirely safe way, allocate the memory, lock it, and then forget about the global handle, if convenient. To release the memory, first call the GlobalHandle() API, discussed later in this chapter, which retrieves the original handle value from a passed-in far pointer. Pass this handle to GlobalFree. The Windows 3.1 WINDOWSX.H file provides some nice macros, like GlobalPtrHandle(), for automating this process.

To further optimize the program, GlobalLock() the handle to get the selector, and then GlobalUnlock() the handle immediately afterwards. Why does this work? Doesn't a block have to be locked to keep it from moving around in memory? The answer is no. Windows can move MOVEABLE blocks around in linear memory to its heart's content. It always updates the base address field in the Local Descriptor Table so that once you get a pointer to the memory, you can use it whenever, regardless of whether it's locked or not. In fact, we'll see in this chapter that locking a MOVEABLE block has *no effect*, other than to return the associated selector value. KERNEL only maintains lock counts for DISCARDABLE objects. In other words:

```
HANDLE h = GlobalAlloc (GMEM_MOVABLE, size);
void far * fp = GlobalLock(h);
GlobalUnlock(h);
//use fp to your heart's content...
GlobalFree (GlobalHandle (SELECTOROF (fp));
```

Memory Ownership

Along with the FIXED, MOVEABLE, and DISCARDABLE attributes, the global heap manager maintains information on the ownership of a memory block. The owner of a block is typically itself a memory handle. A module table handle owns blocks allocated for sharing by all users of a module, for example, USER or PROGMAN. These blocks include code segments and resources. You can also allocate shareable memory with the GMEM_SHARE or GMEM_DDESHARE flags. Blocks that are allocated this way are also owned by an hModule remain in memory until KERNEL unloads the module, at which point it also discards the memory blocks.

When a specific instance of an application uses memory objects, for example, memory allocated by GlobalAlloc(), the PDB of the task that allocated the memory objects owns the memory. PDBs, which are just DOS PSPs under another name, are discussed in detail in Chapter 3. The termination of the task and its PDB frees all segments the terminating task owns.

An important point that many programmers stumble across bears drawing out here. Memory allocated inside of a DLL belongs to the PDB of the current task, that is, to the task that made the call to the DLL function. When the task terminates, KERNEL walks through the global heap and frees up any global blocks that the task forgot to free. If another task then comes along and uses the DLL, the allocated block is no longer valid, resulting in a GP fault. The WEP() routine of C++ DLLs suffers especially with this problem. Windows doesn't call the WEP() function until after KERNEL has freed memory owned by a task. The only way to force KERNEL to associate the block with the DLL, rather than to the current task, is to allocate the memory as GMEM_SHARE, alternatively known as GMEM_DDESHARE. By allocating memory this way, KERNEL will not free up the block until after the DLL unloads from memory.

To keep ownership straight, remember this rule: Blocks that are allocated as GMEM_SHARE/GMEM_DDESHARE are owned by the calling module. The calling module is the module that owns the code segment which called GlobalAlloc(). Memory that isn't allocated as GMEM_SHARE/GMEM_DDESHARE is owned by the current task at the time of the allocation.

In addition to global heap objects that modules or PDBs own, the global heap also contains a few objects which KERNEL uses to manage the heap. For instance, when KERNEL allocates a new block of memory from DPMI, it also creates global heap blocks that reference the beginning and end of the block. KERNEL uses these beginning and end blocks to determine if any portion of the main block is in use, as well as to do other housekeeping chores. The WINKERN.INC file from the DDK defines the special predefined constants with names such as "BurgerMaster," "Phantom," and "Wraith" which "own" these blocks. More on this later.

The Layout of the Global Heap

When KERNEL allocates a block of memory from the global heap, it takes into account the type of memory it's allocating, in order to keep its options free for as long as possible. KERNEL allocates MOVEABLE and FIXED blocks from the lowest free address in the heap that will hold the block; and it allocates DISCARDABLE blocks from the highest possible free address. DISCARDABLE takes precedence over MOVEABLE. The global heap starts somewhere below 1Mb, in the DOS transient program area and extends up to the limit of physical or virtual memory.

There are a couple of reasons for allocating FIXED blocks as low as possible. First, GlobalDOSAlloc() allocates memory that is FIXED, and must be below 1Mb so that real mode DOS can access it. Second, the high end of the global heap expands as KERNEL allocates more memory from the DPMI layer. It wouldn't do to have FIXED blocks be at the high end of the heap because as the high end of the heap grew, the FIXED blocks still wouldn't be moveable. The result would be a lower heap and an upper heap, with the FIXED blocks wedged in between. This is quite obviously not the same as having one big free area.

To get the feel of the global heap, run HEAPWALK from the SDK, or one of the several equivalent programs. Have the program sort the heap by address, and then take a look at the bottom portion of the heap. Notice that the heap is not as tidy as described above. For instance, you might see a group of FIXED blocks, a MOVEABLE segment or two, and then some more FIXED blocks, which seems at odds with the heap description above, but it's really not. In this case, a request for a FIXED allocation that would fit the space currently occupied by the MOVEABLE block would cause KERNEL to place the MOVEABLE block higher up in memory. This is precisely what the MOVEABLE attribute means. Put another way, a block may not start out in the best possible spot, but as applications come and go, and as segments get allocated and freed, the entropy of the system causes blocks to shift and eventually settle in a satisfactory manner. The one fly in the ointment here is the presence of FIXED segments. Where KERNEL allocates them is where they stay. Allocation of FIXED segments in spots that MOVEABLE blocks would ordinarily use (high up in the heap) fragments the heap until the blocks are freed. Fortunately, Windows 3.1 goes to some lengths to make sure this fragmentation doesn't happen.

Never Too Big or Too Small

In Enhanced mode, KERNEL attempts to keep the global heap just slightly bigger than the actual amount of memory Windows is actually using at the moment. When a request for more memory than is currently available in the global heap is made, KERNEL first tries to grow the heap by allocating a new, larger block of memory from the DPMI server. If the DPMI server comes up with this requested larger block (possibly from non-physical virtual memory), KERNEL sets up two boundary markers that point to the beginning and end of the block in linear memory. KERNEL then links the new block into the linked list of heap objects (see below).

If KERNEL cannot grow the heap via DPMI allocations, only then will KERNEL start to move MOVEABLE blocks around in memory in an attempt to coalesce enough free space to satisfy the memory request. Finally, if growing the heap and moving blocks around still doesn't yield enough memory, KERNEL starts discarding DISCARDABLE segments until it frees enough memory. This process leads to a rather startling conclusion. The virtual memory system in Enhanced mode may be maxed out and oftentimes thrashing wildly before KERNEL even starts to think about discarding segments. In a way, KERNEL is a pack rat, adding more and more rooms to its house, rather than getting rid of the junk filling up the rooms. Only when the house can't get any bigger does KERNEL start hauling things to the dump.

On the other hand, the global heap can shrink in size as well. When a a global heap object is freed, KERNEL checks the surrounding heap objects for the boundary markers that demarcate a block allocated from DPMI. If KERNEL finds these markers, it frees the entire block back to the DPMI server. In other words, if KERNEL has an entire six-pack of empties, it brings it back to the store. Doing this makes KERNEL a good neighbor to other DOS extenders that run in DOS boxes and depend on DPMI services, as well.

The Components of the Global Heap

The global heap is composed of several different components. Because you'll be examining detailed pseudocode for the global heap functions, now is a good time to become familiar with the data of the global heap.

Burgermaster

The key to the global heap kingdom is Burgermaster. To dispense with the obvious question, Burgermaster refers to a hamburger restaurant near Microsoft in Redmond that was popular with the early Windows developers. In the context of KERNEL, Burgermaster refers to the segment that contains all the vital statistics used to maintain the global heap. The undocumented GlobalMasterHandle() API returns with the Burgermaster selector in DX and the less useful handle in AX. The Burgermaster selector allows you to construct far pointers to the various pieces of data in the Burgermaster segment, as well as to dissect the global heap quite nicely, thank you. The WINKERN.INC file that comes with the Windows 3.1 DDK demonstrates the Burgermaster segment, and all the wonderful data in it. WINKERN.INC, however, is very dense in information content and not well commented. This section tries to remedy that situation. The Burgermaster segment contains three sections, which are discussed on the following pages. Figure 2-1 shows its layout so you can refer to it during discussion.

The GlobalInfo Header

The first item in the Burgermaster segment, the GlobalInfo structure, is the master database for the global heap and well worth taking the time to understand. The GlobalInfo STRUC

Figure 2-1: The Burgermaster Segment.

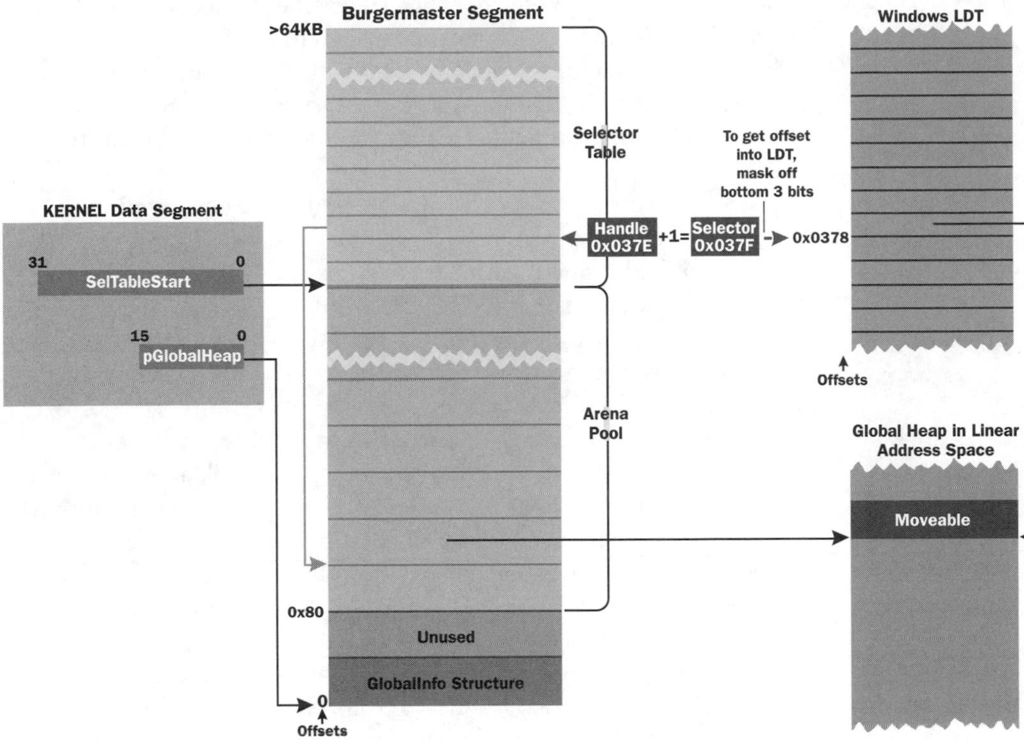

The Burgermaster Segment diagram is reprinted with permission from Microsoft Systems Journal, March 1993,

definition in WINKERN.INC (see below) gives the layout of the structure. The first portion of the GlobalInfo structure contains a HeapInfo STRUC. Both the global and local heaps use the HeapInfo structure, so some fields are used in the global heap but not in the local heap, and vice versa. Other than the size of various fields, the KRNL286 and KRNL386 HeapInfo structures are very similar. For those who don't have access to the 3.1 DDK, the 386 version of the HeapInfo structure is shown in Table 2-2.

Table 2-2: HeapInfo Structure (386).

Offset	Type	Description
00h	WORD	hi_check. If this value is nonzero, the debug version of KERNEL verifies the heap. This field appears to be used only for the local heap, not for the global heap.
02h	WORD	hi_freeze. If this is nonzero, KERNEL should not compact the heap. For the global heap, this value appears to be set only while inside the INT 24h handler. The local heap is frozen during LocalAlloc() and LocalRealloc().
04h	WORD	hi_count. The total number of blocks in the heap.
06h	DWORD	hi_first. A far pointer to the arena header for the first block in the heap. The first block is always a sentinel and points to itself.

Table 2-2: HeapInfo Structure (386). (continued)

0Ah DWORD	hi_last. A far pointer to the arena header for the last block in the heap. The last block is always a sentinel and points to itself.
0Eh BYTE	hi_ncompact. The number of compactions that have been performed on the heap to try and free up memory for a particular allocation. Some code appears to use this field as a count, while other code seems to use it as bitfields.
0Fh BYTE	hi_dislevel. According to WINKERN.INC, it is the current discard level. Both the local and global heaps use it. The global heap treats the value as a bitfield, using it with flags such as GA_NODISCARD. See the CMP_FLAGS equate in WINKERN.INC.
10h DWORD	hi_distotal. Only used by the global heap. When discarding begins, this field contains the number of bytes that need to be discarded. As the global heap discards blocks, it subtracts their sizes from this field. When the field reaches zero or below, discarding stops.
14h WORD	hi_htable. This field contains a near pointer to a handle table for the heap. Only the local heap uses this field. To get the equivalent information for the global heap, you have to read the values from the KERNEL data segment values contained in the KERNEL data segment, using THHOOK to find where to read from. See *Undocumented Windows* and the HEAPFUN program (below) for details.
16h WORD	hi_hfree. Near pointer to the free handle table. Only local heap uses it.
18h WORD	hi_hdelta. When the local heap needs to increase the number of handles it has, it allocates the number of handles specified in this field. The default value is 20h. KRNL286 also initializes this field to 20h, but does not appear to use it.
1A WORD	hi_hexpand. A near pointer to the function that KERNEL uses to increase the number of handles for the local heap. Because it's a near pointer, the function must reside in the KERNEL code segment. Thus, there's no way to hook this function. The Global heap does not use it.
1Ch WORD	hi_pstats. A near pointer to a LocalStats structure which the local heap uses in the debug KERNEL. As the local heap does various things, such as search for free blocks, it increments fields in the structure. The structure is defined in WINKERN.INC.

After the HeapInfo structure, the GlobalInfo structure contains the additional fields shown in Table 2-3.

Table 2-3: Global Structure Additional Fields (386).

1Eh WORD	gi_lrulock. If this value is nonzero, KERNEL doesn't perform LRU sweeping on DISCARDABLE segments. Almost all global heap functions increment this value when they start and decrement it when they finish. The heap is locked while inside the scheduler and during critical times. The section on global arenas discusses the LRU list and sweeping.

Table 2-3: Global Structure Additional Fields (386). (continued)

Offset	Type	Description
20h	DWORD	gi_lruchain. A 32-bit offset in the Burgermaster segment to the first arena in the LRU list. In KRNL386, the Burgermaster segment is greater than 64K in size.
24h	WORD	gi_lrucount. The number of blocks in the LRU list.
26h	DWORD	gi_reserve. The number of bytes of memory required for DISCARDABLE code segments at the high end of the heap. In KRNL286, the equivalent field contains the value in paragraphs.
2Ah	DWORD	gi_disfence. This is a 32-bit linear address. The code fence occupies the memory between this address and the end of the heap. KERNEL appears to use only the least significant word from this field. The most significant word of the address comes from the gi_disfence_hi field at offset 42h.
2Eh	WORD	gi_free_count. The number of free blocks in the heap.
30h	WORD	gi_alt_first. Initialized but apparently not used.
32h	WORD	gi_alt_last. Initialized but apparently not used.
34h	WORD	gi_alt_count. Initialized but apparently not used.
36h	WORD	gi_alt_lruchain. Initialized but apparently not used.
38h	WORD	gi_alt_lrucount. Initialized but apparently not used.
3Ah	WORD	gi_alt_reserve. Initialized but apparently not used.
3Ch	WORD	gi_alt_disfence. Initialized but apparently not used.
3Eh	WORD	gi_alt_free_count. Initialized but apparently not used.
40h	WORD	gi_alt_pPhantom. Initialized but apparently not used.
42h	WORD	gi_disfence_hi. The high half of the 32-bit linear address of the code fence. Combine this value with the bottom word of gi_disfence to get the linear address of the code fence.
44h	WORD	gi_flags. In CVWBreak(), if the gi_lrulock value is not equal to one, KERNEL sets a bit in this field. The GLeave() routine (called when a global heap function is finishing up) checks this field, and if a bit is set, generates an INT 2 (NMI). This process appears to be a method of forcibly stopping the system when an unexpected condition arises, for example, if gi_lrulock is not equal to one. Since the INT 2 is generated in the GLeave() routine, the heap isn't in a critical section of code, and it's therefore safe for the debugger to poke around in it.
46h	DWORD	gi_stats. The start of an array of DWORD values that are incremented when certain global heap functions are called in KRNL286.

A final note on the GlobalInfo structure before moving on. Upon entry to almost all the global heap functions, the functions call GEnter(). Besides locking the heap by increasing the value of the gi_lrulock field, GEnter() also sets the DS:EDI registers to the base of the GlobalInfo structure. Many of the internal functions then rely on these registers to contain the Burgermaster address, rather than loading the address each time they need it. You can think of it as a register variable that extends across many functions.

The Global Heap Arenas

KERNEL tags each block of memory in the global heap, be it an in-use segment or a free block, with a block arena. These arenas are a sort of miniature database of information about each heap block. A global heap arena contains information such as the block's size, its owner, its attributes, pointers to the next and previous arenas in the list (the global heap is a doubly linked list), and so on.

Despite what some writers seem to think, all of this information about a segment is not storable in a descriptor entry in the LDT. There's just too much information that KERNEL needs to keep track of. These arenas, along with the selector table (below), are auxiliary data structures to the Local Descriptor Table. When KERNEL allocates a new block of memory, it searches through the arenas, rather than through the actual blocks themselves. The format of a KRNL386 arena block is shown in Table 2-4.

Table 2-4: Format of KRNL386 Arena Block.

Offset	Type	Description
00h	DWORD	pga_next. The 32-bit offset in the Burgermaster segment of the next arena in the list. In the first heap arena, this field points to itself.
04h	DWORD	pga_prev. The 32-bit offset in the Burgermaster segment of the previous arena in the list. In the last heap arena, this field points to itself.
08h	DWORD	pga_address. The 32-bit linear address of the memory block that this arena belongs to. The Alloc_Sel() routine sets the base address of the returned descriptor to the value of this field.
0Ch	DWORD	pga_size. The size of the block. This is always a multiple of 32 bytes.
10h	WORD	pga_handle. The global handle that was allocated for this memory block, or zero if the block is free.
12h	WORD	pga_owner. The owner of this memory block. Usually the owner is a module handle or a PDB selector. However, there are certain other reserved values: -1 GA_SENTINEL: Either the first or last block. -3 GA_BURGERMASTER: The CheckGlobalHeap() routine tests for this value, but in 3.1 no heap blocks ever appear with this value. -4 GA_NOT_THERE: For every block allocated from the DPMI layer, there are two GA_NOT_THERE blocks at either end of the block, that have pga_address fields that point at the block ends.
14h	BYTE	pga_count. The number of times GlobalLock() has operated on the block. A value of nonzero prevents the compaction routines from discarding the block and prevents MOVEABLE blocks from moving in linear memory. GlobalLock() *won't* increment this field for MOVEABLE blocks, but GlobalFix() will.

Table 2-4: Format of KRNL386 Arena Block. (continued)

Offset	Description
15h BYTE	pga_pglock. The number of times that GlobalPageLock() has pagelocked the block in physical memory.
16h BYTE	pga_flags. Various flags that describe the block. Note the similarity of these flags to the GMEM_ flags in WINDOWS.H. 0001h GA_ALLOCHIGH From the top end of the heap. 0002h GA_MOVEABLE A MOVEABLE block. 0004h GA_DGROUP Block is a data segment. 0008h GA_DISCCODE Discardable code block. 000Ch GA_SEGTYPE GA_DGROUP | GA_DISCODE 0010h GA_NOCOMPACT Don't compact to free space. 0020h GA_NODISCARD Don't discard this block. 0040h GA_ZEROINIT Initialize block with zeros. 0080h GA_MODIFY Just modify the other flags.
17h BYTE	pga_selcount. The number of tiled selectors needed to access all of this block's memory.
18h DWORD	pga_lruprev, pga_freeprev. The 32-bit offset in the Burgermaster segment of the first arena in the LRU list. In the first heap arena, this field points to itself. When an arena is not in use, pga_lruprev is one of the fields that maintain the free list.
1Ch DWORD	pga_lrunext, pga_freenext. The 32-bit offset in the Burgermaster segment of the next arena in the LRU list. In the last heap arena, this field points to itself. When an arena is not in use, pga_lrunext is one of the fields that maintain the free list.

In KRNL386, the arenas are in 8K corrals inside the Burgermaster segment; they physically adjoin other arenas. However, instead of treating the arenas as an array, KERNEL accesses the arenas as a doubly-linked list. The head and tail pointers are stored in the GlobalInfo structure at the beginning of Burgermaster. The arenas are completely separate from the memory blocks themselves, which improves performance when paging is enabled because otherwise, if arenas were contiguous to their blocks, not-present blocks would have to be paged in, just to use their arenas (for example, to walk the linked list of arenas, looking for a free block).Therefore, in the traditional computer science sense of the word, they really aren't arenas, because arenas precede the actual memory they manage. However, KRNL386 refers to them as arenas, so this book does, as well.

The first 8K of arenas comes immediately after the GlobalInfo structure in the Burgermaster segment. If necessary, KERNEL allocates more arenas in 8K chunks, 256 at a time, and inserts them into the list of arenas.

In KRNL286, the arenas take a slightly different form (see WINKERN.INC) and come immediately in memory before the block that they refer to. Thus, the arenas are not located in chunks inside of the Burgermaster segment, but instead, are scattered throughout the linear memory space. This is somewhat akin to the way the DOS INT 21h, function 48h, memory allocation works, though in fact DOS memory blocks are contiguous, rather than arranged in a true linked list.

We've mentioned the LRU list several times, and now we can finally explain it. LRU is an acronym for Least Recently Used, a concept that predated Windows. A system that supports any kind of virtual memory can use more memory than is actually present in main memory. Obviously some of this "memory" must be somewhere else beside in main memory—on a hard disk, for instance. When the program needs this memory, it has to bring it from the secondary storage into main memory. This in turn forces the memory management to take something that's currently in main memory and either discard it or swap it to the hard disk, as the case may be. The trick here is to figure out what to toss. It doesn't take a doctorate in computer science to know that you probably don't want to swap out something that's being heavily used, at least not if performance is important to you. By that reasoning, the ideal candidate for discarding or swapping is the *least recently used* block—hopefully! The thinking here is that if the program hasn't used a block for a while, it hopefully won't need to again for a while, and so it can toss that block out of main memory if needed. In most cases, the LRU algorithm yields good performance results and is easy to implement.

In KRNL286, and in KRNL386 when paging is not enabled, the LRUSweep() function is called every 1/2 a second. LRUSweep() iterates through the DISCARDABLE heap blocks (segments). If the program has accessed (touched) a segment since the last time LRUSweep() was invoked, the function puts the segment at the head of the LRU list, thereby making the segment the least likely to be discarded if KERNEL needs to free up memory. In 386 Enhanced mode with paging enabled, there is no need to go through this process because WIN386 already uses an LRU scheme with the memory pages themselves. LRU sweeping is discussed in more detail in the pseudocode for LRUSweep().

In order to speed up searching for an available block of memory during allocation, the global heap code maintains a free list of arenas. In a clever move, the designer(s) of the global heap take advantage of the fact that a DISCARDABLE block cannot also be free. Thus, the pga_lrunext and pga_lruprev fields are used as the previous and next pointers for the free list. In fact, WINKERN.INC equates pga_freeprev and pga_freenext to pga_lruprev and pga_lrunext, respectively. A question immediately arises at this point. Since there's no hi_first_free field in the GlobalInfo structure, how does KERNEL find the start of the free list? As it happens, the free arena list starts with the pga_freenext field of the first block in the heap (which is never free itself).

The Selector Table

One of the tasks that the KERNEL memory manager needs to perform quickly and efficiently is to obtain the vital statistics of a selector or handle for a segment. In other words, KERNEL needs an efficient method to go from a handle to the associated arena. Towards this end, KERNEL maintains a selector table in the Burgermaster segment. The starting offset and length of the selector table is given in two KERNEL variables, SelTableLen and SelTableStart. To get at these variables in Windows 3.1, you need to know about the undocumented THHOOK entry point. In Windows 3.0, ToolHelp uses hard coded offsets in the KERNEL module to obtain the values. The HEAPFUN example shows how to use THHOOK to obtain the values in 3.1.

Note that the selector table *is not* the same thing as the Local Descriptor Table, or LDT for short. Instead, the selector table operates in parallel with the descriptors in the LDT. For each in-use descriptor in the LDT, a corresponding selector table entry points to an arena. The arena contains KERNEL-specific information about the segment referenced by the descriptor table entry.

In KRNL386, the selector table is up to 32K in size (8,192 selectors in the LDT times four bytes per entry in the table). Each entry in the table is simply the 32-bit offset of the associated arena from the base of the Burgermaster segment. Because all the arenas are in a contiguous block, KRNL386 can quickly map a selector handle to its corresponding entry in the selector table. Since the bottom three bits of a selector aren't used to index the descriptor, KERNEL simply masks off those bits and then shifts that value right by one to get an offset into the selector table. Once KERNEL knows the offset in the selector table, a simple memory dereference gives the address of the desired arena.

In KRNL286 under Windows 3.1, the selector table is 8K in size (4,096 selectors times two bytes per entry in the table). Each entry in the table is a selector value for the arena of the memory block. The arenas for each KRNL286 memory block immediately precede the block in memory, which explains why there are only 4,096 selectors available in Standard mode. Each block in the heap takes up two selectors, one to reference the block itself, and one to reference the arena. If you were to try to reference the arena and the memory block with the same selector, you couldn't use the full 64K of each segment. The first part of the segment would need to be reserved for the arena portion.

In Windows 3.0, there was no selector table in KRNL286. In order to find the arenas therefore, ToolHelp determines the base address of the memory block from its selector and then subtracts 10h to get the address of the associated arena. Remember, in KRNL286, arenas immediately precede their blocks. To access the arena, ToolHelp sets the base address of a temporary selector to the calculated base address of the arena.

HEAPFUN Example

The following program demonstrates some of the concepts of arenas and selector tables. It starts out by allocating a HUGE block of memory, more than 64K, and then uses the block's global handle to find the appropriate entry in the selector table. With that, HEAPFUN creates a pointer to the arena for the block and then shows selected values in the arena, along with the same information obtained through different means. This display proves that the arena we found is really the correct one. The program is written in Borland C++ 3.1 small model. It requires no special .DEF files or .RC files to build it.

```
//==================================
//  HEAPFUN, by Matt Pietrek, 1992
//  File: HEAPFUN.C
//==================================
#include <windows.h>
#include <stdlib.h>
```

```
#include <stdio.h>
#include <dos.h>

typedef struct
{
    DWORD   pga_next;       // 00
    DWORD   pga_prev;       // 04
    DWORD   pga_address;    // 08
    DWORD   pga_size;       // 0C
    WORD    pga_handle;     // 10
    WORD    pga_owner;      // 12
    BYTE    pga_count;      // 14
    BYTE    pga_pglock;     // 15
    BYTE    flags;          // 16
    BYTE    pga_selcount;   // 17
    DWORD   pga_lruprev;    // 18
    DWORD   pga_lrunext;    // 1C
} ARENA32;

// An undocumented function, so we must prototype it ourselves.
// If the linker complains about an undefined symbol, you'll
// need to add it (KERNEL.28) to the IMPORTS in the .DEF file
DWORD FAR PASCAL GlobalMasterHandle(void);

// Called when something unexpected happens. Tells the user
// why the program isn't going to procede before exiting.
void Failure(char *reason)
{
        MessageBox(0, reason, "Uh-Oh!", MB_OK);
        exit(1);
}

int PASCAL WinMain( HANDLE hInstance,  HANDLE hPrevInstance,
                    LPSTR lpszCmdLine, int nCmdShow)
{
    DWORD far * SelTable;        // The "array" of arena offsets
    DWORD far * SelTableStart;   // For extracting a KERNEL var.
    DWORD far * THHookStart;     // For extracting a KERNEL var.
    ARENA32 far *arena;          // Will point at an arena
    WORD hMaster;                // The handle of the heap segment
    WORD hKernel;                // KERNEL's module handle
    WORD ourBlock;               // Handle of a GlobalAlloc block
    WORD ourBlockIndex;          // Index into arena offset array
    char buffer[256];            // For displaying info

    if ( !(GetWinFlags() & WF_ENHANCED) )
        Failure("Cannot run in Standard mode");
```

```
// The selector of the global info block is returned in DX.
// Save that value away, as well as KERNEL's module handle
hMaster = HIWORD( GlobalMasterHandle() );
hKernel = GetModuleHandle("KERNEL");

// The 32-bit offset of the selector table is kept in a DWORD
// that's 0x18 bytes past the address of THHOOK. This is
// the same method that TOOLHELP uses, so don't complain...
THHookStart = (DWORD far*)GetProcAddress(hKernel, "THHOOK");
if ( !THHookStart )
    Failure("Couldn't find THHOOK");

// Add 0x18 to the THHookStart to obtain a pointer to the
// SelTableStart variable.
SelTableStart =
    (DWORD far *)((char far*)THHookStart + 0x18);

// We can't generate 32-bit pointers easily with normal C
// compilers, so give up if the start of the selector table
// exceeds the limit reachable with a 16-bit offset
if ( *SelTableStart > 0xFFFF )
    Failure("SelTableStart > 64K");

// Make a far pointer to the selector table
SelTable = MK_FP(hMaster, *SelTableStart);

// Allocate a huge block of memory for our demonstration.
ourBlock = GlobalAlloc(GMEM_FIXED, 0x1F000L);
if ( !ourBlock )
    Failure("Couldn't Allocate global block");

// The upper 13 bits of a selector are the index into the
// selector table. Thus, we shift right by 3 to get rid of
// the bottom 3 bits.
ourBlockIndex = ourBlock >> 3;

// Verify that we won't be trying to read offsets > 64K
if (((DWORD)FP_OFF(SelTable) + ourBlockIndex*4) > 0xFFFF)
    Failure("Selector table entry > 64K");
if ( SelTable[ourBlockIndex] > 0xFFFF )
    Failure("Arena offset > 64K");

// Point "arena" at the address in the selector table
arena = MK_FP(hMaster, (WORD)SelTable[ourBlockIndex] );
```

```
    // We now display various pieces of information from the
    // arena structure, validating it by obtaining the same
    // values by different means.

    // Verify that the base address in the arena matches the
    // base address given in the descriptor
    sprintf(buffer, "GetSelectorBase(): %08lX\r"
                    "arena->pga_address: %08lX",
                    GetSelectorBase(ourBlock),
                    arena->pga_address);
    MessageBox(0, buffer, "Results", MB_OK);

    // Verify that the block handle we got back from GlobalAlloc()
    // matches what's in the arena
    sprintf(buffer, "ourBlock: %04X\r"
                    "arena->pga_handle: %04X",
                    ourBlock, arena->pga_handle);
    MessageBox(0, buffer, "Results", MB_OK);

    // Verify that the owner of the block as given in the arena
    // is the same as the PDB of the current task.
    sprintf(buffer, "GetCurrentPDB(): %04X\r"
                    "arena->pga_owner: %04X",
                    GetCurrentPDB(), arena->pga_owner);
    MessageBox(0, buffer, "Results", MB_OK);

    // Since the block is > 64K, more than 2 selectors are
    // "tiled" to allow offsets > 64K to be read. Verify
    // that the size and number of selectors jive with what
    // we allocated.
    sprintf(buffer, "Size: %08lX  Selectors: %04X",
                    arena->pga_size, arena->pga_selcount);
    MessageBox(0, buffer, "Results", MB_OK);

    GlobalFree(ourBlock);   // Done with our demo block

    return 0;
}
```

The Global Memory Blocks

The actual memory blocks that your program uses are managed at two different levels. At the lower level, KERNEL allocates large regions of memory from the DPMI server. At startup time, the DPMI server either allocates all available memory from an XMS provider (HIMEM.SYS) or from a 386 memory manager, such as QEMM386. In the latter case, a fairly obscure interface allows the Windows DPMI server to import the paging tables from the memory manager.

At a higher level, KERNEL takes these large DPMI blocks and subdivides them into smaller regions that are accessible with selectors. We know these regions as segments. The aforementioned GlobalInfo structure, global arenas, and selector table are necessary elements of the bookkeeping for the segments.

When KERNEL allocates a memory region from DPMI, it initially takes up three arenas, marking the first and third arenas as owned by GA_NOT_THERE. They point to the beginning and end of the DPMI block. KERNEL marks the second arena as free. It starts out encompassing the entire region. The three arenas are linked into the normal and free global heap lists. Subsequently, when the allocation routine looks for a block, it comes across the second (free) block and decides to use it. However, it would be wasteful to use up the whole block of memory if the routine needs only a small portion of it. In this case, the routine splits the free block into two blocks. The first block occupies the amount of space the allocation needs and the second block contains the remaining memory. The allocation routine then marks the original arena as busy, allocates a new arena, initializes it for the left over block, and marks the remainder block as free.

If memory needs to shrink later on, the original DPMI block can be released back to the DPMI layer. When KERNEL frees a segment, it examines the surrounding arenas. If the preceding and next arenas are both owned by GA_NOT_THERE, there aren't any in-use segments contained within the larger DPMI block. In this case, KERNEL frees the block back to the DPMI layer.

Although Windows is thought of as a 16-bit operating system, there is oftentimes a need to use memory regions greater than 64K. As was mentioned earlier, the selector tiling mechanisms can reference HUGE segments. What is not well known, is that in KRNL386, the 64K blocks of memory that make up a huge segment are contiguous in memory. Thus, if you have a compiler that can generate 32-bit code, or if you don't mind using some assembler, you can call GlobalAlloc() to allocate huge blocks and ignore the selector tiling mechanism. You don't need to create a 32-bit selector that has the same base address of the allocated segment because the first selector for the first 64K region *is* a 32-bit selector. You can see this yourself using the HEAP function in Soft-Ice/W in conjunction with the HEAPFUN program. The segment limit for the ourBlock handle is 1EFFFh, definitely more than 64K.

Segment Attributes in the Global Heap

Perhaps the easiest way to get a group of Windows programmers to disagree is to ask them about segment attributes. There are many different stories about the way things work, many of them contradictory. The following description disregards real mode and discusses attributes as they are currently implemented.

FIXED Versus MOVEABLE Segments

The most important thing to state right off the bat is that there is really no reason for FIXED memory, with one exception. Because of the level of indirection provided by the protected mode descriptors, KERNEL could move your segments around continuously, and your program would continue to use the same selector, blissfully unaware of the segment's movement in linear memory. In fact, in Windows 3.1, it is impossible (or at least very difficult) to allocate FIXED memory in your program. (FIXED memory in DLLs is okay.)

When the KERNEL loader brings your program's segments into memory, it turns off the FIXED flag in all the segments before allocating the segments' memory. You can specify FIXED for all your segments in the .DEF file, but you won't get it. KERNEL also guards the back gate as well. We will see below that, when GlobalAlloc() allocates some memory, it turns the GMEM_FIXED flag off if it was originally on. KERNEL really does not want you to allocate FIXED memory. In Windows 3.0, too many programs (including the Microsoft C run-time library) indiscriminately used FIXED segments, which used up all the low memory below 1Mb very quickly. Remember, FIXED memory comes from the lowest possible address in the heap. Windows was then unable to load more programs, because there was no conventional memory below 1Mb from which to allocate a Task Database. See Chapter 3 for more information on why it's important to have memory below 1Mb. There was also a bug in the Windows 3.0 KERNEL that forced all writeable data segments to be FIXED if there was more than one such segment in the program, a situation that added to the problem, needless to say.

Since we now know why FIXED memory is typically not necessary and should be used sparingly, when do we need it? The primary reason for FIXED memory is for protected mode interrupt handlers in DLLs. An interrupt can occur at any time, which may leave the operating system in an unstable state. If the code for an interrupt handler were currently paged out to disk by WIN386, it would cause a "page not present" fault, which in turn would require DOS to read in the appropriate page from disk. Doing this when the operating system is in an unstable state to begin with is not the best of ideas and leads to system crashes. The obvious solution is to make sure that the interrupt handler code *can't* be paged out. Ever. The way to do this is to pagelock the memory using DPMI services. Pagelocking the memory tells the DPMI server that you always want the page to be physically present in memory; that is, the page should map to real physical memory.

So what does this have to do with FIXED memory? As it turns out, any memory that KERNEL does allow to be allocated as FIXED is also pagelocked. For some dubious reasons of portability, Microsoft strongly urges that the program place all interrupt handlers in DLLs. To "assist" you in coming to this decision, only DLLs can have FIXED segments. The loader and memory allocation functions leave the GA_MOVEABLE bit alone if the memory request comes from a DLL.

Another reason for having FIXED memory in a DLL is to work around the Windows 3.0 WEP problem. Windows 3.0 calls the WEP (DLL termination) procedure while running on a very small KERNEL stack. If the segment containing the WEP procedure had been previously discarded, a "segment not present" fault would occur when WEP was called, leading to a situation similar to the interrupt handler problem described above. The Microsoft approved solution is to locate your WEP in a FIXED segment in the DLL. In Windows 3.1, the KERNEL stack is larger, so WEP doesn't have to be in a FIXED segment. According to Microsoft, it's OK to have WEP in a MOVEABLE, but not DISCARDABLE segment.

Besides using a DLL, there are other methods for getting FIXED memory. GlobalDOSAlloc() is a special case and can allocate FIXED memory, below 1Mb, for an application program. If you want pagelocked memory, and it's not important that it be low, the GlobalPageLock() API may be a better choice.

When using KRNL286, the above pagelocking discussion is moot because KRNL286 never pages or swaps memory. A segment that's been allocated is *always* present in memory, unless allocated as DISCARDABLE. Remember, the 286 doesn't support paging.

DISCARDABLE Segments

DISCARDABLE segments have only a few, narrowly defined uses. Although you can use GlobalAlloc() to obtain DISCARDABLE memory for things like bitmaps, you rarely want to, due to the hassle of not knowing whether your segment's data is present or not. The KERNEL code is willing to cope with this situation, and it stores resources, as well as profile data in DISCARDABLE data segments. For application programmers, the only real reason to be aware of DISCARDABLE memory is for code segments. Because protected mode offers a method for demand loading application segments when needed, there's really no need to have all of a program's segments always in memory. Thus, in most cases, you can specify in the .DEF file that all of your program's code segments are DISCARDABLE. For DLLs, the same applies, with the one exception—the segment containing WEP shouldn't be DISCARDABLE.

To be evenhanded on this issue, some people will argue that it's better to make the most heavily used segments NONDISCARDABLE for the reason that you take a performance hit by having to constantly reload the segment from disk. However, memory is discarded on a least recently used basis. Therefore, if a segment really is being heavily used, it will be far down on the list of segments that get discarded. The only time KERNEL would discard the segment before its time is in low memory situations. And in this case, having the memory be NONDISCARDABLE just makes the situation worse for other applications, since even less memory is available. Incidentally, if you're running in Enhanced mode, but without virtual memory and paging enabled, running a DOS box causes all your DISCARDABLE segments to be discarded. WINOA386.MOD, the DOS shell program, does a Global Compact (0xFFFFFFFF) in this situation. The reason for this is unknown.

If you do choose to work with DISCARDABLE data segments in your program, you have a few facilities at your disposal. First, GlobalLock() prevents a segment from being discarded. DISCARDABLE segments are the *only* segments that have lock counts maintained for them. You typically would GlobalLock() a segment before you start working with it and then GlobalUnlock() it when you're done.

Another facility for dealing with DISCARDABLE segments is the GlobalNotify() callback. When KERNEL is about to discard a segment, GlobalNotify() gives you the option of choosing not to discard the memory. The GlobalNotify() pseudocode later in this chapter describes GloballNotify() in more detail.

Because DISCARDABLE segments can be tossed out at any time, there's no guarantee that the original linear address of a segment will be available when you reload. So any segment that is DISCARDABLE is also implicitly MOVEABLE. It's hard to envision any reason why you'd ever want a DISCARDABLE FIXED block.

With all this in mind, your typical .DEF file should have a section that looks something like this:

```
CODE    MOVEABLE DISCARDABLE
DATA    MOVEABLE
```

If you have certain segments to PRELOAD, specify them separately. The idea is that the default for segments should be the preceding values. Unfortunately, these are not the linker defaults. Thy really should be.

The Code Fence

In order to ensure that there is always enough memory to run any program that's currently loaded, KERNEL maintains a swap area at the high end of the global heap. The swap area is for DISCARDABLE code segments and is at least twice the size of the largest DISCARDABLE code segment in any of the currently loaded modules. By doing this, KERNEL ensures that there will always be enough memory to load a segment that was called, but is currently discarded. The address in memory where the swap area starts is called the code fence. KERNEL recalculates the swap area size and code fence every time a module loads or unloads. The SetSwapAreaSize() function also sets them.

The Global Heap Functions

Now that we've examined the global heap from a high level perspective, let's look at the individual functions that deal with the global heap. Those of you who are familiar with run-time libraries or operating system internals may notice that quite a bit of code in the global heap is fairly stock code and not specific to Windows. If you're interested in generic heap management code, an often cited book is K&R's *The C Programming Language*, which includes an example storage allocator. Another place to look is in the source code for the run-time library of your favorite compiler.

Throughout the pseudocode, notice a variable called GlobalInfo, which refers to the GlobalInfo structure at the beginning of the Burgermaster segment, discussed previously.

GlobalInit()

In order for any of the global heap functions to do anything, there first has to *be* a global heap to act upon. The GlobalInit() function creates the data structures necessary to maintain the global heap. The initialization of the KERNEL module calls GlobalInit() early because so many subsequent actions depend on the presence of a global heap. Chapter 1 shows where this occurs.

GlobalInit() first grabs its parameters off the stack and calls GInit(). The parameters to GlobalInit() specify the starting and ending addresses for the heap. In addition, GlobalInit() passes a selector for the memory containing KERNEL's NE header, as originally loaded by the DOS loader (see Chapter 1). GInit() is covered after the discussion of GlobalInit(). After returning from GInit(), which has allocated the Burgermaster segment and the other initial blocks, all that remains is to connect the wires and tighten down some screws.

The first step of this process is to fill in various fields of the GlobalInfo structure, such as the first and last block fields. These values depend on the results from the GInit() routine. Next, KERNEL sets up selected elements in the first and last arenas to establish the free list. Remember, there are no free list fields in the GlobalInfo structure, so the free list has to be found by examining the first and last blocks in the main list. Perhaps the free list code was added after the initial global heap code was written, and the programmers were loathe to modify the format of the GlobalInfo structure. Before GlobalInit() returns, KERNEL tries to grow the heap. Up to this point, the global heap contains only the conventional memory between the position of WIN.COM and the beginning of video memory (see Chapter 1 for details). Growing the heap now forces the heap to start allocating memory from the DPMI server.

After GlobalInit() finishes, the global heap looks like Figure 2-2.

Figure 2-2: Initial Layout of the Global Heap.

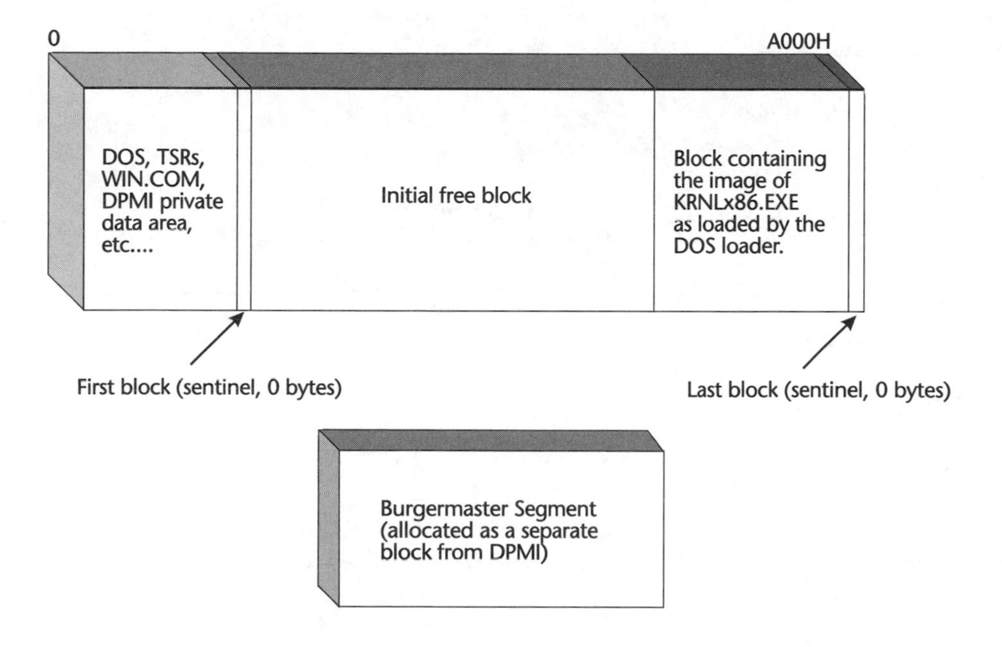


```
pseudocode for GlobalInit() - 3GMEMINI.OBJ
// Parameters:
//      WORD    unknown         // Set to 0x200 in BootStrap()
//      WORD    SegLoadBlock    // Selector to 'NE' header region
//      WORD    StartSelector   // Selector to region above WIN.COM
//      WORD    EndSegment      // Typically A000H
// Locals:
//      DWORD   arenaPointer

    // Load the parameters into registers, and call GInit(),
    // which does much of the real work. Pseudocode for
    // GInit() follows this code.
    if ( !GInit() )
        return with carry flag set
```

```
// GInit() returns DS pointing to the Burgermaster segment
// The GlobalInfo structure is at the base of this segment
GlobalInfo.hi_first = EBX   // Ginit() returned first block
GlobalInfo.hi_last = EDX    // Ginit() returned last block
GlobalInfo.hi_count = 4     // 4 items in the global heap
GlobalInfo.gi_lruchain = 0
GlobalInfo.gi_lrucount = 0
GlobalInfo.gi_lrulock = 0
GlobalInfo.gi_reserve = 0

// Set the "code fence" to point at the last block in the heap
GlobalInfo.gi_disfence =
    LOWORD( GlobalInfo.hi_last->pga_address )
GlobalInfo.gi_disfence_hi =
    ( GlobalInfo.hi_last->pga_address ) >> 16

GlobalInfo.gi_alt_first = -1    // Initialize some less
GlobalInfo.gi_alt_last  = -1    // commonly used fields in
GlobalInfo.gi_alt_count =  0    // the GlobalInfo structure
GlobalInfo.gi_alt_lruchain = 0
GlobalInfo.gi_alt_lrucount = 0
GlobalInfo.gi_alt_free_count = 0
GlobalInfo.gi_alt_reserve = 0
GlobalInfo.gi_alt_disfence = 0
GlobalInfo.gi_alt_pPhantom = -1

// Set the global variable used by GlobalMasterHandle()
// ESI contains the arena pointer to the Burgermaster block
HGlobalHeap = ESI->pga_handle

ESI->pga_count = 0    // Set lock count on Bugermaster to 0
ESI->pga_selcount = 1 // Burgermaster segment uses 1 selector
                      // (it is a 32 bit selector, however)

// Point at the large free block that's before the last,
// "sentinel" block in the global heap. Decrement the
// selector value in the pga_handle field of its arena
arenaPointer = GlobalInfo.hi_last->pga_prev
BX = arenaPointer->pga_handle   // Get selector for block
BX--                            // decrement it to make it
                                // a handle
arenaPointer->pga_handle = BX   // Store back in the arena
arenaPointer->pga_count = 0     // set lock count to zero
```

```
// Now building the "free" list in the global heap.
GlobalInfo.gi_free_count = 1

// Get pointers to the first, last, and "free" blocks in
// EAX, ECX, and EBX respectively
EAX = GlobalInfo.hi_first   // EAX is pointer to first arena
ECX = GlobalInfo.hi_last    // ECX is pointer to last arena
EBX = EAX->pga_next         // EBX is pointer to 2nd arena

// Tweak the first block's "free list" fields
EAX->pga_freeprev = -1      // First block has no "freeprev"
EAX->pga_freenext = EBX     // "next" free block is 2nd block

// Tweak the last block's "free list" fields
ECX->pga_freeprev = EBX     // "freeprev" of last block is 2nd
                            // block
ECX->pga_freenext = -1      // No "freenext" for last block

// Tweak the free blocks "free list" fields
EBX->pga_freeprev = EAX     // Previous block is first block
EBX->pga_freenext = ECX     // Next block is last block

if ( !GrowHeap( 0x60000 ) ) // Try to grow the heap by 60000
{
    // If we couldn't grow by 60000h bytes, then try again,
    // but with only 20000h bytes. Return failure if we
    // still couldn't grow the heap
    if ( !GrowHeap( 0x20000 ) )
        return to caller with carry flag set
}
```

GInit()

GInit() is called by GlobalInit() and has the responsibility for allocating memory from DPMI for the Burgermaster segment. Additionally, GInit() creates the arenas for the sentinel blocks that indicate the start and end of the heap. To use an analogy, GInit() cuts up the fabric pieces (the initial memory blocks) and stitches them together. After returning from the GInit() call, GlobalInit() sews on the buttons (sets up the GlobalInfo fields and so forth).

GlobalInit() passes GInit() the starting and ending addresses for the heap. The initial global heap is located in the memory between WIN.COM and the start of the video memory, typically paragraph A000h. New sections of cloth (DPMI memory blocks) will be sewn onto the heap later, as needed.

The first portion of GInit() figures out how big the Burgermaster segment should be and then allocates an appropriately sized block of memory from DPMI. The size of the Burgermaster segment depends on the size of the arena pool, as well as on the size of the selector table. Based upon how much memory is available, GInit() assigns sizes for those two tables. Using those values, GInit() determines the size of the Burgermaster segment and allocates memory for it from the DPMI server. The 32-bit selector that references the Burgermaster memory has its base address and limit updated accordingly.

The second part of GInit() is devoted to allocating and initializing arenas for the bare minimum global heap. Most significantly, GInit() creates the blocks that indicate the starting, ending, and free blocks of the heap. This routine is also where KERNEL makes the SegLoadBlock segment (see the parameters to GlobalInit, in the pseudocode for GlobalInit()) into an official segment in the global heap. Chapter 1 describes how the DOS loader reads KRNL386.EXE into memory in one shot. Loaded along with everything else was the NE header portion of the file. The BootStrap() routine sets up a selector to this section of memory. Later on, KERNEL uses this segment as the initial module table. GlobalInit() sends this selector to GInit() with the intent that GInit() will allocate an arena for the segment.

```
pseudocode for GInit() - 3GMEMINI.OBJ
// Parameters:
//      WORD    startAddressSel // Selector of heap start (BX)
//      WORD    endAddressPara  // End of heap, in paras (DX)
// Locals:
//      WORD    BurgermasterSel
//      DWORD   BurgermasterArena

    // Get the real mode address from startAddressSel
    EAX = Get_Selector_Address32( startAddressSel )
    Round EAX up to nearest 32 byte boundary

    // Now store the new base address back into startAddressSel
    Set_Selector_Address(startAddressSel, EAX)

    ArenaSel = startAddressSel          // ArenaSel is a global
    BurgermasterSel = startAddressSel

    // Ask DPMI to see how much memory is available. If there's
    // less than 1Mb free, we don't want to create a full sized
    // selector table. Function fills DPMI_buff.
    INT 31h, AX = 0500h         // DPMI get free mem info

    if ( carry flag set )       // call failed
    {
        BX = 0          // Number of pages
        EAX = 16384     // Size of selector table
    }
    else        // Call returned success
    {
        BX = DPMI_buff.total_unlocked_pages
```

```
    if ( BX < 0x100 )     // Less than 0x100 pages free (1Mb)?
        EAX = 16384       // EAX = size of selector table
    else
        EAX = 32768
}

InitialPages = BX          // Another global variable

if ( DPMI_buff.paging_file_size is not 0 or - 1 )
    turn on WF_PAGING bit in WinFlags

// Now establishing the initial size of the arena pool.
ECX = DPMI_buff.largest_free_block
ECX >> 7     // Divide by 32. Why?
ECX++
ECX += 31              // Round up to nearest 32 byte boundary
ECX &= FFFFFFE0

// EAX still contains the size of the selector table
Round EAX up to nearest 32 byte boundary
SelTableLen = AX     // Store the size of the selector table

if ( ECX > 0x8000 ) // If arena pool size > 0x8000 bytes,
    ECX = 0x8000     // reduce to 0x8000

// The Burgermaster segment is comprised of the GlobalInfo
// structure, the arena pool, and the selector table. Here
// we calculate the total size of the Burgermaster segment,
// along with the starting offset of the selector table.
EBX = 80h
ECX += EBX  // start of Arena pool + Arena pool
SelTableStart = ECX
ECX += EAX  // Start of Selector table + SelTableLen =
            // end of the Burgermaster segment

// Now that we know how big Burgermaster must be, it's time
// to allocate some memory for it. An important note: The
// memory for the Burgermaster segment is allocated directly
// from the DPMI server. In 3.1, the Burgermaster segment is _not_
// included in the global heap list, even though an arena
// will be built for it below. In Windows 3.0, Burgermaster
// was part of the Global heap, and showed up if you ran the
// HEAPWALK program.
Convert ECX into BX:CX for DPMI call
```

```
INT 31h, fn. 0501h. // Allocate memory block for Burgermaster
if ( carry flag set )
    return with carry flag set

HBmDPMI = SI:DI     // Store DPMI handle into a global var

// Set up the selector and limit for the Burgermaster segment
Convert returned linear address of block (in BX:CX) to EBX

Set_Selector_Address32( BurgermasterSel, EBX )

Convert ECX (the end of the Burgermaster segment) to CX:DX
INT 31h, fn. 0008h.   // DPMI set segment limit
if ( carry flag set )
    return with carry flag set

DS = BurgermasterSel    // DS points at Burgermaster segment

InitialiseArenas()  // Create the initial state of the arena
                    // pool, with each entry linked with
                    // its immediate neighbors

ESI = Alloc_Arena_Header( ESI ) // ESI is first block in list
EAX = Alloc_Arena_Header( EDI ) // EDI is Burgermaster address

BurgermasterArena = EAX
BurgermasterArena->pga_handle = DS
BurgermasterArena->pga_size = ECX  // ECX ->Burgermaster size

Zero out the Selector table

// Insert the Burgermaster selector into its arena
AssociateSelector32( BurgermasterSel, BurgermasterArena )

Allocate selectors and arenas for the other blocks in the
heap (the free block, the last sentinel block, etc.) and
initialize them. This is a fair amount of fairly routine
code, and not worth going into explicit detail here.

// Set the other global variable used by GlobalMasterHandle()
// GlobalInit() sets HGlobalHeap
PGlobalHeap = BurgermasterSel
```

GlobalAlloc()

Even though the GlobalAlloc() function is very important for Windows programming, the code for GlobalAlloc() is uninteresting. Its helper functions, which we'll come to shortly, do the real work of allocating a block of memory. GlobalAlloc() goes through the standard motions of calling GEnter() to set up the registers so that the internal KERNEL functions can do the actual work. Next, GlobalAlloc() examines and modifies any passed-in allocation flags that weren't proper. For instance, application programs aren't allowed to allocate FIXED memory. If the FIXED flag is set in this case, the GbTop() helper routine turns off the FIXED flag before the memory is allocated. The task of finding the memory falls to the GAlloc() function, which is described later on. Upon return from GAlloc(), the GLeave() function resets things to the way they were upon entry to the routine.

```
pseudocode for GlobalAlloc() - 3GINTERF.OBJ
// Parameters:
//      WORD    flags
//      DWORD   cBytes

    GEnter()    // Prevent LRU (Least Recently Used) sweeping.
                // Point registers at the GlobalInfo struct.
    // Get the "compatibility" flags for the current task. These
    // flags tell Windows 3.1 which 3.0 behaviors should be
    // retained because an application relies on them.
    MyGetAppCompatFlags()   // Described in "Undocumented Windows"

    if ( GACF_IGNORENODISCARD flag is set in compatability flags)
    {
        // For modules that have the above compatability flag set,
        // turn off the GA_NODISCARD flag, unless it is KERNEL
        // itself that is allocating the memory. The allocator
        // of the memory is determined by looking at the return
        // CS value on the stack.
        if ( !IsKernelCalling() )
            turn off GA_NODISCARD bit in flags
    }

    GbTop()     // Tweaks the allocation flags to be "proper,"
                // rounds the block size up to a paragraph
                // boundary, and determines who is going to "own"
                // the new block

    // GAlloc() is a wrapper routine around GSearch(), which
    // does whatever it can to get a block from the global heap,
    // subject to the allocation flags. (GSearch() is really the
    // heart of global heap memory allocation, and is discussed
    // below.) Returns a handle/selector to the allocated block
    GAlloc()

    if( !CheckGlobalHeap() )    // Only does this in debug KERNEL
    {
        AX |= 0x0200    // An error code ???
        NearKernelError("GlobalAlloc: Invalid global heap")
    }
```

```
    GLeave()    // Reenable LRU sweeping

    if ( the Galloc() failed )  // Only does this in debug KERNEL
    {
        // #bx#AX gets filled in with real values from BX and AX
        _KRDebugTest
            ("Kernel: GlobalAlloc(#bx#AX) failed for %ss2" )
    }
```

GbTop()

GbTop() is an internal routine that has three tasks to perform. First, it takes the block size as given in the GlobalAlloc() or GlobalRealloc() call, and rounds the size up to a multiple of 16 bytes. GbTop() then checks to see if the requested size is some impossibly high value (greater than 16Mb); if the size is too big, the function sets the requested size to an even larger value, which guarantees that the memory request will fail.

Next, GbTop() roughs up the allocation flags that were passed to it, especially if the caller was an application program, rather than a DLL. GbTop() has very definite ideas about what kind of attributes your segment can have. If GbTop() doesn't think you really need a particular attribute, it tosses it.

Finally, GbTop() determines and returns the handle that becomes the owner of the block that's under construction. A piece of Windows folk wisdom says, "Memory allocated in a DLL is owned by the calling application, unless allocated as shareable." The actual rule that applies here is as follows. If the block is shareable, then its owner is the module handle of the calling segment. Otherwise, the owner is the PDB of the current task. In other words, the heap code doesn't ask, "Is this allocation in a DLL?" Instead, it always applies the above rule about shareable blocks, and the above DLL folk wisdom drops out as a result.

```
pseudocode for GbTop() - 3GINTERF.OBJ
// Parameters:
//      AX = allocation flags ( GlobalCompact() calls with -1 )
//      BX = DWORD near * (pointer to requested allocation size)
//      DX = handle to reallocate, if called from GlobalReAlloc()
//      DS:DI pointer to global heap's GlobalInfo block
// Returns:
//      AX = allocation flags after modification
//      EBX = rounded allocation size
//      CX = handle of the owner of the block
//      DX = reallocated handle, if called from GlobalReAlloc()
//
// Locals:
//      DWORD   arenaPointer    // the ESI register in reality

    Dereference BX to get the allocation size. Put into EBX
```

```
    EBX += 15          // first part of rounding up to a paragraph

Round the size (in EBX) up to the nearest paragraph. If it overflows (i.e.,
it's a really BIG size!), goto GBTop1

    // The largest block you can allocate in Enhanced mode is
    // slightly less than 16 Mb.
    // 256 selectors * 64K per selector = = ~16Mb
    if ( EBX < 0x00FF0000 )      // 16Mb - 64K Is block small
        goto GbTop_2              //enough???

GbTop_1:    // Come here if the allocation should fail

    EBX = 7FFFFFFFh      // A huge value, guaranteed to fail

GbTop2:     // We now have a rounded up block size to allocate

    if ( flags == - 1)       // Is this a GlobalCompact() call?
        goto GbTop_done

    arenaPointer = Get_Arena_Pointer32( return CS on stack )

    // Here, we're going to start playing around with the
    // allocation flags, to make sure that you don't ask for
    // something that you really don't need (KERNEL knows best!)
    if ( !fBooting )         // Don't do this while booting
    {
        // HExeHead is always the KERNEL module handle, so this
        // block only executes if the owner isn't the KERNEL
        if ( arenaPointer->pga_owner != HExeHead )
        {
            Turn off GA_ALLOCHIGH, GA_DGROUP, GA_DISCODE, GA_CODE_DATA,
            and GA_ALLOC_DOS bits in allocation flags

            Turn off GA_ALLOCHIGH bit in allocation flags // ?
            if ( no "NE" signature in arenaPointer->pga_owner )
              {
                //Owner is a PDB handle (i.e., a task)
                Turn on GA_MOVEABLE bit in flags
              }
            else        //Owner is a module handle
            {
               // IMPORTANT POINT!!!  This code prevents an
               // application from allocating FIXED memory
               // (except via GlobalDOSAlloc()). If you want
               // FIXED memory, the code either must be in a
               // DLL, or you have to "FIX" it with GlobalFix()
```

```
            if ( arenaPointer->pga_owner isn't a DLL module )
                Turn on GA_MOVEABLE bit in flags
        }
    }
}

AND the allocation flags with GA_SEGTYPE bits. Store the
result in GlobalInfo.hi_dislevel

GlobalInfo.hi_dislevel |= 40h    // ???

if ( handle to realloc != 0 ) // Is it a GlobalRealloc()?
{                             // Yes?  Muck with more flags
    if ( GA_MOVEABLE && GA_DISCARDABLE bits set in
        the allocation flags )
    {
        Turn on GA_ALLOCHIGH bit in flags
        GlobalInfo.hi_dislevel |= GA_ALLOCHIGH
    }
}

// Some fiddling about with discardable bits

// If the block is being allocated as SHAREABLE, then the
// owner of the block is the current module. If the block
// is not shared, then GBTob() branches to a piece of code
// that returns the same things as GbTop, but with the block
// owner field set to the PDB of the current task.
if ( GA_SHAREABLE bit not set in allocation flags )
    goto GetDefOwner()
arenaPointer = Get_Arena_Pointer32( return CS on stack)

// Set CX to contain the handle that will own the block
CX = arenaPointer->pga_owner

GbTop_done:

    return
```

GAlloc()

GAlloc() is a middle level internal routine. While it is not directly responsible for finding a free block of memory, it does perform other vital tasks. The first important thing it does is call GSearch(), which searches for a free block. Once GSearch() finds a free block, however, there is still work to be done. GAlloc() next calls Alloc_Sel() to allocate the selector which eventually becomes the handle returned to your program when it calls GlobalAlloc(). When GAlloc() calls Alloc_Sel(), it passes it the address of the memory block it just allocated with GSearch().

Inside Alloc_Sel(), the address of the memory block is stored into an allocated descriptor table entry, thus welding the memory to a particular selector. The important point being stressed is that memory blocks and selectors/descriptors are allocated *separately*, and then joined together to form a usable segment.

After creating the new segment from the two distinct parts (the memory block and the selector), GAlloc() stores the address of the arena in the appropriate slot in BurgerMaster's selector table. This is important for later on when KERNEL needs to know the attributes of the segment, given just its selector. It's a simple matter to take the selector value and convert it to an offset in the selector table. At that offset is the address of the segment's arena. From the segment arena, you can find out just about anything you need to know about the segment.

What happens next in GAlloc() depends on the attributes of the allocated memory. If the memory is FIXED (after passing through GbTop()'s gauntlet to see if you *really* should get FIXED), GAlloc() calls DPMI to pagelock the block into physical memory. If the memory is MOVEABLE, its lock count is set to zero, enabling the segment to be moved around in memory. Also, GAlloc() subtracts one from the selector value for MOVEABLE segments to convert the selector to a handle. Finally, GAlloc() adds the new block to the LRU list.

At the end of GAlloc() is code for handling the special case of allocating a zero length segment. Although you might consider this strange, this actually happens when a segment is discarded. The segment simply becomes a zero length segment, and there is no arena pointer stored in the selector table.

```
pseudocode for GAlloc() - 3GMEM.OBJ
// Parameters:
//      AX = allocation flags after modification
//      EBX = rounded allocation size
//      CX = handle of the owner of the block
//      DS:EDI pointer to global heap's GlobalInfo block
// Returns:
//      AX = handle to allocated object
//      BX = largest block size if call fails
// Locals:
//      DWORD   arenaPointer
//      WORD    newSelector
//      WORD    newBlockFlags

    // If the segment being allocated is not discardable code,
    // then call CheckGAllocBreak(), which tells Galloc() to fail
    // after being called a certain number of times in the
    // context of a particular task.
    if ( GA_DISCODE not set in allocation flags )
        if ( CheckGAllocBreak() returns carry flag set)
            goto GAlloc_failure_3

    if ( EBX > 00FF0000h )        // is size >> (16Mb - 64K)?
        goto GAlloc_failure_3
```

```
if ( EBX == 0 )
    goto Galloc_zero_length_block

arenaPointer = GSearch()    // Find an available block

newBlockFlags = DX          // Set by GSearch()

if ( arenaPointer == 0 )    // GSearch() didn't find anything?
    goto GAlloc_done

EDX = arenaPointer->pga_address // Get information on the
ECX = arenaPointer->pga_size    // block out of its arena

// Get a selector to reference the new memory block
newSelector = Alloc_Sel(EDX, ECX)

if ( !newSelector )         // Fail if no selector available
    goto GAlloc_failure_2

// Determine how many 64K blocks were allocated
ECX = (ECX + 0FFFFh) >> 16

arenaPointer->pga_selcount = CL   // Save # of selectors used
                                  // into the arena header

// Copy the arena's address into the correct spot in the
// selector table.
AssociateSelector32(newSelector, arenaPointer)

// We now have to do different things, based upon what kind
// of block was allocated (MOVEABLE, FIXED, or DISCARDABLE).
// All three block kinds end up going through the code for
// DISCARDABLE blocks.
if ( GA_MOVEABLE flag set in newBlockFlags )
    goto GAlloc_moveable

if ( GA_DISCARDABLE flag set in newBlockFlags )
    goto GAlloc_discardable

// If the segment is not MOVEABLE or DISCARDABLE, then it
// must be FIXED. All FIXED blocks are page-locked in
// Enhanced mode, so pagelock it now.
BX = newSelector          // Supposedly obsolete DPMI function.
INT 31h, AX = 0004        // Locks the pages of the selector
if ( carry flag set )     // specified by BX
    goto GAlloc_failure_1
```

```
    // Indicate that the block is pagelocked
    arenaPointer->pga_pglock++

    goto Galloc_discardable

GAlloc_moveable:

    arenaPointer->pga_count = 0 // lock count is 0

    // The handle for a FIXED memory block is the same as its
    // selector. The handle for a MOVEABLE memory block is
    // one less than the selector value
    newSelector--       // Convert a selector to a handle

GAlloc_discardable:

    arenaPointer->pga_handle = newSelector

    // Add the block to the LRU list. All block types come
    // through here, but GLRUAdd() is smart enough to only
    // add DISCARDABLE blocks to the LRU list.
    GLRUAdd()

    return to caller   //Normally exit here.

GAlloc_zero_length_block:
    If the block is DISCARDABLE, it must also be MOVEABLE

    if ( GA_MOVEABLE flag not set in allocation flags )
        goto GAlloc_failure_3

    Calculate the selector attribute byte for a zero-length,
    non-present selector

    newSelector = Alloc_Sel(0, 0)   // Address & length == 0

    if ( !newSelector )
        goto GAlloc_failure_3

    // Copy the arena's address into the correct spot in the
    // selector table. MK_FP( 0, CX ) part is supposed to be
    // a 32 bit offset for an arena. Strange!
    AssociateSelector32(newSelector, MK_FP(0, CX) )

    newSelector--   // Convert selector to a handle

GAlloc_done:
```

```
    CX = AX
    return to caller

GAlloc_failure_1:

    FreeSelArray()  // Page-locking failed. Free selectors

GAlloc_failure_2:

    GMarkFree()     // Mark the block's arena as free again

GAlloc_failure_3:

    _KRDEBUGTEST("GlobalAlloc failed"s)

    DX = AX = 0

    goto GAlloc_done
```

GSearch()

GSearch() is the low level internal routine that performs all the nasty work of finding a free block of memory, taking into consideration the allocation flags. This is one of the most critical, workhorse routines of the entire global heap system, so we'll dwell on it for a bit.

GSearch() starts by checking to see if there are any free blocks at all. If there are, it next looks to see if any of them are large enough in size to accomodate the request. If either of these conditions is not met, GSearch() goes straight to the heap reorganization code, which we'll discuss momentarily.

Having verified that it's even worth looking for a free block in the heap as it currently exists, GSearch() looks at the allocation flags to see what kind of block is being requested. If the block is DISCARDABLE, GSearch() starts searching at the high end of the heap, working backwards (downwards in memory) until it encounters a sufficiently large block. If the flags indicate a MOVEABLE block, there's no need to search any further. The first block found during the initial scan will do just fine.

The most complex type of memory to find is a FIXED block. The search starts at the low end of the heap, working towards higher memory addresses. When GSearch() finds a free block, the routine attempts to slide the block downwards in linear memory to exchange places with a MOVEABLE block that is even lower in memory. The reason for this is that it's important to pack every FIXED block as low in memory as possible. Once the block has been moved to the lowest possible address, it remains at that address for its entire life. When the FIXED block is in its final resting place, GSearch() tests the GA_ALLOC_DOS flag. If the flag is set, GSearch() examines the address of the block to see if it falls below 1Mb in linear address space. If it is not below 1Mb, GSearch() fails the request because the block must be below 1Mb so that DOS programs can access it. As you can see, there's no need for KERNEL to call DPMI function 0100h to allocate conventional memory. All memory below 1Mb is already in the global heap, so it's a simple matter of finding the lowest address block and verifying that it's below 1Mb in the linear address space.

Once a block is found by any of the above three methods, GSearch() determines if the found block is bigger than the allocation request. If so, the polite thing to do is to take only what it needs, and return the excess to the global heap. GSearch() handles this by creating a new, free arena header for the excess portion of the block and initializing it appropriately. Afterwards, GSearch() returns the address of the arena describing the found block. The calling function eventually binds the address of the found block to a selector to create a complete segment.

As mentioned earlier, KERNEL can reorganize the global heap if there's not enough memory to fulfill the allocation request. You can think of this phase as the implementation of increasingly drastic measures. The first and least painful course of action is to attempt to grow the heap by allocating additional memory blocks from the DPMI server. If the DPMI server comes through with more memory (actually, just more linear address space), GSearch() starts over again at the top of its code, looking for a free memory block. In KRNL286, the global heap starts out at its maximum size. Therefore, this step of growing the heap does not occur in KRNL286.

If growing the heap does not help the situation, the GCompact() routine (described in more detail below) takes over. It shuffles around MOVEABLE blocks in an attempt to coalesce enough free blocks to fill the request. Finally, if that still doesn't do anything to improve the situation, this routine undertakes the most drastic step, the discarding of DISCARDABLE segments. These last two steps occur inside GCompact().

```
pseudocode for GSearch() - 3GALLOC.OBJ
// Parameters:
//      AX = allocation flags
//      EBX = rounded allocation size
//      CX = handle of the owner of the block
//      DS:DI pointer to global heap's GlobalInfo block
// Returns:
//      EAX = address of the allocated block
//      EDX = largest free block, if failure
// Locals:
//      DWORD   arenaPointer
// Static:
//      NEARPROC npfnNextSearchAction   // Near function pointer

    // npfnNextSearchAction is a function pointer that always
    // points at the function to be called when the current steps
    // don't work. After each usage, it's set to the code that
    // takes the next most "drastic" action.
    npfnNextSearcAction = Grow_Heap // Grow_Heap() is a function

Start_GSearch:  // Start searching through the heap

    GAlign()    // Rounds a size request up to nearest paragraph
```

```
    if ( GlobalInfo.gi_free_count == 0 )  // Any free blocks?
        goto Space_Not_Found

    // Start iterating through the entire free list, looking
    // to see if there's any block that big enough to satisfy
    // the memory request. If not, compact immediately
    arenaPointer = GlobalInfo.hi_first  // Point at first block

    while ( not at end of free list )
    {
        if ( a big enough block found )
            goto found_a_free_block

        // point at next free block in list
        arenaPointer = arenaPointer->pga_freenext
    }

    goto Space_Not_Found    // No block found. Time to compact

found_a_free_block:

    // The GA_ALLOCHIGH bit is set for discardable allocations,
    // and indicates that the block should be allocated from
    // the high end of the global heap. If GA_ALLOCHIGH is
    // not set, then the block is MOVEABLE or FIXED, so it
    // should be allocated from the low end of the heap.

    // Decide which end of the heap we're going to start
    // looking from:
    if ( GA_ALLOCHIGH bit not set in flags )
        goto Alloc_Low      // else, fall through to Alloc_High

Alloc_High:

    // Point at the last entry in the heap. DISCARDABLE blocks
    // are at the high end of the heap, so we start at the end,
    // and work backwards, looking for a free block
    arenaPointer = GlobalInfo.hi_last

    while ( not at end of free list )
    {
        if ( a big enough block found )
            goto found_a_free_block_2

        // point at the preceding free block
        arenaPointer = arenaPointer->pga_freeprev
    }
```

```
    // Nothing good found. Time to compact
    goto space_not_found

Alloc_Low:

    // if the GA_MOVEABLE bit is set in the flags, then we can
    // just use the block that was found at the beginning of the
    // GSearch(). Otherwise, we go through the special code to
    // allocate a fixed block.
    if ( GA_MOVEABLE bit not set in flags )
        goto Alloc_Fixed

    // Make sure block fits underneath the code fence, if
    // it's not a DISCARDABLE code segment

    if ( !GCheckFree() )
        goto Space_Not_found
    else
        goto found_a_free_block_2

Alloc_Fixed:

    // Point at the FIRST entry in the heap. FIXED blocks
    // are at the low end of the heap, so we start at the
    // beginning, and work forwards, looking for a free block
    arenaPointer = GlobalInfo.hi_first

    // Skip the first block, because it's a sentinel
    arenaPointer = arenaPointer->pga_next

    // Iterate through all of the blocks in the global heap,
    // looking for a block that is either free, or that
    // can be made free by shuffling things around.
    // Yes, these are really function names in the loop!
    while ( not at end of heap list )
    {
        if ( Is_There_Theoretically_Enough_Space() is less than
            the allocation size  )
            goto next_alloc_fixed

        if ( !Can_We_Clear_This_Space() )
            goto next_alloc_fixed

        // Make sure block fits underneath the code fence, if
        // it's not a DISCARDABLE code segment
```

```
        if ( !GCheckFree() )
            goto next_alloc_fixed

        if ( !PreAllocArena() ) // Allocate arena for GSlide()?
            goto alloc_fixed_done_sliding

alloc_fixed_slide:

        // If possible, GSlide() will "slide" a block downwards
        // in the heap, exchanging places with blocks that are
        // at lower address. This loop moves the block down
        // a far as possible
        if ( GSlide() )
            goto alloc_fixed_slide

alloc_fixed_done_sliding:

        // If we're being called from GlobalDOSAlloc(), then the
        // GA_ALLOC_DOS bit is set in the allocation flags. Make
        // sure that the block we found is below 1Mb.
        if ( GA_ALLOC_DOS bit not set in flags )
            goto found_a_free_block_2

        if ( arenaPointer->pga_address > 1Mb )
            goto GSearch_Fail
        else
            goto found_a_free_block_2

next_alloc_fixed:

        arenaPointer = arenaPointer->pga_next

    }       // End of while() loop

Space_Not_Found:

    // Go do whatever the next course of action is, i.e.,
    // Grow_Heap(), Do_Compact(), or GSearch_Fail()
    npfnNextSearchAction()  // Call through the function pointer
                            // The first time through, GrowHeap()
                            // is what's called. IMPORTANT:
                            // Only after this fails is the heap compacted.

    // The heap couldn't be grown. Try to compact the heap
    // by removing free blocks between in-use blocks, and by
    // getting rid of discardable blocks.
```

```
Do_Compact:

    // If the compaction fails, the next thing to do is fail the
    // allocation request
    npfnNextSearchAction = GSearch_Fail

    GCompact()      // Compact the global heap

start_again_at_top:

    goto Start_GSearch  // Start looking through the heap again

Grow_Heap:

    // If the heap can't be grown (i.e., by paging), the next
    // thing to do is to compact the global heap
    npfnNextSearchAction = Do_Compact

    // Try to allocate memory from DPMI (function 0501h) to
    // expand the global heap.
    if ( GrowHeap() )                   // If heap can be grown,
        goto start_again_at_top         // start search anew

    // Free blocks to the DPMI server. If this doesn't
    // work, then go straight to the compaction step. Perhaps
    // this is to help out with large allocations???
    if( !InnerShrinkHeap() )  // Discussed with GlobalCompact()
        goto Do_Compact()

    // If blocks could be freed by InnerShrinkHeap(), try
    // to expand the global heap again
    if ( GrowHeap() )
        goto start_again_at_top

    // GSearch_Fail is reached when the allocation request
    // still fails after attempting to grow the global heap
    // and compacting the heap.

GSearch_Fail:

    // Iterate through the free list, storing the size of the
    // largest free block in EDX. The intent is to find the size of
    // the largest free block, which is returned if the call fails.
    arenaPointer = GlobalInfo.hi_first  // Point at first block
```

```
    while ( not at end of free list )
    {
        if ( EDX < arenaPointer->pga_size )
            EDX = arenaPointer->pga_size

        // point at next free block in list
        arenaPointer = arenaPointer->pga_freenext
    }

    EAX = 0
    return to caller

    // We get here if a block big enough to satisfy the
    // request is found. The block may be too big, in which
    // case it will need to be split into 2 pieces.

found_a_free_block_2:

    if ( size of allocated block > requested size )
    {
        // Create an arena header for the soon to be created
        // "remainder" block
        if ( PreAllocArena() == 0 )
        {
            // If the arena couldn't be allocated, take
            // appropriate corrective action
            if ( npfnNextSearchAction == GSearch_Fail )
                goto GSearch_Fail

            Turn off GA_NODISCARD and GA_NOCOMPACT flags in
            the GlobalInfo compaction flags.

            Turn on the COMPACT_ALLOC flag in the GlobalInfo
            compaction flags.

            Do_Compact(-1)       // Discard everything
        }
    }

    GDel_Free(arenaPointer) // Remove the block from the free list

    if ( size of allocated block > requested size )
    {
        GSplice()    // Split the block into 2 blocks, one being
                     // big enough for the requested allocation.
                     // The unneeded portion will be added to the
                     // free list.
    }
```

```
GMarkFree()     // Mark the "remainder" block as free
                // Store away the blocks flags. They can later
                // be retrieved
                // via the GlobalFlags() API
arenaPointer->pga_flags = AL

if ( GA_ZEROINIT flag )
{
    Get_Blotto()     // Gets the "blotto" selector, used to
                     // zero out memory segments.

    GZero()          // Zero out the new block
}

OR EAX with EAX to set the Zero flag, indicating success
or failure

return arenaPoniter to caller
```

GrowHeap()

GrowHeap() is the low level KERNEL routine responsible for allocating additional memory from the DPMI server and adding it into the global heap. GrowHeap() initially tries to allocate at least 64K (usually 128K) from DPMI. If that fails, GrowHeap() falls back and tries to allocate the amount of memory actually needed, if less than 64K. If it successfully allocated a DPMI block, GrowHeap() creates the two bounding GA_NOT_THERE arenas that mark the ends of the block. It also creates the free arena that the higher level functions allocate from.

```
pseudocode for GrowHeap() - 3GALLOC.OBJ
// Parameters:
//       DWORD   growSize    // Actually in EDX

    if ( FreeArenaCount < 4 )    // At least 4 arenas are needed
        Set the carry flag and return

    Save growSize on the stack

    if ( growSize < 64K ) // Always allocate at least 64K from DPMI
        growSize = 128K   // 128K is usually the case.

    round growSize to a multiple of 4K

    INT 31h, fn. 0501h       // DPMI allocate memory
```

```
if ( allocation failed )
{
    growSize = original growSize from the stack

    // Find out if DPMI is holding memory "in reserve". If
    // so, go allocate some now. GetDPMIFreeSpace() is
    // discussed later.
    if ( GetDPMIFreeSpace() < growSize )
        set carry flag and return

    INT 31h, fn. 0501h      // DPMI allocate memory

    if ( allocation failed )
        set carry flag and return
}

// If we get here, we were able to get enough memory
// to satisfy the allocation request.
Alloc_Arena_Header()    // Allocate the 1st bracket arena
Set GA_NOT_THERE bit in the pga_owner field

Alloc_Arena_Header()    // Allocate the usable arena
Set GA_NOT_THERE bit in the pga_owner field

Alloc_Arena_Header()    // Allocate the 2st bracket arena
Set GA_NOT_THERE bit in the pga_owner field

Add the new arenas into the linked list of arenas

GMarkFree()     // Mark the middle arena as being free
```

GCompact()

GCompact() is a low level internal routine that, besides being called from GSearch(), is also called from GlobalCompact() (via the GAvail() function). The code starts out by obtaining the timer tick count. This might seem a bit strange, unless you know that GCompact() sends a WM_COMPACTING message to all tasks when an excessive amount of time is spent compacting the global heap.

Next GCompact() calls GCmpHeap(), another low level routine, but we won't go into its details. It is sufficient to say that it shuffles MOVEABLE blocks around in memory and tries to create the largest possible free memory block. If the act of reorganizing the MOVEABLE blocks frees up enough space, GCompact() skips the next and most drastic step of discarding segments.

For the work of discarding segments, GCompact() calls GDiscard(), yet another low level routine that we won't examine here because of its length and complexity. In brief, GDiscard() starts discarding the least recently used segments until it has freed up enough space. Then, since the act of discarding segments may have created additional opportunities for GCmpHeap() to free up even more space, GCompact() calls GCmpHeap() yet again.

All routes of exit from GCompact() lead through a code sequence at the end of the function, where GCompact() calculates the amount of time spent compacting the global heap. If more than 1/8 of the time is spent compacting, the WM_COMPACTING message is broadcast to all tasks in the system. As described in Chapter 1, KERNEL is not quite as self-sufficient as you might think because it has to know about USER routines in order to broadcast the message.

```
pseudocode for GCompact() - 3GCOMPAC.OBJ
// Parameters:
//      DWORD   bytes_requested

    Get timer tick count from BIOS segment area (0040H:006Ch),
    and save the value in GCompact_Timer global variable

    Save the original value of GlobalInfo.gi_cmpflags on stack

    // Set flags to not compact the heap when looking for memory.
    // This flag may be turned off in subsequent passes through
    // the global heap, if the initial pass fails.
    if ( WF_PAGING bit set in WinFlags )
        Turn on GA_NOCOMPACT flag in GlobalInfo.gi_cmpflags

GCompact_start:

    if debug KERNEL
        ValidateFreeSpaces()    // Just RETF's.

    // If there is a discardable code segment reserve area,
    // compact the bottom portion of the heap
    if ( GlobalInfo.gi_reserve != 0 )
    {
        ESI = GlobalInfo.hi_first   // First block in heap
        EBX = offset of pga_next field in GlobalInfo

        GCmpHeap(ESI, EBX)  // compact the bottom portion of the
                            // heap. Move around MOVEABLE blocks
                            // to coalesce free spaces
    }

    // compact the top portion of the heap and see if enough
    // space was created.
    ESI = GlobalInfo.hi_last    // Last block in heap
    EBX = offset of pga_prev field in GlobalInfo
    GCmpHeap(ESI, EBX)
```

```
    if ( GCmpHeap() was able to compact anything )
    {
        if ( GCheckFree() > bytes_requested )   // Enough freed?
            goto GCompact_do_timer_check        // Yes? All done.
    }

    if ( GlobalInfo.hi_freeze != 0 )    // if the heap is "frozen"
        goto GCompact_do_timer_check    // it can't be compacted

    // Did the memory request say "Don't discard to satisfy"?
    // If so, skip over the discarding step
    if ( GA_NODISCARD bit set in GlobalInfo.gi_cmpflags )
        goto GCompact_no_discard

    if ( WF_PAGING bit set in WinFlags )
        goto GCompact_do_discard

    if ( GA_NOCOMPACT bit set in GlobalInfo.gi_cmpflags )
        goto GCompact_no_discard

CCompact_do_discard:

    // We couldn't come up with enough space by moving around
    // segments and coalescing blocks. It's finally time to
    // start discarding segments until there's enough room
    // left. GDiscard() does this.
    if ( GDiscard() )           // If segments were discarded,
        goto GCompact_start     // then the heap may also now be
                                // amenable to coalescing again,
                                // so go try it again
GCompact_no_discard:

    // This section appears to be some sort of state machine.
    // Based upon the values of various flags, it either gives
    // up on the allocation request, or changes some flags and
    // starts anew the process of coalescing and discarding
    // memory blocks to meet the request.
    if ( WF_PAGING bit not set in WinFlags )
        goto GCompact_do_timer_check

    restore original gi_cmpflags on stack to GlobalInfo

    push GlobalInfo.gi_cmpflags on stack, and turn on the
    GA_NOCOMPACT and GA_NODISCARD bits in the compaction
    flags that are saved on the stack
```

```
    if ( GA_NOCOMPACT bit not set in GlobalInfo.gi_cmpflags )
        goto GCompact_start

GCompact_do_timer_check:

    // See if the address of PostMessage() has been obtained
    // yet (KERNEL startup does this). If it's still 0, then
    // we don't have a function pointer to call PostMessage()
    // with. Thus, don't calculate the compaction time ratio
    if ( FP_SEG(PPostMessage) == 0 )
        goto GCompact_done

    Get timer tick count from BIOS segment area (0040H:006Ch)

    Calculate how much time is spent compacting the heap

    // If more that 1/8 of the recent time has been spent
    // compacting the heap, broadcast a message to all programs
    // advising them that memory is low, and that they should
    // free up any unneeded memory. The call is done via the
    // function pointer obtained during KERNEL startup.
    if ( time threshold has been reached (12.5%) )
        PostMessage(-1, WM_COMPACTING, AX, 0L)

    Set GCompact_Start from the current tick count

GCompact_done:

    restore GlobalInfo.gi_cmpflags off the stack

    return to caller
```

GlobalFree()

Like GlobalAlloc(), the code for GlobalFree() is mostly uninteresting. It has the standard GEnter() prologue and GLeave() epilogue code. GlobalFree() checks the handle being freed for a few special conditions and undertakes appropriate remedies if necessary (see the pseudocode). The real work is done inside GFree(), which we cover next.

```
pseudocode for GlobalFree() - 3GINTERF.OBJ
// Parameters:
//      WORD    handle

    push DS on the stack after setting up stack frame

    GEnter()    // Prevent LRU sweeping. Point at GlobalInfo
```

```
    if ( handle == 0 )    // Can't free a NULL handle!
        goto GLeave()

    // Some programs written for Windows 3.0 converted a selector
    // to a handle by just adding 1 to the selector value. In
    // Windows 3.1, the privilege level changed, and hence, the
    // bottom 3 bits should always be on. If a program uses
    // the 3.0 hack, the bits will "wrap" around, and become 0's.
    // If this is the case, GlobalFree() tries to correct the
    // situation by decrementing the value back to (hopefully)
    // its correct value. The debug KERNEL prints out a message:
    // "A program has attempted an invalid selector-to-handle
    // conversion\r\nAttempting to correct this error."
    if ( bottom 3 bits of handle are 0 )
        handle--

    PDref(handle)    // Returns AX = selector, DX = handle
                     // (or 0 if the segment is fixed )

    // The WORD at [BP-2] is the DS that was pushed upon entry
    // to GlobalFree(). Check to see if that selector is the
    // one being freed. If so, set the DS value on the stack
    // to zero, so that we don't GP fault when we restore the
    // value from the stack
    if ( AX or DX equal the WORD at [BP-2] )
        set the WORD at [BP-2] to 0

    if ( running the debug KERNEL )
        If handle being freed is locked, emit an error message

    GFree()     // Takes care of the details of deallocation

GlobalFree_done:

    if( !CheckGlobalHeap() )    // Only does this in debug KERNEL
    {
        AX |= 0x0200     // An error code ???
        NearKernelError("GlobalFree: Invalid global heap")
    }

    GLeave()

    pop DS from the stack
```

GFree()

GFree() is a middle level internal routine. If the segment being freed has not been discarded, then Free_Object() handles the details of freeing the block and releasing its associated selector. If the object has been discarded, there's no block to worry about freeing up; all that remains is setting the selector table entry to zero, and releasing the selector(s) that referenced the block back to the LDT free list.

```
pseudocode for GFree() - 3GMEM.OBJ
// Parameters:
//      WORD    handle  // handle to free (in DX register)
// Locals:
//      DWORD   arenaPointer     // These two vars are really
//      WORD    owner            // in registers

    PDref() // Returns the address of the selector's arena and the
            // block owner's handle. These values are used as
            // the "arenaPointer", and "owner" local variables.
            // The Zero flag is set if object has been discarded.

    if ( object has been discarded )
        goto Object_Discarded

    Free_Object(owner, arenaPointer)    // Release the object
                                        // from the global heap
    return to caller

Object_Discarded:

    // Apparently, if the block has been discarded, the bottom
    // WORD of its "arena pointer" in the selector table is a
    // selector value of some kind. Here, we null out the entry
    // in the selector table.
    AssociateSelector32( LOWORD(arenaPointer), 0 )

    FreeSelArray( LOWORD(arenaPointer) ) // Free up the selector
```

Free_Object()

Free_Object(), called from GFree(), is a low level internal routine. It begins by removing the memory object from the LRU list. If the block is pagelocked, Free_Object() repeatedly invokes the supposedly obsolete DPMI function 0005h until it un-pagelocks the block. Afterwards, Free_Object() examines the surrounding arenas and, if the conditions are right, frees the entire DPMI block back to the DPMI server. If this isn't the case, Free_Object() informs the DPMI server that the memory for the block is no longer needed and can be discarded, rather than paged to disk. The final two bits of housekeeping involves NULLing out the arena pointer in the selector table and freeing up the selector(s) that were used to reference the block.

```
pseudocode for Free_Object() - 3GMEM.OBJ
// Parameters:
//      WORD    owner (in DX register)
//      DWORD   arenaPointer (in DS:ESI)

    // if "owner" is nonzero, then the block will be freed
    // only if it matches the real owner of the block, as
    // specified in the "pga_owner" field in the arena
    if ( owner !== 0 )
        if ( arenaPointer->pga_owner != owner )
            return -1

    GLRUDel()    // Remove this object from the LRU list. FIXED
                 // objects aren't in the LRU list.

    if ( arenaPointer->pga_pglock != 0 )
    {
        loop arenaPointer->pga_pglock times, calling INT 31,
        fn. 0005h to completely unlock the block. This DPMI
        function is listed as "reserved" in the DPMI
        specification. It unlocks all the pages associated with
        a selector. It's similar to INT 31h, fn. 0601h, and in
        fact, both functions call _LinPageUnlock in VMM.
    }

    arenaPointer->pga_pglock = 0    // No longer pagelocked

    GMarkFree()    // Mark the block's arena as free

    // We now begin testing the block being free to see if it's
    // an entire block previously allocated from DPMI. If so
    // we will free the block back to the DPMI server.

    if (owner of arenaPointer->pga_prev block isn't GA_NOT_THERE)
        goto Free_Object_A

    if (owner of arenaPointer->pga_next block isn't GA_NOT_THERE)
        goto Free_Object_A

    if (block _after_ arenaPointer->pga_next block is a sentinel)
        goto Free_Object_A

    // Use INT 31h, fn. 0502 to free the DPMI block back to the
    // DPMI server. Also removes the block from the heap list.
    // pseudocode for this function is given later in the chapter.
    UnlinkWin386Block(arenaPointer)
```

```
    goto Free_Object_B

Free_Object_A:

    // Calls DPMI function 0703h. This tells the DPMI server
    // that the memory region is no longer needed, and that it is
    // O.K to discard the memory, rather than swap it to disk.
    // The DPMI function in turn calls _PageDiscardPages in VMM,
    // which clears the "accessed" and "dirty" bits in the
    // page table entry. This tells the LRU mechanism that it
    // doesn't have to move the memory to disk, and instead can
    // just discard it.
    GWin386Discard( arenaPointer->pga_size,
                    arenaPointer->pga_address )

Free_Object_B:

    // somewhere prior to this part, DX is set to the selector
    // of the segment that's being freed.
    AssociateSelector32(DX, 0)  // Null out arena pointer in
                                // the selector table.

    FreeSelArray(DX)            // Free up the LDT entries
```

GlobalLock()

GlobalLock() is probably one of the most misunderstood of the Windows APIs. The code is actually fairly simple, so it's somewhat surprising how much confusion arises from its use.

GlobalLock() accepts -1 as a handle value and locks whatever the current DGROUP segment is. If the caller passed in -1 therefore, GlobalLock() changes the handle value to the current DS value.

Before the program enters the main body of the function, the LAR instruction obtains the access rights bits for the passed handle. When a memory block is discarded, its "present" bit is cleared. In this case, there's no way to lock the block. The caller must somehow be made aware of this situation. GlobalLock() will return 0 if the segment you told it to lock has already been discarded. When using DISCARDABLE memory, the caller is responsible for checking the return value from GlobalLock() to see if the block has been discarded. If so, the caller is responsible for recreating the memory block.

After the initial preprocessing that we just described, GlobalLock() copies the handle parameter to the DX register (upon return, DX contains the selector portion of a far pointer). Then, it turns the bottom bit of DX on. If the block is already FIXED, then its handle *is* its selector value, and the bottom bit is already on. If the handle is for a MOVEABLE block, the handle value is one less than the selector value. Turning on the bottom bit has the effect of adding one. In all cases, DX ends up with a valid selector value. Now comes the extremely important part. If the block is not DISCARDABLE, GlobalLock() simply returns to the caller.

That's it! For the vast majority of your allocations, the only thing GlobalLock() does is convert your handle to a selector through some bit-twiddling. No lock counts are incremented. *Nothing*. It's really that simple.

If the block being locked is DISCARDABLE, which is fairly rare in most programs, all GlobalLock() does is increment the lock count in the block's arena. This prevents the block from being discarded when the heap manager is scavenging around, looking for something it can toss to free up a few bytes. No pagelocking or anything else fancy goes on.

```
pseudocode for GlobalLock() - 3GINTERF.OBJ
// Parameters:
//      WORD    handle

    if ( handle == -1 ) // Lock DGROUP if passed -1
        handle = DS

    // Return 0 if the segment has been discarded!
    if ( PRESENT bit not set in the LDT entry )
        return NULL

    DX = handle      // Upon return, DX will contain the seg value

    OR the bottommost bit of DX on  // Converts a handle
                                    // to its selector.

    // The 1000h bit in the LDT descriptor (which is 'available'
    // for use by system software) is used to mark whether the
    // segment is discardable or not
    if ( segment is non-discardable )
        return DX:AX          // a usable far pointer. AX=0

    // Important point:  Only DISCARDABLE segments continue
    // past this point. This means that for almost every
    // segment that a program typically allocates, calling
    // GlobalLock() does nothing but convert the handle to
    // a selector.

    // Get handle's arena pointer. DX still contains a selector
    // version of the handle parameter.
    if ( Get_Arena_Pointer32(DX) == 0 )
        return 0
    // Prevent the block from being discarded.
    increment the pga_count field in the found arena

    return DX:AX          // a usable far pointer. AX=0
```

GlobalUnlock()

As you might expect, the GlobalUnlock() code is almost a mirror image of the GlobalLock() code. In other words, it's extremely simple. After testing for and dealing with some special cases (the same ones that GlobalLock() checks for), GlobalUnlock() just returns if the block is not DISCARDABLE. Putting aside questions of aesthetics and portability, there's really no reason to call GlobalUnlock() if the segment isn't DISCARDABLE. If the segment is DISCARDABLE, then you should of course call GlobalUnlock(), as appropriate. All it does in this case is decrement the lock count in the block's arena. When the lock count reaches 0, the segment can be discarded.

```
pseudocode for GlobalUnlock() - 3GINTERF.OBJ
// Parameters:
//      WORD    handle

    if ( handle == -1 ) // Unlock DGROUP if passed -1
        handle = DS

    // Attempt to fix bad selector-> handle conversions by
    // application programs. See pseudocode for GlobalFree()
    // for details.
    if ( bottom 3 bits of handle are 0 )
        handle--

    // Return 0 if the segment has been discarded
    if ( segment is not present )
        return NULL

    if ( segment is non-discardable ) // See GlobalLock() pseudo
        return 0                      // code for how this is
                                      // determined

    // Important point:  Only DISCARDABLE segments continue
    // past this point. This means that for almost every
    // segment that a program typically allocates, calling
    // GlobalUnlock() does nothing.
    if ( Get_Arena_Pointer32(handle) == 0 ) // Get handle's arena
        return 0                            // pointer

    decrement the pga_count field in the found arena, and
    check to see if the lock count has "underflowed"

    return the current lock count
```

GlobalHandle()

GlobalHandle(), which returns the Windows global heap handle that corresponds to a passed-in protected mode selector, just functions as a wrapper around MyLock(). MyLock() (described below) returns its values in the opposite registers than GlobalHandle(), so the GlobalHandle() code switches the values of DX and AX before returning.

```
pseudocode for GlobalHandle() - 3GINTERF.OBJ
// Parameters:
//      WORD    selector

    MyLock(selector)     // Returns handle in DX, Selector in AX
                         // Doesn't "lock" anything.

    XCHG    AX, DX
```

MyLock()

MyLock() is a mid-level internal routine. It first verifies whether the handle passed into it is valid and returns a zero if the handle is invalid. Then, if the block is present in memory, MyLock() retrieves the handle out of its arena. If the block isn't present, XHandle() gets the handle value. Since no locking goes on here, the name MyLock() is misleading. Perhaps it's named this way because in real mode Windows, locking a handle was the same as dereferencing it, which is what MyLock() really does.

```
pseudocode for MyLock() - 3GINTERF.OBJ
// Parameters:
//      WORD    selector

    if ( using LAR on the selector failed (ZF set) )
        return NULL

    if ( selector is marked not-present in the LDT )
        goto MyLock_XHandle

    if ( Get_Arena_Pointer32(selector) == 0 ) // Get the arena
        return NULL                           // pointer for the
                                              // selector param

    get pga_handle field from arena pointer, and store in AX

    Copy AX to DX, and OR the bottom bit of AX on to make a
    selector value out of it.

    return to caller (DX = handle, AX = selector)

MyLock_XHandle:

    XHandle()    // See pseudocode below

    XCHG AX, DX

    return to caller
```

XHandle()

XHandle() is a heavily used internal routine. It takes a global handle and returns various registers that point at relevant data structures and useful values. Most of the values returned by XHandle() are actually obtained by PDRef(), which is another internal routine.

```
pseudocode for XHandle() - 3GINTERF.ASM
// Parameters:
//      WORD    handle
// Returns:
//
//  if Zero flag is not set:
//      AX = handle
//      BX = pointer to the selector table entry for the handle
//      CH = lock count of block (0 if the block is FIXED)
//      CL = flags in arena
//      DX = selector
//      ES:ESI = arena for the memory block
//
// If Zero flag is set:
//      AX = handle

    if ( handle == -1 )
        handle = DS

    DS:EDI = &GlobalInfo    // Point at the GlobalInfo structure

    GlobalInfo.gi_lrulock++ // Prevent LRU sweeping

    PDRef(handle)       // Sets up register to point at, or contain,
                        // various relevant values for the passed in
                        // handle. XHandle() returns these values

    if ( PDRef() returned with the Zero flag set )
        return

    if ( bottom bit set in AX )
        Zero flag = 1           // Segment is FIXED
    else
        Zero flag = 0           // Segment isn't FIXED
```

GlobalReAlloc()

GlobalReAlloc() is a wrapper routine around the internal GReAlloc() function. The beginning and end of the function looks very similar to the GlobalAlloc() code, with the GReAlloc() function sandwiched in between.

The GReAlloc() routine is extremely large and convoluted. Because of its size and complexity, pseudocode is not included here. However, we did notice that GReAlloc() uses the same GSearch() function that's at the core of the GlobalAlloc() routine. The code appears to shift memory blocks around in memory. This may be an attempt to grow a block in place, rather than to allocate a larger block then copy the original contents into it and free the old block (known as the bozo-realloc algorithm). As a side note on GReAlloc(), there was a bug in the Windows 3.0 GlobalReAlloc() that caused reallocations to fail when you tried to reallocate your memory block to a larger size. According to various sources, this was due to a bug in the DPMI server.

```
pseudocode for GlobalReAlloc() - 3GINTERF.OBJ
// Parameters:
//      WORD    handle
//      DWORD   num_bytes
//      WORD    flags

    // Attempt to fix bad selector-> handle conversions by
    // application programs. See pseudocode for GlobalFree()
    // for details.
    if ( bottom 3 bits of handle are 0 )
        handle--

    // This section of code, down to, but not including
    // GReAlloc() is similar to the start of GlobalAlloc()
    // See the GlobalAlloc() pseudocode for more details.
    GEnter()    // Prevent LRU sweeping. Point at GlobalInfo

    MyGetAppCompatFlags()   // Described in Undocumented Windows

    if ( GACF_IGNORENODISCARD flag is set )
    {
        if ( !IsKernelCalling() )
            turn off GA_NODISCARD bit in flags
    }

    GbTop()     // Tweaks the allocation flags to be "proper"

    GReAlloc()  // Does all the hard work. A _LARGE_ function!

    if( !CheckGlobalHeap() )    // Only does this in debug KERNEL
    {
        AX |= 0x0200    // An error code ???
        NearKernelError("GlobalReAlloc: Invalid global heap")
    }
```

GlobalDOSAlloc()

GlobalDOSAlloc() is primarily used by programs for obtaining memory below 1Mb in order to communicate with TSRs, and by KERNEL when allocating a new Task Database. It's important to remember that memory allocated from GlobalDOSAlloc() can only be accessed in the system Virtual Machine (VM). You cannot allocate memory with GlobalDOSAlloc() for use with DOS boxes that were invoked inside Windows. Also, when using virtual memory, memory obtained from GlobalDOSAlloc() is only located below one megabyte in the *linear* address space. It's quite possible that the memory may actually be above one megabyte in physical memory.

GlobalDOSAlloc() starts out by calling GlobalAlloc(), using the undocumented GA_ALLOC_DOS flag. This flag tells GlobalAlloc() that the memory needs to be below 1Mb and FIXED. If GlobalAlloc() is able to come up with the memory, GlobalDOSAlloc() calls Get_Physical_Address() to obtain the linear address of the block in memory. GlobalDOS-Alloc() performs some segment arithmetic with that address in order to calculate the value of a real mode segment that it can pass to DOS or to other real mode code that needs to access the block. This value, as well as the protected mode selector that Windows programs use to access the block, is returned to the caller.

```
pseudocode for GlobalDOSAlloc() - 3GINTERF.OBJ
// Parameters:
//      DWORD   num_bytes

    // Allocate the memory, using an undocumented flag
    if ( !GlobalAlloc(GA_ALLOC_DOS, num_bytes) )
        return 0

    save handle from GlobalAlloc() on stack

    // Reads the base address of the segment out of the LDT
    // descriptor. Note that the returned address is not
    // a physical address that can be put on the address bus.
    // Instead, it's a _linear_ address.
    Get_Physical_Address()

    use SHR and RCR instructions to create a real mode segment
    address in DX

    restore handle from GlobalAlloc() into AX   // On the stack
```

GlobalDOSFree()

GlobalDOSFree() is just a shell around the GlobalFree() API. There does not appear to be any special reason for its existence, other than to maintain continuity of the Windows API naming. In some versions of Windows 3.0, GlobalDOSFree() is just an exported alias for GlobalFree().

```
pseudocode for GlobalDOSFree() - 3GINTERF.OBJ
// Parameters:
//      WORD    handle

    GlobalFree(handle)
```

GlobalCompact()

GlobalCompact() starts out by determining how much free memory is available from the DPMI server. If the amount of free memory is less than the number of bytes requested, or if the free memory size is below 512K, GlobalCompact() calls GAvail(). GAvail(), which is not described here, calls GCompact(), which we examined as part of GlobalAlloc(). Then, GlobalCompact() uses ShrinkHeap() to free up any DPMI blocks that don't have segments allocated in their space. ShrinkHeap() is just a wrapper around InnerShrinkHeap(), which we examine next.

```
pseudocode for GlobalCompact() - 3GINTERF.OBJ
// Parameters:
//      DWORD   bytes_requested
// Locals:
//      DWORD   bytes_free

    GEnter()    // Prevent LRU sweeping. Point at GlobalInfo

    if( !CheckGlobalHeap() )    // Only does this in debug KERNEL
    {
        AX |= 0x0200     // An error code ???
        NearKernelError("GlobalCompact: Invalid global heap")
    }

    // Figure out how much free space there is, round it down
    // to a paragraph boundary, and store it. See
    // GetDPMIFreeSpace() to see how DPMI is queried.
    EAX = bytes_free = galign( GetDPMIFreeSpace() )

    if ( (bytes_free < bytes_requested) || (bytes_free < 512K) )
    {
        if in debug KERNEL, display:
            "%SS2 GlobalCompact(#ax#BX), discarding segments"
        where #ax#BX displays the value of "bytes_requested"

        GBTop(-1)   // Convert bytes_requested to paragraphs

        GAlign()    // Rounds a size request to nearest paragraph

        EAX = GAvail()  // Returns the amount of available free
                        // space. Calls GCompact().
```

```
        if ( EAX < bytes requested )    // Is the amount of free
            EAX = bytes_requested       // space enough???
    }

    Convert EAX into DX:AX representation

    GLeave()    // Reenable LRU sweeping

    ShrinkHeap()    // Wrapper around InnerShrinkHeap() call
```

InnerShrinkHeap()

InnerShrinkHeap() is the function that releases blocks that were previously allocated from DPMI back to DPMI, if no one is suballocating any of the memory in the block. InnerShrinkHeap() iterates through the global heap arenas, and if an arena's pga_prev and pga_next fields both point to blocks that are owned by GA_NOT_THERE, it's safe to free the block. This task is handled by UnlinkWin386Block() (discussed momentarily). After the entire heap has been examined, InnerShrinkHeap() checks to see if any blocks were in fact released to DPMI and sets the ZERO flag accordingly.

```
pseudocode for InnerShrinkHeap() - 3GCOMPAC.OBJ
// Locals:
//      DWORD   arenaPointer (actually in ESI)

    save value of Win386_Blocks on stack

    if ( Win386_Blocks == 0 )   // Win386_Blocks is a global
        return                  // variable, containing the
                                // number of blocks that have
                                // been allocated via DPMI

    arenaPointer = GlobalInfo.hi_first  // Start at list head

next_arena:

    arenaPointer = arenaPointer->pga_freenext // Goto next block

    // Check for the last sentinel. We know it's the last block
    // if its pga_next pointer points to itself
    if ( arenaPointer->pga_next == arenaPointer )
        goto done_looping

    if ( arenaPointer->pga_prev != GA_NOT_THERE )
        goto next_arena
```

```
    if ( arenaPointer->pga_next != GA_NOT_THERE )
        goto next_arena

    if (block _after_ arenaPointer->pga_next block is a sentinel)
        goto done_looping

    // Use INT 31h, fn. 0502 to free the block back to the DPMI
    // server. Also removes the block from the heap list
    UnlinkWin386Block(arenaPointer)

    goto next_arena     // keep looking for more blocks to free

done_looping:

    pop value of Win386_Blocks of the stack, and compare to the
    new value of Win386_Blocks. This causes the Zero flag to
    be set if the heap didn't shrink at all.
```

UnlinkWin386Block()

The KERNEL memory manager is "environmentally aware," and knows that recycling is a good thing. Once KERNEL has determined that a block should be released back to DPMI, UnlinkWin386Block() is responsible for undoing the scaffolding set up when the block was first allocated. The first order of business is to remove the block from the free list. Next, DPMI function 0502h frees the block back to the DPMI server. Then, KERNEL decrements the global variable containing the number of allocated DPMI blocks. The three arenas for the block (two GA_NOT_THEREs and one free arena) are then removed from the regular arena chain. Finally, it releases the three arenas themselves to the free arena pool.

```
pseudocode for UnlinkWin386Block() - 3GCOMPAC.OBJ
// Parameters:
//      DWORD   arenaPointer (in ESI)
//      DWORD   prevArena    (in EBX)
//      DWORD   nextArena    (in ECX)

    // See if we're about to do something nasty with the last
    // sentinel block. Abort now, if so.
    if ( block _after_ nextArena points to itself )
        return

    if debugging version of KERNEL, display a message:
        "UnlinkWin386Block: releasing #dx#AX bytes",
    where #dx#AX displays the value of arenaPointer->pga_size

    GDel_Free(arenaPointer) // Remove block from the free list

    Get DPMI block handle from prevArena->pga_lrunext
```

```
    INT 31h, fn. 0502h to release the memory back to DPMI server
    The DPMI server in turn calls the VMM _PageFree function.

    Win386_Blocks--     // Decrement the global variable

    fix-up pointers so that prevArena->pga_prev points to
    nextArena->pga_next, and vice-versa. (In other words,
    remove the 3 arenas from the global heap list)

    Free_Arena_Header(prevArena)     // Free up the headers for
    Free_Arena_Header(arenaPointer)  // the 3 arenas that were
    Free_Arena_Header(nextArena)     // used to manage the block
                                     // allocated from DPMI
    GlobalInfo.hi_count -= 3

    if debug KERNEL
        CheckGlobalHeap()   // Make sure heap is still correct
```

GlobalFix()

GlobalFix() is a shell around the GLock() routine. GLock() itself is very simple and just increments the pga_count field of the block's arena. You typically never need, or want, to call GlobalFix() because it locks the block in linear memory. This is rarely necessary in protected mode, and it can lead to heap fragmentation. However, you do want to fix a block in memory when you're aliasing data segments to code segments, or vice-versa. Except, as seen in the pseudocode for AllocDStoCSAlias(), in this situation KERNEL already takes care of calling GlobalFix() for you.

```
pseudocode for GlobalFix() - 3GINTERF.OBJ
// Parameters:
//      WORD    handle

    if (!XHandle(handle))   // Points registers at GlobalInfo
        return              // structure, the arena for 'handle',
                            // etc. Returns Zero flag set if
                            // not a valid block to fix
            // Disallow moving of the block
    GLock() // Increments pga_count in the arena for 'handle'
```

GlobalUnfix()

GlobalUnfix() is the mirror image code for GlobalFix(), using the GUnLock() function, which is slightly more interesting than the GLock() code. Thus, we'll cover it below.

```
pseudocode for GlobalUnfix() - 3GINTERF.OBJ
// Parameters:
//      WORD    handle
```

```
    if (!XHandle(handle))   // Points registers at GlobalInfo
        return              // structure, the arena for 'handle',
                            // etc. Returns Zero flag set if
                            // not a valid block to fix
                // Allow block to be moved
    GUnLock()   // Decrements lock count in the arena for 'handle'
```

GUnLock()

Besides doing the obvious task of decrementing the pga_count field in the block's arena, GUnLock() also puts in its two cents to optimize performance. If calling GUnLock() caused the lock count to drop to zero, meaning that the block is now unlocked, and if the block is DISCARDABLE, GUnLock() puts the block at the head of the LRU list, making it the least likely block to be discarded. The LRU list is discussed in the section on global arenas and in the description for LRUSweep().

```
pseudocode for GUnLock() - 3GMEM.OBJ
// Parameters
//      DWORD   arenaPointer (in ESI)

    if ( arenaPointer->pga_count == 0 )
        return

    decrement arenaPointer->pga_count  // If nonzero, block can't
                                       // be moved or discarded
    if ( arenaPointer->pga_count == 0 )
    {
        if (GA_DISCARDBABLE bit set in arenaPointer->pga_flags)
            GLRUTop()   // Put object at head of the LRU chain
                        // (least likely to be discarded)
    }
```

LockSegment()

LockSegment() and UnlockSegment are the environmentally-aware versions of GlobalFix() and GlobalUnfix(). The code is identical, with only one difference. These functions only lock or unlock the segment if it's DISCARDABLE. Since DISCARDABLE segments are the only ones you generally need to lock, LockSegment()/UnlockSegment() do the intelligent thing and don't lock or unlock the segment if it's not DISCARDABLE. See the description of AllocDStoCSAlias() for why fixing segments is sometimes (albeit rarely) necessary.

```
pseudocode for LockSegment() - 3GINTERF.OBJ
// Parameters:
//      WORD    handle

    if (!XHandle(handle))   // Points registers at GlobalInfo
        return              // structure, the arena for 'handle',
```

```
                                // etc.  Returns Zero flag set if
                                // not a valid block to fix

    if ( GA_DISCARDABLE bit not set in pga_flags )
        return
            // Prevent block from being discarded
    GLock() // Increments pga_count in the arena for 'handle'
```

UnlockSegment()

UnlockSegment() is almost identical to GlobalUnfix(), with the exception that it calls the GUnLock() routines only if the segment is DISCARDABLE. See LockSegment() for more information.

```
pseudocode for UnlockSegment() - 3GINTERF.OBJ
// Parameters:
//      WORD    handle

    if (!XHandle(handle))       // Points registers at GlobalInfo
        return                  // structure, the arena for 'handle',
                                // etc. Returns Zero flag set if
                                // not a valid block to fix

    if ( GA_DISCARDABLE bit not set in pga_flags )
        return
                //Allow block to be discarded
    GUnLock()   // Decrements lock count in the arena for 'handle'
```

GlobalPageLock()

GlobalPageLock() is not a function that you commonly need to use. It is intended for pagelocking dynamically allocated data segments that are accessed inside of an interrupt handler. If the segments are not pagelocked, a “not present” fault could occur at interrupt time and potentially hang the system.

Because a pagelocked segment is unmoveable in memory, it makes sense that the block be moved down to as low an address as possible, that is, with the FIXED blocks. Therefore, before calling the (supposedly obsolete) DPMI function 0004h to pagelock the memory, GlobalPageLock() calls GWire() to move the block down in memory (GWire() is described as part of the GlobalWire() description below). After GWire() moves the block down and function 0004L pagelocks it, GlobaPageLock() increments the pga_count and pga_pglock fields in the block’s arena.

```
pseudocode for GlobalPageLock() - 3GINTERF.OBJ
// Parameters:
//      WORD    handle
// Locals:
//      DWORD   arenaPointer    ( set by XHandle() )
```

```
    if ( !XHandle() )    // See pseudocode for XHandle()
        return 0

    if ( arenaPointer->pga_pglock == 0FFh )
    {
        if debug KERNEL, display a message:
            "GlobalPageLock: Lock count overflow"

        return 0
    }

    GWire()     // Move the block down as low as possible

    INT 31h, AX = 0004        // Supposedly obsolete DPMI function.
    if ( carry flag set )     // Locks the pages of the selector
        return AX = 0         // specified by BX. Calls the VMM
                              // _LinPageLock() function.

    arenaPointer->pga_count++   // Increment the two lock count
    arenaPointer->pga_pglock++  // fields for the arena

    return  arenaPointer->pga_pglock   // Return new lock count

    return to caller
```

GlobalPageUnlock()

As its name implies, GlobalPageUnlock() undoes the work that GlobalPageLock() did by calling the corresponding supposedly obsolete DPMI function to unpagelock the memory. GlobalPageUnlock() then decrements both the pga_count and pga_pglock fields to restore them to their values before the segment was GlobalPageLock()'ed.

```
pseudocode for GlobalPageUnlock() - 3GINTERF.OBJ
// Parameters:
//      WORD    handle
// Locals:
//      DWORD   arenaPointer    ( set by XHandle() )

    if ( !XHandle() )    // See pseudocode for XHandle()
        return 0

    if ( arenaPointer->pga_pglock == 0 )
    {
        if debug KERNEL, display a message:
            "GlobalPageUnlock: Lock count underflow"

        return 0
    }
```

```
INT 31h, AX = 0005        // Supposedly obsolete DPMI function.
if ( carry flag set )     // Unlocks the pages of the selector
    return AX = 0         // specified by BX

arenaPointer->pga_count--    // Decrement the two lock count
arenaPointer->pga_pglock--   // fields for the arena

AX = arenaPointer->pga_pglock    // Return the new lock count

return to caller
```

GlobalWire()

GlobalWire() is another function that you rarely need to use. In fact, the debug KERNEL displays a warning if you use it, suggesting that you use GlobalLock() instead. GlobalWire() is a much more potent function than GlobalLock(). Some programmers were overusing GlobalWire(), and therefore using up precious low memory below 1Mb, when a GlobalLock() would have been sufficient.

GlobalWire() has the net effect of making a block FIXED. However, blocks that are GlobalWire()'ed can later be un-FIXED by calling GlobalUnwire(). Although this function is somewhat similar to GlobalPageLock(), there are key differences. GlobalWire() does not call the DPMI server to pagelock the segment. Additionally, if the segment being wired is a DISCARDABLE code segment, GLRUDel() removes the segment from the LRU list so that the compaction routines will not try to discard it in low memory situations.

```
pseudocode for GlobalWire() - 3GINTERF.OBJ
// Parameters:
//      WORD    handle
// Locals:
//      DWORD   arenaPointer    ( set by XHandle() )

    if debug KERNEL
        if ( !fBooting )
        {
            output a message:
            "GlobalWire(#BX of %BX2) (try GlobalLock)"
        }

    if ( !XHandle() )    // See pseudocode for XHandle()
        return 0

    GWire()      // Moves the block's memory down low, if possible

    arenaPointer->pga_count++    // Lock the block in memory
```

```
    if ( GA_DISCODE flag set in arenaPointer->pga_flags )
    {
        GLRUDel()   // Remove from the LRU list

        Turn off GA_DISCODE flag in arenaPointer->pga_flags
    }

    AX = arenaPointer->pga_handle
    OR bottom bit of AL on to convert to a selector

    DX = AX     // Return a far pointer
    AX = 0
```

GWire()

GWire() is an internal routine that's used by both GlobalWire() and GlobalPageLock(). Its job is to find the lowest possible address for a block in the global heap and to move the block there if possible. GWire() does this by relying on GSearch(), the all knowing, all powerful searching routine for the global heap that we examined earlier. If GSearch() finds a new location for the block, GMoveBusy() moves the block to the new spot. It is not considered a failure condition if GWire() cannot move the block down low. The calling routine just has to live with the fact that the block might end up getting locked somewhere in the middle of the global heap, rather than down low with the FIXED blocks.

```
pseudocode for GWire() - 3GINTERF.OBJ
// Parameters:
//      DWORD   arenaPointer (In ESI)
// Locals:
//      DWORD   newArena

    // If the block is DISCARDABLE, prevent it from being
    // discarded. This is probably because GSearch() is called
    // later on in the routine, and GSearch() can cause blocks
    // to be discarded. We don't want the block we're wiring
    // to be discarded!
    if ( GA_DISCARDABLE bit set in arenaPointer->pga_flags )
        arenaPointer->pga_count++

    // Look for a FIXED block that the current block can
    // be copied into.
    newArena = GSearch(arenaPointer->pga_size)

    if ( GA_DISCARDABLE bit set in arenaPointer->pga_flags )
        arenaPointer->pga_count--   // Undo the preceding lock

    if ( newArena == 0 )
        return          // Couldn't allocate a new block
```

```
PreAllocArena()         // Create an arena for the new block

GMarkFree()             // Make sure the new block is free???

GMoveBusy()             // copy the old block to the new block,
                        // frees up the old block, and adjusts
                        // the selector table pointers
```

GlobalUnwire()

GlobalUnwire() starts out by determining if the object being unwired was previously a DISCARDABLE code segment. If it was, GlobalUnwire() turns the GA_DISCODE bit back on in the block's arena and adds the block to the LRU list. After that, GlobalUnwire() uses GUnLock() to decrement the pga_count field in the block's arena.

```
pseudocode for GlobalUnwire() - 3GINTERF.OBJ
// Parameters:
//      WORD    handle
// Locals:
//      DWORD   arenaPointer    ( set by XHandle() )

    if ( !XHandle() )   // See pseudocode for XHandle()
        return 0

    if ( DISCARDABLE bit set in LDT descriptor for handle )
    {
        if ( CODE bit set in LDT descriptor for handle )
        {
            Turn on GA_DISCODE bit set in arenaPointer->pga_flags

            GLRUAdd()   // Put the segment back in the LRU list
        }
    }

    if debug KERNEL
        if ( arenaPointer->pga_count == 0 )
        {
            display a message:
                "GlobalUnWire: Object usage count underflow"
        }
                // Allow block to move again
    GUnLock()   // Decrements lock count in the arena for 'handle'
```

LRUSweep()

In discussing the LRU functions, it makes more sense to first present what happens during an LRU sweep rather than to show the exported APIs. The LRU (Least Recently Used) list is a list of the blocks in the global heap that are DISCARDABLE. Again, NONDISCARDABLE segments are not in the LRU list. Most DISCARDABLE blocks are code segments, and resources from EXEs and DLLs, but it is possible to have DISCARDABLE data segments of your own for any data you don't mind losing.

To improve performance when discarding blocks, a very common technique is to first discard items that haven't been used recently, on the theory that they will hopefully continue not to be needed anytime soon. The trick here is determining what the least recently used segments were. Luckily, in protected mode there is a mechanism to help in this determination. In each descriptor, the CPU sets a bit each time the segment is accessed. The LRUSweep() routine tests and clears the accessed bit to record if a particular segment has been accessed since the last time LRUSweep() was called. The routine then puts any segment that's been accessed since the last sweep at the head of the LRU list where it becomes the last to be discarded. The routine leaves segments that haven't been accessed since the last sweep in their original positions in the list. It's not a highly accurate method, but it's better than just discarding blocks at random.

Now that we know why the LRU list is maintained, how does it actually work? The first part of the mechanism is set up at KERNEL bootstrap time. KERNEL calls CreateSystemTimer() in the SYSTEM driver, and tells it to call LRUSweep() every half second. *Note that this process does not happen if paging is enabled.* In the debug KERNEL, you can adjust the sweep time by setting the profile LRUSweepFrequency in the [KERNEL] section of WIN.INI. The time is specified in milliseconds. Specifying zero disables LRU sweeping.

With a method in place to sweep the LRU list periodically, the next question is what happens inside the sweep routine? First LRUSweep() looks for any excuse to abort out of the routine early (see the pseudocode). Then it walks the LRU list where it tests and clears the accessed bit for each descriptor. LRUSweep() adds any segments that were accessed since the last sweep to the head of the LRU list, while it leaves non-accessed segments alone. What's somewhat interesting is that there are two different sequences of code that do the same procedure just described. One does it without using DPMI functions, while the other one does use DPMI functions. It is not known why the coder(s) didn't just pick one method and stick with it. Well, variety is the spice of life, and all that.

```
pseudocode for LRUSweep() - 3GLRU.OBJ
// Locals:
//      DWORD   arena   // Current arena under examination
//      WORD    handle  // handle to block under examination

    if ( Kernel_InDOS != 0 )  // Don't sweep if inside DOS
        goto LRUSweep_done

    if ( LoadTDB != 0 )       // Don't sweep if loading a program
        goto LRUSweep_done
```

```
    if ( GlobalInfo.gi_lrulock != 0 )    // Don't do if inside a
        goto LRUSweep_done               // memory manager routine

    if ( GlobalInfo.gi_lrucount == 0 )
        goto LRUSweep_done               // Nothing to sweep!

    arena = GlobalInfo.gi_lruchain  // Point at head of LRU list

    // If KERNEL hasn't obtained the LDT selector for some reason,
    // then use DPMI to set the access bits in the descriptor
    if ( GDTDsc == 0 )      // GDTDsc == selector of the LDT
        goto use_DPMI_loop

loop_top_1:

    arena = arena->pga_lrunext  // Goto next LRU list entry
    handle = arena->pga_handle  // Get handle of this block

    Turn off bottom 3 bits in handle to obtain the offset of
    the descriptor in the LDT

    test and clear "accessed" bit in  // Uses BTR instruction (386)
    the descriptor for handle

    // If the selector hasn't been accessed, then just leave
    // the arena in its current spot in the LRU list, and
    // go on to the next arena in the LRU list.
    if ( accessed bit not set )
        goto loop_top_1

    // The selector has been accessed. Put it at the head
    // of the LRU list, making it least likely to be discarded.
    GLRUTop(arena)

    if ( at end of LRU list )
        goto LRUSweep_done  // All done. Return to caller
    else
        goto loop_top_1     // Go on to the next arena

use_DPMI_loop:

    arena = arena->pga_lrunext  // Goto next LRU list entry
    handle = arena->pga_handle  // Get handle of this block

    Use LAR to get the access rights byte from the descriptor
    entry for handle
```

```
    // If not accessed, just leave in its current spot
    if ( accessed bit not set )
        goto use_DPMI_loop      // Go on to next arena

    // Was accessed. Clear the accessed bit in the descriptor
    // via DPMI, and then put arena at the head of the LRU list
    INT 31, AX = 0009   // DPMI set access rights

    GLRUTop(arena)      // put at head of LRU list

    if ( not at end of LRU list )
        goto use_DPMI_loop      // Go on to next arena

LRUSweep_done:
```

GlobalLRUNewest()

GlobalLRUNewest() lets you play favorites with DISCARDABLE memory blocks. It's just a wrapper around GLRUTop(). GLRUTop() deletes the block from the LRU list and then inserts it at the beginning of the LRU list making this block the least likely to be discarded. You might use this function on one of your code segments if you knew that it was going to be heavily used in the near future.

```
pseudocode for GlobalLRUNewest() - 3GINTERF.OBJ
// Parameters
//      WORD    handle

    if (!XHandle(handle))   // Points registers at GlobalInfo
        return              // structure, the arena for 'handle',
                            // etc. Returns Zero flag set if
                            // not a valid block to fix

    GLRUTop()   // Puts the object at the head of the LRU list
                // (last to be discarded)
```

GlobalLRUOldest()

GlobalLRUOldest() lets you pick on particular DISCARDABLE memory blocks. It's just a wrapper around GLRUBot(). GLRUBot() deletes the block from the LRU list and then inserts it at the end of the LRU list, making this block the most likely to be discarded. You might use this function on one of your code segments if you knew that it wasn't going to be used after a certain point (for example, on a code segment used only during initialization).

```
pseudocode for GlobalLRUOldest() - 3GINTERF.OBJ
// Parameters
//      WORD    handle
```

```
    if (!XHandle(handle))      // Points registers at GlobalInfo
        return                 // structure, the arena for 'handle',
                               // etc. Returns Zero flag set if
                               // not a valid block to fix

    GLRUBot()    // Puts the object at the tail of the LRU list
                 // (first to be discarded)

        // Remember, none of this LRU stuff is used in 386 Enhanced mode
        // when paging is enabled, which is on at least 75 percent of
        //  Windows machines.
```

GlobalFlags()

GlobalFlags() uses the versatile XHandle() function (discussed earlier under GlobalHandle()) to extract the GA_xxx flags and the lock count of a segment from its arena header.

```
pseudocode for GlobalFlags() - 3GINTERF.OBJ
// Parameters
//      WORD    handle

    XHandle()   // Returns lock count in CH, flags in CL

    XCHG CL, CH // reverse the flags & lock count

    AX = CX     // Return value in AX
```

GlobalSize()

Like GlobalFlags(), GlobalSize() is extremely simple; it just returns the size of the memory block, as read out of its arena header. If for some reason performance is an issue, bypass this function and just use the LSL instruction, which should always return the same information. If you do use the LSL instruction, make sure to use the 32-bit form of the instruction because the first selector in a tiled block has a 32-bit limit. It might also be a good idea to check the granularity bit, which reflects whether the limit is the number of bytes or the number of 4K pages, although it's not currently necessary. It might become necessary with Win32s.

```
pseudocode for GlobalSize() - 3GINTERF.OBJ
// Parameters
//      WORD    handle
// Locals:
//      DWORD   arenaPointer    ( set by XHandle() )

    if ( !XHandle() )    // See pseudocode for XHandle()
        return 0L        // We call it for the arena pointer here

    if ( arenaPointer == 0 )    // Make sure we got back a valid
        return 0L               // arena pointer
```

```
    // Undocumented: CX returns the # of paragraphs in block
    cx = arenaPointer->pga_size >> 4

    DX:AX = arenaPointer->pga_size
```

GlobalNotify()

GlobalNotify() is of interest to you only if you use DISCARDABLE data segments. GlobalNotify() takes the passed-in function pointer to your notification handler and stores the pointer in the TDB of the current task. Later on, if KERNEL needs to discard a block that belongs to your task, it calls your notification routine. If your notification routine doesn't want the block to be discarded, it should return zero. If it's OK to discard the block, the routine should return a nonzero value.

According to the SDK documentation, your notification handler should be in a FIXED segment in a DLL. It is probably just fine to have the handler in an application, but ensure that the code segment can't be discarded. The GlobalFix() function appears to be the most suited for doing this. Also, your notification procedure is called in the context of the current task (it may not be your task!). The code that calls your notification handler sets DS and ES registers to the value in the SS register. If you do want the notification function in your application, it is important that you export your callback function and use MakeProcInstance(). It is not enough to use smart callbacks, FIXDS, or other methods that assume that DS == SS.

An interesting historical oddity shows up if you examine WINKERN.INC from the DDK. It actually lists two notification codes, GN_MOVE and GN_DISCARD, for the GlobalNotify() callback function. The SDK documentation, on the other hand, says that you're only called when a segment is about to be discarded. As it turns out, the internal routine responsible for calling the notification function, GNotify(), is in fact called when a segment is moved in memory. Unfortunately, GNotify() filters out the GN_MOVE calls, which are much more frequent than GN_DISCARDs. There's surely some sort of performance tuning tool that could be written if you were allowed to receive the GN_MOVE notifications.

```
pseudocode for GlobalNotify() - 3GINTERF.OBJ
// Parameters:
//      DWORD   lpfnNotifyProc

    // Store the function pointer into the slot reserved for
    // in in the current task's TDB. It will be called later
    // when the compaction routines are about to discard a
    // block ( inside GDiscard() ).

    CurTDB.TDB_GNotifyProc = lpfnNotifyProc
```

GetFreeSpace()

GetFreeSpace() determines the amount of memory available for use at the current time. The numbers GetFreeSpace() returns are what the Program Manager About Box displays.

GetFreeSpace() has to take into account both memory that the DPMI server is holding in reserve, as well as free or DISCARDABLE global heap blocks. First GetFreeSpace() calls

GetDPMIFreeSpace() to see how much more memory can be allocated from the DPMI server. Second, it figures out what memory is usable in the global heap. Despite what the documentation says, GetFreeSpace() *does* pay attention to the value of the flag passed in, which is typically zero. If the flag is zero, GetFreeSpace() scans the global heap and adds in the size of all DISCARDABLE and free blocks. The routine then subtracts the size of the reserve or swap area (the memory above the code fence) since the reserve area isn't really free space. Last, it subtracts 64K from that total (a fudge factor?).The calculation looks like this:

+ GetDPMIFreeSpace()
+ Size of all DISCARDABLE segments
+ Size of all free blocks
- size of the swap area
- 64K

If bit 1 of the flag's parameter is set (that is, the flag's value is 2), GetFreeSpace() ignores DISCARDABLE segments. In this case, the calculation looks like this:

+ GetDPMIFreeSpace()
+ Size of all free blocks
- 64K

```
pseudocode for GetFreeSpace() - 3GINTERF.OBJ
// Parameters:
//      WORD     flags  (0 or 2)
// Locals:
//      DWORD    arenaPointer
//      DWORD    nextArena
//      DWORD    freeSize

    GEnter()    // Prevent LRU sweeping. Point at GlobalInfo

    freeSize = GetDPMIFreeSpace()    // Returns in EDX

    arenaPointer = GlobalInfo.hi_first

loop_top:

    nextArena = arenaPointer->pga_next

    // Look for the 'Z' signature, indicating the end of the
    // list. This is a carryover from DOS memory allocation
    // which uses 'M' and 'Z' signatures for arenas
    if ( arenaPointer->pga_sig == 0x5A )
        goto loop_done

    if ( arenaPointer->pga_owner == GA_NOT_THERE )
        goto loop_top   // Don't bother with "internal use" blocks
```

```
    if ( arenaPointer->pga_owner == 0 )   // A free block?
        goto include_this_block

    if ( flags & 2 )     // 3.1 SDK documentation says the flags
        goto loop_top    // are ignored. Doesn't look like it!

    if ( bottom bit set in arenaPointer->pga_handle )
        goto loop_top    // A FIXED block. Ignore it.

    if ( arenaPointer->pga_sig != 0 )   // ???
        goto loop_top

    if ( DISCARDABLE bit not set in blocks descriptor )
        goto loop_top    // Only count discardable blocks

include_this_block:

    // Add the block size to our running total, and continue on
    // to the next block
    freeSize += arenaPointer->pga_size

    goto loop_top

loop_done:       // All done looping now

    // If bit 1 in flags is set, don't count the memory above the
    // code fence in the free memory total
    if ( !(flags & 2) )
        freeSize -= GlobalInfo.gi_reserve

    freeSize -= 0x10000  // Remove another 64K from the total. Why?

    if ( freeSize < 0 )
        freeSize = 0

    DX:AX = freeSize    // put return value in DX:AX

    GLeave()    // Reenable LRU sweeping
```

GetDPMIFreeSpace()

GetDPMIFreeSpace() isn't just a simple call to INT 31h, function 0500h. Instead, the call takes into account whether the system is running with virtual memory support. This means that the size of the swap file needs to be added to the amount of physical memory in this system. The code is somewhat strange, in that it doesn't assume that the reported linear address size is the sum of the swap file and physical memory sizes. Instead, the routine calculates both values and uses the lesser value. A similar situation occurs at the end of the function, when the code has calculated the number of free pages. It compares this value to the largest available block, as reported by DPMI, and returns the lesser of the two. Totally confusing, yet the amount of free memory displayed in the Program Manager About Box is ultimately based on this calculation. Oh well, the returned value seems close enough for government work.

```
pseudocode for GetDPMIFreeSpace() - 3GINTERF.OBJ
// Locals:
//      DWORD   freePageCount
//      DWORD   freePagesInBytes
//      DWORD   largestBlockSize
//      char    DPMIBuff[0x30]

    INT 31h, AX = 0500, ES:DI = DPMIBuff
    if ( carry flag set )   // Did DPMI call fail?
        return 0

    freePageCount = DPMIBuff.free_pages // Start out by trusting
                                        // the value DPMI returns

    if ( DPMIBuff.paging_file_size > 0 )    // Virtual memory???
    {
        // Add the space in the swap disk to the physical
        // memory in the system. Note that the value of
        // freePageCount is used as the _total_ page count until
        // the end of this block of code, where it's adjusted
        // downwards to become the actual _free_ page count.
        freePageCount = DPMIBuff.paging_file_size +
                        DPMIBuff.total_physical_pages

        // If DPMI reports a smaller total linear address space
        // than the above calculation, use it instead.
        if ( freePageCount > DPMIBuff.total_linear_address_pages )
            freePageCount = DPMIBuff.total_linear_address_pages

        // Add in the free page count, and subtract out the
        // total linear address in pages. The result should
        // be the number of pages available for use by KERNEL.
        freePageCount += DPMIBuff.free_linear_address_pages
        freePageCount -= DPMIBuff.total_linear_address_pages
    }

    // Get the largest available contiguous block size
    largestBlockSize = DPMIBuff.largest_available_block
```

```
// Convert the number of free pages into a byte total.
freePagesInBytes = freePageCount << 12  // 2^12 == 4096

if ( sign bit set in freePagesInBytes ) // value is negative?
    freePagesInBytes = 0

// Subtract out 64K from the free page size for safety
freePagesInBytes -= 64K

if ( freePagesInBytes < 0 )      // Did it go below 0?
    freePagesInBytes = 0

// Return either the largest contiguous block, or the free
// page size in bytes, whichever is smaller.
if ( freePagesInBytes < largestBlockSize )
    return freePagesInBytes
else
    return largestBlockSize
```

GetFreeMemInfo()

This undocumented function uses DPMI function 0500h to get the number of free pages and unlocked pages. It is not known why it is undocumented, since the DPMI function 0500h from which it gets the information is fully documented. Additionally, the MemManInfo() function in ToolHelp uses the same DPMI function, and returns all the information returned by the DPMI call, rather than just the two pieces returned here.

This function returns 0xFFFFFFFF as an error condition code if paging is disabled (in Standard mode, or in Enhanced mode with virtual memory disabled).

```
pseudocode for GetFreeMemInfo() - 3GINTERF.OBJ

    DX:AX = -1        // Set default return value to error value

    if ( WF1_PAGING flag set in WinFlags )
    {
        INT 31h, fn. 0500h  // See DPMI doc for buffer description

        if ( DPMI call succeeded )
        {
            AX = unlocked pages
            DX = free pages
        }
    }
```

SetSwapAreaSize()

SetSwapAreaSize() allows Windows to set the size of the swap area. Duh! The swap area is described above in the section on DISCARDABLE segments. SetSwapAreaSize() is mainly a performance tuning mechanism, although there is a tendency for developers to set really large swap areas in the hope that they'll get better performance. Unfortunately, the maximum swap size is 128K, and specifying values greater than 128K still only generates a 128K swap area.

The function starts by comparing the new desired swap size to a KERNEL global variable containing the maximum allowable swap area size. If the desired size is greater than the maximum allowable, SwapSetAreaSize() trims it down to the maximum allowable size. This value is stored into the ne_swaparea field of the task's module database. Next the function calls CalcMaxNRSeg(), which walks through all the modules in the system and finds the one with the largest minimum swap size value. SetSwapArea() passes this value to GReserve() to change the swap area size and code fence if necessary.

```
pseudocode for SetSwapAreaSize() - 3GMOREME.OBJ
// Parameters:
//      WORD    paragraphs
// Locals:
//      WORD    maxSwapSize

    maxSwapSize = MaxCodeSwapArea   // Said something once, why say it again?

    if ( paragraphs > MaxCodeSwapArea )
        paragraphs = MaxCodeSwapArea

    maxSwapSize = MaxCodeSwapArea  // A KERNEL global variable

    if ( paragraphs > maxSwapSize )
        paragraphs = maxSwapSize

    point DS register at module table of current task

    if ( paragraphs == 0 )
        goto set_return_vars

    module_table.ne_swaparea = paragraphs

    CalcMaxNRSeg()  // returns maximum size in CX

    if ( CalcMaxNRSeg() failed )
        restore original value of module_table.ne_swaparea

set_return_vars:

    AX = module_table.ne_swaparea
```

```
    if ( CalcMaxNRSeg() return value > maxSwapSize )
        DX = maxSwapSize
    else
        DX = CalcMaxNRSeg() return value
```

CalcMaxNRSeg()

CalcMaxNRSeg() is an internal function that walks through all the modules in the system and finds the module with the largest minimum swap area size. CalcMaxNRSeg() passes this value to GReserve(), which adjusts the swap area size and code fence if necessary. An interesting thing about CalcMaxNRSeg() is that it walks through the module list twice. The first time, CalcMaxNRSeg() only examines DLL modules. The second time it only looks at task modules. It's not known why the function works this way, as it seems that it would be fairly easy to do both things in one loop.

```
pseudocode for CalcMaxNRSeg() - MODULE.OBJ
// Locals:
//      WORD    currentModule
//      WORD    currentTask
//      WORD    largestSwapSize

    if ( fBooting )
        return 0            // 0 = failure

    largestSwapSize = 0

    // First walk through the module list, and get the largest
    // swap size, counting just the DLLs
    currentModule == HExeHead   // First module in list (KERNEL)

    while ( not at end of module list (currentModule != 0) )
    {
        if ( currentModule is a DLL )
        {
            if ( currentModule.ne_swaparea > largestSwapSize )
                largestSwapSize = currentModule.ne_swaparea
        }

        currentModule = module.ne_pnextexe  // go to next module
    }

    // Next, walk through the task list, and get the largest swap
    // size from the associated module tables. Since this
    // function is called during the creation/destruction of
    // modules (AddModule() / DelModule()), it is important that
    // we only consider modules that are "healthy."
    currentTask = HeadTDB   // Point at first task in list
```

```
while ( not at end of task list ( currentTask != 0 ) )
{
    currentModule = currentTask.TDB_pModule

    if ( LSL on currentModule is O.K. )   // selector limit
    {
        if ( 'NE' signature found in currentModule )
        {
            if ( currentModule.ne_swaparea > largestSwapSize )
                largestSwapSize = currentModule.ne_swaparea
        }
    }

    currentTask = currentTask.TDB_next  // go on to next task
}

// Set the size of the discardable code area (the code fence)
GReserve( largestSwapSize )    // Actually in AX register
```

GReserve()

GReserve() is an internal routine that is passed the minimum size (in paragraphs) that the swap area should be. In KRNL386, GReserve() immediately converts the paragraphs to bytes, whereas in KRNL286, GReserve() deals with the swap area in terms of paragraphs. As part of the process of converting the paragraphs to bytes, GReserve() also doubles the size, allowing for two of the largest DISCARDABLE segments in memory to be present at the same time. This value however, cannot be greater than 128K and is rounded down if 128K is exceeded.

The current swap area size may already be greater than the size passed into GReserve(). In this case, GReserve() just returns the size of the current swap area size. If the swap area needs to be increased, the hard work begins. The best thing that can happen to GReserve() is that the code fence can just be moved downwards in memory to create a bigger swap area. The Will_Gi_Reserve_Fit() function takes care of this. Will_Gi_Reserve_Fit() simply scans backwards from the end of the global heap until it finds a block that is neither free nor DISCARDABLE code. If this block is above the new proposed code fence, Will_Gi_Reserve_Fit() fails. If the block is below the new code fence, it's clear sailing to move the code fence downward.

If the code fence cannot just be moved down, GReserve() tries the opposite tactic. It calls GrowHeap() to expand the top end of the heap upward. If growing the heap doesn't help out, GReserve() compacts the heap, using GCompact(). If none of these methods create a big enough area for the swap space, GReserve() returns zero, indicating failure.

```
pseudocode for GReserve() - 3GMOREME.OBJ
// Parameters:
//      WORD    newDiscardParas
// Locals:
```

```
//      DWORD   newDiscardSize  // new minimum size of swap area
//      DWORD   lastArena       // Last arena in global heap
//      DWORD   newFence        // address of new code fence

    GEnter()    // Prevent LRU sweeping. Point at GlobalInfo

    newDiscardSize = newDiscardParas * 32  // 2 * number of Paras

    if ( newDiscardSize > 0x20000 )     // Limit the maximum size
        newDiscardSize = 0x20000        // to 128K

    round up newDiscardSize to a 32 byte boundary

    // See if the existing code fence is already sufficient
    lastArena = GlobalInfo.hi_last
    newFence = lastArena->pga_address - newDiscardSize

    if ( newDiscardSize > GlobalInfo.gi_reserve )
        goto setup_return_vars      // Yes! Almost done

    // Call a routine to scan backwards from the end of the heap,
    // checking to make sure that all blocks above the proposed
    // new code fence are either FREE, or contain discardable code
    if ( Will_Gi_Reserve_Fit( newFence ) )
        goto setup_return_vars  // It fits!  Almost done

    if ( GrowHeap( newDiscardSize ) )    // Can the heap expand up?
    {
        lastArena = GlobalInfo.hi_last
        newFence = lastArena->pga_address - newDiscardSize

        if ( Will_Gi_Reserve_Fit( newFence ) )
            goto setup_return_vars  // It fits!  Almost done
    }

    if ( GCompact( newDiscardSize ) )    // Try compacting
    {
        GUncompact( newDiscardSize )    // ???

        if ( Will_Gi_Reserve_Fit( newFence ) )
            goto setup_return_vars  // It fits!  Almost done
    }

    if debug KERNEL
        output a message: "greserve doesn't fit"
```

```
    return 0        // Indicate failure to caller

setup_return_vars:

    GlobalInfo.gi_disfence_lo = LOWORD( newFence )
    GlobalInfo.gi_disfence_hi = HIWORD( newFence )
    GlobalInfo.gi_reserve = newDiscardSize

    GLeave()    // Reenable LRU sweeping
```

The Local Heap

Besides global heap management, KERNEL also provides facilities for creating and maintaining local heaps. Local heaps in Windows are somewhat similar to the malloc() heap maintained by the C runtime library. In both cases, large blocks of memory are allocated from the operating system and parceled out in smaller blocks, as needed. The reason for having two methods is that there's a high overhead associated with allocating blocks from the operating system. On the other hand, the price you pay for using the "less expensive" local heap is increased complexity. Should you allocate from the global heap or the local heap? That is the question facing each programmer.

As explained in Chapter 3 on modules, every program contains a DGROUP segment. Besides containing the global data and stack, the DGROUP also contains a local heap. DLLs can optionally have their own local heap, as well. The HEAPSIZE line in the .DEF file can specify the minimum size of the default local heap, subject to the 64K limitation on DGROUP size. A local heap can expand and contract if necessary.

All allocations from the local heap are returned as two-byte (near) offsets. The segment portion of the address is implicitly assumed to be the selector for the segment containing the heap. In the general case, application programs set up their DS to point to the DGROUP so that memory allocated from the local heap can be referenced by just the two-byte offset. However, as will be explained more completely later on, an application can create multiple local heaps. In this case, it's necessary to use far pointers when referencing the memory and passing around pointers.

The local heap is similar to the global heap in many ways. Thus, much of what was discussed in the section on global heaps applies to locals heaps as well. Like the global heap, the local heap has the notions of FIXED, MOVEABLE, and DISCARDABLE memory. The arrangement of memory allocations (FIXED memory from the bottom) also holds true for the local heap. There is even an undocumented LocalNotify() function for DISCARDABLE memory, similar to the GlobalNotify() function for the global heap.

What is slightly different about the local heap is its notion of a MOVEABLE handle. The local heap deals with memory blocks in terms of handles to memory. Like the global heap functions, allocating FIXED memory from the local heap gives you direct address that can be used without any translation. However, when it comes to MOVEABLE memory, the story is different. Unlike the global heap, the local heap includes no mathematical relationship between a MOVEABLE handle and the actual address used to reference the memory. The handle for a MOVEABLE block in the local heap is just an offset to a data structure somewhere inside the local heap. The actual address of the block is contained within this data structure, along with the block's lock count and flags. Knowing the format of these data structures, it is possible to get the address of the memory from its handle. In fact, LMEM_MOVEABLE handles in Windows are exactly like handles on the Macintosh—pointers to pointers, which the program can doubly dereference to get to the data. Several parts of Windows rely on this trick. However, it's easier, though slower, to just call LocalLock() and let it handle the details of locking the block.

Unlike the global heap, if you allocate MOVEABLE memory from the local heap, lock it and keep it locked until finished with it. Since there's no layer of indirection provided by the descriptor table, if the block moves around in memory, there's no way for KERNEL to make this transparent to you. Also, unlike the global heap, your program can easily allocate FIXED memory. The downside is that you can accidentally fragment your own local heap. You have to decide whether to allocate FIXED memory and deal with potential fragmentation or whether to allocate MOVEABLE memory and take care of locking and unlocking as needed.

The LocalInfo Structure

Every segment with a local heap contains an instance of a HeapInfo structure, the same structure the global heap uses and that WINKERN.INC defines. Since the fields are listed above in the global heap discussion, this section does not repeat them. The method of finding the HeapInfo structure for a local heap is fairly straightforward. In a segment containing a local heap, offset 6 contains a WORD value. This WORD is the offset of the HeapInfo structure in the segment.

Immediately after the HeapInfo structure come additional fields of information about the heap. The combination of the HeapInfo structure and these additional fields is called the LocalInfo structure (defined in WINKERN.INC). In the pseudocode that follows, the global variable LocalInfo refers to this structure.

A LocalInfo structure has the format shown in Table 2-5 (see Table 2-2 for the first 1Eh bytes).

Table 2-5: LocalInfo Structure.

Offset	Type	Description
00h	HeapInfo Structure	(1Eh bytes in length). See the description in the Global Heap section for field descriptions.
1Eh	DWORD	li_notify. A far function pointer to a routine that called either when a heap block is about to be moved or discarded or when the heap is out of memory. This value is initialized to point at the LocalNotifyDefault() procedure.

Table 2-5: LocalInfo Structure. (continued)

22h	WORD	li_lock. The lock count of the local heap. A nonzero value prevents blocks from moving or being discarded.
24h	WORD	li_extra. When the local heap is expanded, this is the minimum amount it should be grown by. The default is 200h.
26h	WORD	li_minsize. The minimum size of the local heap, as specified by the HEAPSIZE line in the .DEF file.
28h	WORD	li_sig. The signature word. Set to 484Ch, which, when viewed in a hex dump, show up as 'LH' for Local Heap. Various routines in Windows use this signature word to verify the integrity of the local heap.

The Local Heap Arenas

The arena for a local heap block immediately precedes the block in memory. The local heap code thinks of each block as being in one of three categories: FIXED, MOVEABLE, or free. There are three kinds of arenas, but two of them are just extensions to the first kind.

The simplest arena in the local heap is for a FIXED block shown in Table 2-6.

Table 2-6: FIXED Block Arena.

00h	WORD	la_prev. A near pointer to the preceding arena, also flags (see below).
02h	WORD	la_next. A near pointer to the next arena.

The handle for a FIXED block is the address of the block itself. Therefore, there's no need for a handle field in the arena. You can find the arena of a FIXED block by subtracting 4 from its address.

The next arena type is for a MOVEABLE block. It's just a slight extension of the FIXED block arena, shown in Table 2-7.

Table 2-7: MOVEABLE Block Arena.

00h	WORD	la_prev. A near pointer to the preceding arena, also flags (see below).
02h	WORD	la_next. A near pointer to the next arena.
04h	WORD	la_handle. The offset of the handle table entry for this memory block. The format of a handle table entry is discussed shortly.

The la_handle field provides for two-way mapping between a MOVEABLE block and its handle table entry. Given the address of the block, you can find the address of the arena by subtracting 6. The la_handle field in the arena gives the offset of the handle table entry. Given a handle table entry, you can obtain the address of the memory block, which is the first field of the handle entry.

Finally, for a free block of memory in the local heap, the arena looks like Table 2-8.

Table 2-8: Free Memory Block Arena.

00h	WORD	la_prev. A near pointer to the preceding arena, also flags (see below).
02h	WORD	la_next. A near pointer to the next arena.
04h	WORD	la_size. Size of the block, including the arena.
06h	WORD	la_free_prev. Offset of the previous free arena.
08h	WORD	la_free_next. Offset of the next free arena.

In all three kinds of arenas, notice the complete lack of flags that would indicate what kind of arena it is. Hmm. As it turns out, every arena starts on a four-byte boundary. That means that the bottom two bits of every arena address are always zero. It really would be a pity to waste those two bits. Therefore, the designers of the local heap decided to use the bottom two bits of the la_prev field as flags for that arena. This means that you cannot just use the la_prev field as is. You must first mask off the bottom two bits to get the real previous arena address.

So what do the bottom two bits indicate? The bottommost bit is set if the block is in use and not set if the block is free. The second bit is set if the block is MOVEABLE and not set if it's FIXED. Thus there are four possible combinations, but only three of them are used (you can't have a MOVEABLE block that's free). By examining these bits, KERNEL knows which of the above arena forms to use.

The First Local Heap Block

The first block in the local heap is somewhat special. It actually precedes the LocalInfo structure in memory. Although the bottommost bit of its la_prev field is set, indicating that it's a FIXED, in-use arena, the local heap routines treat the arena as if it were a free arena. Thus, the start of the free list is contained in the la_free_next field of the first local heap block.

The Local Handle Entry

As mentioned earlier, for MOVEABLE blocks, the block's handle gives the offset of the block's associated data structure. These handle data structures are allocated and stored in blocks that are themselves local heap blocks. Free handle table entries are threaded together so that when a new handle table entry is needed, it can be found quickly. The first handle table is found by using the hi_htable field in the HeapInfo structure (see Table 2-2 earlier in the chapter). Each handle table starts out with a WORD indicating how many handle table entries are to follow. The last WORD, after all the entries, is the offset of the next handle table.

The format of an in-use handle table entry is shown in Table 2-9.

Table 2-9: Format of Handle Table Entries.

In-use handle table entry:

00h	WORD	lhe_address. The address of the memory block that the handle references. This field is allows the doubly dereferenced pointer trick mentioned earlier for LMEM_MOVABLE blocks.

Table 2-9: Format of Handle Table Entries. (continued)

In-use handle table entry:

Offset	Type	Description		
02h	BYTE	lhe_flags. The flags for the memory block:		
		0Fh	LHE_DISCARDABLE	Discard level of the object. The meaning of this flag is unclear. Perhaps at one time the discardability of the block was given by this value.
		1Fh	LHE_USERFLAGS	Presumably these values are available for use by the programmers for whatever they want. The SDK document ation however does not mention them.
		40h	LHE_DISCARDED	The block has been discarded.
03h	BYTE	lhe_count. The lock count of the block. Nonzero values prevent the block from being moved or discarded if the block is DISCARDABLE.		

Free handle table entry:

Offset	Type	Description
00h	WORD	lhe_link. The offset of the next free handle table entry.
02h	WORD	lhe_free. If this value is FFFFh, then this entry is free. Otherwise, it's in-use and described by the above structure.

The LHEAP Example

The following program demonstrates some of the local handle and arena concepts discussed above. It also demonstrates how to find the LocalInfo structure. Bear in mind that much of this information can be obtained through the documented ToolHelp APIs. This program walks the heap directly in this case only to demonstrate the concepts involved.

LHEAP starts out by finding the offset of the LocalInfo structure and creating a far pointer to it. LHEAP then allocates a MOVEABLE block to guarantee seeing all three kinds of arenas. The main body of the program is centered around the ShowHeap() function. ShowHeap() first calls DumpHeapHeader() to display information in the LocalInfo structure. Then DumpNode() is called repeatedly to display information about each node in the heap. DumpNode() returns a pointer to the next item in the heap, with NULL indicating that the last block has been reached. The program is written in Borland C++ 3.1 small model and uses the WINIO libraries from *Undocumented Windows.* If you don't have these libraries, it's extremely easy to add a few lines of code that use fopen() to open an output file. Instead of using printf(), use fprintf(). No special .DEF files or .RC files are required to build LHEAP.

```
//==================================
//  LHEAP, by Matt Pietrek, 1992
//  File: LHEAP.C
//==================================
#include <windows.h>
#include "winio.h"
#include "dos.h"

typedef struct
{
    WORD    hi_check;       // 00   // This portion has the same
    WORD    hi_freeze;      // 02   // layout as the GlobalHeap
    WORD    hi_count;       // 04   // info structure in the
    DWORD   hi_first;       // 06   // "Burgermaster" segment
    DWORD   hi_last;        // 0A
    BYTE    hi_ncompact;    // 0E
    BYTE    hi_dislevel;    // 0F
    DWORD   hi_distotal;    // 10
    WORD    hi_htable;      // 14
    WORD    hi_hfree;       // 16
    WORD    hi_hdelta;      // 18
    WORD    hi_hexpand;     // 1A
    WORD    hi_pstats;      // 1C
    DWORD   li_notify;      // 1E   // This portion is specific
    WORD    li_lock;        // 22   // to the local heap, and is
    WORD    li_extra;       // 24   // not in the GlobalHeap info
    WORD    li_minsize;     // 26   // structure
    WORD    li_sig;         // 28
} LHEAPINFO32;

typedef struct      // Arena header for an LMEM_FIXED block
{
    WORD    la_prev;    // Bottom 2 bits are arena flags
    WORD    la_next;
} LOCAL_ARENA_FIXED;

typedef struct      // Arena header for an LMEM_FIXED block
{
    WORD    la_prev;    // Bottom 2 bits are arena flags
    WORD    la_next;
    WORD    la_handle;
} LOCAL_ARENA_MOVEABLE;

typedef struct      // Arena header for an unallocated block
```

```
{
    WORD    la_prev;    // Bottom 2 bits are arena flags
    WORD    la_next;
    WORD    la_size;
    WORD    la_free_prev;
    WORD    la_free_next;
} LOCAL_ARENA_FREE;

typedef struct  // A local handle is an offset to one of these
{
    WORD    lhe_address;
    BYTE    lhe_flags;
    BYTE    lhe_count;
} LOCALHANDLEENTRY;

#define LA_BUSY             1   // Bit 0 on indicates in use
#define LA_MOVEABLE         2   // Bit 1 on indicates MOVEABLE

#define LA_FREE             0
#define LA_BUSY_FIXED       LA_BUSY
#define LA_BUSY_MOVEABLE    ( LA_BUSY | LA_MOVEABLE )
#define LA_FLAGS_MASK       0x0003

WORD    HeapSegment;    // Contains the value of our DS segment

/*==================================================================*/
// Display the information for one node in the local heap
/*==================================================================*/
void far *DumpNode(void far *node)
{
    LOCAL_ARENA_FIXED far *fixedArena;
    LOCAL_ARENA_MOVEABLE far *moveableArena;
    LOCAL_ARENA_FREE far *freeArena;
    LOCALHANDLEENTRY far *locHand;
    WORD arenaType;

    // we assign 'fixedArena' to 'node' so that we can extract
    // the fields that are common to all three kinds of blocks
    fixedArena = (LOCAL_ARENA_FIXED far *)node;

    // Mask off the address portion, leaving just the arena flags
    arenaType = fixedArena->la_prev & LA_FLAGS_MASK;

    printf("%04X  ", FP_OFF(node));

    // If this block's 'next' pointer is point to itself, then
    // it's the last block. Indicate this, and return NULL,
```

```
    // which stops the walk of the nodes
    if ( (WORD)fixedArena->la_next == (WORD)fixedArena )
    {
        printf("END SENTINEL");
        return NULL;
    }

    // Display relevant information, based upon the block type
    switch ( arenaType )
    {
        case LA_FREE:
            // For free blocks, we include the size of the
            // arena in its total size.
            freeArena = (LOCAL_ARENA_FREE far *)node;
            printf(
            "FREE      Size: %04X  Next free: %04X\n",
                freeArena->la_size, freeArena->la_free_next);
            break;

        case LA_BUSY_FIXED:
            printf("FIXED     Size: %04X\n",
                (WORD)fixedArena->la_next - (WORD)node
                - sizeof(LOCAL_ARENA_FIXED) );
            break;

        case LA_BUSY_MOVEABLE:
            moveableArena = (LOCAL_ARENA_MOVEABLE far *)node;
            printf("MOVEABLE  Size: %04X  Handle: %04X  ",
                (WORD)moveableArena->la_next - (WORD)node
                - sizeof(LOCAL_ARENA_MOVEABLE),
                moveableArena->la_handle);

            // Moveable block arenas contain a back link to
            // their handles. Use this to display the lock
            // count for this block.
            locHand=MK_FP(HeapSegment, moveableArena->la_handle);
            printf("Locks: %04X\n", locHand->lhe_count);
            break;

        default:
            // There should never be a moveable block that isn't
            // busy (free). Complain if we find one.
            printf("Invalid arena entry");
    }

    // Return the address of the next node to display
    return MK_FP( HeapSegment, fixedArena->la_next );
}
```

```
/*=================================================================*/
// Verify and display information in the local heap header
/*=================================================================*/
int DumpHeapHeader(LHEAPINFO32 far *lheapinfo)
{
    // Look for the 'LH' signature in the HeapInfo structure
    if ( lheapinfo->li_sig != 0x484C )
    {
        printf("Incorrect local heap signature\n");
        return 0;
    }

    #define FW 20   // Width of description strings

    printf("Local heap Information\n\n");
    printf("%-*s: %Fp\n" ,FW,"Starting Address",lheapinfo);
    printf("%-*s: %04X\n",FW,"Items in heap",lheapinfo->hi_count);
    printf("%-*s: %04X\n",FW,"Handle Delta",lheapinfo->hi_hdelta);
    printf("%-*s: %04X\n",FW,"Minimum size",lheapinfo->li_minsize);

    return 1;
}

/*=================================================================*/
// Displays the HeapInfo information, and then walks the nodes
/*=================================================================*/
void ShowHeap(LHEAPINFO32 far *lheapinfo)

{
    void far * node;

    if ( DumpHeapHeader(lheapinfo) == 0 ) // If the header looked
        return;                            // bad, don't continue

    printf("\nNODE  TYPE\n\n");

    // Get a pointer to the first node in the heap, and then
    // walk through each node until the end is reached
    node = MK_FP( HeapSegment, (WORD)lheapinfo->hi_first);
    while ( node )
        node = DumpNode(node);
}
```

```
/*==============================================================*/
// Helper routine to get WINIO stuff out of main program flow
/*==============================================================*/
void WinioHelper(int mode)
{
    if ( mode == 0 )    // Disable drawing (stop flicker)
    {
        winio_setbusy();
        winio_setpaint(winio_current(), FALSE);
    }
    else    // Turn output back on (all done with output)
    {
        winio_setpaint(winio_current(), TRUE);
        winio_resetbusy();
        winio_home(winio_current());
    }
}

int main()
{
    LHEAPINFO32 far *lheapinfo; // Pointer to HeapInfo struct
    HANDLE localMoveableHandle; // A handle for a moveable block
    WORD heapStart;             // offset of HeapInfo struct

    // Set up some variables related to finding the local heap
    // In this program, we're working with our own local heap
    // This variables here could be altered to refer to a
    // different heap, without affecting the rest of the code
    asm MOV HeapSegment, DS
    heapStart = *(WORD far *)MK_FP(HeapSegment, 6);
    lheapinfo = MK_FP(HeapSegment, heapStart);

    // Allocate an LMEM_MOVEABLE block for our demonstration.
    // The heap doesn't normally contain MOVEABLE blocks unless
    // the program specifically allocates them. While we're
    // at it, we'll lock the moveable block twice so that we
    // can see the effect when we display the heap blocks.
    localMoveableHandle = LocalAlloc(LMEM_MOVEABLE, 128);
    LocalLock(localMoveableHandle);
    LocalLock(localMoveableHandle);

    WinioHelper(0);         // Turn off screen repainting

    ShowHeap(lheapinfo);    // Go to it!!!

    WinioHelper(1);         // Turn screen repainting back on
```

```
    LocalUnlock(localMoveableHandle);    // Unlock the moveable
    LocalUnlock(localMoveableHandle);    // block we allocated,
    LocalFree(localMoveableHandle);      // and free it.

    return 0;
}
```

Sample output from LHEAP is as follows:

```
Local heap Information

Starting Address     : 1A9F:2BB0
Items in heap        : 000C
Handle Delta         : 0020
Minimum size         : 1FFE

NODE  TYPE

2BA0  FIXED     Size: 0008
2BAC  FIXED     Size: 004C
2BFC  FIXED     Size: 0200
2E00  FREE      Size: 0058  Next free: 2F2C
2E58  FIXED     Size: 00B4
2F10  FIXED     Size: 0018
2F2C  FREE      Size: 000C  Next free: 2FE8
2F38  FIXED     Size: 0024
2F60  FIXED     Size: 0084
2FE8  FREE      Size: 1B24  Next free: 4B94
4B0C  MOVEABLE  Size: 0082  Handle: 2F66  Locks: 0002
4B94  END SENTINEL
```

LocalAlloc()

LocalAlloc() begins by checking to see if the request is for a zero length DISCARDABLE block. If so, it allocates a handle table entry and fills in the appropriate fields before returning. Once past this special case, LocalAlloc() either allocates a MOVEABLE block or a FIXED block. For a FIXED block, all LocalAlloc() needs to do is call the internal LAlloc() routine to find a free block. If the block is supposed to be MOVEABLE, however, LocalAlloc() calls HAlloc() (not covered here) to allocate a handle table entry for the block. If a new handle table entry is successfully allocated, LocalAlloc() uses LAlloc() to obtain a memory block that the new handle will refer to.

```
pseudocode for LocalAlloc() - LINTERF.OBJ
// Parameters:
//      WORD    allocFlags
```

```
//      WORD    allocLen
// Locals:
//      WORD    handle
//      WORD    newAddress (in AX)

    if debug KERNEL
        CheckLocalHeap()
                                    // Uses DS:[6] (see Figure 2-3)
    if ( LEnter() != 0 )            // Makes DS:DI point at the
    {                               // LocalInfo structure.
        AX = 0                      // Increment li_lock field
        goto LocalAlloc_return
    }

    if ( allocFlags & LA_NOCOMPACT )    // Prevents heap from
        LocalInfo.hi_freeze++           // being compacted

    if ( allocLen == 0 )    // Allocating 0 length, DISCARDABLE
    {
        // 0 length blocks are only useful for MOVEABLE and
        // DISCARDABLE memory. A zero length FIXED block is
        // meaningless. Abort now if this is the case.
        if ( LA_MOVEABLE bit not set in allocFlags )
            goto LocalAlloc_cleanup

        if ( (handle = Halloc()) == 0 ) // Allocate a new handle
            goto LocalAlloc_cleanup     // Abort if we couldn't

        handle->lhe_address = LA_MOVEABLE   // high 14 bits are 0
        handle->lhe_flags = LHE_DISCARDED

        goto LocalAlloc_cleaup
    }

    if ( allocFlags & LA_MOVEABLE ) // Allocating MOVEABLE memory.
    {
        // LMEM_MOVEABLE memory needs a handle allocated for it
        if ( (handle = Halloc()) == 0 ) // Allocate a new handle
            goto LocalAlloc_cleanup     // Abort if we couldn't

        newAddress = LAlloc(allocLen, allocFlags) // Find a block

        if ( newAddress == 0 )  // Couldn't find a free block
        {
            LHFree()    // Free the allocated handle
            goto LocalAlloc_cleanup
        }
```

```
        handle->lhe_address = newAddress
        store handle in the arena for newAddress
        turn on LA_MOVEABLE bit in the la_prev field of the arena

        if ( allocFlags == LHE_DISCARDABLE )
            turn on LHE_DISCARDABLE in handle->lhe_flags
    }
    else        // Allocating FIXED memory. Don't need handle
    {
        newAddress = LAlloc(allocLen, allocFlags)
    }

LocalAlloc_cleanup:

    if ( allocFlags & LA_NOCOMPACT )    // Unfreeze heap (OK
        LocalInfo.hi_freeze--           // to compact)

    LLeave()            // Decrement LocalInfo.li_lock

LocalAlloc_return:

    if ( newAddress == 0 )
        LogError("LocalAlloc failed")

    // Some functions rely on CX also containing the return value,
    // because JCXZ is faster than OR AX,AX/JZ. Set CX accordingly

    CX = newAddress     // newAddress is really AX
```

LAlloc()

LAlloc() is the internal routine that knows how to walk the local heap and find a block that satisfies an allocation request. It really is two routines in one. At first, LAlloc(), conditionally branches to code that either finds a FIXED block from the low end of the heap or a MOVEABLE block from the high end of the heap.

If walking the heap does not find a block that's suitably sized, LAlloc() calls the LCompact() routine. LCompact() first tries to move unlocked MOVEABLE blocks around to coalesce enough space. If moving blocks doesn't help the situation, LCompact() discards DISCARDABLE blocks until there's enough room. If after all this, there still isn't sufficient memory, LAlloc() invokes LNotify() to call the LocalNotify() callback function.

Once LAlloc() finds a suitable block, its examines it to see if it's large enough to bother making two blocks out of, one for the allocation request, the other, a new free block. The new free block must be at least 16 bytes long to be worth allocating. If it's not, the extra space becomes wasted space at the end of the newly found block.

```
pseudocode for LAlloc() - LALLOC.OBJ
// Parameters:
//      WORD    allocLen    (in BX)
//      WORD    allocFlags  (in AX)
// Locals:
//      NEAR *  currentArena
//      NEAR *  nextArena, *prevArena

    if ( LA_MOVEABLE bit set in allocFlags )
        goto LAlloc_find_moveable

    allocLen += 4   // 4 == size of FIXED arena header

    allocLen = LAlign() // Round size up to a multiple of 4 bytes

    currentArena = LocalInfo.hi_first   // Start with first
                                        // block in the heap
    while ( 1 )
    {
        // Work forward from the start of the heap, because
        // fixed blocks belong at the beginning of the heap
        nextArena == currentArena->la_free_next

        // The la_free_next pointer of the last arena points
        // to itself. It's time to compact if we hit it
        if ( nextArena == currentArena )
            goto LAlloc_compact_fixed

        if ( currentArena->la_size > allocLen )  //Found a big
            break                                //enough block

        currentArena = nextArena
    }

LAlloc_found_block_fixed:

    if debug KERNEL
        if ( LCheckCC() )   // Verify debug signature still there
        {
            Output a message:
                "LocalAlloc: Local free memory overwritten"
        }

    // We're going to have to slice the found block in two. The
    // first part will become the allocated memory. The second
    // part will me made a new, free block. Make sure that the
```

```
    // new free block will be at least 16 bytes long, or else
    // it's not worth creating the new block.
    if ( (currentArena + allocLen) >
         (currentArena->la_next - 16) )
    {
        // All we have to do is mark the found block as busy
        goto LAlloc_mark_block_busy
    }
    else
    {
        // We have to add the "new" free block to the free list
        // before we can mark the found block as busy
        goto LAlloc_have_two_blocks
    }

LAlloc_compact_fixed:

    if ( LCompact() > allocLen )  // LCompact() returns number of
        goto LAlloc_found_block   // bytes free after compaction

LAlloc_notify:

    // If the program installed a LocalNotify() handler, call it
    LNotify( LN_OUTOFMEM, allocLen )

    if ( LocalNotify() handler returned 0 )
        return 0                        // failure
    else
        goto the top of LAlloc()      // Play it again, Sam

LAlloc_find_moveable:

    allocLen += 6   // 6 == size of MOVEABLE arena header

    allocLen = LAlign() // Round size up to a multiple of 4 bytes

    currentArena = LocalInfo.hi_last    // Start with last
                                        // block in the heap
    while ( 1 )
    {
        // Work backwards from the end of the heap, because
        // moveable blocks belong at the end of the heap
        prevArena == currentArena->la_free_prev

        // The la_free_prev pointer of the first arena points
        // to itself. It's time to compact if we hit it
```

```
        if ( prevArena == currentArena )
            goto LAlloc_compact_moveable

        currentArena = prevArena

        if ( currentArena->la_size > allocLen )
            goto LAlloc_found_block_moveable
    }

LAlloc_compact_moveable:

    if ( LCompact() < allocLen )  // LCompact() returns number of
        goto LAlloc_notify        // bytes free after compaction

    // See if we need to make 2 blocks, or just 1. (See above)
    if ( (currentArena + allocLen) >
         (currentArena->la_next - 16) )
    {
        // All we have to do is mark the found block as busy
        goto LAlloc_mark_block_busy
    }

LAlloc_found_block_moveable:

    if debug KERNEL
        if ( LCheckCC() )   // Verify debug signature still there
        {
            Output a message:
                "LocalAlloc: Local free memory overwritten"
        }

LAlloc_have_two_blocks:

    // First add the unused portion of the new block to the free list
    LFreeAdd( currentArena + allocLen )
    // Then fall through
LAlloc_mark_block_busy:

    LFreeDelete( currentArena ) // Remove block from free list

    turn on LA_BUSY flag in currentArena->la_prev

    if debug KERNEL
    {
        if ( LA_ZEROINIT not set in allocFlags )
            LAllocFill()    // Fill block with debug signature
    }

    if ( LA_ZEROINIT set in allocFlags )
        LZero()     // Fill the block with 0's
```

LocalFree()

LocalFree() starts out by calling the internal LDref() function to load the registers with various values related to the passed-in handle. In this respect, LDref() is similar to the XHandle() and PDref() routines for the global heap. Next LocalFree() uses LFree() to mark the arena for the block as free, as well as to add it back to the free list of heap blocks. Finally, LocalFree() calls LHFree() to free up the handle table entry for the block. LHFree() is smart enough to detect if the block is FIXED, and therefore doesn't have a handle.

```
pseudocode for LocalFree() - LINTERF.OBJ
// Parameters:
// WORD     handle

    if ( !Lenter() )     // Points DS:DI at the LocalInfo struct
        return 0         // increments the li_lock field

    if debug KERNEL
        CheckLocalHeap()

    LDref(handle)    // Puts address of arena, lock count, etc.
                     // in registers

    if debug KERNEL
        if ( TDB_expWinVer >= 0x201  )    // Windows 2.01 or later?
            if ( lock count of handle > 0 )
            {
                output a message:
                    "LocalFree: freeing locked object"

                LDref() // Get addresses again. Why???
            }

    LFree(handle)  // Free up the memory / coalesce blocks
    LHFree(handle) // Free up the associated handle (if any)

    LLeave()    // decrement the li_lock count field
```

LocalRealloc()

LocalRealloc() is a rather large and complex routine. After doing the usual setup by calling LEnter(), it looks to see if just the flags need to be modified. If so, LocalRealloc() jumps to a section of code that patches the new flags into the handle table entry and returns. If the new requested size of the block is less than ten bytes, the size of the request is bumped up to ten bytes. If the original requested new size was zero, however, LocalRealloc() figures that the block is being discarded. In this situation, it jumps to code that frees up the blocks of memory; then it sets the LHE_DISCARDED flag in the associated handle table entry. If on the other hand, the handle passed in is for a block that's already been discarded, LocalRealloc() allocates new memory for it and turns on the LHE_DISCARDED bit in the handle table entry.

If LocalRealloc() is called for the more mundane task of simply changing the size of a block, then it does what it can to keep the heap coherent. If the block needs to be grown, the next block in the heap is tested to see if it's free and big enough. If so, LocalRealloc() combines the current block with the free block to form the new block. If this isn't possible, MOVEABLE blocks are shuffled around in an attempt to find a way to satisfy the request. If the block is being shrunk, LocalRealloc() tests to see if it's worth the effort of splitting the block in two, with the now unneeded memory becoming a new free block.

```
pseudocode for LocalRealloc() - LINTERF.OBJ
// Parameters:
//      WORD    reallocHandle
//      WORD    newSize
//      WORD    flags

    if debug KERNEL
        CheckLocalHeap()

    if ( !Lenter() )        // Points DS:DI at the LocalInfo struct
        return 0            // increments the li_lock field

    if ( LA_NOCOMPACT flags set in flags )
        LocalInfo.hi_freeze++   // prevent compaction

    if ( !LDref() )             // Puts address of arena, lock
        goto create_new_block   // count, etc. in registers.

    if ( LA_MODIFY bit set in flags )
        goto modify_flags

    if ( newSize < 10 )     // 10 = size of free arena header???
        newSize = 10

    if ( newSize wasn't 0 upon entry to LocalRealloc() )
        goto move_things_about

    // Only blocks being "reallocated" to zero bytes come
    // through here. If this is the case, then the block
    // should be discarded.
    if ( lock count of reallocHandle == 0 )
        goto discard_block

LocalRealloc_fail:

    LogError("LocalReAlloc failed"s);

    return
```

```
discard_block:  // Here if discarding a block

    if ( LA_MOVEABLE not set in flags ) // DISCARDABLE blocks must
        goto LocalRealloc_fail          // also be MOVEABLE

    if ( LNotify( LN_DISCARD, reallocHandle, 0 ) returns 0 )
        goto LocalRealloc_fail

    LFree( reallocHandle )      // Free up the block's memory

    reallocHandle->lhe_address = 0

    turn on LHE_DISCARDED bit in reallocHandle->flags

    return reallocHandle      // Actually, goto LocalRealloc_done

modify_flags:

    if ( block is fixed )      // Can't modify FIXED blocks
        return reallocHandle

    copy flags to reallocHandle->lhe_flags

    return reallocHandle

create_new_block:

    if ( LHE_DISCARDED bit not set in reallocHandle->lhe_flags )
        return reallocHandle

    turn on LA_MOVEABLE bit in flags

    if ( !LAlloc(newSize, flags) )
        goto LocalRealloc_fail
    else
        turn off LHE_DISCARDED flag in reallocHandle->lhe_flags

    goto LocalRealloc_fixup_new_arena

move_things_about:

    if ( newSize > size of current block )
        goto grow_block

shrink_block:
```

```
    If the block will be shrunk enough to create a new, free block
    then split the current block in 2. The new, free block must
    be at least 16 bytes long. If the block is split in 2, add
    the new, free block to the free list. If there's not enough
    room to split the block into 2 blocks, then don't bother
    splitting the block. Just return the original handle.

    return reallocHandle

grow_block:

    If the next block is free and big enough, join the current
    block to the free block. Otherwise, start shuffling blocks
    around in memory. When blocks get moved, call
    LNotify( LN_MOVE ).

LocalRealloc_fixup_new_arena:

    reallocHandle->lhe_address = new block address

    Turn on LA_MOVEABLE bit in la_prev field of new blocks arena

    Set the la_handle field of new blocks arena to reallocHandle

LocalRealloc_done:

    // All prior "return" statements actually come through here!!
    if ( LA_NOCOMPACT bit set in flags )
        LocalInfo.hi_freeze--

    LLeave()    // decrement the li_lock count field

    return CX = AX  // Caller can test either CX or AX
```

LocalLock()

LocalLock() relies on the way handle tables are laid out to quickly determine if the value passed in is for a MOVEABLE handle or for the address of a FIXED block. FIXED blocks always have memory addresses that are a multiple of four. MOVEABLE blocks always have handles with their second bit set (0002h). For instance, 2, 6, 0xA, 0xE.

If the passed in value is for a FIXED block, LocalLock() simply returns the handle, which is the same as the block's address. If the block is MOVEABLE, LocalLock() adds one to the value in the handle's lhe_count field, making sure the count doesn't overflow. The address it returns is the first field of the handle table entry.

```
pseudocode for LocalLock() - LINTERF.OBJ
// Parameters:
// WORD     handle

    // MOVEABLE block handles are always values like 2, 6, 10,
    // 14, etc. Thus, bit 1 is always set. If the handle passed
    // to us does not have this bit set, then it's an LMEM_FIXED
    // block, in which case we just return its address.

    if ( ! (handle & 0x0002) )      // Is it a MOVEABLE block?
        return handle       // Not a handle. Must be an address

    if ( LHE_DISCARDED bit set in handle->lhe_flags )
        return handle->lhe_address

    handle->lhe_count++             // Increment the lock count

    if ( handle->lhe_count == 0 ) // Did it overflow past 0xFF???
        handle->lhe_count--

    return handle->lhe_address     // return address of data block
```

LocalUnlock()

LocalUnlock() simply decrements the lhe_count field in the handle table entry of a MOVEABLE block, making sure the field doesn't underflow. See the discussion of LocalLock() above for more details on how the block type is determined. The return value is either the new lock count for the block or zero if the block is FIXED or discarded.

```
pseudocode for LocalUnlock() - LINTERF.OBJ
// Parameters:
// WORD     handle

    // Handles are always 4x+2 values like 2, 6, 10, 14, etc.
    if ( !(handle & 0x0002) )     //return NULL if a FIXED block
        return 0

    if ( LHE_DISCARDED bit set in handle->lhe_flags )
        return 0

    // If the handle is already unlocked, or the lock count has
    // been maxed out, don't do anything, and return 0
    if ( (handle->lhe_count == 0) || (handle->lhe_count == 0xFF) )
        return 0

    handle->lhe_count--

    return handle->lhe_count
```

LocalHandle()

LocalHandle() starts out by verifying that the address passed in is that of a MOVEABLE block. If not, the address is a FIXED or free block, in which case LocalHandle() returns the passed handle unchanged. Next, it subtracts six from the address to get a pointer to the MOVEABLE arena. The handle value that it returns is extracted from the arena. As an additional sanity check, LocalHandle() compares the passed address to the handle table entry, to make sure it matches.

```
pseudocode for LocalHandle() - LINTERF.OBJ
// Parameters:
//      WORD    memPtr

    // The addresses of MOVEABLE blocks are always values like 2,
    // 6, 10, 14, etc. Thus, bit 1 is always set. If the address
    // passed to us does not have this bit set, then it's an
    // LMEM_FIXED or free block, in which case we just return
    // the address passed to us.
    if ( !(memPtr & 0x0002) )
        return memPtr

    memPtr -= 6      // Make it point at the MOVEABLE arena header

    // Make sure the address stored in the handle structure
    // matches the address passed in.
    if ( lhe_address field in memPtr->la_handle == memPtr )
        return memPtr->la_handle
    else
        return 0         // Something is wrong if this happens!
```

LocalSize()

LocalSize() is extremely simple. It calculates the address of the block from the passed-in handle. It's then a simple matter to subtract that value from the offset of the next arena. The result is the size of the block.

```
pseudocode for LocalSize() - LINTERF.OBJ
// Parameters:
//      WORD    handle
// Locals:
//      WORD    arenaPtr
//      WORD    memPtr

    if ( !LDref() )     // Sets arenaPtr to block's arena, and
        return 0        // memPtr to address of block
```

```
    // Block size is the address of the next block minus the
    // address of this block.
    return ( arenaPtr->la_next - memPtr )    // Also sets CX
```

LocalFlags()

LocalFlags() uses the LDref() function to verify that the handle parameter is for a MOVEABLE block (only MOVEABLE blocks have flags). If the block is MOVEABLE, LocalFlags() extracts the flags and lock count from the handle table entry.

```
pseudocode for LocalFlags() - LINTERF.OBJ
// Parameters:
//       WORD    handle

    if ( !LDref() )       // Dereference the handle
        return 0

    CX = handle->lhe_flags

    XCHG    CL, CH        // Lock count in low byte, flags in high

    return AX = CX        // Set both CX and AX
```

LocalInit()

LocalInit(), although documented, is typically not called by application programs unless they're doing suballocation. Instead, the startup code for an EXE or .DLL calls LocalInit().

LocalInit() starts by determining if it was passed a zero as the segment in which the heap is to be initialized. If this is the case, LocalInit() assumes the current DS value. Otherwise, it sets DS to the segment value that was passed. After some housekeeping, the next major step is to pin down the addresses of the first block in the heap, as well as the address of the LocalInfo structure. The LocalInfo structure always comes after the first block. As was mentioned earlier in the chapter, the first block in the local heap is considered special and is treated differently than the other blocks.

Once LocalInit() knows the address of the LocalInfo structure, LocalInit() zeroes out that memory and initializes certain fields with default values (see the pseudocode). Then it performs some validity testing to make sure that the LocalInfo structure doesn't go past the end of the heap region. Once the LocalInfo structure passes all the tests, it sets the WORD at offset 6 in the segment to the address of the LocalInfo structure. (See the entry for "Instance Data" in *Undocumented Windows,* Chapter 5.)

The next step in initializing the local heap is to set up the arenas for the initial four blocks in the heap. The arenas for the blocks are initialized in their order in the heap. Thus, the first block arena is initialized, followed by the arena for the block containing the LocalInfo structure. Next comes the arena for the one block containing all the free space, and finally, the sentinel arena, which is an arena with no associated memory. It exists only to indicate the end of the heap. See Figure 2-3 on the next page for the initial layout of the local heap.

Figure 2-3: Initial Layout of the Local Heap.

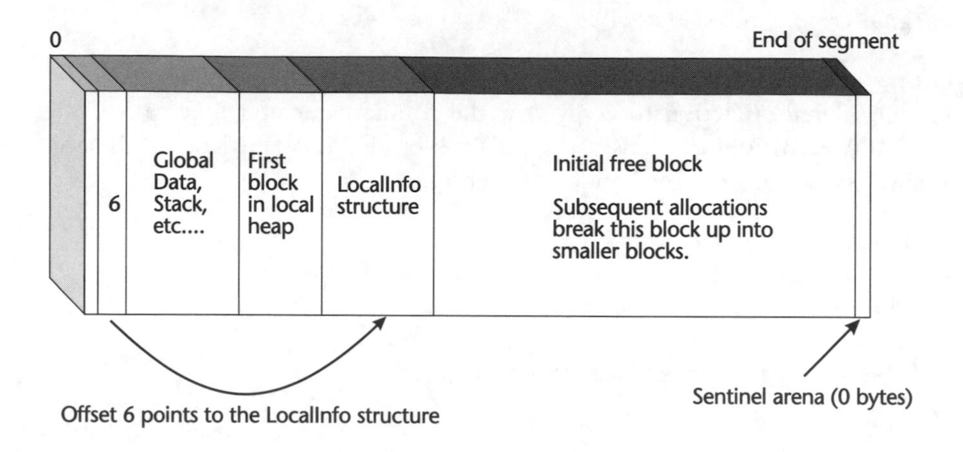


```
pseudocode for LocalInit() - LINTERF.OBJ
// Parameters:
//      WORD    heapSegment
//      WORD    heapStart
//      WORD    heapEnd
// Locals:
//      DWORD   globalBlockLen
//      WORD    LocalInfoArena  // arena for LocalInfo
//      WORD    freeBlockArena
//      WORD    heapEndArena

    Save DS on stack

    if ( heapSegment != 0 )
        DS = heapSegment

    if ( heapStart == 0 )      // use the whole segment?
    {
        globalBlockLen = GlobalSize( DS )

        if ( globalBlockLen >= 64K )
            globalBlockLen = 0xFFFE

        heapEnd = globalBlockLen

        heapStart = heapEnd - globalBlockLen    // always 0???
    }
```

```
heapStart = LAlign(heapStart)  // Round up to nearest 4 bytes

// Reserve 10 bytes for the first arena (size of a FREE
// arena???), and then round up to find the arena address
// for the LocalInfo block that we'll be creating
LocalInfoArena = LAlign(heapStart + 10)

// Make sure the LocalInfo block doesn't go past the
// specified end of the heap
if ( (LocalInfoArena + 4 ) > heapEnd )
    return 0    // Jumps to end to restore DS

Zero out the LocalInfo block

// Fill in various fields of the LocalInfo block
LocalInfo.hi_hdelta = 0x20      // # handles to grow by (More Masters)
LocalInfo.hi_count = 4          // 4 blocks in initial heap
LocalInfo.hi_first = heapStart  // Point at first node
LocalInfo.li_notify = LocalNotifyDefault
LocalInfo.li_hexpand = offset lhexpand
LocalInfo.li_extra = 0x0200     // Minimum amount to grow
LocalInfo.li_sig = 'LH'         // Magic signature (484ch)

freeBlockArena =    // Get address of the free block in heap
    LAlign( LocalInfoArena + sizeof(LocalInfo) )

heapEndArena = heapEnd - 10     // 10 bytes for a free arena

// Make sure the arena for the last block doesn't come before
// the start of the free block. If it does, abort
if ( heapEndArena < freeBlockArena )
    return 0    // Jumps to end to restore DS

LocalInfo.hi_last = heapEndArena

// Set up the pLocalHeap pointer at the base of the segment
*(WORD far *)MK_FP(DS, 6) = &LocalInfo

// Initialize all the fields in the first heap block arena
turn on LA_BUSY flag in heapStart->la_prev
heapStart->la_prev = heapStart      // Points to itself
heapStart->la_next = LocalInfoArena
heapStart->la_free_prev = heapStart // Points to itself
heapStart->la_free_next = freeBlockArena
heapStart->la_size = 10             // size of free arena
```

```
// Initialize fields in the LocalInfo arena
turn on LA_BUSY flag in LocalInfoArena
LocalInfoArena->la_prev = heapStart
LocalInfoArena->la_next = freeBlockArena

// Initialize the free block arena
freeBlockArena->la_prev = LocalInfoArena
freeBlockArena->la_next = heapEndArena
freeBlockArena->la_free_prev = heapStart
freeBlockArena->la_free_next = heapEndArena
freeBlockArena->la_size = heapEndArena - freeBlockArena

if debug KERNEL
    LFillCC()   // Put debug signatures in free block

// Initialize the last block (sentinel) arena
heapEndArena->la_next = heapEndArena        // Point at itself
heapEndArena->la_prev = freeBlockArena
turn on LA_BUSY bit in heapEndArena->la_prev
heapEndArena->la_free_prev = freeBlockArena
heapEndArena->la_free_next = heapEndArena   // Point at itself
heapEndArena->la_size = 10      // size of a free arena

// Set the "minimum allowable heap size" to the size of the
// current heap
LocalInfo.li_minsize =
    LocalInfo.hi_last - LocalInfo.hi_last + 10

GlobalLock( DS )    // Lock the segment ( not really needed )

restore DS from stack

return 1
```

LocalHeapSize()

The undocumented LocalHeapSize() function simply subtracts the address of the first block from the address of the last block and returns the result.

```
pseudocode for LocalHeapSize() - LINTERF.OBJ

    return LocalInfo.hi_last - LocalInfo.hi_last
```

LocalHandleDelta()

LocalHandleDelta() is an undocumented function. It changes the number of handle table entries to be allocated when the local heap needs to allocate more of them for MOVEABLE blocks. LocalHandleDelta() uses the heap in the current DS segment, so you must set DS before calling it. You rarely need to use this function, as the default value of 20h seems to work fine. If you pass it a value of zero, LocalHandle Delta() does not set the handle delta, but instead, returns the current value.

```
pseudocode for LocalHandleDelta() - LINTERF.OBJ
// Parameters:
//      WORD    newHandleCount  (0 means return current value)

    if ( newHandleCount != 0 )
        LocalInfo.hi_hdelta = newHandleCount

    return LocalInfo.hi_hdelta
```

LocalShrink()

LocalShrink() first checks to see if the passed-in heap segment is zero. If so, LocalShrink() calls GlobalHandle() to get the handle of the current data segment. The real work is done inside LShrink(), which moves blocks around and compacts the local heap in an attempt to fit all the NONDISCARDABLE blocks into the amount of memory specified in the LocalShrink() call. LShrink() is a very long, complicated function, and it does not appear to add much to understanding the local heap. Therefore, it is not covered here.

```
pseudocode for LocalShrink() - LINTERF.OBJ
// Parameters:
//      WORD    heapSegment
//      word    newSize

    Save DS on stack

    if ( heapSegment != 0 )
    {
        if ( !GlobalHandle(heapSegment) )   // Sets DX = selector
            return 0

        DS = DX
    }

    if debug KERNEL
        CheckLocalHeap()

    if ( !Lenter() )      // Points DS:DI at the LocalInfo struct
        return 0          // increments the li_lock field

    LShrink( newSize )

    LLeave()    // decrement the li_lock count field

    restore DS from stack
```

LocalCompact()

LocalCompact() is a wrapper around the LCompact() function. LCompact() is responsible for moving blocks around in memory and discarding DISCARDABLE blocks if necessary. The goal is, of course, to free up a block large enough to satisfy the amount of memory needed. Like LShrink(), LCompact() is a long and winding function and not particularly illuminating. It is omitted here.

```
pseudocode for LocalCompact() - LINTERF.OBJ
// Parameters:
//      WORD    bytesNeeded
// Locals:
//      WORD    bytesFreed

    if debug KERNEL
        CheckLocalHeap()

    if ( !Lenter() )     // Points DS:DI at the LocalInfo struct
        return 0         // increments the li_lock field

    bytesNeeded = LAlign(bytesNeeded) // Round up to multiple of 4

    bytesFreed = LCompact( bytesNeeded )
    if ( bytesFreed != 0 )
        return bytesFreed - 6        // 6 = sizeof(arena header)?
    else
        return 0
```

LocalNotify()

LocalNotify() is undocumented in Windows 3.x, but was documented in Windows 2.x. As part of its normal duties, the local heap may need to expand or move memory around. When it does this, it calls the address that your program specifies with LocalNotify(). Expanding the local heap, a tricky business, is probably the reason that this function went undocumented in Windows 3.x. The default handler function knows how to expand a local heap, and that is described below.

LocalNotify() itself is extremely simple; it simply copies the address passed in to the LocalInfo structure and returns the old handler address.

It is the responsibility of the installed callback function to indicate what action should be taken when called. A return value of nonzero indicates it is OK to move or discard the block. A return value of zero means the block should be left alone. If the notification indicates that the heap needs to be expanded, a nonzero return value indicates that the heap was expanded, while zero means that the heap couldn't be grown.

```
pseudocode for LocalNotify() - LINTERF.OBJ
// Parameters:
//      LPFN    newNotificationFunction
// Documented in Windows 2.x, but not in Windows 3.x
```

```
MOV     BX,SP
MOV     AX,WORD PTR SS:[BX+04]      ; Get new handler address
MOV     DX,WORD PTR SS:[BX+06]      ; off stack into DX:AX

MOV     BX,WORD PTR [pLocalHeap]    ; Point to LocalInfo

XCHG    WORD PTR [BX+li_notify],AX      ; Switch new address
XCHG    WORD PTR [BX+li_notify+2],DX    ; with old address

RETF    0004    ; Return with old address in DX:AX
```

LocalNotifyDefault()

LocalNotifyDefault() is the internal function that gets called when the local heap moves or discards a block, or when the local heap needs to be grown to satisfy a memory request. It does no handling if the condition code indicates a block move or block discard; if the LocalNotifyDefault() receives these "notifications," it returns to the caller immediately.

The real job of LocalNotifyDefault() is to handle the nasty business of growing the local heap. The function first determines if the heap can even be grown to the requested size, yet still keep the DGROUP below 64K in size. If not, the function returns failure immediately. If there's enough room to grow the heap, the code hopes for the best and tries for a new heap size that is not only the size requested, but continues to have a large free block. If this wraps around the 64K limit, then 64K minus 16 is used as the new size of the global block.

Once the new size of the encompassing global heap block is known, the function uses GlobalRealloc() to expand the block. If GlobalRealloc() succeeds, LocalNotifyDefault() creates a new sentinel block at the end of the heap and adds the space gained by expanding the global heap block to the free list. Finally, the code returns 1, indicating to the caller that more memory was successfully allocated and that it should re-attempt whatever it was doing.

```
pseudocode for LocalNotifyDefault() - LINTERF.OBJ
// Parameters:
//      WORD    msg_code
//              0 = LN_OUTOFMEM
//              1 = LN_MOVE
//              2 = LN_DISCARD
//      WORD    arg1  for:
//              LN_OUTOFMEM -> size of largest free block
//              LN_MOVE     -> handle
//              LN_DISCARD  -> handle
//      WORD    arg2  for:
//              LN_OUTOFMEM -> #bytes needed
//              LN_MOVE     -> old_location
//              LN_DISCARD  -> discard flags
// Locals:
//      WORD    globalBlockHandle
//      WORD    globalBlockFlags
```

```
//      DWORD   globalBlockSize
//      WORD    reallocFlags

    if ( msg_code != 0 )    // Only provide default handling for
        return msg_code     // LN_OUTOFMEM

    // Get the critical statistics that we need to know about the
    // global block containing the local heap. These values are
    // necessary to know if we can resize it to meet the request
    globalBlockHandle = GlobalHandle(DS)

    if ( globalBlockHandle == 0 )
        return 0

    globalBlockFlags = GlobalFlags(globalBlockHandle)
    globalBlockSize = GlobalSize(globalBlockHandle)
    reallocFlags = 0

    // Calculate how big the global heap block must be to
    // accommodate the allocation request.
    globalBlockSize -= size of largest free local block
    globalBlockSize += #bytes needed    // Carry flag set if this
                                        // "wraps" > 64K

    if ( globalBlockSize > 64K )
        return 0        // We couldn't free up any memory

    globalBlockSize += 0x18      // Need an additional 18h bytes
    if ( globalBlockSize > 64K ) // to resize properly???
        return 0

    // Add in the minimum amount to grow heap by
    globalBlockSize += LocalInfo.li_extra  // typically 0x200
    if ( globalBlockSize > 64K )
        globalBlockSize = 0xFFF0

    // Add the largest free block back in hopes that it'll fit
    globalBlockSize += size of largest free block
    if ( globalBlockSize > 64K )
        globalBlockSize = 0xFFF0

    if ( bottom bit not on in globalBlockHandle )
    {
        if ( lock count in globalBlockFlags != 1 )
            turn on GA_MOVEABLE in reallocFlags
    }
```

```
// Reallocate the heap block to a bigger size
GlobalRealloc(globalBlockHandle,globalBlockSize,reallocFlags)

if ( GlobalRealloc() failed )
    return 0;

globalBlockSize = GlobalSize(globalBlockHandle)

if ( globalBlockSize >= 64K )
    globalBlockSize = 0xFFFF

// Do the grunt work required to add this new space to the
// end of the heap list. This include making a "sentinel"
// block at the end of the heap, as well as freeing up
// the original sentinel block.
Create a new LA_BUSY node at the offset given by
(globalBlockSize - 4).

newNode->la_next = newNode  // Indicates it's the last block

LocalInfo.hi_last->la_next = new_node   // add new node

LocalInfo.hi_last = newNode // Adjust "last block"s pointer

LFree() the original sentinel block

return 1    // Tell the caller we obtained more memory
```

Memory Management at the Application Level

Having examined the inner workings of the memory managers provided by Windows, it's time to step back and look at the broader issues of how they relate to the application programs written in high-level languages. In addition, we'll discuss some other issues that involve memory, but aren't directly related to the heaps or selector functions.

The Windows Address Space

An important concept in operating systems of any complexity is the notion of the address space. Understanding address space fundamentals is often the difference between tracking down a bug and searching for it seemingly without hope.

In simple terms, an address space is the memory that a particular program can see. On one end of the spectrum, there is MS-DOS, which does almost nothing to maintain a formal address space. The operating system, device drivers, applications, and TSR's all use the same 1Mb of real mode address space. Any byte belonging to one application or device driver can easily be read from and written to by other programs. On the other end of the spectrum, operating systems like OS/2 and Windows NT provide a separate address space for each task.

No task can see the memory of another task without its permission. Additionally, the operating system kernel runs in code that's not accessible to tasks, except through very controlled mechanisms. In theory, a properly written operating system using this model would be uncrashable. The operating system couldn't be inadvertently overwritten, nor could one task corrupt another task. In practice, it's not quite this simple, but that's a topic for a different book. Windows 3.1 lies somewhere between these two extremes. In the current implementation of Windows, all programs and DLLs share the same address space and run at the same privilege level. This includes the core Windows DLLs (KERNEL, USER, and GDI). The address space is shared by all programs, using the same LDT for all tasks. In opposition, OS/2 1.x uses a separate LDT for each task, which creates a separate address space for each task. A similar situation existed in earlier real mode versions of Windows using bank-switched EMS memory. Every byte of memory was precious in those days, so Windows mapped the code and data for each task into and out of an EMS bank as needed. In this situation, each task had its own separate address space. It couldn't see the memory of another task because that task had been bank switched out. The correct way to guarantee that your code would always be mapped in was to put it in a DLL, which wasn't subject to EMS bank switching. If you wanted to share data with another application, you had to specifically allocate the memory as SHARED memory. Mercifully, those days are behind us.

The disadvantage to the current, non-EMS Windows address space scheme is that a malicious program can get the selector of, say, a KERNEL code segment, create a data alias for it, and write its own code over KERNEL's. On the other hand, this shared address space allows for easy sharing of data. You can simply pass a far pointer for some data to another application, and the receiving program can use the pointer directly. It's a mixed blessing, at best.

In Enhanced mode, multiple DOS sessions can run at the same time as Windows programs and DLLs. In this situation, all the Windows programs and DLLs are considered to be in one virtual machine and share an address space amongst themselves. Each DOS session is a different virtual machine and has a separate address space from other DOS sessions, as well as from the Windows virtual machine. This is the underlying reason why it's exceptionally difficult to share data between a Windows program and a DOS program that is invoked after starting Windows. It isn't impossible, but that's a topic for a different book.

Use the Runtime Libraries!

One of the reasons that many programmers new to Windows have such a difficult time is due to a simple misunderstanding. Specifically, many programmers see literally dozens of memory management APIs and figure that they *have* to use them. Thus, they dutifully plow through all the standard texts, which leave them thoroughly confused. It was so much easier under DOS, wasn't it? You just called malloc() and free() and you were done with it, right?

Stand back and look at the facts, however, and a different story emerges. DOS has a set of crude memory management APIs. There are INT 21h subfunctions to allocate and free memory, but almost no one uses them. Instead, they let the C (or Pascal, or whatever language you like) runtime library handle the messy work. That's precisely what runtime libraries are to be used for.

The same story exists in Windows. The authors of the runtime libraries for the various compilers have already done the hard work. In the general case, C programmers can continue to call malloc() and free() and not worry about using GlobalAlloc() or LocalAlloc(). Even the memory models are essentially the same. In the small and medium memory models, you use near pointers; and your data, stack, and heap are all in the DGROUP. In the compact and large memory models everything is done in terms of far pointers.

The point here is that you do not *have* to use all the heap functions that KERNEL provides. If you want to, they're there, but it's certainly not a requirement. Unless your program makes thousands and thousands of allocations, or unless you have special memory management needs, the runtime library functions are usually just fine for the job at hand.

The Large Model is Bad Myth

Another big misconception programmers have is that the large model under windows is BAD. Thus, they often go to great lengths to avoid having a large-model program. The reason for this myth has to do with two situations that are now long behind us. First, the Microsoft C 6.0 large model created a separate data segment for each source module in the program. As explained in Chapter 3 on the loader, Windows cannot run more than one instance of a program that has more than one writeable data segment. Chapter 3 gives the details, but the short story is that if there's more than one data segment, the compiler and linker must place hard-coded selector value fix-ups into the code segments of the program. This in turn, makes it impossible for two instances of the program to share the same code because the second instance would be reading and writing to the data segments of the first instance. The problem however is not the large model. Instead, the problem is having multiple data segments in your program. It's quite easy to create multiple data segments in *any* memory model!

The second reason for the paranoia about large models has to do with a bug in Windows 3.0. If the Windows 3.0 loader encounters a program that has multiple data segments, it makes each of the extra data segments FIXED and pagelocked. This causes all the low memory below 1Mb to be eaten up very quickly. At the start of every program, you need a certain amount of memory below 1Mb for the TDB of the new task (see Chapter 3). Thus, the more large model programs you run, the less likely you are to be able to start new programs in Windows 3.0.

The resolution to these problems came in two forms. The first breakthrough involved a more intelligent large model. The Borland C++ large model uses far pointers for code and data, but it places all ordinary data in the DGROUP segment. The result is that when linked, assuming you have less than 64K of data, there's only one data segment. Both Microsoft C/C++ 7.0 contains an option that allows you to do the same thing. The important thing is that you have only one data segment if you want to run multiple instances of your program. In any memory model, you can declare far data (not the same as far pointers), with the result being a multi-data segment program. It's important to understand the reasons for this limitation, rather than to try to live with sound-bite solutions.

The second part of the fix for the large model problem came about with Windows 3.1. The loader in Windows 3.1 is much more intelligent and does not fix and pagelock multiple data segments. Instead the segments are MOVEABLE, as they should be. Although you can't run multiple instances of the application, at least you don't have to worry about a program being a low memory hog.

The Mapping Myth

Another common myth is that Windows maps malloc() to LocalAlloc() in the small data models and to GlobalAlloc() in the large data models. This is simply not true. Windows knows nothing about malloc() or memory models. This is a decision made entirely by the compiler runtime library.

As it turns out, the Microsoft C 6.0 and Borland C++ 2.0 libraries do call LocalAlloc() for the small data model malloc() and GlobalAlloc() for large data model malloc(). However, these programs were certainly not bound to do this. Instead, at the time it seemed to be the easiest and most obvious thing to do.

One of the key problems in these versions is that in the large data models, programs that make lots of allocations run out of selectors very quickly because there are only about 8K selectors available in the LDT (and only 4K when using KRNL286). To remedy this, Microsoft C/C++ 7.0 and Borland C++ 3.x use a suballocator scheme in the large data models so that each malloc does not turn into a GlobalAlloc() and thereby chew up a selector. We'll discuss suballocation shortly. In the small data models, these compilers still allocate memory from the local heap, so the heaps are limited to somewhat less than 64K, but that's, of course, always true in the small data models.

If the memory management provided with your compiler is not sufficient for your needs, you might check out some of the many third-party memory management libraries. These libraries often offer significant functionality above and beyond what comes with your compiler. A glance at the ads in almost any programmers' magazine is likely to yield quite a few alternatives.

What About New and Delete?

In the general case, the C++ operators new and delete map directly to the C malloc() and free() functions. Thus, the above discussion about malloc() and free() in the small and large data models applies here as well.

Suballocation

Just as the global heap code allocates memory from DPMI and subdivides it, and just as the local heap allocates memory from the global heap and subdivides it, so can you. The process of allocating memory from the global heap and then managing a heap within the block is called suballocation. Typically, a suballocator allocates multiple blocks from the global heap as needed and then manages local heaps within them. When your program requests memory, the suballocator checks each of the heaps to see if it can accommodate the memory request. If so, the block is allocated in one of the local heaps, and a far pointer to the memory is returned to the caller. If none of the heaps can fulfill the request, another global block may be allocated for use as a new heap, thereby ensuring that the requested block size fits in it. Alternatively if the requested size is above a certain limit, the request might be fulfilled by using GlobalAlloc() on a block just for that request, without constructing a local heap for it.

Suballocation is so useful that even the USER module uses it. In Windows 3.0, the USER local heap contains all sorts of items. All the window class names, resources, and other various things are allocated from USER's local heap. Like all local heaps, the USER local heap is limited to 64K. This leads to the infamous problem of the Free System Resources, which always seem to dwindle away the more you use Windows. In Windows 3.1, the problem has been alleviated somewhat because USER maintains three local heaps. It stores the menus in one local heap, the menu strings in another, and takes the remaining things from the default DGROUP heap. Thus, USER is suballocating.

Since suballocators have been discussed in so many other publications, we won't be building our own here. If you're interested in building your own suballocator, the LocalInit() will certainly take care of a lot of the work and is certainly worth investigating. Alternatively, you might look at the source code from the Borland C++ runtime library, which includes a suballocator, as well as the many third-party Windows memory management libraries.

Sharing Memory

As in all multitasking systems, Windows oftentimes needs to communicate between different tasks. One of the easiest ways to communicate is through shared memory, wherein more than one task can access the same memory location(s). Windows 3.x makes it extremely easy to share memory between applications because there is a single address space. Any program can read and write the data segments of another program, as long as it knows which selector to use or knows the base address of the segment so that it can synthesize a selector. However, the proper way to share memory for future compatibility is actually a relic from the past. In older versions of Windows that used EMS, only the current task was mapped into memory. All the other tasks were "bank switched" out and were not available. If you wanted to share memory between tasks, you had to make sure that it was in a memory region that wasn't banked out. The way to do this was to allocate the memory as GMEM_SHARE or GMEM_DDESHARE. This memory is guaranteed to be always available to all tasks because it is never bank switched out. In Windows 3.x, you can still allocate memory with this attribute, but it doesn't gain you anything in the way of shareability. All segments are equally accessible. Other operating systems, such as OS/2 2.0 and Windows NT are not like Windows 3.x, however, as they have separate address spaces for each task. If you want to share memory between tasks, you've got to play by the rules. Future versions of Windows might again require GMEM_SHARE.

What about sharing memory between Windows and DOS programs? This is a little more complicated, and there is no one answer. The easiest way to share memory between DOS and a Windows program is to use GlobalDOSAlloc() to allocate memory that's below 1Mb. This memory is guaranteed to be accessible by real mode code in the system virtual machine (VM). You then need to somehow communicate the real mode address to the program (TSR) in the system virtual machine. A good way to do this is by hooking and using interrupts, and passing values in the registers. There are several good Microsoft Knowledge Base articles that show how to do this. An important point is that only programs that were run before Windows started up (that is, TSR's) or run from WINSTART.BAT are visible in the system virtual machine. Starting up a DOS session inside Windows and then trying to share memory with a program in that session is a whole different can of worms that we won't go into here.

Another alternative is to have the TSR program allocate memory before it goes resident, and before Windows is started. It can then pass the real mode address of the memory to the Windows program or DLL (again, interrupts are a good method). The Windows program or DLL can then use the selector functions to create a selector to access the real mode memory.

The downside to this approach is that the memory that the TSR allocates is wasted in every other virtual machine (DOS box) that's started.

Use the Debug KERNEL

As you may have noticed from the preceding pseudocode, the debug KERNEL does quite a bit of checking and testing for error conditions. It can be quite verbose in its output at times. I highly recommend that you use the debug KERNEL *all* the time. In addition to catching errors in your program—and in others—it is often enlightening to watch the various diagnostic traces as you do your normal work in Windows. It's an interesting peek into the maze of memory management code that we've just examined so thoroughly.

CHAPTER 3

Starting a Process: Modules and Tasks

The primary focus of any operating system is to control the execution of programs, known more formally as tasks, or processes. This includes creating tasks, as well as terminating them. A good operating system can manage the execution of multiple programs and allow different instances of the same program to share code and read-only data, thereby conserving precious memory. In this chapter, we examine in detail how Windows performs these chores. We also examine some of the fundamental data structures used for process management.

In order to really grasp what goes on in Windows, it's essential to have a solid understanding of modules and tasks. We discuss modules first, then tasks. Once modules and tasks are solid in our mind, we can dive into the mechanics of how a program file on disk becomes a running process in memory. The shutdown of a program will be covered as well. Lastly, we peer into the poorly understood area of self-loading applications.

Modules

A "module," in Windows parlance, refers to all of the code, data, and resources that a particular file "brings to the party." A module can either be an executable program or a dynamic link library (DLL) used by a program. The term module technically does not refer to the actual bytes on the disk or to the file itself. Rather, a module is the in-memory representation of the information in the disk file. The information from the disk file is read into memory and the module is created from that. Much of the code for creating a new process involves translating the disk version of the information into the in-memory version.

An executable file is one source of a module. Typically, it has code segments, data segments, and resources. A DLL file can also be the basis for a module, as it can also contain code, data, and resources. It is important to note that a DLL does not need to have a .DLL extension. For instance, font files (.FON and .FOT) are DLLs and can be used as the basis for modules, although they typically contain only resources. The numerous device driver files (.DRV) in the \WINDOWS\SYSTEM directory are also DLLs. And just to make life interesting, the core Windows files (USER.EXE, KRNLx86.EXE, and GDI.EXE) are also DLLs! The important thing for EXEs and DLLs is that the file be in the standard New Executable (NE) file format, which we discuss in a moment. Windows knows the format of NE files and uses that knowledge to locate and read the code, data, and resources from a file.

NE files are one generation newer than the old DOS Mark Zbikowski (MZ) executable file format, hence the New in the name. NE files are also called "segmented executables" because the file format defines distinct segments. Each segment can easily be located and loaded separately from the other segments. DOS MZ files, on the other hand, lump the whole program into one blob. The result is that the DOS loader has to read in the whole file, minus the .EXE header, at once.

Windows programs have used the NE format since version 1.0; it is also used for OS/2 1.x programs. The NE format is also the format of choice for many 16-bit DOS extended programs. For instance, several of the executables from Borland C++ 3.0 are DOS extended and use the NE format. The NE format is now fairly well documented, with the most up-to-date information being in the File Formats section of the Windows 3.1 documentation.

If you're interested in examining the contents of an NE file, TDUMP from Borland or EXEHDR from Microsoft can break apart and display NE files. For an interesting experiment, run TDUMP or EXEHDR on all the files in the \WINDOWS\SYSTEM directory and see which ones really are NE files. Incidentally, there are even newer file formats than the NE format, such as LE files (Linear Executables) used in Windows Virtual Device Drivers, LX files for OS/2 2.0 executables and DLLs, and PE files for Win32 and Win32s executables and DLLs. The WIN386.EXE file, which is a collection of LE files, uses an ad hoc W3 format. All of these formats target 32-bit operating systems, while the NE format is tied to the 16-bit world.

The most important part of any NE file is its header. The NE header is a 40h-byte region that acts as a database for the other sections in the file. Any valid NE file starts out with an old style MZ header. If the WORD value at offset 18h is 40H, then the DWORD value at offset 3Ch is an offset to a header *of some kind*. It might be an NE header, but it could also be an LE, an LX, or a PE header, so check! The first two bytes in the header are a signature such as 'NE' (454Eh), 'LE' (454Ch), 'PE' (4550h), and so on.

The NE header points to information such as the number of segments, their attributes and length, and where the segments' data can be found in the file. The header points to other information as well, such as the location of the resources and the addresses of exported functions. For example, to find the file offset of a given segment, use the NE header to find the location of the segment table. Then read the appropriate section of the segment table to find the file offset of the desired segment.

When Windows needs information in an NE file (that is, when you run a program or load a DLL), KERNEL reads the NE header, and several of the tables that it refers to into an allocated segment. This segment is called the module table, or module database (MDB). The global memory handle of the segment is none other than the module handle. Although the module table is similar in format to the NE header and its associated tables, there are key differences. For instance, the entry table, where exported functions are listed, is optimized to save space in the NE file. When the entry table is loaded into memory, it's converted to a larger format that's optimized for quick lookup of a given entry ordinal. Another example in which the disk image is smaller than the memory version is the segment table. In addition to the segment information, such as attributes and lengths, the module table also remembers which selector accesses the various segments. This applies to resources as well.

Once a module table has been created for the first instance of a program or a DLL, there's no need to create additional module tables for a second instance of a program or for the use of a DLL that's already in memory. As long as the module table exists in memory, it fulfills all future requests to use information in the module. Another one is not created from the NE file. When the last instance of a program using a module terminates, KERNEL removes the module table, along with the segments and resources it points to, from memory. Similarly, when the number of programs or DLLs using a particular DLL drops to zero, the DLL's code, data, and resources are removed from memory by KERNEL. "The last one out turns off the lights!"

If you were to run four copies of CALC.EXE, it wouldn't make sense to have four copies of CALC's code segments in memory. The code segments should be identical for each instance, unless modified with a data alias (see AllocCStoDSAlias() in Chapter 2). The same argument applies to resources, such as bitmaps. This is where the idea of modules really starts to help out. Code segments and resources can be loaded once, and then used by any number of programs and DLLs. Windows uses the module table to coordinate the sharing. In addition to memory savings from reusing code and resources, another benefit of modules is faster loading time for the second instance of a program or for the user of a DLL. When a module is already in memory, there's no need to read the information in from the NE file again. The one exception is writeable data segments in EXEs. These segments may have initialized data in them, so every time another instance of a program runs, the data segment (that is DGROUP) is read in fresh from the NE file.

Debugging in Shared Code Environments

The method of sharing code between different instances of a program in Windows is very simple, compared to other operating systems. Windows makes the assumption that code segments won't ever be modified, so it's OK to share them. This presents a problem when debugging. If you load a program under a Windows debugger and set a breakpoint, *any* instance of the program can hit the breakpoint, causing the debugger to wake up. In more advanced operating systems, there's a concept called "copy on write" that prevents this situation. On these systems, multiple instances share code *until* a section of code (for example, a page) is written to. When this happens, a copy of the affected section is made and mapped only to the process that needs the modified version (with the breakpoint in place).

Unfortunately, OS/2 2.0 does not have a copy on write mechanism. This makes hook procedure debugging a show-stopping situation. Each OS/2 2.0 task has its own separate address space, implemented by switching page tables around. However, DLL code is in the address space of all tasks in the system (the DLL code is in pages that map to the same address in each task). System-wide Presentation Manager hooks (for example, an HK_SENDMESSAGE hook) *must* be in a DLL, since the hook procedure can be called in the context of any task. The problem is that an OS/2 2.0 debugger is not restricted from placing a breakpoint in DLL code. If a task besides the one being debugged hits the breakpoint, the debugger is not notified of the breakpoint exception. Instead, the default system exception handler is invoked, and the task is terminated, along with your use of the machine until you cold reboot. So much for crash protection!

Windows does not have copy on write, but it also doesn't have this particular problem. Windows allows one task to intercept exceptions destined for another task. In the situation above, a Windows debugger can check to see if the task that hit the breakpoint is the task being debugged. If it isn't, the debugger can just single step past the breakpoint and then resume running the task.

Multiple Instances and Windows Memory Models

An unpopular restriction in Windows arises because of its fundamental assumption that code can be shared by multiple invocations of the same program. If a program has more than one DATA segment that's non-read-only, just one instance of the program is allowed to run. The reason for this has to do with fixups in CODE segments. In a typical program with one data segment, the CODE segments don't need to contain any explicit references to the DGROUP segment. As Chapter 8 describes, the DS register in callback functions is usually set by loading it from the AX register in the prologue code of the function. Alternatively, the DS register can be set from the SS register (termed Smart Callbacks by Borland). In any case, no hardwired selector values are placed into the CODE segments as a result of a fixup. The CODE segments in this case are called pure and can be used by multiple instances of the same program. When a program has two or more non-read-only DATA segments, however, the CODE segments might end up with hardwired selector values in them referring to the second data segment (once the KERNEL loader loads the code segment into memory and applies the relocations). These hardwired values are the selector values of the data segments of the *first* instance of the program. If a second program is allowed to run, it would use CODE segments with hardwired data segment selectors for the *first* instance of the program, obviously a recipe for disaster. Windows disallows a second instance of the program from running in this case.

Despite what Charles Petzold says in *Programming Windows*, and despite the oft-repeated Microsoft mantras, the large model is not bad and does not prevent multiple copies of the program from running. Windows knows nothing about C compiler memory models. Windows knows about CODE and DATA segments. Before Microsoft C/C++ 7.0, all Microsoft C-compiled large model programs typically had multiple data segments. Thus, you couldn't run multiple instances of most large model Microsoft C programs. However, you could just as easily have created multiple data segments in any of the other memory models by declaring some far data. The Borland C++ large model puts all data into the DGROUP by default and, therefore, doesn't create multiple segments unless you have more than 64K bytes of static data. Thus, a Borland C++ large model program can run multiple times. Microsoft C/C++ 7.0 introduced a new switch to do the same thing. The key point is that it's not which memory model you use. Instead, it's how many DATA segments you end up with in the EXE file. You can find out how many data segments you have by looking at the linker's .MAP file or by examining the output from TDUMP or EXEHDR.

Windows maintains a linked list of all of the modules currently loaded in the system. Each module table holds a selector to the next module in the list. The head of the list can be found by calling GetModuleHandle() (any valid module name will do). Although not documented, upon return from this call, DX contains the module handle of the first module in the system. There are several programs in *Undocumented Windows* which walk the module table list and display information about each module. TOOLHELP.DLL has a set of documented functions that allow you to obtain information about any or all of the modules in the system.

There is often a great deal of confusion between a module handle and an instance handle. Much of this confusion comes from the fact that the Windows API asks for instance handles, where you'd really expect it to want a module handle, or vice versa. For example, when your program starts up, its instance handle (its DGROUP selector) is passed to WinMain(). If you want to obtain the full pathname of your program's EXE file, you should call GetModuleFilename(). Unfortunately, GetModuleFilename() takes a module handle (or hModule), rather than an instance handle. What do you do? You don't have the hModule of your program. As it turns out, you can pass your hInstance to GetModuleFileName(), and it will work just fine. Another example is that resources are shared by every user of a module. Why then, do functions like LoadIcon() expect an instance handle, rather than a module handle? A good question. In any case, you can pass in either one, even though module handles and instances are totally different.

A module handle is simply the selector of the segment containing information about the code, data, and resources of an NE file that has been read into memory. An instance handle is not a module handle. Instead, an instance handle is the handle of the segment containing the EXE's or DLL's DGROUP segment. How are these two things related? How can certain Windows functions take either a module handle or an instance handle? The answer lies in a wonderfully useful but undocumented function, GetExePtr(), which is described in detail in

Chapter 8. GetExePtr() takes an instance handle (or practically any other global handle) and returns the module handle of the program or DLL that the passed handle belongs to. In this case, the instance handle (DGROUP segment) is associated with a particular instance of a program. Since all programs are created from a module table, it's a simple matter to map an instance handle back to a module handle.

GetExePtr() is not the only function that knows about and uses module tables. The GetModuleFilename() function simply returns the complete path for the NE file that's stored in each module table. GetModuleUsage() returns the number of programs or DLLs that are referencing a module and obtains the value by reading it directly out of the module table.

In much of Windows, Microsoft refers to module tables as EXEs, even for modules that are DLLs. For instance, the GetExePtr() function sounds like it would return a pointer to an EXE, whatever that means. In fact, the function returns the selector of a module table. Once you start mentally translating EXE to mean module, understanding the internals of Windows becomes a bit easier.

Logical and Physical Addresses

There are two ways to refer to an address inside a code or data segment in memory. The first method is to specify the selector and an offset. This is called a physical (or actual) address because it refers to an address that exists inside the CPU.

What happens, however, when a physical address is required for some reason, but the selector value is not available? Take the example of a program making a FAR call to a function in a different code segment. When the CALL instruction is executed, an actual selector value and offset are required as part of the instruction. When the program was compiled and linked, however, the selector value of the target segment could not have been known. To remedy this situation, the Windows loader applies fixups or patches to the code and data segments as they're loaded so that they contain actual selector values and offsets that can be used by the CPU. In order to do these fixups, some way of specifying an address without using real selector values is needed. This form of addressing is called logical addressing. Incidentally, DOS programs also have fixups but they're much simpler than Windows fixups, and are covered in numerous books, including the *MS-DOS Encyclopedia*. (Chapter 8 describes Windows fixups.)

A complete logical address consists of a segment value, an offset in the segment, and some way of uniquely specifying which module the segment came from. The module portion of the address can be specified by either the module name (the NAME/LIBRARY field in the DEF file) or a module handle. The segment portion of a logical address specifies a segment number, such as 1, 2, and so on. The first segment in the segment table of a module database is considered to be logical segment 1, not 0. The second segment in the table is logical segment 2, and so on. The offset portion of a logical address is the offset within the specified segment and is exactly the same as its corresponding physical address counterpart.

Let's look at a hypothetical example of logical and physical addresses. Assume a program with one code segment, one data segment, and a module name of FOO. The main() procedure in this example starts at offset 235h in the code segment. This program is WinExec()'ed, causing KERNEL to load the code segment into memory and assign it a selector value of 13C7h. The physical memory address of main() is therefore 13C7h:0235h. The logical address of main() is FOO 0001:0235h, meaning module FOO, 235h bytes into its first segment.

The mapping between the logical and physical addresses is done two different ways. Given a logical address, the selector value assigned to it can be found in the segment table inside of the module database. Going from a selector value back to a logical address is a little trickier. The owner of a GlobalAlloc()'ed block of memory can be found in the header that precedes the data for each block (see Chapter 2 for more details). If the block is owned by a module, the block's arena also contains its logical segment number. It is important to note that any given logical address can be mapped to a physical address, but the converse is not true. Blocks that were dynamically allocated by a program (by calling GlobalAlloc() for instance) are not owned by a module. Instead, they're owned by the DOS PSP (PDB) that's associated with each task. More on PDBs later.

Logical addresses are most often encountered in the MAP file of a program and in the output from programs like TDUMP and EXEHDR. They're also used in debugging information and SYM files. Just as the linker can't fill in genuine selector values when it creates the program, debug information can't be filled in with genuine segment values. When you debug a program symbolically, there's always a series of address translations going on to convert logical address in the debug information to physical addresses, which can be read and shown to the user. Another place where you see logical addresses is in a postmortem tool like WinSpector or Dr. Watson. These programs often show you both the logical address and the corresponding physical address in their LOG files.

Having discussed the module table in the abstract, we now present the module table as it exists in memory. Since the NE file format is readily available elsewhere (such as the Windows 3.1 SDK), it will not be presented here. You may notice similarities between the file format and the format shown in Table 3-1.

Table 3-1: Format of the In-Memory Module Table in Windows 3.1.

00h	WORD	'NE' signature (454Eh)
02h	WORD	Usage count of module. The number of times this module has been used to create a program, or been linked to, or been loaded using LoadLibrary().

Table 3-1: Format of the In-Memory Module Table in Windows 3.1. (continued)

04h WORD

Near pointer to entry table inside the module table. The entry table is a linked list of bundle headers. Each header specifies the range of entry points that are in this bundle. They are immediately followed by an array of entry structures, one structure per entry, in the bundle. Note that the structure described here is quite a bit different from the NE file version.

Entry table bundle header:

WORD	First entry ordinal in bundle - 1.
WORD	Last entry ordinal in bundle (number of entries = last - first).
WORD	Near pointer to next bundle.

Each entry:

BYTE	Type	(actual segment number for fixed entry, or 0FFh for moveable entry).
BYTE	Flags	(1 = exported, 2 = shared data entry).
BYTE	SegNum	(logical segment for entry).
WORD	Offset	(offset of entry in segment).

06h WORD — Selector of next module table. Zero indicates end of list.

08h WORD — Near pointer to the segment table entry for DGROUP. See offset 22h for the format of segment table entries.

0Ah WORD — Near pointer to load file information (an OFSTRUCT).

Load file info:

BYTE	Length of load file information section, not counting itself.
BYTE	0 = file on removable media; 1 = fixed media (hard drive).
WORD	Error code of some kind.
WORD	File date, in MS-DOS date format.
WORD	File time, in MS-DOS time format.
BYTE	Filename, in ASCIIZ format.

0Ch WORD

Module flags (based on NE file flags). Over time, there have apparently been many different interpretations of the module flags. The NE file format contains a complete list of flags. Following are the flags which Windows 3.1 appears to use:

Table 3-1: Format of the In-Memory Module Table in Windows 3.1. (continued)

Offset	Type	Description
0Ch	WORD (cont.)	**Flags:** 8000h — Library module (0=task 1=DLL). This bit is the only thing that differentiates a program from a DLL. You can flip this bit and fool various routines internal to Windows, such as GetProcAddress(), which won't work if it thinks the target is a program module. 4000h — WEP procedure should be called (different meaning than flag for NE file). 2000h — Errors in file image. 0800h — A self-loading application. 0002h — Each instance of this module gets its own DGROUP segment (a task). 0001h — Each instance of this module shares the DGROUP segment (a DLL).
0Eh	WORD	Logical segment number of DGROUP (1 based).
10h	WORD	Initial local heap size, in bytes.
12h	WORD	Initial stack size in bytes. Loader sets to 5K if NE file specifies less.
14h	DWORD	Starting CS:IP as a logical address.
18h	DWORD	Starting SS:SP as a logical address.
1Ch	WORD	Number of segments in the segment table.
1Eh	WORD	Number of entries in module reference table. See offset 28h for the format of the table.
20h	WORD	Size of non-resident names table on disk. The format of non-resident names table is the same as the resident names table. Entry zero is the module description specified in the .DEF file when linking.
22h	WORD	Near pointer to segment table in the module table. Segment table consists of a series of entries. The number is given by the WORD at offset 1Ch. Entries are sequentially numbered, starting at one. Format of a segment table entry is similar to the segment table entry in the NE file, but with the addition of a WORD at the end of each entry. **Segment table entry:** WORD — Offset in the file of the segment, in sectors. A sector is defined as one shifted left by the alignment shift. The alignment shift is found in offset 32h. See offset 32h for a description of how the alignment shift works. WORD — Size of segment on disk in bytes (65,536). WORD — Flags: (bitfield) 0001h DATA segment (zero indicates CODE) 0008h Iterated segment 0010h Moveable

Table 3-1: Format of the In-Memory Module Table in Windows 3.1. (continued)

Offset	Type	Description
	WORD	Flags: (bitfield) (cont.). 0020h Shareable (should not be modified). 040h Preload (0 indicates LOADONCALL). 0080h Execute/read only (depends on code or data bit). 0100h Has relocations. 1000h DISCARDABLE.
	WORD	Minimum size of segment in memory (0 = 64K).
	WORD	Handle or selector of segment in memory. For fixed segments, this is the actual selector. Otherwise, it's the global handle. 0 indicates that the segment isn't loaded. This field is missing from the NE file on disk.
24h	WORD	Near pointer to resource table in module table.
		Resource Table Format:
	WORD	Alignment shift (4 = 16 byte alignment, 9 = 512 byte alignment). This value is always supposed to be the same as the alignment shift in offset 32h.
		Immediately followed by:
		Format of the resource type structure:
	WORD	ID If high bit set, an ordinal resource, and the bottom eight bits indicate the type of the resource: Cursor 1 Bitmap 2 Icon 3 Menu 4 Dialog 5 String table 6 Font directory 7 Font 8 Accelerator 9 RC data 10 (User data) Error table 11 Group cursor 12 Unknown 13 Group icon 14 Name table 15 (Eliminated in Windows 3.1 NE files) Version info 16 (Used by Win 3.1 VER.DLL) TrueType font 204

Table 3-1: Format of the In-Memory Module Table in Windows 3.1. (continued)

Offset	Size	Description
		Format of the resource type structure (cont.):
	WORD	ID If high bit not set (a named resource), the value is the offset of the resource name in the resource table, inside the module table.
	WORD	Number of info structs following this struct.
	WORD	Far pointer to function containing resource handler.
		Format of the resource info struct:
	WORD	Offset in file, in sectors (see offset 32h).
	WORD	Length in file, in sectors.
	WORD	Flags: 1000h Discardable 0040h Preload 0020h Read only 0010h Moveable 0004 Loaded in memory
	WORD	Resource identifier. If high bit is set, then the value is treated as an integer identifier. If it's not set, then the value is the offset of a string identifier, relative to the resource table start.
	WORD	Handle to segment containing the resource in memory.
	WORD	Usage count.
26h	WORD	Near pointer to resident name table in the module table. A series of Pascal-style strings, one after the other. The length is found by subtracting the resident names table offset from the module reference table offset. Each string is suffixed by a WORD containing the associated entry ordinal. Entry zero in the table contains the module name, as specified in the NAME or LIBRARY entry in the .DEF file.
28h	WORD	Near pointer to module reference table in the module table. Module table reference table is an array of WORDs. Each WORD is the module handle of a referred-to module (note the difference from the NE file on disk). The indexing of the module handles starts with 1.
2Ah	WORD	Near pointer to imported names table in the module table. This always points to a zero byte, which according to the documentation should indicate the end of the table. However, the imported names table always starts with a zero byte, and then follows with Pascal-style strings. The first zero byte may be there so that the first valid offset in the table is 1, rather than 0. The imported names are usually the names of the modules that this module links to.

Table 3-1: Format of the In-Memory Module Table in Windows 3.1. (continued)

Offset	Type	Description
2Ch	DWORD	File offset of non-resident name table, in bytes.
30h	WORD	Number of moveable entries in the entry table.
32h	WORD	The alignment shift count. The file offsets for segments and resources is given in units of sectors. The size of a sector in bytes can be found by shifting the value 1, left by the value in this field. For example, an alignment shift of 4 causes a sector size of 16 (1 << 4 == 16). The other common sector size is 512 bytes (alignment shift = 9).
34h	WORD	Set to 2 if a TrueType font.
36h	BYTE	Operating system flags. 0 Unknown (Windows 1.0 files use this value) 1 OS/2 2 Windows 3 European DOS 4 4 Windows/386
37h	BYTE	Other flags. 0002 Windows 2.x application MARK'ed OK for proportional font. 0004 Win 2.x application MARK'ed OK for protected mode. 0008 File has gangload area (area with all preload code segments ganged together, so they can be loaded in one read).
38h	WORD	Contains the same value as offset 2Ah (the Imported Names Table offset).
3Ah	WORD	Contains the same value as offset 2Ah, except KERNEL.
3Ch	WORD	The minimum swap area size for this module.
3Eh	WORD	Expected Windows version (minimum version required).

The Windows modules are like the physical components of a computer. By themselves, they don't do anything; but when you add electricity to the equation, they come to life. The electricity in the world of Windows is a task, which we describe next.

Tasks

A Windows task can loosely be described as a running program. More precisely, a task is a thread of execution through code segments loaded by Windows. As described earlier, code segments in Windows are usually pure, allowing more than one task to use the same code segments and read-only data segments at the same time. Modules are the code segments and resources loaded from an NE file. A task is the CPU executing through the module's code. In OOP parlance, modules are like member functions or methods, useless without data to act upon. Tasks correspond to actual objects. They use the same code (module) for each instance of an object, but differentiate between objects by using different 'this' or 'self' pointers. The role of the 'this' pointer is played by the data segment or DGROUP segment. Each object or task has its own 'this' pointer (DGROUP), but shares the same member function code (module code and resources).

Not all information about a process can be stored in a module table. The primary example of this is the selector of the DGROUP (the automatic data segment). As shown in our previous example, it is desirable that each of the four copies of CALC have its own data segment; otherwise, it would be useless to run four copies of CALC. It wouldn't be a good idea to put the DGROUP segment's selector in the module database, where it might get overwritten by a subsequent invocation of the same program. Likewise, each instance of a program needs its own Disk Transfer Area (DTA), separate and distinct from other instances. Information like this is task-specific and needs to be stored on a per-task basis.

Each task in Windows has a data structure that contains its per-task data. The data structure is in a globally allocated segment and is called the Task Database, or TDB, for short. The global memory handle of a task database is known as a task handle or hTask. Contained within each task database is information specific to that invocation of the program, including the handle of the module the task was created from, the handle of the task's DGROUP segment (aka, the hInstance), and the thunks created by MakeProcInstance().

The second half of each task database contains a DOS Program Segment Prefix (PSP) for the task. Windows still lives some of its life in the shadow of MS-DOS, especially with regard to file I/O. Since each DOS program needs its own PSP, it's not surprising that each Windows task needs to drag along its own PSP, as a relic from the past. In fact, as discussed in Chapter 2 on memory management, if a program uses GlobalAlloc() on a memory block, the owner of the block is considered to be the PSP, rather than the task itself. This is a throwback to the days of DOS, where Memory Control Blocks (MCBs) were marked with the PSP of the program that allocated them. Why this was continued in Windows, where task handles are much more prevalent than PSP handles, is not known. Incidentally, Microsoft refers to the PSPs of Windows programs as Process Databases (PDBs), even though most programmers are much more familiar with the term PSP. The Process Database term may be solely for symmetry with the Task Database (TDB) and Module Database (MDB).

At any given moment, Windows is running only one task. All other tasks in the system are frozen. The main function of the Windows scheduler is to switch among the various tasks in the system. All the information needed to start up a frozen task is present in its task database. Contrary to popular belief though, the TDB for a frozen task does not contain the complete register set of the task. Chapter 6, on the Windows scheduler, discusses these topics in much more detail than we go into here.

There is a popular belief among programmers that each task in the system has a window. Carrying the assumption further, each task could be found by looking at the Task Manager window (TASKMAN.EXE) or by enumerating all the windows in the system with EnumWindows(). This is, quite simply, not true. A task is not required to have a window. In fact, a task does not have to contain a GetMessage() loop either, although such a task would hog the CPU until it ran to completion or yielded in some way.

How then can you determine all the tasks in the system? Like modules tables, the task databases are maintained in a linked list, with each TDB containing the selector of the next TDB. The first task in the linked list can be obtained by (yet again) some undocumented functionality. The handle of the current task, meaning the hTask of your program, can be obtained by calling GetCurrentTask(). What's not usually documented is that upon return, DX contains the hTask of the *first* TDB in the list. As mentioned in Chapter 6, the ordering of tasks within the list is subject to change from instant to instant. ToolHelp contains a variety of functions for examining and changing each of the tasks in the task list.

As was mentioned in the section on modules, both tasks and DLLs are based on modules. Both tasks and DLLs can have code segments, data segments, and resources. What differentiates a task module from a DLL module is one bit. Offset 0Ch in Table 3-1 shows this difference, which is the setting of a single bit in the flags field of the module header. However, it is a very key distinction. For example, LoadModule() can be used to both create new tasks, as well as to load DLLs into the system. It is this single bit that tells LoadModule() if a new Task Database should be created. Remember, DLLs aren't tasks, and therefore can't have TDBs. And as Chapter 8 on dynamic linking describes, it is this one bit that determines whether GetProcAddress() succeeds or fails. As we already saw in Chapter 2, this bit also determines whether Windows honors a GMEM_FIXED memory allocation request.

The format of the Task Database was finally documented, although obscurely, in the Windows 3.1 DDK, in the file TDB.INC. Since many people don't have this file, and since it's terse at best, the format is given in Table 3-2, with substantially more information than will be found in TDB.INC:

Table 3-2: Format of a Windows 3.1 Task Database.

Offset	Type	Description
00h	WORD	Selector of Next Task. Zero indicates end of list.
02h	DWORD	SS:SP of the task when last switched away from.
06h	WORD	Number of events waiting for the tasks. Used by the Windows scheduler. See Chapter 6 for more information.
08h	BYTE	Priority. The linked list of TDBs is kept in sorted order, based on the priority. Lower numbers are higher priority. The scheduler uses this field.
09h	BYTE	Appears to be unused in Windows 3.1. Probably left over from OS/2. This field and the other unused fields may be used for thread information in OS/2 1.X tasks.
0Ah	WORD	Appears to be unused in Windows 3.1. Probably left over from OS/2.
0Ch	WORD	Selector for this task database (it points to itself).
0Eh	WORD	Appears to be unused in Windows 3.1. Probably left over from OS/2.
10h	WORD	Appears to be unused in Windows 3.1. Probably left over from OS/2.
12h	WORD	Appears to be unused in Windows 3.1. Probably left over from OS/2.
14h	WORD	80x87 control word (FLDCW/FSTCW). Saved and restored during task switches.
16h	WORD	Task flags. TDB.INC lists: TDBF_WINOLDAP 0001h TDBF_OS2APP 0008h TDB_WIN32S 0010h

Table 3-2: Format of a Windows 3.1 Task Database. (continued)

18h	WORD	Error handling flags: 0001h = Don't display critical error box. Return a default response. 002h = Don't put up GP fault box. 8000h = Don't display a dialog box asking for the file if it couldn't be found.
1Ah	WORD	Expected Windows version for task. The minimum version of Windows required to run this program.
1Ch	WORD	Instance handle (DGROUP) for task.
1Eh	WORD	Module handle for task.
20h	WORD	Selector of the task message queue. See Chapter 7 on the messaging system.
22h	WORD	Selector of TDB of parent task. The initial shell application (for example, PROGMAN) has a valid selector in this field, but it is not a valid TDB.
24h	WORD	Some sort of flag relating to the task signal handler. See offset 26h for more information.
26h	DWORD	Application signal handler address. This field can be set by calling SetSigHandler(). It's used to allow a task to install its own Ctrl-Break handler. See *Undocumented Windows* for details.
2Ah	DWORD	USER signal handler address. This function is called when significant events happen. Known values: 0020h Task is terminating normally 0040h DLL is loading 0080h DLL is unloading 0666h Task is terminating by GP fault
2Eh	DWORD	GlobalDiscard() notification handler.
32h	DWORD	Interrupt 0 handler address (divide by zero).
36h	DWORD	Interrupt 2 handler address (NMI).
3Ah	DWORD	Interrupt 4r handler address (INTO).
3Eh	DWORD	Interrupt 6 handler address (invalid opcode).
42h	DWORD	Interrupt 7 handler address (coprocessor N/A).
46h	DWORD	Interrupt 3Eh handler address (80x87 emulator).
4Ah	DWORD	Interrupt 75h handler address (80x87 error).
4Eh	DWORD	Application compatibility flags. Set by calling: GetProfileInt(modName, Compatibility, zero).
52h	BYTE[0Eh]	Appears to be unused in Windows 3.1.
60h	WORD	Selector to PSP (PDB).
62h	DWORD	DOS Disk Transfer Address (DTA) pointer.
66h	BYTE	Current drive of task + 80h (80 = A:, 81 = B:, etc.).

Table 3-2: Format of a Windows 3.1 Task Database. (continued)

Offset	Type	Description
67h	BYTE[41h]	Current directory of task (see previous field for drive letter). Windows maintains a separate current directory for each task.
A8h	WORD	Set to the initial value of AX in the task as a validity test for the TDB. Does not appear to be actually used, however.
AAh	WORD	hTask of task that should be scheduled next. Set by DirectedYield().
ACh	DWORD	Selector:Offset of referenced DLL list. Before the program calls InitApp(), this segment contains a list of module handles for modules that haven't had their initialization functions called.
B0h	WORD	Code segment alias selector for this task database. Used for MakeProcInstance() thunks.
B2h	WORD	Selector to segment with additional MakeProcInstance() thunks. Contains zero if no segment necessary. Segment has the same format as offsets B2h - F1h.
B4h	WORD	'PT' (5450h) signature for MakeProcInstance thunks.
B6h	WORD	Appears to be unused in Windows 3.1.
B8h	WORD	Next available slot for MakeProcInstance() thunk. Subtract six from this value to get the actual offset where the next thunk will be stored.

BAh	BYTE[38h]	Space for up to seven MakeProcInstance() thunks. If more thunks are needed, they're put in another segment (see offset B2h). Each thunk contains the original parameters to MakeProcInstance():
		`mov ax, hInstance selector`
		`jmp far lpProc`

F2h	BYTE[08h]	Module name for task. No terminating zero character if the module name is eight bytes in length.
FAh	WORD	'TD' (4454h) Task Database signature.
100h	BYTE[100h]	PSP for task. The WORD at offset 60h is a selector that points here (100h bytes into the TDB segment).

A point worth taking away from the above description of the task database is that each running process has both a task database (a Windows data structure) and a PSP/PDB (a DOS data structure). Windows does everything it can to maintain the illusion that each running process is really a DOS program with special capabilities. In a manner of speaking, each Windows process leads a dual life. Part of the time it's a graphical, protected mode program, while other times it's just a run of the mill DOS application, which uses a PSP and runs in real mode to do file I/O. The separate task database and PSP reflect this dual identity. The fact that the PSP sits at the end of the TDB's segment appears to be just a matter of convenience. There doesn't seem to be any reason why the PDB couldn't be in an entirely different segment. Figure 3-1 shows the relationship between a TDB and a PDB.

Figure 3-1: Relationship Between a TDB and a PDB.

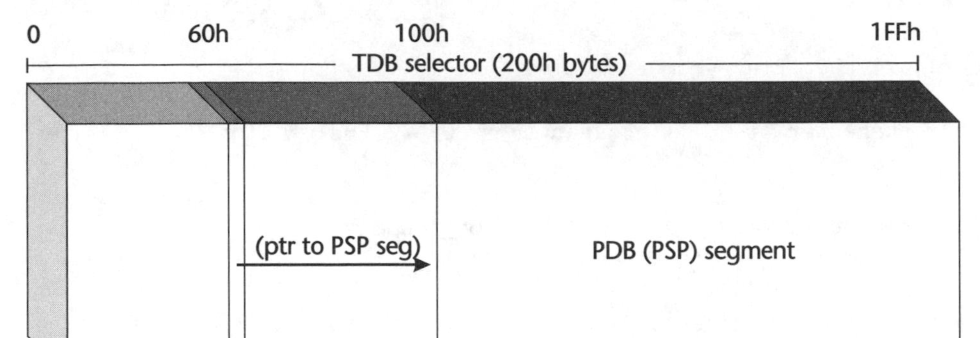

From a File to a Process, in 28 Easy Steps

Now that we're familiar with the two key data structures relating to process management, we can start examining how a new process is created. The Windows API manual looks like a good place to start. WinExec() pops outs initially as the first function worth taking a closer look at. WinExec() expects to be passed a filename and arguments, just as you would type them on a DOS command line. In this respect, it's sort of like the C system() function, in that you just pass it strings. This is much simpler to use than DOS INT 21H, function 4Bh (EXEC), which requires a rather complicated data structure, as well as loading CPU registers with far pointers. Let's look at pseudocode for WinExec:

```
Pseudocode for WinExec() - WINEXEC.OBJ

// Parameters:
//      LPSTR lpCmdLine, int nCmdShow
// Locals:
//      char localCmdLine[0x108] // Local copy of the command line
//      char near *parameters    // start of parameter section in
//                               // localCmdLine buffer
//      BOOL period_found        // Was there a '.' in the name?
//      EXECBLOCK   exec_block   // The standard MS-DOS exec block
//                               // (INT 21h, fn. 4Bh)
//      WORD        cmd_show[2]

    period_found = 0;   // No '.' in the filename so far

    // Start looping through the command line string, looking
```

```
    // for the end of the filename portion.
    while ( 1 )
    {
        get next character from lpCmdLine

        if ( character == ' ' || character == 0) // End of line?
            break

        if ( character == '.' )       // period_found = TRUE
            period_found = character // Why not just set to 1?

        // if we found a directory separator, the period can't be
        // part of the 8.3 filename.
        if ( character is '\' or '/' )
             period_found = 0;

        copy character to next spot in localCmdLine[]
    }

done_with_filename:

    if ( !period_found )    // In case an extension wasn't specified
        add ".EXE" to end of localCmdLine[]

    null terminate the localCmdLine[] string

    parameters = next character after the null terminator
    in localCmdLine[].

    parameters[0] = 0        // provide an "empty" parameter area
    parameters[1] = 0Dh      // in case no params were provided

    if ( command line params were specified in lpCmdLine )
    {
        Copy parameters from lpCmdLine to parameters[].
        Add a 0Dh (linefeed) to the end of parameters[].
        Fix parameters[0] to contain the correct length,
        as required by the DOS EXEC function.
    }

    cmd_show[0] = 2     // Doc for LoadModule() says must be 2
    cmd_show[1] = nCmdShow

    // Set up things like a normal DOS INT 21h, 4B00h call.
    // The difference here is that the first FCB holds the
    // cmd_show info.
```

```
exec_block.envseg = 0           // Use current environment
exec_block.fcb2 = NULL
exec_block.cmdline = &localCmdLine[]
exec_block.fcb1 = &cmd_show

DS:DX = &localCmdLine[]
ES:BX = &exec_block    // Start the program up. This
AX = 4B00H             // INT is trapped and handled by the
INT 21H                // KERNEL INT 21h handler, not DOS
```

WinExec() parses the passed-in command line and breaks it into a filename and, possibly, some arguments. It then goes through the tedious process of setting up everything for a DOS EXEC call; finally WinExec() calls INT 21h. Hmm. We're not much closer to an answer than we were before. We know that when we're not running under Windows, DOS doesn't know anything about Windows files. The error message, "This program requires Microsoft Windows," is all too familiar. Obviously, something is going on behind the scenes, but what?

One of the many roles that Windows plays is that of a DOS extender. A DOS extender is responsible for intercepting interrupt calls that an application might make and doing the correct thing in the protected mode environment. The Windows KERNEL hooks INT 21h. KERNEL has special handlers for certain INT 21h subfunctions, including the EXEC function (4Bh). For the rest of this discussion, we'll assume that the goal is to load a Windows NE file. DOS .EXE, .COM files, and .PIF files require different handling, which unfortunately we don't have the space to cover in this book.

So then, what goes on inside the INT 21h function 4Bh handler in Windows? Basically, the KERNEL handler takes the parameters passed into the registers and invokes the LoadModule() function. We're still not much closer to our goal of finding out how a disk file becomes a running program. If we're going to really understand what goes on, we're going to have to dive into the LoadModule() function (not surprisingly). Time to strap on those air tanks and put on the goggles!

LoadModule

Before diving into the vast chasms of code in LoadModule(), we'd like to first comment on the style of the LoadModule() code. From examining the disassembly listings, it is quite obvious that it's highly optimized assembler code. There doesn't appear to be any consistent structure to the code. There are JMP instructions that traverse hundreds of instructions. Quite a few variables and buffers are used for multiple, unrelated purposes. In Windows 3.0, LoadModule() was one rather gargantuan function. In Windows 3.1, it appears that the 3.0 LoadModule() code was ripped into smaller parts and placed in separate procedures. We say ripped because it doesn't appear to be a well-thought-out rewrite of the code. The new helper procedures do not have their own stack frames, but instead use the stack frame of LoadModule(), which means that LoadModule()'s local variables are also used in the helper procedures. You'll see this reflected in the pseudocode. Another indicator that the code was arbitrarily ripped apart is the use of registers. At various points through the code, heavily used values are stored in registers. Many of the new 3.1 helper procedures must be called with certain values in certain registers and must exit with other values in other registers. If you were to paste together the various 3.1 LoadModule() helper routines into one large routine, you'd notice that the use of register variables at critical points is almost identical to the 3.0 LoadModule() code. This code is probably a nightmare to maintain!

In retrospect, it's not terribly surprising that the LoadModule() code is a mess, at least to the viewer of a disassembly listing. Over the years, LoadModule() has been asked to handle many different situations. OS/2 1.x and Windows share the same executable format. It is certainly possible that at some point, the LoadModule() code was used for both OS/2 and Windows programs. Prior to version 3.0, EMS was heavily used by Windows. This most likely added additional requirements to the code. Windows 3.0 introduced gangload segments (discussed below). As you can see from the pseudocode listings, this one change permeates most of the LoadModule() code and logic. In Windows 3.1, Win32 (PE) executables have to be checked for and handled specially, in order to invoke the Win32s subsystem. On top of all this, LoadModule() is recursive! LoadModule() is responsible not only for loading tasks, but also for loading DLLs. When a new program is loading, any DLLs it uses also have to be loaded before the program can be started. These DLLs may themselves load other DLLs. Nasty! With all the various weird cases and requirements that LoadModule() has, it's a wonder it works at all!

Another subject that should be investigated before examining the pseudocode is the gangload area (also known as the fastload area, probably a name from the marketing types). As mentioned earlier, an NE file stores the individual program segments and resources in various places in the executable. If there are numerous segments and resources that need to be loaded upon startup (if they're PRELOAD), it can take a significant amount of time to seek to and read each of the individual segments and resources. In Windows 3.0, the gangload area was introduced to deal with this problem. When you invoke the resource compiler after linking your program, it searches the executable file and finds all the PRELOAD segments and resources. It then rewrites the executable file, placing all PRELOAD segments and resources into a contiguous region of the file. The executable header is updated to reflect the new position of the segments and resources and to indicate that the file has been gangload optimized. This brings up an important point. Regardless of whether an NE file has a gangload area, it can always be loaded by LoadModule(). The gangload area is simply an optimization. It takes no additional space and can be ignored if desired. If you do not wish for your file to have a gangload area for some reason, you can use the -K switch with the resource compiler.

How does having a gangload area improve the loading time? Fairly early, the LoadModule() code checks for the presence of a gangload area in the file. If it finds one, LoadModule() allocates a HUGE segment that's big enough to hold the gangload area, up to 1Mb in size. LoadModule() then reads in the whole area with one _hread() (huge read) call. When it comes time to load segments or resources, LoadModule() copies the raw bytes out of the gangload memory block, rather than seeking to and reading the data from the NE file. If a failure occurs at any point during preparations for using the gangload area, LoadModule() continues on as normal, reading the information from the file. The gangload area is certainly beneficial, but LoadModule() doesn't consider it a serious error if it fails for some reason.

In addition to the gangload area, another optimization KERNEL performs is to cache the open file handles for the most recently used NE files. The cache is a simple array of structures. Each structure contains a module handle, as well as an open file handle for the module's NE file. The handles for the open files are in the context of the PDB (PSP) that was in effect when Windows started up (the TopPDB global variable). Windows always switches to the TopPDB when loading segments and resources from an NE file. After the initial load of the program, KERNEL can quickly obtain an open file handle for a given NE file by simply passing the module handle to the GetCachedFileHandle() function. If the specified module is not in the cache, GetCachedFileHandle() opens the file and adds it to the cache, bumping another entry if necessary. An example of when the KERNEL might need a file handle after the NE file has been loaded is when a LOADONCALL segment has been touched for the first time and needs to be brought into memory. NE files that were loaded from floppies or other removable media are not cached.

Another important point that needs to be made about LoadModule() is that it executes in the task context of its caller. For instance, LoadModule() is most often called from PROGMAN.EXE, when the user has either double-clicked on an icon or picked the menu item FILE | RUN. In this situation, PROGMAN (or whatever program called WinExec() or LoadModule()) is the current task throughout the whole LoadModule() sequence. When a GP fault occurs, the current task is blamed by the KERNEL and terminated. In Windows 3.0, there was a bug in the gangload code of LoadModule() that caused a GP fault if the gangload area was a multiple of 64K in size. When the GP fault was reported to the user, it indicted PROGMAN as the cause of the fault and terminated PROGMAN. The result was usually a confused programmer or user, who had no idea that there was nothing wrong with PROGMAN or their code.

Now that we've properly introduced the subject we can look at pseudocode for LoadModule(). Note that LoadModule() uses several helper functions. The helper functions, in turn, use other helper functions. In order to present the material in an orderly fashion, there are numerous forward references to other functions. If you come across a function that hasn't been discussed yet, don't panic. It is most likely covered further on in the discussion.

```
Pseudocode for LoadModule - LD.OBJ
// Parameters:
//      LPSTR lpModuleName, LPVOID lpParameterBlock
// Globals:
//      WORD fLMdepth       // Number of nested invocations
// Locals:
//      WORD    file_handle
//      WORD    module_table
//      WORD    ret_value
//      WORD    implicit_link_failure
//      WORD    failure_code
//      WORD    font_flag
//      WORD    exe_flag
//      WORD    gangload_handle
```

```
//      WORD    allocAllSegs_ret
//      WORD    TDB_handle
//      WORD    old_PDB
//      WORD    winoldap_flag
//      WORD    on_hard_drive
//      OFSTRUCT    ofs_buffer      // used as a scratch area
                                    // and as an OFSTRUCT

    Check KERNEL flags to see if WINOLDAP is what is being
    loaded. Set winoldap_flag accordingly. Turn off WINOLDAP
    flag in kernel flags. The WINOLDAP flag is set in KERNEL
    when it recognizes that it needs to load the WINOLDAP module
    to run a DOS program.

    // Keep track of the nesting level of LoadModule() calls
    // This is necessary when there are circularly dependent
    // DLLs. You have to make sure that the DLL reference count
    // doesn't get incremented too many times.
    fLMdepth++

    // Write out some trace diagnostics. See Chapter 1.
    if ( fBooting and fDiagMode )
        write out "LoadStart = <modulename>" string

    // Zero out some of the local variables
    TDB_handle = gangload_handle = exe_flag = 0
    font_flag = failure_code = module_table = 0

    // Some others vars need to be initialized to -1
    old_PDB = file_handle = -1

    // An undocumented use of LoadModule. Instead of passing
    // an LPSTR to a filename, you can pass MK_FP(0, gHandle),
    // where gHandle is a global memory handle. The module
    // handle that owns gHandle is found, and another instance
    // of the module is started.
    if ( HIWORD(lpModuleName) == 0 )
    {
        // GetExePtr() takes a global handle, and returns
        // the module handle it's associated with
        if ( GetExePtr( LOWORD(lpModuleName) ) )
            goto module_already_loaded
        else
        {
            AX = 2  // File not found
            goto LoadModule_done
        }
    }
```

```
    // Determine if there's already an instance of the module in
    // memory. LMAlreadyLoaded() returns AX = previous module
    // handle if it's loaded, and < 32 if not.
    if ( LMAlreadyLoaded(lpModuleName) < 32 )
        goto module_not_loaded

module_already_loaded:

    // Start up another instance of a previously loaded module
    // returns with AX == instance handle or error code
    LMPrevInstance()
    goto LoadModule_done

module_not_loaded:

    // Attempts to open the exe/dll file. Sets "file_handle"
    // if successful, returns "file not found" if not.
    if ( LMLoadExeFile() < 32 )
        goto LoadModule_done

    // Create a module table from the "New EXE" header in
    // the exe/dll file. Also loads the "gangload" segments
    if ( LoadExeHeader() < 32 )
        goto LoadModule_done

    // Do some sanity checks on the header to see if everything
    // is legal and valid. If so, create the data
    // structures necessary for a new task to be added.
    if ( LMCheckHeader() < 32 )
        goto LoadModule_done

    // Allocate the segment selectors for the module, although the
    // segments are not actually read in yet. Also looks for
    // links to modules that require special handling.
    if ( LMRamNMods() < 32 )
        goto LoadModule_done

    // Load any imported libraries the module might need.
    // The startup routines for the libraries are not called yet.
    // LoadLibrary() can be called in LMImports(), causing
    // LoadModule() to become recursive ( LoadLibrary() calls
    // LoadModule() )
    if ( LMImports() < 32 )
        goto LoadModule_done
```

```
    // Load the segments for the module, and perform relocations
    if ( LMSegs() < 32 )
        goto LoadModule_done

    // Load any necessary resources, and start running
    // the module if it's a task (not a DLL).
    LMLetsGo()

LoadModule_done:    // When we get here, AX contains the error
                    // code that will be returned

    // Cleans up things, such as deallocating the gangload_handle,
    // destroying the TDB if was allocated but something failed
    // later on, etc.
    LMCleanUp()

    return to caller

    // When any of the Abort_x labels are called, AX contains the
    // error code that will be returned to the caller.
Abort_1:

    if ( flMdepth == 1 )            // Decrement usage count for
        DecExeUsage(module_table)   // this module, modules that
                                    // refer to this module

Abort_2:

    My_lclose(file_handle)      // We don't need this file
                                // handle anymore!
    push module_table.ne_flags

    DelModule(module_table)     // Remove this module from memory

    module_table = 0

    pop module_table.ne_flags value off the stack

Abort_3:
    if ( module_table.ne_flags indicate module was a DLL )
        goto Abort_4

    if ( Old_PDB )          // Restore PSP variables to their
    {                       // initial values.
        Win_PDB = OldPDB
        Old_PDB = -1
    }
```

```
    CloseApplEnv()  // Clean up unsuccessful load.

Abort_4:
    return failure_code to caller
```

Although the Windows SDK doesn't mention it, LoadModule() is responsible for loading *all* modules in the system, not just programs. The LoadLibrary() function uses LoadModule() to load DLLs by passing it -1L as the pointer to the parameter block. Throughout LoadModule() and its helper functions, the value of -1L for lpParameterBlock is used to test whether LoadModule() is loading a EXE or a DLL.

Another undocumented use of LoadModule() is to pass it a module name pointer, with 0 in the high WORD and an instance handle in the low WORD; for example, MK_FP(0, hInstance). LoadModule() maps the instance handle back to its module handle and then loads another instance of the module. This functionality does not appear to be used in either the KERNEL or USER modules, so it may be dead code from a previous version of Windows. On the other hand, the KERNEL bootstrap routines (Chapter 1) use stripped down versions of the LoadModule() function. In that code, the KERNEL module is created from the memory image of the file, rather than by reading it in from the file.

The first order of business in LoadModule() is to determine if the application being loaded is WINOLDAP. WINOLDAP is the Windows program responsible for running DOS applications under Windows. Starting with the INT 21h, function 4Bh handler in KERNEL, and throughout all of the module loading code, WINOLDAP is treated as a special case. The WINOA386.MOD file has multiple data segments, which ordinarily would limit the program to one executing instance. WINOA386.MOD is handled specially however, and allowed to run multiple times.

Next, LoadModule() increments the global variable fLMdepth. This variable is used to keep track of how many levels of recursion LoadModule() is currently in. Ordinarily, the value of fLMdepth is 0. When LoadModule() is called to load a program, it increments this value to 1. If the program has implicitly linked libraries, LoadModule() will be recursively called, and fLMdepth increases to 2 or more. Interestingly, in many spots in the code, the value of fLMdepth is saved on the stack, and then fLMdepth is set to 0 before calling a function. Afterwards, fLMdepth is restored off the stack. It's a miracle the code works at all with all these hijinks going on.

After finishing the obligatory startup and special case code, LoadModule() calls LMAlreadyLoaded() to determine if the module is already loaded in the system. If it is, LoadModule() calls LMPrevInstance() to either start up a new instance of a program or increment the usage count of a DLL. We'll come back to the case where the module already exists later. For know, we're going to concentrate on the more interesting mechanics of creating a new module from a disk image.

The first step in creating a new module is to make sure you have an appropriate file to build from. The LoadExeHeader() function performs several tests on the file to verify that it really is an NE file. This is where many of the error codes for LoadModule(), such as the warning for a still-compressed file, are detected. If the file passes all the tests, LoadExeHeader() loads the file's header section and some of its tables into memory and synthesizes a module table out of the raw data. An important step in this process involves iterating through the segment table, modifying any attributes of segments that weren't set properly when the file was linked. If the file has a gangload area, this is where it's detected and loaded.

Having built the module table, LoadModule() now calls LMCheckHeader(). The name LMCheckHeader is a bit of a misnomer. Although some validity testing does occur, the most important thing that LMCheckHeader() does is call the helper functions that ultimately create the task database for the new program (see the CreateTask() description). If the loading module is a DLL rather than an EXE, LMCheckHeader() performs the validity testing, but creates no TDB. That one little bit in the module database sure makes a lot of difference!

Once the module table and task database are in place, the next step in loading a module is to bring in the code and data needed to give the module the smashing send-off it truly deserves. LMRamNMods() (what a pain to type!) first adds the module table to the linked list of modules described earlier. It then loops through all of the segments in the segment table, allocating appropriate selectors, and storing them in the selector field of each segment table entry. Based upon their GMEM_XXX attributes, some segments have memory allocated for them at this same time, while others only get a selector without any associated memory. No data is read in by LMRamNMods(). That job goes to the LMSegs() routine. LMSegs() coordinates the actions of allocating memory for the segments, where necessary, bringing in the segment's data, and applying any relocations. If the module's gangload area was successfully loaded, the data for the segments is copied out of the in-memory gangload area, rather than reading the data from the file.

In between allocating space for the segments in LMRamNMods() and bringing in the data for the segments in LMSegs(), LMImports brings any DLLs referenced by the loading module into memory. LMImports() examines the module references in the newly created module table. If any DLLs are needed but not yet loaded, LMImports() calls LoadLibrary() to load them. Since LoadLibrary() is just a wrapper around a call to LoadModule(), the obvious implication, as mentioned previously, is that LoadModule() is a recursive function.

After all the referenced DLLs have been loaded and all the PRELOAD segments of the primary module are in place, the preparatory work is pretty much done. It's now time to pop the cork and launch the newly created module to fulfill its destiny as a new member of the community of Windows modules. This honor goes to LMLetsGo(). Inside LMLetsGo(), any PRELOAD resources are brought into memory. If the module is for a task, the initial register values for the task, including the starting CS:IP, are set up on the stack; and the new task is started up by yielding to it through DirectedYield(). A more detailed description of this procedure comes later, so don't worry just yet. If the loading module is a DLL, and unless the DLL is being loaded implicitly by a new task, LMLetsGo() causes the module's initialization routine to be called. Again, a more detailed description comes later.

Any successful launching party involves a cleanup afterwards. LoadModule() is no exception. This janitorial work falls to LMCleanUp(). If a gangload area was allocated, it's freed up now. If the module was loaded from a floppy disk, its file handle is closed. It doesn't make sense to keep an open file handle for something that might change at any time. If the loading of the module was aborted for some reason, LMCleanUp() closes the NE file and frees up the task database segment.

The LOADMODULE Helper Routines

You've now seen, from a fairly high vantage point, what happens when a new module is brought into the system. While high level overviews are nice, it's also important to understand the details. To enhance our understanding of the module and task creation processes, we now dig down into the helper routines. These routines appear roughly in the order discussed in the previous section.

LMAlreadyLoaded()

LMAlreadyLoaded() determines if a module is already present in memory, and if it is, LMAlreadyLoaded() returns its module handle. If the asked-for module name contains an .EXE or .FON extension, LMAlreadyLoaded() sets one of two flags used by other helper routines. To determine if a module is already present in the system, it makes two passes through the module list. The first pass is performed by FindExeFile(), which takes the passed-in base filename and extension (for example, MYPROG.EXE) and compares it to the base filename and extension of every module in the system (for example, USER.EXE). As noted earlier, the complete path and filename for every module's NE file is stored in the module table. If no matches are found, LMAlreadyLoaded() calls FindExeInfo() to make a second pass through the module list. FindExeInfo() takes just the passed in base filename (C:\MYPROG.EXE becomes MYPROG) and compares it to the module name of every loaded module (the module name corresponds to entry 0 in the resident names table; see offset 26h in Table 3-1).

The implications of this search are not always obvious and have bitten more than a few Windows programmers. One assumption LMAlreadyLoaded() makes is that the module name, specified by the NAME or LIBRARY field in the DEF file, is the same as the base filename of the executable file. Microsoft itself violates that assumption, with the KERNEL module having filenames of KRNL286.EXE and KRNL386.EXE. Other examples are the various device drivers (VGA.DRV has a module name of DISPLAY). It's somewhat surprising that the LoadModule() code doesn't extract the module name from the NE file and compare it to entry zero in the resident names table of the loaded modules.

Another assumption in LMAlreadyLoaded() is that you never have two different EXE or DLL files with the same filename, but in different directories. Try this simple experiment. Find a Windows program in a directory other than the main Windows directory. Make a copy of this executable file and name the copy CALC.EXE. Run the regular Windows CALC by clicking on its icon. From the Program Manager, type in the full pathname to the copy of the program that you named CALC.EXE. You end up with two copies of the Windows CALC. When you invoked your dummy CALC.EXE, LMAlreadyLoaded() determined that CALC was already loaded, and so another copy of the Windows CALC was started, rather than your dummy CALC.EXE.

Next, shut down your renamed program and the Windows CALC, thereby removing the CALC module from memory. Now from the PROGMAN RUN menu, type in the complete path to your renamed program. It will run the correct program, even though its name was changed to CALC.EXE.

Obviously, Microsoft is hoping that no two EXEs or DLLs end up with the same name. The odds of this are pretty slim, given the success of Windows. In addition, there are a limited number of useful eight-byte names, many of which are already taken by existing programs and DLLs. Many a programmer has spent frustrating hours while they figured out that you can't have an EXE and a DLL with the same base filename (like PLAY.EXE and PLAY.DLL). Similarly, SHELL.EXE is a perfectly nice name for a program in Windows 3.0, but it can't be used in Windows 3.1, where there's a SHELL.DLL.

```
Pseudocode for LMAlreadyLoaded() - LD.OBJ

// Determines if the module specified by lpModuleName already
// exists in the system. Shares its locals with LoadModule()
// (it uses the same stack frame). If the module already is
// loaded, returns the module handle, 0 otherwise

    // Check for zero length strings
    if ( strlen( lpModuleName ) == 0 )
        return 2    // File not found

    Extract the base filename and extension from lpModuleName,
    and uppercase it (i.e., "c:\work\test.exe" -> "TEST.EXE").
    Store the extracted string in ofs_buffer.

    // See if the file is a font file. Normally, Windows 3.x
    // will refuse to work with Windows 2.x files that haven't
    // been MARK'ed as O.K. to run in 3.0. However, it's a
    // fairly safe assumption that a font file won't have code
    // segments that won't run in protected mode. Thus, we'll
    // make a special exception, and load these files.
    if ( filename extension in ofs_buffer == ".FON" )
        font_flag = TRUE    // actually set to whatever BP is

    if ( filename extension in ofs_buffer == ".EXE" )
        exe_flag = TRUE     // actually set to whatever BP is

    // FindExeFile() iterates through each module in the module
    // table list. It compares the base filename.ext of each
    // module with the passed in base filename.ext. If a match
    // is found, it returns the matching module handle,
    // 0 otherwise.
    if ( FindExeFile(ofs_buffer) != 0 )
        return AX   // AX = already loaded module handle

    // FindExeInfo() iterates through each module in the module
    // table list. It compares the module name of each module
    // (entry 0 in the resident names table), with the base
    // filename (no extension) passed to it. If a match is
    // found, it returns the found module handle, 0 otherwise.
```

```
    // The difference between FindExeFile(), and FindExeInfo()
    // is that one compares the filenames, while the other
    // compares the module names (the NAME/LIBRARY field in the
    // .DEF file).
    return FindExeInfo()
```

LMLoadExeFile()

LMLoadExeFile() is responsible for opening the NE file for subsequent reading by other helper routines. It first switches the Windows PDB (or PSP, if you prefer) to the PSP that was in effect when Windows started up (TopPDB). It next creates the flags used to open the file. If the file is for a DLL, LMLoadExeFile() sets OF_CANCEL and OF_PROMPT in the Open-Field() flags. If SetErrorMode() has been called to disable prompting for the file, the OF_PROMPT flag is not set, however. A third, unknown flag (value 0x0080) is also turned on in the open-file flags. Once the open file flags are set up, MyOpenFile() opens the file. MyOpenFile() is a wrapper function around the OpenFile() function.

```
Pseudocode for LMLoadExeFile() - LD.OBJ

// Locals:
//      WORD    openFile_flags

    old_PDB = Win_PDB
    Win_PDB = topPDB          // topPDB = PDB of KERNEL when loaded
                              // by the DOS loader
    openFile_flags = 0

    // Set flags so that if a DLL isn't found, it's prompted
    // for. If an EXE can't be found, don't prompt for it
    // See also: SetErrorMode() in WINDOWS.H
    if ( !exe_flag )
    {
        openFile_flags = OF_CANCEL
        if (SEM_NOOPENFILEERRORBOX bit not set in TDB_ErrMode)
            openFile_flag = OF_CANCEL | OF_PROMPT
    }

    openFile_flags |= 0x0080    // ???

    file_handle = MyOpenFile(lpModuleName, &ofs_buffer, openFile_flags)

    on_hard_drive = ofs_buffer.fFixedDisk

    if ( file_handle != - 1 )
        return 0    // Success
    else
        return 2    // File not found
```

LoadExeHeader()

As the name implies, LoadExeHeader() is responsible for bringing the NE header in from the disk and creating a module table. The first step in creating a module table is to ensure that the file being loaded really is a Windows NE file. Since every NE file has an old style DOS header, LoadExeHeader() checks the first two bytes of the file for the 'MZ' signature. If the signature is not there, LoadExeHeader() looks for the signature of a Windows compressed file. If it finds this signature ('SZDD'), the function returns the "compressed file" error code. (You need to run EXPAND.EXE before executing the file.) Otherwise, LoadExeHeader() returns the "invalid EXE" error code. What's interesting is that LoadExeHeader() completely ignores the WORD at offset 18h in the file. According to all Microsoft documentation, this WORD must contain 40h to be a valid NE file; the 3.1 SDK says it must be 40h or greater. The Microsoft Excel 3.0 EXCEL.EXE file contains the value 1Eh at offset 18h, yet Windows still loads it without a complaint.

Having established that the file is at least a DOS executable, the next step is to find and read the NE header, verifying its presence by the 'NE' signature in the first two bytes. If LoadExeHeader() finds a 'PE' signature for a so-called Portable Executable, instead of the expected 'NE' signature, the file is a Win32 application, and LoadExeHeader() returns an appropriate error code. The KERNEL INT 21h handler that called LoadModule() checks for this specific return value; if it sees this value, the handler loads the Win32s subsystem, if present, to run the program as a Win32s application. More on this later.

Since the size and format of some of the NE file tables are different in memory than on disk, a fairly lengthy sequence of code calculates the size that the module table needs to be, in order to accommodate them all. Tables that are different include the segment table, where entries go from eight bytes on disk to ten bytes in memory, and the entry table, which trades compactness on disk, for ease of look-up in memory. In addition, an OFSTRUCT, used to access the file, contains the complete pathname to the executable, and adds to the size of the module table. When all the calculations are completed, LoadExeHeader() calls GlobalAlloc() to allocate the memory for the module table.

Once LoadExeHeader() has the selector for the new module table, it reads the disk image of the NE header and certain tables into memory. The strange thing is that the data is not read in starting at offset zero, but is instead read into the middle of the segment. We'll come back to this in a moment.

Using the copy of the NE header in memory, LoadExeHeader() checks to see if it should abort the load because either the "errors in image" flag is set, or the linker version number is less than 4. The first version of the Microsoft linker to produce NE files had a version number of four, so this is a form of sanity checking. LoadExeHeader() then examines the operating system field and returns error codes if the field doesn't contain an acceptable value. Surprisingly, if the NE file is an OS/2 1.X file, and if the "Windows 2.x application runs in 3.x protected mode" flag is set, the Windows loader accepts the file as a *Windows* NE file. This hidden capability is not documented anywhere, nor are there any known OS/2 1.X files that meet the criteria. It appears that Microsoft may have been experimenting with running OS/2 programs under Windows, but that it never came to fruition.

Once the module header has been validated, LoadExeHeader() copies the NE header (read in previously) to the beginning of the module table. Immediately after the NE header portion (40h bytes) comes the segment table. The segment table is an array of ten-byte entries, each entry corresponding to one segment in the NE file. The first eight bytes of each segment entry are copied from the eight-byte segment entries which were stored in the NE file and read in previously. When copying the flags WORD of a segment entry, the MOVEABLE bit is turned on if the module is an executable module as opposed to a DLL module. Since Windows 3.1 only runs in protected mode, there's no need for applications to have FIXED segments, unless you're mucking about with CODE or DATA aliases, or with interrupt handlers, which need to be in pagelocked memory. If a segment's data gets moved in memory, the Local Descriptor Table is updated to reflect this, and the application is none the wiser. The last two bytes of each segment entry are initialized to zero. The global memory handle allocated to hold the segment's data will be stored in those bytes later.

With the NE header and segment table portions of the module table completed, LoadExeHeader() makes a temporary detour to find and read in the gangload area. The Windows 3.1 SDK documentation refers to the gangload area as the fast-load area; they are one and the same thing. LoadExeHeader() first checks to see if the file has a gangload area. If one is present and it is less than 1Mb in size, LoadExeHeader() calls GlobalAlloc() to obtain a huge segment. If the allocation request succeeds, the undocumented _hread() function reads in the block. Later on in the LoadModule() call, segments and resources will be copied out of this memory block, rather than read from the NE file. If for some reason, an error occurs during the processing of the gangload area, the loading of the module is *not* affected. The gangload area can speed things up, but it is definitely not required.

With the temporary gangload area diversion out of the way, LoadExeHeader() resumes processing the remainder of the raw data in the middle of the module table, working from lower offsets to higher offsets. The result of this processing is copied to the start of the module table with lower offsets near the beginning and higher offsets further up in memory. The processing builds towards higher addresses. At some point, the finished version of the module table starts overwriting the beginning of the raw portion, but everything works out OK in the end. It's a cute optimization, but it wreaks havoc on those trying to figure out what the code does. This was probably not a concern of Microsoft's programmers when the code was written. The code may have been written during the days of real mode Windows, where every byte counted.

After all the tables are copied, LoadExeHeader() fills in the remaining fields in the module table's NE header with appropriate values. For instance, this is where the complete filename of the NE file is copied into the module table.

Near the end of LoadExeHeader(), the function iterates through the segment table again, with the intention of fixing any segment flags that might have been set incorrectly by the careless or unknowing programmer. (Gee, a KERNEL that knows what's good for you. Just like Mom!) All code segments that are MOVEABLE and NONDISCARDABLE have their PRELOAD flags turned on. Any FIXED CODE segment has its PRELOAD flag turned on as well, unless Windows is still in the process of booting. Finally, all data segments are forced to be NONDISCARDABLE, and their PRELOAD flag is turned on. While it might seem that almost every segment is now PRELOAD, this is usually not the case. A well-written program has its code segments marked as MOVEABLE and DISCARDABLE. LoadExeHeader() doesn't add the PRELOAD attribute to these segments.

```
Pseudocode for LoadExeHeader() - LDHEADER.OBJ

// Returns AX = module_table, BX = gangload_handle

    Read in old style .EXE header. Verify read was successful

    if ( 'MZ' signature found )
        goto old_header_ok

    // Check for compressed files, in case they accidentally
    // weren't decompressed when they installed the program.
    if ( compressed file signature found, i.e., "SZDD...." )
    {
        AX = 19     // compressed file
        goto LoadExeHeader_cleanup
    }
    else
        goto invalid_exe

old_header_ok:

    if ( oldheader.new_exe_offset == 0 )
        goto invalid_exe

    Seek to the start of the "new exe" portion of the file, and
    read in the 'NE' header (40h bytes) into a spot on the stack.

    if (seek or read failed)
        goto invalid_exe

    if ( 'NE' signature found in header )
        goto have_new_exe_header

    if ( 'PE' signature found in header )
    {
        AX = 21     // Win32s extensions required
        goto LoadExeHeader_cleanup
    }

invalid_exe:

    AX = 11     // Invalid exe
    goto LoadExeHeader_cleanup
```

```
have_new_exe_header:

    Calculate the size of the new module table. This includes:
        - The new exe header from the file
        - The entry table (larger in memory than on disk)
        - 10 byte segment table entries (only 8 bytes on disk)
        - The OFSTRUCT, including the exe/dll filename

    GlobalAlloc() a piece of memory big enough to hold the
    calculated size of the module table. The flags are:
    ( GMEM_ZEROINIT  | GMEM_MOVEABLE )

    if ( GlobalAlloc() fails )
        goto invalid_exe_2

    GlobalLock()/GlobalUnlock() the module table handle to get
    a selector

    // At this point, we have a copy of the new exe header on
    // the stack, and an allocated segment that the module table
    // will be built in. In order to minimize disk reads, the
    // new exe header, and other sections of the exe file will
    // be read into the middle of the allocated segment. Then,
    // this "raw" data is processed and copied to the beginning
    // of the segment. The end result is a new module table.

    copy new exe header from the stack image into upper portion of new module table

    Read in the rest of the in-memory portions of the file into
    the upper portion of the module table. This includes the:
        Segment table
        Resource table
        Resident names table
        Module reference table
        Imported names table
        Entry table

    if ( successfully read in resident portions of file )
        goto test_new_exe_header

invalid_exe_2:
    AX = 11      // Invalid exe error code

free_module_table:
```

```
    // Control comes here if the module can't be loaded for
    // whatever reason. AX holds the error code that will
    // be returned to the LoadModule() caller.
    GlobalFree() the allocated module table, preserving the
    error code in AX

    goto LoadExeHeader_cleanup

test_new_exe_header:

    // The following section of code "checks out" the values in
    // the 'NE' header portion of the file. If something doesn't
    // look right, LoadExeHeader() returns an error code that
    // eventually is returned by LoadModule() or WinExec().
    // The following tests are performed:
    //
    // Is the "errors in image" flag set?  Abort if so.
    // Is the linker version number less than '4'?  Abort if so.
    // Is the file a Windows or NE_UNKNOWN file?  Continue if so.
    // Is the file an OS/2 file? (Having a particular bit set
    //     tells Windows to try and load the file anyhow)
    // Is the file a "European DOS 4" file? (an OEM version
    //     with limited multitasking abilities). Abort if so.
    // Is the OS type of the file none of the above? Abort if so.
    if ( "errors in image" flag set in module table )
        goto invalid_exe_2

    if ( linker_version in module_table < 4 )
        goto invalid_exe_2

    Turn off "protected mode required" flag in module_table

    // Windows 1.X files were NE_UNKNOWN, so we can't just
    // punt if the OS type isn't NE_WINDOWS. Isn't backwards
    // compatibility great???
    if ( exetype in module table == NE_UNKNOWN or NE_WINDOWS )
        goto windows_exe

    if ( exetype in module table == NE_OS2 )
    {
        // Apparently this means certain OS/2 apps can be
        // run under Windows.
        if ( "2.X app runs in 3.X protected mode" flag is set )
        {
            Turn off "self-loading application" flags in module
            flags. Turn on "protected mode required" flag in
            module table
```

```
            // The "expected OS version" field is going to be
            // out of whack if we're loading an OS/2 module.
            // We'll call it a 3.0 compatible module, and hope
            // for the best.
            module_table.expected_winver = 3.0

            goto windows_exe     // Continue on as if this were
                                 // a normal Windows module.
        }
        else
        {
            AX = 12   // Normal OS/2 app. Can't run it. Sorry!
            goto free_module_table
        }
    }
    else if ( exetype in module table == NE_DOS4 )
    {
        AX = 13     // European DOS 4 app
        goto free_module_table
    }
    else
    {
        AX = 14     // Unknown application type
        goto free_module_table
    }

windows_exe:

    Copy the 'NE' header from its position on the stack to offset
    0 of the module table.

    if ( module has no segments )   // A resource .DLL
        goto do_gangload

    Build the segment table in the low end of the module. The
    8 byte disk segment entries are transformed into 10 byte
    versions, with the last WORD being the handle for the
    segment. Several internal flags are twiddled in the flags
    field of the segment record. All segments not in a DLL are
    marked as MOVEABLE, regardless of their flags in the 'NE'
    file. See Chapter 2 for more information on FIXED vs.
    MOVEABLE segment issues.

do_gangload:
```

```
    if ( gangload bit not set in "other flags" of module_table )
        goto gangload_done

    if ( gangload_start offset == 0 )
        goto gangload_done

    calculate the starting offset in the file of the gangload
    area, as well as its length

    // Huge memory blocks can't exceed 1Mb in length
    if ( gangload length > 1Mb)
        goto gangload_done

    GlobalAlloc() space for the gangload area to be read into
    if ( GlobalAlloc() fails )
        goto gangload_done

    GlobalLock() the gangload memory

    Seek to the start of the gangload area, and _hread() it into
    the allocated block

    if ( read of gangload area was successful )
        goto gangload_done

gangload_read_failed:

    GlobalUnlock()/GlobalFree() the allocated gangload area

gangload_done:

    Start creating the new module table by processing the raw
    information in the upper portion of the module table, and
    storing the finished product in the lower portion (offset 0).
    The segments table was built previously.

    copy the resource table to final position in module_table

    copy the resident names table to final position in
    the module_table

    upper-case the module name (the 0'th entry in the resident
    names table). This is why the NAME or LIBRARY field in your
    .DEF file should always be uppercased. In Windows 3.0, not
    doing this could cause a DLL to be loaded, but to not be
    unloaded later on.
```

```
copy the module reference table to final position in
module_table

copy the imported names table to final position in
module_table

Build the entry table. The in-memory form is substantially
different than the table on disk. See the beginning of
the chapter for its in-memory format, and the Windows 3.1
SDK for its NE file format.

if ( linker version in module_table < 5 )
    rework the resource table   // Reason: Unknown

module_table.next_module = module_table.usage = 0

copy the filename into module table

set module_table.ne_autodata to point at the segment entry
of the automatic data segment (DGROUP)

if ( module_table.expected_winver == 0 )
    module_table.expected_winver = 2.01

// Abort if an app that requires a newer version of Windows
// is trying to load on this version.
if ( module_table.expected_winver > current version )
{
    GlobalFree() the module table
    goto LoadExeHeader_cleanup
}

Iterate through the segment table, applying these rules:
    - If (MOVEABLE and NONDISCARDABLE) CODE segment
        set to PRELOAD
    - If FIXED CODE segment    // Should only happen in DLLs
        set to PRELOAD (except at boot time)
    - if DATA segment
        set to NONDISCARDABLE and PRELOAD.

Set the entry point code segment to PRELOAD
Set the DGROUP segment to PRELOAD
// Note that MOVEABLE/DISCARDABLE segments aren't
// set to PRELOAD.
```

```
    if ( not a DLL )
        Make sure stack size in module_table is at least 5K

    if ( heapsize != 0 )    // Allow for programs with no heap
    {
        if ( heapsize in module table < 100 )
            heapsize = 100  // slightly more in debug version
    }

    FarSetOwner()   // Set owner of module_table to be itself

LoadExeHeader_cleanup:
    // When we reach here, AX contains the return value

    GlobalUnlock() the gangload block if necessary

    if ( a segment that should have been PRELOAD wasn't marked
        as such)
    {
        GlobalFree() the gangload area  // Don't use it
        gangload_handle = 0
    }

    if ( AX < 32 )      // AX < 32 is an error code
        GlobalFree() the gangload area  // Doesn't appear to
                                        // zero out the
                                        // gangload_handle here

    return AX   //  BX contains handle of gangload block
```

LMCheckHeader()

LMCheckHeader() performs some additional tests beyond those in LoadExeHeader() to make sure that there's smooth sailing ahead for the module. The first test determines if the module was originally written for Windows 2.x, but doesn't have the "OK to run in Windows 3.x protected mode" flag set. If a 2.x application is tested and found to run successfully in Windows 3.x protected mode, use MARK.EXE from the Windows SDK to set a flag in the NE file. This flag indicates that it's OK to run this application in Windows 3.x. If the flag isn't set, a dialog box pops up, warning the user of this potential problem and asking whether to proceed anyway, at the user's own risk. If the file is a Windows 2.x font file, this step is skipped. The likely assumption is that fonts don't have any protected mode sensitive code, so it's OK to use them.

Another test LMCheckHeader() performs is to make sure there are enough "free system resources." LMCheckHeap() is a very simple function that just calls GetFreeSystemResources(0) and returns 0 if there is less than ten percent available. This test is ultimately responsible for the dreaded PROGMAN error, "Insufficient memory to run this application. Quit one or more Windows applications and then try again." *Undocumented Windows* discusses various aspects of the infamous free system resources.

Last, if the module is for an executable file, LMCheckHeader() calls OpenApplEnv() to handle the details of creating a new task database.

```
Pseudocode for LMCheckHeader() - LD.OBJ

    module_table = AX       // These 2 registers set by LoadExeHeader
    gangload_handle = BX

    if ( module_table.expected_winver < 3.0 )
        if ( "3.X protected mode compatible" flag not set )
            if ( not font_flag )
                if ( WarnRealMode() == IDCANCEL ) // Ask user if OK to proceed.
                    return 15   // Attempt to load real mode app

    if ( module_table is for an EXE )
    {
        // if lpParameterBlock == -1, the loading module
        // is a DLL
        if ( lpParameterBlock != -1 )
            goto LMCheckHeader_application
        else
            return 5 // The module_table flags are indicating
                     // that it's an .EXE, but lpParameterBlock
                     // is -1, which it can only be for a DLL;
                     //  5 is the "can't link to task" error
    }
    else                // Module is a DLL
        return  33  // First non-error return value?

    // Execution won't continue past this point for DLL modules

LMCheckHeader_application:

   // Make sure at least 10% free system resources
    if ( LMCheckHeap() == 0 )
        goto Abort_2    // In LoadModule() code

    // Calls CreateTask() to create the TDB, and allocates a
    // segment to store the hModules of the DLLs that will
    // need to be initialized when the program starts.
    if ( OpenApplEnv() == 0 )
        goto Abort_2    // In LoadModule() code
    else
        return AX from OpenApplEnv() call
```

OpenApplEnv()

OpenApplEnv() calls CreateTask() to allocate and initialize the Task Database segment. In addition, it creates a segment that contains the module handles of all the DLLs that the loading executable module brought into memory. Modules that were already present in memory are not added to the list. When the new application calls InitTask() in its startup code, it causes the module handles in this segment to be iterated through and their startup routines to be called. The code was originally written this way because back in the bad old days of real mode code, the DLL startup routines had to execute in the EMS bank of the application being loaded. Therefore, their initialization routines couldn't be called until the new task was completely done loading and bank switched into memory. This is no longer true, but it hangs around as interesting historical baggage in Windows; it might come in handy again some day if Windows switches over to giving each task its own address space.

```
Pseudocode for OpenApplEnv() - LD.OBJ

// Locals:
//      WORD    return_value
//      WORD    initseg_handle, initseg_selector

    if( (return_value = CreateTask()) == 0 )
        return 0;

    if ( not booting )
    {
        initseg_handle = GlobalAlloc(2048)
        initseg_selector = GlobalLock(initseg_handle)

        loadTDB.LibInitSeg = initseg_selector;
        loadTDB.LibInitOff = 10h

        *(WORD far*)MK_FP(initseg_selector, OxA) = 0x12
    }

    return return_value
```

CreateTask()

CreateTask() is one busy function! Its first duty is to calculate how big the Task Database segment should be. Once the size has been determined, it allocates memory for the segment with GlobalDosAlloc(). Why GlobalDosAlloc() instead of regular old GlobalAlloc()? A good question. GlobalDosAlloc() allocates memory below 1Mb in the linear address space. That means that real mode DOS, which Windows sits on top of, can access the same memory. Why is this important? The second half of the TDB (offsets 0100h to 1FFh) is actually a DOS Program Segment Prefix (PSP). (Remember, a PSP is often called a PDB in Windows terminology.) The PSP contains the Disk Transfer Area (DTA), which DOS uses for certain file I/O services. It's essential that real mode DOS be able to access that memory, thus, the requirement that the memory be below 1Mb in the linear address space. In addition, DOS services are used to fill in the current drive and directory fields in the TDB (offsets 66h and 67h), so the same argument applies there as well. Because each task requires at least 200h of memory below 1Mb, it's a good idea to keep your own use of GlobalDosAlloc() to a minimum. Eating up memory below 1Mb can make it impossible to create more tasks, even if there's plenty of free memory elsewhere. Figure 3-1 shows the relationship between a TDB and a PDB.

After allocating the TDB segment, the next major step is to set up the PSP (or PDB if you prefer). CreateTask() allocates a selector using AllocSelector() and sets its base address to the start of the PDB, 100h bytes into the TDB segment. Then, BuildPDB() fills in the fields of the PDB. The rest of the CreateTask() routine involves filling in the various fields of the TDB, including the MakeProcInstance() thunk area.

```
Pseudocode for CreateTask() - TASK.OBJ
// Parameters:
//      LPVOID  lpParameterBlock
//      WORD    module_table
//      WORD    hPreviousInstance
//      WORD    winoldap_flag
// Locals:
//      WORD    environment_segment
//      WORD    tdb_alloc_size
//      WORD    TDB
//      WORD    pdb_alias

    environment_segment = 0

    if ( FP_SEG(lpParameterBlock) != 0 )   //Was an environment specified?
    {
        // Returns environment seg in AX
        Pass_Environment(module_table, lpParameterBlock)

        environment_segment = AX

        tdb_alloc_size = 100h   // 100h = size of the PDB

        // DOS applications can have command lines greater than
        // 127 characters. Windows apps can't. *Sigh*
        if ( winoldap_flag )
        {
            if ( length of command line > 127 )
                bump up tdb_alloc_size by the additional bytes
                beyond 127, and then round up to the nearest
                paragraph boundary.
        }
    }
```

```
    // In most cases, the TDB segment is 200h bytes. However,
    // in the case of an unusually long command line (above),
    // the TDB segment can be larger.
    tdb_alloc_size += 100h      // 100h = sizeof the TDB
    round tdb_alloc_size up to a multiple of 16

    // Allocate the TDB below 1Mb, so that it can be accessed by DOS
    // for file I/O
    TDB = GlobalDosAlloc(tdb_alloc_size)
    Zero out TDB's segment

    FarSetOwner(TDB,TDB)    // Set owner of this TDB to itself

    if ( winoldap_flag )                    // Not the same thing
        set TDBF_WINOLDAP flag in TDB       // as the PDB flag
                                            // at offset 48h

    if ( lpParameterBlock == 0 )
        goto CreateTask_a

    if ( task is protected mode only (from module_table flags) )
        set some bits in TDB_flags and TDB_ErrMode

    pdb_alias = AllocSelector()
    call LongPtrAdd() to point pdb_alias to the start of the PDB
    inside the TDB segment. For LongPtrAdd(), see "Undocumented
    Windows," Chapter 5.

    BuildPDB()      // Set up the fields for the PDB

    copy first FCB from lpParameterBlock to the PDB we just built

    TDB.PDB_environ = environment_segment

CreateTask_a:

    // fill in some fields of the TDB
    TDB.TDB_pModule = module_table
    Copy module name from module_table to TDB.TDB_ModName
    Copy interrupt handler addresses from KERNEL's DS into the TDB

    // Puts the current drive/dir/FPU state into the TDB. Inserts
    // the new TDB into the task list.
    FarCreateTask()
```

```
    Set TDB.TDB_DTA at offset 80h in the PDB section
    TDB.TDB_sig = 'TD'
    TDB.TDB_ASignalProc = &Default_Sig_Handler  // In USER

    Call AllocDStoCSAlias() to create a code alias to the TDB for
    use by the MakeProcInstance() thunks. Store the alias in
    TDB_MPI_Sel field of the TDB. Afterwards, initialize the
    area used for MakeProcInstance() thunks.


Pseudocode for Pass_Environment() - TASK.OBJ
// Returns environment seg in AX
// Parameters:
//      LPVOID  lpParameterBlock
//      WORD    module_table

    if ( fBooting )     // Are we bootstrapping KERNEL?
        return 0

    if ( lpParameterBlock.envseg == 0 )     // No environment
        return AX = 0

    Scan lpParameterBlock.envseg, looking for the 2 consecutive
    0's, indicating the end of the environment. Remember the
    length of the environment.

    GlobalAlloc() a new block big enough to hold a copy of the
    previously scanned environment.

    Copy the environment from lpParameterBlock.envseg to the
    new block

    return handle of allocated block in AX
```

BuildPDB()

BuildPDB() relies on the undocumented DOS subfunction 55h to build a new PDB, using the segment/selector specified in DX. In this case, BuildPDB() sets DX to the selector allocated to point at the PDB portion of the newly created TDB. Then BuildPDB() copies the command line, which was specified in the lpParameterBlock and passed to LoadModule() into offset 80h in the PDB. This space is reused later as the disk transfer area (DTA). If you're unfamiliar with PSPs, *Undocumented DOS* contains a good description of them.

```
Pseudocode for BuildPDB() - MODULE.OBJ
// Parameters:
//      WORD    parent_PDB, new_PDB
//      LPVOID  lpParameterBlock
```

```
//      WORD    size
//      WORD    winoldap_flag

    Save Win_PDB on stack
    Win_PDB = parent_PDB

    // Create the new PSP. This DOS subfunction is undocumented.
    INT 21H, Fn. 55H

    // cur_dos_PDB is a Windows global variable that contains
    // the value that DOS thinks the current PSP is set to.
    cur_dos_PDB = handle of new PDB

    restore Win_PDB from stack

    Plug in new parent, block length, & exit address into new PDB

    if ( winoldap_flag )
        copy lpParameterBlock.lpCmdLine to DTA of new PDB. Moves
        as many characters as specified in the first byte of the
        command line
    else
        copy lpParameterBlock.lpCmdLine to DTA of new PDB. Copy
        80h characters, ignoring the length specified in the
        first byte of the command line
```

LMRamNMods()

Before we started investigating how tasks are created, we were examining the various helper functions that LoadModule() uses. We'll pop our stack and return to that investigation. We left off having examined the LMCheckHeader() function, which ultimately causes a task to be created. We therefore resume our trek through LoadModule() with the LMRamNMods() function, which adds the new module to the module list and allocates its CODE and DATA segments.

LMRamNMods() begins by calling AddModule() to add the new module table to the list of system modules. LMRamNMods() then adds the file handle that's been used to access the NE file to the Windows file handle cache and sets the local copy of the file handle to -1 so that it can't be used anymore. Next, LMRamNMods() calls AllocAllSegs() and passes to it the module handle of the loading module. AllocAllSegs() iterates through the segment table and, where appropriate, fills in the selector/handle field in each segment table entry. All PRELOAD DATA segments and all PRELOAD FIXED segments have memory allocated for them. Otherwise, all MOVEABLE segments have selectors allocated, but no memory is committed. FIXED segments in DLLs are left alone entirely. There shouldn't be any FIXED segments in EXEs at this point because any FIXED flags were turned off when the module table was originally created in LoadExeHeader().

The remainder of LMRamNMods() is devoted to checking for two special cases involving referenced modules. The first check is to be sure the operating system field in the module header does not have a value (NE_UNKNOWN). Early Windows 1.x programs, as well as some OS/2 programs have NE_UNKNOWN as their operating system type. To attempt to weed out the OS/2 programs, Search_Mod_Dep_List() (Search Module Dependency List) is called with a pointer to the string "DOSCALLS". Search_Mod_Dep_List() iterates through the imported names table of the module, looking for the passed-in string. Since DOSCALLS is an OS/2 DLL used by almost all OS/2 programs (it's the equivalent of KERNEL in Windows), finding it in the imported names table is a good indicator that the NE file is an OS/2 file.

The second special case involves looking for references to the WIN87EM module in EXEs and DLLs built for Windows versions prior to 3.0. If WIN87EM is found in the imported names table, LoadLibrary() loads WIN87EM.DLL into memory. It is not clear why this module, which does 80x87 floating-point emulation, is handled specially.

```
Pseudocode for LMRamNMods() - LD.OBJ

    // Adds a new module table to the list of system modules
    if ( AddModule(module_table) == 0 )
    {
        unlink module_table from list
        goto Abort_3     // In LoadModule code
    }

    implicit_link_failure = -1    // Assume no error for now.

    // Windows maintains a cache of module handles, and the
    // associated file handle for the 'NE' file. Add the
    // loading module to the cache.
    FarGetCachedFileHandle(module_table, -1, file_handle)

    // The file handle is now cached by windows. LoadModule() doesn't
    // need its file handle anymore
    file_handle = -1

    Win_PDB = old_PDB
    old_PDB = -1

    if ( application is self loading ) // 0800h bit in module
        goto done_allocating_segs      // flags (offset 0Ch)

    if ( seg count in module_table == 0 )    // A resource DLL?
        goto done_allocating_segs

    module_table.usage_count = 1
```

```
    // Allocate selectors for the module's segments. In some
    // cases just selectors are allocated. In others cases,
    // selectors are allocated and memory associated with them.
    // Some segments don't get a handle at this time. The
    // PRELOAD / LOADONCALL attribute is what distinguishes
    // between the two cases.
    allocAllSegs_ret = AllocAllSegs(module_table)

    module_table.usage_count = 0x8000   // ?

    if ( preceding AllocAllSegs() returned 0 )
        goto Abort_1

done_allocating_segs:

    if ( module_table.num_modules == 0 )   // Any links to DLLs?
        goto LMRamNMods_done

    if ( module_table.exe_type == NE_UNKNOWN )
    {
        Call Search_Mod_Dep_List() to examine the imported names
        table for the string "DOSCALLS". This identifies the
        file as an OS/2 application. In this case, we don't want
        to run it. On the other hand, if it's not an OS/2
        program, it could be a Windows 1.X app, in which case we
        should try to load it.

        if ( "DOSCALLS" found  in imported names table)
        {
            failure_code = 11   // invalid exe
            goto Abort_1
        }
    }

    if ( module_table.expected_winver < 3.0 )
    {
        Call Search_Mod_Dep_List() to examine the imported
        names table for the string "WIN87EM".

        if ( "WIN87EM" found )      // May be related to the old
            LoadLibrary("WIN87EM")  // WIN87EM.EXE. We'd rather
                                    // use the newer WIN87EM.DLL?

        if ( LoadLibrary() failed  to load WIN87EM)
            implicit_link_failure = LoadLibrary() return value
    }

LMRamNMods_done:
    return
```

LMImports()

LMImports() is responsible for loading any DLLs that the loading program implicitly links to. The majority of the code loops through the imported names table, extracting each referenced module in turn. For each module it finds, LMImports() calls GetModuleHandle() to see if the module is already loaded. If not, LMImports() calls LoadLibrary() to load the module. Before going on to the next module in the imported names table, the module handle of the referenced module is added to the module reference table (see offset 28h in Table 3-1), overwriting the offset into the imported names table that the NE file contained.

IncExeUsage(), a complex routine near the end of LMImports(), handles the details of incrementing the usage count of each DLL that the passed-in module handle references. Adding complexity to the situation, DLLs can link to other DLLs, and those DLLs can in turn link to still other DLLs. IncExeUsage() handles all those details with code that acts recursively on the list of DLLs. There is a corresponding DecExeUsage() function that's called when a module is freed. It performs the opposite job of decrementing the usage count of all DLLs that are directly or indirectly referenced by a module.

```
Pseudocode for LMImports() - LD.OBJ
// Locals:
//  WORD    dll_handle  // module handle of loaded/loading DLL

    if ( number of imported modules == 0 )
        goto LMImport_done

    // See offsets 1Eh and 28h in Table 3-1
    for ( count = 0; count < number of imported modules; count++ )
    {
        Extract module name from imported names table      // offset 2Ah

        dll_handle = GetModuleHandle( module name )

        if ( dll_handle == 0 )
        {
            if ( module_table.expected_winver < 3.0 )
                append ".EXE" to module name
            else
                append ".DLL" to module name

            dll_handle = LoadLibrary( module name )
            if ( dll_handle < 32 )
                implicit_link_failure = dll_handle
        }

        // Convert dll_handle to a module handle, if it's not a
        // module handle already
        dll_handle = GetExePtr( dll_handle )
```

```
        // The module reference table in memory is a list
        // of module handles, rather than offsets into
        // the imported names table (NE file on disk).
        add dll_handle to next spot in module reference table
    }

LMImport_done:

    // If in first level call to LoadModule, call IncExeUsage()
    // to bump up the usage count of the loading modules, and
    // all DLLs that it refers to
    if ( fLMdepth == 1 )
        IncExeUsage( module_table )

    if ( implicit_link_failure != -1)
        failure_code = implicit_link_failure
```

LMSegs()

The job of LMSegs() is to get all the PRELOAD segments into memory so that the module can start up. Since segments for self-loading applications are loaded differently than normal modules, LMSegs() first checks to see if the module is self-loading. If so, it calls BootAppl() (described later) to handle the self-loading duties. For normal modules, the code iterates through the segment table. Any segment marked as PRELOAD is brought into memory and fixed up by the FarLoadSegment() function. (Dynamic linking and fixups are covered in Chapter 8). If a gangload area was loaded, the segments are copied from it. Otherwise the segments are loaded from the NE file. Segments that aren't loaded at this time are LOADONCALL segments. They're also loaded by FarLoadSegment(), but not until they're accessed for the first time. Protected mode Windows can rely on a processor segment-not-present exception to notify it when a segment that's not currently loaded is touched. This is a much cleaner mechanism than the awful mechanism used in real mode, wherein all far calls passed through a thunk.

```
Pseudocode for LMSegs() - LD.OBJ

    // Self loading applications bring their segments into memory
    // by themselves. BootAppl() initiates this sequence of
    // events. This is discussed towards the end of the chapter.
    if ( self loading app )
    {
        FarGetCachedFileHandle()

        if( !BootAppl() )
            goto Abort_1

        FlushCachedFileHandle()
    }

    // Abort now if the segments couldn't be allocated
```

```
    if ( allocAllSegs_ret == 0 )
        return

    // See offset 1Ch in Table 3-1.
    for ( count=0; count < number of segments; count++ )
     { //  See offset 22h in Table 3-1.
        if ( segment[count] is not PRELOAD )
            goto next_segment

        // if possible, copy the segments from gangload area
        if ( gangload_handle != 0 )
        {
            if ( !global_lock(gangload_handle) )
            {
                GlobalFree(gangload_handle)
                gangload_handle = 0
                goto read_from_disk
            }

            Calculate address of segment's data in gangload block

            // Copy the memory to the allocated selector, and
            // perform the relocations. FarLoadSegment() can
            // work with either a file handle to read with,
            // or a pointer to copy memory from.
            FarLoadSegment()

            GlobalUnlock(gangload_handle)
        }
        else    // Read segment in from disk
        {
read_from_disk:

            // Load the segment's data, and do the relocations.
            // Here, we pass a file_handle, so the segments are
            // read in from the disk image.
            FarLoadSegment()
        }

next_segment:
    }
```

LMLetsGo()

LMLetsGo() is where the module begins to sprout its wings and take off. First, however, it brings the module's PRELOAD resources into memory using PreloadResources(). With that out of the way, LMLetsGo() calls StartModule(). StartModule() sets up the initial register values for program modules and calls StartLibary() for DLLs. Lastly, if the module is for a program, LMLetsGo() calls CloseApplEnv(). CloseApplEnv(), despite its backwards-sounding name, is where the new task is finally launched. Upon return from CloseApplEnv(), the new program has executed its startup code and run until it yielded—for your average Windows program, the first yield is inside a GetMessage() call, with the main window already created.

```
Pseudocode for LMLetsgo() - LD.OBJ
// Locals:
//      WORD    fhandle

    push current Win_PDB    // save the current PDB, and switch
    Win_PDB = topPDB        // to the PDB of KRNLx86.EXE when
                            // Windows loaded

    fhandle = FarGetCachedFileHandle()   // Get file handle of loading module

    // If we have a gangload area, use it to create the preload
    // resources. Else, read the resources from the 'NE' file.
    if ( gangload_handle != 0 )
        PreloadResources(gangload_handle)
    else
        PreloadResources(fhandle)

    pop back the current Win_PDB

    if ( lpParameterBlock == -1 )   // -1 indicates a DLL load
        lpParameterBlock = 0

    // Do some setup work. EXE modules will get their initial
    // registers set up on the initial stack of the task. DLLs
    // have their initialization routine called if appropriate
    // loading via LoadLibrary().
    ret_value = StartModule()

    if ( module is a task (not a DLL) )
    {
        // CloseApplEnv() is where the task is "launched".
        // The call does not return until the app has yielded,
        // typically in its GetMessage() loop. CloseApplEnv()
        // is a very strange name, considering that it _starts_
        // the new task, rather than "closing" it. This may
        // be a throwback to the weirdness of EMS Windows, and
        // the need to "open" and "close" EMS banks.
        ret_value = CloseApplEnv()
    }
```

StartModule()

StartModule() is a fairly minor routine. The code probably could have been inlined inside LMLetsGo() with no loss of clarity. It performs two functions: First, it makes sure that the module's automatic data segment (DGROUP) is present in memory. Since this segment was loaded previously in LMSegs(), it's not understood why it's loaded again here. StartModule()'s second job is to call either StartTask() for program modules or StartLibrary() for DLL modules. One of the arguments to StartTask() is the initial SS:SP of the task. It obtains this value by calling GetStackPtr().

GetStackPtr() is an even simpler routine. It retrieves the stack size value out of the module table and adds it to the size of the DGROUP segment. The result is the initial SP value. The DGROUP selector is used for the initial SS value.

```
Pseudocode for StartModule() - LD.OBJ
// Parameters:
//      WORD    hPreviousInstance
//      WORD    lpParameterBlock
//      WORD    module_table
//      WORD    file_handle
//      DWORD   start_address

    // Make sure the automatic data segment is in memory
    if ( module_table.starting_CS != 0 )
        if ( module_table.autodata_segment != 0 )
            if (!FarLoadSegment(module_table,autodata_segment))
            {
                _lclose(file_handle)
                return 0;
            }

    start_address = StartProcAddress(module_table);

    if ( file_handle != -1 )
        _lclose(file_handle)

    if ( module is a task )
    {
        GetStackPtr()       // Return result sent to StartTask()
        StartTask()         // Set up registers for the task
    }
    else
    {
        Set flag in module_table.ne_flags indicating that WEP
        needs to be called.

        StartLibrary()
    }
```

StartTask()

StartTask() is where the magic sleight-of-hand of starting a new task occurs. Chapter 6, on the scheduler, discusses how one task is always running, while all other tasks are parked inside the scheduler routine. The register values for each parked task are saved on the stack and are restored when the task is scheduled to run again. StartTask(), rather than call a program's entry point, instead arranges for the new task to get scheduled. You might be asking, "Why can't the entry point for the program just be called directly?" Like any other Windows function, LoadModule() is executing in the context of the calling task. If we were just to JMP to the entry point, we'd still be running as the task that called LoadModule(), which is no good. The scheduler doesn't know anything about task creation or destruction. We need a new task, and the only way to do this is to fool the scheduler into thinking that the task has been there all along.

StartTask() performs this fakery by storing the initial startup values on the new task's stack, *just like the scheduler would have done* if the task had been switched away from previously. Without the scheduler knowing it, a new task has been inserted into the task list. Actually, the new task was added to the task list in CreateTask(), but the real magic is making the new task looks like it's just another task parked inside the scheduler. The task will actually run for the first time inside of CloseApplEnv(), which we will discuss momentarily. Incidentally, there is nothing Windows-specific to the procedure. Many multitasking operating systems start new tasks by making them look like old switched-away-from tasks.

Another interesting bit of trickery occurs when the ToolHelp or WinDebug DLLs need to be notified about task creations for debugging purposes. Notifications are discussed in detail in Chapter 5 of *Undocumented Windows*. For now, it is sufficient to say that the notification handler function needs to be called *in the context of the new task*, when a new task starts up.

This is the NFY_STARTTASK notification in ToolHelp. It's not sufficient to call the notification handler before starting the new task up. The new task has to be *running* when the handler is called. The handler also has to be called before any instructions in the new task are executed. The only feasible way to do this is to patch things so that the notification handler is called in the context of the new task, but before the entrypoint of the task is called. This is done by setting the initial CS:IP values of the new task to the address of a routine, CVW_Hack(), which calls the notification handler and then JMPs to the correct entry point in the new task. The name CVW_Hack() obviously refers to Microsoft's own Code View for Windows, as though this were the only Windows debugger. So much for Chinese Walls.

```
Pseudocode for StartTask() - TASK.OBJ
// Parameters:
//      WORD    hPreviousInstance
//      WORD    module_table
//      DWORD   starting_sssp
//      DWORD   starting_csip
// Locals:
//      WORD    instance_handle, dgroup_selector

    // A task must have a valid stack and a valid entry point
```

```
// These values come from offsets 14h and 18h in Table 3-1
if ( (starting_sssp.ss == 0) || (starting_csip.cs==0) )
    return 0

// Check the signature bytes to make sure it's a real TDB
if ( loadTDB.TDB_sig != 'TD' )
    return 0

// Set the SS:SP field in the TDB. Adjust SP downward to
// accommodate the saved registers stackframe in Reschedule()
// See Chapter 6 for more information on Reschedule()
loadTDB.TDB_taskSS = starting_sssp.ss
loadTDB.TDB_taskSP = starting_sssp.sp - 0x16

instance_handle = GetInstance(module_table)

starting_csip.cs = HIWORD( GlobalHandle(starting_csip.cs) )
dgroup_selector = HIWORD( GlobalHandle(instance_handle) )

TDB.TDB_ExpWinVer = module_table.expected_winver

// Start filling in "register values" on the stack. The
// registers themselves aren't being modified. Instead,
// we're setting up a stack frame that looks like it was
// created by a call to Reschedule(). When the new task is
// scheduled, it will "resume" from this call to Reschedule(),
// and start executing at the specified starting address with
// the register values "set" here.
AX = 0
ES = TDB.TDB_PDB
DI = instance_handle
DS = dgroup_selector
SI = hPreviousInstance
BX = stacksize
CX = heapsize
BP = 1                    // indicate a Far frame?

// Still setting register values in initial task stack.
//For RegisterPtrace, etc. See "Undocumented Windows," Chapter 5.

if ( RegisterPtrace/ToolhelpHook flag set in KERNEL_Flags )
{
    // Set the initial CS:IP of the stack to start at
    // CVW_Hack(). CVW_Hack() generates the appropriate
    // start-task "notification", and then calls the
    // real entry point of the task (which are saved below
    // in the global variable ptrace_app_entry).
```

```
        CS:IP = CVW_Hack
        FP_SEG( ptrace_app_entry ) = starting_csip.cs
        FP_OFF( ptrace_app_entry ) = starting_csip.IP
    }
    else    // The scheduler will return to the task directly.
    {
        CS = starting_csip.cs
        IP = starting_csip.ip
    }
```

StartLibrary()

StartLibrary() is responsible for setting up a library to be initialized. An important point here is the initialization sequence for DLLs depends on the circumstances of the DLL load. If the global variable loadTDB is 0, the DLL is being loaded at run-time, as the result of a LoadLibrary() call during the execution of a program. In this case, the DLL's initialization routine, which eventually calls LibMain(), is invoked.

The other scenario involves DLLs that are loaded because they're implicitly linked to (that is, an import library was used). In this case, the DLL initialization routine is *not* called inside of StartLibrary(). Instead, the module handles of all new, implicitly linked DLLs are stored in a special segment called the LibInitSeg. The application startup sequence calls InitTask(), which iterates through the list of module handles. InitTask() finds the entry point of each module and calls it, eventually causing LibMain() to be called.

The fact that the entry point of an implicitly linked DLL isn't called until after the task starts executing may have some of its roots in the need to debug DLL initialization routines. Normally, debuggers like TDW load a program and, if it has debug information, run the program to the WinMain() procedure. By this point, the LibMain() of each DLL has been invoked, and it's too late to debug them. However, if you tell the debugger not to run to WinMain(), such as by specifying "-l" on the TDW command line, the debugger stops at the very first instruction. At that point, you can set breakpoints in any DLL initialization routine.

```
Pseudocode for StartLibrary() - TASK.OBJ
// Parameters:
//      DWORD   starting_csip
//      LPVOID  lpParameterBlock
//      WORD    module_table

    // loadTDB != 0 indicates an implicitly loaded DLL. Don't
    // call the initialization function, as the application will
    // do that inside its startup code.
    if ( loadTDB != 0 )
        if ( !booting )
        {
            insert module_table into array of module handles for which
            InitApp() will call the entry point.
        }
```

```
if ( FP_SEG(pSignalProc) )     // pSignalProc is a global variable.
    pSignalProc(40)            // Undocumented. 40 means DLL load. See
                               // "Undocumented Windows" for details.

convert starting_csip.cs from a handle to a selector
with GlobalHandle().

Set up CX:BX to starting_csip for DLL load notification
Send the DLL load notification  // NFY_STARTDLL in TOOLHELP

if ( FP_SEG( starting_csip ) == 0 )    // No initialization code?
    return

// Set up registers for calling the DLL entry point
CX = heapsize    // from module_table.ne_heap
DX = selector of hInstance segment
ES:DI = lpParameterBlock.lpCmdLine

call [starting_csip]     // Actually calls a "wrapper"
                         // function which does the call
```

CloseApplEnv()

CloseApplEnv() sounds as though its job is to shut something down. Exactly the opposite is true. CloseApplEnv() is where a new task joins the ranks of other running tasks. The first order of business is to clean up a few things. If no module handles were added to the LibInitSeg for initialization by InitTask(), the segment is deleted. The global variable loadTDB indicates whether a task is in the process of being created. Once the task is fully formed, loadTDB is set back to 0, indicating that no task is being created at the moment. Before it's set to 0, a local copy of the TDB selector value is made because CloseApplEnv() isn't quite done with the loading TDB just yet.

CloseApplEnv() is called both for successful and unsuccessful module loadings. If the module is successfully loaded, CloseApplEnv() gets the honor of starting up the new task. In order to ensure that the new task will be scheduled and, therefore, run, CloseApplEnv() sets the event count in the task database (offset 6 in Table 3-2) to 1. Next, CloseApplEnv() increments the global variable Num_Tasks to reflect the fact that a new task has joined the system. If the TDBF_OS2APP flag is set in the TDB, and if the function pointer dressed_for_success is nonzero, CloseApplEnv() calls the address stored in dressed_for_success. Presumably this is some sort of notification to someone that an OS/2 application is about to be launched under Windows. Finally, CloseApplEnv() starts the new task by calling Yield(). Yield() eventually calls the core scheduling routine, which sees the nonzero event count in the newly created TDB and schedules the task to run. Break out the cigars!

```
Pseudocode for CloseApplEnv() - LD.OBJ
// Called for both successful and unsuccessful loads
// Locals:
//      WORD current_TDB
//      WORD local_loadTDB

    current_TDB = curTDB    // curTDB is a global variable, and the
                            // return value from GetCurrentTask()

    local_loadTDB = loadTDB

    if ( local_loadTDB  )
        if ( no module handles in local_loadTDB.TDB_LibInitSeg )
        {
            GlobalUnlock(local_loadTDB.TDB_LibInitSeg)   // Don't need
            GlobalFree(local_loadTDB.TDB_LibInitSeg)     // the LibInitSeg.
        }

    loadTDB = 0;    // A KERNEL global variable, so put it back
                    // to zero when all done with it.

    if (ret_value > 32 )      // A successful load?
    {
        // Making the event count nonzero ensures that the
        // scheduler will schedule the task
        local_loadTDB.event_count = 1;

        Num_Tasks++     // A system global variable. The
                        // GetNumTasks() API returns this value.

        // This following sequence looks like something having
        // do with running OS/2 applications.
        if ( TDBF_OS2APP set in TDB_flags )
            if ( dressed_for_success != 0 )
                dressed_for_success()   // A function pointer

        // Start the program up, and let it run until it yields,
        // typically inside its message loop
        if ( not booting )
            Yield()
    }
    else    // Task load failed for some reason
    {
        FarDeleteTask()     // Remove the TDB from the memory
        FarUnlinkObject()   // chain and delete its memory
        FreeTDB()
    }
```

LMCleanUp()

The final act of LoadModule() is to clean up after itself. LMCleanUp() performs these chores, both for successful and unsuccessful loads. The function begins by closing the file handle that was used by LoadModule() to read in the various parts of the 'NE' file. Since Windows maintains a cache of module handles, which are paired with the file handles of the associated 'NE' files, closing the original file handle that LoadModule() used doesn't hurt anything.

If there's still a gangload area selector still floating around, LMCleanUp() calls GlobalFree() to release its memory back to the system. If a task database was created, but didn't make it all the way to an actual task, LMCleanUp() deallocates its memory by invoking CloseApplEnv(). Lastly, if the module was loaded from a floppy disk or other removable media, its file handle in the previously mentioned cache file handle is closed. Presumably, this is done because the floppy may be changed at any moment and it doesn't make sense to keep an open file handle for a removable file.

```
Pseudocode for LMCleanUp() - LD.OBJ

    // On entry, AX contains the error code (or instance handle)
    // that will be returned by LoadModule()
    if ( AX < 32 )      // Was it successful?  < 32 means NO!
    {
        close file_handle;
        file_handle = -1
    }

    if ( old_PDB != -1 )
        Win_PDB = old_PDB

    if ( gangload_handle != 0 )    // Free the gangload memory.
        GlobalFree(gangload_handle)

    if ( AX >= 32 )
        goto LMCleanup_app_ok    // <32 is an error code.

    if ( loadTDB != 0 )    // If we get here, unsuccesful load.
        if ( module_table > 32 )
            if ( module is a task )
                CloseApplEnv()  // Free up stuff allocated for the task

LMCleanup_app_ok:

    // if a module was loaded, and it was loaded from removable
    // media (e.g., a floppy), then flush the file handle (don't
    // keep it around in the cache).
```

```
if ( AX > 32 )    // Succesful load.
{
    if ( !on_hard_drive )
    {
        // If we get here, AX is an instance handle

        // Close the file in KERNEL's cache
        FlushCachedFileHandle( GetExePtr(AX) )
    }
}

if ( fBooting and in diagnostics mode )
    write out all kinds of stuff about what happened.
```

Loading a Second Instance of an EXE or DLL

We've seen the details of how a new module is created in the system. The next thing to examine is how an existing module is reused. Near the beginning of LoadModule(), it checks to see if the requested module is already loaded. If so, it calls LMPrevInstance().

LMPrevInstance()

LMPrevInstance() is a combination of previously seen routines, and new code. Like LMCheckHeader(), LMPrevInstance() uses LMCheckHeap() to ensure that there's at least ten percent free system resources before attempting to load the module. The new code in LMPrevInstance() is necessary because of the problem with programs containing multiple data segments. This situation was discussed previously in the section on the module table.

To prevent an application that has multiple data segments from running a second time, the code loops through the module's segment table, counting the total number of DATA segments that aren't read-only. If there is more than one such segment, LMPrevInstance() returns an appropriate error code. Multiple read-only data segments are allowed because the application can't write to the segment unless it goes to the trouble of creating an alias selector. Therefore, it doesn't matter if more than one instance of an application *reads* from the same segment. Resources work on the same concept.

Once LMPrevInstance() has certified the module as having only one read/write DATA segment, it calls some functions that we've seen already. OpenApplEnv() creates a new task database; IncExeUsage() bumps up the reference count of all implicitly linked DLLs; AllocAllSegs() creates a new DGROUP for the loading task; StartModule() sets up the initial register values on the stack of the new task; and CloseApplEnv() eventually causes the new task to be scheduled.

If the LMPrevInstance() is called for a previously loaded DLL, LMPrevInstance() makes sure that the DLL's DGROUP segment is loaded. It then calls IncExeUsage() to bump up the usage count of the implicitly linked DLLs. Yawn...

```
Pseudocode for LMPrevInstance() - LD.OBJ
// Starts up another instance of a previously loaded module
// On startup, AX contains the module handle of the previous
// instance of the module
//
// Locals:
//      WORD previousInstanceHandle

    module_table = AX
    ret_value = 0

    // Undocumented use of LoadModule(). LoadLibrary() uses
    // LoadModule() to load the DLL, and passes it -1 for the
    // lpParameterBlock
    if ( lpParameterBlock == -1 )
    {
        if ( DLL flag not set in the module table )
            return 5    // Can't dynamic link to a task
        else
            lpParameterBlock = 0
    }

    if ( MULTIPLEDATA flag not set in module table )
        goto no_instance_data

    // LMCheckHeap() checks to make sure there is enough space
    // in the USER/GDI heaps by calling GetFreeSystemResources(0)
    // "Enough" in this case means 10%.
    if ( LMCheckHeap() == 0 )
        return 0    // Out of memory

    if ( winoldap_flag )    // WINOA386.MOD contains 2 data segs
        goto only_one_data_seg  // Reason: Unknown

    iterate through the segment table in the module table.
    Count how many non-read-only DATA segments there are.

    If ( number of non-read-only DATA segments > 1 )
        return 16   // Multiple data segments in application

only_one_data_seg:

    // OpenApplEnv() calls CreateTask() to create the TDB, and
    // allocates a segment to store the hModules of the DLLs that
    // will need to be initialized when the program starts. Since
    // there already is a previous instance, there won't be any
```

```
    // DLLs that are initialized by this instance of the program.
    OpenApplEnv()

    // The previousInstanceHandle is needed by StartModule(),
    // below. The instance handle (the DGROUP handle) is
    // obtained from module_table's segment table.
    previousInstanceHandle = GetInstance(module_table);

    // Bumps up the usage count in the module table. Makes
    // sure that modules referenced by this module have their
    // usage count incremented as well.
    IncExeUsage(hModule)

    // Allocate the code/data segments that this instance will
    // use. Since there is already a previous instance of the
    // program, and since code segments are shared between
    // instances, AllocAllSegs() will only allocate a
    // new automatic data segment in this case.
    if ( AllocAllSegs(hModule) == -1 )    // -1 -> failure.
    {
        // If AllocAllSegs() failed, then we need to restore
        // the module usage count to its previous value
        DecExeUsage(hModule)

        return 0    // Not enough memory
    }

    // StartModule sets up the register values for the new task
    if ( StartModule() == 0 )
    {
        FreeModule();   // Decrements the usage count of the module
        return 0        // Not enough memory
    }

    // Start execution of the new task, by Yield()'ing
    return CloseApplEnv()

no_instance_data:   // DLL modules come here

    if ( auto data segment selector == 0 )
        if ( FarLoadSegment(auto data segment) == 0 )
            return 0    // Not enough memory

    IncExeUsage()       // Increment the module usage count

    return GetInstance()    // Gets DGROUP of DLL.
```

The Application Startup Code

Up to this point, we've focused on what happens in the Windows KERNEL to load a new task and call its entry point (or get the scheduler to do so). While WinMain() is where your own code begins executing, you are probably aware that WinMain() is not called directly by Windows itself. Instead, the entry point of your program is in the startup code that's supplied by your compiler vendor (assuming you're not one of the dying breed who still hand codes everything, even Windows programs and DLLs, in assembler). If you're a C or C++ programmer, the startup code is in the OBJ file that's the first OBJ file linked into the EXE or DLL. For Borland C and C++, the source code for this OBJ can be found in \BORLANDC\LIB\STARTUP. For EXEs, the file is C0W.ASM, for DLLs, C0D.ASM. Microsoft C/C++ users can find the startup code in CRT0.ASM and WINSTART.ASM. Zortech supplies its startup code in the \ZORTECH\SOURCE\CLIB directory.

The C/C++ startup code does thc normal things you'd expect, such as parsing the command line to create argv and argc arguments, and calling any C++ static constructors. In Windows EXEs and DLLs, the startup code plays the additional role of calling some critical initialization functions that do things such as creating a message queue for the new task and calling the DLL initialization routines for implicitly linked DLLs.

If you're interested in what happens in the startup code, examine the actual code supplied by your compiler vendor. However, if you're not an assembler wizard, or if you just want to know the general concepts, we present the startup code for Borland C++ EXEs and DLLs in pseudocode form.

Windows EXE Startup Code

For EXEs, the important parts of the startup code involves calling InitTask() and then InitApp(), which we cover momentarily. After those functions have been called, the EXE is completely initialized and ready to start its work as a Windows program. This is where WinMain is called. Assuming that the application terminates normally, (i.e., that a UAE doesn't terminate it abruptly) WinMain() returns with the program's exit code. After some cleanup, the startup code eventually calls the DOS terminate function, INT 21h function 4Ch. It's somewhat strange that Windows uses functions like LoadModule() and WinExec() to start a program, but uses a DOS interrupt to shut them down. The DPMI specification states that DPMI clients must exit by doing an INT 21h function 4Ch in protected mode; perhaps this has something to do with it.

```
Pseudocode for COW.ASM

    // Give KERNEL an opportunity to initialize things related
    // to the task, such as the instance data area.
    InitTask()

    Save off register return values from InitTask() into global
    and local variables that can be referenced by the C code
```

```
// Lock the DGROUP segment
if ( near data memory model )   // Decided at assembly time
    LockSegment(-1)             // rather than at run time

Initialize the BSS area of DGROUP to zeroes

// CloseApplEnv() had to "fake" an event (with PostEvent())
// to force this task to be scheduled. WaitEvent() "eats"
// the event, thus putting the task in its "natural" state.
WaitEvent()

// Creates the queue for the new task, sets the signal proc
// handler, and so on.
InitApp()

Determine and save off various global variables, such as
the date, time, DOS version number, etc.

Call any C++ static constructors. Note that this is done
_after_ InitApp() is called. If this wasn't the case, calls
to MessageBox() (and other routines that require a message
queue to be present) would blow up in the constructors.
_Windows++_ by Paul DiLascia (Addison-Wesley, 1992)
describes a bug related to this in the startup code of one
the major C++ vendors.

// This is it!!! Call the user supplied WinMain(). This
// routine won't return until the program has been told to
// terminate by the user. The parameters to WinMain() were
// given to us in various registers after returning from
// InitTask(), and are pushed on the stack for WinMain().
WinMain(hInstance, hPrevInstance, lpCmdLine, nCmdShow)

// Calls any static destructors, and eventually terminates
// the program via INT 21h, fn. 4Ch
_exit( AX )     // AX set to return value from WinMain()
```

Windows DLL Startup Code

The startup code for DLLs is much simpler than for EXEs. If the programmer requests a local heap, the startup code calls LocalInit() to set up the data structures that maintain the heap. After invoking any static constructors the startup code finally calls LibMain().

```
Pseudocode for COD.ASM

    // Setup the local heap in the DGROUP
    LocalInit()
```

```
if ( near data memory model )    // Decided at assembly time
    LockSegment(-1)              // rather than at run time

Initialize the BSS area of DGROUP to 0's

Call any C++ static constructors.

LibMain(hInstance, wDataSeg, wHeapSize, lpCmdLine)

// Unlike the application startup code, static destructors are
// not called after the "main" routine. Instead, they are
// called by the run time library before the user-supplied WEP()
// routine is called.
```

InitTask()

While the startup code for EXEs is mildly enlightening, the real question is, What goes on inside InitApp(), InitTask(), and WaitEvent()? These functions were first documented as part of the Microsoft Open Tools initiative. While a good start, this information was not freely available to just anyone. Luckily, these functions are now documented in the Microsoft Windows 3.1 SDK, in Chapter 22 of Volume 1 of the *Programmer's Reference*. Pseudocode for InitApp() and InitTask() is presented here. WaitEvent() is covered in Chapter 6 on the scheduler.

InitTask() starts by calculating the lowest and highest SP values that should occur in this task and stores them in the "instance data" area of the DGROUP. The instance data area is 10h bytes in length, and starts at offset 0 of each DGROUP. Along with stack values, the instance data area contains near pointers to the local heap and atom tables. The instance data area is described in the InitTask() documentation in the 3.1 SDK, as well as in Chapter 5 of *Undocumented Windows*. Afterwards, InitTask() calls LocalInit() to initialize the local heap and store some additional values, like a pointer to the local heap and atom tables, into the instance data area. LocalInit() is discussed in Chapter 2 on memory management.

The next item on the work list of InitTask() is to call the entry points of all DLLs which were just loaded and which are implicitly linked to by this task. This chore is performed by Do_LibInit(). As described in the description for StartLibrary() earlier in this chapter, a special segment is created that contains an array of module handles for each DLL that needs to be initialized. Do_LibInit() iterates through the list, finding the entry point of each module and calling it. If for some reason a library initialization returns 0, indicating failure, Do_LibInit() terminates the task by calling INT 21h function 4Ch, with the exit code in AL set to F0h.

InitTask() next calls SetAppCompatFlags(), which, despite its name, retrieves the compatibility flags for an application. The compatibility flags enable certain behaviors that existed in Windows 3.0, but which were changed in Windows 3.1. Certain applications depended on a particular behavior in Windows 3.0 and broke when the initial beta releases of Windows 3.1 were introduced. To keep these applications working in Windows 3.1, the [Compatibility] section of the WIN.INI file contains a list of the module names for the programs and the associated flags that tell Windows which behavior, including bugs, to reenable. The individual compatibility flags are discussed in *Undocumented Windows.* SetAppCompatFlags() extracts the module name from the task database and uses the profile functions to determine if the module is in the [Compatibility] section. The compatibility flags only apply to Windows 3.0 applications, so if the expected Windows version in the TDB is greater than 3.0, SetAppCompatFlags() returns 0. The return value from SetAppCompatFlags() is stored in the task database for fast retrieval by the GetAppCompatFlags() function.

If the task being initialized in InitTask() is the first task to be loaded into the system, some additional code is executed. It's at this point that CalMaxNRSeg() is called to set up the initial minimum value for the swap area size. The global heap is then compacted twice. It's not clear why it's done twice; one would hope that the GlobalCompact() would work correctly the first time it's called. The USER module needs a chance to initialize a few things after the first task has loaded, and so it is called through the PUserInitDone() function pointer. Finally, if the KERNEL is running in Enhanced mode, InitTask() calls KRebootInit() to set up the local reboot handling. (In Windows 3.1, you can use CTRL-ALT-DELETE to reboot out of a non-responding application).

After the "first task only" code is out of the way, InitTask() finishes by setting up the registers with the return values that InitTask() is documented to return. This includes some mucking about with the command line and retrieving the value for the nCmdShow parameter out of the first file control block (FCB) in the PDB. The application's startup code passes these values on the stack as the parameters to WinMain().

```
Pseudocode for InitTask() - TASK.OBJ
// Locals:
//      WORD    TDB

    pop return address off the stack into DX:AX

    Save SP value into pStackMin and pStackBot. These are
    variables at the base of the DGROUP seg, and indicate
    the _highest_ address that the SP register can contain.

    Calculate the lowest address that the stack will contain,
    by subtracting the stack size (in BX) from the SP value.
    Add 0x96 to that value (unsure as to why). Store this
    value in pStackTop. This is the _lowest_ address that the
    SP register should be able to use without incurring a stack
    overflow.

    BP = 0
    PUSH BP

    Push the return CS:IP back onto the stack (from DX:AX)
```

```
// If there's a local heap for this task, initialize it
if ( CX != 0 )    // CX = heap limit
{
    if ( !LocalInit() )
        goto InitTask_done      // AX == return code == 0
}

TDB = GetCurrentTask()

// Do_LibInit() calls the initialization routines of any
// implicitly linked DLLs loaded by this task. Only call
// if there is a LibInitSeg
if ( TDB.LibInitSeg )
    Do_LibInit()

// Get the compatibility flags, and store them in
// the TDB for quick look-up
TDB.TDB_CompatFlags = LOWORD(SetAppCompatFlags())
TDB.TDB_CompatFlags2 = HIWORD(SetAppCompatFlags())

if ( some bit set in KERNEL_Flags ) // Indicates booting?
{
    fBooting = 0  // a global variable (0 = not booting)

    // Unlock the DGROUP segment
    UnlockSegment(GlobalHandle(DS))

    CalcMaxNRSeg()  // Calculate the minimum swap area needed

    // Compact system memory
    GlobalCompact(0)
    GlobalCompact(0)    // again

    // Lock the DGROUP segment
    LockSegment(GlobalHandle(DS))

    // Give USER a chance to initialize some things after
    // the first application has started up.
    if ( FP_SEG(pUserInitDone) )
        pUserInitDone()

    KRebootInit()   // Enhanced mode only
}

// Set up return register values from InitTask().
```

```
    Scan through the command line in the PDB. Null terminate
    the string after the filename. Set ES:BX to the next
    character afterwards (the start of the command line, i.e.,
    lpszCommandLine).

    CX = pStackTop

    // Set up the nCmdShow value in DX. This value was passed
    // to loadModule() via the lpParameterBlock, and was squirreled
    // away in the first FCB of the PDB. This explains the need
    // for the magic value '2' when setting up the parameter block
    if ( first WORD in first FCB == 2 )
        DX = second WORD in first FCB
    else
        DX = 1    // (SW_NORMAL)

    AX = selector of PDB  // Set in ES upon entry to InitTask()

InitTask_done:

    return
```

InitApp()

The InitApp() function resides in USER and performs initializations that are more specific to USER than to KERNEL. InitApp(), to a much larger degree than InitTask(), contains special code that's only executed for the first task to be loaded (typically, PROGMAN).

The Windows boot sequence creates a message queue that doesn't belong to a specific task. The desktop window gets its messages from this queue and contains the queue handle in its WND structure (see Table 4-2 in Chapter 4, offset 18h). InitApp() sets the queue of the first program to be this queue, rather than creating a whole new message queue for it. No sense leaving the original message queue (see Table 7-1 in Chapter 7, offsets 2 and 36h) laying around unused. At the same time, InitApp() sets the hTask and "expected Windows version" fields in this message queue to the hTask and expected Windows version of the first task. For any other task besides the first one, InitApp calls CreateQueue() to allocate and initialize a queue for the new task.

Next, InitApp() installs some callback functions. The task signal procedure is set up by SetTaskSignalProc(). These signals indicate the termination of tasks and the loads and unloads of DLLs. ToolHelp hooks this signal to allow it to shut down interrupt and notification handlers for tasks that did not or could not do it for themselves.

The next handlers installed are the resource handlers. Resource handlers are callback functions that load particular resources from the NE file. The SDK documentation implies that resource handlers are only for custom resources, but this is not the case. InitApp() sets the resource handlers for cursors and icons. There are different installed handler functions, based upon the expected Windows version in the TDB (Windows 3.1 has DIBs, or device independent bitmaps). Finally, InitApp() calls SetDivZero() to change the divide-by-zero exception handler to point to a routine in USER. The new handler pops up a message box informing the user of the situation and then terminates the program.

The last portion of the InitApp() code is devoted to more code that only executes for the first task in the system. Thus, we're back to watching the Windows initialization sequence, which we examined in Chapter 1. InitApp() calls SetSystemTimer() to set up a timer routine that's invoked every ten seconds. The timer callback routine simply calls IsUserIdle(), which determines if a screen saver should be started up. The core scheduling routine, Reschedule() also calls IsUserIdle().

InitApp() next calls LoadDrivers() to load any drivers (DLLs) that were specified in the "drivers=" entry in the [boot] section of SYSTEM.INI. In a related vein, InitApp() calls LW_InitNetInfo() to load the network driver, if one is specified in the SYSTEM.INI file.

After loading the drivers, InitApp() uses GetProfileInfo() to see if there is a "SETUPWIN" entry in the [windows] section of WIN.INI. If SETUPWIN is found, InitApp() calls WriteProfileString() with a NULL pointer, causing SETUPWIN to be deleted from the WIN.INI file. By deleting the SETUPWIN entry when it's found, the Windows setup procedure can be made to run only once. If SETUPWIN isn't found, then presumably the setup program isn't running, and some additional initializations need to be performed. The code now calls WNetRestoreConnection() to reconnect to the network if the connection was broken for some reason. Following that, InitApp() calls AutoLoadTSRApps() to give installed TSRs an opportunity to request that WinExec() execute a program or load drivers and DLLs. The drivers are queried with a DPMI "simulate real-mode INT" call that does an INT 2Fh function 160Bh. (The 3.1 DDK describes this interrupt in INT2FAPI.INC, with the helpful comment, "Identify TSRs." There is a lengthy description on the MSDN CD-ROM.) Finally, InitApp() calls SetCursor() to set the cursor to the normal cursor instead of the hourglass cursor that's shown during the load process.

```
Pseudocode for InitApp() - TMINIT.OBJ (USER)
// Uses a global WORD variable that's initialized to 1. We'll
// call it "first_program" here.
//
// Parameters:
//      WORD    hInstance
// Locals:
//      char    stringBuff[20]
//      char    is_setup
//      QUEUE   FAR * queuePtr; // Pointer to a message queue

    if ( first_program != 0 )   // Do only if the first task
    {
        SetTaskQueue(0, HWndDesktop.hQueue);

        // Plug the queue created for the desktop window with the
        // current task and expected Win version for this task.
        queuePtr = MK_FP( HWndDesktop, 0 )
        queuePtr->hTask = GetCurrentTask()
        queuePtr->ExpWinVersion = GetExeVersion()
    }
```

```
// Create a queue for all programs besides the first one
if ( first_program == 0 )
    if ( CreateQueue(DefQueueSize) == 0 )
        return 0;

// Set the task signal proc to the default handler in USER
SetTaskSignalProc(0, SignalProc)

// Install the callback routines that will be used to load
// cursors and Icons from the NE file. See the SDK
// documentation for details.
if ( GetAppVer() >= 3.0 )
{
    SetResourceHandler(hInstance, RT_CURSOR,
        LoadDibCursorHandler)

    SetResourceHandler(hInstance, RT_ICON,
        LoadDibIconHandler)
}
else
{
    SetResourceHandler(hInstance, RT_CURSOR,
        LoadCursorIconHandler)

    SetResourceHandler(hInstance, RT_ICON,
        LoadCursorIconHandler);
}

SetDivZero()                // Set divide-by-zero handler to a routine
                            // that pops up a message box if a division
                            // by zero occurs.

if ( first_program != 0 )     // First program in system.
{
    first_program = 0        // Don't let happen again

    // See "Undocumented Windows" for a description of the
    // system timers, and SetSystemTimer().
    SetSystemTimer(hWndSwitch, 0xFFFD, 10000, IdleTimer)

    LoadDrivers()              // Load installable drivers.

    LW_InitNetInfo()

    // Loads stringBuff with "Windows"
    LoadString(HInstanceWin, 0, stringBuff, 20);
```

```
        // Determine if windows is being run for the very first
        // time. It does this by looking for "SETUPWIN" in the
        // WIN.INI file. If found, it's the first time. To
        // prevent it from being found subsequently, the string
        // is deleted from WIN.INI.
        is_setup = GetProfileInt(stringBuff, "SETUPWIN", 0)

        if ( is_setup == 0 )            // Not the first invocation.
        {
            WNetRestoreConnection(0, MK_FP(0,1))

            UserDiagOutput(0, "TSRQuery")

            AutoLoadTSRApps()       // Int 2Fh function 160Bh

            UserDiagOutput(1, "TSRQuery")
        }
        else
        {
            WriteProfileString(stringBuff, "SETUPWIN", 0)  // Remove it.
        }

        SetCursor(HCursNormal)
    }

    return 1
```

Application Shutdown

The startup code for a Windows application is also responsible for shutting it down. Just as WinMain() isn't the true entry point to a Windows program, returning from WinMain() does not immediately terminate the Windows program. If you recall, the startup code called WinMain(), and so when WinMain() is exited, the startup code takes over again. After doing any necessary shutdown procedures, such as calling C++ static destructors, the startup code terminates the program the same way as a DOS application, with INT 21h function 4Ch.

At this point, you may be thinking, "But DOS doesn't know anything about Windows programs!" Once again, we're faced with the dual personality of Windows. Sometimes Windows acts like DOS, with system services provided by INT 21hs; and other times you forget about DOS and make Windows calls. When WinExec() starts a program, Windows translates the call into a DOS style INT 21h call. But then the INT 21h in KERNEL intercepts the INT 21h request and transforms it back into a series of Windows function calls. As you might expect, application shutdown is nearly as twisted. Like the INT 21h, function 4Bh that starts a Windows program, KERNEL intercepts INT 21h, function 4Ch and transforms it into a series of Windows calls. The routine that performs process terminations in KERNEL is ExitCall().

ExitCall()

ExitCall() is one busy routine! It starts by setting the WExitingTDB global variable to the selector value of the exiting TDB, indicating to Windows that a task is in the process of exiting. Next, ExitCall() invokes DebugExitCall(), which sends the extremely important process termination notification. This notification is essential for debuggers, which need to know when the process they're debugging has exited. However, one problem related to this seems to bite quite a few programmers. Look a bit further in the code, and see where the module for the task is freed, causing the WEPs for the implicitly loaded DLLs to be called. Why is this a problem? When a debugger gets the task termination notification, it considers the process to be dead and therefore shuts down its internal tables and cleans up. It's turned a deaf ear towards Windows. Unfortunately the WEP()s haven't been called yet. Thus, programmers who set a breakpoint in their WEP code are somewhat surprised when their WEP() is called, but the debugger doesn't stop at the breakpoint. Although there is a fairly ugly way to work around this problem in TDW, the best solution is to use a system level debugger like Soft-Ice/W, or if desperate, WDEB386 from the Microsoft SDK.

After the task termination notification is sent, ExitCall() checks to see if the terminating task is the last one in the system. In this case, ExitCall() needs to shut down Windows. Windows without a task is like a car without an engine. In this case, the local rebooting feature of Enhanced mode Windows 3.1 is first disabled. Then, ExitCall() invokes the infamous Bunny_351(). Bunny_351() is described in *Undocumented Windows*, but here, suffice it to say that it changes KERNEL's GP fault handling routine to a function that prints out, "Fault at Exit Time!!!" if the debug version of KERNEL is running. Finally, ExitCall() invokes ExitWindows(). If for some strange reason ExitWindows() manages to return from this call, ExitCall() invokes ExitKernel(). ExitWindows() and ExitKernel() are examined in detail in Chapter 1. It's unlikely that Windows will exit through the code sequence just described, however. Typically, the user selects "Exit Windows" from PROGMAN, or else closes PROGMAN. In either case, ExitWindows() is called by PROGMAN, and the code sequence just described doesn't get a chance to execute. The actions of ExitWindows() are also covered in Chapter 1.

Naturally, most invocations of ExitCall() are not for the last task in the system. ExitCall() calls the task signal procedure with a parameter of 20h. This indicates that the task is terminating normally, as opposed to a code of 666h, which indicates the task has died violently in a UAE (draw your own conclusions about the appropriateness of the signal value). This is USER's opportunity to do any cleanup that needs to be done on a task specific basis. We'll come back to this shortly.

After sending the termination signal, ExitCall() goes through a rather strange sequence of code that points the exception 6 (illegal opcode) handler at the final portion of the ExitCall() code. It then intentionally generates an exception 6. This causes the rest of ExitCall() to be executed as a DPMI exception handler. Why is this? It's been hypothesized that a DPMI exception handler is a quick and easy way to get a "cheap" stack. In Windows 3.0, the extremely small stack used during program exits cause severe problems. It wouldn't do to have the application exit on its own stack either, since its stack segment is going to be tossed as part of its cleanup process. Running the program cleanup sequence on an exception handler stack seems a bit odd, but the problems with Windows 3.0 do seem to have gone away.

Inside ExitCall()'s "exception handler," a call to the GlobalFreeAll() function walks the global heap and frees any segments owned by the exiting PDB. DeleteTask() removes the TDB from the linked list of TDBs. TerminatePDB() shuts down any filehandles that the task may have open. FreeModule() removes the module database of the exiting tasks and decrements the usage counts of any DLLs that were implicitly linked to. If the usage count of the DLL falls to 0, KERNEL removes the DLL from memory. The details of FreeModule() are covered shortly. DOS function 50h sets the current PSP to the PSP that was in effect when Windows loaded. The selector allocated to point at the PDB (the WORD at offset 60H in the TDB) is freed; and immediately after that, ExitCall() frees the TDB itself.

Also inside this exception handler, ExitCall() sets the exception 6 handler address back to its original value. It then sets the saved SS:SP value in the DPMI stack frame to point to a small stack inside KERNEL. The CS:IP in the stack frame is set to a label inside the core scheduling routine. When ExitCall() RETFs from the exception handler, the CPU ends up executing in the scheduler, looking for a task to schedule, and running on the temporary KERNEL stack. Once a new task is scheduled, the exiting task is completely gone.

The final act before RETF'ing to the scheduler is to set the global variable WExitingTDB to 0, indicating that the task termination is complete.

```
Pseudocode for ExitCall() - I21TASK.OBJ
    WExitingTDB = CurTDB     // Both are global variables
                             // A non-zero WExitingTDB indicates
                             // that a task is terminating

    // Send RegisterPtrace() / ToolhelpHook() notification
    // for debuggers/TOOLHELP
    DebugExitCall()

    // If in graphics mode, call DISPLAY.500
    // ( UserRepaintDisable() ) to suspend screen updates
    // This only occurs in the Enhanced mode KERNEL
    if ( graphics )
        PDisplayCritSec(1)

    pStackTop = 0   // See InitTask() for description

    UnlinkObject()  // Remove the PDB from the list of PDBs

    Num_Tasks--     // Global variable returned by GetNumTasks()

    // If the number of task drops to 0, exit Windows. This
    // section appears to be a "safety-hatch" (e.g., if PROGMAN
    // was the only task, and GP faulted). Windows is normally
    // exited by calling ExitWindows()
```

```
    if ( Num_Tasks == 0 )    // Last task in system?
    {
        // Calls the reboot VxD via 2F/1684 to shut down local reboot
        if ( FP_SEG( LPReboot ) )
            LPReboot()

        // Set FaultHandler() to a different handler for exiting
        Bunny_351()

        // Calls ExitWindows(). This call doesn't return
        PExitProc()

        // In case the previous call _did_ return?
        ExitKernel()
    }

    // Usually come here: _not_ the last task in the system

    // Send the "task-exiting" signal. This is where USER gets
    // its opportunity to clean up things, such as window classes
    // that need to be unregistered.
    if ( FP_SEG( WExitingTDB.TDB_USignalProc ) != 0 )
        WExitingTDB.TDB_USignalProc(20h)

    // This next section is somewhat strange. It deliberately
    // generates an exception 6 (invalid opcode) and handles
    // it. It's been theorized that the reason for this is to
    // make sure that there's a "safe stack" to terminate the
    // task with (i.e., we can't run on the original stack
    // anymore)  There were problems in Windows 3.0 with very
    // small stacks at program exit time.
    Use DPMI fn. 202h to get the current exception 6
    handler. Push this address on the stack

    Use DPMI fn. 203h to set the exception 6 handler to
    ExitCall_exception_6_handler

    pop the original exception 6 handler off the stack into CX:DX

    An invalid 0fh 0FFh "opcode" appears here. This triggers an
    exception 6, that's now vectored to
    ExitCall_exception_6_handler

ExitCall_exception_6_handler:

    MOV BP, SP
```

```
Use DPMI fn. 203h to set the exception 6 handler to CX:DX
Before the intentional exception 6, CX:DX contained the
address of the original exception 6 handler.

Patch the SS:SP values at [BP+12] to point to GMOVE_STACK

Patch the CS:IP values at [BP+6] to point at ExitSchedule(),
which is inside the scheduler.

// O.K. We're all done with that strange section that did
// the deliberate exception 6, and handled it. Note however,
// that we're still in the exception 6 handler, and will be
// throughout the rest of this function.
GlobalFreeAll() // GlobalFree() segments belonging to task

DeleteTask()    // Remove task from the list of tasks

TerminatePDB()  // Closes open files, etc.

// Look for a private file handle table
if ( WExitingTDB.TDB_PHT )
    WExitingTDB.TDB_PHT = 0

// Free up the task's module. This in turn decrements
// the usage count of implicitly linked DLLs, and frees
// the DLLs whose usage count has gone to zero
FreeModule( WExitingTDB.TDB_Module )

Free up the file handle table segment if it's not inside the PDB

// topPDB = PDB of DOS when Windows loaded
Cur_DOS_PDB = Win_PDB = topPDB

PrevInt21Proc( AH = 50 )    // Set PDB to cur_DOS_PDB

Free_Sel()    // Free the PDB selector stored in the TDB

FreeTDB()     // Free up the TDB selector

WExitingTDB = 0     // Indicate task is done terminating

RETF    // Returns to ExitSchedule in the scheduler
        // We're _still_ in the exception 6 handler.
```

AppExit()

We can now come back to the details of the USER task cleanup that we temporarily deferred. Inside the SignalProc() task signal handler routine in USER, if the signal number is either 20h (normal task termination) or 0666h (termination by GP fault), SignalProc() calls AppExit().

AppExit() is a particularly interesting routine. The code has to completely remove all traces of a task, at least from the perspective of the USER module. To make matters interesting, the task that's exiting could be dying as the result of a UAE or GPF. AppExit() can't make any assumptions concerning the state of the exiting task. For instance, the exiting task may have put Windows into a system modal state. Or it may have captured the mouse cursor. Or any number of other things. As a result, examining AppExit() gives us a pretty good idea of USER's worry list, that is, things that USER doesn't trust an application to have shut down properly. The operational motto of AppExit() seems to be, "Better safe than sorry."

```
Pseudocode for AppExit() - TMDSTROY.OBJ
// Parameters:
//      WORD    hTask
//      WORD    hInstance
//      WORD    hQueue
//      WORD    termByGPFault
// Locals:
//      WORD    hModule
//      DWORD   lpfnFileCDR

    hModule = GetInstanceModule(hInstance)  // Need the hModule

    if ( HQAppExit != 0 )        // See if we're recursing
        if debug KERNEL
            output a message: "Reentrant application termination"

    HQAppExit = hQueue       // HQAppExit is a global variable.
                             // Is non-zero if a task is exiting

    if ( fTaskIsLocked )     // If exiting task is system modal,
        LockMyTask(0)        // unlock it now

    CloseCommPorts( hTask ) // Don't need these anymore!

    DestroyTimers( hQueue, 0 )  // Undo any timers we have going

    Loop through some sort of linked list. If certain flags are
    set, and if a field in the structure matches the hInstance,
    call ReleaseCacheDC(). This would appear to be
    freeing up any DC's that weren't freed up by the program.
```

```
// Make sure nobody is waiting for us to reply to their
// sent message, because we certainly won't be.
FlushSentMessages()

UnhookHooks( hQueue, 1 )    // Release any installed hooks

//Did the app GP fault? Is it a 3.1 or later application?
if ( termByGPFault || GetExpWinVer(hInstance) = 0x30A )
    DeactivateQueue( hQueue )   // ???

// Change the queue handle of the desktop window to the
// queue of the parent of the exiting task.
PatchQueueModuleWindows( HWndDesktop, hQueue, 0 )

// Get rid of any windows or menus owned by the queue
// of the exiting task.
DestroyQueueWindows( HWndDesktop, hQueue )
DestroyQueueMenus ( hQueue )

// if the exiting queue "owns" the clipboard, reset
// values relating to the clipboard
if ( hQueue == hqClipLock )
{
    hwndClipOpen = 0
    hwndClipOwner = 0
    EmptyClipboard()
    hqClipLock = 0
}

// Do USER cleanup things that should be done on a per-module
// basis, rather than on a per-task basis (e.g. unhook
// installed hooks). Pseudo-code is below.
ModuleUnload( hModule, 1, termByGPFault )

fDragIcon = 0       // Not dragging icons anymore

// If the terminating application (e.g., WINFILE) is using
// FileCDR() disable the FileCDR() callbacks (see
// "Undocumented Windows" for FileCDR() description.
lpfnFileCDR = FileCDR( 0xFFFF )
if ( lpfnFileCDR )
    if ( GetProcModule( lpfnFileCDR ) == hModule )
        FileCDR( 0 )
```

```
Some kind of menu cleanup ( i.e, EndMenu() )

if ( termByGPFault )
{
    ClipCursor( 0 )      // Undo any cursor clipping the
                         // faulting app may have set up?

    fMessageBox = 0
    fInt24 = 0           // No longer in critical error handler

    EnableHardwareInput( 1 ) // Turn mouse on (just in case?)

    hCurCursor = 0                // Nobody has the cursor now
    SetCursor( hCursNormal )      // Restore to normal cursor

    if ( hTask == hTaskGrayString )       // The meaning of the
    {                                     // hTaskGrayString
        SelectObject( hDCGray, hBmGray )  // variable is
        SelectObject( hDCGray, hFontSys ) // unknown.
        hTaskGrayString = 0
    }
}
else    // The task is terminating normally (No GP fault)
{
    // If there's sufficient space in the DGROUP heap,
    // shrink all 3 heaps used by USER
    if ( LocalCountFree() > 4096 )
    {
        LocalShrink( 0,
            LocalHeapSize() - LocalCountFree() - 0x0400 )
        LocalShrink( hMenuHeap, 0 )
        LocalShrink( hMenuStringHeap, 0 )

        fShrinkGDI = 1  // GDI heap needs to shrink?
    }
}

if ( fPaletteDisplay )  // Does palette need to be changed?
    Tweak some palette values

// If the terminating app has the mouse capture, or is system
// modal, put the system back into a "normal" state
if ( HQAppExit == hQCapture ||
     HQAppExit == hQSysModal )
```

```
    {
        Capture( 0 )
        hwndSysModal = 0
        hqSysModal = 0
    }

    DeleteQueue()    // Don't need our message queue anymore!

    // Give GDI a chance to check for unfreed objects, etc?
    GDITaskTermination()

    // Tell installable drivers that an application is going away?
    InternalBroadcastDriverMessage()

    HQAppExit = 0    // AppExit() is done, and can now be
                     // entered again
```

ModuleUnload()

ModuleUnload() is a helper routine to AppExit(). It's called every time AppExit() is called, but only does something if this is the last task using the module, and the module is about to be unloaded. For instance, if you were running four copies of Solitaire (slow day, huh?), and exited each of them in turn, ModuleUnload() would be called each time. It doesn't spring into action, however, until the last instance terminates, and the Solitaire *module* is about to be unloaded.

ModuleUnload() performs the USER cleanup needed when a module (as opposed to a task using the module), is leaving the system. The two items that fall into this category are callback hooks like WH_JOURNALPLAYBACK and windows classes. It wouldn't do to undo hooks or unregister classes every time an application terminates. Another instance of the same program might be using them. Therefore, these two cleanup chores aren't performed until the last instance of a particular module terminates.

```
Pseudocode for ModuleUnload() - TMDSTROY.OBJ
// Parameters:
//      WORD    hModule
//      WORD    isApplication
//      WORD    termByGPFault
// Locals
//      WORD    usageCount

    usageCount = GetModuleUsage( hModule )
    // If this is the last instance of the module, or if the
    // app GP faulted, remove any installed hooks.
    if ( usageCount == 1 || termByGPFault )
        UnhookHooks( hModule, 0 )
```

```
    if ( usageCount == 1 )        // Is module going away?
    {
        // Patches queue handles in WND structures. Why?
        PatchQueueModuleWindows( hwndDesktop, 0, hModule )
        // Get rid of all classes registered by this module
        PurgeClass( hModule )      // see end of chapter 4
    }
```

FreeModule() and FreeLibrary()

Awhile ago, we handwaved past the details of FreeModule(). Now it's time to put it under the microscope. FreeModule() and FreeLibrary() are one and the same function, with the FreeLibrary() name being more widely known. There are two entry ordinals, but they both JMP to the same internal code. The code for FreeModule() is fairly straightforward. It starts by calling DecExeUsage() to decrease the usage count of the module. If the usage count drops to 0, FreeModule() removes the module from the system by calling DelModule(), which will be examined momentarily.

If the module isn't removed from the system, there's still work to be done in FreeModule(). If the module being freed has MULTIPLE data segments (that is, it is a task), the selector for the DGROUP segment might need to be updated in the module table. If you recall, each module table contains a table of the segments from the NE file, along with their associated selectors (see offset 22h in Table 3-1). Since multiple copies of a program can be running, the selector of the DGROUP segment in the segment table contains the selector value for the most recently run instance of the program. If this selector value is that of the DGROUP for the instance being freed, the selector value is invalid after the instance is freed. To remedy this, DelModule() iterates through the task list, looking for a task with a DGROUP that was created from the same module as the freed instance, but which is not the instance that's being freed. When a qualified DGROUP is found, FreeModule() plugs the selector into the DGROUP selector's spot in the module table.

```
Pseudocode for FreeModule() - MODULE.OBJ
// FreeLibrary() is an alias for FreeModule()
// Parameters:
//      WORD    instance_handle
// Locals:
//      WORD    module_table

    // GetExePtr takes an hInstance, and returns an hModule
    module_table = GetExePtr(instance_handle)    // Is module valid?
    if ( !module_table )
        return

    // Decrement the usage count of the module. If the usage
    // count becomes 0, it's time to remove the module from the
    // system.
    if ( DecExeUsage(module_table) == 0 )
```

```
    {
        DelModule(module_table)
        return
    }

    if ( module is MULTIPLE instance ) // More than one task using this module?
    {
        FarMyFree(instance_handle)    // Free the DGROUP.

        if ( instance_handle != current instance handle  // No need to worry?
             in the module_table )
            return

        // The instance handle in module_table has been freed.
        // It needs to be replaced with an hInstance for a
        // different instance of the same program.
        loop through the task list, looking for a task whose
        hModule == module_table, and whose hInstance is not the
        same as instance_handle. When one is found, store its
        hInstance into the instance_handle of module_table.
    }
```

DelModule()

DelModule() is responsible for undoing all the work that LoadModule() did. DelModule() calls FarDebugDelModule(), which causes the module deletion notification, NFY_DELMODULE in TOOLHELP.DLL, to be sent. Next, DelModule() uses CallWEP() to handle all the messy details of calling DLL WEP() functions. After whatever WEP() processing occurs, DelModule() calls the task signal procedure with a signal value of 80h, indicating that a DLL unload is taking place. DelModule() then frees the DGROUP segment of the DLL, if one is present. Self-loading applications have their ExitProc() called at this time. Continuing on, DelModule() closes the module's NE file handle in the KERNEL file handle cache. Next, DelModule() removes the exiting module from the list of modules. The global heap is locked during this procedure. Afterwards, the GlobalFreeAll() function walks through the global heap, freeing any global memory blocks owned by the outgoing module. (Global memory blocks that were owned by the process were freed previously, in the ExitCall() routine). Finally, DelModule() adjusts the maximum swap area size of the system by invoking CalcMaxNRSeg().

```
code for DelModule() - MODULE.OBJ
// Parameters:
//      WORD    module_table

    // Perform the RegisterPtrace/ToolhelpHook module deletion
    // notification.
    FarDebugDelModule()
```

```
CallWEP()   // Calls the WEP if necessary.

if ( module_table is for a DLL )
{
    if ( FP_SEG(pSignalProc) )
        pSignalProc(80) // Undocumented. 80 = DLL unload
}

if ( module_table has a DGROUP segment )
    FarMyFree(DGROUP segment)

if ( module is self loading )
    ExitAppl()                              // ExitProc()

FlushCachedFileHandle()                     // Remove from KERNEL cache

Far_GEnter()        // locks the global heap

// Remove module_table from the module list
FarUnlinkObject()

// Undoes the Far_GEnter()
Decrement the lrulock in the global heap

// Free any global blocks owned by the exiting module_table
GlobalFreeAll(module_table)

CalcMaxNRSeg()  // See if the swap area needs to be adjusted
```

What About Win32s Programs?

Having seen how normal Windows NE programs and DLLs are loaded and unloaded from memory, we can now take a little time and examine how Win32s allows programs designed for Win32 and Windows NT to be run on top of Windows 3.1.

The first difficulty with running Win32 programs that springs to mind is the fact that these programs aren't in the NE format. Instead, they're in the Portable Executable (PE) format. Indeed, when LoadModule() encounters one of these files, it doesn't load it. Instead, the error code (21) returned from LoadExeHeader() indicates to the caller that the file is a PE file. The INT 21h 4Bh (EXEC) handler in KERNEL sees "Windows 32-bit extensions required" error code and springs into action, calling the ExecPE() function.

ExecPE()

The ExecPE() function is responsible for loading W32SYS.DLL and transferring control to it. The ExecPE() code does nothing with regards to the 'PE' file. It's therefore obvious that the loader for 'PE' applications that run under Windows 3.1 is somewhere inside the Win32s system. This loader is responsible for doing everything that LoadModule() does, including creating module tables and task databases.

```
Pseudocode for ExecPE() - I21TASK.OBJ
// Command line and nCmdShow are on the stack when ExecPE is
// called. ExecPE does not set up its own stack frame
//
// Locals:
//      WORD hInstW32Sys
// Globals:
//      DWORD lpfnW32Sys_startprog

    // Don't prompt if the file can't be found
    SetErrorMode(8000h)
    Save the returned error mode on the stack

    // Load the Win32s support DLL
    hInstW32Sys = LoadLibrary("W32SYS.DLL")

    pop the returned error mode, and call SetErrorMode() again
    with the original error mode value

    // Get address of 3rd entry in W32SYS.DLL.
    lpfnW32Sys_startprog =
        GetProcAddress(hInstW32Sys, MK_FP(0, 3) )

    push lpfnW32Sys_startprog on stack, and RETF to it. This
    eliminates the return CS:IP from the stack, thereby making
    the stack in lpfnW32Sys_startprog look just like the stack
    frame that was passed to ExecPE()
```

The Win32s environment itself continues the grand tradition of hacks on top of hacks. When DOS programs started outgrowing the confines of real mode, DOS extenders were invented. A small stub program sits in real mode DOS and acts as a proxy for the protected mode code. The protected mode code ignores DOS and enjoys its newfound freedom, except when it needs to do certain things, at which point it temporarily converts back to a normal DOS program. The Win32s environment is a Windows Extender. A Win32s implementation has some EXEs and DLLs (for example, W32SYS.DLL), plus a virtual device driver, W32S.386, that give the appearance to 16-bit Windows that just another 16-bit Windows application is running. Meanwhile, the meat of a Win32s application runs in 32-bit flat mode and acts like a Win32 application. When it needs to put something on the screen or otherwise interact with lowly 16-bit Windows applications, it reverts temporarily to acting like a normal Windows application.

Self-Loading Windows Applications

This chapter wouldn't be complete if we didn't say a few words about the historical oddity of self-loading Windows applications. At one point in time, the Microsoft applications developers felt that the Windows loader, which we've just discussed so extensively, wasn't adequate for their needs. *Amazingly*, the Windows development team was able to provide a back door to the KERNEL, allowing a program to provide its own loader and rely only on very minimal KERNEL services. One might speculate as to whether this back door would have appeared had at least two of Microsoft's most successful products not been involved.

At this time, the only self-loading programs known to us are Microsoft Word 1.x, Microsoft Fortran, and early versions of Microsoft Excel. With Microsoft Word 2.0, self-loading appears to have been abandoned. Microsoft Fortran produces programs that use the self-loading mechanism because of the lack of proper support for huge (greater than 64K) data segments in Windows 3.0. The large data segments were necessary for Fortran COMMON block support. Additionally, Microsoft Excel 3.0 appears to have self-loading fingerprints, perhaps left over from a previous version. However, Excel 3.0 does not use the self-loading facilities of Windows 3.X. In version 4.0 of Excel, the fingerprints are gone. The obvious conclusion is that Microsoft itself is moving away from self-loading applications.

At this point, you might be thinking, "Oh well, they're a thing of the past. History is bunk. End of story." This is not the case. With the Microsoft Open Tools initiative of 1991, the requirements for a self-loading application were laid out. This documentation, while a huge step in the right direction, was amazingly lacking in some key details and concepts that would be necessary for someone to implement a self-loading application. The Open Tools documentation later reappeared in the Windows 3.1 SDK (Chapter 24, Overviews), with *even less* detail provided. Microsoft representatives on CompuServe have stated that self-loading applications were documented because Microsoft itself uses them, and that Open Tools was intended to create a level playing field. At the same time however, they strongly discouraged anyone from actually writing one. The fact that Microsoft discourages self-loading applications, along with the incomplete documentation, may be related. Everything associated with self-loading applications seems to generate lots of heat, but not much light. It has been suggested that the self-loading documentation is so poor because no one in Redmond admits to knowing anything about it!

Why would a program purposely forego using the loader provided by KERNEL, especially when one considers the substantial amount of work self-loading requires? The Microsoft documentation itself gives two very good examples of why performing your own loading might be beneficial. The first reason is that your program might wish to use different code or data segments for different machine configurations or environments. The Microsoft documentation gives the case of a Windows compiler that generates different code for machines with a coprocessor than for those without. The other example given is that of a program where data segments have been compressed and need to be expanded to be read into memory. Self-loading has a tendency to make life more difficult for those people who try to disassemble everything in sight. In fact, a third use of self-loading applications would be for encrypting sensitive data and allowing it to be loaded only if the proper password, dongle, or whatever was present.

Despite the previous comments on the quality of the SDK documentation regarding self-loading applications, it's still the first place to go if your application just *has* to be self-loading. Rather than rewriting everything that's in the SDK documentation, we'll assume that you have it and will comment on various spots where the documentation is unclear or lacking.

The first spot in the SDK documentation that bears closer examination is the sentence, "For a complete description of an executable file before it is altered by the loader and loaded into memory..." This information is analogous to describing a butterfly by discussing the details of the cocoon. Since Microsoft hasn't divulged the details of the in-memory module table, the documentation assumes that you know that file offsets in the NE header translate to offsets in the module tables segment. In addition, there are tables in the in-memory module table that have a different format than those in the NE file. Luckily, in most cases, a self-loading application doesn't need to use any tables beside the segment table, which is addressed momentarily. If you do need to know the format of the other tables, see Table 3-1 on the in-memory module table.

Next, there is a spot in the documentation referencing the self-loading flag, which must be set to 0x0800. There are two different sets of flag in the NE header. The module table description early in this chapter refers the flags at offset 0Ch in the NE header. What's completely missing in the documentation is just how those flag values get set. The Open Tools documentation is somewhat clearer on this, stating that starting with LINK version 5.15, APPLOADER is a new keyword in the DEF file that causes the bit to be set. Borland's TLINK does not support this feature. However, it would be rather trivial, given the NE file spec, to write a 30 line C program that would find the NE header and toggle on the bit. There does not appear to be anything else special required, besides setting the bit and having a proper loader data table set up in segment 1.

Continuing our hit parade we find the section that says, "After the segment table for an executable file is loaded in memory, each entry contains an additional 16-bit value. This value is a segment selector (or handle) that the loader created." This refers to the eight-byte segment table entries for an NE file. What the documentation is trying to say is that each eight-byte entry on disk becomes a ten-byte entry when loaded into memory. The last two bytes contain the selector handle used to reference the CODE or DATA in the segment. This topic was discussed previously in the section on the module table (see offset 22h in Table 3-1). In addition, the documentation implies that the module table is handed to the self-loading application, with the selectors already allocated for each of the segments. This is not the case. BootApp() is a function that must be provided as part of a self-loading executable. When BootApp() is called, it's expected to allocate the selectors for each of the segments in the NE file and patch the segment table itself.

In the section, Reloading Segments, the documentation says, "...the LoadAppSeg function should resolve any far pointers that occur in the segment." This seems to contradict an earlier statement, "All of the pointers in this table must point to locations within the first segment. There can be no fixups outside this segment." The intended meaning might be this: All functions pointed to in the Loader Data Table must be in the first segment. Otherwise, there'd be relocations to segments that the Windows loader isn't loading, but which you are.

Now that we've beaten up on the documentation, let's take a look at what KERNEL does to assist self-loading applications. Self-loading programs are required to provide three functions, BootApp(), ExitApp(), and LoadAppSeg(), which Windows calls at the appropriate time. Each of these functions has a corresponding wrapper function in KERNEL. Thus, BootApp() is called by KERNEL's BootAppl(); LoadAppSeg() is called by LoadApplSeg(); and ExitProc() is called by ExitAppl(). As it turns out, however, ExitAppl() is an empty function. It doesn't do anything, which means that the user-supplied ExitProc() isn't called. The KERNEL-supplied functions that a self-loading application uses is discussed in other chapters of this book. That leaves BootAppl() and LoadApplSeg(), for which we can show pseudocode.

BootAppl()

BootAppl() starts by verifying that the segment attributes for segment 1 are what they should be for a self-loading application. BootAppl() then loads the first segment, just as if it were a regular segment in any normal Windows EXE. One result is that the fixups for the first segment are applied. This is how the addresses of the user-supplied functions in the loader data table get filled in. Next, a data segment selector that aliases the newly loaded code segment is created. This allows BootAppl() to put in the addresses of the KERNEL-supplied functions without GP faulting by trying to write to a code segment. After verifying the "A0" signature at offset 0 in the segment, BootAppl() calls the user supplied BootApp() function using the function pointer in the loader data table.

```
Pseudocode for BootAppl() - LDAPPL.OBJ
// Parameters:
//      WORD    module_table
//      WORD    file_handle

    // LoadModule() sets all code segments to moveable,
    // so if the first segment is fixed, something funny
    // is going on.
    if ( first segment in module_table is FIXED )
        return 0

    if ( first segment in module_table isn't PRELOAD )
        return 0

    FarLoadSegment(1)          // Load segment 1 normally

    // Allocate a data segment alias for the newly load code
    Far_Get_Temp_Sel()

    If ( first 2 bytes in the segment != "A0" )
        return 0

    Fill in the "self-loading" table with the addresses of
    FarMyAlloc(), AppLoaderEntProcAddress(), and MySetOwner().
    Another far pointer not mentioned in the documentation is
    also filled in.

    Far_Free_Temp_Sel() // Free the data segment alias
```

```
    call BootApp() in the application's code, via the function
    pointer in the self-loading app table.
```

LoadApplSegment()

LoadApplSeg() begins by calling the user-supplied LoadAppSeg() function with the pointer in the loader data table. On its first attempt, LoadApplSeg() passes LoadAppSeg() the file handle that it was passed as a parameter. If that procedure fails for some reason, LoadApplSeg() tries to open up the EXE file itself and calls LoadAppSeg() again with its newly opened file handle. Before LoadApplSeg() returns, it checks to see if it did open the file, and if so, it closes the file.

```
Pseudocode for LoadApplSegment() - LDAPPL.OBJ
// Parameters:
//      WORD    module_table
//      WORD    segment_number
//      WORD    file_handle
// Locals:
        WORD    local_file_handle

    local_file_handle = -1

start:

    if ( "AO" signature not in segment 1 )
        goto error

    call program supplied LoadAppSeg() function with the function
    pointer stored in the self-loading table

    if ( LoadAppSeg() returned non-zero )   // Selector in AX
        goto done

    // Open the file specified in the module table. The flags
    // are OF_PROMPT | OF_REOPEN | OF_CANCEL | OF_VERIFY
    if ( local_file_handle == -1 )
    {
        local_file_handle = MyOpenFile()

        // Try to call LoadAppSeg() again with this file handle
        if ( local_file_handle )
            goto start
    }

error:
```

```
    AX = 0

done:

    if ( local_file_handle )
        INT 21h, fn. 3Eh to close local_file_handle

    return AX
```

Summary

In this chapter, we've examined modules, tasks, and the Windows loader.

A module is comprised of a module table and the associated code, data, and resources that the module table refers to. A module table is somewhat similar to the New Executable header found in NE files. The global memory handle used to access the module table is called a module handle, or hModule. Both programs and DLLs are built from modules. The automatic data segment (DGROUP) for program and DLL modules is called the instance handle, or hInstance.

A task is a thread of execution through code. Every task has a task database (TDB) associated with it. The task database stores information about the task, such as the number of events waiting for the task, a handle to the task's message queue, the current directory, and so on. The global memory handle used to access the task database is called a task handle, or hTask. There can be more than one task created from a program module. Tasks based on the same module can be differentiated by their DGROUP segment (hInstance).

The Windows loader consists of the LoadModule() function and its helper functions. LoadModule() loads both programs and DLLs. Much of the work of the Windows loader involves reading in the NE file, and creating a module from it. If the module is for a program file, the loader also creates a task database and inserts the new task into the list of tasks to be scheduled.

CHAPTER 4

The Windowing System

Of all the Windows components, the most immediately visible is the windowing system. Understanding the fundamentals of the windowing system is crucial, as this is how you convey information to and from the user. Any interactive DOS program must deal with the specifics of the keyboard, mouse, and video display mode. One of the goals of Windows is to remove the need to worry about these hardware-specific areas and let you concentrate on your program. Chapter 7 on the messaging system concentrates on how messages are passed around between windows and applications. Here, we examine the internal data structures for windows and classes and see what happens during the lifetime of a window.

The implementation of the windowing system in USER.EXE could easily be the subject of an entire book. Therefore, the functions discussed here are in no way supposed to represent the whole of the windowing system. We cannot hope to cover all the intricacies of such things as controls, the dialog manager, or Multiple Document Interface (MDI) windows. Instead the focus is on covering areas that even the simplest generic application encounters.

You might be surprised to learn that, like the messaging system, the windowing system in Windows is quite similar to its OS/2 counterpart. Therefore, many of the concepts in this chapter apply equally to Presentation Manager (PM) and to Windows. Experts in this area give the idea that the PM implementation is purer. Its API doesn't have as many special cases and doesn't try to overload parameters to mean different things in different circumstances. Since OS/2 PM was designed and developed after the original Windows implementation, it's reasonable to assume that Microsoft and IBM, one-time partners who developed PM, incorporated many of the lessons learned from Windows.

Many programmers keep the core Windows DLLs straight by associating their primary functionality with them. For instance, KERNEL (KRNL286 and KRNL386) is considered to be the memory manager, while the Graphics Device Interface (GDI) is considered the graphics engine. In this simplified scheme, USER is the windowing system. Although USER performs other duties such as resource handling, string manipulation, and atom management, the vast majority of USER appears to deal with displaying and managing windows in one form or another.

Window Classes

One of the first and most daunting things new Windows programmers encounter is the RegisterClass() function. The WNDCLASS structure you pass as a parameter sure has a lot of fields! Why do you have a WNDCLASS, and why do you need to call RegisterClass() with the WNDCLASS, if all you want to do is put a simple window on the screen?

The WNDCLASS structure reflects Window's habit of sharing as much commonality as possible. Rather than forcing the programmer to specify all the attributes of a window whenever a new window is created, the attributes are collected into a central place, the WNDCLASS structure. When you need to create a new instance of a particular kind of window, USER can retrieve much of the required information out the WNDCLASS structure, which is described below.

A window class is similar in some ways to the module table (Chapter 3). It acts as a central database of information and can be reused by different programs. Just as tasks are created from information in a module table, windows are created from information stored in a window class. When the last task created from a module table goes away, so does the module table. When the last window using a class goes away, so does the window class (sort of: see the discussion of PurgeClass() at the end of this chapter). The use of the term class is rather unfortunate, as a class in Windows has a completely different meaning from a C++ class.

A disturbing aspect of window classes is that you need to contend with them immediately upon writing your first non-trivial Windows program. There are typically lots of window classes already registered when your program starts up, such as the USER control classes described below. Unfortunately, none of these classes is either suitable or available for popping up a simple window and printing "Hello World" in it. Instead, most programmers' first Windows programs usually create a very predictable generic window class. There doesn't appear to be any reason why Windows couldn't have a predefined generic window class. It would certainly be helpful to beginning programmers.

In order to provide a slick look, as well as to include a modicum of basic functionality, Windows provides a collection of predefined window classes for certain well-defined tasks. These window classes are commonly known as controls; they include standard user-interface components such as scroll bars, list boxes, edit boxes, and so on. These controls are registered inside the USER module at bootstrap time (see Chapter 1) and are CS_GLOBALCLASS classes, making them available to all applications. The standard windows control classes are as follows:

ComboBox
ComboLBox
ScrollBar
ListBox
Edit
Static
Button

When you specify the layout of a dialog box in a resource script (.RC) file, you use names like PUSHBUTTON, SCROLLBAR, or LISTBOX. The resource compiler converts the strings into integer IDs that are stored in the RES and EXE or DLL files. When you create a dialog box using the dialog template, USER takes these integer values and uses them to look up the appropriate WNDCLASS structure in a list of window classes. USER then passes the selected window class as an argument to CreateWindowEx(), which creates the control window. In addition to the control classes, USER creates some additional classes for its own use as well:

```
MDIClient
#32768 (PopupMenu)     // These windows are named using the
#32769 (Desktop)       // integer atom method. The names in
#32770 (Dialog)        // parentheses are just descriptions.
#32771 (WinSwitch)     // WinSwitch is the ALT-TAB window.
#32772 (IconTitle)     // IconTitle is the title below an icon.
```

Window classes can either be application local or global. You typically create an application local class when you call RegisterClass(). Only instances of your program or DLL can use this window class to create windows. If a different program registers a class using the same name, USER creates a different class. The module handle is used to differentiate between application local classes with the same name. A global window class (CS_GLOBALCLASS) is a class that's available for use by all applications. The USER control classes are the best examples of global classes. When an application specifies a class name to CreateWindow(), the code first searches for an application local class. If the class isn't found, CreateWindow() repeats the search, but this time, global classes are also included in the search.

Format of the WNDCLASS Structure.

The parameter to RegisterClass() is a pointer to a WNDCLASS structure, defined in WINDOWS.H. RegisterClass() creates a data structure in the USER local heap that's a combination of the WNDCLASS and some additional information about the class. Here, we call the data structure an INTWNDCLASS (for INTernal WNDCLASS). The first part of an INTWNDCLASS consists of fields initialized by USER internally. The second part of the INTWNDCLASS structure is a copy of the WNDCLASS passed to RegisterClass(), although USER modifies a few fields after it copies the WNDCLASS.

The format of an INTWNDCLASS is shown in Table 4-1.

Table 4-1: Format of an INTWNDCLASS.

Off	Type	Name	Description
00h	WORD	hcNext	USER local handle of next class in linked list.
02h	WORD	wSig	Signature word - 4B4Eh. (4B4Eh = 'NK' for Neil Konzen, the original author of USER.)
04h	ATOM	atomCls	USER local atom for class name.
06h	WORD	hDCE	USER local handle to device context entry (DCE) (see *Undocumented Windows*).
08h	WORD	cClsWnds	Number of windows of this class.

From this point, the rest of an INTWNDCLASS is just a WNDCLASS and can be accessed with the GetClassWord() and GetClassLong() APIs:

Off	Type	Name	Description
0Ah	WORD	style	WS_XXX style bits.
0Ch	WNDPROC	lpfnWndProc	Address of window procedure.
10h	WORD	cbClsExtra	Extra bytes needed by class, allocated at end of structure and accessed by GetClassWord() or GetClassLong().
12h	WORD	cbWndExtra	Extra bytes needed by each window of this class (allocated at end of WND structure).
14h	HMODULE	hModule	Module handle of registering module (not an hInstance!).
16h	HICON	hIcon	Icon handle associated with instances of this window.
18h	HCURSOR	hCursor	Cursor handle associated with instances of this window.
1Ah	HBRUSH	hBrBackground	Background Brush handle for window instances.
1Ch	LPSTR	lpszMenuName	Menu name for class.
20h	LPSTR	lpszClassName	Name of class (zeroed by RegisterClass).

Of particular interest here is the hcNext field, used by USER to keep all window classes in a linked list. The TOOLHELP API provides functions for walking the list of registered window classes. If you're feeling adventurous, call the undocumented UserSeeUserDo(5) function to get the first class in the list; then walk the class list yourself. This function only works under Windows 3.1. When running under Windows 3.0, TOOLHELP finds the head of the class list using hard-coded offsets into a USER data segment.

Another thing worth noting in the INTWNDCLASS is the use of ATOMs to manage the class name. For instance, the GetClassName() API simply obtains the handle to the INTWNDCLASS stored in the passed HWND's data structure. The atomCls stored in the INTWNDCLASS can be fed to GetAtomName() to retrieve the class name, assuming DS is set to USER's DGROUP. This use of atoms is similar to how GDI manages device driver names (see Chapter 5).

Class Registration

The first step in creating a new window is to create a new class, or at least to know the name of a suitable, existing class. Look below at how RegisterClass() adds a new class to the windowing system.

RegisterClass()

```
ATOM    WINAPI RegisterClass(const WNDCLASS FAR*);
```

At its highest level, RegisterClass() checks to see if the class to be registered is already present in the system. If not, it allocates memory for it out of a USER local heap and fills in the INTWNDCLASS fields.

RegisterClass() first calls GetClassPtr() (covered next) to see if an application local class that was registered by the calling module is already present in the system. If so, RegisterClass() aborts immediately. The next step is to determine if the class will be a global class, accessible to all applications. In Windows 3.0 and greater, the CS_GLOBALCLASS flag indicates that the class should be global. Prior to version 3.0, however, all classes were global, so the expected Windows version of the calling module needs to be determined, to allow the appropriate global class things to be done in all cases. (Yes, there really were Windows applications before version 3.0, and some people still run them!).

With this initial inspection out of the way, RegisterClass() now allocates memory for the INTWNDCLASS structure. It block-copies the data in the passed WNDCLASS structure to the end of the newly allocated INTWNDCLASS. Afterwards, RegisterClass() starts filling in and modifying fields in the INTWNDCLASS.

RegisterClass() calls AddAtom() to add the class name to the USER local atom table. The returned atom handle is stored in the atomCls field of the INTWNDCLASS. If a valid menu name is passed, the function allocates memory for a local copy of the menu name, and copies the menu name string into the local copy. This is necessary because the calling task many not keep the menu name string around for the entire existence of the class. It's necessary to make a local copy of the name to ensure that you've got a valid pointer at all times.

The hInstance passed in the WNDCLASS structure is now converted into the module handle associated with the hInstance. Despite the fact that the Microsoft documentation refers to it as an instance handle, after the class is registered, it's really a module handle. It doesn't make sense to tie a class to a particular *instance* of a program. Another instance of a program could be using the window class when the first instance shuts down. If USER deleted the class when the registering *instance* went away, the results could be disastrous. Information like this is *per module*, not per instance.

The remaining code just fills in a few more fields in the INTWNDCLASS and uses hcNext to link the new INTWNDCLASS into the list of classes. The return value of RegisterClass() is either 0, 1, or the atom handle of the class name.

```
Pseudocode for RegisterClass() - WMCLASS.OBJ
// Parameters:
//      WNDCLASS far * lpWndCls
// Locals:
```

```
//      INTWNDCLASS *intWndCls      // Pointer to internal class
//      WORD        isGlobalClass   // is it a CS_GLOBALCLASS ?
//      WORD        expWinVersion   // expected Windows version
//      LPSTR       menuName        // local copy of menu name

    // Look up the class in the list of existing classes.
    // GetClassPtr() walks the list of classes (using the
    // next field of the INTWNDCLASS structure). The
    // hInstance parameter is necessary for identifying
    // application local classes.
    intWndCls = GetClassPtr(lpWndCls->lpszClassName,
                    lpWndCls->hInstance, 0 )

    if ( intWndCls )  // Abort if the class is already registered
    {
        _DebugOutput(
            "USER: RegisterClass failed: class already exists")
        return 0
    }

    if ( lpWndCls->style & CS_GLOBALCLASS ) // Set a flag
        isGlobalClass = 1                   // indicating if this
    else                                    // will be a global
        isGlobalClass  = 0                  // class

    // Get the minimum version of Windows required for module
    expWinVer = GetExpWinVer( lpWndCls->hInstance )

    if ( expWinVer < 0x0300 )   // Before Windows 3.0, all
        isGlobalClass = 1       // classes were global, so set
                                // isGlobalClass appropriately
    if ( isGlobalClass )    // Are we registering a global class?
    {
        // Look up the class name to be registered in the USER
        // local atom table. Pass this, along with the module
        // handle of the registering module to GetClassPtrAsm().
        // The idea is to see if the class is already registered
        // by walking the list of registered classes.
        intWndCls = GetClassPtrAsm(
            FindAtom( lpWndCls->lpszClassName ),
            GetModuleHandle(MAKELP( 0, lpWndCls->hInstance)), 1 )

        if ( intWndCls )  // Abort now if the class already exists
        {
            _DebugOutput( "USER: RegisterClass failed: global "
                          "class already exists" )
            return 0
        }
    }
```

```
// Allocate memory for the new class. The first parameter
// tells the debug USER that the allocation is for a class
// (see TOOLHELP.H). The allocated memory is zero filled and
// FIXED (since LMEM_MOVEABLE isn't specified). The returned
// "handle" is really a near pointer to the class's memory.
// The third parameter takes into account any "extra bytes"
// specified in the WNDCLASS structure.
intWndCls = UserLocalAlloc(LT_USER_CLASS, LMEM_ZEROINIT,
                sizeof(INTWNDCLASS) + lpWndCls->cbClsExtra)

if ( !intWndCls )    // Make sure we successfully allocated
    return 0         // memory for the new class

// Copy the passed WNDCLASS structure into the middle
// of the INTWNDCLASS structure (starting at offset 0xA)
LCopyStruct( lpWndCls, intWndCls + 0xA, sizeof(WNDCLASS) )

// If the user specified the ugly IDI_APPLICATION icon,
// switch it now to the more colorful Windows "flag" icon.
// HIconWindows is a USER global variable
if ( intWndCls->hIcon == HIconSample )
    intWndCls->hIcon = HIconWindows

// Turn on CS_GLOBALCLASS flag for applications that don't
// know to do it for themselves (i.e., pre-3.0 programs)
if ( isGlobalClass )
    turn on CS_GLOBALCLASS in intWndCls->style

// Add the new class name to the USER atom table (The DS
// register must be set to the DGROUP segment whose atom
// table you want to add to (in this case, USER's)
intWndCls->atomCls = AddAtom( intWndCls->lpszClassName )
if ( !intWndCls->atomCls )
    goto RegisterClassNoMem

// Null out the pointer to the class name. From now on,
// you can only get the name by dereferencing the atom.
// ( GetClassName() does this )
intWndCls->lpszClassName = 0

if ( FP_SEG(intWndCls->lpszMenuName) )  // Was a menu given?
{
    if ( strlen(intWndCls->lpszMenuName) == 0 )
    {
        menuName = 0  // No menu if the "empty" string given
    }
```

```
    else                // Menu name string looks OK
    {
        // Time to go allocate space so that we can retain
        // a local copy of it in the USER local heap.
        menuName = UserLocalAlloc( LT_USER_CLASS,
                        LMEM_ZEROINIT,
                        strlen(intWndCls->lpszMenuName) )

        if ( menuName == 0 )    // Did allocation fail?
        {
            DeleteAtom( intWndCls->atomCls ) // Not needed
            goto RegisterClassNoMem          // anymore
        }

        // Copy the string to the allocated memory (in the
        // USER heap), and update the menu name pointer in
        // the INTWNDCLASS data structure.
        lstrcpy( menuName, lpWndCls->lpszMenuName )
        intWndCls->lpszMenuName = menuName
    }
}

// Make the background brush private if it's greater
// than or equal to 0x15
if ( intWndCls->hbrBackground >= 0x15 )
    MakeObjectPrivate( intWndCls->hBrBackgound, 1 )

// The hInstance field in the WNDCLASS is seriously
// mislabeled. It is really a module handle, not an
// instance handle. In fact, GetClassWord() accesses this
// field with a GCW_MODULE constant, instead of as
// GCW_INSTANCE. Here, the code converts the passed
// hInstance into the corresponding hModule.
intWndCls->hModule = GetModuleHandle(
            MAKELP( 0, intWndCls->hModule) )
intWndCls->wSig = 0x4B4E    // 'NK' = Neil Konzen

intWndCls->hcNext = PClsList    // Add class to the head of
PClsList = intWndCls            // the list of classes
                                // PClsList is a USER var

if ( expWinVersion > 0x0300 )   // If Win 3.1 app or later,
    return intWndCls->atomCls   // return the atom of the
else                            // class name. Otherwise,
    return 1                    // just return 1
```

```
RegisterClassNoMem:

    // "generic" failure label. Tell the programmer there's
    // no memory, then free up memory allocated for INTWNDCLASS.
    _DebugOutput( "USER: RegisterClass failed: out of memory" )

    LocalFree(intWndCls)  // Don't need this memory anymore!
    return 0
```

In a nutshell, RegisterClass() creates a new instance of an INTWNDCLASS data structure and links it into the list of INTWNDCLASSes maintained by USER.

GetClassPtr()

GetClassPtr() is the high-level routine that encapsulates the algorithm for looking up a class. If it finds the specified class, GetClassPtr() returns a pointer to a pointer to an INTWNDCLASS (an INTWNDCLASS **). GetClassPtr() relies heavily on the lower level GetClassPtrAsm() function, described next.

After some initial validity tests, GetClassPtr() converts the passed hInstance into the correct hModule. This is necessary because an INTWNDCLASS has an hModule, not an hInstance, stored in it. If the global-class flag wasn't specified, GetClassPtr() calls GetClassPtrAsm(), telling it to only look for application local classes. If such a class isn't found, or if we're only interested in global classes, GetClassPtr() uses GetClassPtrAsm() again, this time directing it to look for global classes. If that search fails, GetClassPtr() uses GetClassPtrAsm() one more time, directing it to look up the class using USER's module handle. This is how the control classes (e.g., buttons) are found by applications and DLLs, even though their hModules don't match USER's hModule.

```
Pseudocode for GetClassPtr() - WMCLASS.OBJ
// Parameters:
//      LPSTR   lpszClassName
//      HANDLE  hInstance
//      WORD    checkGlobalClasses  // Look for global classes?
// Locals:
//      ATOM    atom
//      INTWNDCLASS   near * near *intWndCls
//      HANDLE  hModule

    atom = FP_OFF( lpszClassName )  // In case MAKELONG(0, atom)
                                    // was passed

    // If a valid name pointer was passed (the selector portion
    // is nonzero), look up the name in the USER atom table.
    if ( FP_SEG(lpszClassName) )
        atom = FindAtom( lpszClassName )
```

```
    if ( atom == 0 )            // if a valid atom or name wasn't passed to
        return 0                // us bail out now.

    // Get the module handle associated with the hInstance. Note
    // the undocumented usage for GetModuleHandle(). FMessageBox
    // is a USER global variable that's set to 1 inside
    // SysErrorBox() (a critical state!). It's not known why
    // FMessageBox comes into play here.
    hModule = hInstance
    if ( FMessageBox == 0 )
         hModule = GetModuleHandle( MK_FP(0, hInstance) )
    else

        goto LookupGlobalClasses

    // Look for the class in the class list, but only look
    // for application local classes for now (the 0 param)
    intWndCls = GetClassPtrAsm( atom, hModule, 0 )
    if ( *intWndCls != 0 )      // Return the pointer we got, if
       goto GetClassPtr_exit    // it points to nonzero value

LookupGlobalClasses:  // End up here when we want global classes
    if ( checkGlobalClasses == 0 )  // *intWndCls == 0 if we
        goto GetClassPtr_exit       // get here (see above)

    // Look for classes again, but this time, we'll accept
    // a CS_GLOBALCLASS (the 1 parameter)
    intWndCls = GetClassPtrAsm(atom, hModule, 1)
    if ( *intWndCls != 0 )       // Return the pointer we got, if
        goto GetClassPtr_exit    // it points to nonzero value

    // Our last hope. Look for classes registered by the USER
    // module (e.g., dialog boxes, buttons, etc.). If we get
    // to this point, whatever GetClassPtrAsm() returns to us is
    // what GetClassPtr() returns. hModuleWin is USER's module handle.
    intWndCls = GetClassPtrAsm(atom, hModuleWin, 0 )

GetClassPtr_exit:
    return intWndCls
```

GetClassPtrAsm()

GetClassPtrAsm() is the dumb, low-level routine that simply iterates through the class list, looking for a class that matches the passed parameters. The one bit of intelligence it has is that it knows it's OK if the hModule fields don't match up when directed to look for a global class.

```
Pseudocode for GetClassPtrAsm() - CLASS.OBJ
// Parameters:
//      ATOM    atom
//      HANDLE  hModule
//      WORD    globalClassFlag
// Locals:
//      INTWNDCLASS near * near * intWndCls

    if ( atom == 0 )        // Must be passed a valid atom!
        return 0

    intWndCls = &PClsList   // Get pointer to pointer to class list
                            // PCls List is a USER Global variable that
                            // points to the head of the class list.

    // Start walking through the linked list of INTWNDCLASSs
    // in the USER local heap.
    while ( *intWndCls )
    {
        // Do the class name atoms match?  If they do, drop out
        // of the loop for further testing to see if it's the
        // class we're after.
        if ( (*intWndCls)->atom == atom )
            break;
NextClass:
        intWndCls = &(*intWndCls)->classNext    // Go on to
    }                                           // next class

    if ( *intWndCls == 0 )  // Was something found?  Return
        return intWndCls    // "empty" pointer if not

    // We get to this section of the code if the above loop
    // found a class whose atom handle matches the atom
    // handled passed as a parameter. It's necessary to do
    // further testing on the class to see if it's really the
    // class we're looking for.

    if ( hModule == 0 )     // If hModule parameter is null, we
        return intWndCls    // don't need to compare hModules,
                            // so just return the found class.

    // Does the passed in hModule match that stored in the
    // INTWNDCLASS?   We're done if they do.
    if ( (*intWndCls)->hModule == hModule )
        return intWndCls
```

```
// If we get here, the atom names matched up, but the
// hModules don't. This would happen if two applications
// registered application local classes with the same name.

// If we're not looking for global classes, continue iterating
// through the list, looking for a class whose module does
// match the passed module handle (and whose atom matches)
if ( globalClassFlag == 0 )
    goto NextClass

// If we are looking for global classes, see if the class for which we
// broke out of the loop is a CS_GLOBALCLASS. If not
// go back and continue searching through the other classes.
if ( (intWndCls->style & CS_GLOBALCLASS ) == 0 )
    goto NextClass

return intWndCls    // All tests passed. Ship it!
```

In summary, a window class is a convenient way to store information that's common between windows. An application can register new window classes as needed. In addition, there are predefined window classes that USER provides (the control windows). We now turn our attention to the process of creating windows from a registered class.

Windows and the WND Data Structure

The windowing system in USER can be thought of as a tree. All windows fall somewhere in the hierarchy, with the desktop window at the root of the tree. Each window has its own data area to maintain the window's state. You change the state of a window by sending messages to it (for instance, the WM_PAINT message tells a window to go into its paint state). We discuss both the window tree and the state that each window maintains in the following sections.

Perhaps the most pervasive handle in all of Windows is the HWND. An HWND is a local handle to a WND data structure in the USER local heap. Unfortunately, Microsoft doesn't document the format of the WND data structure that the HWND refers to. As mentioned in *Undocumented Windows*, the window structure changes dramatically between Windows 3.0 and 3.1. Some people might see this as evidence that you really should heed Microsoft's warnings not to use undocumented data structures. Other people, however, might see this as evidence that Microsoft deliberately broke misbehaving applications that used undocumented fields. There may have been a legitimate reason for this dramatic change, but none is known at this time.

Although the WND structure wasn't formally documented under Windows 3.0, certain parts of it could be derived by looking at the GetWindowWord() and GetWindowLong() constants in WINDOWS.H. These could be treated as negative displacements from the end of the WND structure. As people found out about other undocumented fields in the WND structure (for example, Paul Bonneau's June 1992 *Windows/DOS Developer's Journal* column), they could easily be extracted by defining new constant values to pass to GetWindowWord() or GetWindowLong(). In Windows 3.1, the ordering of the WND fields changed, which means that the constant values in WINDOWS.H no longer work as offsets. In order to be backwards compatible, the USER authors were forced to continue using the same WINDOWS.H values and to use a table to convert the WINDOWS.H constants to usable offsets in the 3.1 WND structure. Why would they take a simple system, as implemented in Windows 3.0, and make it slower and more complicated? Go back and read the preceding paragraph and draw your own conclusions.

The format of a WND structure under Windows 3.1 is shown in Table 4-2.

Table 4-2: Format of a WND Structure Under Windows 3.1.

Off	Type	Name	Description
00h	HWND	hWndNext	(GW_HWNDNEXT) window handle of next sibling window.
02h	HWND	hWndChild	(GW_CHILD) First child window.
04h	HWND	hWndParent	(GWW_HWNDPARENT) Parent window handle.
06h	HWND	hWndOwner	(GW_OWNER) Owning window handle.
08h	RECT	rectWindow	Rectangle describing entire window.
10h	RECT	rectClient	Rectangle for client area of window.
18h	HANDLE	hQueue	Application message queue handle.
1Ah	HRGN	hrgnUpdate	window region needing an update.
1Ch	HANDLE	wndClass	handle to an INTWNDCLASS.
1Eh	HANDLE	hInstance	(GWW_HINSTANCE) hInstance of creating application.
20h	WNDPROC	lpfnWndProc	(GWL_WNDPROC) Window procedure address.
24h	DWORD	dwFlags	internal state flags.
28h	DWORD	dwStyleFlags	(GWL_STYLE) Flags holding window style (the WS_XXX values in WINDOWS.H).
2Ch	DWORD	dwExStyleFlags	(GWL_EXSTYLE) Flags holding extended window style (the WS_EX_XXX styles in WINDOWS.H).
30h	HANDLE	hMenu	Menu handle for window.
32h	HANDLE	hBuffer	Alternative DS value for window text.
34h	WORD	scrollBar	WORD associated with the scroll bars.
36h	HANDLE	properties	Handle for first window property.
38h	HWND	hwndLastActive	Last active owned popup window.
3Ah	HANDLE	hMenuSystem	handle to the system menu.

The WND structure has quite a few interesting fields. The structure starts out with the parent, next, child, and owner window fields. These fields allow USER to maintain the window hierarchy, which we examine shortly.

USER employs the hQueue field to know which message queue a message should go to, given just an HWND. This is an extremely important point. As Chapter 7 discusses, each application has its own message queue. Since each window is associated with a specific message queue, windows are implicitly connected to a particular task as well. It doesn't matter whether the window was created inside a DLL or an application. All that matters is what the current message queue was at the time of the window's creation. Whatever task owns that message queue implicitly owns all the windows associated with the queue. When the task goes away, so will its windows. Knowing this, we can answer the commonly asked question, "Who owns the window if CreateWindow() is called in a DLL?" The application that called the DLL owns the window. This is what GetWindowTask() returns.

The wndClass field allows the window to refer back to its class, just as each task database maintains a selector to the module table from which it came.

The hInstance field stores the DGROUP associated with the DLL or EXE that created the window. As shown in the pseudocode for DispatchMessage() in Chapter 7, the AX register is loaded with the value in the hInstance field before calling the window function. A normally exported window function in an EXE loads the data segment register (DS) from the AX register in its prologue. This is why you don't need MakeProcInstance() thunks for window functions. As a sidenote, at creation, a global memory handle can be passed to edit controls as the hInstance value. Doing this allows edit controls to contain up to 64K of text.

The lpfnWndProc field holds the address that is called to handle a message for the window (the window procedure). You might notice that a window class contains a window procedure address as well. What's the difference? In object-oriented terms, the window class is like a base class. It provides default values and default behavior for classes derived from it. In this case, during the creation of the WND structure, its lpfnWndProc is set to whatever the corresponding value is in the window class. You can go in later and override the default lpfnWndProc() with another function (i.e., "derive" from the base class). Changing the value of the lpfnWndProc is how window subclassing is implemented. If the window procedure address were only stored in the window class, it would be rather difficult to subclass a standard control because *every* control would be affected, rather than just the one you were interested in. By storing a window procedure address in each WND structure, you can alter the behavior of just the desired window. If you do subclass a window, it's important that your application retain the original window procedure address so that messages you don't handle can be passed on to the original procedure.

Another obscure but interesting field in the WND structure is the property list. Each window can maintain a linked list of properties. This allows an application to store an arbitrary collection of named 16-bit values on a per-window basis. For instance, you could allocate a global memory block and store its handle in a property. The SetProp() and GetProp() APIs are the exported interface to this functionality. Most programmers are aware that a window can have extra bytes where they can store information. While this is fine for your own windows that you create, it may not be possible for windows created by other applications. The window properties neatly circumvent this problem, assuming you can come up with unique property names, which shouldn't be hard.

Windows styles

All windows can be categorized in terms of three basic styles. These styles are defined in WINDOWS.H, and are:

WS_OVERLAPPED
WS_POPUP
WS_CHILD

A WS_OVERLAPPED window is the most basic window style. WS_OVERLAPPED windows are used as the main, or top level, window in a program. WS_OVERLAPPED windows always have a title bar because the CreateWindow() code turns on the WS_CAPTION bit.

WS_POPUP windows are typically used for dialog boxes, but they have many of the same attributes as main windows (for example, they can have titlebars and such). It is not a requirement that WS_POPUP windows have a titlebar, however.

WS_CHILD windows are most often used as controls for dialog boxes. Examples of child windows include buttons, edit boxes, scroll bars, and list boxes. Note, however, that it is perfectly legitimate to have child windows that aren't in dialog boxes. A child window is often used to send WM_COMMAND messages to its parent, informing it of user actions.

There are other window styles such as WS_CLIPCHILDREN and WS_GROUP that can be OR'ed in with the three main styles. There are quite a few styles, so we defer to a comprehensive discussion of them to the Windows SDK. When specifying controls for a dialog box in an RC file, the last entry on each control line contains the style bits for the window. When you create a dialog box, for instance, with DialogBox(), each control is created with the style bits specified in the RC file definition. We cover the inner workings of window creation shortly.

The Window Hierarchy: the Parent/Child/Sibling Relationships

Of all the concepts in the windowing system, the most fundamental is the parent/child/sibling relationship. As we saw in the description of the WND data structure, every window maintains a handle to its parent window, a handle to its first child window, and a handle to the next window, also known as a sibling. HWND values are really just near pointers in a USER local heap, so you can consider these HWNDs as linked-list pointers that allow hierarchy traversal. The hierarchies that USER creates look like Figure 4-1.

The window hierarchy is traversed extensively in all three directions, parent to child, child to parent, and sibling to sibling. Examples of traversing the hierarchy include the following:

- When destroying a window, USER must destroy all of its children and their descendants, as well. USER traverses the entire hierarchy using the hWndChild and hWndNext fields. Remember, window handles are just near pointers in a USER local heap.

Figure 4-1. Window Hierarchies Created by USER.

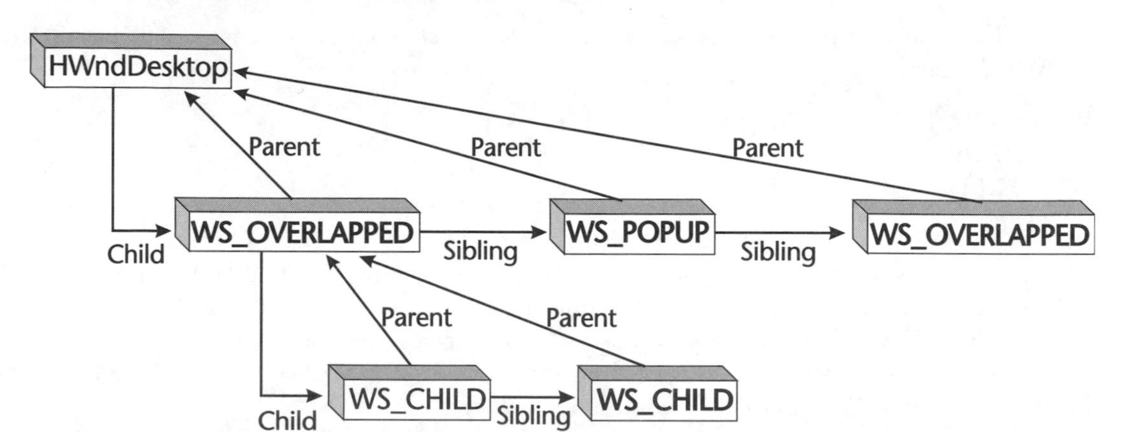

- When tabbing through the controls in a dialog box (which are child windows of the dialog box window), the sibling pointer (or hWndNext field) is what links the controls. In addition, the ordering of windows in the hWndChild and hWndNext list mirrors the Z-order of the windows on screen. The Z-order is the relative position of windows in the third dimension (coming out of the screen, towards you). As you click on various main windows to bring them to the top of the Z-order, their relative positions in the hWndNext list are shifted about.
- When clicking on a dialog control window, you cause the dialog manager to walk up the parent pointer chain to see if the top level (main) window of the application needs to be made the active window.

At the root of the window tree is the desktop window. This window covers the entire screen and is always at the bottom of the Z-order, meaning that it is always behind all other windows. The desktop window is always the first window created, and it is the only window in the system that does not have a parent or owner window. (Owner windows are described next). The painting of the desktop window is responsible for the Windows wallpaper.

There is nothing special about the desktop window in terms of special bits or such. At creation, its style bits (discussed below) are WS_POPUP and WS_CLIPCHILDREN. There is nothing like an undocumented WS_DESKTOP style bit. Instead, the handle to the desktop is stored in a USER global variable, HWndDesktop. When the windowing system needs to know if it's dealing with the desktop window, it just compares the HWND in question to HWndDesktop. You can get the value of HWndDesktop using the documented GetDesktopWindow() API.

Window Ownership

Along with the parent/child relationship, Windows also maintains an entirely different notion of window ownership. Each window has a field in its data structure that contains the window handle for the window that owns the window. Unlike the parent/child relationship, the window owner relationship is one-directional. A window knows the handle of its owner window, but it doesn't know the handles of the windows it owns.

The owner of a window is the window that receives notifications for the owned window. For instance, when you create a WS_POPUP menu window with TrackPopupMenu(), you specify an owner window. The owner window receives the WM_COMMAND message generated when a menu item is selected. It's important to note that in the general case, the parent window and the owner window are completely distinct. The parent/child relationship defines where the window is in the window hierarchy, while the owner window determines which windows receives the owned window's notifications.

A twist to the above rule involves WS_CHILD windows. For WS_CHILD windows, the owner HWND in the child window's WND structure is zero, and notification messages are instead sent to the *parent* window. For instance, a button in a dialog box is the child of the main dialog box window. When you press the button, the button window notifies its parent, the main dialog window, of the event. You can think of the hWndOwner of WS_CHILD window as one and the same as the hWndParent, even though they really are different. In Presentation Manager, there's no need for WS_CHILD or WS_POPUP bits. Both the hWndParent and hWndOwner fields are filled in. This completely defines who gets the child's notification messages and the location of the window in the hierarchy. Under Presentation Manager, the hWndOwner and hWndParent fields typically contain the same HWND value.

In addition to sending notifications to its owner, an owned window is also always in front of its owner window. If a window is iconized, all windows it owns are iconized. If the owning window is destroyed, all windows it owns are destroyed, as well. Since a window doesn't keep track of the windows it owns, the child/sibling pointer lists must be walked and the owner of each window compared to the HWND of the window being destroyed.

What's somewhat strange in all this is that Windows doesn't make the owner relationship very explicit. Although the SDK documentation discusses ownership briefly, you have to look pretty hard to see where the owner relationship is differentiated from the parent/child relationship. In OS/2 PM, you specify both a parent window and an owner window when you create a window. In Windows, you only specify a parent.

If CreateWindow() only accepts a parent HWND, how then do you specify an owner window in Windows? One of the parameters to CreateWindow() is the style bitmask. If the windows style is WS_CHILD, the hWndParent parameter is indeed interpreted as the parent window. If you specify WS_OVERLAPPED or WS_POPUP, however, the hWndParent parameter is actually used as the *owner* HWND, which is made clear later in some pseudocode. The parent window of a WS_OVERLAPPED or WS_POPUP windows is always the desktop HWND (HWndDesktop).

The relationship between style bits, parents, and owners is shown in Table 4-3.

Table 4-3: Relationship Between Style Bits, Parents, and Owners.

WS_STYLE	Parent	Owner
WS_OVERLAPPED	HWndDesktop	hWndParent parameter.
WS_POPUP	HWndDesktop	hWndParent parameter.
WS_CHILD	hWndParent param	0 (messages go to hWndParent).

hWndParent parameter is the hWndParent argument to CreateWindow() or CreateWindowEx().

Window Creation

An area that frequently confuses programmers is the order of messages during window creation. Many programmers know that WM_CREATE is *not* the first message that a window receives, but there's much more to it than that. Here, we examine the sequence of events that is set off by a CreateWindow() call.

In the following pseudocode, note the numerous calls to REvalSendMessage(). This function is just a debugging wrapper function around a normal SendMessage() call. The parameters to both functions are identical, so you should just mentally translate REvalSendMessage() to SendMessage().

CreateWindow()

From the pseudocode below, you can see that CreateWindow() doesn't do much. The real work is shunted off to the documented CreateWindowEx() API, which we look at next. In pre-Windows 3.0 days, there was no CreateWindowEx(), and CreateWindow() contained much of the code that's now in CreateWindowEx(). To prevent having two similar copies of the code, the USER authors moved the original CreateWindow() code into CreateWindowEx() and made CreateWindow() a stub to transfer control to CreateWindowEx().

```
Pseudocode for CreateWindow() - WMCREATE.OBJ

    Use REP MOVSW to copy the entire stack frame (including the
    return address) 4 bytes down in memory. Fill in the 4 byte
    "hole" at the highest address with 0's. The stack frame
    now looks like a call to CreateWindowEx(), with 0 passed as
    the dwExStyle parameter.

    JMP CreateWindowEx  // Begin executing in CreateWindowEx()
```

CreateWindowEx()

```
HWND        WINAPI CreateWindowEx(
   DWORD        dwExStyle,
   LPCSTR        lpszClassName,
```

```
    LPCSTR          lpszWindowName,
    DWORD           dwStyle,
    int             x,
    int             y,
    int             nWidth,
    int             nHeight,
    HWND            hwndParent,
    HMENU           hmenu,
    HINSTANCE       hinst,
    void FAR*       lpvCreateParams);
```

CreateWindowEx() is quite a large function! So large in fact, that we're going to break it up into logical sections, and discuss each in turn.

The first portion of CreateWindowEx() deals with validity checking of the parameters, allocation of the memory for a WND structure, and filling in some of the WND's fields. The first validity test determines if a parent window was specified when you requested a WS_CHILD style window. In addition, the hInstance parameter must be nonzero unless the requesting application is pre-Windows 3.1. In this case, the stack segment is used as the instance handle, with appropriate bit twiddling. The next test determines if the specified window class has been registered, with the expected whining in the debug USER if it's not found.

CreateWindowEx() now allocates memory for the WND structure, taking into account the extra byte size specified when registering the class. It then fills in several fields that don't depend on anything else. These fields include the current task's message queue and both style DWORDs. The last bit of this section is to call the Computer Based Training (CBT) hook to see if the window creation should proceed. The CBT hook is new to Windows 3.1, and is barely documented. USER calls the CBT hook callback function at key points throughout the life of the window (creation, destruction, etc.). For some events, the hook callback can direct USER to continue with the event or abort it.

```
Pseudocode for CreateWindowEx() - WMCREATE.OBJ
// Parameters:
//      DWORD   dwExStyle
//      LPCSTR  lpszClassName
//      LPCSTR  lpszWindowName
//      DWORD   dwStyle
//      short   x, y, nWidth, nHeight
//      HWND    hWndParent
//      HMENU   hMenu
//      HANDLE  hInstance
//      LPVOID  lpvCreateParams
// Locals:
//      INTWNDCLASS *intWndCls
//      HWND    hWnd                    // Return HWND value
//      short   localX, localY
```

```
//      short   localWidth, localHeight
//      WORD    isChild                     // Is it a child window?
//      WORD    showWindow = SW_SHOW
//      RECT    localRect                   // a "scratch" RECT
//      WORD    someFlag = 0
//      WORD    moreStyleBits = 0           // default to nothing

    // First, make sure child windows have a parent specified
    if ( WS_CHILD bit set in style  && ( hWndParent == 0 ) )
    {
        _DebugOutput("USER: CreateWindow(): Invalid parent hwnd")
        return 0
    }

    if ( hInstance == 0 )
    {
        _DebugOutput("USER: CreateWindow(): NULL instance handle")

        hInstance = GlobalHandle( SS )  // Get instance handle
                                        // from SS register

        // Only pre 3.1 apps get away with supplying a
        // NULL instance handle. 3.1 and later apps must
        // supply a correct hInstance.
        if ( GetExpWinVer( hInstance ) >= 0x030A )
            return 0
    }

    // Determine if the specified class has been registered.
    // If the last param is nonzero, GetClassPtr() searches for
    // global classes if an application local class isn't found.
    intWndCls = GetClassPtr(lpszClassName, hInstance, 1)
    if ( !intWndCls )   // If not registered, return failure
    {
        _DebugOutput("USER: CreateWindow failed: "
                     "Window class not found" )
        return 0
    }

    // Allocate space for the new WND structure, taking into
    // account the extra bytes specified in the class structure.
    // LT_USER_WND == 2, and is defined in TOOLHELP.H. Note
    // also that since LMEM_MOVEABLE isn't specified, the memory
    // is fixed, thus allowing you to use HWNDs as offsets into
    // a USER heap.
```

```
hWnd = UserLocalAlloc( LT_USER_WND, LMEM_ZEROINIT,
            sizeof(WND) + intWndCls->cbWndExtra )

if ( !hWnd )    // Abort call if memory isn't available
{
    _DebugOutput("USER: CreateWindow failed: Out of memory")
    return 0
}

hWnd->hQueue = HQCurrent()  // Set the window's message queue
                            // to the current message queue
                            // (see Chapter 7)

hWnd->wndClass = intWndCls          // Start filling in the
hWnd->dwStyleFlags = dwStyle        // fields of the newly
hWnd->dwExStyleFlags = dwExStyle    // allocated WND

if (GetExpWinVer(hInstance) >= 0x030A)  // Windows >= 3.1?
{
    // This bit is used in several places, indicating the
    // window belongs to a 3.1 (or greater) compatible app
    Turn on bit (0x0004) in the HIWORD of hWnd->dwFlags
}
else        // A 3.0 or earlier app
{
    // Get the task handle associated with this window out of
    // the new window's message queue structure. It's unclear
    // why GetCurrentTask() isn't used instead. Use the task
    // handle to determine if this program needs a
    // "compatibility" hack to keep 3.0 apps working in 3.1.
    // GetAppCompatFlags() is described in Undocumented
    // Windows.
    AX = GetAppCompatFlags( hWnd->hQueue->hTask )
    if ( AX & GACF_ALWAYSSENDNCPAINT )
        Turn on bit (0x0008) in HIWORD of hWnd->dwFlags
}

// CallHook() is the function that handles calling the
// installed filter functions (hooks). In this case,
// it appears to be calling any installed Computer Based
// Training hooks to find out if the window creation
// should proceed. 5=WH_CBT, 3 = HCBT_CREATEWND
if ( !CallHook(3, hWnd, &some_local_buff, 5) )
    goto CreateWindowEx_out_of_mem
```

The next section of CreateWindowEx() calculates the initial position and size of the new window. Judging from the amount of code involved, there is quite a complex algorithm for determining these values. The style of the window (WS_CHILD, WS_OVERLAPPED, or WS_POPUP) plays an important role here. For instance, when creating child windows, the coordinates given are relative to the parent window. These values need to be adjusted to screen coordinates, since at the lowest level it all comes down to putting pixels on the screen, and the display driver doesn't know anything about windows.

There is quite a bit of code here that appears to be related to positioning WS_OVERLAPPED (or main) windows on the screen. If you specify CW_USEDEFAULT for the size and position parameters, notice that successive invocations of the same program cause the initial positioning to move slightly down and to the right. To see this, try invoking Solitaire several times in a row, exiting it each time before starting it again. (No, don't play it now!)

```
Continuation of Pseudocode for CreateWindowEx() - WMCREATE.OBJ

    // If the window is a CHILD or a POPUP, CW_USEDEFAULT isn't
    // allowed for x, y, width, height. Reset them to 0.
    if ( hWnd->dwStyleFlags & (WS_CHILD | WS_POPUP) )
    {
        if ( x == CW_USEDEFAULT )
            x = y = 0;
        if ( nWidth == CW_USEDEFAULT )
            nWidth = nHeight = 0
    }

    localX = x                  // Save off the position parameters
    localY = y                  // into local copies
    localWidth = nWidth
    localHeight = nHeight

    // Set a variable indicating a child window is being created
    isChild = ( hWnd->dwStyleFlags & WS_CHILD ) ? 1 : 0

    // If we're creating a child window, the X,Y coordinates are
    // relative to the parent window, so adjust them to use
    // screen coordinates.
    if ( isChild )
    {
        localX += hWndParent->rectClient.left
        localY += hWndParent->rectClient.top
    }

    // If the window is WS_OVERLAPPED, do some adjustments
    if ( (hWnd->dwStyleFlags & (WS_CHILD | WS_POPUP)) == 0 )
    {
        // Force on the WS_CLIPSIBLINGS and WS_CAPTION bits for
```

```
    // WS_OVERLAPPED windows
    hWnd->dwStyleFlags |= WS_CLIPSIBLINGS
    moreStyleBits = 0x00C0

    SetTiledRect(hWnd, &localRect)  // Fill in LocalRect with
                                    // the initial x,y values?
    if ( x == CW_USEDEFAULT )
    {
        someFlag = 1
        x = localX = rc.left
        y = localY = rc.top
    }
    else
    {
        if (iWndStack != 0) // iWndStack is a global var.
            iWndStack--     // The "window stack" depth?
    }

    if ( localWidth = CW_USEDEFAULT )
    {
        localWidth = localRect.right - x
        localHeight = localRect.bottom - y
    }
    else if ( someFlag )
    {
        a long string of calculations that's not entirely
        understood.
    }
}                        // End of WS_OVERLAPPED 'if' statement
```

The next section of CreateWindowEx() fills in some more fields in the WND structure and sets up other things related to menus. If a menu was specified for a non-WS_CHILD window, the code calls LoadMenu() to load the menu from the EXE or DLL file. In addition, if the CS_NOCLOSE flag was given when the class was registered, CreateWindowEx() removes the Close menu item, as well as its separator.

```
Continuation of Pseudocode for CreateWindowEx() - WMCREATE.OBJ

// If the window is a popup window, and isn't the desktop
// window, turn on the WS_CLIPSIBLINGS flag
if ( hWnd->dwStyleFlags & WS_POPUP )
    if ( hWnd != HWndDesktop )
        hWnd->dwStyleFlags |= WS_CLIPSIBLINGS

OR in moreStyleBits into the HIWORD of hWnd->dwStyle. For
WS_OVERLAPPED windows, this has the effect of turning on the
WS_CAPTION flag.
```

```
hWnd->hBuffer = 0          // Initial value is zero.

// If no menu was specified to CreateWindow, and if the
// window isn't a child window, load the default menu
// specified in the window class.
if ( hMenu == 0 )
    if ( isChild == 0 )
        if ( intWndCls->lpszMenuName != 0 )
        {
            hMenu = LoadMenu( intWndCls->hModule,
                              intWndCls->lpszMenuName )
        }

hWnd->hMenu = hMenu        // Store whatever menu was picked
                           // (either the default class menu, or
                           // the menu passed to CreateWindow)

if ( CS_NOCLOSE bit set in hWnd->wndClass )
{
    // Remove the "close" selection, and its separator
    // from the system menu. Note that in both cases, the
    // item to delete is specified by its relative position
    // in the menu. 5 is used for both items, because after
    // the first DeleteMenu(), the menu items shift up by 1.
    hMenu = GetSystemMenu( hWnd, FALSE )
    DeleteMenu( hMenu, 5, MF_BYPOSITION )
    DeleteMenu( hMenu, 5, MF_BYPOSITION )
}

// Store the hInstance and window procedure address into
// the WND structure.
hWnd->hInstance = hInstance
hWnd->lpfnWndProc = intWndCls->lpfnWndProc
```

This next section of CreateWindowEx() concerns setting up the parent/child/owner window relationship. See the discussion of this earlier in the chapter for the details of what the end result should be. One thing worth noting here is that if the window being created has an owner, and if the owner is a topmost window (WS_EX_TOPMOST), the new window will also become WS_EX_TOPMOST. This is apparently to make sure that the owner window Z-ordering rules are adhered to.

The second part of this section ensures that the WS_CLIPCHILDREN and WS_CLIPSIBLING flags are set correctly. Perhaps to remain compatible with applications written before Windows 3.1, CreateWindowEx() turns off the WS_CLIPCHILDREN and WS_CLIPSIBLINGS flags for these applications if the CS_PARENTDC flag is specified in the window class. The CS_PARENTDC style makes WS_CLIPCHILDREN and WS_CLIPSIBLINGS meaningless, since it says to use the parent window's DC and clipping region instead of calculating one for this window.

Continuation of Pseudocode for CreateWindowEx() - WMCREATE.OBJ

```
    // Do things related to top level windows and owners
    if ( isChild == 0 )     // If not a child window...
    {
        hWnd->hWndLastActive = hWnd

        // The owner of a top level window is specified by
        // passing an HWND as the hWndParent parameter. Check
        // for this special case here.
        if ( (hWndParent != 0) && (hWndParent != HWndDesktop) )
        {
            // Set the owner of the new window to the HWND
            // specified as the hWndParent parameter. If
            // the hWndParent isn't a "top level" window,
            // GetTopLevelWindow() walks up the parent list
            // till it finds a top level window.
            hWnd->HWNDOwner = GetTopLevelWindow(hWndParent)

            // If the owning window is a TOPMOST style window,
            // make sure this window is TOPMOST as well?
            if ((hWnd->HWNDOwner != 0) &&
                (hWnd->HWNDOwner->dwExStyleFlags & WS_EX_TOPMOST))
            {
                Turn on WS_EX_TOPMOST in hWnd->dwExStyleFlags
            }
        }
        else                          // No owner window specified
            hWnd->HWNDOwner = 0       // The window isn't owned

        hWndParent = HWndDesktop      // All non-WS_CHILD windows
                                      // are children of the desktop
                                      // HWndDesktop is a USER
    }                                 // global variable.

    hWnd->hWndParent = hWndParent     // Copy parent HWND into
                                      // hWndParent field of
                                      // the WND structure

    // Earlier, we saw that bit 0x0004 was set only for
    // apps that required Windows 3.1 or greater. Here, we
    // check to see if the app is a pre-Windows 3.1 app.
```

```
if ( bit 0x0004 NOT set in HIWORD(hWnd->dwFlags) )
{
    // If the class uses its parent DC, and if the parent
    // doesn't use WS_CLIPCHILDREN, CreateWindowEx() turns
    // off and ignores the WS_CLIPXXX flags.
    if ( (intWndCls->style & CS_PARENTDC) &&
         !(hWndParent->dwStyleFlags & WS_CLIPCHILDREN) )
    {
        if ( hWnd->dwStyleFlags & WS_CLIPCHILDREN )
        {
            _DebugOutput( "USER: WS_CLIPCHILDREN overridden"
                          "by CS_PARENTDC" )
        }

        if hWnd->dwStyleFlags & WS_CLIPSIBLINGS )
        {
            _DebugOutput( "USER: WS_CLIPSIBLINGS overridden"
                          "by CS_PARENTDC" )
        }

        Turn off WS_CLIPSIBLINGS and WS_CLIPCHILDREN flags
        in hWnd->dwStyleFlags
    }
}
```

The first part of the next portion of CreateWindowEx() concentrates on more issues involving sizing and positioning the window. Of special interest is the call to CheckByteAlign(), which if specified with the CS_BYTExxx flags, causes the window borders and client area to be placed on pixel boundaries that allow the video board to perform optimizations when accessing video memory. This is primarily useful for boards that have more than one pixel per byte of memory, such as EGA and VGA boards in 16-color mode.

Then CreateWindowEx() increments the usage count of the window class. By keeping track of how many windows are using the class, the class can be deleted from memory when it's no longer in use. The final act of this section is to create or obtain the device context (DC) for the window if the CS_OWNDC or CS_CLASSDC flags were specified at class registration time. Device contexts are described in Chapter 5.

```
Continuation of Pseudocode for CreateWindowEx() - WMCREATE.OBJ

    // It appears that AdjustSize() can alter the width and
    // height parameters passed to it. This routine presumably
    // does some calculations to "tweak" the size of the windows
    // with messages; see below.
    AdjustSize( hWnd, &localWidth, &localHeight )
```

```
// Now store the window coordinates (including the title and
// borders) into a RECT in the WND struct under construction.
hWnd->rectWindow.left   = localX
hWnd->rectWindow.right  = localX + localWidth
hWnd->rectWindow.top    = localY
hWnd->rectWindow.bottom = localY + localHeight

// CheckByteAlign() appears to be responsible for dealing with
// the CS_BYTEALIGNCLIENT and CS_BYTEALIGNWINDOW details. The
// goal of byte alignment is to place the window so that the
// client area and/or borders don't fall in the middle of a
// byte in video memory. This can create performance speedups
// with some video boards.
CheckByteAlign( hWnd, &hWnd->rectWindow )

intWndCls->cClsWnds++    // Indicate that another window
                         // instance was created from class

// Since the reference count is stored in a 16 byte value, it
// places a limit of 32K windows in the system. It's likely
// that the USER heap will run out of space before then!
if ( intWndCls->cClsWnds < 0 )
    _DebugOutput("USER: Window class reference count overflow")

// If the class uses its own private DC, or the class's DC,
// go get the DC now.
if ( CS_OWNDC or CS_CLASSDC bits set in
    intWndCls->style )
{
    // CreateCacheDC() creates a DC, and adds it to the list
    // of DC's that USER maintains. See the entry for DCE
    // in chapter 6 of Undocumented Windows for details.
    if ( !CreateCacheDC(hWnd, 2, 0 ) )
        goto CreateWindowEx_out_of_mem
}
```

CreateWindowEx() now turns its attention to sending the initial startup messages to the new window. Due to a design error in Windows 2.0, the first message actually sent to the window is sometimes WM_GETMINMAXINFO, which is sent from a routine called by AdjustSize(). In the pseudocode below, CreateWindowEx() sends the intended first message, WM_NCCREATE (non-client create), to the new window. If the window returns nonzero from this message, the window creation proceeds.

At this point, the window is sufficiently created that the HWndDesktop USER global variable can be filled in. The desktop window is always the first window to be created (see Chapter 1), so if HWndDesktop's value is 0, CreateWindowEx() must be creating the desktop window. After this special case code, CreateWindowEx() links the new window into the parent/child hierarchy with the LinkWindow() function. This function is given enough information for it to walk the child list of the parent window and insert the new window accordingly.

With this administrative work completed, the code goes back to the task of sending the startup messages to the new window. First, it sends the WM_NCCALCSIZE message. Upon return, the passed RECT structure contains the size of the client area of the window, which is the portion of the window that you normally draw in. Next, CreateWindowEx() sends the WM_CREATE message. The handler for WM_CREATE is usually where applications do their work that needs to be done at window-creation time. If the handler returns -1 in response to the WM_CREATE message, CreateWindowEx() destroys the window using DestroyWindow() (described later) and aborts the creation process. The last sequence of this section is to send WM_SIZE and WM_MOVE messages to the new window, if a certain (unknown) bit is set in the windows dwFlags field.

```
Continuation of Pseudocode for CreateWindowEx() - WMCREATE.OBJ

    // Send the WM_NCCREATE message to the new window. If the
    // window handler returns failure, the memory for the WND
    // structure is freed, and the function returns failure.
    // REvalSendMessage() is just a "wrapper" around a
    // SendMessage() call that verifies the hWnd after
    // the SendMessage() call. The retail version calls
    // SendMessage() directly.
    if (!REvalSendMessage(hWnd,WM_NCCREATE,0,&lpvCreateParams))
    {
CreateWindowEx_out_of_mem:  // Can get here from several places

        FreeWindow( hWnd )
        _DebugOutput("USER: CreateWindow: Out of memory")
        return 0
    }

    if ( HWndDesktop == 0 ) // If HWndDesktop is 0, this
        HWndDesktop = hWnd  // is the first window being created,
                            // and is therefore, the desktop

    // If a parent window was specified, splice it into the
    // parent/child hierarchy.
    if ( hWndParent )
    {
        if ( isChild == 0 )
        {
            A long sequence of code that appears to relate to
            to the WS_EX_TOPMOST flag.
        }
```

```
        // Use LinkWindow() to add the window to the list of
        // child windows maintained by the window's parent.
        // LinkWindow() needs to know the address of the pointer
        // to the first child in the list, so that it can
        // insert the new window at the head of the list.
        LinkWindow(hWnd, some_local_var, &hWndParent->hWndChild)
    }

    // Send the WM_NCCALCSIZE message to the new window, passing
    // it the coordinates of the full window rectangle. The
    // message returns the size of the client area, which we
    // copy into the WND under construction.
    copy hWnd->rectWindow to localRect
    REvalSendMessage( hWnd, WM_NCCALCSIZE, 0, &localRect )
    copy localRect to hWnd->rectClient

    // Send the WM_CREATE message to the new window. If it
    // returns failure for some reason, abort the creation.
    if ( REvalSendMessage( hWnd, WM_CREATE, 0, &lpvCreateParams)
            == -1 )
    {
        DestroyWindow( hWnd )
        return 0
    }

    // Send WM_SIZE and WM_MOVE messages to the new window.
    if ( bit 0x0010 not set in hWnd->dwFlags )
    {
        SendSizeMessage( hWnd, 0 )  // Sends WM_SIZE message

        if ( hWndParent )
        {
            localRect.left = rc.left - hWndParent->rectClient.left
            localRect.top  = rc.top - hWndParent->rectClient.top
        }

        REvalSendMessage( hWnd, WM_MOVE, 0,
            MAKELONG( localRect.left, localRect.top ) )
    }
```

The last section of CreateWindowEx() begins by handling the special cases where a window is supposed to start out minimized (WS_MINIMIZE) or maximized (WS_MAXIMIZE). The code calls the MinMaximize() function and lets it handle the dirty work.

If the WS_EX_NOPARENTNOTIFY flag wasn't given, the code sends the WM_PARENTNOTIFY message to the window's parent, informing it of the child window's creation. If the WS_VISIBLE flag was specified, a ShowWindow() call takes care of the initial display of the window. The last step before CreateWindowEx() returns is to call the

WH_SHELL hook, informing it of the window's creation. However, this is only done if the window is not a child window and isn't owned by anyone (a WS_OVERLAPPED window). The WH_SHELL hook is new for Windows 3.1 and is intended for use by applications that want to replace PROGMAN.EXE as the Windows shell. The WH_SHELL hook is called when a top level window is created or destroyed and when the shell program should activate itself.

```
Continuation of Pseudocode for CreateWindowEx() - WMCREATE.OBJ

    if ( hWnd->dwStyleFlag & WS_MINIMIZE )
    {
        Turn off WS_MINIMIZE in hWnd->dwStyleFlags )
        MinMaximize( hWnd, 7, 1 )   // Minimize or maximize it
    }
    else if (hWnd->dwStyleFlag & WS_MAXIMIZE )
    {
        Turn off WS_MAXIMIZE in hWnd->dwStyleFlags )
        MinMaximize( hWnd, 3, 1 )   // Minimize or maximize it
    }

    // If the window is a child window, and it's O.K. to send
    // messages to the parent, send the WM_PARENTNOTIFY message
    // to the new window's parent. The WPARAM indicates that
    // a new window has been created.
    if ( isChild )
        if ( !(hWnd->dwExStyleFlags & WS_EX_NOPARENTNOTIFY) )
        {
            REvalSendMessage( hWnd->hWndParent, WM_PARENTNOTIFY,
                WM_CREATE, MAKELONG( hWnd, hWnd->hMenu) )

            if ( IsWindow(hWnd) == 0 )  // Make sure window is
                return 0                // still valid!
        }

    // If the caller specified that the window should be visible
    // immediately upon creation, show the window now.
    if ( dwStyle & WS_VISIBLE )
        ShowWindow( hWnd, showWindow )

    // If the window just created is a top level window, call the
    // WH_SHELL hook, and tell it about the new window.
    if ( isChild == 0 )
        if ( hWnd->HWNDOwner == 0 )
        {
            // 1 -> HSHELL_WINDOWCREATED, 0xA -> WH_SHELL ?
            CallHook( 1, hWnd, 0, 0xA )
        }

    return hWnd     // All done!  Return window handle to caller
```

We're now done with the arduous journey through the creation of a window. The net result of CreateWindowEx() is the creation a new data structure linked into the appropriate spot in the window hierarchy. The initial startup messages are then sent. Depending on the value of the dwStyle parameter to CreateWindowEx(), the window may or may not be visible on the screen.

Window Manipulation

Now that we've created a window, look at the mechanics of some common window manipulation functions. As we examine the various routines, notice that almost all window manipulation boils down to a small set of functions.

ShowWindow()

```
BOOL    WINAPI ShowWindow(HWND, int nCmdShow);
```

ShowWindow() is perhaps the most immediately useful window manipulation routine. This is an API that allows you to minimize, maximize, show and hide a window, as well as to restore it to its original screen position and size. As you might imagine, the code is somewhat lengthy.

The first portion of ShowWindow() is where the specifics for each of the possible SW_xxx arguments, like SW_HIDE, are dealt with. Each possible SW_xxx case boils down to one of two actions. One action is to call the MinMaximize() function, let it do the work, and then return from ShowWindow(). The other SW_xxx cases build an appropriate set of SWP_xxx flags to be used in a subsequent SetWindowPos() call.

The second portion of ShowWindow() is invoked only for the commands that weren't handled by a MinMaximize() call. The highlight of this section is the call to SetWindowPos(). Although SetWindowPos() might look like it contains the brains to manipulate window positions and such, it doesn't. We put SetWindowPos() under the microscope momentarily, to see who's doing the real work.

If the window isn't currently visible, ShowWindow() doesn't bother to call SetWindowPos(). It wouldn't have any effect, since the window couldn't be seen. Instead, it adjusts the WS_VISIBLE flags to give the effect of having called SetWindowPos(), without incurring the overhead.

Besides calling SetWindowPos(), this portion of ShowWindow() is responsible for sending the messages that indicate a change in window state. Specifically, it sends the WM_SHOWWINDOW, WM_SETVISIBLE, WM_MOVE, and WM_SIZE messages.

```
Pseudocode for ShowWindow() - WMSHOW.OBJ
// Parameters:
//        HWND     hWnd
//        int      nCmdShow
// Locals:
//        WORD     setWndPosFlags
```

```
//      WORD    wasVisible
//      WORD    showFlag

    // Set the initial value of wasVisible. We'll be returning
    // this value. It indicates whether the window was
    // previously visible.
    wasVisible = hWnd->dwStyleFlags & WS_VISIBLE

    // This next if statement is for backwards compatibility with
    // the "icon parking lot" values that could be passed to
    // ShowWindow() in Windows 1.x. The values for nCmdShow
    // were from 0xFF80 to 0, and allowed you to specify a
    // particular "parking lot space" for your icon.
    if ( HIBYTE(nCmdShow) & 0xFF )
    {
        // If the upper byte of nCmdShow is nonzero, convert it
        // to a more reasonable value
        if ( HIBYTE(nCmdShow)==0xFF) && (LOBYTE(nCmdShow)&0x80) )
            nCmdShow = SW_SHOWMINNOACTIVE
        else
            nCmdShow = SW_SHOW
    }

    if ( (WORD)nCmdShow > 9 )    // Get rid of SW_xxx values
    {                            // that are out of range.
        _DebugOutput("USER: Invalid ShowWindow command")
        goto ShowWindow_done
    }

    convert nCmdShow into an offset into a JMP table. This may
    be a compiler optimization of a switch statement, as the code
    looks similar to other switch statements produced by the
    Microsoft C compiler. We'll show it as one here:

case SW_HIDE:
    if ( wasVisible == 0 )       // We're done if it was already
        goto ShowWindow_done     // invisible

    setWndPosFlags |= SWP_HIDEWINDOW | SWP_NOSIZE | SWP_NOMOVE

    // If hWnd is not the active window, don't cause it to
    // be activated when we call SetWindowPos()
    if ( hWnd != hWndActive )
        setWndPosFlags |= SWP_NOACTIVATE | SWP_NOZORDER
    break
```

```
case SW_SHOWNORMAL:
case SW_SHOWNOACTIVATE:
case SW_RESTORE:
    if ( hWnd->dwStyleFlags & WS_MINIMIZE ||  // Is window already
         hWnd->dwStyleFlags & WS_MAXIMIZE )   // min/maximized?
    {
        MinMaximize( hWnd, nCmdShow, 0 )  // minimize or maximize
        goto ShowWindow_done              // as appropriate
    }
    else    // Window isn't min/maximized
    {
        if ( wasVisible )       // The window is already visible!
            goto ShowWindow_done

        setWndPosFlags |= SWP_NOSIZE | SWP_NOMOVE | SWP_SHOWWINDOW

        if ( nCmdShow == SW_SHOWNOACTIVATE ) // Do this extra
        {                                    // step only if
            setWndPosFlags |= SWP_NOZORDER   // SW_SHOWNOACTIVATE
                                             // was selected
            if ( hWndActive )
                setWndPosFlags |= SWP_NOACTIVATE
        }
    }
    break

case SW_SHOWMINIMIZED:
case SW_SHOWMAXIMIZED:
case SW_MINIMIZE:
case SW_SHOWMINNOACTIVE:
    MinMaximize( hWnd, nCmdShow, 0 )    // Make it so.
    goto ShowWindow_done

case SW_SHOW:
    if ( wasVisible )            // Window is already visible!
        goto ShowWindow_done

    setWndPosFlags |= SWP_NOSIZE | SWP_NOMOVE | SWP_SHOWWINDOW
    break

case SW_SHOWNA:
    setWndPosFlags |= SWP_NOSIZE | SWP_NOMOVE | SWP_SHOWWINDOW

    if ( hWndActive )   // If there's an active window, don't
    {                   // cause it to lose its "active" status
        setWndPosFlags |= SWP_NOACTIVATE
        break
    }
```

```
//
// End of pseudo switch statement
//

// Set showFlag to 0 if the window should be hidden
// when we're done, 1 if it should be visible
showFlag = (nCmdShow == SW_HIDE) ? 0 : 1

// If the desired window visibility is different than its
// current state, change it now. Note that this section
// of code sends messages, but the actual display of the
// window comes later (a SetWindowPos() call).
if ( showFlag != wasVisible )
{
    REvalSendMessage(hWnd, WM_SHOWWINDOW, showFlag, 0 )

    // If the application is not 3.1 compatible, send
    // a WM_SETVISIBLE message to the window
    if ( bit 0x0004 set in HIWORD(hWnd->dwFlags) )
        REvalSendMessage( hWnd, WM_SETVISIBLE, showFlag, 0 )
}

if ( IsWindow(hWnd) == 0 )  // Is window still around?
    goto ShowWindow_done

if ( hWnd->dwStyleFlags & WS_CHILD )    // Is it a child wnd?
{
    if ( CS_SAVEBITS specified in hWnd->wndClass )
    {
        if ( nCmdShow is SW_SHOWNORMAL or SW_SHOW )
        {
            ActivateWindow( hWnd, 1 )

            if ( IsWindow(hWnd) == 0 )  // Is window still
                goto ShowWindow_done    // valid?

            setWndPosFlags |= SWP_NOACTIVATE | SWP_NOZORDER
        }
    }
}
else        // Not a child window
{
    setWndPosFlags = SWP_NOACTIVATE | SWP_NOZORDER
}
```

```
// If the window should be visible, use SetWindowPos() to
// make it visible on the screen. FChildVisible() walks up
// the parent window chain, testing to see if each parent
// window is WS_VISIBLE. If not, it returns 0. If all
// parents are visible, it returns 1.
if ( FChildVisible(hWnd) )  // All parents are visible
{
    // SetWindowPos() does the real work. Call it now.
    // Pseudocode for SetWindowPos() is below.
    SetWindowPos( hWnd, 0, 0, 0, 0, 0, setWndPosFlags )

    if ( IsWindow(hWnd) == 0 )  // Is window still valid?
        goto ShowWindow_done
}
else    // Parents aren't visible, so neither are we. Just
{       // set the appropriate style bits, and go on.
    if ( nCmdShow == SW_HIDE )
        Turn off WS_VISIBLE flag in hWnd->dwStyleFlags
    else
        Turn on WS_VISIBLE flag in hWnd->dwStyleFlags
}

// Send some sizing message to the window, if necessary
if ( bit 0x10 set in LOBYTE(hWnd->dwFlags) )
{
    Turn off bit 0x10 set in LOBYTE(hWnd->dwFlags)

    // Send an appropriate WM_SIZE message to the window
    if ( hWnd->dwStyleFlags & WS_MINIMIZED )
        SendSizeMessage(hWnd, SIZE_MINIMIZED)
    else if ( hWnd->dwStyleFlags & WS_MAXIMIZED )
        SendSizeMessage(hWnd, SIZE_MAXIMIZED)
    else
        SendSizeMessage(hWnd, SIZE_RESTORED)

    // Now send a WM_MOVE message.
    REvalSendMessage( hWnd, WM_MOVE, 0,
        MAKELONG( hWnd->rectClient.left
                  - hWnd->hWndParent->rectClient.left,
                  hWnd->rectClient.top
                  - hWnd->hWndParent->rectClient.top) )

    // Verify that the window is still valid. Perhaps it's
    // possible that the window could have been destroyed
    // during the preceding manipulations?
```

```
        if ( IsWindow(hWnd) == 0 )  // Is window still valid?
            goto ShowWindow_done
    }

    // If we're hiding the active window, do something special
    // to get out of whatever state we're in.
    if ( nCmdShow == SW_HIDE )
        if ( hWnd == hWndActive )   // are we the active window?
        {
            ActivateWindow( hWnd, 3 )   // Make it inactive?

            if ( IsWindow(hWnd) == 0 )  // Is window still valid?
                goto ShowWindow_done
        }

    if ( nCmdShow == SW_HIDE )  // If HWND parameter has the
        CheckFocus( hWnd )      // focus, and is a child, set
                                // focus to the parent HWND

    // Send a WM_SHOWWINDOW to the icon title window if the
    // window is minimized
    if ( hWnd->dwStyleFlags & WS_MINIMIZED )
        ShowIconTitle( hWnd, nCmdShow != SW_HIDE )

ShowWindow_done:
    return wasVisible
```

As you can see, ShowWindow() is a high level function that takes any SW_xxx parameter and dispatches it to an appropriate MinMaximize() or SetWindowPos() invocation. It isn't the last time we encounter SetWindowPos().

MoveWindow()

```
BOOL    WINAPI MoveWindow(HWND, int left, int top,
                          int width, int height, BOOL fRepaint);
```

From the pseudocode below, it's apparent that MoveWindow() is just a wrapper routine around a SetWindowPos() call. Like too many other routines in Windows, there is one path that's executed for pre-Windows 3.1 applications, and another for Windows 3.1 or above compatible applications.

```
Pseudocode for MoveWindow() - WMSWP.OBJ
// Parameters:
//      HWND    hWnd
//      int     left, top, width, height
//      BOOL    fRepaint
```

```
// Locals:
//      WORD    returnValue
//      WORD    setWndPosFlags

    // if we're not the desktop window, and not a 3.1 app, and
    // our parent is the desktop (i.e., a top level window)...
    if (    (hWnd != HWndDesktop)
         && (bit 0x0004 not set in HIWORD(hWnd->dwFlags))
         && (hWnd->hWndParent == HWndDesktop) )
    {
        returnValue = SetWindowPos(hWnd, 0, left, top, width,
            height, SWP_NOZORDER | SWP_NOACTIVATE)

        if ( fRepaint == 0 )            // Remove entire window
            ValidateRect( hWnd, 0 )     // from update region
    }
    else
    {
        setWndPosFlags = SWP_NOZORDER | SWP_NOACTIVATE
        if ( fRepaint == 0 )
            setWndPosFlags |= SWP_NOREDRAW

        returnValue = SetWindowPos(hWnd, 0, left, top, width,
            height, setWndPosFlags )
    }

    return returnValue
```

SetWindowPos()

```
BOOL WINAPI SetWindowPos(HWND hwnd,
                HWND hwndInsertAfter,
                int x, int y, int width, int height,
                UINT fuFlags);
```

We've seen how ShowWindow() and MoveWindow() use SetWindowPos(). As it turns out, there are many routines (for instance, DestroyWindow() and BringWindowToTop()) that also boil down to a call to SetWindowPos(). It's becoming readily apparent that SetWindow-Pos() is a key routine that other windowing routines are built upon.

Taking a look at the pseudocode for SetWindowPos(), we quickly discover that the code can be summarized as:

BeginDeferWindowPos()
DeferWindowPos()
EndDeferWindowPos().

For good measure, SetWindowPos() throws in a RedrawWindow() call and some flag twiddling. The core of the routine however, is just the above three functions. SetWindowPos() is just another layer on the onion. All SetWindowPos() does is encapsulate the three stages of the *actual* window-manipulation APIs into one function call. The DeferWindowPos functions allow you to collect all of your changes together and tell USER to update the screen once with the final results. We'll look at them next.

```
Pseudocode for SetWindowPos() - WMSWP.OBJ
// Parameters:
//      HWND    hWnd, hWndInsertAfter
//      int     left, top, width, height
//      WORD    flags
// Locals:
//      HDWP    hDWP    // handle to DeferWindowPos structure
//      WORD    needsRedraw = 0

    // Is the window being shown or hidden?
    if ( flags & (SWP_SHOWWINDOW | SWP_HIDEWINDOW) )
    {
        // Is it a 3.1 compatible app window?
        if ( bit 0x0004 not set in HIWORD(hWnd->dwFlags)
        {
            flags |= SWP_NOMOVE | SWP_NOSIZE

            if ( flags & SWP_SHOWWINDOW )
                if ( hWnd->dwStyleFlags & WS_VISIBLE )
                    needsRedraw = 1
        }
    }

    // Tell USER that we're going to start giving it our changes.
    // The return value is a handle to a USER internal structure
    // Note that the 1 parameter value tells USER that we
    // only expect to change one window.
    if ( (hDWP = BeginDeferWindowPos(1)) == 0 )
        return 0

    // tell the windowing system about the window that we want to
    // move, but don't cause it to be drawn yet.
    hDWP = DeferWindowPos(hDWP, hWnd, hWndInsertAfter, left, top,
            width, height, flags)
    if ( hDWP == 0 )    // Make sure we're still O.K.
        return 0
```

```
if ( EndDeferWindowPos(hDWP) )
{
    // Repaint the window now, if it needs it
    if ( needsRepaint )
        RedrawWindow(hWnd, 0, 0, RDW_INVALIDATE | RDW_ERASE
            | RDW_ALLCHILDREN | RDW_FRAME)

    return 1          // Success!
}
else
    return 0          // EndDeferWindowPos() failed!
```

The DeferWindowPos() APIs

At the heart of all routines that position or resize windows on the screen are three functions. All three must be used in conjunction with each other, and luckily, all are documented. If you want maximum performance when moving around multiple windows on the screen, these functions are what you're looking for.

The process of manipulating one or more windows occurs in three steps. The first step is to call BeginDeferWindowPos(). BeginDeferWindowPos() allocates a data structure called a DWP, for DeferWindowPos. BeginDeferWindowPos() returns a handle to a DWP (an HDWP). The DWP acts as a container for all the changes made in the next step. Think of the DWP structure as a blank piece of paper on which to record your window changes. If more than one window is changed as a result of the next step, the DWP structure can grow as needed. The format of a DWP is shown in Table 4-4.

Table 4-4: Format of a DWP.

Off	Type	Name	Description
00h	WORD	actualWndCount	// # of windows we're managing
02h	WORD	suggestWndCount	// Suggested number of windows
04h	WORD	isValid	// 1 if usable, 0 if not
06h	WORD	signature	// 5057h = 'WP' (WindowPos?)
08h	?	windowData	// Start of window data area

The second step of moving windows on the screen is to invoke DeferWindowPos() one or more times. The arguments to DeferWindowPos() include the DWP handle, the HWND to be changed, the position and size coordinates, and the SWP_xxx flags. It's important to note that no visible action takes place at this time. You won't see anything move about as a result of calling DeferWindowPos(). As its name implies, it *defers* action. The function, although not well understood enough to provide pseudocode for, does not call any functions which would cause display updates. Instead, the DeferWindowPos() just adds the specified changes to the DWP structure allocated in the first step. These changes are taken care of in the third step, below. If more windows need to be positioned than there are room for in the DWP structure, DeferWindowPos() calls LocalReAlloc() to resize the structure. The goal of DeferWindowPos() is to collect all the changes to all the windows in one place, without repainting anything. When all the changes are complete, the screen can be updated just once, minimizing the amount of window flash.

After all the calls to DeferWindowPos() have completed, EndDeferWindowPos() steps in and calls the necessary internal routines to enforce Z-ordering, clipping, and so on. The DWP structure is passed to these returns, which might cause even more windows to be added to the list of windows needing to be repainted. When all windows affected by the DeferWindowPos() calls in step two have been accounted for, EndDeferWindowPos() redraws them. It appears that DoSyncPaint() may play a large part in this procedure also.

As we saw earlier, SetWindowPos() is just a convenient wrapper around the trio of calls. Besides SetWindowPos(), the three functions are called as a group from several other places in USER, such as in the NW_DrawSwitchWindow() function, which draws the small window you see when using ALT-TAB in your programs. You too can gain performance improvements at the expense of a little complexity. If your program needs to move around more than one window at a time, consider using the DeferWindowPos functions, instead of SetWindowPos().

Now that we understand what goes on at a high level, let's examine pseudocode for BeginDeferWindowPos() and EndDeferWindowPos(). We aren't able to show you DeferWindowPos() because its actions aren't well understood. However, it doesn't appear to do anything besides add data to the DWP structure in preparation for the eventual call to EndDeferWindowPos().

BeginDeferWindowPos()

```
HDWP    WINAPI BeginDeferWindowPos(int cWindows);
```

It's the responsibility of BeginDeferWindowPos() to return a local handle to a DWP structure for DeferWindowPos() to fill in. It's somewhat unusual that BeginDeferWindowPos() gives the caller the opportunity to suggest how many windows will be affected by subsequent DeferWindowPos() calls. It appears that USER keeps around two permanent DWP structures. Only if a permanent DWP structure can't be used will a new DWP structure be allocated. Once the local handle for the DWP structure has been determined, the code initializes the known fields before returning the DWP handle.

```
Pseudocode for BeginDeferWindowPos() - WMSWP.OBJ
// Parameters:
//      WORD    suggestWndCount
// Locals:
//      DWP near *  hDWP

    if ( FMessageBox )  // Normally 0. Set to 1 by SysErrorBox()
    {
        hDWP = Msg_Workspace     // a "permanent" DWP structure
                                 // Used when a message box is up?
```

```
        if ( (hDWP->isValid) || (suggestWndCount > 2) )
        {
            _DebugOutput("USER: Too many windows positioned "
                         "with tasks locked" )
            return 0
        }

        suggestWndCount = 2     // Msg_Workspace has 2 windows?
    }
    else if ((suggestWndCount <= 4) && (Workspace->isValid == 0))
    {
        hDWP = Workspace    // "Workspace" appears to be yet
        suggestWndCount = 4 // another "permanent" DWP structure,
                            // with 4 "update" windows
    }
    else
    {
        // Allocate a new DWP structure in the USER heap. Take
        // into account the suggested number of windows given by
        // the caller. LT_USER_MWP is defined in TOOLHELP.H
        hDWP = UserLocalAlloc( LT_USER_MWP, LMEM_ZEROINIT,
                    (suggestWndCount * 0x26) + 8 )
    }

    if ( hDWP != 0 )    // If we have a DWP pointer to work with,
    {                   // fill in the fields now
        hDWP->isValid = 1
        hDWP->actualWindowCount = 0 // No windows modified yet!
        hDWP->suggestWndCount = suggestWndCount
        hDWP->signature = 'WP'
    }

    return hDWP         // Return handle to caller
```

DeferWindowPos()

```
HDWP    WINAPI DeferWindowPos(
            HDWP,
            HWND hWnd,
            HWND hWndInsertAfter,
            int x, int y, int cx, int cy,
            UINT flags);
```

DeferWindowPos() is where you submit window changes. These changes can include the window's size, position on the screen, position in the Z-order, and so on. DeferWindowPos() adds these changes to the running list of changes stored in the DWP structure. As "defer" implies, these changes do not affect the current windows on the screen. All DeferWindowPos() does is manipulate some data in memory. The actual WND structures and on-screen images don't change till later.

If the DWP structure becomes too small to hold all the changes, DeferWindowPos() reallocates the memory block to a larger size. If it can't reallocate the memory, DeferWindowPos() returns NULL, and you should abort the sequence of window changes. When you've completed all your changes, the final DWP structure is turned over to EndDeferWindowPos() so that it can update the screen in one operation.

EndDeferWindowPos()

```
BOOL    WINAPI EndDeferWindowPos(HDWP);
```

EndDeferWindowPos() is passed the handle to a DWP structure that contains the information for all windows the caller wants modified. There are several calls that handle the dirty work of recalculating and updating the affected windows. The first of these routines is ZOrderByOwner(), which takes care of determining the order of windows in the third dimension. Another important routine is CalcValidRects(), which presumably takes care of calculating which windows overlap other windows, and deciding what portions of the various windows are to be visible. Also important is DoSyncPaint(), which appears to take care of the task of forcing the affected windows to repaint.

```
Pseudocode for EndDeferWindowPos() - WMSWP.OBJ
// Parameters:
//      HDWP    hDWP
// Locals:
//      WORD    doPaint
//      WORD    someWnd
//      WORD    anotherWnd
//      WORD    SwpActivateResult

    if ( hDWP->actualWndCount == 0 )        // nothing to do!
        goto EndDeferWindowPos_free_exit    // Vacation time!

    // ValidateSmwp() appears to set the doPaint variable
    // (if the DWP is valid???).
    if ( ValidateSmwp(hDWP, &doPaint) )
    {
        someWnd = some unknown field in the hDWP structure

        // Do Z-ordering things if the desktop window was
        // included in the DWP structure.
        If ( someWnd != 0 )
            if ( someWnd == HWndDesktop )
```

```
        {
            hDWP = ZOrderByOwner(hDWP)
            if ( hDWP == 0 )
                return 0
        }

    // Find out which portions of the various windows
    // referenced by the DWP structure are valid.
    // CalcValidRects() is a lengthy routine, and
    // appears to contain a fair amount of the "logic"
    // behind window placement and ordering.
    CalcValidRects( hDWP, &anotherWnd )

    if ( BltValidBits(hDWP) != 0 )  // If bitmaps are saved,
        doPaint = 0                 // no need to repaint?

    SwpActivateResult = SwpActivate( &anotherWnd )

    // Do we need to do any painting? DoSyncPaint() is
    // another large routine that appears to contain even
    // more update logic.
    if ( doPaint )
        if ( IsWindow(someWnd) != 0 )
            DoSyncPaint( someWnd, 0, 4 )

    if ( SwpActivateResult )    // ??
    {
        if ( HWndActive )
            Turn off bit 0x0100 in HWndActive->dwFlags
        if ( HWndActivePrev )
            Turn off bit 0x0100 in HWndActivePrev->dwFlags
    }

    SendChangedMsgs( hDWP ) // Send WM_WINDOWPOSCHANGED
                            // messages
    if ( someWnd )
        if ( someWnd == HWndDesktop )
        {
            // Walks top level windows. Something having
            // to do with WS_EX_TOPMOST?
            ValidateTopmost()
        }
}                   // End of ValidateSmwp() == TRUE

EndDeferWindowPos_free_exit:

    @FreePsmwp( hDWP )      // Free the hDWP if it's not the
                            // permanent "Msg_Workspace" or
                            // "Workspace" DWP structures
```

The three functions just described, BeginDeferWindowPos(), DeferWindowPos(), and EndDeferWindowPos(), comprise the core routines that window manipulation is built on. As we saw earlier, other window manipulation routines are really just layers built upon the three DeferWindowPos functions.

Window Focus

Until now, we've not paid much attention to the subject of window focus. It certainly bears mentioning here, as the notion of window focus is important to many aspects of the windowing system.

The focus window receives messages related to keyboard activity, for instance, WM_CHAR messages. The most immediate example of window focus is the edit control window in a dialog box. An edit control with the focus has a blinking cursor which indicates that the window will receive the characters typed at the keyboard. If the focus switches away from the dialog box, the cursor disappears from the edit control. Note however that almost any window can have focus, including the window for a simple generic program.

USER maintains a global variable, HWndFocus, that holds the HWND of the current focus window. The HWndFocus value can be obtained using the GetFocus() API. It's possible not to have a current focus window, in which case HWndFocus is zero. You can enter this state by calling SetFocus() (described below) with an HWND of zero. In the Win32 API, the notion of focus has a somewhat different meaning, as one application isn't allowed to interfere with another application (for example, to steal the focus away from it). In Win32, the windowing system maintains a focus in a per-application manner.

Besides the focus window, USER maintains a global variable, HWndActive, containing the HWND of another special window called the active window. While the focus window can be any window in the system, the active window is always a top level window (WS_OVERLAPPED or WS_POPUP). The active window is either the focus window, or an ancestor (parent, grandparent, great grandparent, and so forth) of the focus window. The active window HWND can be set with the SetActiveWindow() API and retrieved with GetActiveWindow(). The pseudocode for ShowWindow() and DestroyWindow() shows examples of how HWndActive is used.

The active window is indicated to the user by the color of its title bar. The active window title bar is color, while the title bars of all the other, inactive colors are gray—that is, unless you've played with the color schemes in the Control Panel.

SetFocus()

The first portion of SetFocus() takes care of the special case where the focus is to be taken away from all windows (HWndFocus set to zero). The code first queries the Computer Based Training hook (WH_CBT) to see if it's OK to change the focus; if it is OK, the code calls SendFocusMessages(), described later.

If the new focus window won't be zero, the expected Windows version of the windows task comes into play. Depending on whether it's a pre-Windows 3.0 application or not, SetFocus() determines the top level window for the new focus, using different methods, then

SetFocus() saves the HWND. The rest of SetFocus() is similar to the code where the focus HWND is set to zero. The code calls the Computer Based Training hook, and then invokes SendFocusMessages(). The one difference between the two calls to SendFocusMessages() is that SetFocus() makes the previously found top level window into the new active window, if it's not already active.

```
Pseudocode for SetFocus() - WINLOOP2.OBJ
// Parameters:
//      HWND    hWnd
// Locals:
//      HWND    hWndPrevFocus    // WND with focus at time of call
//      HWND    hWndScratch      // A scratch HWND

    if ( hWnd == 0 )    // Taking focus away from everybody...
    {
        // Call a hook function. 9==HCBT_SETFOCUS, 5==WH_CBT ?
        if ( CallHook(9, hWnd, MAKELONG(HWndFocus, hWnd), 5) != 0 )
            return 0

        hWndPrevFocus = HWndFocus   // Remember the old focus wnd

        // Send the WM_KILLFOCUS and WM_SETFOCUS messages
        SendFocusMessages( HWndFocus, hWnd )

        return hWndPrevFocus
    }

    if ( GetAppVer() < 0x0300 )     // pre 3.0 windows app?
    {
        // Walk up the parent window list to get the topmost
        // window (the "main" window).
        hWndScratch = GetTopLevelWindow(hWnd)

        if ( hWndScratch & WS_DISABLED )  // Don't set focus to
            return 0                      // a disabled parent
                                          // window
    }
    else
    {
        // we walk up the parent window list, checking to see
        // if the state of any parent window would prevent us
        // from being able to get the focus.
        hWndScratch = hWnd                // start at focus window
        while ( hWndScratch & WS_CHILD )  // Stop when we reach
        {                                 // the top level window
```

```
            // Check to see if any parent window is minimized or
            // disabled. We can't set the focus if so.
            if ((hWndScratch & WS_MINIMIZED) ||
               (hWndScratch & WS_DISABLED) )
                return 0

            hWndScratch = hWndScratchParent // Now check the parent
                                            // window...
        }
    }

    if ( hWnd != HWndFocus )    // Is focus WND changing?
    {
        // Call a hook function. 9==HCBT_SETFOCUS, 5==WH_CBT ?
        if ( CallHook(9, hWnd, MAKELONG(HWndFocus, hWnd), 5) != 0 )
            return 0

        // hWndScratch should be pointing to the top level
        // window of the application receiving the focus. If
        // this top level window is  different than the currently
        // active top level window, call ActivateThisWindow()
        // to switch the active window.
        if ( hWndScratch != HWndActive )
            if ( ActivateThisWindow(hWndScratch, 0, 0) == 0 )
                return 0

        if (IsWindow(hWnd)== 0) // Was new focus WND destroyed?
            return 0

        hWndScratch = HWndFocus // Remember previous focus HWND,
                                // because we need to return it!

        // Send the WM_KILLFOCUS and WM_SETFOCUS messages
        SendFocusMessages( HWndFocus, hWnd )
    }
    else                                // Focus not changing
        hWndScratch = HWndFocus

    return hWndScratch      // contains previous focus HWND
```

SendFocusMessages()

SendFocusMessages() has three duties. It sets the HWndFocus global variable to the new focus HWND; it sends the WM_KILLFOCUS message to the window that's about to lose focus, and send the WM_SETFOCUS to the new focus window. It's interesting to note that before sending the WM_SETFOCUS message, the value of the new focus HWND is compared to its value upon entry into SendFocusMessages(). This is most likely needed because some applications handle the WM_KILLFOCUS message, calling SetFocus() with their HWND to prevent themselves from losing the focus. It's conceivable that without this code, applications that call SetFocus() in their WM_KILLFOCUS handler could cause an infinite recursion.

```
Pseudocode for SendFocusMessages() - WINLOOP2.OBJ

// Parameters:
//      HWND    hWndOldFocus
//      HWND    hWndNewFocus

    HWndFocus = hWndNewFocus // Set USER global variable. This
                             // precedes the WM_KILLFOCUS msg!!!

    if ( hWndOldFocus != 0 )    // If there was a previous focus
    {                           // HWND, send WM_KILLFOCUS
        FRevalidate = 0         // A USER Global variable

        REvalSendMessage( hWndOldFocus, WM_KILLFOCUS,
                hWndNewFocus, 0 )
    }

    // If we're setting the focus to a new window (i.e., not
    // NULL), send the WM_SETFOCUS message to the new window
    // Note that the hWndNewFocus is compared to its original
    // value (stored in HWndFocus). This is probably necessary
    // because an application might have trapped the
    // WM_KILLFOCUS message, and set the focus back to itself.
    if ( hWndNewFocus )
        if ( HWndFocus == hWndNewFocus )
        {
            SendMessage( hWndNewFocus, WM_SETFOCUS,
                hWndOldFocus, 0 )
        }
```

Message Processing

Our discussion of the windowing system would be sorely lacking if we didn't cover at least some of the most basic functions for handling window messages. Therefore, we discuss the BeginPaint() and EndPaint() functions, as well as DefWindowProc().

BeginPaint()

Of all the messages your program could handle, WM_PAINT is typically the most important. The standard response to the WM_PAINT message is to call BeginPaint() to get a device context from the list of five cached DCs USER maintains (DCs are discussed in Chapter 5). With the device context, you do whatever screen updating is necessary and release the DC when you're done using it. Since there's a set of functions that acquire and release DCs (GetDC() and ReleaseDC(), also discussed in Chapter 5), you might think that it's OK to bypass BeginPaint() and EndPaint() in favor of calling the DC functions. This is not the case. While BeginPaint() does acquire a DC for your use, it performs other necessary actions that GetDC() doesn't. We'll see what these actions are when we examine the pseudocode.

We won't be presenting pseudocode for BeginPaint(), as it's just a stub routine. All it does is push another value on the stack frame created when BeginPaint() was called, and then JMP to InternalBeginPaint().

InternalBeginPaint() begins by zeroing out the PAINTSTRUCT structure whose address was passed. Next, it turns off a flag inside of the HWND that was set inside DispatchMessage(). This indicates to DispatchMessage() that BeginPaint() was called in response to the WM_PAINT message. Chapter 7 discusses the DispatchMessage() part of this process.

A bit later, InternalBeginPaint() sends the WM_NCPAINT (non-client paint) message to the window, if necessary. If the window wants to paint its own custom frames, it would handle this message and paint accordingly. Then, if the window being painted is the caret window, InternalBeginPaint() hides the caret so that it doesn't interfere with subsequent painting.

The next task for InternalBeginPaint() is a key step that distinguishes it from a call to GetDC(). If the window has an update region, InternalBeginPaint() calls DecPaintCount() for it. As described in Chapter 7 on the Windows messaging system, DecPaintCount() decrements the paint count field in the application's message queue, and clears the QS_PAINT bit if the count drops to zero. If DecPaintCount() wasn't called, the application would continue to see that a WM_PAINT message needs to be generated whenever GetMessage() or PeekMessage() is called. GetDC() doesn't clear the QS_PAINT bit or call DecPaintCount().

InternalBeginPaint() now turns it attention to obtaining a device context handle from USER's cache of DCs (see the discussion of DCEs in Chapter 6 of *Undocumented Windows*, and the discussion of LW_DCInit() in Chapter 1 of this book), for the application to paint with. It uses the GetDCEx() function to get the device context which it stores in the PAINTSTRUCT field. Some other PAINTSTRUCT fields are cleared at this point.

Before BeginPaint() can return the DC to the caller, two more steps remain. If the window has a background area to be erased, the code calls SendEraseBkgnd() to send either WM_ICONERASEBKGND or WM_ERASEBKGND, whichever is needed. The second task is to call SendChildNCPaint(), which sends WM_NCPAINT messages to the window's child windows.

```
Pseudocode for InternalBeginPaint() - WMPAINT.OBJ
// Parameters:
//      HWND     hWnd                // WND to be painted
//      PAINTSTRUCT far *lpps        // PAINTSTRUCT pointer
//      WORD     windowDC            // Should DCX_WINDOW be used?
// Locals:
//      HRGN     hUpdateRgn
//      WORD     needBkgErase
```

```
//      HDC     hDC
//      DWORD   DCFlags

    // Write a consistent memory pattern to the PAINTSTRUCT
    // for debugging purposes (only in the debug USER)
    // Undocumented Windows list K329() as "DebugFillBuffer()"
    K329( lpps, sizeof(PAINTSTRUCT) )

    // Clear the flag set inside of DispatchMessage(). This
    // flag indicates that painting did occur for the window. If
    // DispatchMessage() see that this flag is still set after
    // dispatching the message, it will do default painting, and
    // in the debugging version, whine at the caller that painting
    // didn't occur properly.
    Turn off bit 0x02 in HIWORD(hWnd->dwFlags)

    // if not the desktop window AND not a 3.1 compatible app
    // AND the window is minimized AND there is an hIcon for
    // class, set windowDC to 1.
    if ( hWnd != HWndDesktop )
        if ( bit 0x04 not set in HIWORD(hWnd->dwFlags) )
            if ( hWnd->dwStyleFlags & WS_MINIMIZED )
                if ( hWnd->wndClass->hIcon != 0 )
                    windowDC = 1    // It's a window DC

    if ( 0x0800 bit set in LOWORD(hWnd->dwFlags) )
    {
        // Get a handle to a RGN containing the non-client areas
        // that need to be painted
        hUpdateRgn = GetNCUpdateRgn( hWnd, 0 )

        SendNCPaint( hWnd, hUpdateRgn ) // Send WM_NCPAINT to hWnd

        DeleteNCUpdateRgn( hUpdateRgn ) // All done with the RGN
    }

    if ( hWnd == Caret )     // Turn off the caret before painting
        InternalHideCaret() // The _real_ HideCaret() code

    needsBkgErase = (BYTE at hWnd->dwFlags+1) & 0x0002
    if ( needsBkgErase )
        Turn off bits 0x0004 & 0x002 in (BYTE at hWnd->dwFlags+1)

    // If the window has an update region, decrement the paint
    // count stored in the application's message queue
```

```
if ( hWnd->hRgnUpdate ||
     bit 0x1000 set in LOWORD(hWnd->dwFlags) )
{
    DecPaintCount( hWnd )
}

hUpdateRgn = hWnd->hrgnUpdate   // Remember update RGN handle

// Null the window update region stored in the WND structure.
// We've already saved the handle in a local variable.
hWnd->hrgnUpdate = 0
lpps->fRestore = 0    // Zero out fields in the PAINTSTRUCT
lpps->fIncUpdate = 0

if ( windowDC )
    DCFlags = DCX_WINDOW | DCX_INTERSECTRGN | DCX_USESTYLE
            | some undocumented flag
else
    DCFlags = DCX_INTERSECTRGN | DCX_USESTYLE
            | some undocumented flag

// Get a DC (from USER DC cache) that'll be used for painting
// the window. Put the DC in the PAINTSTRUCT, as well as in
// a local variable.
hDC = GetDCEx( hWnd, hUpdateRgn, DCFlags )
lpps->hdc = hDC

// Fill in the rcPaint field of the PAINTSTRUCT with the
// rectangle coordinates that need painting.
if ( UT_GetParentDCClipBox( hWnd, hDC, &lpps->rcPaint ) )
{
    // Send either WM_ICONERASEBKGND or WM_ERASEBKGND to
    // the window, as appropriate.
    if ( needsBkgErase )
        SendEraseBkgnd( hWnd, hdc, hUpdateRgn )

    if ( IsWindow(hWnd) == 0 )  // Make sure the window is
        return 0                // still valid.
}

SendChildNCPaint( hWnd )    // Send WM_NCPAINT msgs to the
                            // child windows, as appropriate

// Set the flag that indicates that the application needs
// to erase the background. This will be nonzero if the
// application didn't specify a background brush in the
```

```
    // window class.
    lpps->fErase = LOWORD(hWnd->dwFlags) & 0x0400

    return hDC      // Return DC that caller will paint with
```

Upon completion of BeginPaint() and InternalBeginPaint(), the application has a device context to draw and paint its window (see Chapter 5 on GDI). When the application completes its work, it releases the device context back to the USER device context cache using the EndPaint() function.

EndPaint()

The EndPaint() code is very straightforward. It first releases the device context used for painting back to the cache of display DCs that USER maintains. If the window had the caret before painting began, InternalShowCaret() turns it back on. The last step is to zero out the PAINTSTRUCT, if the program is running under the debugging USER.

```
Pseudocode for EndPaint() - WMPAINT.OBJ
// Parameters:
//      HWND     hWnd
//      PAINTSTRUCT far *lpps

    // Release the painting DC back to the pool of 5
    // display DCs that USER keeps around.
    ReleaseCacheDC( lpps->hdc, 1 )

    if ( hWnd == Caret )          // Now that painting is done, we
        InternalShowCaret()       // can reshow the caret, if the
                                  // window is the caret window

    K329( lpps, sizeof(PAINTSTRUCT) )    // blow away the
                                         // PAINTSTRUCT fields
                                         // (debug USER only)
```

DefWindowProc()

The way an application handles messages is somewhat similar to inheritance in object-oriented languages such as C++. The idea behind inheritance is that a derived class retains all the functions of the base class and only overrides or adds the functions it needs to. In Windows programming, your window procedure is the derived class; it handles only the messages it needs. The role of the base class is played by DefWindowProc(). DefWindowProc() is responsible for handling all messages that *must* have some sort of action taken for them.

With the hundreds of messages that Windows slings around, it's bound to be somewhat interesting to see what messages absolutely must have some form of special processing. Luckily, we don't have to dig much to find this out. The source code for DefWindowProc(), as well as the default dialog procedure, DefDlgProc(), can be found in the Windows SDK. In the Windows 3.1 SDK, the files can be found in the DEFPROCS directory (for example,

C:\SDK\SAMPLES\DEFPROCS\) as DEFWND.C and DEFDLG.C. We highly recommend that you look at the code if you have it, as it can be very enlightening. However, we wouldn't recommend that you base your own window procedure code on the code in DefWindowProc(). It's one *very long* switch statement. Contrary to what some people seem to think, you don't have to write all of your program's code to fit inside a single switch statement.

If you do examine the DefWindowProc() code, you might notice the TestWF() function. According to the CodeView information, as well as the disassembly listings, there is no TestWF() function. Instead, it appears that TestWF() is really a C macro. What's somewhat strange is that the TestWF() macro appears able to access the WND structure's dwFlags, dwStyleFlags, and dwExStyleFlags fields, all from the same macro. The TestWF() macro must be ugly indeed!

An interesting aspect of DefWindowProc() is that it calls numerous internal functions (and the comments in the code don't explain them very well). Since the internal functions aren't exported, you can't just compile DefWindowProc() and include it in your application.

Also of some note is that DefWindowProc() openly handles a set of messages that aren't documented in the SDK or DDK. One would think that if they absolutely required some sort of response, they'd be documented. The undocumented messages are described in *Undocumented Windows* and are as follows:

WM_SYNCPAINT
WM_ISACTIVEICON
WM_GETHOTKEY
WM_SETHOTKEY
WM_QUERYDROPOBJECT
WM_DROPOBJECT

DestroyWindow()

When you're finished with a window, you need to remove it from the windowing system. The disposal of a window is much more than just undoing the work of CreateWindowEx(). DestroyWindow() is another large function, so we have broken it up into subsections to cover individually.

DestroyWindow() is usually not directly called as often as CreateWindow(). In many cases, it's called for you by DefWindowProc() in response to the WM_CLOSE message.

The first section of DestroyWindow() determines if it's OK to shut down the window; then it gets out of any states during which it wouldn't be good to shut down. The first test determines if the window being destroyed is associated with the current message queue. If not, the function returns a failure code. This prevents one application from destroying the windows of another application, be it malicious or not.

Next, DestroyWindow() exits out of a locked state if the system is in such a state. The locked state is a special mode of the scheduler that only allows the current task to run (Chapter 6 discusses this in more detail). If the system were to remain in a locked state, a potential deadlock situation could arise later on if a message was sent to another task.

Afterwards, DestroyWindow() invokes the Computer Based Training hook, asking it if it's OK for the window destruction to proceed. Assuming the return is zero (okay to proceed) and that the right conditions are met, DestroyWindow() uses EndMenu() to get out of a menu state.

```
Pseudocode for DestroyWindow() - WMDSTROY.OBJ
// Parameters:
//      HWND    hWnd

    // Find out if the window we're destroying is owned by the
    // current task/queue. If not, slap the caller on the wrist.
    if ( hWnd->hQueue != HqCurrent() )
    {
        _DebugOutput( "USER: DestroyWindow: hwnd not created "
                      "by the current task" )
        return 0
    }

    // If the scheduler is only letting the current task run, get
    // out of that state now, as intertask SendMessage()'s may be
    // sent later on.
    if ( FTaskIsLocked != 0 )
        LockMyTask( 0 )

    // Call a hook. 4-> HCBT_DESTROYWND, 5 -> WH_CBT
    // CBT -> "Computer Based Training"
    if  ( CallHook(4, hWnd, 0, 5) != 0 )
        return 0

    // Do something related to getting out of a menu state if
    // we're in one. PGlobalPopupMenu is a USER global variable
    if ( PGlobalPopupMenu )
        if ( hWnd == some field in PGlobalPopupMenu )
        {
            set PGlobalPopupMenu field to 0
            EndMenu()
        }
```

The second part of DestroyWindow() concerns itself with broadcasting the fact that the window is shutting down and that various states may need to be updated. If the window is a top level window, DestroyWindow() calls the WH_SHELL hook procedure. This gives the owner of the shell hook a chance to do whatever it needs to do when a top level window goes away. This section is also where DestroyWindow() updates the palette and tells other applications of the new palette, using a WM_PALETTECHANGED message.

If the window is a WS_CHILD window, and if it is not prevented from notifying its parents, the code sends a WM_PARENTNOTIFY message to the hWndParent window. It's apparently undocumented that the high WORD of the LPARAM field is the menu handle for the window being destroyed. This section of DestroyWindow() ends by using SetWindow-Pos() to remove the window entirely from the screen.

```
Continuation of pseudocode for DestroyWindow() - WMDSTROY.OBJ

    if ( hWnd->dwStyleFlags & WS_CHILD == 0    // If not a child
         && hWnd->HWNDOwner == 0  )            // or owned window
    {
        CallHook(2, hWnd, 0, 0xA)    // 2-> HSHELL_WINDOWDESTROYED
                                     // 0xA -> WH_SHELL

        if ( 0x0001 bit set in HIWORD(hWnd->dwFlags) )
        {
            RealizeDefaultPalette( HDCBits )    // HDCBits is a
                                                // global var

            // HQAppExit is normally 0. When an app is exiting,
            // HQAppExit is set to its message queue
            if ( HQappExit == 0 )
            {
                // Tell all top level windows, and the desktop
                // that the palette has changed
                REvalSendMessage( HWND_BROADCAST,
                                WM_PALETTECHANGED, hWnd, 0)
                REvalSendMessage( HWndDesktop,
                                WM_PALETTECHANGED, hWnd, 0)
            }
        }
    }

    // If the app isn't exiting, and the window is a child window,
    // and the window isn't WS_EX_NOPARENTNOTIFY, send the
    // WM_PARENTNOTIFY message to its parent
    if ( HQAppExit == 0 )
        if ( hWnd->dwStyleFlags & WS_CHILD )
            if ( !(hWnd->dwExStyleFlags & WS_EX_NOPARENTNOTIFY) )
            {
                REvalSendMessage(hWnd->hWndParent, WM_PARENTNOTIFY,
                        WM_DESTROY, MAKELONG(hWnd, hWnd->hMenu))
            }

    // DestroyWindow() is recursive, so it always makes sure
    // the window it's working on is still valid at this point.
```

```
if ( IsWindow(hWnd) == 0 )  // If the window isn't valid
    return 1                // anymore, return success

if ( hWnd->dwStyleFlags & WS_VISIBLE )  // Is window visible?
{
    if (hWnd->dwStyleFlags & WS_CHILD)  // A child window?
    {
        ShowWindow( hWnd, SW_HIDE )     // Hide it!
    }
    else                                // Not a child window
    {
        // We're a top level window. Call SetWindowPos()
        // to hide the window. If we're the app that's
        // currently exiting, add in the SWP_DEFERERASE flag.
        if ( HQAppExit == hWnd->hQueue )
        {
            SetWindowPos( hWnd, 0, 0, 0, 0, 0,
                SWP_DEFERERASE | SWP_HIDEWINDOW |
                SWP_NOACTIVATE | SWP_NOZORDER |
                SWP_NOMOVE | SWP_NOSIZE )
        }
        else
        {
            SetWindowPos( hWnd, 0, 0, 0, 0, 0,
                SWP_HIDEWINDOW | SWP_NOACTIVATE |
                 SWP_NOZORDER | SWP_NOMOVE | SWP_NOSIZE )
        }
    }

    if ( IsWindow(hWnd) == 0 )  // If the window isn't valid
        return 1                // anymore, return success
                                // SetWindowPos() may have
}                               // destroyed the window?
```

The final section of DestroyWindow() breaks apart the various components of the window and deallocates them. The first thing to be disposed of is some window whose handle is stored in the destroying window's property list. DestroyWindow() recurses into itself to complete this.

Next DestroyWindow() throws away any windows owned by the window undergoing destruction. DestroyOwnedWindows() handles the job of walking the list of child windows, looking for appropriate windows. Since DestroyOwnedWindows() calls DestroyWindow(), you can see that these two functions recurse into each other in order to walk the window hierarchy. We cover DestroyOwnedWindows() after our discussion of DestroyWindow().

At this point, all windows that were owned by the destroying window should be gone from the window hierarchy. Only non-owned WS_CHILD windows should remain.

DestroyWindow() calls SendDestroyMesssages() to send a WM_DESTROY message to the window being destroyed and to each of its descendants.

The next step taken depends on whether the window has a parent or not. If the window doesn't have a parent, meaning it's a top level window, DestroyWindow() changes the queue associated with the desktop window to the queue of the active application. This may be an attempt to keep down the number of intertask SendMessage()s. By keeping the queue of the desktop window the same as the queue of the active window, most messages sent to the desktop window can be handled within the context of the active application. This reduces the number of time-consuming task switches needed.

If the window does have an hWndParent, it needs to be removed from the hierarchy of windows. UnlinkWindow() takes care of this.

DestroyWindow() finishes up by calling FreeWindow(). FreeWindow() does more than its name implies; it frees up not only the memory for the HWND passed to it, but also that of the window's children. We discuss FreeWindow() in a bit.

```
Continuation of pseudocode for DestroyWindow() - WMDSTROY.OBJ

    if ( hWnd->properties )
    {
        HANDLE hProp

        // This could possibly be the destruction of the icon
        // title window if the window is minimized (iconic).
        // AtomCheckPointProp is a USER global variable.
        hProp = GetProp( hWnd, MAKELP(0, AtomCheckPointProp) )
        if ( hProp )
            if ( hProp->someWindow )
            {
                // The DestroyWindow() call below implies that
                // DestroyWindow() can be recursively entered.
                if ( IsWindow( hProp->someWindow ) )
                    DestroyWindow( hProp->someWindow )
                hProp->someWindow = 0
            }
    }

    // If the window is not a child window, it's time to get
    // rid of all windows that it owns. See pseudocode below.
    if ( hWnd->dwStyleFlags & WS_CHILD == 0 )
        DestroyOwnedWindows( hWnd )

    if ( FMessageBox == 0 ) // FMessageBox set to 1 inside
    {                       // SysErrorBox() (a critical state!)

        A long sequence of nested code branches. The code
```

```
        calls ActivateWindow(), InternalDestroyCaret(), and
        RedrawIconTitle(). At various points, it sets
        the global variables HWndActive, HQActive, and HWndFocus
        to 0. It appears that this sequence is related to
        activating some other window.
    }

    // Recursively send WM_DESTROY messages to ourself, and all
    // our child windows. See pseudocode below.
    SendDestroyMessages(hWnd)

    if ( IsWindow(hWnd) == 0 )  // If the window isn't valid
        return 1                // anymore, return success

    if ( hWnd->hWndParent == 0 )    // If there's no parent...
    {
        // And if the queues match...
        if ( hWnd->hQueue == HWndDesktop->hQueue )
        {
            // Change the hQueue of the second window to the
            // hQueue for the first window. Don't bother
            // doing this if the two queues are the same.
            // This is presumably done so that the desktop
            // window always gets its messages from the queue
            // of the currently active window, thereby avoiding
            // expensive intertask SendMessage() calls.
            ChangeToCurrentTask( hWndActive, HWndDesktop )
        }
    }
    else    // There is a parent window...
    {
        // Unlink the window from the list of child windows
        // maintained by the parent. The second parameter points
        // to the first child window of the parent. UnlinkWindow()
        // iterates through its child windows until it finds
        // the hWnd (the first parameter), and then unlinks it.
        UnlinkWindow( hWnd, &hWnd->hWndParent->hWndChild )
    }

    FreeWindow( hWnd )  // Deallocate the window's memory, as well
                        // as that of its children.

    return 1
}
```

DestroyOwnedWindows()

Because the window structure only contains information for its child and sibling windows and doesn't include any owned window information, the method used by DestroyOwnedWindows() to destroy all the owned windows of a particular HWND is somewhat inefficient.

DestroyOwnedWindows() starts at the desktop window and iterates through every window in the child hierarchy. If it finds a window that's owned by the destroying window, the hierarchy traversal stops so that the found window can be destroyed. Perhaps in an attempt to be safe, the found window isn't destroyed if the window's queue doesn't match the queue of the destroying window.

If an owned window is found and destroyed, DestroyOwnedWindows() begins searching for more owned windows *at the desktop window* making no attempt to remember where the search left off. This may be necessary because a window could be owned by a window that itself was owned by yet another window. Since the owner of a window could conceivably be deeper in the hierarchy than a window it owns, the search has to begin at the root of the hierarchy each time.

```
Pseudocode for DestroyOwnedWindows() - WMDSTROY.OBJ
// Parameters:
//      HWND    hWndDestroying
// Locals:
//      HWND    hWnd

    while ( 1 )
    {
        // We're going to iterate through all the top level
        // windows. We start with the first child window of the
        // desktop window, and follow the 'hWndNext' pointers
        hWnd = HWndDesktop->hWndChild
        while ( hWnd )
        {
            if ( hWnd->HWNDOwner == hWndDestroying )
            {
                // Check hQueues to see if we rightfully "own"
                // the window we just found. If we don't, just
                // set the owning window to 0, rather than
                // destroy the window.
                if ( hWnd->hQueue == hWndDestroying->hQueue )
                    break
                else
                    hWnd->HWNDOwner = 0
            }

            hWnd = hWnd->hWndNext        // Go on to next window
        }
```

```
        if ( hWnd == 0 )      // When there are no more top level
            return            // windows owned by 'hWndDestroying',
                              // This test will be true, and the
                              // function will return.

        // Destroy the found window. Afterwards, we start looping
        // through the children of the desktop window again,
        // looking for more windows owned by 'hWndDestroying'.
        DestroyWindow( hWnd )
    }
```

SendDestroyMessages()

SendDestroyMessages() sends a WM_DESTROY message to a window and all of its children. It does this by recursing through the child window hierarchy. Besides sending WM_DESTROY messages, SendDestroyMessages() performs two other tasks. The first is to ensure that the focus doesn't remain with a window that's about to receive the WM_DESTROY message. The second is to disown the clipboard if it's owned by the window about to receive the WM_DESTROY.

A point worth noting is the relationship between WM_DESTROY and WM_NC-DESTROY (see FreeWindow(), below). The WM_DESTROY messages are sent to the windows in the hierarchy in top-down order, that is, the parent window always sees the WM_DESTROY message before its children. The WM_NCDESTROY message is exactly the opposite. It propagates through the hierarchy from the bottom up. The child windows see their WM_NCDESTROY messages before their parents.

```
Pseudocode for SendDestroyMessage() - WMDSTROY.OBJ
// Parameters:
//      HWND    hWndDestroying
// Locals:
//      HWND    hWnd

    CheckFocus( hWndDestroying )  // If HWND parameter has the
                                  // focus, and is a child, set
                                  // focus to the parent HWND.

    if ( hWndDestroying == hWndClipOwner )  // If we own the
        SDM_DisownClipboard()               // clipboard, get
                                            // rid of it now.

    // Send WM_DESTROY to ourselves. For main windows, the usual
    // response to WM_DESTROY is to call PostQuitMessage().
    REvalSendMessage( hWndDestroying, WM_DESTROY, 0 , 0 )

    // Make sure we didn't lose ourselves in the process of
```

```
    // handling the WM_DESTROY message...
    if ( IsWindow( hWndDestroying ) == 0 )
    {
        _DebugOutput( "USER: Window destroyed itself during "
                      "WM_DESTROY processing" )
        return
    }

    // Iterate through all the children of 'hWndDestroying',
    // calling SendDestroyMessages() for each of them. This means
    // that SendDestroyMessages() is recursive.
    hWnd = hWndDestroying->hWndChild    // Start with first child
    while ( hWnd )
    {
        SendDestroyMessages( hWnd )
        hWnd = hWnd->hWndNext           // Go on to next sibling
    }

    CheckFocus( hWndDestroying )        // See above description
```

FreeWindow()

From its name, FreeWindow() would seem to be a simple routine that just deallocates the memory for a WND structure. This is certainly not the case. FreeWindow() is a large function that handles many chores you'd think would be handled in DestroyWindow(). In fact, it's FreeWindow(), rather than DestroyWindow(), that's really the opposite of CreateWindow(). Since it's so big, we broke it up into sections and discuss each in turn.

The first important duty of FreeWindow() is to recurse through the child window hierarchy, calling FreeWindow() for each child window. This ensures that all children of the window being freed are themselves freed. When all the child windows are destroyed, FreeWindow() sends a WM_NCDESTROY (non-client destroy) message to the window being freed.

```
Pseudocode for FreeWindow() - WMFREE.OBJ
// Parameters:
//      HWND    hWnd
// Locals:
//      HWND    hWndFree, hWndFreeNext
//      MSG     msg

    // Verify a valid hWnd was passed. It seems rather unlikely
    // that there's a real assert() in the code, since no source
    // file and line number is given. The program isn't exited
    // either, like a real assert() would do.
```

```
if ( IsWindow( hWnd ) == 0 )
    _DebugOutput( "USER: Assertion failed" )

if ( hWnd == HWndCbDlgExtra )   // Dialog extra bytes ???
    HWndCbDlgExtra = 0

Iterate through some sort of linked list, setting fields
to 0. The head of the list is pointed to by PBWLList.

// Recursively iterate through all the child windows, calling
// FreeWindow() on each of them. FreeWindow() is recursive.
hWndFree = hWnd->hWndChild  // Start with first child window
while ( hWndFree )
{
    // Remember hWndNext, because we won't be able to get
    // it after we free the current hWndFree.
    hWndFreeNext = hWndFree->hWndNext
    FreeWindow( hWndFree )      // Isn't recursion great!
    hWndFree = hWndFreeNext     // Go on to next window
}

// Send a non-client destroy message to the window that's
// presently being freed.
REvalSendMessage( hWnd, WM_NCDESTROY, 0, 0 )
```

FreeWindow() now examines various USER variables that represent states of the windowing system. If the window being freed is associated with the state, FreeWindow() resets the state to "none," since the window won't be valid when FreeWindow() completes. The window being freed is compared to the following USER global variables in Table 4-5.

Table 4-5: Some USER Global Variables.

HWndCursor	The Window with the cursor over it.
HWndSysModal	The system modal window.
HWndActivePrev	The previous active window.
HWndActive	The current active window.
HWndClipViewer	The clipboard viewer window.
HWndFocus	The window with input focus.
HWndCapture	The window with the mouse capture.

Continuation of pseudocode for FreeWindow() - WMFREE.OBJ

```
// We now start a long sequence where we compare the window
// being freed to USER global HWND variables. If the window
```

```
// being freed is stored in any of these variables,
// appropriate action is taken to "reset" the state. It
// wouldn't do to have global variables referring to an HWND
// after it was deallocated.

// Here, if the window being freed is the one with the cursor,
// call FarSetWakeBit(). This causes "events" in a queue,
// and causes the scheduler to "wake" the task associated
// with the queue. See Chapter 6 for details.
if ( hWnd == HWndCursor )
{

    HWndCursor = 0
    if ( HQKeyboard )
        FarSetWakeBit( HQKeyboard, QS_MOUSEMOVE )

}

// If the window is owned by another window, do something
// involving resetting the last active window.
if ( hWnd->HWNDOwner )
    if ( hWnd->HWNDOwner->hWndLastActive == hWnd )
        hWnd->HWNDOwner->hWndLastActive = hWnd->HWNDOwner

if ( hWnd == HWndSysModal ) // If we're system modal, get
    SetSysModalWindow( 0 )  // get of that state.

if ( hWnd == HWndActivePrev )    // If we were the previous
    hWndActivePrev = 0           // active window, we can't
                                 // be anymore!
if ( hWnd == HWndActive )
{

    hWndActive = 0
    _DebugOutput("USER: Attempt to activate destroyed window")
}

if ( hWnd == HWndClipViewer )
    HWndClipViewer = 0

if ( hWnd == HWndFocus )    // If we're leaving, it wouldn't
    HWndFocus = 0           // be nice to keep the focus...

if ( hWnd = HWndCapture )   // Release the mouse capture if
    ReleaseCapture()        // we currently have it

if ( hWnd == PSBISB->someWindow )   // Popup Save Bits?
    PSBISB->someWindow = 0
```

FreeWindow() begins the next section by destroying any timers that would be a source of messages for the window being freed. (Note that as explained in Chapter 7, timer messages aren't sent or even posted. They're created when the application asks for another message.) If the exiting window has an update region stored in a block in a USER local heap, FreeWindow() deletes the update region at this time. There's certainly no need to update a window that's soon to be nonexistent!

A very important task of this section of FreeWindow() is to flush out any messages in the application's message queue that were destined for the window being freed. If this weren't done, GetMessage() could be called later on and return a message for a window that no longer existed. It would be rather difficult to dispatch such a message! All messages read from the queue are "dropped on the floor," with the exception of WM_QUIT. If this message is seen, FreeWindow() reposts it back to the application's queue so that the task will still get it. Remember, messages are kept in the *task's* message queue, rather than with a particular window. When GetMessage() encounters the WM_QUIT message in the queue, it returns zero, which indicates to the program that it should drop out of its main loop and exit.

This section of FreeWindow() ends by destroying, as appropriate, the regular menu and system menus for the window.

```
Continuation of pseudocode for FreeWindow() - WMFREE.OBJ

    DestroyTimers( 0, hWnd )     // Get rid of timers associated
                                 // with the freeing window?

    // If the window needed painting, it's too late now. Free
    // up the GDI region associated with the window.
    if ( hWnd->hRgnUpdate ||
         bit 0x1000 set in LOWORD(hWnd->dwFlags) )
    {
        DecPaintCount( hWnd )    // What if paint count > 1 ???

        if ( hWnd->hRgnUpdate > 1 )
            DeleteObject( hWnd->hRgnUpdate )
    }

    // Flush out any messages in the queue for this window.
    while ( 1 )
    {
       // Read messages (and toss them) until there's no more
       // in the queue.
        if ( !ReadMessage( hWnd->hQueue, &msg, hWnd, 0, -1, 1) )
            break;
        if ( msg.message == WM_QUIT )        // Except!  Don't lose
        {                                    // WM_QUIT messages!
            PostQuitMessage( msg.wParam )
            break;
        }
    }
```

```
// If not a child window, and if there's a menu for it,
// go destroy the menu.
if ( hWnd->dwStyleFlags & WS_CHILD == 0 )
    if ( hWnd->hMenu != 0 )
    {
        if ( IsMenu( hWnd->hMenu )
            DestroyMenu( hWnd->hMenu )
        else
            _DebugOutput("USER: DestroyWindow: Window menu "
                         "no longer valid" )
    }

// If the window has a system menu, go destroy it now.
if (hWnd->hMenuSystem )
{
    if ( IsMenu(hWnd->hMenuSystem) )
    {
        DestroyMenu( hWnd->hMenuSystem )
    }
    else
    {
        _DebugOutput("USER: DestroyWindow: System menu "
                     "handle no longer valid" )
    }
}
```

The last section of FreeWindow() finally gets the opportunity to free up things. First to go are any DCs that weren't released by the window beforehand. The pseudocode shows other things of interest, including the window properties, being deleted.

Near the very end, FreeWindow() decrements the reference count of the window class, indicating that one less window is using it. You might think that the class would be freed here if its count dropped to zero. This is not the case, however. The window class is freed in the PurgeClass() routine, called from ModuleUnload(), called from AppExit(). As its name implies, AppExit() (see Chapter 3) is invoked when a program is terminating. No-longer-in-use window classes hang around in memory until the program terminates.

The last act of FreeWindow() is to do what its name implies, free the WND structure in the USER local heap.

```
Continuation of pseudocode for FreeWindow() - WMFREE.OBJ

    Iterate though the list of Device Contexts (DCs), and based
    upon various flags, clean up things. The head of the DCE
    (Device Context Entry) list is given by the global variable
    'PDCEFirst'. The following functions are called:
    DeleteHRgnClip(), DestroyCacheDC(), and ReleaseCacheDC().
    At one point, the message: "USER: GetDC without ReleaseDC"
    can be printed out. DCs are explained in chapter 5.
```

```
if ( hWnd->dwStyleFlags & WS_CHILD == 0 )
    SetHotKey( hWnd, 0 )    // Get rid of hotkeys for window?

if ( hWnd->hBuffer != 0 )       // Free up memory used
    TextFree( hWnd->hBuffer )   // by text controls?

if ( hWnd == HWndLockUpdate )   // ???
{
    FreeSPB( FindSPB(hWnd) )    // Free "Saved Popup Bits"

    HWndLockUpdate = 0
    HQLockUpdate = 0
}

if ( 0x80 bit set in LOBYTE( hWnd->dwFlags ) )
    FreeSPB( FindSPB(hWnd) )    // Free Saved Popup Bits?

// If there's a scrollbar for the window, delete it.
// UserLocalFree() is equivalent to LocalFree() with USER's DS.
if ( hWnd->scrollBar )
    UserLocalFree( hWnd->scrollBar )

// Get rid of any properties that may have been added
// to the widow.
if ( hWnd->properties )
    DeleteProperties( hWnd )

Decrement the reference count field in hWnd->wndClass

if ( reference count field in hWnd->wndClass < 0 )
{
    _DebugOutput( "USER: Window class reference "
                  "count underflow" )
}

hWnd->wndClass = 0      // Zero out the INTWNDCLASS pointer

UserLocalFree( hWnd )   // All done with the WND's memory
```

Summary

This chapter has examined the basic structure and mechanics of the windowing system. To create a window, you need a class. A window class specifies information that all windows of the class have in common. The controls (buttons, scrollbars, and so forth) are predefined classes.

Windows are arranged in a parent/child/sibling linked list. The root of the hierarchy is the desktop window. Each window has its own state, given by the fields of the WND data structure. When updating windows on the display, everything boils down to the three DeferWindowPos functions.

CHAPTER 5

The Graphics Device Driver Interface (GDI)

Systems programmers are often divided into two camps. The first group are quite happy spelunking around in the depths of program loaders, schedulers, memory management, and so on. Sometimes it seems like their attitude is, "Hey, we take a file on disk and create a running process. We give you scheduling and memory management and the ability to put characters on the screen. What more is there?" This group of programmers gave us operating systems such as UNIX and MS-DOS.

The second group of programmers are those who build on top of the work of the first group. These are the programmers who created things such as X-Windows for UNIX, and the USER and GDI portions of Windows. They often see the work of the first group as an "implementation detail."

The design of many operating systems reflects this two-camps sort of thinking. In his extremely accessible book *Inside OS/2*, Gordon Letwin describes the workings of OS/2 for several hundred pages. However, when he comes to the topic of the graphical user interface (Presentation Manager), Letwin has this to say:

> These packages are complex; explaining them in detail is beyond the scope of this book.

Guess which camp Gordon Letwin is in! To your benefit, your intrepid editor won't let the same thing happen here. Unlike OS/2, Windows doesn't give the developer the choice to ignore the graphical portions of the operating system. To do anything significant in Windows, with a very few exceptions, you have to confront its graphical nature very early in the game.

The intent of this chapter is to give you an overview of the internal workings of some of the main GDI concepts, in other words, how things get put on the screen.

The graphics engine module in Windows is GDI.EXE. GDI is an acronym for Graphics Device Interface. The GDI was conceived to be a device independent subsystem, like its OS/2 sibling, the GPI. With the profusion of faster and more complex output devices, it would be a nightmare trying to maintain a code base that knew that a VGA card provides 640x480 resolution, while an HP Laser-Jet provides 300 dots per inch and a given list of fonts. The GDI works around this problem by providing a generic interface that in theory generates the same results on a Super VGA board as on a plotter. Actions common to any output device, such as calculating clipping regions, are handled by the GDI. Actions requiring knowledge of the output device are shunted off to GDI device drivers. The GDI doesn't work to the lowest common denominator abilities of the device driver, however. For instance, if the driver knows how to draw lines, GDI tells the driver to draw a line. If the driver doesn't know how to draw lines, but it knows how to plot pixels, GDI simulates the line by calculating which pixels need to be drawn and then calls the driver's pixel-drawing routine. How does GDI know what the device is capable of? As you'll see later, there's a well-defined interface for obtaining the capabilities (caps) of GDI device drivers.

In Windows, there are two kinds of screen output. The first kind of output is the displaying and drawing of window frames, icons, title bars, and so forth. At the very highest level, you control these actions by calling the windowing routines in USER (CreateWindow(), ShowWindow(), MoveWindow(), and so forth, which are discussed in Chapter 4). The USER module maintains an internal picture of what the window looks like, and USER calls GDI routines such as BitBlt() to update the display as necessary. You don't deal with the GDI at all for this kind of output.

The second type of screen output occurs when your program interacts with GDI directly. The primary example of this is when your code responds to a WM_PAINT message. This may involve calling TextOut(), LineTo(), BitBlt(), or any of a multitude of GDI calls. At this level, it is very helpful to know what's going on underneath the covers. The intent of this chapter is to give you a top-level overview of some of the main GDI concepts.

Compared to the KERNEL module, GDI is quite large. KERNEL weighs in at roughly 64K of code, while GDI's code is over 200K. KERNEL does an amazing amount of work in 64K, so GDI must *really* have a full plate. (In all fairness, the KERNEL module code is apparently mostly in assembler, while GDI does have some C modules.) When you think about it, just implementing all the various font mechanics that Windows supports in a device-independent manner is daunting. Then, add in all the machinery to draw lines, circles, and arcs. Now throw in all the code that deals with BitBlt'ing and stretching bitmaps. Don't forget that GDI supports recording your actions to a metafile for later playback. And don't forget all the work required to deal with logical and physical palettes. GDI supports multiple coordinate systems. In short, there's a lot going on here!

Adding to the complexity and size of GDI is the possibility that when it isn't feasible for the device driver to implement a particular function, GDI decomposes the operation into simpler parts that the device driver can handle. That means GDI must also include the ability to perform many operations that may never be needed because the DISPLAY driver and printer driver are sufficiently capable. No matter, GDI must be prepared for the worst. An interface exists between the device driver and the GDI that enables the driver to specify what its capabilities are.

The flexibility that GDI provides to the device driver also has its downside. In the course of looking at disassembled code for many GDI functions, it became evident that the GDI code is incredibly complex and convoluted. In order for Windows to provide a device-independent interface, yet still deal with the special capabilities and idiosyncrasies of various devices, somebody had to bite the bullet, and handle all the possible permutations and combinations. GDI is that somebody.

For instance, trying to trace through a simple TextOut() call becomes an exercise in madness. Then, consider that some devices handle text rotation, while others don't. Windows supports both bitmap and vector fonts, which adds complexity. Likewise, some devices know about fonts and can generate characters directly, while others don't. For devices that don't handle fonts directly, GDI has to simulate the font, either with bitmaps or lines. If the device doesn't do lines, GDI has to break the operation into calls to draw individual pixels. The GDI code must be a monster to maintain.

Because we have no hope of covering everything that GDI does, we have picked a few important functions and go into some detail with them. Before jumping into pseudocode for these functions though, let's first explore some general concepts that GDI is built upon.

GDI Device Drivers

Despite all of the code in GDI, it still knows nothing about the details of any particular output device. To the user of a GDI function, it shouldn't matter whether the output goes to the screen, a printer, a plotter, or a metafile. To enable this device independence, GDI dynamically loads device drivers as needed and expects the device drivers to export a predefined set of functions. Even the DISPLAY device is loaded dynamically, although it happens at USER initialization time, so it's effectively a predefined device. The Windows Device Development Kit (DDK) enumerates the functions that a GDI compatible device driver must implement, as well as some optional functions.

The most commonly used GDI device driver is the DISPLAY device (the "display.drv=" entry in SYSTEM.INI such as VGA.DRV). Another common GDI device driver is the printer driver (for instance, EPSON9.DRV). If you use TDUMP or EXEHDR to dump their exported functions, notice that there's a series of exported entries, starting at ordinal #1 that are the same, or nearly identical, for each device. As we'll see later when we look at the GetLog() function, GDI loads the driver module with LoadLibrary() and calls GetProcAddress() to dynamically link to the driver's entry points. The functions exported by the driver constitute a sort of logical device with a consistent interface, regardless of the differences, illogicalities, inconsistencies, and idiosyncrasies of the underlying hardware. More on this later.

A complete logical device exports the functions shown in Table 5-1.

Table 5-1: Functions Exported by a GDI Logical Device.

Entry	Name	Description
01	BitBlt	Transfer bits from src to dest rect.
02	ColorInfo	Converts between logical and physical colors.
03	Control	Handles "Escape" extensions.
04	Disable	Disables device driver actions.
05	Enable	Enables device driver actions.
06	EnumDFonts	Enumerate driver fonts.
07	EnumObj	Enumerate driver pens, brushes.
08	Output	Draw lines, arcs, and so forth.
09	Pixel	Draw a pixel or get its color.
10	RealizeObject	Create device specific data structures.
11	StrBlt	String BLT. Superseded by ExtTextOut.
12	ScanLR	Find nearest non-matching pixel.
13	DeviceMode	Shows configuration dialog box.
14	ExtTextOut	Write text to device.
15	GetCharWidth	Gets widths of character ranges.
16	DeviceBitmap	Do nothing stub function.
17	FastBorder	Fast drawing of window frames.
18	SetAttribute	Do nothing stub function.
19	DeviceBitmapBits	Converts between DIBs and DDBs.
20	CreateBitmap	Create a device-independent bitmap.
21	SetDIBitsToDevice	Copy DIB to device.
22	SetPalette	Set hardware palette values.
23	GetPalette	Get logical RGB color values.
24	SetPaletteTranslate	Set palette translation table.
25	GetPaletteTranslate	Get palette translation table.
26	UpdateColors	Redraws pixels with translated colors.
27	StretchBlt	Shrinks or grows src bitmap as needed.
28	StretchDIB	Converts between DIB and DDB, stretching as needed.
29	SelectBitmap	Select a new bitmap into the device.
30	BitmapBits	Sets, retrieves, copies bitmap data.

It is important to note however, that a GDI device driver does not have to implement all of these functions. For instance, the EPSON9.DRV file only exports the first 18 functions; the SUPERVGA.DRV that comes with Windows 3.1 implements the first 21 functions; while an ATI 800x600 driver contains the first 27 functions. In addition, some GDI device drivers like the SUPERVGA driver implement even more than the standard set of functions.

GDI Objects

In its interface to the programmer, GDI maintains the Windows tradition of relying heavily on handles. The KERNEL module has HTASKS (handles to tasks) and HMODULES (handles to modules). The USER module has HWNDs (handles to windows). Likewise, the GDI uses handles to device contexts (HDCs), handles to pens (HPENs), and so on. As with the rest of Windows, Microsoft has tried to implement "information hiding" and has not fully documented the full nature of what GDI handles really refer to. *Undocumented Windows* discloses many of these data structures, but some of the information bears repeating here. In addition, we have some new information to add to that covered in *Undocumented Windows.*

GDI objects are just standard LMEM_MOVEABLE memory blocks in the GDI local heap (local heaps are covered in Chapter 2). Each GDI object starts its data structure with a standard set of fields that we call a GDIOBJHDR and have the format shown in Table 5-2.

Table 5-2: Data Structure of GDI Objects.

Offset	Type	Name	Description
00h	WORD	nextinchain	Next object in linked list.
02h	WORD	ilObjType	The type of object (see below).
04h	DWORD	ilObjCount	Number of previous objects.
08h	WORD	ilObjMetaList	Something to do with metafiles?
0Ah	WORD	ilObjSelCount	Number of DCs selected into (debug only).
0Ch	WORD	ilObjTask	Task that created the object (debug only).

Note that in the nondebug GDI, the ilObjSelCount and ilObjTask fields are not present, thereby shifting all subsequent fields backwards by four bytes.

GDI defines the following types of objects, shown with their corresponding signatures in the ilObjType field in Table 5-3.

Table 5-3: GDI Objects and Signatures.

Object	Signature
PEN	0x4F47 ('GO')
BRUSH	0x4F48 ('HO')
FONT	0x4F49 ('IO')
PALETTE	0x4F4A ('JO')
BITMAP	0x4F4B ('KO')
REGION	0x4F4C ('LO')
DC	0x4F4D ('MO') (Device context)
IC	0x4F4E ('NO') (Information context)
META_DC	0x4F4F ('OO')
METAFILE	0x4F50 ('PO')
METAFILE_DC	0x4F51 ('QO')

The PEN, BRUSH, and FONT objects are all very simple in structure. They consist of the GDIOBJHDR, followed by their logical data structure, as given in the SDK. For instance, the data structure referred to by an hBrush is just a GDIOBJHDR followed immediately by a LOGBRUSH structure, as shown in Table 5-4.

Table 5-4: BRUSH Object Structure.

Offset	Type	Name	Description
00h	WORD	nextinchain	These fields are the GDIOBJHDR described above
02h	WORD	ilObjType	
04h	DWORD	ilObjCount	
08h	WORD	ilObjMetaList	
0Ah	WORD	ilObjSelCount	
0Ch	WORD	ilObjTask	
0Eh	WORD	lbStyle	These fields are a LOGBRUSH structure, as given in the Windows SDK
10h	DWORD	lbColor	
14h	WORD	lbHatch	
16h	DWORD	ilBrushBkColor	Background painting color
1Ah	WORD	ilBrushhBitmap	Bitmap for painting with

The above BRUSH object is somewhat special in that it adds two extra fields after the GDIOBJHDR and LOGBRUSH structures. The pen and font objects do not have any corresponding extra fields.

As you would expect, GDI objects are referred to, both internally by GDI and externally in your program, by their local handles. Since GDI objects are MOVEABLE, their handles are not just offsets into the GDI local heap. Instead, GDI needs to lock the handles with LocalLock() whenever it needs to access the data contained therein. Or so you would think. The GDI routines, perhaps in an attempt to increase performance, make an assumption about the format of a local heap data structure. Specifically, a MOVEABLE object's handle is a near pointer to a structure in the local heap (Chapter 2). The first field of this structure contains the offset in the GDI heap of the handle's data. By treating the GDI object's handle as a near pointer to a near pointer (near **) and dereferencing the handle, GDI does a quick LocalLock() without the overhead of calling LocalLock(). Note that this action does not actually lock the data, so it can still move around. This doubly-dereferenced pointer trick is just like handles on the Macintosh; parts of USER employ this technique, also. Microsoft is quite adamant about telling developers not to rely on undocumented data structures, because they might change in the future. In this case, it doesn't look like they practice what they preach. Since this kind of pointer trickery is common in the GDI code, as well as elsewhere, it's probably a safe bet to assume this feature won't change in the future. Too much of Windows would break if it did.

Device Contexts (DCs)

The central structure that much of the GDI revolves around is the device context, more often known by its DC acronym. A device context is also sometimes referred to as a display context. That's incorrect, however, because the GDI is designed *not* to tie you to a particular output device. A DC for a printer or a plotter is just as valid as a DC for the display device. Unfortunately, Microsoft muddied the issue by referring to DCs as display contexts in certain portions of their documentation up through Windows 3.0 (for example, the return value from GetDC()). The 3.1 documentation uses the proper name, device context.

Picture a DC as a virtual canvas, upon which you draw without knowing what the underlying surface is. Other graphical systems, such as the Macintosh, use similar concepts; on the Mac, it's called a GrafPort. Think of the device context as a magic cookie that you need in order to perform output operations. When it comes time to output some text, draw a circle, fill a region, or whatever, you need to obtain a handle to a DC (an hDC). You then call the appropriate GDI routines, handing them the DC handle (hDC) as part of the request. When your program receives a WM_PAINT message and you call BeginPaint() in response, you most commonly get a device context. You do whatever repainting is necessary, using the DC, and when you're finished, you give the DC back with the EndPaint() function. You can obtain and use DCs outside of WM_PAINT message handler by calling GetDC() and ReleaseDC():

```
case WM_TIMER:
{
    HDC hDC;
    hDC = GetDC(hWnd);
    if ( hDC )
    {
        LineTo(hDC, newX, newY);
        ReleaseDC(hWnd, hDC);
    }
}
```

A DC is a fairly large data structure because it needs to retain quite a bit of "state" information. Of primary interest in the DC are the handles to the logical device and the physical device block. The logical device is the set of core primitive functions that a GDI device driver provides. Part of the logical device is an array of function pointers to the devices entry points. The physical device block is a data structure describing the actual capabilities of the device, for example, what kind of device it is, its pixel resolution, and its color capabilities. We'll come back to these topics later.

Also of particular interest in the DC are the handles to the current pen, brush, font, and bitmaps. When you give a command to display text, draw a line, and so on, GDI uses the currently selected pen, brush, font, or bitmap, as appropriate. If you want to use a different object, select a new object into the device context with the SelectObject() API. If current values weren't stored in the device context, the programmer would always have to specify which font, pen, brush, and bitmap to use for each GDI operation. Storing current values is much easier in general. It's important to note that calling SelectObject() can result in calls to the GDI device driver and can fail in low memory situations. We'll see the details of this later.

When Windows boots, there are no device contexts. DCs (like any other GDI object) need to be created. This is done with the CreateDC() API. During its initialization, USER creates five DCs for the display device (see LW_DCInit() in Chapter 1) and keeps them in a cache. These are the DCs that your program sees when it calls BeginPaint() or GetDC() (unless you are using CS_CLASSDC or CS_OWNDC, a situation which is described in the SDK documentation). Unless your program does printing, these cached DCs are typically the only DCs you encounter. If your program needs to do printing, you need to create a device context for the desired printer, using CreateDC().

Chapter 8 of *Undocumented Windows* gives a fairly complete description of the various fields in the DC. However, we felt that the DC was so important that it warranted giving a condensed version of it here. The fields of type INT16 indicate a signed 16-bit integer value. The format of a Windows 3.1 debug GDI DC, as extracted from the debug information, is shown in Table 5-5.

Table 5-5: Format of Debug GDI DC.

Offset	Type	Name	Description
00h	GDIOBJHDR	SayWhatBro	This is the real name!
0Eh	BYTE	DCFlags	flags (e.g., needs repaint).
0Fh	BYTE	DCFlags2	more flags.
10h	WORD	hMetaFile	metafile handle if meta DC.
12h	WORD	hClipRgn	handle to clipping region.
14h	WORD	hPDevice	handle to PDEVICE.
16h	WORD	hLPen	handle to logical pen.
18h	WORD	hLBrush	handle to logical brush.
1Ah	WORD	hLFont	handle to logical font.
1Ch	WORD	hBitMap	handle to selected bitmap.
1Eh	WORD	dchPal	handle to selected palette.
20h	WORD	hLDevice	handle to LOGDEV (below).
22h	WORD	hRaoClip	handle to Rao clipping region.
24h	WORD	hPDeviceBlock	handle to PHYSDEVBLOCK (below).
26h	WORD	hPPen	handle to physical pen.
28h	WORD	hPBrush	handle to physical brush.
2Ah	WORD	hPFontTrans	handle to font xlate table.
2Ch	WORD	hPFont	handle to physical font.
2Eh	LPBYTE	lpPDevice	far ptr to PDEVICE.
32h	LOGDEV near *	pLDevice	near ptr to LOGDEV (below).
34h	PBYTE	pRaoClip	near ptr to Rao clip region.
36h	PHYSDEVBLOCK near *	pPDeviceBlock	(see field 24h).

Table 5-5: Format of Debug GDI DC. (continued)

Offset	Type	Name	Description
38h	PBYTE	pPPen	near ptr to physical pen.
3Ah	PBYTE	pPBrush	near ptr to physical brush.
3Ch	PBYTE	pPFontTrans	near ptr to font xlate table.
3Eh	FONTINFO far *	lpPFont	far ptr to FONTINFO (see DDK).
42h	WORD	nPFTIndex.	
44h	POINT	Translate.	
48h	DRAWMODE	phDrwMode	DRAWMODE struct (see DDK).
68h	INT16	LCurPosX	logical cursor X position.
6Ah	INT16	LCurPosY	logical cursor Y position.
6Ch	INT16	WndOrgX	window origin X.
6Eh	INT16	WndOrgY	window origin Y.
70h	INT16	WndExtX	window extent X (width).
72h	INT16	WndExtY	window extent Y (height).
74h	INT16	VprtOrgX	viewport origin X.
76h	INT16	VprtOrgY	viewport origin Y.
78h	INT16	VprtExtX	viewport extent X (width).
7Ah	INT16	VprtExtY	viewport extent Y (height).
7Ch	INT16	UserVptOrgX	user viewport origin X.
7Eh	INT16	UserVptOrgY	user viewport origin Y.
80h	INT16	MapMode	mapping mode - SetMapMode().
82h	INT16	XformFlags	transform flags?
84h	INT16	RelAbsmode	
86h	INT16	PolyFillmode	polygon fill mode.
88h	INT16	StretchBltMode	stretch BLT mode.
8Ah	BYTE	dcPlanes	number of color planes.
8Bh	BYTE	dcBitsPixel	bits per pixel.
8Ch	INT16	PenWidthX	logical pen width.
8Eh	INT16	PenWidthY	logical pen height.
90h	INT16	dcTextAlign	SetTextAlign() flags.
92h	DWORD	dcMapperFlags	SetMapperFlags() flags.
96h	INT16	BrushOrgX	logical brush origin X.
98h	INT16	BrushOrgY	logical brush origin Y.
9Ah	INT16	FontAspectX	font aspect ratio X value.
9Ch	INT16	FontAspectY	font aspect ratio Y value.
9Eh	WORD	hFontWeights	font weights.
A0h	INT16	DCSaveLevel	nesting level of saved DCs.
A2h	INT16	DCLockCount	lock count of DC.
A4h	WORD	hVisRgn	handle to visible region.
A6h	INT16	DCOrgX	DC origin X (in pixels).
A8h	INT16	DCOrgY	DC origin Y (in pixels).

Table 5-5: Format of Debug GDI DC. (continued)

Offset	Type	Name	Description
AAh	FARPROC	lpPrintProc	far pointer to printing procedure.
AEh	INT16	DCLogAtom	driver name atom.
B0h	INT16	DCPhysAtom	device name atom.
B2h	INT16	DCFileAtom	DOS filename atom.
B4h	INT16	PostScaleX	
B6h	INT16	PostScaleY	
B8h	RECT	BoundsRect	bounding rectangle.
C0h	RECT	LVBRect	Logical Video Buffer rect.
C8h	FARPROC	lpNotifyProc	SetDCHook() callback proc.
CCh	DWORD	HookData	data to give to hook callback.
D0h	INT16	globalDCFlags	more flags for the DC.
D2h	WORD	hNextDC	next DC in linked list.

As you can see, there is quite a bit of state information, as well as quite a bit of redundant information in a DC. For instance, the DC stores both a handle and a near pointer to the LOGDEV structure. This may be another stab at improving performance, although it violates the principal of not keeping two copies of the same information.

The GDI Logical Device

At some level, the GDI stops calculating, and hands off the results to a GDI display driver for rendering. Where the rubber meets the road is the point at which GDI calls the functions exported by the GDI device driver. By forcing a GDI display driver to have a well-defined set of interface functions with given entry ordinal values, the GDI can load device drivers at run time and not worry about what the device driver connects to.

To use an OOP analogy, the Logical Device holds the public member functions of a class. It is essentially a big table of virtual function pointers. GDI works (it puts stuff on the screen) by calling the virtual functions. The public data for the object corresponds to the Physical Device Block (described later). The private data is the driver-defined PDEVICE structure. After examining the Physical Device Block (PHYSDEVBLOCK) to see what the device is capable of, GDI calls the appropriate logical device (LOGDEV) member functions. The PDEVICE pointer is passed as a sort of "this", or "self", pointer, which gives the device driver's member functions access to any data that the driver defines to do its job. Like a well designed class interface that uses virtual functions, the GDI can interact with an output device object without knowing about its underlying internal data structures.

The format for the Windows 3.1 debugging GDI for the LOGDEV structure, as extracted from the debug information, is shown in Table 5-6.

Table 5-6: Format for Debugging GDI for LOGDEV Structure.

Offset	Type	Name	Description
00h	FARPROC	OEMBitblt	(For fields 0-74h, see Table 5-1.)
04h	FARPROC	OEMColorInf	
08h	FARPROC	OEMControl	
0Ch	FARPROC	OEMDisable	
10h	FARPROC	OEMEnable	
14h	FARPROC	OEMEnumDFonts	
18h	FARPROC	OEMEnumObj	
1Ch	FARPROC	OEMOutput	
20h	FARPROC	OEMPixel	
24h	FARPROC	OEMRealizeO	
28h	FARPROC	OEMStrblt	
2Ch	FARPROC	OEMScanLR	
30h	FARPROC	OEMDeviceMode	
34h	FARPROC	OEMExtTextOut	
38h	FARPROC	OEMCharWidths	
3Ch	FARPROC	OEMDevBitmap	
40h	FARPROC	FastRectBorder	
44h	FARPROC	SetAttrs	
48h	FARPROC	OEMDIBBits	
4Ch	FARPROC	OEMCreateBit	
50h	FARPROC	OEMDIBtoScreen	
54h	FARPROC	OEMSetPalette	
58h	FARPROC	OEMGetPalette	
5Ch	FARPROC	OEMSetPalTrans	
60h	FARPROC	OEMGetPalTrans	
64h	FARPROC	OEMUpdateCol	
68h	FARPROC	OEMStretchBlt	
6Ch	FARPROC	OEMStretchDIB	
70h	FARPROC	OEMSelBitmap	
74h	FARPROC	OEMBitmapBits	
78h	FARPROC	RealOEMRealizeO	Genuine address of RealizeObject(). Bypasses Adobe Type Manager GetProcAddress() hook in ATM versions prior to 2.5.
7Ch	INT16	DevDCRefCnt	Number of DCs using this LOGDEV.
7Eh	UINT16	hPDevBlock	Handle to PHYSDEVBLOCK (below).
80h	UINT16	LDevAtom	Logical (driver) atom.
82h	UINT16	hModule	Module handle of device driver.
84h	UINT16	hNextLogDev	Next logical device in GDI chain.
86h	UINT16	hPhysPalette	Handle to physical palette.
88h	UINT16	RealTime	???
8Ah	UINT16	fPaletteUse	???

The GDI Physical Device Block

The Physical Device Block (PHYSDEVBLOCK) is a data structure that GDI device drivers fill in with information concerning the attributes and capabilities of the device. The structure is filled in when GDI calls the driver's Enable() function with a particular parameter flag set. The Enable() function is a standard routine in all GDI device drivers. GDI calls Enable() to tell the device that it's time to start up. GDI also calls Enable() to obtain information, such as the PHYSDEVBLOCK, from the device.

The information in the PHYSDEVBLOCK tells GDI what kind of device it's dealing with, its pixel resolution, what graphics primitives it can handle itself, what type of palette management is available, and so on. When a GDI function is called by your program, GDI examines what capabilities the device has by looking at the PHYSDEVBLOCK structure. If the device can handle sophisticated commands, like outputting fonts directly or clipping, GDI does only the work it has to, and lets the device driver do everything else. On the other hand, if the device driver only handles a simple set of primitive instructions (for example, if it can only output pixels), GDI breaks the high-level command down to simpler instructions that it feeds to the device driver. Having a smart device driver is often beneficial because it can often use special hardware or make assumptions that the GDI code can't, thereby increasing the speed of graphics operations.

The first part of the PHYSDEVBLOCK consists of a GDIINFO structure, as documented in the DDK. If you don't have the DDK, take a look at the GetDeviceCaps() function in the SDK. Each of the capabilities listed corresponds directly to a field in the GDIINFO structure. In fact, the #define values you pass as the iCapability parameter happen to be, "coincidentally," the offset of the matching field in the GDIINFO structure. For instance, DRIVERVERSION, HORZSIZE, and so on.

The second part of the PHYSDEVBLOCK holds fields that GDI uses for "internal housekeeping." For instance, the atom handles that refer to the device name, like EPSON FX-80, and the output filename (e.g., LPT1:) are stored here.

The format for the Windows 3.1 debugging GDI version of the PHYSDEVBLOCK structure, as extracted from the debug information, is shown in Table 5-7.

Table 5-7: Format for Debugging GDI for PHYSDEVBLOCK Structure.

Offset	Type	Name	Description
00	GDIINFO	PhysGDIINFO	See DDK or GetDeviceCaps().
6E	UINT16	hNextPhysDev	Next PhysDevBlock in chain.
70	UINT16	PDevRefCnt	Number of references by DCs
72	UINT16	PDevMemRefCnt	???
74	UINT16	PDevAtom	Physical (device) atom
76	UINT16	PDOSAtom	filename atom (i.e., "LPT1:")
78	UINT16	hPDevData	Global handle to PDEVICE
7A	UINT32	PDevCount	???

Pseudocode for Selected GDI Functions

Now that we've covered some of the key concepts and data structures in GDI, it's time to dig into some pseudocode to illustrate what we've just learned. The following functions are in no way intended to show you all the various facets of the GDI. GDI is just too large and convoluted. Instead, they were selected to give you a feel for some of the fundamental ideas.

Parameter Validation

A bit of explanation is in order before examining the various GDI functions. Windows 3.1 added a parameter validation layer, which ensures that all parameters passed to a Windows API are valid and won't cause a GP fault somewhere down inside the Windows DLLs. While we don't have the space to discuss parameter validation in any detail, for now it is sufficient to say that the core Windows DLLs (USER, KERNEL, and GDI) each have a source module, LAYER.OBJ, that includes the entry points for many of their exported functions. The parameter validation occurs in the appropriate LAYER module, before JMP'ing to the real function. The real function is never exported, but has the name of the API preceded by an "I". For instance, if you call CreateDC(), the CreateDC() function in the GDI LAYER module validates the parameters. If the CreateDC() LAYER function decides the parameters are OK, it JMPs to the ICreateDC() function in some other GDI source module. If the parameters are invalid, the LAYER module may print out a debugging message in the debugging DLLs before returning a failure code to the application.

Throughout this book, many of the functions described are really the internal version of the function (for example, IGetMessage(), rather than the real GetMessage() function). Attempting to show the parameter validation everywhere it's encountered would quickly obscure the main point of the discussion. However, the CreateDC() function has an interesting twist embedded in the parameter validation layer, which makes it worth examining. Plus, we felt it was important to show parameter validation at least once.

CreateDC()

The three strings passed to CreateDC() are the name of the GDI driver to be loaded, the device name (if the driver supports more than one kind of device), and the name of the file that output should be sent to (for example, "LPT1:"). The second and third strings can be NULL if necessary. For instance, upon initialization, USER creates five DCs for the display, using the "display.drv=" entry in the SYSTEM.INI file as the driver name. The calls to CreateDC() from LW_DCInit() in USER probably look something like this:

```
CreateDC( "DISPLAY", NULL, NULL, NULL)
```

If, on the other hand, you are creating a DC to print with, you might use:

```
CreateDC("EPSON9", "Epson FX-80", "LPT1:", NULL);
```

which specifies that you want to load the EPSON9.DRV device driver, that the printer is an FX-80 model, and that the device driver output should be sent to the DOS device, LPT1:. In most applications printing is usually the only time that you need to call CreateDC(), since you use the USER-created DCs when doing screen output.

The pseudocode for the CreateDC() function below has nothing to do with creating a device context. Instead, it's the one example we give of what parameter validation looks like. The real code for creating a DC is in the InternalCreateDC() function, which we cover next.

What is especially interesting about CreateDC() is the way it deals with Adobe Type Manager (ATM). Here, we're going to concentrate on the technical details, but see Chapter 1 of *Undocumented Windows* for the horrifying story about Michael Geary, Adobe Type Manager, and the Microsoft legal department. The original ATM for Windows 3.0 provides a system for giving the user access to better fonts than Windows 3.0 could provide. To do this, ATM needs to tap into the calls to various Windows functions, substituting its own information relating to fonts for that which would normally go back and forth between the GDI, the GDI device drivers, and the application. ATM taps into the function calls by searching *in the GDI's code segments* for the calls to the functions and patching them to point to its own functions. This is very distasteful, as Mike Geary willingly admits. According to Mike, several cleaner methods were tried, but they were more difficult for the user to install. The code that was finally decided on made the assumption that the GDI code wouldn't change or that ATM would need to be updated if the GDI code did change. As we just mentioned, however, the code *did* change in Windows 3.1 when the parameter validation layer was added.

More recent versions of ATM, starting with version 2.5, add yet another layer to this tangled mess. These versions intercept all GetProcAddress() calls and hook even more routines (for example, the EngineXXX functions). Interestingly, some of the hooking is made simpler by directly modifying certain entries in GDI's entry table to point to the ATM code, rather than to the intended GDI code. This negates the need to patch the actual code. Table 3-1 in Chapter 3 shows the structure of entry table.

To Microsoft's credit, the GDI developers did go the extra mile and made the Windows 3.1 GDI compatible with ATM versions prior to 2.5. To do this, they had to trick ATM into thinking it had found the functions it needed to patch, while still maintaining the CreateDC()/ICreateDC() separation needed for the validation layer. To accomplish this, they placed bait code, which looks exactly like what ATM wants, at the start of the CreateDC() code. When these older ATM versions start up, they scan through the CreateDC() code looking for calls to LoadLibrary(), GetProcAddress(), and FreeLibrary(). ATM patches these calls to point at ATM code, which does whatever it needs to do, then ATM chains on to the original function. ATM searches the DeleteDC() code for a FreeLibrary() call, as well.

This bait code never gets executed directly. Instead, the GDI developers took advantage of the way direct and indirect CALL's are encoded, to fake out ATM. The destination field of a direct FAR CALL instruction (which ATM looks for) can also be used as a DWORD memory location for an indirect (through memory) FAR CALL. When GDI needs to call one of the functions that ATM may have hooked, it calls indirectly through the memory location. If ATM has patched the direct FAR CALL, control goes to ATM. If ATM isn't around, the indirect FAR CALL goes to the correct Windows function, which was fixed up with the proper address when GDI was loaded. It's a sick world out there.

If the general flow of CreateDC() is confusing, don't feel bad. It is contorted enough that it is not immediately obvious what goes on. Just remember that the code eventually makes its way to InternalCreateDC(), where the code gets down to the business of creating and initializing a new device context structure.

The parameter validation is reasonably simple here. The first parameter must be a valid far pointer to a string. CLPSZText() ensures that accessing any of the characters of the string won't cause a GP fault. The second two parameters to CreateDC() can be either NULL or valid far pointers to a string. CLPSZ0Text() performs the same test as CLPSZText(), but it first checks for a NULL pointer, letting it go through if it's NULL. The last parameter can either be NULL or a far pointer to a data structure. If it's non-NULL, a few fields in the data structure are tested to see if they'll cause problems later on. Once the parameter validation layer verifies that things are OK, the code eventually ends up at InternalCreateDC(), which we cover next.

```
pseudocode for CreateDC() - LAYER.OBJ
// Parameters:
//      LPSZ    lpszDriver      // (e.g., "EPSON9")
//      LPSZ    lpszDevice      // (e.g., "Epson FX-80")
//      LPSZ    lpszOutput      // (e.g., "LPT1:")
//      LPVOID  lpvInitData     // typically NULL

    goto CreateDC_2         // Skip over the "bait" code placed
                            // for Adobe Type Manager (ATM) to find.

    CALL FAR LoadLibrary()      // ATM patches these function calls
    CALL FAR GetProcAddress()   // Inside InternalCreateDC(),
    CALL FAR FreeLibrary()      // indirect calls are made
                                // through these "function pointers".

ATMInternalCreateDC:            // A real label name

    Set up a standard INC BP / PUSH BP / MOV SP,BP stack frame.
    Then, immediately undo the above stack frame. ATM looks
    for this prologue code.

    goto InternalCreateDC   // JMP to the real CreateDC() code

CreateDC_2:

    // Parameter validation. String must be a valid far pointer
    // that doesn't GP fault when accessed. If the string fails
    // the test, the function returns without doing anything.
    CLPSZText( lpszDriver )

    // Parameter validation. String must either be null OR a
    // valid far pointer that doesn't GP fault when accessed.
    CLPSZ0Text( lpszDevice )
    CLPSZ0Text( lpszOutput )
```

```
    if ( lpvInitData == 0 )      // if lpvInitData == NULL, no
        goto Real_CreateDC       // need to do param validation

    perform more validation checks on the lpvInitData structure

Real_CreateDC:

    JMP ATMInternalCreateDC // This actually jumps to ICreateDC(),
                            // which just zeros CX, DX, BL, then
                            // JMPS to ATMInternalCreateDC (above)
```

InternalCreateDC()

In the most general terms, InternalCreateDC() loads a GDI device driver DLL into memory, allocates space for a device context, and initializes its fields. Along the way, it allocates space for the LOGDEV and PHYSDEVBLOCK structures, described earlier, and initializes their fields as well.

The function starts by obtaining atom handles for the three string parameters that are passed in. Storing the strings in the atom table allows the GDI to simplify a lot of code that would have to maintain and compare strings like device driver names, in favor of just storing a 16-bit handle. If you're not familiar with atoms, they can be extremely useful, and reading the SDK documentation for AddAtom() and GlobalAddAtom() is highly recommended (there is also a lengthy discussion of atom tables in Chapter 5 of *Undocumented Windows*). In addition, because atom tables are hashed, determining if a string is already in use is much faster than doing a linear search through all the possible strings.

Once the atom work is done, InternalCreateDC() allocates space for the device context out of the GDI local heap. Very soon after creating the space for the DC, the code calls GetLog() and GetPhys() to create and initialize the LOGDEV and PHYSDEVBLOCK data structures. Their local handles are stored in the DC under construction. GetLog() is discussed a bit later. GetPhys() is a lengthy routine that's not easily taken apart; pseudocode for GetPhys() is not given here.

After the above three data structures are created, InternalCreateDC() goes through a lengthy stretch where it fills in various fields of the device context with initial values. This includes calling the documented SetBkColor(), SetTextColor(), and SelectObject() APIs.

```
pseudocode for InternalCreateDC() - DCMAN1.OBJ
// Parameters:
//      LPSZ    lpszDriver      // Note that these are the same as
//      LPSZ    lpszDevice      // the parameters to CreateDC()
//      LPSZ    lpszOutput
//      LPVOID  lpvInitData
// Locals:
//      ATOM    driverAtom, deviceAtom, outputAtom
//      BYTE    DCKind
//      WORD    AChain[9]
//      WORD    logDevHnd, physDevBlkHnd    // local handles
```

```
//      DC near *dc       // Pointer to space allocated for DC
//      LOGDEV near *logdev
//      PHYSDEVBLOCK near *physDevBlk

    // Get the kind of DC to be created (in BL register)
    // 0 == normal        -> CreateDC()
    // 1 = memory         -> CreateCompatibleDC()
    // 80h = info DC      -> CreateIC()
    DCKind = BL

    physDevBlkHnd = DX        // CX and DX are initialized by the
    logDevHnd = CX            // caller of InternalCreateDC()

    driverAtom = MyAddAtom( lpszDriver )  // e.g., "EPSON9"
    deviceAtom = MyAddAtom( lpszDevice )  // e.g., "Epson FX-80"

    // SansColon() strips any trailing ':', and calls
    // GDIAddAtom() with the resultant string. For instance,
    // "LPT1:" becomes "LPT1".
    outputAtom = AX = SansColon( lpszOutput )

    if ( AX != 0 )  // AX==outputAtom. Was an output file given?
    {
        if ( outputAtom != NullPortAtom )   // ??
            goto decided_on_atom

        if (DCKind == 0)  // 0 -> normal DC
            goto RetAtoms // Calls MyDeleteAtom() for driverAtom,
                          // deviceAtom, and outputAtom. It then
                          // zeros AX, and JMPs to CreateDCExit
    }
    else
        AX = deviceAtom

decided_on_atom:

    some local var = AX // Either deviceAtom or outputAtom. The
                        // local var doesn't seem to be used.

    Zero out the 12h bytes of the "AChain" structure (a local var)

    AX = GetCurrentTask()
    if ( AX == 0 )
        goto RetAtoms         // Abort. RetAtoms is described above.
    Store AX (current hTask) into a field in AChain
```

```
    // Here's where we allocate space for device context!  The
    // return value is a handle, rather than a near pointer.
    // In general, the code likes to deal with handles to local
    // memory blocks (in the GDI heap), and dereference them to
    // near pointers as needed.
    AX = MyAlloc( 0xD4 )            // sizeof (DC)--see Table 5-5.
    Store AX into field in AChain   // AX = DC handle
    if ( AX == 0 )
        goto RetAtoms       // Abort. See above for details

CreateDC10:     // These labels are real names in the debug info!
                // Perhaps Bill originally wrote this in BASIC?

    if ( DCKind != 1 )      // 1 -> memory (compatible) DC
        goto CreateDC15

    if ( !GetPhys300() )        // Calls CreateRectRgn(), and
        goto CreateDC20         // stores handle in AChain

    SI = logDevHnd          // Atoms obtained at top of function
    DI = physDevBlkHnd
    goto CreateDC30

CreateDC15:

    // Create the logical device. This includes loading the
    // driver DLL module, and obtaining the entry points for
    // various functions in the driver. Pseudocode below.
    CX = GetLog()
    if ( CX == 0 )
        goto CreateDC20     // Failure!
    else
        logDevHnd = CX

    // Obtain a handle to a previously created "physical device"
    // block. It appears that GetPhys() walks through some sort
    // of list of physical devices, and compares their deviceAtoms
    // and outputAtoms to the corresponding atoms obtained above.
    // If no matching physical device blocks are found, a new one
    // is created.
    if ( GetPhys() )
        goto CreateDC30

CreateDC20:     // We get here if something failed. This is
                // where handles are freed up.
```

```
    goto RetAChain       // Free all the local handles in AChain
                         // structure. Calls GlobalFree() for
                         // one of the handles. Returns to the
                         // InternalCreateDC() caller.

CreateDC30:

    logdev = *(WORD *)SI     // SI is logical device local handle.
                             // Dereference to get LOGDEV pointer.

    logdev->DevDCRefCnt++    // Increment the LOGDEV reference count

    // Get a pointer to the PHYSDEVBLOCK structure that was
    // allocated and initialized inside the GetPhys() function.
    physDevBlk = *(WORD *) PHYSDEVBLOCK handle from GetPhys()

    // Get a pointer to the DC we're creating. We're going to
    // start filling in its fields now. Remember, GDI uses the
    // "quick LocalLock" trick to dereference local handles.
    dc = *(WORD *) DC handle allocated earlier

    // Start filling in fields in the DC
    dc->hPDevice = physDevBlk->hPDevData
    dc->hVisRgn = some field in AChain structure
    dc->globalDCFlags = 2
    dc->hNextDC = hFirstDC        // hFirstDC is a global var
                                  // Put this DC at the head of
                                  // the GDI DC list

    // GDIOBJHDR is the standard header that all GDI objects
    // start with. IC = 4f4Eh, DC = 4F4D, 80h = info DC
    dc->GDIOBJHDR.ilObjType = DCKind & 80h ? IC : DC

    dc->GDIOBJHDR.ilObjCount = physDevBlk->PDevCount
    dc->GDIOBJHDR.ilObjMetaList = 0
    dc->GDIOBJHDR.ilObjTask = 0
    dc->DCFlags = BX | 80h          // BX = ???
    dc->hMetaFile = some field in AChain
    dc->hBitMap = hStaticBitmap     // A global var
    dc->dchPal = LDefaultPalette    // A global var
    dc->hLDevice = logDevHnd    // logDevHnd set at fn. entry
    dc->hRaoClip = some field in AChain
    dc->hPDeviceBlock = physical device handle // from GetPhys()
    dc->phDrwMode.Rop2 = 0Dh
    dc->phDrwMode.bkMode = 2
    dc->WndExtX = dc->WndExtY = 1
```

```
    dc->VprtExtX = dc->VprtExtY = 1
    dc->MapMode = 1
    dc->XformFlags = 1
    dc->RelAbsmode = 1
    dc->PolyFillmode = 1
    dc->StretchBltMode = 1
    dc->SaveLevel = 1
    dc->BitsPixel = some local variable
    dc->DCLogAtom = driverAtom      // These 3 atoms were created
    dc->DCPhysAtom = deviceAtom     // at the top of the function
    dc->DCFileAtom = outputAtom

    if ( some field in AChain != 0 )
        GlobalUnlock( field in AChain )

CreateDC40:

    if ( !LockDC( dc ) )     // Lock the DC being created?
        goto CreateDC50      // Failure!

    // Start selecting defaults into the DC under construction.
    if ( !SetBkColor( dc, 0xFFFFFF ) )  // Set color to WHITE
        goto CreateDC50      // Failure!

    if ( !SetTextColor( dc, 0xFFFFFFFF ))   // Set to WHITE
        goto CreateDC50      // Failure!

    // StockObj is a global structure variable
    if ( !SelectObject( dc, some field in StockObj ) )
        goto CreateDC50      // Failure!

    // Set the logical pen field. Then, get the physical pen,
    // which involves calling the device driver's RealizeObject()
    // function.
    dc->hLPen = some field in StockObj
    if ( !GetPPen( dc ) )
        goto CreateDC50      // Failure!

    Compare "DisplayAtom" (a global variable), with a local
    variable. Depending on whether they're equal or not,
    set AX with one field or another from StockObj.

CreateDC45:

    dc->hLFont = AX      // AX is some field from StockObj
```

```
    if ( GetPFont( dc, 0 ) )      // "Get physical font"
        goto CreateDC60           // Success!

CreateDC50:          // Some error has occurred. Clean up things.

    DeleteMetaStuff()    // Kill things related to metafiles?
    DeleteDC( dc )       // Kill the DC items allocated so far.

    AX = 0
    goto CreateDCExit

CreateDC60:

    Turn off 80h bit in dc->DCFlags if set

    if ( driverAtom == MGXWMFAtom )      // MGXWMFAtom ???
        Turn on some bit in dc->DCFlags2

    if ( some field in AChain == 0 )
        goto CreateDC70

    if ( !SaveDC(dc) )        // ??
        goto CreateDC50       // Failure!

    dc->GDIOBJHDR.ilObjType = Metafile      // 4F50h

CreateDC70:

    AX = DC local handle allocated earlier (stored in AChain)

CreateDCExit:

    if ( debug GDI and AX == 0 )
        output a message: "CreateDC failed"

    if ( AX != 0 )
        hFirstDC = AX         // Put new DC at head of chain
```

GetLog()

GetLog() is where the GDI device driver specified as the first argument to CreateDC() is loaded into memory. GetLog() also creates the LOGDEV data structure that's used throughout GDI to call the device driver's routines.

Because the specified device driver may already have been loaded (for example, after the first DISPLAY DC is created), GetLog() first walks the linked list of LOGDEVs, comparing their LDevAtom field to the driver atom found or created at the beginning of InternalCreateDC(). If a match is found, the driver has already been loaded, and GetLog() just returns its local handle. If the driver is not in the list, GetLog() has more work ahead of it.

The first task of creating a new LOGDEV is to allocate space for it. With this done, GetLog() loads the device driver with LoadLibrary(), using the device driver name specified as the first argument to CreateDC(). Thus, calling CreateDC() does an indirect LoadLibrary(). Assuming the driver is safely loaded, the next step is to hook up the LOGDEV to the functions exported by the driver. This is an amazingly simple task. Starting with ordinal value 1, and incrementing up through ordinal 30, GetLog() calls GetProcAddress() for the newly loaded driver, specifying the current ordinal value. The return addresses from GetProcAddress() are stored in the first part of the LOGDEV structure (see Table 5-6). After the loop completes, you can think of the LOGDEV structure as an array of 30 function pointers. If the driver doesn't export a particular function, GetProcAddress() returns NULL. Since the device can use the device capabilities to specify what functionality it exports, there shouldn't be any danger of GDI trying to call through a NULL pointer. Each capability corresponds roughly to a function pointer.

Interestingly, after the standard 30 functions are imported, GetLog() calls GetProcAddress() for the driver's RealizeObject() routine one more time. This time, however, it calls GetProcAddress() directly, rather than indirectly through the function pointer that ATM may have patched to point to itself. In ATM 2.5 and later, even this GetProcAddress() call gets intercepted. If these hacks on top of hacks on top of hacks continue, somebody's going to get hurt!

The last portion of GetLog() simply fills in the other, non-function pointer fields of the LOGDEV with appropriate values.

It is important to note when looking at the pseudocode that GetLog() does not create its own stack frame. Instead, it uses the stack frame from InternalCreateDC(). Put another way, GetLog() shares the same parameters and local variables as InternalCreateDC(). This is similar to the LoadModule() helper functions in Chapter 3.

```
pseudocode for GetLog() - DCMAN1.OBJ
// Returns CX set with a local handle to a logical device block,
// or 0, if it couldn't be loaded/created.
//
// Locals:
//   LOGDEV  *logdev      // Alternately either a local handle or
//                        // a near *

    // First have to see if the requested device is already
    // loaded. Walk the chain of logical device blocks,
    // looking for one whose atom matches "driverAtom" inside
    // the InternalCreateDC() function.
    logdev = HLDevHead  // HLDevHead is a global, and the "head"
                        // handle in the logical device chain.

GetLog10:               // A real label name

    CX = logdev         // Retain handle of current LOGDEV handle
                        // being examined in CX
```

```
    if ( logdev == 0 )  // If at end of chain, it wasn't found,
        goto GetLog20   // so we need to try loading the driver.

    logdev = *(WORD *)logdev    // Convert the local handle to
                                // a near pointer. HACK!!!
                                // Assumes knowledge of local
                                // heap data structures.

    // See if the LDevAtom for this block matches "driverAtom"
    // (from the InternalCreateDC() stack frame). If it does,
    // return now. CX contains the handle of the logical device
    // local heap block.
    if ( logdev->LDevAtom == driverAtom )
        return              // CX contains driver local handle
    logdev = logdev->hNextLogDev    // Try the next logical
    goto GetLog10                   // device block in the chain

GetLog20:

    // Allocate space for a new LOGDEV structure. AChain is a
    // local variable from InternalCreateDC().
    Some field in AChain = MyAlloc( sizeof(LOGDEV) )

    if ( MyAlloc() call failed )
        goto GetLog30               // Return failure

    // Figure out how long the driver name is, and make a copy
    // of it on the stack. Add on the ".DRV" extension,
    // in preparation for calling LoadModule()
    CX = HowLongIsIt( lpszDriver )  // A strlen() clone
    CX += 5                         // For ".DRV" ???
    CX &= 0FEh                      // Make the result even?
    copy lpszDriver onto temporary space on stack
    strcat() on ".DRV" extension

    // Load the library using the driver name created on the stack.
    // But don't call LoadLibrary() directly. Adobe Type Manager
    // might have "hooked" what it thinks is the call to
    // LoadLibrary(). Thus, call through the LoadLibrary()
    // "bait" function call that was conspicuously placed at the
    // start of CreateDC()'s code so that ATM would find it.
    if ( CreateDC_lpfnLoadLibrary() > 32 )
        goto GetLog40       // Success. Continue on.

GetLog30:       // Failure. Time to clean up
```

```
    return with CX = 0

GetLog40:       // Things are going well. Continue on.

    store AX (the LoadLibrary() instance handle) into another
    field in AChain

    Retrieve local handle obtained by earlier MyAlloc() call, and
    convert to a near *. Put value into DI. DI will be a near
    pointer to the LOGDEV structure just allocated.

    // Now going to call GetProcAddress() for the first 0x1E
    // entries in the driver. Call indirectly through the
    // "bait" GetProcAddress() call. (See earlier ATM comments.)
    // The address of each function is stored in a corresponding
    // field in the LOGDEV structure. (See Table 5-6)
    for ( WORD i=1; i < 0x1E; i++ )
    {
        CreateDC_lpfnGetProcAddress( hInstanceLib, MK_FP(0, i) )
        * (DWORD far *) ES:DI = DX:AX   // Save function address
        DI += 4                         // point at next fn. ptr field
    }

    // Circumvent any ATM hooking, and get the "real" address of
    // RealizeObject() by calling GetProcAddress() directly.
    // This is an escalation in the "war of hacks"!  ATM seems
    // to be winning though!(It patches the following too.)
    logdev->RealOEMRealize0 =
        GetProcAddress( hInstanceLib, MK_FP( 0, 0xA ))

    // Start filling in various fields in the second part of the
    // LOGDEV structure (the first part is all function pointers).
    logdev->LDevAtom = driverAtom   // driverAtom is local var
                                    // from InternalCreateDC()

    logdev->hModule = hInstance returned from LoadLibrary() call

    logdev->hNextLogDev = hLDevHead // Add the new device to the
    hLDevHead = logdev              // head of the device list

    logdev->hPhysPalette = 0        // No physical palette?
    logdev->RealTime = 0            // ?
    logdev->fPaletteUse = 1         // ?
```

To sum up the above, device contexts are created on the fly as needed. They testify to the enormous power and flexibility you can achieve with runtime dynamic linking using LoadLibrary() and GetProcAddress().

ICreatePen()

CreatePen() (actually, ICreatePen()) is covered here because it's a fairly essential GDI function if you need to do anything that the stock objects don't provide. A typical call to make a new GDI pen would look something like this:

```
// Create a pen with the PS_DOT style, width == 1, and the
// specified color.
HPEN hPen = CreatePen( PS_DOT, 1, RGB(10,20,30) );
```

The ICreatePen() pseudocode below is extremely simple. It takes the style, width, and color parameters and constructs a LOGPEN structure on the stack. (The LOGPEN is described in the CreatePenIndirect() section of the SDK documentation.) ICreatePen() then calls ICreatePenIndirect(), which we cover next. Essentially, CreatePen() is just a user friendly version of CreatePenIndirect(). Note that CreatePen() and siblings don't actually create a physical object. That comes later when we invoke SelectObject().

```
pseudocode for ICreatePen() - OBJMAN.OBJ
// Parameters:
//      WORD    style
//      WORD    width
//      DWORD   color

    // Take the passed parameters, and create a LOGPEN structure
    // on the stack.
    push    HIWORD(color)
    push    LOWORD(color)
    push    0                   // Y part of POINT structure is  0
    push    width
    push    style

    ICreatePenIndirect( SS:SP ) // Pass far pointer to LOGPEN
                                // created above.

    ADD     SP, 0Ah             // Clean off things pushed on stack
```

ICreatePenIndirect()

ICreatePenIndirect() is either called indirectly from ICreatePen() or directly by the user (actually, CreatePenIndirect() goes through the CreatePenIndirect() parameter validation layer first, but you get the idea). The code is a model of simplicity. It takes a pointer to a LOGPEN structure and immediately hands it off to the MoveObject() helper routine, along with the PEN signature, 4F47h='GO' (see Table 5-3). The MoveObject() routine (below), takes the LOGPEN structure and copies it into the GDI local heap, making it an official GDI object.

```
pseudocode for ICreatePenIndirect() - OBJMAN.OBJ
// Parameters:
//      LOGPEN far *logpen

    SI = 04F47h          // PEN signature
    BX = DI = 0Ah        // size of LogPen

    MoveObject( logpen )    // Move object into GDI local heap
```

MoveObject()

MoveObject() is called by ICreatePenIndirect(), ICreateBrushIndirect(), and ICreateFont-Indirect(). Its job is to take a far pointer to a logical object somewhere in the caller's address space and make a GDI object in the GDI local heap based on the logical object. MoveObject() doesn't care about what kind of object it's creating. If MoveObject() were a C++ member function, it would be operating on a pointer to a base class, ignoring the data members specific to the derived classes (for example, the PEN, BRUSH, and FONT "classes").

As we noted in the discussion of GDI objects, each object starts out with a standard GDIOBJHDR structure (see Table 5-2). When MoveObject() allocates memory from the GDI local heap for the new object, it has to add the size of the GDIOBJHDR to the size of the logical object. After the memory is allocated, it's a simple matter to initialize the GDIOBJHDR fields and copy the logical object's data immediately after the end of the GDIOBJHDR.

```
pseudocode for MoveObject - OBJMAN.OBJ
// Parameters:
//      LPVOID  object
//      SI      = object type
//      DI      = size of object
//      BX      = size to allocate
// Locals:
//      WORD    hTask
//      WORD    GDIObjHandle
//      GDIOBJHDR near *GDIObjPtr

    if ( !(hTask = GetCurrentTask()) ) // bail out if hTask == 0
        goto MoveObject_done

    // Allocate the specified memory size + 0Eh. The extra 0Eh
    // is for the GDIOBJHDR (at the beginning of all GDI objects)
    // (0Ah bytes in non-debug Windows)

    if ( ! (GDIObjHandle = GDILocalAlloc( BX + 0Eh ) ) )
        goto MoveObject_done
```

```
    // Dereference the allocated handle to get a pointer to the
    // actual data for the block. Really should use LocalLock()
    GDIObjHeader = *(WORD near *) GDIObjHandle

    GDIObjHeader->nextinchain = 0
    GDIObjHeader->ilObjType=SI  // object type (e.g., 4F47h=PEN)
    GDIObjHeader->ilObjCount = ObjectCount  // A global variable
    ObjectCount++               // A global variable. Indicate
                                // there's one more GDI object

    GDIObjHeader->ilObjMetaList = 0
    GDIObjHeader->ilObjSelCount = 0
    GDIObjHeader->ilObjTask = hTask

    copy the bytes from the passed "object" to the allocated
    block (immediately after the GDIOBJHDR portion). For
    instance, if the passed object was a LOGPEN, the LOGPEN
    would be copied right after the GDIOBJHDR portion.

MoveObject_done:

    return allocated handle to caller
```

CreateSolidBrush()

CreateSolidBrush() is included here because it's also a common GDI function that you are likely to encounter if you do any serious graphics output. It also provides another opportunity to see how simple the GDI logical object concept is.

A typical call to CreateSolidBrush() would be like this:

```
// Create a brush with the specified color given in RGB format
HBRUSH hBrush = CreateSolidBrush( RGB(0,128,255) );
```

CreateSolidBrush() is extremely simple, as it just loads two registers with appropriate values and passes the color parameter off to the internal CreateBrush() function. Note also that there is no parameter validation for this function. Just about any value you could pass as the color parameter will be OK, so there's no need to have separate CreateSolidBrush() and ICreateSolidBrush() functions.

```
pseudocode for CreateSolidBrush() - OBJMAN.OBJ
// Parameters:
//      DWORD   color

    AX = BS_SOLID
    BX = 0
    CX:DX = color
```

```
    // Call the common brush creation entry point. Also called
    // by CreateHatchBrush(), CreatePatternBrush(), and
    // CreateDIBPatternBrush()
    CreateBrush()
```

CreateBrush()

It's somewhat surprising that Microsoft doesn't export this function, as it's very similar in nature to CreatePen(). Instead, Microsoft provides four different CreateXXXBrush() functions that all do essentially the same thing, with only minor variation among them. Perhaps the problem was that one of the parameters would have to be either a hatch code or a bitmap handle, depending on what kind of brush is being created.

Like CreatePen(), CreateBrush() takes the parameters and pushes them on the stack, creating a LOGBRUSH structure. This structure is passed to ICreateBrushIndirect(). Once again, we have a user-friendly front end to another exported function, CreateBrushIndirect().

```
pseudocode for CreateBrush() - OBJMAN.OBJ
// Parameters:
//      AX = Brush style (BS_xxx)
//      BX = hatch index, or hBitmap, or...
//      CX:DX = color scheme (e.g., a COLORREF)

    // Create a LOGBRUSH structure on the stack
    push    BX      // Hatch or hBitmap
    push    CX      // HIWORD( COLOR )
    push    DX      // LOWORD( COLOR )
    push    AX      // style

    ICreateBrushIndirect( SS:SP )   // Pass far pointer to
                                    // LOGBRUSH created above.

    ADD     SP, 8           // Clean off things pushed on stack
```

ICreateBrushIndirect()

ICreateBrushIndirect() starts out very similarly to ICreatePenIndirect(). The far pointer to the LOGBRUSH object is handed off to MoveObject() (covered earlier) to make the BRUSH object in the GDI local heap.

Unlike ICreatePenIndirect() however, there is additional work to be done after MoveObject() completes. GDI gives you the capability to make brushes that use bitmaps. It's not safe to use a bitmap that the application manages because it might be deleted at an inopportune time. Therefore, if the brush being created depends on a bitmap (a DIBBrush or PatternBrush), ICreateBrushIndirect() makes a copy of the bitmap information. Presumably, the "object manager" code takes care of deleting GDI's copy of the bitmap when the brush is deleted. Note in the code below that this is *not* the same bitmap as was passed to CreateDIBBrush(). The caller of CreateDIBBrush() is responsible for deleting the bitmap it passed.

```
pseudocode for ICreateBrushIndirect() - OBJMAN.OBJ
// Parameters:
//      LOGBRUSH far * logbrush
//      HANDLE   brushHandle
//      BRUSHOBJ near *brushObj
//      WORD    bitmapSize
//      WORD    bitmapHandle

    SI = 04F48h         // BRUSH signature
    DI = 8h             // size of LOGBRUSH
    BX = 0Eh            // Allocate this many bytes (for extra
                        // data at the end of the structure)

    // Move the brush object into the GDI local heap
    brushHandle = MoveObject( logbrush )
    if ( !brushHandle )
        return 0

    brushObj = *(WORD *)brushHandle // Hack dereference of local
                                    // handle to a near *

    if ( brushObj->LOGBRUSH.lbStyle == BS_DIBPATTERN )
        goto CreateBrushIndirect_DIBBrush

    if ( brushObj->LOGBRUSH.lbStyle == BS_PATTERN )
        goto CreateBrushIndirect_Pattern

    return with AX == brushHandle

CreateBrushIndirect_DIBBrush:   // Come here to create a DIB brush

    // The lbHatch field is really holding a global memory handle
    // for a bitmap, rather than a hatch ID.
    bitmapSize = GlobalSize( brushObj->LOGBRUSH.lbHatch )

    if ( bitmapSize > 64K )
        goto Free_brushHandle_and_exit  // Bitmap is too big!

    bitmapHandle =      // Allocate space for the GDI copy
        GlobalAlloc( GMEM_MOVEABLE | GMEM_SHARE, bitmapSize )

    if ( !bitmapHandle )                // Couldn't get memory in
        goto Free_brushHandle_and_exit  // the global heap. Abort.
```

```
    // Lock the block just allocated, and the handle of the bitmap
    // passed in. We're going to make a copy of the passed in
    // bitmap into our own local copy.
    GlobalLock( bitmapHandle )
    GlobalLock( brushObj->LOGBRUSH.lbHatch )

    Copy the memory of the passed in bitmap to the global memory
    block just allocated.

    // Can now unlock the bitmap's global memory handles
    GlobalUnlock( bitmapHandle )
    GlobalUnlock( brushObj->LOGBRUSH.lbHatch )

    // Copy the original bitmap handle (from the lbHatch field)
    // into another field in the BRUSHOBJ header (so that we
    // don't forget its value). Then, store the global bitmap
    // handle just allocated into the LOGBRUSH structure,
    // overwriting the original brush handle that we copied from.
    brushObj->ilBrushBitmap = brushObj->LOGBRUSH.lbHatch
    brushObj->LOGBRUSH.lbHatch = bitmapHandle

    return AX = brushHandle

CreateBrushIndirect_Pattern:    // Here to create a pattern brush

    Get the bitmap handle out of the brushObj->LOGBRUSH.lbHatch
    field. Dereference the handle to get a pointer to a bitmap.

    LockBitmap( brushObj->LOGBRUSH.lbHatch )

    Based upon various fields in the bitmap structure, call either
    ICreateCompatibleBitmap() or ICreateBitmapIndirect().

    if ( CopyBitmap() )
        goto PatternBrush_OK

    // Couldn't copy the bitmap. Start cleaning things up for
    // an error return.
    UnlockBitmap( brushObj->LOGBRUSH.lbHatch )

Free_brushHandle_and_exit:

    FreeObject( brushHandle )
    return AX = 0

PatternBrush_OK:
```

```
    FreeObject( AX )          // AX = ???

    // Can now unlock the bitmap passed in the lbHatch field.
    UnlockBitmap( brushObj->LOGBRUSH.lbHatch )

    // Move the original bitmap handle to a new spot in the
    // BRUSHOBJ structure, and replace it with the handle of
    // the bitmap just created and copied into.
    brushObj->ilBrushBitmap = brushObj->LOGBRUSH.lbHatch
    brushObj->LOGBRUSH.lbHatch = bitmapHandle
```

ISelectObject()

The ISelectObject() API is one of the more important APIs in GDI. Rather than making you always specify the attributes of every GDI object used for every GDI call, the device context has a set of current objects, like a solid BLUE brush, or a PS_DOT pen, that it uses for drawing. When you need to use a different object, you select it into the device context like this:

```
// Select the new object, and remember the old object so that it
// can be restored later.
HGDIOBJ oldObject = SelectObject(hDC, newObject);
```

At its highest level, ISelectObject() changes the appropriate field in the device context structure to contain the handle of the object passed to ISelectObject(). The previous handle value is returned to the caller. ISelectObject() determines the appropriate field by examining the ilObjType field of the passed object. For instance, if the passed object is a PEN, it changes the DC's hLPen field to the passed object handle and returns the previous hLPen value to the caller.

At a lower level however, some GDI objects need a little more preparation. To prevent a long series of tests and branches, ISelectObject() uses a JMP table to quickly transfer control to the appropriate code for the object.

It's important to note that ISelectObject() is where the GDI device driver's RealizeObject() function is called from. It's the RealizeObject() call that tells the device driver to set up whatever data structures are needed to actually do the output. Up till now, the logical objects were tentative. The RealizeObject() call is where these logical objects are finally committed. The routines that select pens, brushes, and fonts all eventually call the device driver's RealizeObject() function.

```
pseudocode for ISelectObject() - OBJSEL.OBJ
// Parameters:
//      WORD    hDC
//      WORD    hObj
// Locals:
//      DC near *dc             // Pointer to device context structure
//      GDIOBJHDR object        // Pointer to GDI object
```

```
//      WORD pbrushHandle   // Handle to physical(?) brush

    object = *(WORD *)hObj  // Get a pointer to the data for the
                            // object being selected. Quick
                            // replacement for LocalLock()

    Do something related to testing if the DC is a metafile. The
    functions CheckMetaFile(), and SendInvalidVisRgn() are called
    in this section, based upon some unknown criteria. If
    CheckMetaFile() is called, ISelectObject() returns immediately
    afterwards.

    dc = *(WORD *)hDC   // Get a pointer to the DC's data. Quick
                        // replacement of LocalLock()

    BX = object->ilObjType  // Get object type (4f47h=Pen, etc.)
    BX &= 0x5FFF            // Mask off high bit flags???

    if ( BX > 4F4Ch )           // Don't bother with objects with
        goto SelectObject_done  // ID's > 4F4C (e.g., DCs)
                                // Note that a test is not
                                // performed on the "lower bound"

    BX = (BX - 0x4F47) << 1     // Convert object type into a JMP
                                // table offset

    JMP [SelectObjectJmpTable + BX] // Go through the JMP table
                                    // Control ends up at one of
                                    // the select_xxx labels below
select_rgn:
    SelectClipRgn( hDC, hObj )      // A documented API
    goto SelectObject_done

select_palette:
    goto SelectObject_done      // Nothing needs to be done

select_brush:
    pBrushHandle = GetPBrush(hDC, hObj) // Get Physical Brush.
    if ( !pBrushHandle )                // Calls RealizeObject()
        goto SelectObject_done          // in device driver

    if ( dc->hPBrush != 0 )          // Unlock the old Phys Brush
        LocalUnlock( dc->hPBrush )   // Doesn't really call
                                     // LocalUnLock(). Just
                                     // decrements the lock count
```

```
    dc->hPBrush = pBrushHandle      // Stuff in new brush handle.

    LocalLock( pBrushHandle )   // "Lock" the new brush by
                                // incrementing its lock count

    // Set the pointer to the physical brush data 0x10 bytes into
    // the data structure returned by GetPBrush()
    dc->pPBrush = LocalLock( pBrushHandle ) + 0x10

    AX = hObj                 // Swap the original logical brush
    XCHG dc->hLBrush, AX      // handle with the new one, leaving
                              // AX with the original handle.

    goto SelectObject_success

select_pen:
    XCHG hObj, dc->hLPen            // Swap the old and new pens

    // Get a physical pen. Calls RealizeObject() in device driver
    if ( GetPPen( hDC ) )           // Test to see if the new pen
        goto SelectObject_success   // works?  If so, return
                                    // success.

    XCHG dc->hLPen, hObj            // Something went wrong. Put
    AX = 0                          // things back the way they
    goto SelectObject_done          // were, and return 0

select_font:
    XCHG hObj, dc->hLFont           // Swap the old and new font

    if ( GetPFont( hDC ) )          // Get physical font. Looks
        goto SelectObject_success   // like a lot of pointer
                                    // manipulation!

    XCHG dc->hLFont, hObj           // Something went wrong. Put
    AX = 0                          // things back the way they
    goto SelectObject_done          // were, and return 0

SelectObject_success:
    object = *(WORD *)hObj  // Get a pointer to the data for the
    object->iLObjSelCount++ // object just selected. Increment the
                            // selection count.

    object = *(WORD *)AX    // Get a pointer to the data for the
    object->iLObjSelCount-- // object just deselected. Decrement
                            // the selection count. AX contains
```

```
                              // the old object handle

    if ( AX == 0 )            // Make sure we return "success",
        AX++                  // even if AX is 0 (???)

SelectObject_done:
    return AX to caller

select_bitmap:                // Why is this code separate???
    // The undocumented SelectBitmap() function JMPs to a spot
    // a few instructions past the select_bitmap label.

    if ( hDC == 0 )       // We must have a valid DC!
        return 0

    dc = *(WORD *)hDC     // Get a pointer to the DC's data

    if ( hDC is not for a memory DC )
        return 0

    // A long sequence of code follows that's not well understood.
    // The following functions are called, and are apparently
    // necessary to properly select a new bitmap object.
    LockBitmap() / UnlockBitmap()
    MakeBitmapCompatible()
    SetRectRgn()
    GetBkColor() / SetBkColor()
    GetTextColor() / SetTextColor()
    ComputeRaoRgn()

    // At various points along the way, tests are performed, if
    // the tests fail, 0 is returned. If the code makes it
    // all the way to the end, it JMPs to the
    // SelectObject_success label.
```

If you're interested in digging even deeper into the GDI/device driver interface, you should look at the device driver source code included in the DDK. For instance, at several place in the ISelectObject() code, you see function calls that eventually call the device driver's RealizeObject() function. The code for RealizeObject() in the four-plane display device (including the VGA driver) is a real yawner. It's a large amount of bit twiddling and copying of data from one place to another. Nothing dramatic here. The different objects that can be realized are handled by dispatching through a JMP table to a suitable routine. If these things are up your alley, you'll certainly get a kick out of the code.

ISetPixel()

When we started this chapter, we wanted to show a function that put something on the screen. The original first choice was TextOut(). Unfortunately, the obvious flow of control quickly got lost in the labyrinth of the GDI font engine. Rectangle() looked like the next logical choice. Rectangle(), however, goes through an amazingly long series of computations before it gets anywhere near putting something on the screen. The same is true for even the seemingly-simple LineTo(). We are now proud to present pseudocode for the ISetPixel() routine, which displays a single dot. Even this is pretty complicated!

ISetPixel() begins by converting the logical coordinates, which were passed to it, to device context coordinates. ISetPixel() then checks the new coordinates to make sure they won't be clipped away (for example, by the current window borders, or by windows overlapping the window we're drawing in). If the pixel wouldn't be visible, ISetPixel() returns -1 indicating that the pixel is outside the clipping region.

Once ISetPixel() knows the pixel will be drawn, its next task is to convert the logical RGB value parameter to a physical palette color that the device can render. The user may have specified a palette index instead of an RGB value, so this is handled before the color mapping occurs.

The core of the SetPixel() function is the call to the GDI device driver's Pixel() routine. The device driver is responsible for handling whether the output surface is a physical device or a memory bitmap. After the pixel's been drawn, ISetPixel() calls LVBUnion() (Logical Video Buffer Union) to force the device context to include the pixel just drawn in its "dirty region" to be updated. The last thing ISetPixel() does is find the actual RGB value of the plotted pixel. It may differ from the input RGB value if the device had to map the input RGB value to make it fit in the current palette. The actual RGB value is needed for SetPixel's return value.

```
pseudocode for ISetPixel() - SETPIXEL.OBJ
// Parameters:
//      WORD    hDC
//      WORD    x, y          // window coordinates of pixel
//      COLORREF color
// Locals
//      DC near * dc          // Pointer to DC struct
//      LOGDEV near *logdev // Pointer to LOGDEV structure for DC
//      POINT lPoint          // Local POINT structure
//      COLORREF outColor     // Display driver

    Do something related to testing if the DC is a metafile. The
    functions CheckMetaFile(), and SendInvalidVisRgn() are called
    in this section, based upon some unknown criteria. If
    CheckMetaFile() is called, ISetPixel() returns immediately
    afterwards.

    dc = *(WORD *) hDC  // Get a pointer to the DC's data

    lPoint.x = x        // Copy the X,Y parameters into a
```

```
lPoint.y = y            // local POINT structure.

FarLC2DC()              // Convert logical coordinates to DC
                        // base coordinates???

// Make sure the point won't get clipped away. If it will,
// just return -1 now.
if ( !InRegion( dc->hRaoClip, &lPoint) )
    return -1

// If a palette index was specified, convert it now to a
// real color value.
if ( topmost byte of color is nonzero )
    color = FarPalIndexToPhysical( hDC, color )

logdev = dc->pLDevice   // Get pointer to LOGDEV from the DC

// Call the device driver to do color mapping
logdev->OEMColorInf( dc->lpPhysDevice, color, &outColor )

// Call the device driver to draw the pixel. The whole
// point of this exercise!
logdev->OEMPixel(dc->lpPhysDevice, lPoint.x, lPoint.y,
                      outColor, dc->lpDrawMode )

// LVBUnion() relates to updating the rectangle in the
// device context that needs to be redrawn. See
// _Undocumented Windows_ for details. Note also that the
// device context pointer is being passed, rather than the
// handle to the device context (the hDC).
if ( some bit set in dc->GlobalDCFlags )
    LVBUnion(dc, lPoint.x, lPoint.y, lPoint.x+1, lPoint.y+1)

// Call the device driver to convert the physical color
// that was drawn, into a logical color. The function
// returns the value in DX:AX, which is just what SetPixel()
// needs to return with.
logdev->OEMColorInf( dc->lpPhysDevice, outColor, OL )   // return
```

As mentioned earlier, you can go down even another level into the pixel display process by examining the sources in the Windows DDK. The four-plane VGA driver code takes care of putting the pixel to either a memory bitmap or the display device. As you would expect, the code is a large collection of optimized assembler, designed to do scan line computation, handle frame buffers that are greater than 64K in size, sum up bits in color planes, and so on. If the output surface is the display device, the pixels are set and read using OUT instructions. This is as close to the hardware as you can get.

A Word or Two About Names

As a group, programmers have a tendency to inject a bit of humor into their code, especially with regard to function and variable naming. The coders at Microsoft are no exception. In researching this chapter, we came across many humorous names that we felt you might enjoy. If you disdain such practices, you can skip the rest of this section. For those of you who don't think programming has to be dry and dull, we present the following list of symbols extracted from the debugging GDI symbol table:

```
OutMan_HappyPolyLineGutsExit
Lets_See_What_The_Engine_Can_Do
The_Victorious_Font_Is_Returned
Use_Your_Kopf
Bloat
GDISeeGDIDo
Major_Bummer
ScaleThisShit
GiveMeThePrinterAtom
RonHatesThis                    // Ron Gery? (palette function)
```

By no means does GDI have a lock on good names. For instance, the KERNEL module has Display_Box_Of_Doom and PrepareToParty, while USER has MS_FlushWigglies. On the whole however, GDI seems to lead the pack in this particular category.

This small side diversion is not intended as a comment on the professionalism or dedication of anyone at Microsoft. Instead, its goal is to give you a glimpse at the lighter side of the sometimes overwhelming system that is Windows.

CHAPTER 6

The Windows Scheduler

In any multitasking operating system, a scheduler is necessary to switch among the various tasks currently alive in the system. Unlike OS/2, Windows NT, or UNIX, Windows has a nonpreemptive scheduler. A program running under Windows continues to run until it gives up the CPU to another program. If a program enters a tight loop or otherwise hogs the CPU, the system is effectively deadlocked until the application yields the CPU. The act of yielding is either done explicitly, by calling Yield() for instance, or indirectly, by calling a Windows API (such as GetMessage() or MessageBox()) that causes a yield to occur. Because of the non-preemptive nature of the Windows scheduler, you can deadlock the input system if your program doesn't relinquish control in some manner. This renders the computer effectively useless. In this chapter, we examine the Windows scheduler in detail so that you can avoid these situations and even use it to your advantage in some cases.

The scheduler discussed in this chapter is the scheduler that manages Windows applications only; it is part of the KERNEL module. This scheduler is entirely separate from the time-slicing scheduler that's part of the Virtual Machine Manager (VMM) in Enhanced mode Windows. The scheduler we focus on here runs *inside* the system virtual machine. The system virtual machine (VM) is scheduled by the VMM in WIN386. If you run DOS applications from within Enhanced mode, the system VM scheduler preemptively switches between the system VM (the collection of running Windows applications), and the DOS boxes you're running. The KERNEL scheduler described here is only active when WIN386 has given a timeslice to the system VM. In other words, it's a scheduler within a scheduler.

Fundamentals of the Windows Scheduler

To fully understand the scheduler, there are three fundamental concepts you need to know. Once you understand them completely, you can think through almost any situation and accurately predict what the scheduler's behavior will be.

Nonpreemptive Scheduling

The first fundamental aspect of the scheduler is that it's nonpreemptive. While a task is running, it will *never* have control taken away from it by another Windows task without warning. The current task must relinquish control of the CPU to allow other Windows tasks to run. The virtual machine scheduler can switch away from the system VM at almost any time, but when the system VM is scheduled again, the current Windows task picks right up where it left off. Within the system VM, the current task is absolutely in charge until it says otherwise, by yielding. Even if an interrupt occurs in the system VM, any interrupt handler registered by a Windows application or DLL executes *in the context of the current task,* rather than the task that registered the handler.

There is a Yield() call in the Windows API, but it is hardly ever called directly. You might be thinking, "I never yield in any of my code, but I'm still able to run other programs." This works because certain Windows API calls yield for you. For instance, when you don't have any more messages waiting for your application, the GetMessage() API yields to other tasks. If your code doesn't call any functions that yield control, your task will run indefinitely. We'll get a better idea of just which functions can yield control a bit later on.

Events

The second concept fundamental to understanding the Windows scheduler is the notion of events. An event indicates that there's some reason for a task to wake up. The scheduler won't wake up a task (schedule it) *unless* there's an event waiting for it. When there are no events for the current task, and when that task relinquishes the CPU, the scheduler puts the task to sleep until the task receives another event.

What causes events? Typically, a task gets an event when there's a new message for it. For instance, when you post a message to a window, the message is put in the message queue of the task associated with the window. In addition, the task's event count is incremented. A nonzero event count indicates to the scheduler that there's a good reason to wake up the task and let it run again. Events and messages are not the same thing, however.

It's important to note that events and messages are tied more to tasks and queues, rather than to the windowing system. As explained in Chapter 3, the windowing system puts new messages in the task's message queue and increments the event count in the task database (TDB). It's only late in the game, inside DispatchMessage(), that the window associated with the message becomes important. Chapter 7, the messaging system, discusses in more detail how the messaging system internals cause tasks to receive events.

Events have no data associated with them. To the scheduler, there aren't different kinds of events. When a task receives a new event, the only thing KERNEL does is increment the WORD at offset 6 (TDB_nEvents) in the TDB (see Table 3-2). Note that the event count in the TDB is *not* the same as the message count stored in the task's message queue, described in Chapter 7 (see Table 7-1).

You can increment the number of events waiting for a task with the undocumented PostEvent() API, which simply increments the value in the TDB_nEvents field in the TDB. PostEvent() is intended for use by the USER messaging system routines to indicate that some kind of message is waiting for the task. In addition, WINDEBUG.DLL and its descendants, CVWIN.DLL and TDWIN.DLL, modify the event count field directly to affect the scheduling behavior of the child being debugged.

Besides PostEvent(), there's a corresponding, barely documented WaitEvent() API that "blocks" until the task has another event waiting for it. The messaging system, especially GetMessage(), calls WaitEvent() to block the current thread of execution until there's another event for the task. As noted in Chapter 3, compiler startup code typically calls WaitEvent(). WaitEvent() doesn't just spin mindlessly in a loop, checking the event counter though. If it did, no other task could run. (The scheduler is nonpreemptive, remember.) Instead, WaitEvent() loops around a call to the core scheduling routine, Reschedule(), until there's a new event for the task. The call to the core scheduling routine allows other tasks to run. We cover Reschedule() in detail later; it is really Reschedule() that we refer to when we say the Windows scheduler.

Task Priorities

It's a little known fact that under Windows, tasks have a priority level. A task's priority is a value between -32 and 15. Lower priority level values indicate a *higher* priority task. Thus, tasks with a priority level of -32 have the highest priority, while tasks at priority level 15 are the lowest priority. The default priority for a task is 0. Since most programmers aren't aware of priority levels or how to change them, almost all tasks run at priority level 0.

When considering priority levels and which task will be scheduled next, you need to constantly keep in your mind the earlier discussion concerning events. A task running at a high priority (say, -8), but with no events, will *not* be scheduled ahead of a task at average priority (0), that has an event. Put another way, the priority level only comes into play when two or more tasks have events waiting for them.

To use an analogy, consider the CPU to be a pay phone. Only one person (task) can use it at a time, and nobody else can use it until the current user is done with it. Now imagine that each task is a person waiting in line to use the pay phone (the CPU). The people closer to the front of the line have the highest priority (lowest priority level values). In this scenario, a task event is like the dime that you need to use the phone. Not every person waiting in line has a dime to use the phone. When the person using the phone (the currently running task) finishes, the first person in line *who has a dime* gets to use the phone next. In scheduler terms, when the task currently using the CPU gives it up, the scheduler has to examine each task, in priority order, to find the first one that has an event for it. That task gets to use the CPU next and becomes the current task.

In the above discussion, we implicitly assumed the existence of a sorted list of tasks. How is this implemented? As shown in Chapter 3, each task database contains a field holding the selector of the next task database in the list. Each TDB also has a field at offset 8 that remembers the current priority level of the task (see Table 3-2). One of the jobs of the core scheduling function Reschedule() is to keep this list in priority sorted order, with the highest priority tasks at the list's front. Thus, all the tasks with priority level -32 come first in the list, followed by tasks at priority level -31, and so on. The head of the list is referenced by the HeadTDB global variable, which resides in the KERNEL module. The current value of HeadTDB can be found in the DX register after a call to GetCurrentTask(). As we see later, all the main scheduling routine has to do is walk through the task list until it sees a task with an event. The relative priority levels of the tasks are thus handled implicitly. There's no need to compare priority levels when trying to find the correct task to run next. This is shown in Figure 6-1.

Figure 6-1: Priority Levels.

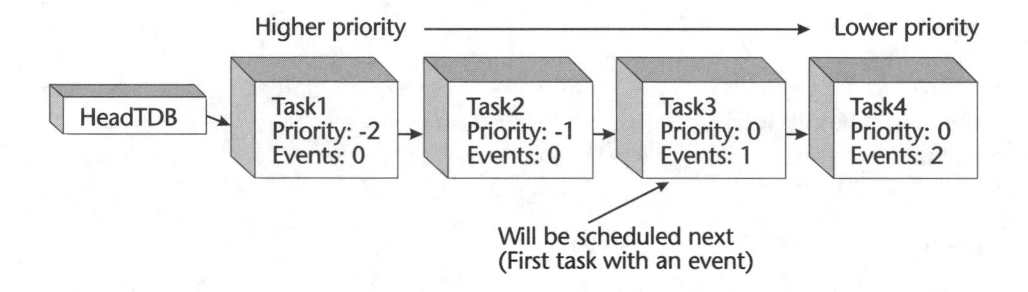

The priority level of a task can be adjusted using the undocumented SetPriority() API. A description of this function appears in *Undocumented Windows*, but it is unfortunately incorrect for the most part. The real behavior of SetPriority() can be seen in the following pseudocode:

```
Pseudocode for SetPriority() - CONTEXT.OBJ
// Parameters:
//       WORD    hTask
//       WORD    PriorityDelta
// Locals:
//       WORD    newPriority

    // Calculate new priority by adding (possibly negative) PriorityDelta to the
    // current priority of the task.
    newPriority = hTask.TDB_priority + PriorityDelta

    if ( newPriority < -32 )     // Min priority is -32
        newPriority = -32

    if ( newPriority > 15 )      // Max priority is 15
        newPriority = 15

    if ( newPriority == hTask.TDB_priority )  // If priority isn't
        if ( hTask == CurTDB )                // changing, and
            return                            // it's the current
                                              // task, we're done!
```

```
// We're going to reposition hTask in the task list
// immediately after all tasks that are at hTask's new
// priority level. We do this by temporarily making its
// new priority 1 higher than what it really should be.

hTask.TDB_priority = newPriority + 1

DeleteTask( hTask )      // Delete and Insert the task to put
InsertTask( hTask )      // it in priority sorted order.

hTask.TDB_priority--     // Reset to the correct new priority.
```

A couple of things are worth noting in the SetPriority() code. First, the priority value passed as the second parameter is a relative priority delta, not an absolute priority value. If a task currently has a priority of -4, and SetPriority() is called with a priority level of -3, the new priority of the task will be (all together now!) -7.

Second, observe that the code deletes, then reinserts, the task in the list. The InsertTask() function knows about priority levels and always inserts a task in the correct position in the list. Correct means immediately *before* any tasks at the same priority level. By adding one to the priority level of the task before inserting it, the task can be forced to appear *after* all other tasks of the same priority. Then, to ensure that the task ends up with the correct priority level, decrements the task's priority level, SetPriority(), by one. As we see later, the core scheduling routine also uses this trick.

Now that task priority levels are out in the open, we should point out that they're not that beneficial. Setting your task priority to the lowest numeric value, so that it has the highest priority, usually won't do you a lick of good. The scheduler only cares about finding the first task that has an event. Even if your task is running at the very highest priority, it won't get scheduled until there is an event for it. If there's no event for your task, it will be beaten out every time by a lower priority task that does have an event. The only time task priority would be useful is if there were a flurry of messages going to all the tasks in the system, and you wanted your task to get first crack at them. At this time, we're unaware of any programs that try to modify their priority level.

Yielding to Other Tasks When You Have Messages

One question that draws a lot of confusion concerns yielding to other tasks while you have pending messages. Many programmers are under the impression that Windows will not let you relinquish control to another program if you haven't emptied your message queue. This simply isn't true. If you understand the task event and priority concepts, you can see how it certainly is possible. The following YIELD program demonstrates this.

```
//==================================
// YIELD, by Matt Pietrek, 1992
// File: YIELD.C
//==================================
#include "windows.h"

BOOL FirstInstance = 0;         // Set to 1 if the first instance
HWND OurHWnd, SecondInstHWnd;   // HWNDs we need to know
HANDLE SecondHInstance = 0;     // HInstance value of 2nd instance

#define WM_YIELD_MSG        (WM_USER + 0x1234)  // Our yield test
#define WM_OUR_POSTED_MSG   (WM_USER + 0x1235)  // messages

// SysErrorBox() is undocumented, so we need to prototype it.
// You may need to add it to the IMPORTS section of a .DEF file.
int FAR PASCAL SysErrorBox(LPSTR, LPSTR, WORD, WORD, WORD);

long FAR PASCAL _export YieldWndProc( HWND hWnd,
    unsigned msg, WORD wParam, LONG lParam )
{
    switch( msg )
    {
        case WM_DESTROY : PostQuitMessage(0); break;

        case WM_LBUTTONUP:  // Using left button does the yield
        case WM_RBUTTONUP:  // Using right button doesn't
        if ( FirstInstance )
        {
            // Slimy hack to get the HWND of the 2nd instance
            GetInstanceData( SecondHInstance,
                (BYTE *)&SecondInstHWnd, sizeof(HWND) );

            // Post different messages to our (the 1st
            // instance's) queue, as well as to the queue of
            // the 2nd instance.
            PostMessage( hWnd, WM_OUR_POSTED_MSG, 0, 0 );
            PostMessage( SecondInstHWnd, WM_YIELD_MSG, 0, 0 );

            if ( msg == WM_LBUTTONUP )  // Use left button to show
                Yield();                // effect of Yield()'ing
        }
        break;

        // The 2nd instance of the application gets this msg.
        // SysErrorBox() doesn't yield as MessageBox() will.
        case WM_YIELD_MSG:
```

```
            SysErrorBox("I was Yielded to", "Second Instance",
                0, 1, 0); break;

        // The 1st instance of the application gets this msg
        case WM_OUR_POSTED_MSG:
            SysErrorBox("Got posted message","First Instance",
                0, 1, 0); break;

        default: return DefWindowProc(hWnd,msg,wParam,lParam);
    }
    return 0L;
}

int PASCAL WinMain( HANDLE hInstance, HANDLE hPrevInstance,
                    LPSTR lpszCmdLine, int nCmdShow )
{
    MSG msg;
    char exeName[260];              // Name of our program
    int width = 300, height = 50;   // Window sizes

    if ( hPrevInstance == 0 )   // Register a generic WNDCLASS
    {
        WNDCLASS wndCls;
        wndCls.style = CS_HREDRAW | CS_VREDRAW;
        wndCls.lpfnWndProc = (WNDPROC)YieldWndProc;
        wndCls.cbWndExtra = wndCls.cbClsExtra = 0;
        wndCls.hInstance = hInstance;
        wndCls.hIcon = LoadIcon(NULL, IDI_APPLICATION);
        wndCls.hCursor = LoadCursor(NULL, IDC_ARROW);
        wndCls.hbrBackground = GetStockObject(WHITE_BRUSH);
        wndCls.lpszMenuName = NULL;
        wndCls.lpszClassName = "Yield";
        RegisterClass( &wndCls );
        FirstInstance = 1;  // Remember if we're the 1st instance
    }

    // Create a Window. We use a quick hack to ensure that the
    // windows don't overlap, and are close to each other.
    OurHWnd = CreateWindow("Yield", "Yield", WS_OVERLAPPEDWINDOW,
            10 + width*FirstInstance, 10 + height*FirstInstance,
            width, height, NULL, NULL, hInstance, NULL);

    // Set a global variable. The 1st instance will later grab
    // this value into its own copy via GetInstanceData()
    SecondInstHWnd = OurHWnd;

    // Have both windows indicate which instance they are
    SetWindowText( OurHWnd, FirstInstance
        ? "Yield - 1st instance" : "Yield - 2nd instance");
```

```
    ShowWindow(OurHWnd, SW_SHOWNORMAL);

    // A quick hack to get the exact filename of our .EXE file
    // If this is the first instance, fork the 2nd instance
    GetModuleFileName(hInstance, exeName, sizeof(exeName));
    if ( FirstInstance )
        SecondHInstance = WinExec(exeName, SW_SHOWNORMAL);

    while ( GetMessage( &msg, NULL, 0, 0 ) )  // Standard loop
    {
        TranslateMessage( &msg );
        DispatchMessage( &msg );
    }
    return msg.wParam;
}
```

The above YIELD.C code isn't pretty. It was written with the aim of compressing the generic code as much as possible, in order to draw out the important areas. In other words, there's isn't any error checking like you'd expect in a shipping program. You shouldn't need a DEF file to link the program, unless you're using a LIBW.LIB that doesn't include the undocumented functions. Use IMPLIB to build your own LIBW.LIB if so!

In order to show that yielding can occur between two tasks while there are pending messages, the first instance of YIELD starts a second copy. The catalyst for the yield is when you let go of either the left or the right mouse button while over the first instance.

Releasing either mouse button while over the first instance tells the program to put a user-defined message in its own message queue and a different one in the message queue of the second instance of the program. Upon receipt of these messages, each instance immediately indicates its receipt. By yielding after the messages have been posted, and seeing which message is received first, we can test to see if the scheduler switched tasks or not.

Since both instances have a message waiting for them (and hence, have nonzero event counts), the scheduler should be able to schedule either instance to run next. We can now test the assertion that a task can in fact yield while it has a message waiting for it. Letting go of the left mouse button while over the window of the first instance makes the code post the messages and then call Yield(). Letting go of the right mouse button causes the messages to be posted, but doesn't call Yield(). To provide an unbiased judge as to which task processed its posted message first, and hence, to see if the first instance yielded while it still had an unprocessed message, we used the undocumented SysErrorBox() function. We chose SysErrorBox(), described in *Undocumented Windows*, because it is synchronous. No other task can run while you have a SysErrorBox() up. MessageBox() allows other tasks to run, so using it would skew the results.

What should happen in the case where the left button is used? Both instances of the program have an event waiting for them and are at the same priority level. However, as we saw in the SetPriority() pseudocode, the currently running task always comes later in the list than all other tasks with the same priority level. Inside the Yield() call this should cause the scheduler to see the event for the second instance of the task before it sees the event for the first instance, the currently running task. Therefore, the scheduler should wake up the second task immediately. You should see the SysErrorBox from the second instance pop up before the SysErrorBox for the first instance. Indeed, this is what happens.

If you use the right mouse button instead, the code doesn't perform the Yield() call. In this situation, the first instance returns from the WM_RBUTTONUP handler and eventually calls GetMessage() from its main loop. The GetMessage() invocation sees another message waiting for it, so it doesn't yield the CPU to the second instance. The SysErrorBox for the first instance appears first as a result. Only afterwards, when there are no more messages for the first instance, will GetMessage() yield to the second instance, giving it a chance to run and show its SysErrorBox.

A couple of conclusions can be drawn from the above. First, contrary to popular belief, the messaging system does not maintain some sort of internal flag that prevents one application from retrieving a message while another task is still processing a message. Secondly, it is possible to yield to other tasks while you still have unprocessed messages. The key thing to remember is that in order to yield, there has to be some other task with an event to yield to. You could call Yield() all day long, but if other tasks don't have events, calling Yield() does effectively nothing.

Yielding: How You End Up in the Scheduler

Having seen at a high level the criteria the scheduler uses to make its decisions, we now look at how to get into the scheduler. Specifically, what actions allow the scheduler to switch tasks?

GetMessage() and PeekMessage()

Most programs don't explicitly manage their scheduling. Instead, the scheduling is handled for them "automagically" inside GetMessage2(). As Chapter 7 describes in much more detail, GetMessage2() is just a back end for both GetMessage() and PeekMessage(). If you call GetMessage() and there are no messages waiting for you, GetMessage2() invokes UserYield() (described on the following page). GetMessage2() also calls UserYield() if you call PeekMessage() without specifying PM_NOYIELD.

An important thing to remember is that even if *you* don't call GetMessage() or PeekMessage() yourself, some Windows APIs call those functions behind your back. For instance, the DialogBox() family of routines, including MessageBox(), contains its own set of PeekMessage() loops. Therefore, calling any of these routines can cause your application to hand over control to another task without your explicitly being aware of it.

SendMessage()

Interestingly, another way to end up in the scheduler is to call SendMessage() with a message for another task. An intertask SendMessage() occurs when the window that's receiving the message belongs to a different task than the sending task. Since the code in each window procedure must operate in the correct task context, a convoluted section of code in the messaging system organizes the necessary task switches. The code needs to ensure that the correct task is awakened to handle the message and that the original task is switched back to afterwards. Chapter 7 describes the incredible complexity of intertask SendMessage() calls in much more detail.

There are Windows APIs that use intertask SendMessage() beneath the surface. Programs such as WinSight and Spy help ferret out which messages (such as WM_KILLFOCUS) are commonly sent between tasks.

Yield()

The scheduling API most familiar to programmers is Yield(). Yield() relinquishes control to any applications that have events waiting for them and which are at equal or higher priority to the caller. Pseudocode for Yield() looks like this:

```
Pseudocode for Yield() - CONTEXT.OBJ

    CurTDB.TDB_Yield_to = 0     // Zero out the field indicating a
                                // specific hTask to yield to.

    if ( CurTDB.TDB_QUEUE )     // If there's a message queue for
        goto UserYield()        // the current task, go to the
    else                        // UserYield() routine. Otherwise
        goto OldYield()         // goto OldYield() directly.
```

All Yield() does is clear the "Yield to this task" field used by DirectedYield() (described later) in the current TDB before branching to either UserYield() or OldYield(). In the general case, the application calling Yield() has a message queue which is created as part of the application startup code. UserYield() is what's called in this instance. We look at UserYield() next, followed by OldYield().

UserYield()

UserYield() is an undocumented API exported from USER. Its pseudocode is as follows:

```
Pseudocode for UserYield() - WINSEND.OBJ
// Locals
//      WORD    hQueue

    hQueue = GetTaskQueueES()  // Get current task queue handle

    // Make sure the current task doesn't have any intertask
    // SendMessage()s that are waiting to wake it up. Call
    // ReceiveMessage() until there's no more to process.
```

```
    // This is to prevent potential deadlock situations.
    while ( QS_SENDMESSAGE bit set in hQueue.wakebits )     // InSendMessage
        ReceiveMessage()

    OldYield()      // The actual Yield function (below)

    // Handle any intertask SendMessages to this task that
    // occurred while the task was asleep?
    while ( QS_SENDMESSAGE bit set in hQueue.wakebits )     // InSendMessage
        ReceiveMessage()
```

UserYield() provides a USER-aware wrapper around a call to OldYield(). OldYield() is where the core scheduling routine is invoked, and it is described next. As Chapter 7 explains, PostMessage() simply puts the message in the appropriate message queue and returns, while SendMessage() waits until the message has been replied to. The wrapper code in UserYield() apparently ensures that no other task is blocked while waiting for the current task to respond to a message. If this situation were encountered, potential deadlock situations could arise. UserYield() deals with this by calling ReceiveMessage() to make sure that no intertask SendMessage() calls are waiting for the task about to yield.

OldYield()

OldYield() is an undocumented API that's callable by your program. Based on its name, you might draw the conclusion that OldYield() used to be the real Yield() function, before the USER messaging system became part of Windows. It's been mentioned that the three core modules in Windows (USER, KERNEL, and GDI) were developed separately and then glued together. The fact that there's both a Yield() and an OldYield() could be evidence of this.

```
Pseudocode for OldYield() - CONTEXT.OBJ

    if ( InScheduler != 0 )       // Don't re-enter the scheduler!
        return                    // a KERNEL global variable

    if ( CurTDB != 0 )            // If there's a current TDB, bump
        CurTDB.TDB_nEvents++      // up its event count so that
                                  // it is guaranteed to be
                                  // rescheduled eventually.

    Reschedule()                  // The core scheduling routine

    CurTDB.TDB_nEvents--          // Restore the original event count
```

OldYield() first makes sure that the core scheduling routine won't be re-entered. Since Yield(), UserYield(), and DirectedYield(), discussed on the following pages, all go through OldYield(), it's apparently safe to assume that the core scheduling routine won't be re-entered.

If it's OK to enter the scheduler, OldYield() bumps up the event count for the current task, calls the scheduler, and resets the event count afterwards. If the event count weren't incremented before the Reschedule() call, Reschedule() wouldn't return till there was a real event for the task. Since a task should yield only if some other task has an event, OldYield() fakes an event for the task so that it will be scheduled next if no other task needs to be scheduled. This is a good example of where an event doesn't correspond exactly to a message.

DirectedYield()

DirectedYield() is a specialized and very powerful routine. It's used by SendMessage(), and it is a lifesaver when writing Windows debuggers. DirectedYield() allows you to yield to a specific task. As we see later, if that task doesn't have a waiting event, DirectedYield() turns into an ordinary Yield() call. DirectedYield() existed in Windows 3.0, but wasn't documented until Windows 3.1. DirectedYield() simply stores the HTASK that should be yielded to in a field in the current TDB, before JMP'ing to OldYield(). The Reschedule() function examines this field and, if it's nonzero, Reschedule() attempts to schedule that task next, assuming there's an event for it. To effectively use DirectedYield() therefore, you need to ensure that the task you're yielding to has an event. PostMessage() and PostAppMessage() are the usual means of accomplishing this, but you can also use the undocumented PostEvent().

```
Pseudocode for DirectedYield() - CONTEXT.OBJ
// Parameters:
//      WORD    hTask         // Task to yield to

    CurTDB.TDB_Yield_to = hTask // stash away task to yield to

    goto OldYield()             // The "real" yield code
```

All of the routines we've looked at so far get to the core scheduling function (that is, Reschedule()) through OldYield(). There's one other way to get into the scheduler, so we'll look at it now before we proceed to our discussion of Reschedule().

WaitEvent()

From reading the SDK documentation, you can get the impression that WaitEvent() is a routine that Microsoft didn't want to document, but had to since it's called from the standard Windows startup code. As Chapter 3 shows, the Windows loader has to fake an event with PostEvent() so that the new task gets scheduled. WaitEvent() is where this dummy event is removed, restoring the "level playing field" of tasks. WaitEvent() is also at the core of GetMessage2() (see Chapter 7).

WaitEvent() is as close as you get to a semaphore in Windows. You call WaitEvent() to block your task until there's an event for it. While blocking your task, WaitEvent() still allows other tasks to run. In OS/2 PM, the WaitEvent() routine is replaced by a semaphore, which is much more elegant. *Undocumented Windows* has a sample program, SEMTEST, that demonstrates the use of the WaitEvent() and PostEvent() pair as a pseudo-semaphore.

WaitEvent() is where events are eaten. Each time it's called, WaitEvent() decrements the event count for the task by one. If the event count is 0, WaitEvent() immediately calls

Reschedule(). When Reschedule() returns, there should be an event for the task, causing WaitEvent() to return to its caller. If there's already an event for the task when WaitEvent() is called, WaitEvent() simply decrements the event count and returns.

```
Pseudocode for WaitEvent() - CONTEXT.OBJ
// Parameters:
//      WORD    hTask

    if ( LockTDB == 0 )
        FTaskSwitchCalled = 1

    hTask = get_task(hTask)      // Returns either the passed
                                 // hTask, or the current task
                                 // if 0 is passed.
    while ( 1 )
    {
        hTask.TDB_nEvents--          // Decrement the event count

        if ( hTask.TDB_nEvents >= 0 )
            goto WaitEvent_done      // There was at least 1 event,
                                     // so we're done!

        hTask.TDB_nEvents = 0    // Event count was 0 before we
                                 // decremented it. Reset it to 0

        Reschedule()             // The core scheduling routine
    }

WaitEvent_done:
```

We've now examined the path leading up to the core scheduling routine. It's now time to light the torches, bring the dogs to the front, and slowly push open the door of Reschedule().

The Core Scheduling Routine—Reschedule()

Reschedule() takes no parameters, returns no values, and is not an exported API. When OldYield() and WaitEvent() call Reschedule(), they have no idea what happens inside Reschedule(). Reschedule() may decide that there's no reason to switch tasks and simply return. Alternatively, it may switch away from a task for hours on end. To the caller, Reschedule() is an atomic operation. Time effectively does not exist for the task when it is in Reschedule().

In order to provide this transparency of operation, as well as to keep the system flowing smoothly, Reschedule() has four major duties:

- Find the next task that should be scheduled and make sure that there are no extraordinary conditions that could prevent it from being switched to.
- Save the complete state of the outgoing task, and restore the state of the incoming task.
- Go into an idle loop that allows certain idle time actions to take place if no task needs to be scheduled (has an event).
- Update global variables that KERNEL maintains for the current task.

Unfortunately, the code to do each of these things is not broken up into distinct sections. Instead, the above chores are somewhat interwoven, and are in various states of completion throughout much of Reschedule(). Thus, I have chosen to walk through the sequence of events that occurs when Reschedule() is called, breaking up the code into three distinct sections.

Reschedule() Entry Code

Upon entering Reschedule(), the following registers are saved on the stack of the calling task: BP, DS, SI, DI, AX, CX, ES, BX, and DX. Furthermore, calling Reschedule() implicitly causes the CS and IP registers to be placed on the stack. The TOOLHELP routines, TaskGetCSIP() and TaskSetCSIP(), rely upon the stack frame created by Reschedule() to obtain and set the CS:IP values that will be used when the task starts up again. The 32-bit registers are not saved across task switches. If your code uses the 32-bit registers, it's important that you be aware when a task switch might occur and plan accordingly. Once again, we should stress that the scheduler we're discussing here is the one responsible for scheduling *Windows* applications (including Win32s applications). The preemptive VM scheduler *does* save the full 32-bit register set when it switches between virtual machines.

After Reschedule() saves the registers on the stack, TaskSwitchProfileUpdate() updates the profile (INI) files if they have been changed since the task was last switched to. Following that, Reschedule() verifies the 'TD' signature at offset 0FAh in the current TDB (see Table 3-2). If the 'TD' signature isn't found, Reschedule() assumes that the current TDB is garbage; Reschedule() immediately jumps to the code that searches for a new task to switch to.

If the signature bytes in the TDB look OK, the TDB_Yield_to field in the TDB is zeroed-out, but not before retrieving its value into AX. This field is nonzero if Reschedule() was entered using a DirectedYield() invocation. Its value indicates the hTask that the DirectedYield() caller desires to be scheduled next. Reschedule() is careful, though, and does not just blindly switch to this hTask. It first verifies that the event count for the potential new task is nonzero. If the event count is 0 for the DirectedYield() task, there's no need to schedule it, so Reschedule() treats this invocation as if it were invoked by a regular Yield() call. The implication is that the task specified in a DirectedYield() call is not necessarily the one that's scheduled next. As the Windows 3.1 documentation states, if you want to ensure that a particular task is scheduled, you should do a PostAppMessage() to make sure that the event count field in the TDB is nonzero. If you know what you're doing, you can also use the undocumented PostEvent() API.

```
Pseudocode for Reschedule() - SCHEDULE.OBJ
// Locals:
//      WORD    thisTask    // Task we're currently looking at
//      WORD    newTask     // Task to switch to
//      WORD    USERIsIdle  // Return value for IsUserIdle()
// Statics:
//      WORD    NumIdleIters = 0    // Number of times the idle
                                    // loop has been executed

    save registers on outgoing task stack in the following order:
    DS, SI, DI, AX, CX, ES, BX, DX

BootSchedule:       // The Bootstrap (Chapter 1) routine
                    // JMP's here to start normal scheduling

    TaskSwitchProfileUpdate()   // update task profiles (.INIs)

ExitSchedule:   // The ExitCall() routine (Chapter 3) JMP's
                // here after removing the task from the list

    if ( CurTDB == 0 )                  // No current task? Start
        goto Walk_through_task_list     // looking for a new task
                                        // immediately!

    If ( CurTDB.TDB_sig != 'TD' )       // Signature is bogus.
        goto Walk_through_task_list     // Thus, don't trust the
                                        // DirectedYield() HTASK.

    // Get the task that we're supposed to be yielding to. A 0
    // indicates no one in particular. Reschedule() always zero
    // out the "yield to" field regardless of whether it
    // contains an hTask to yield to or not.
    newTask = CurTDB.TDB_Yield_to
    CurTDB.TDB_Yield_to = 0

    if ( newTask == 0 )             // If no hTask was specified
        goto Walk_through_task_list // a task needs to be found.

    // Does the task we're supposed to yield to have any events
    // waiting for it?  If so, Reschedule() doesn't have to
    // search any further. If not, then don't yield to it.
    if ( event count in DirectedYield TDB != 0 )
        goto startup_this_task
```

Searching for a Task to Schedule, and the Idle Loop

The next section of code is the heart of Reschedule(). It's responsible for finding a suitable task to switch to, spinning in an idle loop if no task with an event is found.

As we now know, all task databases are kept in a linked list. Reschedule() starts at the head of the list and iterates through each TDB, looking for one with a nonzero event count in the TDB_nEvents field. For the remainder of this section, we refer to the code that iterates through the tasks, looking for one with an event, as the Walk_through_task_list code. When a TDB with a nonzero event count is found, Reschedule() attempts to switch the current task to the found TDB. We describe this a bit later.

If all the tasks were examined and none were found with waiting events, the Walk_through_task_list code falls into the idle loop section. The actions of the idle loop depend somewhat on whether you're running Standard or Enhanced mode windows, and if you're using virtual memory. The code described in the next two paragraphs exists only in the KRNL386 version.

Upon entering the idle loop, Reschedule checks some values in the KERNEL paging flags. If conditions are right, it calls ShrinkHeap(). ShrinkHeap() walks the global heap and, if enough free memory is found, it unlinks free blocks from the global heap's list. ShrinkHeap() and the DiscardFreeBlocks() routine are covered in Chapter 2.

If the paging system is in use, and if other paging flags are set, the idle loop code calls DiscardFreeBlocks(). The job of DiscardFreeBlocks() is to find free blocks of paged memory and give them back to the DPMI server. During the call of DiscardFreeBlocks(), hardware events may have occurred, causing new events for the tasks. To deal with this, Reschedule() JMP's back to the Walk_through_task_list code and starts anew the process of looking for a suitable task to switch to.

With the global heap housekeeping out of the way, Reschedule() calls the USER routine IsUserIdle(). In Windows 3.1, this is where USER places its checks to see whether to activate a screen saver. The return value from IsUserIdle() is a BOOL, and it is TRUE if a mouse button is held down, FALSE otherwise. We present pseudocode for IsUserIdle() after examining Reschedule().

If the return from IsUserIdle() was TRUE, and if the FPokeAtSegments global variable is nonzero, then once every 20h times through the idle loop, Reschedule() calls PokeAtSegments(). PokeAtSegments() walks the module list and loads any discardable segments of boot time modules that haven't been previously loaded. The walk of the module list stops when it encounters the SHELL module. This presumably causes PokeAtSegments() to load only segments for modules that are required for Windows to boot up. Once all the boot time segments have been loaded, PokeAtSegments() sets FPokeAtSegments to 0, causing the idle loop not to call PokeAtSegments() any more. If PokeAtSegments() loaded a segment during a particular iteration of the idle loop, a task event may have occurred, so Reschedule() JMP's back to the Walk_through_task_list code.

Next on the play list of the idle loop is a call to INT 28, the MS-DOS idle interrupt. After the INT 28h completes, the IsUserIdle() return value determines what goes in the BX register for an INT 2Fh, AX=1689h call. If IsUserIdle() returns TRUE, BX is 0, otherwise BX is 1. The INT 2Fh, 1689H call is documented in the INT2FAPI.INC file in the DDK, as the "Windows kernel idle" call. When the INT 2Fh returns, one iteration of the idle loop has completed, and it's time to check once again to see if any task has received an event. A JMP to the Walk_through_task_list code takes care of this.

An important point concerning the idle loop needs to be made here. The idle loop interrupts are critical to the proper functioning of power management software, such as POWER.EXE from Microsoft. If the idle loop isn't entered, the power management mechanisms can't kick in, and your laptop's battery drains at the normal rate, rather than at the idle rate. As Chapter 7 explains, applications that use a PeekMessage() loop never fall into the idle loop. The reason for this is that PeekMessage() calls UserYield(), which in turn calls OldYield(). OldYield() always increments the event count of the current task before calling Reschedule(), which means that Reschedule() is *guaranteed* to find a task to switch to and, as a result, it never goes into the idle loop code. GetMessage() on the other hand, calls WaitEvent(), which doesn't muck with the event count. The moral of the story is that you should use PeekMessage() loops as little as possible. If at all possible, use GetMessage() instead. It's much nicer to your laptop battery, and also to any DOS TSRs that depend on INT 28h.

```
Continuation of pseudocode for Reschedule() - SCHEDULE.OBJ

Walk_through_task_list:

    thisTask = HeadTDB  // Point to the first task in the list

Try_next_task:

    if ( thisTask != 0 )     // At the end of the task list?
        goto Does_this_task_have_an_event?  // At end of loop

    // This next section of code is the "Idle loop". When
    // searching for tasks, this code is jumped over repeatedly.
    // only when there's no task with events will execution
    // "fall" into this code.
    if ( bit 0x0008 set in PagingFlags )
        ShrinkHeap()     // In KRNL386 only. See Chapter 2.

    if ( a bit set in WinFlags )
    {
        DiscardFreeBlocks() // In KRNL386 only. An internal
                            // memory management routine.
        goto Walk_through_task_list     // Start again at top
    }

    if ( FP_SEG( PIsUserIdle ) )    // A global function pointer
    {
        USERIsIdle = PIsUserIdle()  // Ask the USER module if
    }                               // it's idle.
```

```
    if ( FPokeAtSegments != 0 ) // A global variable, set from
    {                           // the LOADSEGMENTSATIDLE key in
        if ( USERIsIdle )       // the BOOT section of SYSTEM.INI
        {
            NumIdleIters++  // Remember how many times through

            // Every 0x20 times through, load some boot time
            // segments. This doesn't happen anymore, once
            // they're all loaded.
            if ( (NumIdleIters & 0x1F) == 0 )
                PokeAtSegments()

            goto Walk_through_task_list // Now start looking for
                                        // a task with an event!
        }
    }

    INT 28h      // Generate the DOS "idle" interrupt

    INT 2Fh, AX = 1689h      // KERNEL tells WIN386 of its
                             // idle state. BL is 0 or 1,
                             // depending on IsUserIdle() result

    goto Walk_through_task_list // Maybe a task got an event
                                // while we were doing idle time
                                // things. Go check!

    // This is the other half of the "Walk_through_task_list"
    // loop. Between the top half and this part lies the
    // "idle loop".

Does_this_task_have_an_event?:

    if ( thisTask.TDB_nevents == 0 )    // If there's no events
    {                                   // for this task, go on
        thisTask = thisTask.TDB_next    // to the next one. If
        goto Try_next_task              // there are events, drop
    }                                   // through to the code
                                        // below.

    // If we get here, we've found a task (described later in continued code).
```

We've Found a Task. So Now What?

Once Reschedule() finds a TDB that has a nonzero event count, it begins the process of saving the context of the outgoing task and restoring the context of the incoming task. Before this can be done, Reschedule() needs to make a few tests. If the incoming task *is* the current task, there's no reason to go through the full process of saving and restoring the task context. Instead, Reschedule() just JMP's to the section that restores the registers from the stack frame that was saved upon entry; then it returns.

The next important thing to check is whether there is a locked task. When a task is locked, it is the only task in the system that is allowed to receive messages. All other tasks are shut out until the task is unlocked. A task can be locked by the LockCurrentTask() API in KERNEL or by the LockMyTask() function in USER. A system modal message box is an example of a locked task in action. If the incoming task is not the same as the locked task, Reschedule() should not switch to it. Instead, the saved registers on the stack are restored, and Reschedule() returns without having switched tasks.

The last hurdle to clear before starting the task switching sequence is to check the KERNEL_InDOS flag. The value of KERNEL_InDOS is nonzero if the KERNEL Real_DOS() function has been entered. Real_DOS() is a low level routine that, for the most part, just calls the INT 21h handler established by the DPMI server and DOS extender. KERNEL_InDOS is also checked in other critical sections of code elsewhere in KERNEL. Presumably, switching to a task when KERNEL_InDOS is nonzero would cause DOS re-entrance problems. Therefore, if KERNEL_InDOS is nonzero, Reschedule() won't switch tasks. In place of switching tasks, it resumes walking the task list, where the TDB search left off. If the TDB search started at the beginning, the same task would be found, and we still wouldn't be able to switch to it. Perhaps the hope is that by starting the search farther down the task list, the idle loop code will eventually execute. This might in turn clear the KERNEL_InDOS flag, allowing things to return to normal.

Once past the above gauntlet of idle loops and other checks, Reschedule() starts saving the context of the current task and waking up the incoming task in the same state it was left in when it was last switched away from. The switching code is as much of a critical section as any other piece of code, so it's only fitting that a global variable, InScheduler, is incremented to indicate that this work is in progress.

The first thing the switching section does is readjust the priority of the task. Like the previously discussed SetPriority() function(), Reschedule() keeps the task list in priority sorted order by momentarily deleting the incoming TDB from the task list and then reinserting it.

Because most tasks share the same priority value, it's important to give them each a fair chance to be selected for scheduling. Reschedule() accomplishes this by incrementing the priority value in the incoming TDB before removing and reinserting it into the task list. Then it decrements the priority back to its previous value. The net effect is to place the incoming task later in the list than any other tasks of the same priority value. This gives other tasks running at the same priority level first crack at being scheduled when they receive events. In the much more sophisticated OS/2 scheduler, this is roughly equivalent to the round-robin scheduling of threads at the same priority level.

After reprioritizing the TDB list, Reschedule() locks the global heap. This prevents the Least Recently Used (LRU) sweeping of the global heap from changing the global heap during the remainder of the task switching code. The LRU sweeping only occurs if you're not using paged virtual memory, as Chapter 2 explains.

Now it's time to finish the job of saving the context of the outgoing task. At the beginning of Reschedule(), most of the 16-bit registers for the outgoing task were pushed on the stack. This is where they remain the entire time the outgoing task is asleep.

The remainder of the job involves three steps. The first step is to save the current SS:SP values into the DWORD at offset 2 in the outgoing TDB. These two values are all that connect the outgoing task to its sleeping state in the scheduler (recall that the outgoing task's registers are saved on its stack, not in its TDB). Overwrite either of these two values, and the scheduler goes down in flames the next time the task is switched to.

The next step in saving the state of the outgoing task is to call SaveState(). SaveState() stores the current 80x87 control word and the current drive and directory values into the outgoing TDB. We examine SaveState() later on.

The final act of the outgoing process is to call DebugSwitchOut(), which generates the task switching out notification. This notification can be hooked through TOOLHELP.DLL as an NFY_TASKOUT notification, or by a RegisterPtrace() or ToolhelpHook() callback function with AX = 0Dh. RegisterPtrace() and ToolhelpHook() are crucial to writing a Windows debugger (see *Undocumented Windows*, Chapter 5).

Reschedule() now turns to the job of waking up the incoming task. As you might expect, the steps to reawaken a task are almost a mirror image of the steps to save away the outgoing task. First, Reschedule() sets the CurTDB KERNEL global variable to the value of the incoming TDB. Next, it retrieves the PDB (or PSP if you prefer) of the incoming task and stores it in the Win_PDB KERNEL global variable. Note however that INT 21h, function 50h is not invoked to switch what DOS thinks is the current PSP. Since Windows relies so heavily on the PSP and DOS for file I/O, you might think that it would call DOS to change the current PSP each time a task switch happens. As it turns out, KERNEL delays switching the PSP until it absolutely has to, such as during a file I/O operation. Switching the PSP requires a transition to DOS, a relatively slow process. If the only reason for a particular task switch is to deal with an intertask SendMessage(), it would get expensive. Thus, KERNEL holds out switching the current PSP until it's unavoidable. This causes problems on occasion, as the current PSP in DOS may not match the current TDB in Windows.

If an 80x87 is installed, Reschedule() loads the control word for the incoming task from its TDB using an FLDCW instruction. Before the control word is loaded though, Reschedule() executes an FCLEX instruction. This one instruction is a vital bug fix in Windows 3.1. In Windows 3.0, if a task generated a floating-point exception, it was possible for it to be masked until a new task had been scheduled and was loading its control word. This had the rather unfortunate effect of causing the wrong task to be blamed for the exception and then terminated as a result. Paul Bonneau's column in the May 1992 *Windows/DOS Developer's Journal* describes this in more detail.

At this point, Reschedule() sends the incoming task notification, NFY_TASKIN for TOOLHELP, AX = 0Eh for the RegisterPtrace(), and ToolhelpHook () callbacks. DebugSwitchIn() takes care of this chore.

Reschedule() is now almost done. It's time to start running on the stack of the incoming task. Accordingly, the SS:SP is switched to the SS:SP stored away in the incoming TDB. Reschedule() can now decrement the InScheduler flag, indicating that Reschedule is once again safe to enter. If running KRNL386, Reschedule() calls the UserRepaintDisable() function in the DISPLAY module, indicating that screen updates are now OK. Repainting may have been disabled inside the ExitCall() routine (see Chapter 3), which is invoked when a task is terminating.

Afterwards, the global heap is unlocked, allowing LRU sweeping to resume. As a final act, Reschedule() pops the register values for this task off the new stack and returns to either OldYield() or WaitEvent(). The new task is now awake, and the previous task is now silently sleeping. It will not wake up again till another event arrives for it.

```
Continuation of pseudocode for Reschedule() - SCHEDULE.OBJ

    // When we get here, we've found a potential task to switch
    // to. Make sure it's o.k. to switch to the new task though
    newTask = thisTask

    if ( newTask == CurTDB )      // The current task and the found
        goto Reschedule_done      // task are the same. Just pop the
                                  // registers and return!
startup_this_task:

    if ( LockTDB != 0 )               // If there's a locked task,
        if ( LockTDB != newTask )     // and it's not the task we
            goto Reschedule_done      // selected, don't switch
                                      // to it!

    If ( KERNEL_InDOS flag )
        goto Try_next_task:

    InScheduler++     // The above tests were passed. We're now
                      // definitely committed to switching to the
                      // found task. Increment a flag so that we
                      // don't get re-entered.

    // This next section is responsible for keeping the task list
    // in priority order. It also prevents one task at a given
    // priority from "hogging" the CPU from other tasks at the
    // same priority. The new task always ends up at the end
    // of the list of tasks at the same priority level.
    newTask.TDB_priority++  // Lower the tasks relative priority
    DeleteTask( newTask )   // Remove it from the task list
    InsertTask( newTask )   // Reinsert it in the task list
    newTask.TDB_priority--  // Restore original priority

    GlobalInfo.gi_lrulock++ // lock the global heap (prevent LRU
                            // sweeping) See Chapter 2.

    // This next section is responsible for saving the state of
    // the outgoing task.
```

```
    CurTDB.TDB_taskSS = SS  // Save the SS:SP in the TDB of the
    CurTDB.TDB_taskSP = SP  // outgoing task.

    SaveState( CurTDB )     // Save 80x87 state, Current DOS
                            // disk/directory. See pseudocode
                            // below.

    DebugSwitchOut()        // send task switch out notification
                            // For the outgoing task (the TOOLHELP
                            // NFY_TASKOUT notification)

    // From this point on, we're restoring the context of the
    // new task.
    CurTDB = newTask     // Update KERNEL global variable. We're
                         // now running as the new task!

    Win_PDB = newTask.TDB_PDB   // Update KERNEL global variable

    if ( F8087 )                      // 80x87 present?
    {
        FCLEX                         // Restore the 80x87 state
        FLDCW   [newTask.TDB_FCW]     // of the incoming task
    }

    DebugSwitchIn()      // send task switch out notification for
                         // the incoming task (the TOOLHELP
                         // NFY_TASKIN notification)

    SS = newTask.TDB_taskSS     // Switch stacks to the SS:SP
    SP = newTask.TDB_taskSP     // of the incoming task.

    CurTDB = newTask     // Set CurTDB again for good measure?

    InScheduler--    // Now "safe" to re-enter the scheduler

    if ( a bit set in (Kernel_Flags+2) )
        PDisplayCritSec( 0 )    // Tell the display driver that
                                // it's O.K. to repaint now.

    GlobalInfo.gi_lrulock-- // Unlock the global heap. See above

Reschedule_done:

    Restore registers saved on stack upon entry

    Return to caller
```

That's it for the Reschedule() code. We've seen exactly how Windows switches between tasks. In our coverage of Reschedule(), we came across the IsUserIdle() and SaveState() functions. These functions are especially interesting, so we examine them next.

IsUserIdle()

Besides being called by Reschedule() to determine if anything is happening in the messaging system, IsUserIdle() is also called by the internal IdleTimer() function. IdleTimer() calls IsUserIdle to give it a chance to activate the screensaver (added in Windows 3.1). During its first invocation, InitApp() calls SetSystemTimer(), telling it to call IdleTimer() every 10 seconds. The implication is that the minimum screensaver delay is 10 seconds.

Of some note are the tests in IsUserIdle() that determine whether to activate the screensaver. In order to start the screensaver, the following conditions must be met:

- Enough time has elapsed.
- There's an active window. See Chapter 5 for details on what this entails.
- The active window cannot be a DOS application running in a window if running in Enhanced mode.

If all these tests are passed, IsUserIdle() posts a WM_SYSCOMMAND message with an SC_SCREENSAVE wParam. Assuming the active window doesn't handle the message, DefWindowProc() gets it and calls the internal SysCommand() function to load the screensaver module specified in the SYSTEM.INI file.

```
Pseudocode for IsUserIdle() - WINLOOP.OBJ
// Locals:
//      DWORD   timeDiff

    // See if the user has any of the mouse buttons pressed
    // If so, return 0, indicating that USER isn't idle.
    if ( GetAsyncKeyState(VK_LBUTTON) & 0x8000 )
        return 0
    if ( GetAsyncKeyState(VK_RBUTTON) & 0x8000 )
        return 0
    if ( GetAsyncKeyState(VK_MBUTTON) & 0x8000 )
        return 0

    // Here's where we find out if we need to post the
    // SC_SCREENSAVE message. We won't bother to do this if
    // there's a system modal window up, or if the screen save
    // time interval is set to 0.
    if ( (HWndSysModal==0) && (IScreenSaveTimeout > 0)
         && (TimeLastInputMessage != 0) )
    {
        // TimeLastInputMessage is a USER global variable, which
        // remembers the time (in milliseconds) when the last
        // input message (mouse or keyboard) was received.
        timeDiff = GetCurrentTime() - TimeLastInputMessage
```

```
        // Has enough time elapsed?  Get out now if not.
        if ( (IScreenSaveTimeout * 1000) >= timeDiff )
            goto IsUserIdle_done

        if ( HWndActive == 0 )          // If no active window, don't
            goto IsUserIdle_done        // bother posting the message

        // If running in Standard mode, we'll always post
        // the SC_SCREENSAVE message if we get this far.
        if ( (WinFlags & WF_ENHANCED) = 0 )
            goto IsUserIdle_PostMessage

        // Running in Enhanced mode. See if the active
        // window is for a DOS application in a window. Don't
        // post the SC_SCREENSAVE message if so.
        if ( IsWinOldApTask(GetWindowTask(HWndActive)) )
            goto IsUserIdle_done

IsUserIdle_PostMessage:

        PostMessage( HWndActive, WM_SYSCOMMAND, // Post the
            SC_SCREENSAVE, 0 )                  // screensave msg

        TimeLastInputMessage = 0      // Reset the idle timer
    }

IsUserIdle_done:

    return 1                // Indicate that USER is idle
```

SaveState()

SaveState() is responsible for saving all the context information that a task needs later in order to start back up in the same state as when it was switched away from. A quick look at the pseudocode on the following page tells you that there's not much state to save. The register values for the task are implicitly saved as part of the Reschedule() routine. Therefore, all SaveState() has to do is save the 80x87 control word, if an 80x87 is present, and the current DOS drive and directory. (Remember, Windows runs multiple programs, each with its own drive, directory, and environment, all on top of one copy of DOS.) Of these states, the current drive, directory, and 80x87 control word are saved in fields designated exclusively for them in the TDB of the outgoing task.

From our observations, the current drive and directory information needs to be saved here only once. After the fields are initialized the first time, it appears that the KERNEL INT 21h handler maintains the current drive and directory values, obviating the need to obtain and store away the values here. By testing the high bit of the drive letter field (see offset 66h in Table 3-2), SaveState() decides if it needs to query DOS for these values.

```
Pseudocode for SaveState() - SCHEDULE.OBJ
// Parameters:
//      WORD    hTask       // hTask of outgoing task

    if ( F8087 )                 // If there's an 80x87, save its
        FSTCW   [hTask.TDB_FCW] // control word in the TDB

    if ((hTask.TDB_Drive & 0x80) == 0)  // Only if high bit set
    {
        INT 21h, AH = 19h        // DOS Get current disk in AL
        hTask.TDB_Drive = AL | 80h

        // Get the current DOS directory
        hTask.TDB_Directory[0] = '\'    // prepend root '\'
        INT 21h, AH = 47h, DS:SI = &(hTask.TDB_Drive+1)

        if ( carry flag set )           // Failure? If so, NULL
            hTask.TDB_Directory[0] = 0  // out the dir string
    }
```

CHAPTER 7

The Windows Messaging System

Messages are the lifeblood of a Windows program. To draw an analogy with the human body, the GetMessage()/DispatchMessage() loop is the heart, while the window procedures and their associated functions are the arteries, veins, and capillaries of a Windows program. The role of blood is, of course, played by messages. If the flow of blood stops, the body dies. A Windows program that stops processing messages also dies. Not only does the program halt, all other programs also stop until circulation resumes. As we'll soon see, the central point is that the creation, disposition, and flow of messages must be a smooth, well-oiled process.

In Windows, messages are used for many purposes. There are obvious uses for messages, such as indicating when a mouse moves or a menu item is selected. On a more complex scale, dialog boxes, menus, and other controls make very heavy use of messages, especially for communicating with each other. Messages are used for system-wide inquiries and broadcasts, as well as a form of interprocess communication. For instance, messages are used to query all applications to determine if it's OK to shut Windows down. In fact, the KERNEL module, which is supposed to be *below* the level of the messaging system, uses messages to indicate changes in the global heap. Much of the understanding of how Windows and Windows programs work often comes down to knowing what messages are used, when they're used, and what the proper response to a message is.

In this chapter, we examine how the Windows messaging system works. To return to the circulatory system analogy, we see where the blood is created and examine the chambers of the heart. In addition, Windows messages are commonly sent between different tasks, oftentimes without your knowing it! Imagine if your circulatory system were connected with that of everybody else in the room. All of a sudden, the connections and blood flow become more vital, for *everyone*. Because the messaging system must work with this high level of complexity, while remaining highly reliable, the Windows code that keeps the messages flowing is highly complex. (So what else is new?) We examine these mechanisms to see what kind of ugly tricks go on underneath the surface.

To best demonstrate how the various parts of the messaging system interrelate, it helps to describe smaller chunks of the messaging system individually. The code for the messaging system is implemented throughout much of USER.EXE. The scheduler in the KERNEL module also plays a vital role in keeping the system flowing; it is discussed in Chapter 6. After looking at small sections of the messaging system, we then bring all the pieces together to show how they create a message pump that keeps the program, and ultimately the whole of Windows, alive. The smaller chunks consist of:

- A quick review of the message structure.
- The different types of messages.
- The application message queue (one per program) and the single shared system message queue.
- How Windows implements cooperative multitasking.

A Quick Review of the MSG Structure

The format of a MSG structure, as seen by a program, is as follows:

```
typedef struct tagMSG
{
    HWND        hwnd;
    UINT        message;
    WPARAM      wParam;
    LPARAM      lParam;
    DWORD       time;
    POINT       pt;
} MSG;
```

The hwnd field indicates which window the message should be directed to. It's possible for the field to not contain a valid window handle. For instance, a message posted with PostAppMessage() contains an hwnd of 0. Though almost always processed in a WndProc, messages are in fact independent of the windowing system.

The message field contains a code representing what the message is trying to say. For instance, the value 0x000F is a WM_PAINT message which indicates that a portion of the window should be repainted. Values below WM_USER (0x0400) are reserved by Microsoft for system-wide usage. In Windows, the range of system messages is small enough so that you can sometimes use an array of function pointers to deal with the common messages, thereby eliminating a very long C switch statement. Message values above WM_USER are user-definable messages, meaning you can define them to mean whatever you wish in your application.

The wparam and lparam fields store information that is particular to a given value of the message field. For instance, if the message field contains WM_MOUSEMOVE, wparam contains information about which keys are held down, and lparam contains the (x, y) coordinates of the cursor. For other messages, wparam and lparam may not be meaningful at all.

The time and pt fields contain the time and cursor position when the message was created. The time is represented as the number of milliseconds since the booting of the system.

In Windows 3.1, there is additional information stored with each message. Since backwards compatibility with Windows 3.0 was a requirement for Windows 3.1, the existing APIs for retrieving messages couldn't be changed. Thus, a new API, GetMessageExtraInfo(), retrieves the extra information. Messages that enter the system through the mouse or keyboard drivers appear to be able to pass on this extra information, while posted messages cause zeros to be stored in the extra information field.

The Different Kinds of Messages

There are essentially five different ways for messages to be introduced into a Windows program. The GetQueueStatus() API, newly documented and improved in Windows 3.1, is a thin veneer that exposes some of the internals of the messaging system. In its return values, defined in WINDOWS.H, we see the five types of messages. Each of these message types is represented by a bit in a WORD in the application message queue (discussed momentarily).

- QS_KEY, QS_MOUSEMOVE, and QS_MOUSEBUTTON messages, although considered distinct by GetQueueStatus(), are all examples of input messages. Input messages are generated by hardware devices like the keyboard and mouse; they are stored in the shared system message queue. We discuss the system queue later.
- QS_POSTMESSAGE messages are placed in the application's message queue using PostMessage() or PostAppMessage(). There is one application message queue per program. Application message queues are also discussed later.
- QS_PAINT messages like QS_TIMER messages (see below), don't wait in a queue, but are, instead, generated as needed when an application requests a message. The Windowing system (see Chapter 4) is responsible for knowing if a particular window needs updating. When a window region becomes invalidated, USER informs the messaging system that a repaint is necessary by setting the QS_PAINT flag. When an application asks for a new message, the QS_PAINT flag is checked, and if set, a WM_PAINT message is composed on the spot. An important point worth noting here is that paint messages are not generated until there are no messages in the application's message queue. More on this later.
- QS_TIMER messages, similar to QS_PAINT, cause WM_TIMER messages to be generated on the fly when the QS_TIMER flag is set and an application calls GetMessage() or PeekMessage(). These messages are not stored in either the application's message queue or the system queue. Thus, timer messages cannot back up and fill the application or system queues.

- QS_SENDMESSAGE. The SendMessage() API allows a message to be sent to a window and guarantees that the receiving window replies immediately. To send messages between two windows of the same application is not hard. A simple function call does the job. However, SendMessage() does not always involve a simple function call. The difficult part is when messages are sent between two *different* tasks. Because each window procedure must operate in its normal task context, the Windows scheduler needs to get involved. Doing this correctly involves a large amount of synchronization between the two tasks. Much work goes on underneath the covers to make this appear seamless to the caller of SendMessage(). Because *intertask* SendMessages() are so complex and misunderstood, we examine them in detail at the end of the chapter.

It's important to note that the above distinctions are *not* based on the message number, but rather, on how the message came into existence (no, there's not a message stork!). For instance, consider the WM_PAINT message. Normally, it's generated for you when your application calls GetMessage() while the QS_PAINT flag is set. On the other hand, it's perfectly legal for an application to use SendMessage() to send a WM_PAINT message to another window. Such a message will be seen in the queue status bits as a QS_SENDMESSAGE, rather than as a QS_PAINT type message. Likewise, you can just as easily do a PostMessage() of a WM_PAINT message, which results in a QS_POSTMESSAGE type of message. The message numbers themselves aren't important for this discussion. What is important is that there are multiple ways to introduce messages into the system. Incidentally, you really wouldn't want to send or post WM_PAINT messages. The windowing system generates them automatically. We only picked WM_PAINT as the example message because it could be generated in three different ways.

The IBM OS/2 Presentation Manager (PM) input system is based upon similar message classifications. This isn't surprising when you learn that before the big IBM/Microsoft divorce, Presentation Manager and the Windows input system shared essentially the same source base. In fact, the OS/2 2.0 Presentation Manager implementation is still remarkably similar to the Windows 3.1 input system. This casts an interesting light on the operating system warfare between Microsoft and IBM. Windows and OS/2 are (evil?) twins that were "separated at birth."

The Application Message Queue

To get a firm grip on all that goes on in the Windows messaging system, it's first necessary to understand the two types of queues used by the messaging system. We examine the application message queue first and the system message queue afterwards.

During a program's initialization, USER generates a message queue for the application inside of the InitApp() routine (see Chapter 3 for details on program startup). The memory for the application queue is allocated and initialized by two internal USER routines, CreateQueue() and CreateQueue2(). The message queue is created in a segment of memory allocated from the global heap. A handle to the current message queue (actually a selector, since the segment is FIXED) can be obtained with the undocumented GetTaskQueue() function. The function is prototyped as:

```
HANDLE FAR PASCAL GetTaskQueue(HANDLE hTask);
```

Passing 0 as the hTask returns the queue handle of the current task.

Every window in the system is associated with a particular application message queue. Examine the fields in the WND data structure (see Chapter 4) and you'll notice a message queue handle (see offset 18h in Table 4-2). In fact, when messages are posted, the message queue handle in the WND structure determines which queue the message is added to.

Even the desktop window (your wallpaper, remember?) has a message queue associated with it. The desktop window is somewhat of a special case when it comes to its message queue. The message queue that the desktop window is associated with changes based upon a complex set of conditions that's not fully understood. However, there does seem to be a general pattern that the desktop window's message queue tracks the currently active application. This behavior can be observed by setting a hardware write breakpoint on the message queue field of the desktop window. To do this, you need to determine the data segment in USER that contains the window structures (it's one of the USER local heaps). You also need to find the offset or handle of the desktop window. Programs like WinSight or SPY can tell you the desktop's hwnd. Add 0x18 to the desktop hwnd value to determine the offset in the USER segment that should be used. Once you have the segment and offset, set a hardware write breakpoint at that address and start up Windows again. By clicking on icons, starting up applications, and performing other tasks, you can start to see where the message queue of desktop is switched around.

Messages are placed in an application's queue using PostMessage(). Some internal Windows functions also call PostMessage() behind the scenes, for instance DefWindowProc(). If a program wants to post a message in the queue of another task without knowing its HWND, or if the task has no windows, the program can use PostAppMessage(). PostAppMessage() takes the hTask parameter and finds the associated queue by looking it up in the Task Database (Chapter 3). The message is then placed into the destination queue with the HWND field of the message set to 0.

The default size of an application's message queue is just eight messages. In most cases, this is more than enough to contain all the messages actually posted to an application. This size is usually fine for most programs because, typically, far more messages are sent directly to the window or generated outside of the message queue than are posted. However, if you have more than one top level window, you might consider bumping up the size. If you need to do this, SetMessageQueue() is your friend. It's important that this function be called before any windows are created, since USER deletes the original message queue and creates a new one. This can cause confusion in the messaging system if the original message queue has already been used. Thus, SetMessageQueue() should be called before the message queue is used in any way by the application. An alternative to using SetMessageQueue() is to add to or otherwise alter the "DefaultQueueSize" setting in the [windows] section of the WIN.INI file. This is an undocumented INI key, so you may have to add it to the WIN.INI file yourself. In the general case though, eight messages is perfectly adequate for almost all applications.

The message queue for an application is closely tied to the Task Database (TDB) of the application. A field in the message queue contains the selector of the associated TDB, and vice versa. It's conceivable that the application queue could have been made a part of the TDB, but as we see later, there are reasons for treating them as distinct entities.

It's not possible to have a message queue for a DLL. As mentioned in Chapter 3, DLLs are really just library code that gets linked at run time. Therefore, they cannot own things that Windows associates with a task, like message queues or file handle tables. A common problem programmers encounter is that functions like MessageBox() won't work inside the LibMain() of an implicitly-linked DLL. Why is this? MessageBox() creates and uses windows. As mentioned earlier, each window must be associated with a message queue. Since an application has not yet created its message queue at the time your task calls LibMain() (see Chapter 3), windows cannot be created, and hence, MessageBox() fails.

The format of a message inside a message queue is very similar to the format of a MSG described previously. The difference is that a message held inside the message queue is four bytes larger. The extra four bytes occur at the beginning of the structure and are used by the "extra info" DWORD added in 3.1. A message that's waiting to be read from the application message queue looks like this:

```
DWORD       ExtraInfo
HWND        hwnd
WORD        message
WPARAM      wParam
LPARAM      lParam
DWORD       time
POINT       pt
```

In Windows 3.0, there is no ExtraInfo field, so MSGs inside and outside the message queue are identical.

A message queue structure contains far more than just a queue of messages. Fields are needed to handle intertask SendMessages() and the like. GetTaskQueue() returns a handle to this structure. The format of the message queue structure changed between Windows 3.0 and 3.1. *Undocumented Windows* contains the format for both 3.0 and 3.1. Table 7-1 gives an updated version of the message queue for Windows 3.1.

Table 7-1: Message Queue for Windows 3.1.

00h WORD	Selector of next message queue. Like many data structures in Windows, message queues are stored in a linked list, with each queue containing the selector of the next queue in the list. The system message queue is not included in this list.
02h WORD	hTask of task that owns this queue. GetWindowTask() gets the queue handle from the HWND parameter and gets the associated hTask from this field. (See WND structure in Chapter 4 and TDB in Chapter 3.)
04h WORD	Size of a message in this queue. Contains 22 for application message queues in Windows 3.1.

Table 7-1: Message Queue for Windows 3.1. (continued)

06h	WORD	Number of messages waiting in the message area that have not been removed by a GetMessage() or PeekMessage(PM_REMOVE).
08h	WORD	Offset in the queue segment of next message to be retrieved.
0Ah	WORD	Offset in the queue segment where the next message will be written.
0Ch	WORD	The length in bytes of the queue segment. Used to determine when the (circular) queue needs to wrap back to the beginning of the message area.
0Eh	DWORD	Value returned by GetMessageTime().
12h	DWORD	Value returned by GetMessagePos().
16h	WORD	Unknown. Sometimes contains 1.
18h	DWORD	Information returned by GetMessageExtraInfo().
1Ch	WORD	Unknown.
1Eh	DWORD	Contains the LPARAM of a SendMessage() to another task.
22h	WORD	Contains the WPARAM of a SendMessage() to another task.
24h	WORD	Contains the MSG of a SendMessage() to another task.
26h	WORD	Contains the HWND of a SendMessage() to another task.
28h	WORD	Contains the DWORD result from the SendMessage().
2Ch	WORD	Nonzero if PostQuitMessage() has been called by this program.
2Eh	WORD	PostQuitMessage() exit code.
30h	WORD	Flags of some sort.
32h	DWORD	Unknown.
36h	WORD	Expected Windows version from NE file.
38h	WORD	Queue handle of application that is sending a message to this application. InSendMessage() returns this value.
3Ah	WORD	In an intertask SendMessage(), the sending task sets this field in the receiving task's queue. The value is the queue handle of the sending task. When the receiving task wakes up, it uses this field to determine which task/queue sent the message to it. This field, in conjunction with the next field, allows nested intertask SendMessage() calls to occur.
3Ch	WORD	In an intertask SendMessage(), the sending queue stores the value from offset 3A of the receiving queue into offset 3C of the sending queue. When the receiving queue wakes up, it restores the value it used to contain in offset 3A by reading the field at offset 3C of the sending queue. Put another way, it unlinks the sending queue from the chain of intertask SendMessage() calls.
3Eh	WORD	Number of paints needed by this application.
40h	WORD	Number of timer events waiting for this application.
42h	WORD	Change Bits. Contains the QS_xxx bits that have changed since the last GetMessage(), PeekMessage(), or GetQueueStatus() call. The bits are sets by SetWakebit2() (described later).

Table 7-1: Message Queue for Windows 3.1. (continued)

Offset	Type	Description
44h	WORD	Wake Bits. Contains the QS_xxx bits which indicate what kind of messages are waiting for the application. As the messages are extracted, the appropriate QS_xxx bit is turned off. There are a few other bitfields used for communicating the current status of an intertask SendMessage().
46h	WORD	Wake Mask. Contains the QS_xxx bits that an application is currently waiting for. When the application goes to sleep through SleepHq(), it sets the wakemask bits to indicate which type of QS_xxx messages should wake it up and make it start executing again.
48h	WORD	Used for intertask SendMessages(). Upon return from intertask call, contains the near address on the stack where the SendMessage() result (offset 28h) will be copied.
4Ah	WORD	Used for intertask SendMessages(). Before the intertask call, is initialized with the near address on the stack where the SendMessage() result (offset 28h) will be copied after the intertask call Returns.
4Ch	WORD	Used for intertask SendMessages(). In the ReceiveMessage(), it is set to the value in the WORD at offset 4Ah in the sending queue. Later on in ReplyMessage(), this same value is copied to offset 48h in the sending queue.
4Eh	WORD	Something having to do with hooks.
50h	BYTE[1Eh]	Unknown. Possibly having to do with hooks.
6Eh	WORD	Start of the posted message storage area (the message queue proper). The memory from here to the end of the segment can be thought of as an array of messages, each message being 22 bytes in length (in Windows 3.1).

As can be seen from the preceding description, the message queue maintains data for several different states:

- A circular buffer of messages. This area is similar in concept to the ROM-BIOS keyboard buffer. The queue contains read and write pointers that indicate where the next message will be read from, as well as where the next message will be written to. A pointer pointing at the last available message slot wraps around to the first available slot when it's incremented. When the read and write pointers are equal, there are no messages in the queue. The message queue also maintains data for intertask SendMessage(). The parameters, return values, and current state of the SendMessage() transaction are stored in the message queue, but *not* in the section that's normally used for posted messages since messages sent by intertask SendMessage() are guaranteed to be processed immediately, ahead of any other waiting messages.
- Whether the application has been told to quit and if it has, its exit code.

- A back link to the Task Database. GetWindowTask() uses this field to obtain the task handle associated with a given window.
- The wakebits and other associated status fields. These flags indicate information such as which types of message are waiting to be processed by this queue. These fields play a very important role in multitasking Windows applications. We examine them in detail later.

Because an application message queue contains most of the data that the messaging system uses, the queue can be thought of as a command center for messaging. The application queue is much more than a holding area for posted messages. It's what links a window handle to a particular task, and it is the keeper of the status bits, so vital to GetMessage() and PeekMessage().

The QUEUE Sample Program

The following program demonstrates some of the concepts discussed previously. It uses the WINIO library that was distributed with *Undocumented Windows* to keep the user interface code to a minimum.

```
//==================================
// QUEUE, by Matt Pietrek, 1992
// File: QUEUE.C
//==================================
#include <windows.h>
#include <dos.h>
#include "winio.h"

// If your IMPORT.LIB or LIBW.LIB doesn't include
// GetTaskQueue(), you'll have to add it to the IMPORTS section
// of the .DEF file. The ordinal number is KERNEL.35
WORD FAR PASCAL GetTaskQueue(WORD hTask);

typedef struct
{
    DWORD   extraInfo;
    HWND    hwnd;
    WORD    message;
    WORD    wParam;
    DWORD   lParam;
    DWORD   time;
    POINT   pt;
} QUEUEMSG;
```

```
typedef struct
{
    WORD        NextQueue;
    WORD        OwningTask;
    WORD        MessageSize;
    WORD        NumMessages;
    WORD        ReadPtr;
    WORD        WritePtr;
    WORD        Size;
    LONG        MessageTime;
    POINT       MessagePoint;
    WORD        Unknown1;
    DWORD       ExtraInfo;
    WORD        Unknown2;
    LONG        SendMessageLParam;
    WORD        SendMessageWParam;
    WORD        SendMessageMessage;
    HWND        SendMessageHWnd;
    DWORD       SendMessageResult;
    WORD        QuitFlag;
    int         ExitCode;
    WORD        flags;
    DWORD       Unknown3;
    WORD        ExpWinVersion;
    WORD        SendingHQ;
    WORD        sendmsg_helper1;
    WORD        sendmsg_helper2;
    WORD        PaintCount;
    WORD        TimersCount;
    WORD        ChangeBits;
    WORD        WakeBits;
    WORD        WakeMask;
    WORD        SendMessageResult1;
    WORD        SendMessageResult2;
    WORD        SendMessageResult3;
    WORD        Hook;
    BYTE        Hooks2[30];
    BYTE        MessageArrayStart;
} QUEUE;        // see Table 7-1

// Dumps selected fields of a message queue
void DumpQueueContents(QUEUE far *queue)
{
    QUEUEMSG far *queuemsg;
    unsigned maxMessages, i;

    maxMessages =
```

```
        ( queue->Size - FP_OFF(&queue->MessageArrayStart))
                    / sizeof(QUEUEMSG);

    queuemsg = (QUEUEMSG far *) &queue->MessageArrayStart;

    printf("Messages: %u  ReadPtr: %04X  WritePtr: %04X\n",
        queue->NumMessages, queue->ReadPtr, queue->WritePtr);

    printf("WakeBits: ");
    if ( queue->WakeBits & QS_KEY )
        printf("QS_KEY ");
    if ( queue->WakeBits & QS_MOUSE )
        printf("QS_MOUSE ");
    if ( queue->WakeBits & QS_POSTMESSAGE )
        printf("QS_POSTMESSAGE ");
    if ( queue->WakeBits & QS_TIMER )
        printf("QS_TIMER ");
    if ( queue->WakeBits & QS_PAINT )
        printf("QS_PAINT ");
    printf("\n");

    for ( i=0; i << maxMessages; i++ )
    {
        printf(
            "HWnd: %04X  Msg: %04X  WParam: %04X  LParam: %08lX\n",
            queuemsg->hwnd, queuemsg->message,
            queuemsg->wParam, queuemsg->lParam );

        queuemsg++;
    }
    printf("\n");
}

// Get a pointer to the application message queue. Then, put
// some messages into the queue, and retrieve them. We display
// the contents of the queue at each state, so that we can see
// the principles involved.

void ExamineQueue(void)
{
    QUEUE far *queue;
    MSG msg;

    queue = MK_FP( GetTaskQueue(GetCurrentTask()), 0 );
    if ( !queue )
    {
        printf("Unable to find message queue\n");
        return;
    }
```

```
    printf("Here we have an empty queue:\n\n");
    DumpQueueContents(queue);

    printf(
    "We'll now call PostAppMessage() to put some messages in\n"
    "the queue.  Note that the message count goes up, and that\n"
    "QS_POSTMESSAGE is now set:\n\n");

    PostAppMessage(GetCurrentTask(), 0x1234, 0x5678, 0x12345678L);
    PostAppMessage(GetCurrentTask(), 0x2345, 0x6789, 0x12345678L);
    PostAppMessage(GetCurrentTask(), 0x3456, 0x789A, 0x12345678L);
    PostAppMessage(GetCurrentTask(), 0x4567, 0x89AB, 0x12345678L);

    DumpQueueContents(queue);

    printf(
    "We'll now call GetMessage() to remove a message. The\n"
    "message still appears in the message array, but the Read\n"
    "pointer has been incremented.  We also print out the\n"
    "contents of the retrieved message to show that it matches\n"
    "what was in the queue:\n\n");

    GetMessage(&msg, 0, 0, 0);
    DumpQueueContents(queue);

    printf(
    "The message retrieved into the MSG struct:\n"
    "HWnd: %04X  Msg: %04X  WParam: %04X  LParam: %08lX\n\n",
    msg.hwnd, msg.message, msg.wParam, msg.lParam );

    printf(
    "We now call GetMessage 3 more times to get rid of the\n"
    "remaining messages.  Note that the Read and Write ptrs are\n"
    "equal, the QS_POSTMESSAGE flag is no longer set, and the\n"
    "message count field shows 0.  Thus, the queue is considered\n"
    "to be empty:\n\n");

    GetMessage(&msg, 0, 0, 0);
    GetMessage(&msg, 0, 0, 0);
    GetMessage(&msg, 0, 0, 0);
    DumpQueueContents(queue);
}

int main()
{
```

```
    // This program uses the message queue format for Windows
    // 3.1. Abort if running under any other version.
    if ( LOWORD(GetVersion()) != 0x0A03 )
    {
        winio_warn(FALSE, "QUEUE",
            "This program requires Windows 3.1");

        return 1;
    }

    // Turn off repaints. If we don't do this, the WINIO library
    // will attempt to use the queue while we're in the process of
    // examining it.
    winio_setbusy();
    winio_setpaint(winio_current(), FALSE);

    ExamineQueue();

    // Turn the repaints back on. This allows WINIO to refresh
    // the display with all the output that was created in
    // ExamineQueue().
    winio_setpaint(winio_current(), TRUE);
    winio_resetbusy();
    winio_home(winio_current());
    return 0;
}
```

Here is sample output from QUEUE.EXE:

```
Here we have an empty queue:

Messages: 0  ReadPtr: 006E  WritePtr: 006E
WakeBits: QS_MOUSE QS_TIMER QS_PAINT
HWnd: 0000  Msg: 0000  WParam: 0000  LParam: 00000000
HWnd: 0000  Msg: 0000  WParam: 0000  LParam: 00000000
HWnd: 0000  Msg: 0000  WParam: 0000  LParam: 00000000
HWnd: 0000  Msg: 0000  WParam: 0000  LParam: 00000000
HWnd: 0000  Msg: 0000  WParam: 0000  LParam: 00000000
HWnd: 0000  Msg: 0000  WParam: 0000  LParam: 00000000
HWnd: 0000  Msg: 0000  WParam: 0000  LParam: 00000000
HWnd: 0000  Msg: 0000  WParam: 0000  LParam: 00000000

We'll now call PostAppMessage() to put some messages in
the queue.  Note that the message count goes up, and that
QS_POSTMESSAGE is now set:
```

```
Messages: 4  ReadPtr: 006E  WritePtr: 00C6
WakeBits: QS_MOUSE QS_POSTMESSAGE QS_TIMER QS_PAINT
HWnd: 0000  Msg: 1234  WParam: 5678  LParam: 12345678
HWnd: 0000  Msg: 2345  WParam: 6789  LParam: 12345678
HWnd: 0000  Msg: 3456  WParam: 789A  LParam: 12345678
HWnd: 0000  Msg: 4567  WParam: 89AB  LParam: 12345678
HWnd: 0000  Msg: 0000  WParam: 0000  LParam: 00000000
HWnd: 0000  Msg: 0000  WParam: 0000  LParam: 00000000
HWnd: 0000  Msg: 0000  WParam: 0000  LParam: 00000000
HWnd: 0000  Msg: 0000  WParam: 0000  LParam: 00000000

We'll now call GetMessage() to remove a message. The
message still appears in the message array, but the Read
pointer has been incremented.  We also print out the
contents of the retrieved message to show that it matches
what was in the queue:

Messages: 3  ReadPtr: 0084  WritePtr: 00C6
WakeBits: QS_MOUSE QS_POSTMESSAGE QS_TIMER QS_PAINT
HWnd: 0000  Msg: 1234  WParam: 5678  LParam: 12345678
HWnd: 0000  Msg: 2345  WParam: 6789  LParam: 12345678
HWnd: 0000  Msg: 3456  WParam: 789A  LParam: 12345678
HWnd: 0000  Msg: 4567  WParam: 89AB  LParam: 12345678
HWnd: 0000  Msg: 0000  WParam: 0000  LParam: 00000000
HWnd: 0000  Msg: 0000  WParam: 0000  LParam: 00000000
HWnd: 0000  Msg: 0000  WParam: 0000  LParam: 00000000
HWnd: 0000  Msg: 0000  WParam: 0000  LParam: 00000000

The message retrieved into the MSG struct:
HWnd: 0000  Msg: 1234  WParam: 5678  LParam: 12345678

We now call GetMessage 3 more times to get rid of the
remaining messages.  Note that the Read and Write ptrs are
equal, the QS_POSTMESSAGE flag is no longer set, and the
message count field shows 0.  Thus, the queue is considered
to be empty:

Messages: 0  ReadPtr: 00C6  WritePtr: 00C6
WakeBits: QS_MOUSE QS_TIMER QS_PAINT
HWnd: 0000  Msg: 1234  WParam: 5678  LParam: 12345678
HWnd: 0000  Msg: 2345  WParam: 6789  LParam: 12345678
HWnd: 0000  Msg: 3456  WParam: 789A  LParam: 12345678
HWnd: 0000  Msg: 4567  WParam: 89AB  LParam: 12345678
HWnd: 0000  Msg: 0000  WParam: 0000  LParam: 00000000
HWnd: 0000  Msg: 0000  WParam: 0000  LParam: 00000000
HWnd: 0000  Msg: 0000  WParam: 0000  LParam: 00000000
HWnd: 0000  Msg: 0000  WParam: 0000  LParam: 00000000
```

The System Message Queue

The system message queue is a kind of half-brother to the application message queue. The system message queue holds all the hardware or input messages. Typically this means mouse and keyboard events, but the queue is not restricted to those input devices. There are mechanisms for alternative input devices, such as digitizing tablets, to place messages in the system queue.

Like the application message queue, the system queue is allocated and initialized by USER. The format of the system queue is the same as the application queue, except that the format of their stored messages differ. The fields that store information like the number of messages remain the same. Unlike the application queue, there is only one system queue for all of Windows. In addition, there is no API, documented or undocumented, to obtain the handle of the system queue. Thus, we have to resort to slimy hacks to find its handle. The first WORD in the 0x2C'th segment of USER contains the handle of the system queue. In Windows 3.0, it's the WORD at offset 2 of the 0x2B'th segment. GlobalEntryModule() in TOOLHELP provides a convenient way to obtain the selector or handle to a segment, given its logical number.

Some of the fields used in the application message queue are ignored in the system message queue. For instance, the hTask field (offset 2) is not the owning task, as no one task owns the system queue. In fact, the only parts the system queue uses are the fields used for the circular message buffer portion.

As mentioned earlier, the system queue's job is to save up the hardware messages that are turned into user input. In general, hardware events occur at a pretty good clip. Simply moving your mouse across the screen can cause dozens of WM_MOUSEMOVE messages. To prevent all these events from being lost, the system queue typically can hold many more messages than an application queue. By default, the system queue can hold 120 hardware messages. The number of message slots can be altered by adding or changing the TypeAhead entry in the [windows] section of the WIN.INI file, but this is almost never necessary.

Messages in the system queue are not destined for a particular window, which is a key difference between Windows 3.x and Windows NT. The processing of one system message affects which window or task subsequent messages should go to. For instance, a WM_LBUTTONDOWN message could cause a change of focus. Subsequent messages in the queue should then go to the new focus window, rather than to the previous one.

On the other hand, the system queue can be locked by a task. This ensures that no other task can read messages from the system queue until the locking task is done reading all the messages it needs. For example, a double click message is synthesized out of a series of button up and down messages. It wouldn't do for one task to steal away messages in the middle of the process. The system queue is unlocked when there are no messages left for a task, or when it receives a message that another task must handle.

The format of a message in the system queue is as follows:

```
DWORD   Extra info.
WORD    Meaning varies by message number.
WORD    Message number. This is a real WM_ number, such as
```

```
        WM_MOUSEMOVE
WORD    Meaning varies by message number
DWORD   Time. Number of milliseconds since booting the system.
```

How do events get into the system queue? A good question. In USER.EXE, a routine called EnableInput() (see Chapter 1) calls the mouse driver and keyboard driver Enable() functions (ordinal entry #2). The parameters to the mouse and keyboard driver Enable() functions are the addresses of the exported USER functions, mouse_event() and keybd_event(). The mouse_event() and keybd_event() routines are essentially interrupt-level functions. Moving the mouse or striking a key generates a hardware interrupt. Interrupt handler functions are provided in the mouse or keyboard device driver, typically called MOUSE.DRV and KEYBOARD.DRV. The mouse and keyboard drivers then call mouse_event() and keybd_event(), using function pointers passed to them during their initialization. Inside of mouse_event() and keybd_event(), some processing occurs to place appropriate values in the registers before calling SaveEvent().

SaveEvent() is responsible for placing the message in the system queue by calling WriteSysMsg(). SaveEvent() also attempts to coalesce multiple WM_KEYDOWN messages that result from a key that is repeating because it is being held down. Finally, SaveEvent() calls WakeSomeone(). WakeSomeone() determines which application is the best candidate to receive the message. When WakeSomeone() finds an appropriate application, the appropriate flags are set in its message queue and an event is posted to the application's TDB. As we see later, this causes the chosen application to wake up and receive the message. This looks somewhat interesting, so we'll dig into the WakeSomeone() code.

WakeSomeone()

Of special note in WakeSomeone() is the test for hQCapture. This one innocent looking test contains nearly the entire implementation of the capture mechanism. When your application calls SetCapture(), USER sets the global variable hQCapture to the queue associated with SetCapture()'s hwnd parameter. Inside of WakeSomeone(), if hQCapture is non-null, the hQCapture queue is given the QS_MOUSE event, rather than the queue that ordinarily would have received it. It is also important to note that if Windows is in a system modal state, the hQSysModal queue is always highest in the pecking order, even ahead of the queue with the capture.

```
Pseudocode for WakeSomeone()

// Globals variables:
// hQCursor - The queue "associated" with the cursor
// hQActive - The queue of the "active" window that has focus
// hQCapture - The queue associated with the capture window
// hQSysModal - The queue associated with the system modal window
//
// Local variables:
// "best_queue" contains the current "best guess" as to which
// queue should be woken up to receive the message
```

```
//
// "wakebit" contains the QS_xxx message type (QS_MOUSEMOVE,
// QS_MOUSEBUTTON, or QS_KEY) that will be placed in the
// WakeBits of whatever queue is selected to receive the message

    best_queue = hQCursor

    if ( message is a not a key message )
        goto mouse_event

    wakebit = QS_KEY

    if ( hQActive != NULL )
        best_queue = hQActive

    goto system_modal_check

mouse_event:
    if ( message == WM_MOUSEMOVE )
        wakebit = QS_MOUSEMOVE
    else
        wakebit = QS_MOUSEBUTTON

    if ( hQCapture != NULL )
        best_queue = hQCapture

system_modal_check:
    if ( hQSysModal != NULL )
        best_queue = hQSysModal

    if ( best_queue != 0 )
        goto wake_em_up

    iterate through queue linked list
    {
        if ( queue's WakeMask includes wakebit determined previously )
        {
            best_queue = current queue under examination
            goto wake_em_up
        }

        if ( at end of queue linked list )
            return
    }

wake_em_up:
    SetWakeBit2();      // Sets WakeBits, and posts event; see below

    return
```

If you're especially interested in the mechanisms that transform a mechanical action into a message in Windows, you might wish to examine the DDK. The DDK provides source code for the mouse and keyboard drivers, so you can see for yourself how the interrupts handlers and USER work together to create system queue messages.

If you have your own hardware device and wish to add messages to the system queue, you can use the exported hardware_event() routine. hardware_event() is just a wrapper around a call to WriteSysMsg(). On entry, hardware_event() should contain:

```
SI = hWnd
AX = message number
DI = wParam
DX:CX = lParam
```

Like the application message queue, the system queue is a critical component of the messaging system. Now it's time to find out how the messaging system delivers messages in the application and system queues to waiting applications.

Wakebits, WaitEvent, and the Scheduler

The goal of the next large piece of the messaging system is to wait for a message to appear, but not hold up other programs. If no messages are waiting to be processed inside of GetMessage(), the task should allow other programs to retrieve messages waiting for them. This is where the term cooperative multitasking comes from. If you use the standard GetMessage()/DispatchMessage() loop, cooperative multitasking happens automatically.

As seen earlier, there are five ways for a message to become available to a program. Because it wouldn't do to just spin in a loop, polling for messages, there needs to be a way to wait for a message, while still allowing other tasks an opportunity to run. To show how this is done, we first have to introduce a few terms that are used for much of the remaining discussion. Actually, they are fields in the message queue (see Table 7-1).

- WakeBits—Offset 44 in the message queue. These bitfields indicate that a particular kind of message (QS_PAINT, QS_TIMER, for example) is *available* to the task. For instance, if the QS_PAINT bit is set, it indicates that a paint message is waiting for the application, but hasn't yet been retrieved. Only QS_POSTEVENT messages exist in the application message queue. All other message types need to have messages synthesized or read out of the system queue when a program calls GetMessage().
- WakeMask—Offset 46 in the message queue. A mask of the QS_xxx message types that the application is actively *waiting* for. Typically, GetMessage() is called with uMsgFilterMin and uMsgFilterMax set to 0. This sets the WakeMask to include all the QS_xxx message types. If you specify an actual range of messages in the GetMessage() call, an appropriate set of QS_xxx bits is calculated inside of GetMessage().
- ChangeBits—Offset 42 in the message queue. The QS_xxx bits that have changed since the last call to GetQueueStatus(), GetMessage(), or PeekMessage(). This information is mainly for informational purposes and doesn't appear to be used much by the messaging system.

With those definitions in mind, we now look at pseudocode for SleepHq(), which is called by GetMessage() to wait for a message, but which yields to other tasks if they have messages.

```
//
// WakeMask contains QS_xxx OR'ed together. SleepHq() will not return
// until at least 1 of QS_xxx bits in the WakeMask parameter has been
// set in the ChangeBits.
//

void SleepHq( unsigned WakeMask )
{
    HANDLE currQ

SleepHq_check_flags:

    currQ = GetTaskQueue(0)  // Get current task queue

    // If already have a message then go get it
    if ( WakeMask & currQ.ChangeBits )
        goto SleepHq_done

    // Check for SendMessages and deal with them
    if ( currQ.WakeBits & QS_SENDMESSAGE )
        goto SleepHq_have_SendMessage

    // Always check for SendMessages
    currQ.WakeMask = WakeMask & QS_SENDMESSAGE

    if ( WakeMask & currQ.ChangeBits )
        goto SleepHq_done

    WaitEvent()     // Kernel routine that waits for an event

    goto SleepHq_check_flags:

SleepHq_done:

    zero out currQ.WakeMask

    return

SleepHq_have_SendMessage:

    zero out qWakeMask
```

```
    // Deal with the SendMessage(). Described in the section
    // on SendMessage()
    ReceiveMessage()

    goto SleepHq_check_flags
}
```

There are a couple of interesting things going on inside of SleepHq() that are worth pointing out. First, notice the code that deals with replying to SendMessage() calls. SendMessages() are dealt with at a lower level than the other four message types. The messaging system checks for sent messages in many different spots and deals with them immediately, before continuing with the normal waiting state. When SleepHq() notices that a SendMessage is waiting for the current queue, it calls ReceiveMessage() to deal with it and then goes back to waiting for one of the other QS_xxx type messages. Sent messages are like an annoying phone call. When one happens, you deal with it immediately so that you can go back to whatever you were doing before. SleepHq() really wants to wait for a QS_POSTMESSAGE, a QS_PAINT, or whatever. When it sees a pending QS_SENDMESSAGE flag, it handles it and then goes back to what it's really waiting for. We discuss SendMessage() in detail at the end of this chapter.

Because SendMessage() is dealt with inside SleepHq(), your application doesn't do anything special to receive SendMessage() messages. The handling of sent messages is thrown in for free when you call GetMessage(). As noted earlier, though, it is unsafe to yield during a SendMessage(). For this your application needs to call InSendMessage() and ReceiveMessage(). Another implication of the way SendMessage() is dealt with is that you cannot receive sent messages at just any given time. You only receive sent messages when you're inside of GetMessage() or PeekMessage(), when you call SendMessage() yourself, or when you call a function that uses SendMessage(), such as a dialog box function. If you're in the middle of crunching a long series of numbers, there's no need to worry about a critical message being sent to you and interrupting your work.

The other point worth noting in the SleepHq() code is its use of WaitEvent(). The Windows scheduler and events are described in detail in Chapter 6, but a brief synopsis is needed here: At offset 6 in the Task Database is the event count field. The event count is like a flag on a mailbox. If it's up (if it contains a non-zero value), then there is some reason to switch to the task, because *something* is waiting for it. The something is determined by the WakeBits in the message queue. The scheduler however, knows nothing of why the task should be woken up, just that it should be. WaitEvent() simply waits for the mailbox flag to pop up. SleepHq() checks what's in the mailbox and either waits some more for a desired QS_xxx "letter", or returns when it finds what it wants. If SleepHq() sees a QS_SENDMESSAGE in the mailbox (essentially, an InSendMessage()), SleepHq() takes it out, deals with it promptly, using ReceiveMessage(), and goes back to waiting for the desired QS_xxx letter. In OS/2 Presentation Manager, the act of "sleeping" is simplified by just using a semaphore for each message queue. A Presentation Manager process can have more than one message queue, but only one queue per thread. The equivalent to calling WaitEvent() in OS/2 is to block on a semaphore. When there's input for a particular queue, the semaphore is "tickled," and the thread wakes up. Indeed, it was noted earlier that the WaitEvent()/PostEvent() pair of functions essentially treat offset 6 in the TDB as a counting semaphore.

SetWakeBit2()

Now that we've seen how SleepHq() waits for the QS_xxx messages to appear, let's see where the QS_xxx bits come from in the first place. The SetWakeBit2() function sets the WakeBits in the application's message queue, as well as ensuring that the program gets scheduled so that it can respond to the message.

```
void SetWakeBit2(HANDLE hQueue, UINT WakeBit)
{
    hQueue.ChangeBit |= WakeBit      // Turn on the QS_xxx flags
    hQueue.WakeBit   |= WakeBit

    // If we're setting a QS_xxx bit that the queue is waiting
    // for, force the scheduler to schedule the task
    if ( WakeBit & hQueue.WakeMask )
    {
        hQueue.WakeMask = 0
        PostEvent() to hQueue's task     // See Chapter 6 for info
    }
}
```

SetWakeBit2() is a very popular internal routine. It is called by the following functions in USER:

- WakeSomeone(). This routine is called by the hardware event handlers when a message has been added to the system queue. It sets the QS_MOUSE or QS_KEY bits.
- IncPaintCount(). When a window region is invalidated, IncPaintCount() sets the QS_PAINT bit and increments a counter. There's a corresponding DecPaintCount() that decrements the counter. When the counter value goes down to zero, the QS_PAINT bit is turned off.
- SendMessage(). During an intertask SendMessage(), SetWakeBit2() sets the QS_-SENDMESSAGE bits in the queue of the receiving task, so that the task wakes up and processes the message.
- ReceiveMessage(). During an intertask SendMessage(), when the receiving task is done processing the message and needs to wake up the sending task to receive the result, this function sets a bit that's not included in the previously discussed QS_xxx bits.
- ScanTimers(). Called by the timer interrupt service routine, this routine sets the QS_TIMER bit if sufficient time has elapsed. The USER timer interrupt service routine is installed using CreateSystemTimer(). The CreateSystemTimer() rate is the smallest rate that's been specified in all the SetTimer() invocations.
- WriteMessage(). PostMessage() and PostAppMessage() call PostMessage2(), which uses WriteMessage() to put the message in the application's queue, and sets the QS_POSTMESSAGE bit.

Bringing It All Together—GetMessage(), PeekMessage(), and DispatchMessage()

At this point, we can now put together what we've learned about queues, sleeping, wakebits, and all the rest and show how GetMessage() and DispatchMessage() do their thing. First, in the code below, we see that GetMessage() and PeekMessage() are really just front ends for GetMessage2(), which does most of the actual work. Put another way, GetMessage() and PeekMessage() share most of their code, so the following pseudocode is for the GetMessage()/PeekMessage() front ends and the GetMessage2() back end.

GetMessage() and PeekMessage()

```
// "flags" are the "flags" parameter to PeekMessage()

// "removeFlag" is a local indicating whether a message will be
//  read from the queue.

// WakeMask is a local containing a QX_xxx mask of messages types
// that GetMessage()/PeekMessage() are waiting for.

// WakeBits is a local containing the QS_xxx bits that
// indicate which types of messages are waiting for this task.

PeekMessage:
    Is_GetMessage_call = 0

    goto GetMessage2

GetMessage:
    Is_GetMessage_call = 1

    Insert a flags WORD in the stack frame so that the stack
    frame for GetMessage() is the same as for PeekMessage().
    The flag is set to PM_REMOVE.

GetMessage2:        // This is where GetMessage() and PeekMessage()
                    // start sharing their code

    // See Chapter 6 for more details on locked task
    if ( current task is locked )
        set PM_NOYIELD in flags

    removeFlag = flags & PM_REMOVE

    Unlock the system queue if this task holds it
```

```
    if ( (msgMin != 0) or (msgMax != 0) )
        Call function to set up WakeMask for the specified
        message range
    else
        WakeMask = QS_MOUSE | QS_KEY | QS_POSTMESSAGE
                    | QS_TIMER | QS_PAINT

begin_looking_for_msgs:
    if ( !CheckForNewInput() )      // Pseudocode below
        goto wait_for_input

    if ( system queue not locked )
        goto not_in_system_queue

    if ( system queue not locked by current queue )
        goto not_in_system_queue

    if ( (QS_MOUSE | QS_KEY) set in WakeMask and WakeMask )
        if ( ScanSysQueue() )
            goto GetMessage_have_msg

not_in_system_queue:
    if ( QS_POSTMESSAGE set in WakeBits and WakeMask )
        if ( ReadMessage() )
            goto GetMessage_have_msg

    if ( (QS_MOUSE or QS_KEY) set in WakeBits and WakeMask )
        if ( ScanSysQueue() )
            goto GetMessage_have_msg

    if ( !CheckForNewInput() )
        goto wait_for_input

    if ( QS_PAINT set in WakeBits and WakeMask )
        if ( DoPaint() )
            goto GetMessage_have_msg

    if ( PM_NOYIELD set in flags )
        goto check_for_timer_msg

    UserYield()   // Yield after paint test, before timer test.

    if ( !CheckForNewInput() )
        goto wait_for_input

check_for_timer_msg:
```

```
    if ( QS_TIMER set in WakeBits and WakeMask )
        if ( DoTimer() )
            goto begin_looking_for_msgs

wait_for_input:
    if ( FShrinkGDI )
        ShrinkGDIheap()     // Shrink the GDI heap?

    if ( Is_GetMessage_call == 0 )  // If not in GetMessage(), we
        goto PeekMessage_exit       // must be in PeekMessage()

    SleepHq(wakemask)   // Wait for a message. Calls WaitEvent().

    goto begin_looking_for_msgs

GetMessage_have_message:
    if ( a WH_GETMESSAGE hook is installed )
        call the hook function

    if ( Is_GetMessage_call == 0 )  // If not in GetMessage(), we
        return 1                    // must be in PeekMessage()

    if ( returning msg == WM_QUIT ) // This is responsible for
        return 0                    // making the main
    else                            // "while ( !GetMessage() )"
        return 1                    // loop exit.

PeekMessage_exit:
    if ( ! PM_NOYIELD )
        UserYield()         // Yield to any higher priority app
                            // See Chapter 6 for significance of
    return 0                // PeekMessage() calling UserYield(), instead
                            // of WaitEvent().
```

CheckForNewInput()

```
// Returns Zero Flag set if no desired input flag is set
//
// WakeMask & WakeBits are in registers, and are the same
// thing as WakeMask and WakeBits in GetMessage2()

top:
    Get handle of current queue

    if ( QS_SENDMESSAGE set in the queues wakebits )
    {
        ReceiveMessage()
        goto top
    }
```

```
// AND instruction sets the Zero flag if any bits match
AND WakeMask, WakeBits together

return
```

We can now examine how each of the five types of messages are dealt with in the GetMessage()/PeekMessage() code:

- QS_SENDMESSAGE. GetMessage2() calls CheckForNewInput() several times. Checking for sent messages is its first priority. If GetMessage2() ends up sleeping via SleepHq(), SleepHq() checks for sent messages.
- QS_POSTMESSAGE. ReadMessage() extracts the message from the application message queue. The message fields are copied into the addresses specified in the GetMessage() or PeekMessage() call.
- QS_MOUSE and QS_KEY. ScanSysQueue() extracts the message from the system message queue. The message fields are copied into the addresses specified in the GetMessage() or PeekMessage() call.
- QS_PAINT. DoPaint() extracts the painting parameters from the WND structure. The message fields are copied into the addresses specified in the GetMessage() or PeekMessage() call.
- QS_TIMER. DoTimer() synthesizes, then writes a timer message into the application queue. GetMessage2() then starts at the beginning and finds the timer message as if it were a QS_POSTMESSAGE.

From the GetMessage()/GetMessage2()/PeekMessage() pseudocode, we can draw a couple of conclusions. First, a task calling GetMessage() or PeekMessage() does not yield to any other applications if there are messages waiting for it. (As noted in Chapter 6, a task can call Yield() to relinquish control, even when there are messages waiting for it.)

Secondly, there is a definite pecking order of message priority. Messages sent with SendMessages() always have top priority, which is necessary because the task that did the SendMessage() is cooling its heels, waiting for the reply. Next in priority are messages posted with PostMessage(). Messages from the input system (mouse and keyboard) come next, followed by WM_PAINT messages. Checking for WM_PAINT comes after the other message types because processing the other messages might cause additional paints to be needed. To alleviate the potential for doing unnecessary paints, WM_PAINT messages are handled late in the game, after things have settled down. Bringing up the rear, the last messages checked for before GetMessage2() gives up and goes to sleep are WM_TIMER messages. The ordering of these last two message types is critical. If WM_TIMER messages were handled before WM_PAINT messages, programs like CLOCK wouldn't work! (Exercise for the reader: Why?)

There's a *Microsoft Knowledge Base* article that claims that GetMessage() and PeekMessage() will yield to other tasks if there are messages waiting for these tasks, before they check for WM_PAINT and WM_TIMER messages. Based upon examination of the code in Windows, this does not appear to be entirely accurate. Instead, it seems that the yield occurs before checking for WM_TIMERs, but *not* before checking for WM_PAINTs.

It appears that the above message priorities are cast in stone. However, a clever application can play with the order that messages are received. How? You simply set the values of uMsgFilterMax and uMsgFilterMin to encompass messages of the various types and use PeekMessage (PM_REMOVE) to get the message.

NOTE: the following section relies heavily on knowledge of the scheduler, events, and idling, which are described in detail in Chapter 6.

Many applications use a PeekMessage() loop to do background processing during lengthy sequences, while still allowing other applications to receive messages and respond to the user. There are several *Microsoft Knowledge Base* articles that warn that PeekMessage() loops should be used sparingly, as they never allow the system to idle when no user input is occurring. The idle loop in the scheduler generates an INT 2Fh, Function 1689h, as well as an INT 28h, the DOS idle interrupt. Some power management schemes use these interrupts to determine when the hardware can be put into a low power idle state. Many TSRs also rely on receiving INT 28h. PeekMessage() prevents this idle loop from executing.

From looking at the pseudocode for PeekMessage() and GetMessage(), it might be hard to pick out exactly why GetMessage() allows the system to idle, while PeekMessage() does not. The answer lies in what happens when there are no waiting messages to be processed. If GetMessage() is called, SleepHq() is invoked. SleepHq() calls WaitEvent(), which decrements the event count for the task down to 0 before calling the core scheduling routine in KERNEL, Reschedule(). If the task has no events waiting for it, there's a good chance that Reschedule() will fall into its idle loop and generate the appropriate idle interrupts.

On the other hand, if there are no messages waiting to be processed, and if PeekMessage() was called, the code invokes UserYield() (assuming that the PM_NOYIELD flag wasn't specified). UserYield() checks for sent messages and eventually calls the KERNEL routine OldYield(). OldYield() in turn calls Reschedule(). You might think that this would be enough for Reschedule() to fall into its idle loop, just like when called by WaitEvent(). This is not the case however. OldYield() first *increments* the event count field for the current task before calling Reschedule(). This guarantees that Reschedule() will never enter its idle loop because it always finds that the current task has an event waiting for it. PeekMessage() is documented as returning control to the calling task, whether or not it has messages, and the complicated mechanism just described is simply the way this always-return behavior is implemented. Because the calling task *stays* the current task, whether or not it has messages, obviously the system never goes idle.

DispatchMessage()

Once an application has retrieved a message, it is expected to deal with it. Typically, the message is dealt with by dispatching it to the appropriate window procedure. Luckily, Windows provides the DispatchMessage() function to do this, rather than requiring the programmer to determine the address of the window procedure and call it directly. DispatchMessage() looks like:

```
Pseudocode for DispatchMessage()

LPMSG lpMsg // Pointer to passed in message.
```

```
        // Will be used as scratch variable.

    if ( (msg.msg != WM_TIMER) && (msg.msg != WM_SYSTIMER) )
        goto handle_normally

    if ( msg.lParam == 0 )
        goto handle_normally

    push msg fields onto stack (except lParam)

    GetTickCount()  // Returns DWORD in DX:AX, which becomes the
    push DX:AX      // lParam parameter for the WM_TIMER message.

    lpMsg = msg.lParam  // Timer function callback address

    AX = SS             // Fake a MakeProcInstance() thunk

    goto call_function  // now go call the window procedure

handle_normally:
    if ( msg.hwnd == 0 )
        return;

    push msg fields on stack

    if ( msg.msg == WM_PAINT )
        set "paint" flag in WND structure    // see Chapter 4

    lpMsg = Window proc address // stored in WND data structure
                                // pointed to by msg.hwnd

    AX = hInstance from WND structure   // Pretend there's
                                        // a MakeProcInstance()
                                        // thunk

call_function:
    ES = DS = SS    // Set all segment registers to hInstance
                    // of the application

    call [lpMsg]    // Call the window proceedure (or timer
                    // callback fn). Remember, lpMsg is now
                    // used to store the address of the window
                    // function (or timer callback function)
                    // that needs to be called
```

```
    if ( msg.msg != WM_PAINT )
        goto DispatchMessage_done

    // Check for destroyed window
    if ( ! IsWindow(msg.msg) )
        goto DispatchMessage_done

    if ( "paint" flag in WND structure still set )
        goto No_BeginPaint

DispatchMessage_done:
    return

No_BeginPaint:
    Display debugging message "Missing BeginPaint..."

    Call DoSyncPaint() to handle the painting correctly

    goto DispatchMessage_done
```

The DispatchMessage() code is straightforward, with only a few interesting things worth pointing out. At its beginning, there's special handling for WM_TIMER and WM_SYSTIMER messages. If the lParam field of the message is non-zero, DispatchMessage() calls a user supplied callback, rather than a standard window procedure. The SDK documentation for SetTimer() describes how to use timer callbacks.

Another interesting facet of the DispatchMessage() code is its handling of misbehaving programs that forget to do a BeginPaint() in their handler for WM_PAINT messages. Apparently Microsoft felt that this is enough of a problem such that DispatchMessage() always checks to see if BeginPaint() was called by the message handler. If the program didn't call BeginPaint(), DispatchMessage() goes ahead and does default painting to correct the situation, and whines at you with a debug message if you're running the debug version of Windows.

Last of all, sharp eyes might notice that before the window procedure is called, DispatchMessage() sets DS to the hInstance of the application, a setting that compensates for applications that fail to export their callback functions properly. Under Windows 3.0, if you don't export your functions, there is a good chance that when your window procedure is called, the DS register will be set incorrectly, and you would most likely have a GP fault. Some people have claimed that it's no longer necessary to export your functions and call MakeProcInstance(), as long as your application only runs under Windows 3.1. Whether this is sound advice or not is up for debate, but apparently Microsoft felt that it fixed enough problems to warrant trying it.

Advanced Study: Anatomy of a SendMessage() Call

SendMessage() is one of the most frequently used function calls in Windows and one of the least understood. Even though the SDK documentation is fairly lucid on what a SendMessage() does, many programmers are under the mistaken assumption that SendMessage() simply calls the appropriate window procedure. The fact that a SendMessage() might need to operate in two different task contexts is often forgotten.

The methods for synchronizing two different tasks in order to bounce a message and its response back and forth are highly complex. The receiver of a sent message might need to send a message to another task before it can respond to the original message. This can lead to nested SendMessage()s. We've seen how the messaging system works for normal messages, and we've seen indications that intertask SendMessages() are dealt with in a special way. Now we're ready to tackle the toughest portion of the messaging system and see what happens during an intertask SendMessage().

SendMessage()

```
Pseudocode for SendMessage()

    if ( receiving HWnd == -1 )
        goto BroadcastMessage   // Not included here

    Verify sending app has a message queue

    Get receiving app's queue from receiving hWnd

    // Are the sending and receiving queues the same?
    Intertask = ( receivingHQueue != sendingHQueue )

    Call any installed WH_CALLWNDPROC hooks

    if ( Intertask )
        goto InterTaskSend

    // The next section deals with calling a window proceedure within
    // the same program. This is the simple case, and is much easier
    // than calling between two different programs (below)

    Push address of the wndproc of the receiving WND structure
    on the stack

    Push SendMessage params on stack

    put hInstance into AX   // Fake MakeProcInstance() thunk

    Load DS & ES from the SS register   // In case callee didn't
                                        // export properly!
```

```
    Call through the wndproc address in the window structure //See Chapter 4

SendMessage_done:
    return to caller

SendMessage_error:  // Common JMP location when errors occurr
    put 0 in DX:AX

    goto SendMessage_done

    // SendMessage()'s that go between different tasks come here.
    // This is where the code gets complex.

InterTaskSend:
    If ( A task is locked )
    {
        display a diagnostic in debugging version
        Goto SendMessage_Error
    }

    if ( sending task is terminating )
    {
        display a diagnostic in debugging version
        Goto SendMessage_Error
    }

    If (SendMessage parameter area in sending app is already used)
    {
        display a diagnostic in debugging version
        Sleep until the parameter area is free  // Uses SleepHq()
    }

    Grab parameter area in sending app

    Save the address where the result of the call will be stored

    Copy the SendMessage parameters off the stack into the
    sending hQueue

    Put the receiving queue at the head of the SendMessage() list

    // Set bits to wake up the receiving task
    SetWakeBit2( QS_SENDMESSAGE )
```

```
SendMessage_wakeup_receiving_task:
    if ( a previous SendMessage() has completed )
        goto got_reply

    Turn off "have result" flags in sending queue

    Call DirectedYield() to force the child task to run next

    // When the DirectedYield() returns, the receiving task
    // should have woken up, and called ReceiveMessage() and
    // ReplyMessage(), which are described below.

    Sleep until result is back from child

    // Uses SleepHq(). Part of the code below is probably redundant, because
    // there already should be a result available when the prior
    // DirectedYield() returned.

got_reply:
    Copy the return value to the "result" area on the stack

    Release parameter area in sending queue

    if ( Not replied to )
        goto SendMessage_wakeup_receiving_task

    goto SendMessage_done
```

ReceiveMessage()

```
    Make sure there is a SendMessage waiting for us

    Remove sending queue from list of SendMessage() queues

    Clear QS_SENDMSG bit if the list of queues is empty

    Save copies of the sending hQueue and pointer to area
    where results should be saved in the sending task

    Free the the SMPARAMS area in the sending queue

    make sure target window is still valid

    Copy the ExtraInfo data from sender to receiver
```

```
    Call the target window proc

    Call ReplyMessage() // ReceiveMessage() & ReplyMessage() call
                        // each other!
```

ReplyMessage()

```
// Reply message takes the value that should be returned to
// the sender as a parameter. Here, it's called "return_value"

ReplyMessage_start:
    If ( message has already been replied to, or if no sending queue )
        return

    if ( QS_SENDMESSAGE bit set in receiving queue)
    {
        ReceiveMessage()          // ReplyMessage() and
        Goto ReplyMessage_start // ReceiveMessage()
    }                             // call each other!

    if ( result area in use )
    {
        OldYield()
        Goto ReplyMessage_start
    }

    Copy return_value into sending hQueue

    Restore pointer to result area on stack in the sending hQueue

    Set AlreadyRepliedFlag

    SetWakeBit2( QS_SMRESULT )  // Tell the sending task that
                                // its reply is ready.

    DirectedYield(SendingTask)  // Switch directly to the sending
                                // task.
```

As the code at the top of SendMessage() shows, handling the case where an application sends itself a message is very straightforward. SendMessage() pushes the parameters on the stack, and calls the window procedure. The majority of the code for SendMessage() is for handling SendMessage() calls in which the receiving window is in a different task (an *intertask* SendMessage()). Within the intertask SendMessage(), and in ReceiveMessage() and ReplyMessage(), as well, a large amount of the code is for handling nested SendMessage() calls. As SendMessage() calls are nested, a linked list of queues that are waiting for the SendMessage() to return builds up. The most recent queue is always at the head of the list. As each message is replied to, the head of the list is removed, and the list shrinks down, eventually, to an empty list. (See offsets 38h and 3Ah in the message queue structure in Table 7-1.)

Although not commonly done, ReplyMessage() can be called by application programs. For instance, inside of a WH_CALLWNDPROC hook, ReplyMessage() can be used to prevent the window that ordinarily would get the message from actually receiving it. Another case where you might call ReplyMessage() is when you're handling a message that's been sent to you through SendMessage(). The sending program cannot execute until your program finishes processing the message. If part of your handling of the message involves Windows functions that yield control (MessageBox(), and so forth), a potential deadlock situation can arise. By calling ReplyMessage() before doing anything which might yield control, you can prevent this situation.

Problems with the Windows Input System

The fatal flaw in the Windows input system, as well as in OS/2 PM, has to do with the single threaded input system. If an application fails to call GetMessage() or PeekMessage() in a timely manner, the system deadlocks. The mouse can be moved around, and background processing in enhanced mode DOS boxes continues, but Windows applications do not respond to mouse or keyboard input. The system is as good as hung.

The underlying reason for this is inside GetMessage2() where applications yield to other tasks in the system. Between successive calls to GetMessage2(), no other Windows program can run. For example, let's say a database program gets a WM_COMMAND message, which it interprets to mean, "Go sort this database of 300,000 records." If the program dutifully performs the sort operation and takes 45 minutes, then all applications in the system are deadlocked for 45 minutes until the application calls GetMessage() again. Occasionally an application tries to be helpful and lamely changes the icon to an hourglass. This is not extremely helpful, other than to let you know that it's time to get a cup of coffee.

This wonderful quirk in the messaging system really rears its ugly head when you attempt to write a Windows hosted debugger (also called a GUI debugger). A GUI debugger is a debugger for Windows programs that itself uses the Windows display mechanisms. What's the problem with that? Imagine the following scenario. A GUI debugger places a breakpoint in the debugee's code. Eventually, the program being debugged hits the breakpoint and stops. Now we have a problem on our hands. The program being debugged is stopped so it cannot call GetMessage() to yield control to other tasks. That means no other tasks, *including* the GUI debugger, can get their messages. The debugger can't even respond to mouse clicks telling the debuggee to run again. It's time for the reset button.

Some readers are probably saying, "But there are GUI debuggers available!" How do they deal with this situation? Unfortunately, the answer is, not extremely well. When the debuggee hits the breakpoint, or stops for any reason, the GUI debugger takes over the duties of calling GetMessage() and DispatchMessage() for the debuggee. The debugger must prevent any code in the debuggee process from running. To do this, the debugger must somehow intercept all messages that would normally go to the debuggee windows and deal with them itself.

One way to intercept all messages destined for the debuggee is to subclass all of the debuggee's windows. A major question then arises. How do you deal with all the messages that were originally intended for the debuggee? The debugger surely doesn't know how to paint the debuggee's windows in response to a WM_PAINT message. Situations such as DDE transactions where message ordering is critical are even harder to deal with. Unfortunately, there's no 100% perfect solution. It's up to the designers of the GUI debugger to deal with this situation as best they can. You may now understand why Turbo Debugger for Windows (TDW) and Codeview for Windows (CVW) are text mode debuggers, rather than GUI debuggers.

In Win32, the input mechanism has been redesigned. One of the main goals of the redesign was to eliminate the input system problem. To accomplish this, Win32 has separate input queues for each task. A thread in the Win32 subsystem continually assigns the messages to the appropriate applications queue as the input events occur. This allows programs to deal with messages in their own sweet time, without adversely affecting the responsiveness of the system as a whole. Helen Custer's book, *Inside Windows NT*, describes the details of the NT input system. Unfortunately, this improved functionality is really part of Windows NT, rather than the Win32 API; and so this functionality does not extend to Win32s applications. Under Win32s, the Windows 3.1 USER is still in charge of the input system, thereby causing Win32s applications to be in the same boat as regular 16-bit Windows programs. Sigh!

If you know that your Windows 3.x program will take a significant amount of time to process a message, you can allow it to yield to other programs by using a PeekMessage() loop. A prime example of PeekMessage() loops in action are the Windows hosted development environments that compile your program, while still allowing other applications to be used. The details of implementing a PeekMessage() loop have been covered to death in *Microsoft Knowledge Base* articles, as well as in magazine articles. Thus, I won't go into the details of implementing one here. If you do use a PeekMessage() loop, be sure to read the caveats given earlier concerning power consumption and idling.

WM_QUIT

The Windows input system is a complex beast. It's integrally tied to many other parts of Windows, especially the scheduler (Chapter 6) and the windowing system (Chapter 4). Of all the subsystems discussed in this book, the messaging system is almost certainly one of the most important to understand if you want to really understand Windows.

CHAPTER 8

Dynamic Linking

In the days when DOS was the only game in town, programming was a lot simpler in some respects. You wrote your code, compiled and linked it, and were done with it. All the pieces of your program came together when you invoked the linker. Occasionally you might get fancy and generate or intercept an interrupt to communicate with some other code, such as DOS itself. For the most part, though, your program remained essentially a single, self-contained entity.

With Windows, the situation is much more complex. Your code calls routines in libraries that the linker never sees when it links your program. Put another way, the linker can't possibly fill in the target addresses of the CALLs to these library routines. To take it a step further, your program can even call functions that you and your program had no concept of when you compiled and linked. There's no way to retreat under a rock and ignore this dynamic linking aspect of Windows. *Every* Windows program does dynamic linking of one form or another. Whenever you call a Windows API function in your code, another dynamic link occurs.

With this added complexity comes enormous power and flexibility, however. A prime example of this flexibility is the device drivers used by Windows. The same core Windows files (USER, KERNEL, GDI, and so forth) work with a multitude of different video, mouse, keyboard, sound, communications port, and printer drivers. This feat is achievable because dynamic linking allows the target of CALL instructions to be filled in at the last possible moment, while the program is running. When Windows starts up, KERNEL uses SYSTEM.INI to tell it which drivers should be loaded and fixed up. Instead of having to re-link all of the various Windows components every time you change a driver, instead you just modify a line in the SYSTEM.INI file.

Although Windows is the first exposure to dynamic linking for many PC programmers, it is certainly not the first system with these capabilities. OS/2 uses a dynamic linking implementation which is virtually identical to Windows. For instance, the OS/2 DosGetProcAddr() corresponds exactly to GetProcAddress() under Windows. UNIX, with its shared libraries, has a form of dynamic linking. In fact, almost all real operating systems are fundamentally based on the availability of dynamic linking and have been so for a long time. It's DOS that's out of the mainstream with its need for programs to be entirely self-contained.

In this chapter, we first come to a good definition of dynamic linking. We cover both implicit dynamic linking, as well as explicit dynamic linking using the GetProcAddress() function. Then, we see how dynamic linking is implemented in Windows 3.1 and finish up by examining some of the issues, such as MakeProcInstance() thunks and exporting, that affect how your program performs dynamic linking.

Before we begin our discussion, I'd like to note that the concepts described in this chapter rely heavily on an understanding of the module table described in Chapter 3. If you're not familiar with the basic concepts of NE files and in-memory module tables, you should probably read the appropriate sections of Chapter 3 before continuing.

What is Dynamic Linking?

When thinking about dynamic linking, it helps to remember that everything eventually boils down to machine instructions. When compiling or assembling your program, the compiler or assembler generates machine code and places it in an object file (an .OBJ file on the PC). For instance, a CALL instruction generated by your compiler consists of two parts, the CALL opcode and the address where the CPU should start executing. Your compiler can emit the CALL opcode byte at compilation time. It can't, however, know the exact address to which the CPU should transfer. The compiler simply can't know where in memory the target of the call instruction will be. The target address of the call instruction can vary each time Windows is loaded. The resulting machine instructions are therefore incomplete (see Figure 8-1).

Figure 8-1: A Typical FAR CALL Fixup in an EXE or DLL.

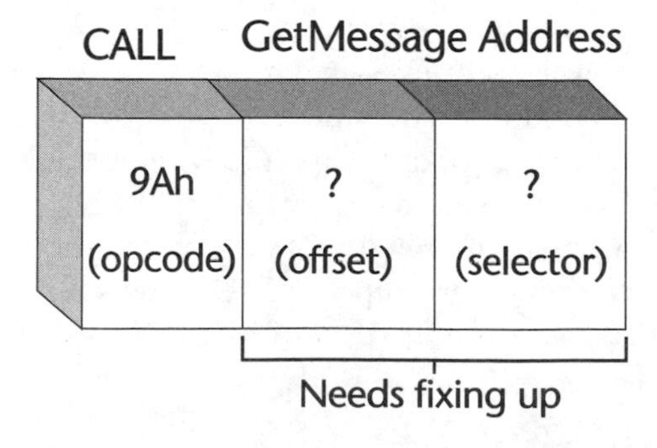

The job of completing the instruction is left to the linker. To assist the linker in finishing the instruction, the compiler emits a fixup record in the OBJ file. The fixup record tells the linker what the intended target routine is. For instance, if you call a function "Foo" in another source file, the fixup record tells the linker to find the code for the Foo function in the list of OBJ or LIB files presented to it. The linker should then put Foo's address into the second part of the CALL instruction, thereby completing the instruction. The *MS-DOS Encyclopedia* has a very good explanation of how this works.

A more physical example of a fixup can be found throughout this book. In writing the chapters, I needed a way to refer to other chapters of the book by their chapter number. However, I was not sure how many chapters there would be or what their order would be. Because I didn't know actual chapter numbers when writing a reference, I placed an XXX wherever a chapter number should go. The XXXs are a form of fixup. Later on, when the book was being prepared for printing, I searched for all the XXXs and replaced them with the correct chapter number. As you'll see later, the Windows loader does something similar to this when it loads an EXE or DLL.

Coming back to the topic at hand (compiler generated fixups), an important point needs to be made. The compiler knows ***absolutely nothing*** about the intended targets of the call instruction. It cannot and should not know that GetMessage() will be in a Windows DLL, while Foo()'s code is in another source module in your program. The compiler is just an ignorant code generator that gives the linker the name of the call target in the fixup record and expects the linker to sort out where the function's code resides.

Also, before we go any further, we do need to make one other point, to be completely accurate. Not *every* dynamic link fixup involves a CALL instruction. Any instruction, including variables in data segments that could be affected by a fixup record, can be handled with dynamic linking. For the most part, though, dynamic linking is used with the FAR CALL instruction, so that's what we focus on here.

The linker's job is to collect all the OBJ and LIB files given to it and create a file that the operating system loader can load into memory. (LIB files are essentially just collections of OBJ files strung one after the other, so we treat them as OBJ files for this discussion.) If there are any instructions that the compiler could not complete (as described earlier), the linker must fill in the target address. This task is called performing the fixups, or resolving fixups.

Now we're ready to see what differentiates dynamic linking from static linking. A static link occurs when the linker is able to find the target of the fixup in one of the OBJ or regular LIB files given to it. In this instance, the linker patches the address portion of the CALL instruction with the correct address and then forgets the fixup record. It's no longer needed. Dynamic linking occurs when the linker can't possibly know the address of the fixup target. These fixups aren't performed until the program or DLL is actually loaded into memory, hence the term dynamic linking.

The emphasis of this chapter is on the intermodule aspect of dynamic linking, that is, CALLs between two separately linked Windows modules. However, the simplest form of dynamic linking is termed base linking; it doesn't involve any outside modules. If your program has more than one code segment, it's very likely that you have FAR CALLs between the two segments. When linking a program like this, the linker doesn't know the actual selector value that the Windows loader will assign to the various segments. Since the linker doesn't know which selectors will be assigned to the EXE or DLL's segments, it has to give up and let somebody else resolve the fixup. The "somebody else" is the Windows loader. More specifically, it's the internal KERNEL SegReloc() function, called by LoadModule(), that performs the fixup. LoadModule() is described in Chapter 3.

Just as the compiler emitted fixups to tell the linker about instructions it couldn't complete, the linker puts information in the EXE or DLL file telling the Windows loader about fixups that the loader needs to resolve. This is nothing more than "passing the buck." The Windows loader resolves all the fixups for a given segment in a module when it loads the segment into memory. How the Windows loader can take the fixup information and find the correct address with which to resolve it is one of the primary focuses of this chapter. If you're interested, the format of fixups in EXE and DLL files are given in the NE file documentation in the Windows 3.1 SDK.

To give an example of base dynamic linking, imagine that you have a program with two code segments. In segment 1, you call a function in segment 2. A FAR CALL instruction is needed. Part of the FAR CALL instruction is the selector value that should be put in the CS register, which in this case, is the selector for the second segment. Since there's no way for the linker to know the actual selector the loader will pick for the second code segment, all the linker can do is emit a fixup record in the EXE or DLL. The fixup tells the loader to figure out what selector it assigned to the second segment and patch the FAR CALL instruction with the selector value. How does the loader remember which selector value it assigned to the second segment? Simple. As Chapter 3 describes, each module table holds a segment table containing information about each logical segment in the module, including the associated selector value.

Another type of dynamic linking happens when the linker is unable to find the code for the target routine anywhere in the OBJ files given to it. This means that the destination of the CALL instruction must lie somewhere *outside* the code in the module being linked. For example, your program can call GetMessage(), but the GetMessage() code is nowhere to be found in the OBJ files passed to the linker. Instead, the GetMessage() code is in the USER.EXE file.

At this point, you may be wondering, "But how does the linker know that a GetMessage() call can be resolved by the Windows loader, while other calls can't be?" Every Windows programmer has had the experience of getting an "Undefined symbol" message when linking a Windows EXE or DLL. What criteria does the linker use for determining which fixups are valid, while others aren't?

The answer lies in the magic of import libraries, which we cover in more detail later on. For now, it's enough to say that an import library associates names (for example, GetMessage), with a set of "magic cookies." For instance, all of the Windows APIs that you typically call have their names and associated magic cookies contained in an import library (usually IMPORT.LIB or LIBW.LIB). If the linker can't find the name it's looking for in the OBJ file list, it searches the import libraries and the IMPORTS section of the DEF file (more on IMPORTS later). If the linker finds the name in an import library or in the IMPORTS section, it puts the magic cookies in the fixup table of the EXE or DLL. When the Windows loader comes along to load this module, it uses the "cookies" to find the correct target address to fixup the instruction with. Only if the linker can't find the name of the function after searching in the OBJ files, the import libraries, and the IMPORTS section, will it give the "Undefined symbol" error. Calling a function in a DLL, and using an import library to tell the linker about it, is called implicit dynamic linking. The Windows loader knows through the module reference table to load the target DLLs, if necessary, before fixing up the call instruction. Once you provide the import library to the linker, your work is done.

A third type of dynamic linking occurs even later, after the program has already been loaded and is executing. This form of dynamic linking involves the program explicitly asking the KERNEL module for the address of a function in a loaded DLL. If KERNEL is able to locate the function, it returns the function's address, so that the requesting program can call it. You can request the address of a function with the GetProcAddress() API. Typically, you call GetProcAddress() and store the result in a function pointer. You then call the function indirectly through the function pointer. We discuss the implementation of GetProcAddress() in a bit.

Requirements for Intermodule Dynamic Linking

In order to perform either kind of intermodule dynamic linking, implicit or with GetProcAddress(), two things are necessary. The first requirement is that you know the Windows module that you're trying to link to. This can be either a module name, specified in the NAME or LIBRARY line in the DEF file, or the associated module handle. For instance, USER is a module name, and you can get its module handle by calling:

```
hModuleUSER = GetModuleHandle("USER");
```

The format of the module table which the module handle refers to is discussed in detail in Chapter 3. As that chapter also mentions, the module tables are kept in a linked list, so all GetModuleHandle() needs to do is walk the list, comparing the passed string argument to the module name stored in the module table. Also, note that sometimes you can hard code in a module name such as USER, while at other times, you may need to get the module name from an INI file. A good example is a printer driver.

When you implicitly link to a function (for example, when you call GetMessage() directly, resolving the fixup with the import library), the module *name* is stored in the imported names table of the executable file. For instance, GetMessage() is in the USER module. If your program calls GetMessage(), "USER" appears in the imported names table of the EXE or DLL. Alternatively, when you dynamically link explicitly with GetProcAddress(), the loader needs to know the module *handle* for the module containing the function you're linking to (see above example). The point is that either a module name or a module handle is sufficient to identify the target module.

Internally, module handles are the only thing KERNEL uses in its dynamic linking functions. If a module is specified by its name, KERNEL automatically finds the corresponding module handle and uses that from then on. For example, when you load a new module in the system, KERNEL takes each module name string in the imported names table and converts it to the corresponding module handle. KERNEL stores the module handles in the in-memory module table and uses the handles from that point on. The imported names table isn't needed anymore.

The second requirement for dynamic linking is that an entry point must exist for the target to which you're fixing up. The entry point can either be an integer value, termed an ordinal here, or an ASCII string. If you do specify a string, KERNEL converts the string to its corresponding entry ordinal. What exactly is an entry ordinal? In each module table resides an entry table (hence, the need to specify which module you're linking to). The entry table maps an entry ordinal value to an address in the module's code or data segments.

To give an example of this, the GetMessage() function is the 108th entry in the USER module. In my copy of USER.EXE, the entry table tells me that the address for the 108th entry is in logical segment 1, offset 0B74Dh. When loading a code segment that contains a call to GetMessage(), the loader sees a fixup for the 108th entry in USER. The fixup also indicates where in the loading code segment the fixup should be applied. Using the example shown in Figure 8-1, the fixup indicates that selector and offset fields in the FAR CALL need to be changed to contain the address of GetMessage(). The offset field (one byte into the instruction) will be set to B74Dh. The segment field (three bytes into the instruction) will be set to the selector for USER's first segment.

The loader goes through the following steps:

1. Figure out the module handle for USER.
2. Use the module handle to access the entry table inside USER's module table. In the entry table, the loader sees that the code for the 108th entry is at logical segment 1, offset 0B74Dh.
3. Use the module's segment table to look up the selector value for USER's first logical segment (for example, 05BFh). The loader now knows that GetMessage() is at the physical address 05BFh:B74Dh.
4. Patch the segment and offset portions of FAR CALL instruction with the physical address of GetMessage().

A moment ago, we mentioned that you can specify a function name, rather than an entry ordinal, when dynamic linking. This is most commonly done when you call GetProcAddress() (although there is also a way to specify an entry ordinal rather than a name to GetProcAddress()). In addition, it is possible to implicitly link to a function by name, rather than by entry ordinal. This is rarely done, however. In all cases, if a function name is specified instead of an entry ordinal, KERNEL converts the name to its matching entry ordinal.

You might be wondering how KERNEL converts names to their matching entry ordinal value. The answer lies in a set of tables contained within the module table. These tables contain the resident and nonresident names. Both tables are just a series of uppercase strings like "GETMESSAGE", with each string followed by its corresponding entry ordinal value. As we see a bit later on, KERNEL scans these tables to match a given string to its entry ordinal. As its name implies, the resident names table is always in memory and is part of the module table. When KERNEL searches for a name, it always looks in the resident names table first. KERNEL loads the *nonresident names* table from disk each time it's needed. Since most dynamic linking is done implicitly, and therefore with entry ordinals, the *nonresident names* table is not loaded that often, so it usually doesn't reduce performance to have the table be nonresident. In fact, if you know that nobody will be linking to your DLL by name (with GetProcAddress() for example), you can remove the nonresident names table altogether.

If you're curious to see real examples of all these tables we've been discussing, run TDUMP (from Borland) or EXEHDR (from Microsoft) on some Windows EXEs and DLLs. Both of these programs give you comprehensive information for the tables contained within Windows EXE and DLL files. TDUMP displays the tables in a fairly raw format, showing you each table exactly as it exists in the file. Figure 8-2 below, shows a portion of the TDUMP output from PBRUSH.DLL. All of the tables discussed above can be seen in the output. Note that WEP is in the nonresident names table, which is a no-no according to Microsoft. It should be in the resident names table so that the nonresident names table doesn't need to be loaded during the DLL termination. EXEHDR tends to combine the information from several tables. You see more information in less space, but don't get quite the feel for what the tables actually look like.

Figure 8-2: Portion of TDUMP Output of PBRUSH.DLL.

```
Segment Table                       offset: 00C0h

    Segment Number: 01h
    Segment Type:    CODE           Alloc Size : 16BAh
    Sector Offset:   0019h          File length: 16B9h
    Attributes: Relocations

    Segment Number: 02h
    Segment Type:    DATA           Alloc Size : 0180h
    Sector Offset:   019Ah          File length: 00CEh
    Attributes: Moveable  Sharable  Preloaded

No Resource table present

Resident Name Table                 offset: 00D0h
    Module Name: 'PBRUSH'

Module Reference Table              offset: 00DAh
    Module  1: KERNEL
    Module  2: GDI

Imported Names Table                offset: 00DEh
    name                                   offset
    KERNEL                                  0001h
    GDI                                     0008h

Entry Table                         offset: 00EAh
  Fixed Segment Records (  8 Entries)   Segment: 0001h
    Entry    1: Offset: 0075h   Exported   Single data
```

Figure 8-2: Portion of TDUMP Output of PBRUSH.DLL. (continued)

```
    Entry    2: Offset: 009Eh   Exported   Single data
    Entry    3: Offset: 0208h   Exported   Single data
    Entry    4: Offset: 0220h   Exported   Single data
    Entry    5: Offset: 0341h   Exported   Single data
    Entry    6: Offset: 0541h   Exported   Single data
    Entry    7: Offset: 0770h   Exported   Single data
    Entry    8: Offset: 0D3Ch   Exported   Single data

Non-Resident Name Table         offset: 0105h
    Module Description: 'Virtual bitmap manager'
    Name: VSTRETCHBLT                      Entry:     6
    Name: WEP                              Entry:     1
    Name: DISCARDBAND                      Entry:     8
    Name: VDELETEOBJECT                    Entry:     7
    Name: VPATBLT                          Entry:     4
    Name: VBITBLT                          Entry:     5
    Name: GETVCACHEDC                      Entry:     3
    Name: VCREATEBITMAP                    Entry:     2

Segment Relocation Records
    Segment 0001h relocations
    type     offset       target
    PTR      0061h        KERNEL.4
    PTR      0831h        KERNEL.132
    PTR      0B8Dh        KERNEL.5
    PTR      0138h        KERNEL.6
    PTR      0BF6h        KERNEL.7

        ... rest of file omitted
```

What can we discern from the TDUMP output? Quite a lot. First off, there are two segments, a code and a data segment. We can also see the size of the two segments and where the raw data for the segments can be found in the file. The first entry in the resident names table is the module name PBRUSH. If we wanted to use GetProcAddress() to call routines in PBRUSH.DLL, we would first get the DLL's module handle in the following way, assuming PBRUSH.DLL is already loaded:

```
hModPBrush = GetModuleHandle("PBRUSH");
```

The module reference table tells us that PBRUSH.DLL calls functions in the KERNEL and GDI modules. From the entry table, we know there are eight functions that PBRUSH exports for use by outside EXEs or DLLs. The entry table also tells us that each of these exported functions is in segment 1, and gives the starting offsets of each function within segment 1.

The nonresident names table gives us the name of each exported function that appears in the entry table. For instance, if we wanted to call VSTRETCHBLT, assuming we knew its parameters, we could get its address like this:

```
lpfnVStretchBLT = GetProcAddress(hModPBrush, "VSTRETCHBLT");
```

or alternatively, as we'll see later:

```
lpfnVStretchBLT = GetProcAddress(hModPBrush, "#6");
```

Last of all, the segment relocation records tell us all the locations where the Windows loader needs to fix up an instruction. The target portion of each fixup is useful for determining which APIs the DLL calls. For instance, KERNEL.4 is LocalInit(), KERNEL.132 is GetWinFlags(), and so on. You can find out these names by running TDUMP or EXEHDR on KRNL386.EXE.

Resolving Dynamic Links

Now that we have a sense of what dynamic linking is, we'll dig into the details of how the Windows KERNEL implements it. In this excursion, we travel through the code of the GetProcAddress() function. We chose to show the GetProcAddress() style of linking because it's much simpler than showing how implicit linking works when you load a new program or DLL. Internally, GetProcAddress() and the Windows loader use the same workhorse routines, so we're really not missing much.

GetProcAddress()

Earlier, we went over the two requirements for dynamic linking, a module and an entry point. It's no coincidence that these are the exact parameters to GetProcAddress(). Actually, that's not quite true, according to the Microsoft documentation. The first parameter to GetProcAddress() is documented as an instance handle (DGROUP). What good is the selector of the module's DGROUP segment? By itself, it's useless. However, as we know from Chapter 3, the instance handle can easily be converted into a module handle. GetProcAddress() calls GetExePtr(), which we cover next, to take care of this conversion. GetProcAddress() really *should* take a module handle. In fact, the Windows 3.0 documentation shows GetProcAddress() taking an HMODULE. Unfortunately, the 3.1 SDK backtracks and specifies an HINSTANCE instead. Perhaps it's currently documented as taking an HINSTANCE because instance handles are more easily obtained than module handles. Your WinMain() or LibMain() function is passed an instance handle, rather than a module handle. When you call LoadLibrary(), you get an hInstance, as well. On the other hand, if you follow the GetProcAddress() documentation exactly and want to get the address of something in USER, you somehow need to get USER's instance handle. Just how are you supposed to do that? It's not immediately clear that one solution is to use LoadLibrary() on a DLL that's already loaded. And as we see from Chapter 3, calling LoadLibrary() has a lot of overhead just to get an instance handle that GetProcAddress() just turns around and internally converts *back* to a module handle anyway. Many seasoned pros don't bother with LoadLibrary() therefore. They just call GetModuleHandle("USER") and give GetProcAddress() what it really wants, a module handle. This is yet another case where Microsoft tried to make things simple for the programmer, but instead made it harder to really understand what's happening.

Once GetProcAddress() knows the module handle it's supposed to work with, it looks to see if the module handle is for a task, as opposed to a DLL. If the module is for a task, GetProcAddress() immediately bails out. The reasoning is that you're not supposed to be linking to a task. It's OK for a task to link to a DLL, and for a DLL to link to another DLL, but Microsoft doesn't want you linking one task to another task, or from a DLL to a task. The reason for this might be that you could make calls to the task's code without having properly switched to the proper task context. For instance, you could end up using the wrong PSP or the wrong SS register. As shown in Chapter 3, the Windows loader makes a similar test when loading implicitly linked modules and returns error code 5, "Attempt to dynamically link to a task," if such a situation arises. If you *really* want to dynamically link to a task, you can turn on the DLL bit in the flags of the module table before calling GetProcAddress(), and then turn the bit back off later. This hack assumes that the module is already loaded in memory. It won't work if you're implicitly linking (there's no module table to modify yet).

An undocumented feature of GetProcAddress() is the ability to pass in 0 as the hInstance. When GetProcAddress() sees this, it uses the module handle associated with the current (calling) task. This enables a task to call GetProcAddress() on its own functions, but still prevents it from linking to other tasks.

With the module handle portion of the dynamic link squared away, GetProcAddress() now turns its attention to the entry point parameter. GetProcAddress() can take an entry point in three different forms:

- The name of the entry point as an ASCII string. It must match the name in the target module's resident or nonresident names table exactly. The string is typically uppercase, for instance, "GETMESSAGE".
- An ASCII string representing the entry ordinal in decimal. For instance, GetMessage(), the 108th entry in USER, would be specified in this form as "#108". This behavior isn't documented for Windows, but is documented for the OS/2 equivalent DosGetProcAddr(). The KERNEL module itself uses this method of specifying the target function when it links to functions in other DLLs.
- An entry ordinal value. In this case, the ordinal value is found in the offset portion of the LPSTR parameter to GetProcAddress(). The segment portion must be zero. For instance, GetMessage() in this form could be created by MAKELP(0, 108).

Regardless of which form is specified, GetProcAddress() does whatever is necessary to get the entry point into its integer (entry ordinal) form. If either of the string forms was specified, the FarFindOrdinal() function, described later, does whatever is necessary to determine the integer entry point value.

After the integer form of the entry point is known, the final step is to pass the hModule and entry ordinal to FarEntProcAddress(), which just passes its parameters to EntProcAddress(). EntProcAddress() uses the hModule and entry ordinal to determine an actual selector:offset that can be returned to the caller of GetProcAddress(). We describe EntProcAddress() in a bit.

```
Pseudocode for GetProcAddress() - LDAUX.OBJ
// Parameters:
//      WORD    hInstance
//      LPSTR   procName
// Locals
//      WORD    buffer[0x82]
//      WORD    hModule           // handle to a module database
//      WORD    entryOrdinal      // Entry ordinal to look for

    if ( hInstance != 0 )         // a nonzero instance handle?
    {
        // Get module handle from hInstance. If an hModule
        // was passed to us, GetExePtr() returns it, unchanged.
        hModule = GetExePtr( hInstance )
        if ( hModule == 0 )           // Bail out if hInstance
            return 0                  // was no good.

        if ( DLL flag not set in hModule's flags )
        {
            // You can't dynamically link to a task. Tell the
            // caller about this.
            FarKernelError("Can not GetProcAddress a task.")
            return 0;
        }
    }
    else    // We were given a 0 instance handle. We'll use
    {       // the module handle of the current task therefore.

        hModule = CurTDB.TDB_pModule  // module handle for a task
                                      // is stored in its TDB.
    }

    // We now check which form the procedure "name" is in. It
    // can either be a LPSTR to a function name, or it can be
    // an entry ordinal value in the LOWORD, and a 0 in the HIWORD.
    if ( FP_SEG(procName) == 0 )    // LOWORD is entry ordinal
    {
        entryOrdinal = FP_OFF( procName )
    }
    else                            // we have a name pointer
    {
        // Copy the name to a local buffer, and prepend a length
        // byte to it.
        CopyName( procName, buffer, 0 )
```

```
        // Look up the name in the resident or nonresident names
        // table for the module. The WORD after each name
        // contains the entry ordinal for the associated name.
        // FarFindOrdinal() just calls FindOrdinal(), which is
        // explored later on.
        entryOrdinal = FarFindOrdinal( hModule, buffer, 0xFFFF )
        if ( entryOrdinal == 0 )
            return 0
    }

    // The real work goes on in this routine. Given a module
    // handle, go look up the address of the specified entry
    // ordinal in the module's entry table.
    return FarEntProcAddress( hModule, entryOrdinal )
```

GetExePtr()

GetExePtr() is one of my favorite undocumented functions. Given almost any kind of global handle, it will find the module handle associated with it. Sadly, it will RIP in the debug KERNEL if you pass it a task handle—a minor blemish on an otherwise wonderfully useful function.

GetExePtr() goes through the following steps in the order given below, to find the associated module handle:

1. If you pass in a module handle, GetExePtr() just returns it. A simple test for the 'NE' signature at the beginning of the segment is all that's needed to test for this.

2. If you pass in an instance handle, GetExePtr() walks through the task list, looking for a task (TDB) whose hInstance field matches the passed handle. If GetExePtr() finds the TDB, it knows the passed handle is an instance handle. It's then a simple matter to return the corresponding module handle that's stored in the task database.

3. If you passed in a handle that is a GMEM_MOVEABLE global handle, GetExePtr() calls MyLock() (Chapter 2) to obtain the associated selector. GetExePtr() tests this selector to see if it points to a module table. If so, it's returned.

4. GetExePtr() then calls GetOwner() to determine the owner of the block. Block ownership is discussed in Chapter 2. A block's owner can be either a module handle, a PDB (PSP), or a task handle. If the owner is an hModule, GetExePtr() returns it.

5. Last, GetExePtr() iterates through the task list again. This time, it compares the owner of the block to the PDB for each task. If GetExePtr() finds a match, it returns the module handle for the task. Blocks that were obtained using GlobalAlloc() and friends are found this way.

```
Pseudocode for GetExePtr() - LDUTIL.OBJ
// Parameters:
//      WORD    handle
// Locals:
//      WORD    hTask
//      WORD    hModule
//      WORD    PDB
//      WORD    blockHandle

    if ( handle & 1 )   // If the handle is in a FIXED segment
    {
        // Treat the handle as a selector, and look for an NE
        // signature (at the beginning of all module tables),
        // meaning that no further work is required.
        if ( handle.ne_magic == 'NE' )
            return handle
    }

    // Perhaps the handle passed to us was an instance handle.
    // Therefore, iterate through every task in the system,
    // comparing the hInstance for the task to the handle that
    // we were passed. If a match is found, the hModule for the
    // task is returned.
    hTask = HeadTDB
    while ( hTask != 0 )
    {
        if (hTask.hInstance == handle)  // Does hInstance of task
            return hTask.TDB_pModule    // match passed handle? If so,
                                        // return hModule for task.
        hTask = hTask.TDB_next          // Try the next task.
    }

    // Call the MyLock() function to obtain the selector for
    // the handle passed to us. See Chapter 2 for details
    // on MyLock().
    blockHandle = MyLock( handle )
    if ( blockHandle == 0 )         // Bail out if not found.
        return 0

    if ( blockHandle.ne_magic == 'NE' ) // Is blockHandle a
        return blockHandle              // module table?  Return
                                        // it if so.

    // Get the owner of the memory block by looking it up in
    // the global memory block's arena (see Chapter 2). The
```

```
// owner of a global heap block is either a module handle or
// a PDB (Process Data Base; a PSP).
hModule = GetOwner( blockHandle )
if ( hModule == 0 )              // Block isn't owned. Abort!
    return 0

if ( hModule.ne_magic == 'NE' ) // If the block is owned by
    return hModule              // an hModule, return the
                                // hModule as the owner.

PDB = hModule     // Maybe it was a PDB, rather than an hModule?
                  // We'll walk the task list again, comparing
                  // the PDB's for each task to find out.

hTask = HeadTDB
while ( hTask != 0 )    // Walking the task list...
{
    // Is the PDB for this task the same as the PDB that owns
    // the passed handle? Return the task's hModule if so.
    if ( hTask.TDB_PDB == PDB )
        return hTask.TDB_pModule

    hTask = hTask.TDB_next      // Nope. Try next task.
}

return 0          // No owner could be found. Return failure
```

FindOrdinal()

In our previous discussion of GetProcAddress(), we saw where it called FarFindOrdinal(), which is just a wrapper around a call to FindOrdinal(). FindOrdinal()'s job is to take an ASCII string and return the associated entry ordinal. In most cases, this involves searching through the resident and nonresident names tables. Besides being called by GetProcAddress(), FindOrdinal() is also invoked from the SegReloc() function, which is the part of the Windows loader that performs all the fixups on a segment when it's loaded into memory.

FindOrdinal() begins by determining if the passed string starts with the pound sign (#). If so, the remainder of the string is supposed to contain an entry ordinal value, in decimal, as a string (for instance, "#123"). If a pound sign is found, FindOrdinal() branches to a section of code that reads the remaining characters of the string and creates the integer value from them. This code is similar to the atoi() function in C.

The more likely case is that the passed string contains the name of a function. For these strings, FindOrdinal() iterates through the resident names table and compares the passed string to the entries in the table. The comparison is quasi case-insensitive. FindOrdinal() uppercases each character of the input parameter string before it's compared to the corresponding character in the name table strings. The linker is supposed to have uppercased the names it put in the table, so in general, you can consider FindOrdinal() and, hence, GetProcAddress() to be case insensitive. FindOrdinal() optimizes the scanning by only comparing strings whose lengths match exactly.

If the name is not found in the resident names table, FindOrdinal() loads the nonresident names table from the NE file and branches back to the code that searched through the resident names table. When the FindOrdinal() finishes with the nonresident names table it discards the table. Thus, every time you call GetProcAddress() with a name that's not in the resident names table, you force the nonresident names table to be brought in, searched, and discarded.

Also worth noting is that FindOrdinal() ignores the first entry (#0) in both the resident and nonresident names table. The first entry in the resident names table contains the module name, as specified in the NAME or LIBRARY line in the DEF file. The first entry in the nonresident names table is the module description, as given in the DESCRIPTION field in the DEF file.

```
Pseudocode for FindOrdinal() - LDUTIL.OBJ
// Parameters:
//      WORD    hModule
//      LPSTR   name    // proc name with prepended length byte
//      WORD    fileHandle
// Locals:
//      WORD    NRTableLoaded = 0   // Have we loaded the non-
                                    // resident name table yet?
//      LPSTR   nameTableEntry  // Current name we're looking at in
                                // iresident/non-resident name
                                // table.

    // *name is the string length. *(name+1) is the first
    // character in the string. Find out if the string begins
    // with a '#', which indicates that an ASCII representation
    // of the ordinal value (in decimal) follows (e.g., "#123" ).
    if ( *(name+1) == "#" )
        goto ConvertStringToInteger

    // Initialize pointer to resident names table. See chapter
    // 3 for the full description of the resident names table.
    nameTableEntry = MK_FP(hModule, hModule.ne_restab)

SearchNameTable:

    // Skip over the module name or module description, which are
    // both the first entries (#0) in the tables.
    nameTableEntry += (*nameTableEntry) + 3  // +3 skips over the length
                                             // byte and entry ordinal WORD.

    // Start searching through all the entries in a name table.
```

```
    // The string passed, as well as the names in the table
    // are preceded by length bytes to make comparisons faster.
    // We stop when we reach an entry whose length byte is 0.
    // This indicates the end of the table.
    while ( 1 )
    {
        if ( *nameTableEntry == 0 )
            goto NoMoreNames

        if ( *nameTableEntry == *name ) // Do lengths of the two
        {                               // strings match?

            Start comparing each byte of the two strings, calling
            MyUpper() on the characters in the procedure name
            passed to us. This has the effect of making the
            string comparison case insensitive. It also assumes
            that the linker uppercased the names it put in the
            resident and non-resident names tables. If at any
            point the strings don't compare, stop the comparison,
            and increment the nameTableEntry pointer to the next
            string in the table.

            If passed in string completely matches the string in
            the resident/non-resident names table, LODSW the
            WORD immediately after the name in the table. This
            is the entry ordinal associated with the name.

            if NRTableLoaded
                goto FindOrdinal_FreeNonResidentNames
            else
                return AX       // Contains the entry ordinal
        }
    }

ConvertStringToInteger:
    Start reading in the bytes past the '#' character. Convert
    the string to it's equivalent machine value. The algorithm
    is the standard atoi() algorithm:

    ordinal = 0
    while ( character is between '0' & '9' )
    {
        ordinal = (ordinal * 10) + (character  - '0')
        get next character
    }
```

```
    When all characters have been read, return the resulting
    ordinal value.

NoMoreNames:
    if ( NRTableLoaded == 0 )
    {
        // Look up the file handle in the cache of file handles
        // that KERNEL maintains.
        AX = GetCachedFileHandle(hModule, fileHandle, 0xFFFF)

        // Now go load the nonresident names table into memory
        LoadNRTable( hModule, AX, &someBuffer, 0x96 )

        nameTableEntry = &someBuffer  // Start searching at
                                      // the beginning of the
                                      // nonresident names.
        NRTableLoaded = DS        // Remember that we've loaded
                                  // the nonresident names.
        goto SearchNameTable      // Go search through the
                                  // non-resident names table.
    }

FindOrdinal_FreeNonResidentNames:
    FreeNRTable( hModule, 0x2C )    // 0x2C -> ???

    return AX                       // AX == entry ordinal or 0
```

EntProcAddress()

EntProcAddress() has the interesting job of determining the selector:offset in memory, corresponding to the passed hModule and entry ordinal combination. In addition to being called from GetProcAddress(), EntProcAddress() is also called from SegReloc(), the routine that handles all fixups for a segment when it's brought into memory.

The first thing EntProcAddress() needs to do is scan through the entry tables contained in the module database. The format of the entry bundles and entries is discussed in Chapter 3. Once EntProcAddress() finds the bundle that matches the entry ordinal passed in, it now has the logical address for the entry point. A logical address consists of a segment number, corresponding to the order of the segments in the file, and an offset within the segment. For instance, the logical address 0003h:1234h means offset 1234h in the third segment in the module's segment table.

EntProcAddress() now has to take the segment portion of the logical address and find out which selector the Windows loader assigned to that segment. However, first there are two special cases that need to be tested for. If the segment portion of the logical address is 0xFE, the offset portion of the logical address is really a constant value, rather than an offset to a segment. For instance, consider the exported symbol __F000H in KERNEL. The value returned by GetProcAddress() in this case is not the address of a function called __F000H. Instead, the offset portion of the returned address can be used as a protected mode *selector* to access the memory at real mode segment F000H. (We saw these selectors constructed in Chapter 1.)

The logical segment value 0xFF is also a special value treated differently by the loader. Entries with a logical segment of 0xFF are termed moveable, even though moveable entries have lost any semblance of significance now that Windows only runs in protected mode. When the logical segment is 0xFF, the actual logical segment needs to be looked up in another field in the entry bundle's data structure. From there on, EntProcAddress() acts the same for moveable entries as it does for fixed entries. Fixed entries are all entries that have logical segments other than 0xFE or 0xFF.

Resuming our original line of thought, EntProcAddress() needs to map the logical segment to the matching selector value. It does this by indexing into the segment table contained within the module database. The one difference between fixed and moveable entries is that fixed entries force the segment to be loaded into memory, if it's not already, while moveable entries don't. Once EntProcAddress() knows the selector value, it combines the value with the offset portion of the address stored in the entry bundle's data structure. EntProcAddress() returns the result to GetProcAddress(), which simply passes the address back to the caller, thereby completing the dynamic link.

```
Pseudocode for EntProcAddress() - LDUTIL.OBJ
// Parameters:
//      WORD     hModule
//      WORD     ordinal
// Locals:
//      DWORD    bundleHeader          // Pointer to entry bundles
//      DWORD    entry                 // Pointer to found bundle
//      WORD     logSeg                // logical segment of entry
//      WORD     selector              // Selector for entry

    ordinal = ordinal & 0x7FFF  // Turn off high bit, so
                                // no entry ordinals > 32768
    if ( ordinal == 0 )
        return 0

    ordinal--            // Entries in module table are zero based
                         // Elsewhere are one-based.

    bundleHeader = hModule.ne_enttab

    do   // Search for the correct bundle.
    {
        if ( ordinal < bundleHeader->firstEntry )
            return 0
```

```
        if ( ordinal < bundleHeader->lastEntry )
        {
            // Point "entry" at the correct entry within the
            // entry point bundle. 6 is the size of the bundle
            // header.
            entry = bundleHeader + 6 +
                (ordinal - bundlerHeader->firstEntry)

            goto foundBundle        // Now get the address!
        }

        bundleHeader = bundleHeader->nextBundle

    } while ( bundleHeader )

    return 0    // We didn't find the entry. Return failure

constantEntry:  // Come here for "constant" entries like __F000H
    BX = &bundle->entryOffset

    return MK_FP( -1, bundle->entryOffset )

foundBundle:    // We found enclosing bundle in entry table

    if ( bundle->entrySegment == 0xFE ) // Check for "constant"
        goto constantEntry              // entries like __F000H

    if (bundle->entrySegment == 0xFF)   // Check for moveable
        goto MoveableEntry              // entries

    // If we get here, the entry is a "fixed" entry, and
    // bundle->entrySegment contains the logical segment of the
    // entrypoint.
    logSeg = bundle->entrySegment

    Given the logical segment specified by logSeg, create a
    pointer to the appropriate entry in the segment table of
    the module table (see Chapter 3 for details).

    if ( MOVEABLE bit set for the segment )
        goto MoveableEntry

    selector = LoadSegment( hModule, logSeg, 0xFFFF, 0xFFFF)
    if ( selector == 0 )
        return 0
```

```
    return MK_FP( selector, entry->entryOffset )

MoveableEntry:
    logSeg = bundle->entrySegment

    Given the logical segment specified by logSeg, create a
    pointer to the appropriate entry in the segment table of
    the module table.

    if ( handle for segment in the segment table == 0 )
        return 0
    else
        return MK_FP(handle in segment table, entry->entryOffset)
```

When loading an EXE or DLL from disk, the Windows loader doesn't call GetProcAddress(). It does, however, use EntProcAddress(), which we just discussed. As we saw in the earlier TDUMP output for PBRUSH.DLL, an EXE or DLL file usually has tables of fixups that need to be applied. The fixup tables are per-segment, allowing the loader to apply all the fixups for a particular segment, without having to filter out fixups for other segments. Whenever KERNEL loads a segment from an NE file, the loader iterates through all of the segment's fixup records. For fixups to outside modules, the loader uses EntProcAddress() to obtain the address of the target function. This address is copied into the specified fixup location in memory, thereby completing the CALL instruction. In other words, this is where the EXPORTed function is connected up to the IMPORTing module. For fixups to other segments within the same EXE or DLL, it's a simple matter to look up the segment's selector value in the module's segment table.

That's it! As you can see from the preceding pseudocode, dynamic linking isn't that hard. We now move on to cover some smaller topics that are directly or indirectly related to dynamic linking.

Import Libraries

An import library tells the linker about routines that are in DLLs, rather than in the program it's linking. Import libraries allow the linker to defer to the Windows loader the job of fixing up calls to these routines. Without an import library, the linker would generate "Undefined symbol" errors for these calls.

It's hard to avoid import libraries. Even if you're creating a simple, self-contained Windows program, the odds are that you're using an import library, even if you don't know it. Each Windows API function you call has an entry in an import library. Borland C++ users use IMPORT.LIB. The equivalent for Microsoft C users is LIBW.LIB. The closest equivalent to an import library for Turbo Pascal for Windows users is the WinProcs unit in the TPW.TPL file. If your program consists of an executable file that implicitly links to your own private DLLs, you need to create import libraries for the DLLs before you can link the main executable.

An import library generally contains no code. Rather, it's just a collection of OBJ file records that connect a function name to a module name and an entry ordinal within the module. You can see this in the following excerpt of TDUMP output of IMPORT.LIB:

```
005D10 THEADR  GETMESSAGE
005D1F COMENT  Purge: Yes, List: Yes, Class: 160 (0A0h)
    Dynamic link import (IMPDEF)
      Imported by: ordinal
      Internal Name: GETMESSAGE
      Module Name: USER
      ordinal: 108
005D39 MODEND
```

The Internal Name: line tells the linker the name of the routine, GETMESSAGE. The next two lines provide the previously described prerequisites for dynamic linking: a module name (USER), and an entry point, 108. The format of IMPDEF and the related EXPDEF records can be found in the Windows 3.1 SDK documentation.

There is a way to avoid using import libraries, if you enjoy doing things the hard way. Rather than tell the linker about DLL routines with an import library, specify the same information in the IMPORTS section of the DEF file. For instance, to implicitly link to GetMessage() without using an import library, you need to have something like this:

```
IMPORTS
    GETMESSAGE = USER.108
```

Alternatively, you could use:

```
IMPORTS
    GETMESSAGE = USER.GETMESSAGE
```

The key point is that you still need to specify both a module and an entry point within the module. It's generally much easier to use import libraries, but if you need to call an undocumented function that's not in your import library, the IMPORTS section can come in handy.

To create import libraries, you use the IMPLIB utility. Borland and Microsoft each ship their own version of IMPLIB, but with the same name. IMPLIB creates an import library from either a DLL file or from a DEF file. This isn't a hard process. As you now know, the records in the import library need to specify a function name, the module containing the function, and the function's entry point. From examining the TDUMP output earlier in the chapter, you can see that this information is readily obtainable in the EXE or DLL file. You can also specify this exact same information in the EXPORTS section of the DEF file, which we discuss momentarily. All IMPLIB has to do is know how to read both NE files and DEF files, and then emit all three pieces of information for each function in the appropriate IMPDEF record and LIB file format.

Exporting and Exportable Functions

So far, we've focused on what's involved in linking to a function in another module. It's now time to turn the telescope around. We need to see what the requirements are for being the *target* of a dynamic link. In the first part of our discussion, we concentrate on exporting functions from EXE files.

In general, a function that will be called from outside the DLL or EXE it was compiled in needs to be exported. If you don't export a function, there's no way that GetProcAddress() or the Windows loader can find it to link up to it. (For those of you familiar with smart callbacks and FIXDS, be patient, we'll get to those later.)

For a function to be properly exported, two steps are essential. First, you need to tell the linker about the function to be exported. Traditionally, you do this by putting the uppercase name of the function, along with the export ordinal value, in the EXPORTS section of the DEF file. For instance:

```
EXPORTS
    MYCALLBACKFUNC          @10
```

Telling the linker to export a function has two effects. First, it creates a new entry for the function in the EXE or DLL entry table. Each entry in the entry table holds the logical address of the function. In the above example, the tenth entry in the entry table of the module being linked contains the logical address of MYCALLBACKFUNC.

Second, exporting a function causes its name to appear in the resident or nonresident names table. Putting the function name in the EXPORTS Section of the .DEF file causes the name to appear in the nonresident names table by default. If you expect this function to be primarily linked by its ordinal value (from import libraries), this is usually what you want. Putting the name, instead, in the nonresident names table saves memory because the name doesn't reside in memory for the entire lifetime of the module, but if you want the name to always be in memory (in the resident names table), either omit the export ordinal value (thereby letting the linker pick one) or use the RESIDENTNAME modifier. For instance:

```
EXPORTS
    MYCALLBACKFUNC
```

or

```
EXPORTS
    MYCALLBACKFUNC          @10  RESIDENTNAME
```

RESIDENTNAME is most often used for the WEP (Windows exit procedure) routine in DLLs. Due to some problems in DLL termination, you could often crash Windows if WEP were in the nonresident names table. When KERNEL tries to load the nonresident names table at a time when the system is in a shaky state, things rapidly go downhill. The solution is to keep WEP in the resident names table, which is always in memory.

The second part of properly exporting a function is to make sure that the function is exportable. An exportable function has the proper prologue and epilogue code to allow it to be called from outside the EXE or DLL it resides in. Note this carefully: Making a function *exportable* is not the same as *exporting* it. Making a function exportable affects the code generated for it, whereas exporting the function is something the linker does. It's quite possible to have exportable functions that aren't exported. The other case, exported functions that aren't exportable, is a bad idea.

So what exactly does making a function exportable entail? In the simplest terms, an exportable function needs to set up the DS register to access the correct data segment. As Chapter 3 describes, each instance of a program has its own data segment. Each DLL also has its own data segment. It's imperative that the DS register be loaded with the correct data segment selector before any code tries to read or write it. The convention Windows follows is that upon entry to an exported function, the original DS value is saved before the correct DS value for the code in question is loaded. You might be aware of a C modifier called _loadds. Wouldn't that do the job? Unfortunately for applications, no. Using _loadds causes an actual data segment selector value for DGROUP to be put in the code segment. For instance:

```
mov     ax,257Fh
mov     ds,ax
```

As Chapter 3 explains, putting the data segment selector value into the code segment is fine if you want to run only one instance of a program. If you want to run two or more copies of a program, however, it just won't work. Because code is shared between multiple instances, and because _loadds puts the data segment selector (DGROUP) right in this shared code, each instance ends up using the same data segment selector, which is obviously not a good thing.

Since we most definitely can run multiple instances of a program, there must be some other method to load the DS register. To find out what it is, let's look at the code generated in an EXE file for two tiny functions, one of which is exported, and the other of which isn't. The C code looks like this:

```
int FAR PASCAL _export ExportMe(void)
{
    return 1;
}

int FAR PASCAL DontExportMe(void)
{
    return 1;
}
```

Ignore the _export modifier for the ExportMe() function. We discuss _export a bit later. For now, it's enough to say that it tells the compiler to generate code to make the function *exportable*. The assembler code generated looks like this:

```
EXPORTME        proc    far
        mov     ax,ds
        nop
        inc     bp
        push    bp
        mov     bp,sp
        push    ds
        mov     ds,ax
        mov     ax,1
        pop     ds
        pop     bp
        dec     bp
        ret
EXPORTME        endp

DONTEXPORTME    proc    far
        inc     bp
        push    bp
        mov     bp,sp
        mov     ax,1
        pop     bp
        dec     bp
        ret
DONTEXPORTME    endp
```

Both the exported and nonexported functions have the INC BP, PUSH BP, MOV SP,BP code, which is used to set up a standard stack frame to reference local variables and parameters. (Some compilers can omit the INC BP, which is only necessary for real mode Windows.) Filtering out the stack frame code shows that the real effect of making a function exportable is to add the following prologue code:

```
mov     ax,ds
nop
push    ds
mov     ds,ax
```

This sure looks redundant! The code loads AX from the DS register, and then three instructions later, it loads DS from AX. It doesn't do anything! And what about that NOP? At best, the code is harmless. It chews up some clock cycles, but it doesn't break anything. As it turns out, this is exactly why the code sequence was chosen. If you make a function *exportable*, but don't *export* it, nothing bad happens, other than a slight performance degradation. In early Windows compilers, all far functions had this prologue code, even if they didn't need it. Luckily the situation has improved and you only need to use the right compiler options to get better code. More on this later.

Returning to the question at hand, we still don't know *why* you would want to add this extra code to a function. To answer this, you need to know about some magic. When the Windows loader brings an EXE's code segment into memory, it looks at the prologue code for all the *exported* functions. If the loader sees:

```
mov     ax,ds
nop
```

or the equivalent:

```
push    ds
pop     ax
```

at the start of an exported function, it patches those instructions with three NOP instructions. The result, ignoring the stack frame code, looks like this:

```
nop
nop
nop
push    ds
mov     ds,ax
```

Now, it's starting to become clearer. The prologue code for an exportable *and* exported function sets the DS register to whatever's in the AX register. This implies that the AX register had better contain the data segment that the exported function, and all of the functions it calls, should be using. In other words, AX needs to contain the DGROUP selector for the instance of the program currently executing.

How does the AX register get set? Usually, it happens in one of two ways. For example, when you call MakeProcInstance() (such as before calling DialogBox()), the address of a thunk is returned to you. (See Chapter 3 for a description of where thunks are stored in the TDB.) This thunk just sets AX to the corresponding selector for the hInstance passed to MakeProcInstance(), before jumping to the address passed to MakeProcInstance(). A MakeProcInstance() thunk, therefore, looks like this:

```
MOV AX, XXXX               ; XXXX -> hInstance selector (DGROUP)
JMP FAR YYYY:ZZZZ          ; YYYY:ZZZZ -> address of function
```

The magic of MakeProcInstance() thunks allows dialog box procedure code for example to be shared between multiple program instances, while still allowing each instance to have its own data segment. Each program instance passes a different MakeProcInstance() thunk to the DialogBox() function, which is why thunks are stored with the task, not with the module. Whenever DialogBox() needs to call your dialog box callback function, it calls through the thunk you passed. This ensures that the callback function always has the correct hInstance selector in AX when it's called and can, therefore, load the DS register with the proper selector value for your hInstance or DGROUP.

The other way of setting the AX register occurs when the exported function being called is a window procedure. DispatchMessage() and friends set AX to the hInstance stored in the WND data structure (Chapter 4) before calling the exportable function, so you don't need to pass a MakeProcInstance() thunk when you call RegisterClass() or CreateWindow(). The MakeProcInstance() thunk is done for you!

What About Exporting and DLLs?

The situation with exporting functions from DLLs is somewhat different. In particular, the code generated for an exportable DLL function differs from that generated for an EXE. In a DLL the prologue for the ExportMe() function looks like this:

```
mov     ax,DGROUP
inc     bp
push    bp
mov     bp,sp
push    ds
mov     ds,ax
```

The DGROUP symbol in the first line causes a fixup record to be generated for the segment. When the loader brings this segment into memory, it patches the first instruction to move the selector value for the DGROUP into AX, for example:

```
mov     ax,134Fh
```

The line at the end just copies the AX register into the DS register. It would be even simpler if the Intel CPUs allowed the segment registers to be loaded from immediate values, for example:

```
mov     DS, 134Fh
```

The implication is that the functions in a DLL always use the same DATA segment, no matter which instance of a task it was called from. Specifically, they use the DLL's DGROUP. Any value in AX upon entry is ignored by an exported DLL function. In fact, if you call MakeProcInstance() with the address of a DLL function, it just returns the original address, unmodified. There's simply no need for a thunk in this case. Likewise, _loadds works from a DLL, so long as you remember to also _export the function.

FIXDS and Smart Callbacks

One of the most common mistakes Windows programmers make is to forget to call MakeProcInstance() when needed. This may be simple oversight, or the programmer may just not be aware of the need for it. In any event, forgetting to call MakeProcInstance() causes your exported function to be called with a meaningless value in AX. This almost always has the fatal effect of causing your program to die ignominiously with a General Protection Fault (or UAE, if you prefer). Isn't there a better way?

One of the most fundamental, but little known, aspects of Windows is that your program's stack resides in its data segment, or DGROUP. In the general case, therefore, you can assume that, while executing *in your EXE's code*, the stack segment register (SS) contains the same value as the data segment register (DS). In other words, SS==DS. As we just saw, the purpose of the prologue code for an exported function in an EXE is to set up the data segment register for the particular instance of the task. Since the stack segment register *is* the same thing as the DS for the task, we should be able to load the DS value from the SS register. By doing this, we can get rid of the need to create a MakeProcInstance() thunk. This is a great idea! The prologue code would look something like this:

```
mov     ax,ss
nop
inc     bp
push    bp
mov     bp,sp
push    ds
mov     ds,ax
```

Although stretched across several instructions, the prologue code has the net effect of loading DS from the SS register. What's very interesting here is that only the first instruction differs from what a normally exported function's prologue would look like. Plus, the first instruction fits into exactly the same number of bytes.

A few years ago, Michael Geary wrote a program that took advantage of this lucky coincidence. The program is called FIXDS; it post-processes executable files after they've been linked. FIXDS scans through the code segments in the EXE file and finds all the routines that start with either of the standard exportable prologues we saw earlier. It then patches those prologues to start with `mov ax,ss` instead.

Programmers who forget to or don't want to call MakeProcInstance() are now free of its tyranny. Subsequently, Borland and Microsoft added the capability to make their compilers generate FIXDS style code directly. Borland terms this option Smart Callbacks. For Borland C++ compilers, -WS enables this option for all far functions, while -WES generates smart callbacks only for functions with the _export modifier (described later). In Microsoft C++ 7.0, use -GA -GEs.

For DLLs, FIXDS and smart callbacks have no effect. If you think about it for a bit, there's no need to call MakeProcInstance() for a function in a DLL. The prologue code for an exported DLL function already sets DS to the module's DGROUP selector. In addition, things would get rather interesting in a hurry if the DLL prologue code *did* switch the DS value to the current stack's value. The DLL would be reading and writing the data in the application's DGROUP, rather than its own. An interesting footnote is that early versions of FIXDS didn't verify that the file was an EXE, as opposed to a DLL, before modifying it. This oversight was subsequently corrected.

Compiler Code Generation Options

Finally, we'd like to clear up some issues concerning code generation and dynamic linking.

The PASCAL and C Calling Conventions Are Both OK

Many programmers are under the mistaken impression that to export a function, it *must* be declared as a PASCAL function. This is simply not true. The PASCAL convention implies two things in Windows compilers. First, function names will be uppercased by the linker (for example, GetMessage() becomes GETMESSAGE()). Second, the PASCAL calling convention dictates that parameters be pushed on the stack in the order they appear in the function definition. The called function pops the arguments before returning. The other common convention is CDECL, where names are case sensitive and have an underbar (_) prefix (Foo() becomes _Foo()). Parameters to a CDECL function are pushed on the stack in right to left order. The CDECL convention also dictates that the calling code remove the arguments from the stack, which is how varargs are implemented. Incidentally, both PASCAL and CDECL are actually #defines in WINDOWS.H; they just map to the compiler keywords _pascal and _cdecl.

The vast majority of the Windows APIs are defined as PASCAL functions. However, this is not a requirement. For instance, the wsprintf() function in USER is *not* a PASCAL style function (it takes a variable number of arguments). One advantage of using functions declared as PASCAL is that the name you declare in your code is the same name you export. If you have a CDECL function, you need to remember to put an "_" at the front of the name when you export it in the DEF file. Since this confuses many people, they tend to stick with the PASCAL convention. There are sometimes size benefits from using the PASCAL convention; specifically, the stack arguments can be cleaned up in one place, at the end of the function, rather than after every *call* to the function. However, if you really need the CDCEL convention, such as for variable argument lists, don't be afraid to use it.

C++ Name Mangling

All too often, C programmers try their hand at writing a DLL in C++, only to get immensely frustrated when the function doesn't export properly. For instance, there are quite a few people who write a C++ based DLL and try to call it from a Visual Basic application. Try as they might, they can't get Visual Basic to recognize the exported DLL function. The compiler and the linker are all too often unfairly maligned when this happens.

The problem these programmers are hitting is called "C++ name mangling" (or "C++ name decoration" for Microsoft users). When you compile a function in C++, the name emitted in the OBJ files is *not* the name you used in the source file. Instead, it's a variation of the name, which includes information on the parameter types and so on. This is how function overloading and type-safe linkage are implemented. This topic is covered in many texts on C++. Here, we're interested in why it causes problems for DLL authors.

Since the name emitted in the OBJ file name is different from the name used in the source file, the first problem programmers usually have is when the linker won't link. For instance, you have the following function in a C++ program:

```
int FAR PASCAL ExportMe(void)
{
    return 1;
}
```

And in the .DEF file, you have:

```
EXPORTS
    EXPORTME    @1
```

The problem is that in the OBJ file, the compiler has mangled (or decorated) the function name:

```
0001C1 PUBDEF  '@EXPORTME$QV'          Segment: _TEXT:0000
```

In other words, thanks to C++ name mangling, your function is really called @EXPORTME$QV, but you're trying to export a function called EXPORTME. Obviously, they aren't the same, and the linker has every right to complain.

There are two solutions to this problem. The first is to use the *extern "C"* modifier when you declare the function, for instance:

```
extern "C" int FAR PASCAL ExportMe(void);
```

This modifier prevents the compiler from mangling the name. The name in the OBJ file will now be EXPORTME, just as you'd expect. The problem with this modifier is that you can no longer overload your functions. The names *have* to be different for the compiler and linker to distinguish between them.

The other solution is to use the _export modifier, which we cover in more detail in a moment. For now, the important thing is that using _export tells the compiler to emit an EXPDEF record in the OBJ. This record indicates to the linker that it should export the function *as is*, regardless of whether or not the name appears in the EXPORTS section of the DEF file. The downside of this approach is that the mangled name appears in the resident or non-resident names table. Thus, any programs that want to use GetProcAddress() on the function (including Visual Basic) need to know that the name is in its mangled form and deal with it accordingly.

The _export modifier

One of the most handy and little known Windows feature in today's C and C++ compilers is the _export or __export (with two underscores) modifier. For instance:

```
int FAR PASCAL _export ExportMe(void)
```

The _export modifier causes two things to happen. First, it *guarantees* that the proper prologue code to make a function *exportable* is generated, no matter what other compilation options are selected. We come back to this important point later. Second, the modifier tells the compiler to emit an EXPDEF record (Exported Definition) for that name. When the linker sees the EXPDEF record, it includes that function in the list of functions to be exported, *regardless* of whether or not you included the function in the EXPORTS section of the DEF file. This is a great aid to programmers like the author, who always forgets to add the exported function names to the DEF file.

There is one slight drawback to using _export. If you don't add the exported function name to the EXPORTS section of the DEF file, the linker picks the entry ordinal for you. This isn't ordinarily a problem, unless you modify a library that other programs or DLLs link to by ordinal values (which is usually the case). If you add a new exported function and use _export, but don't include the nam in the EXPORTS section, there's a good chance the linker will shift around the entry ordinals it assigned to the exported functions. Confusing, to say the least!

There are two solutions in this situation. If you can relink the EXE or DLL that's importing the DLL functions, you can run IMPLIB on the DLL to produce an updated import library and then relink the dependent EXE or DLL file(s). If you can't relink the dependent files (for instance, if you've already distributed files to customers), you'll want to include the exported function names and ordinals in the DEF file EXPORTS section. This can be messy if you have C++ functions with mangled names, but at least the export ordinals won't change.

Making Your Code Optimally Efficient

If you're the type of programmer who worries about clock cycles, you may have noticed something about the prologue and epilogue for both traditionally exportable and FIXDS style functions. Specifically, they both contain two segment register loads, which is, in and of itself, not a problem. However, the compiler doesn't know which functions will actually be called from outside the module. As a result, in some default or worst-case modes, the compiler generates the extra prologue and epilogue code for *every single FAR function.* If you program in the compact or large memory models, this extra code is dead weight that adds up and gets expensive.

In this day, when performance and code size are often the last things on programmer's minds, we see all too many people giving the advice, "Just use smart callbacks. You don't have to worry about MakeProcInstance() or exporting anymore." While this is often a quick and easy solution, you also pay the price in increased code size and slower performance if your program is a compact or large-model program.

If you don't mind applying a little thought to your coding, you can squeeze out this dead weight, creating a smaller, faster program as a result. The key to this technique is the _export modifier and a specific compiler code generation option.

Our goal in this process is to tell the compiler to generate the prologue to make a function exportable *only when it needs to be generated.* In other words, by default, the compiler should *not* generate exportable prologue and epilogue code for *all* far functions. For Borland compilers, this option is -WE or -WES for EXE files, and -WDE for DLL files. For Microsoft C++ 7.0, use -GEs or -GEd with -GA or -GD as appropriate.

When the compiler compiles a function that *needs* the exportable prologue code, it should generate it. How does it know for which functions to generate the prologue? You need to help out the compiler a bit here. As mentioned earlier, one effect of the _export modifier is to always force exportable prologue code to be generated, no matter what the current default is. Therefore, you just need to add _export to the function declaration for functions that need to have the exportable prologue. The use of _export has an additional side benefit—you usually don't have to add the exported function names to the EXPORTS section of the DEF file.

In conclusion, to create optimal compact and large-model programs, you first need to add the _export modifier to any function, like window and dialog procedures, that will be called from outside the module. Next, you need to tell the compiler *not* to make all functions exportable. The final step is to generate smart callback prologue code for all _export functions. Alternatively, create MakeProcInstance() thunks as necessary for all _export() functions. Smart callbacks are easier, but are less portable to earlier Windows compilers. In this case, FIXDS helps out.

If you follow these simple rules and understand the concepts of dynamic linking discussed earlier, you should be well on your way toward fast, efficient code. Dynamic linking is your friend, rather than your misunderstood and feared enemy.

Bibliography

The following is a listing of books, articles, and other sources of information I found particularly useful when writing this book.

Ralf Brown and Jim Kyle, *PC Interrupts: A Programmer's Reference to BIOS, DOS, and Third-Party Calls*, Reading MA: Addison-Wesley, 1991, ISBN 0-201-57797-6

A veritable gold mine for anyone taking apart PC software. Almost every interrupt encountered while examining Windows is covered in PC Interrupts. *It is especially nice to have the DPMI interrupts in quick reference form. The interrupts are ordered somewhat strangely, but the index does a good job of showing where to look for a particular interrupt subfunction.*

Harvey M. Deitel and Michael S. Kogan, *The Design of OS/2*, Reading MA: Addison-Wesley, 389 pp., ISBN 0-201-54889-5

Describes at many points the differences between OS/2 1.x and OS/2 2.0. OS/2 1.x is very similar in implementation to Windows and OS/2 2.0 retains many of these concepts, such as module handles.

DOS Protected Mode Interface (DPMI) Specification, Version 0.9 (May 15, 1990), Intel Order No. 240763-001

The DPMI specification was originally Microsoft's response to the VCPI specification, which provided for cooperative multitasking of 386 DOS extenders. Subsequently,

Microsoft and other companies formed a committee to hammer out a specification on which Windows and other DOS extenders could be built. The 0.9 specification is what Windows 3.0 and Windows 3.1 implement. There is a 1.0 specification, but it's not in wide use because running in a Windows DOS box (with only 0.9 DPMI support) is a design requirement for most applications. Once you're familiar with the DPMI specification, you can use PC Interrupts *as a quick reference to the DPMI functions.*

Ray Duncan et al., *The MS-DOS Encyclopedia*, Redmond WA: Microsoft Press, 1988, 1570 pp., ISBN 1-55615-174-8
Although some of the information is becoming outdated, there's still much good information here. The information in the chapters on the .OBJ file format, and on the inner workings of LINK.EXE is hard to find elsewhere. There's also an appendix describing the New Executable format, and a chapter describing programming for Windows 2.0 (interesting reading if you want to see what a big step forward Windows 3.0 was).

Ray Duncan et al., *Extending DOS: A Programmer's Guide to Protected-Mode DOS, Second Edition*, Reading MA: Addison-Wesley, 1992, 538 pp., ISBN 0-201-56798-9
Windows is one part graphical user interface and one part DOS extender. There aren't many books that really cover the pros and cons of DOS extenders, and how they work. Extending DOS, *now in its second edition, provides a wealth of interesting and useful material for programmers who have to contend with the lower level operating system aspects of Windows. See especially Ray Duncan's chapter on DPMI and Bob Moote's chapter on multitasking and DOS extenders.*

Robert L. Hummel, *PC Magazine Programmer's Technical Reference: The Processor and Coprocessor*, Emeryville CA: Ziff-Davis Press, 1992, 761 pp., ISBN 1-56276-016-5.
A readable guide to the Intel series of CPUs. It's particularly good for its description of chip bugs (termed "errata" by Intel).

Intel i486 Microprocessor Programmer's Reference Manual, 1990, Intel Order No. 240486-001, ISBN 1-55512-101-2
It's been said that this book is only slightly more exciting than reading the phone book. Don't you believe it! If you need the final word on some esoteric or obscure feature of protected mode, there's no substitute for the original documentation. More than just opcode documentation, over half the book is devoted to describing various aspects of how the 80486 works, and how to program for it. There are other books (such as The Processor and Coprocessor*) which might be more readable but, inevitably, small details get lost in the translation.*

Gordon Letwin, Inside OS/2, Redmond WA: Microsoft Press, 1988, 289 pp., ISBN 1-878058-43-6
Although many of its details are somewhat outdated, Letwin does an excellent job of explaining the "religion" of OS/2. Since OS/2 and Windows were so similar in the early days, much of this book is still relevant today.

Microsoft Windows Device Driver Kit, Version 3.1, 1992, Microsoft Part No. 29132
Of particular interest in regards to Windows Internals *are the header files that document the format of the task database (TDB.INC), the module database (NEWEXE.INC), and the local and global heaps (WINKERN.INC). Also, the DDK documents the interface for GDI device drivers and gives several example drivers.*

Microsoft Windows Software Development Kit, Version 3.1, 1992, Microsoft Part No. 30211
Often maligned, the 3.1 SDK is actually pretty good within the confines of what it must do: document the exported APIs and data structures.

Daniel A. Norton, *Writing Windows Device Drivers*, Reading MA: Addison-Wesley, 1992, 434 pp., ISBN 0-201-57795-X
While definitely not a DDK replacement, it's detailed enough to keep within arms reach as a quick reference. If you need more information, use the DDK.

Charles Petzold, *Programming Windows 3.1, Third Edition*, Redmond WA: Microsoft Press, 1990, 983 pp., ISBN 1-55615-395-3
The universally acknowledged standard text on Windows programming. The focus is on showing you how to write Windows programs, rather than on how Windows works. However, both types of books are necessary these days.

Andrew Schulman, "Exploring Dcmand-Paged Virtual Memory in Windows Enhanced Mode," *Microsoft Systems Journal*, December 1992, pp. 17-36.
An in-depth description of how page-based virtual memory is implemented in Enhanced mode windows. Chapter 3 of Windows Internals *describes the virtual memory "sandbox" that the KERNEL memory management layer is built on. Andrew's article describes how the sandbox works.*

Andrew Schulman, et al., *Undocumented DOS: A Programmer's Guide to Reserved MS-DOS Functions and Data Structures*, Reading MA: Addison-Wesley, 1990, 694 pp., ISBN 0-201-57064-5
As chapters 1 and 3 of Windows Internals *show, Windows rests precariously upon the foundation of MS-DOS. As you might expect, what's officially documented about DOS isn't enough for the Windows developers to do everything they need to.* Undocumented DOS *brings this often essential undocumented information to the rest of us. A second edition with greatly expanded coverage on the interaction between DOS and Windows will appear in 1993.*

Andrew Schulman, David Maxey, and Matt Pietrek, *Undocumented Windows: A Programmer's Guide to Reserved Microsoft Windows API functions*, Reading MA: Addison-Wesley, 1992, 715 pp., ISBN 0-201-60834-0
The forerunner of this book. As the title implies, the focus is on documenting the undocumented APIs in KERNEL, USER, GDI, and SYSTEM. In addition, many key data structures in Windows are described as well. Also includes chapters on taking apart Win-

dows, undocumented messages, and the inner workings of TOOLHELP.DLL. There are numerous useful spelunking utilities included on the accompanying disk.

A large amount of the research done for Undocumented Windows *didn't make it into that book, mostly because the findings related to documented APIs or subsystems. In order for something to be in* Undocumented Windows, *it had to be an undocumented data structure or an undocumented exported API. The intent of* Windows Internals *is to explain and document the Windows subsystems as a whole, without regard to whether the functions or topics were documented, undocumented, internal, or exported.*

Index

A

B

C

D

E

G

H

I

J

K

L

P

S

T

W

X

Y

Z

About the Andrew Schulman Programming Series

THE ANDREW SCHULMAN PROGRAMMING SERIES has been designed for PC programmers seeking clarity and direction in a rapidly evolving programming universe. This award-winning series reinforces the idea that a decade of programming experience in MS-DOS need not be abandoned in the brave new age of objects and windows.

All titles in the series are authoritative, timely, and substantive. They encompass every aspect of IBM programming with particular emphasis on Windows and DOS programming.

Andrew Schulman, the series editor, is a software engineer known for his insight on programming issues and his ability to express technical ideas clearly. He has established a reputation as one of the finest writers on programming topics.

Undocumented DOS

"Only one or two books per year stand out as truly worthwhile efforts that we can use every day. Undocumented DOS *is such a book. Serious DOS programmers should own a copy."*
—PC Magazine

"I consider this to be one of the best programming books (Undocumented DOS*) since Zen of Assembly Language."*
—PC Techniques

"Undocumented DOS *is the most informative DOS programming book I have ever read"*
—Dr. Dobb's Journal

Undocumented Windows

"Undocumented Windows *is a must-have guide for developers of serious Windows applications"*
—InfoWorld

"Undocumented Windows *will take a place of honor on your bookshelf"*
—PC Magazine

Windows 3.1 Programming for Mere Mortals

"Windows 3.1 Programming for Mere Mortals *is actually fun to read. It's also highly informative."*
—PC Magazine

"This is a brilliant title and the book (Windows 3.1 Programming for Mere Mortals*) is just a hair short of genuine brilliance."*
—PC Techniques

Windows ++

"No other work I have seen comes close to what Windows ++ *brings to the C++ Windows programmer."*
—Dr. Dobb's Journal

About the Books in the Series

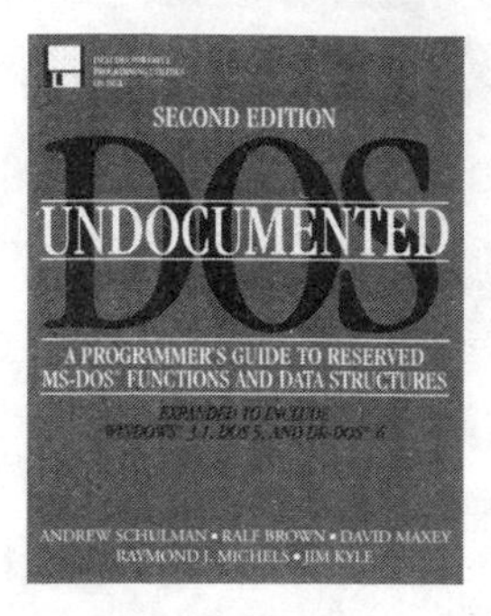

Undocumented DOS: A Programmer's Guide to Reserved MS-DOS Functions and Data Structures, Second Edition
by Andrew Schulman, Ralf Brown, David Maxey, Raymond J. Michaels, and Jim Kyle. *Undocumented DOS* is widely considered one of the best DOS programming books ever published. As the first complete reference to all of Microsoft's reserved DOS functions, it has become an essential addition to any serious programmer's library. This second edition is completely revised to cover DOS 6, Windows™ 3.1, and DR-DOS® 6, with coverage of all the newest interrupts and data structures that have appeared since the first edition.
$44.95, Paperback, 900 pages, 3.5" disk.
ISBN 0-201-63287-X

Windows ++: Writing Reusable Windows Code in C++
by Paul Dilascia describes how to build a C++ class library. Rather than teach you how to use commercially available class libraries, it shows you how to build your own system, one that's tailored to suit your needs. Along the way, you'll learn the benefits and ease of object-oriented programming in C++. Highlighted tips show how to adapt the various tips and techniques to C.
$29.95, Paperback, 571 pages.
ISBN 0-201-60891-X

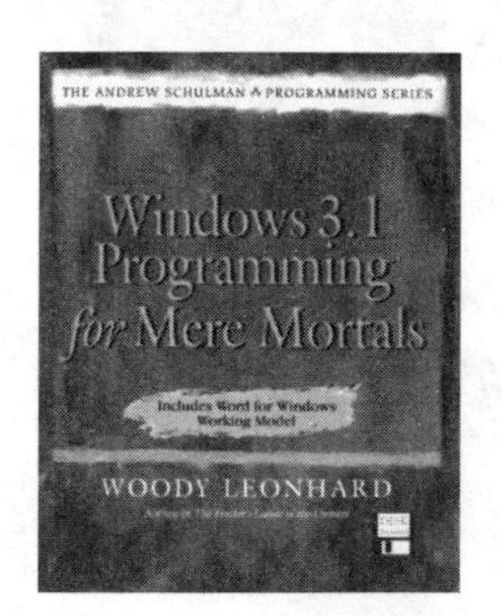

Windows 3.1 Programming for Mere Mortals
by Woody Leonhard uses commonly available Windows tools—most notably WordBasic, the programming language in Word for Windows, and Visual Basic—to develop effective utilities from the ground up. You'll discover the power of creating dialog boxes, moving data between applications with Dynamic Data Exchange (DDE), client/server links, calling Windows API functions, and using Dynamic Link Libraries (DLL) while building these exciting programs.
$34.95, Paperback, 537 pages, 3.5" disk.
ISBN 0-201-60832-4

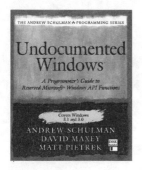

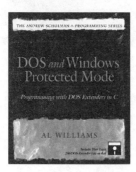

Get Inside WINDOWS!

MICROSOFT® WINDOWS™ COMPATIBLE

Windows 3.1 & C7.0 compatible!

VxD's · WINDOWS DRIVERS · DEBUG FLUID · DOS BOXES

NEW! Soft-ICE/W™

Version 1.1
(free update for registered 1.0 customers)

Debug Windows at the systems level!

Soft-ICE/W takes you inside Windows! Debug and explore with power and flexibility not found in any other Windows debugger! Soft-ICE/W allows you to debug at the systems or applications level or simply learn the inner workings of Windows.

- Debug VxD's, drivers and interrupt routines at source level,
- Debug interactions between DOS T&SR's and Windows Apps
- Debug programs in DOS boxes
- Display valuable system information (from the total memory occupied by a Windows application, to the complex internal structures of Windows)

Soft-ICE/W uses the 386/486 architecture to provide break point capabilities that normally require external hardware. Nu-Mega, which pioneered this technology with the introduction of its award winning Soft/ICE for DOS, now gives Windows programmers the same debugging power... *and still at a software price.*

Own the debugger that combines the best "view" of Windows internals with the most powerful break points of any software debugger.

Soft-ICE/W . . . Only $386

"While you may choose to keep your own favorite debugger for simple work, Soft-ICE/W will soon become mandatory equipment for serious windows debugging."
PC Magazine, June 1992

Undocumented Windows *FREE!*

- Learn Windows Inside & Out -

For a limited time get a great book, Undocumented Windows, a **$39.95** value ***FREE*** with your Soft-ICE/W order (or $39.95 separately while supplies last).

The ideal companion for your Soft-ICE/W Windows debugger!

by Andrew Schulman
David Maxey
Matt Pietrek

Undocumented Windows places, at programmer's fingertips, all the information needed to use the more than 200 reserved Windows functions that Microsoft has left undocumented.

Call: **(603) 889-2386**
FAX: **(603) 889-1135**

RISK = NULL
30 DAY
MONEY-BACK GUARANTEE

P.O. Box 7780
Nashua, NH 03060-7780 U.S.A.

24 HOUR BBS
603-595-0386